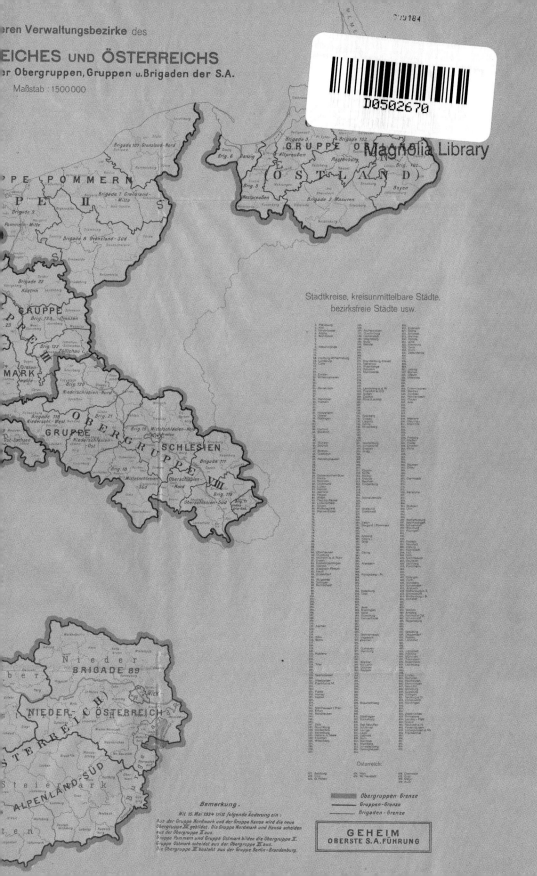

STORMTROOPERS

STORMTROOPERS

A New History of Hitler's Brownshirts

DANIEL SIEMENS

YALE UNIVERSITY PRESS
NEW HAVEN AND LONDON

For information about this and other Yale University Press publications, please contact:
U.S. Office: sales.press@yale.edu   yalebooks.com
Europe Office: sales@yaleup.co.uk   yalebooks.co.uk

Set in Adobe Caslon Pro by IDSUK (DataConnection) Ltd
Printed in Great Britain by TJ International Ltd, Padstow, Cornwall

Library of Congress Control Number: 2017943290

ISBN: 978-0-300-19681-8

A catalogue record for this book is available from the British Library.

10 9 8 7 6 5 4 3 2 1

MIX
Paper from
responsible sources
FSC® C013056

Don't comfort yourself with the fact that the present age is at fault. That it is in the wrong does not yet mean that we are in the right; its barbarity does not imply that we already behave as human beings, just because we do not agree with it.

— Boris Pasternak[1]

It is the experience of violence that unites people.

— Wolfgang Sofsky[2]

CONTENTS

PART IV

PLATES

1. 'Crushing pockets of Spartakists' (photograph, Munich 1919). © Bayerisches Hauptstaatsarchiv IV. [Bestand Freikorps und Höhere Stäbe 387/2]
2. Ernst Röhm in Bolivia (photograph, c. 1928). © Bundesarchiv-Berlin.
3. SA men at a party rally in Weimar (photograph, 1926). © Russian State Military Historical Archive.
4. SA men helping out on a local farm (photograph, 1928). © Russian State Military Historical Archive.
5. SA propaganda in the countryside (photograph, 1929). © Russian State Military Historical Archive.
6. Danzig stormtrooper (poster by Leo von Malotki, c. 1930). © Bundesarchiv-Bildarchiv. [Plak 003-004-023]
7. An SA-*Sturm* marching through the city of Spandau (photograph, 1932). © Bundesarchiv-Bildarchiv. [B 145 Bild P 049500]
8. 'Germany's autarky' by Erich Schilling. © bpk. [# 4849]
9. Advertisement for SA Cigarettes (poster, 1932). © Münchner Stadtmuseum, Sammlung Reklamekunst.
10. and 11. 'The Victory of Faith' and 'The Red Devil Rages' (two woodcuts by Richard Schwarzkopf, 1936), taken from Oberste SA-Führung (ed.), . . . *wurde die SA eingesetzt: Politische Soldaten erzählen von wenig beachteten Frontabschnitten unserer Zeit* (Munich: Eher, 1938).
12. SA boycott action in Cologne (photograph, 1933). © AKG images/Interfoto. [# 7-I1-556778]
13. SA 'sports' in the KZ Oranienburg (photograph, 1933). © Deutsches Historisches Museum, Berlin. [Inv. Nr. F88 527]

14. 'Arbeits-Kommando Schutzhaft-Lager Burg Hohnstein' (photograph, 1933). © Archiv Burg Hohnstein.

15. Selling SA dolls (photograph, December 1933). © Süddeutsche Zeitung Photo. [# 364913]

16. 'When German men part company' (drawing by Felix Hartlaub, 1934). © Hartlaub Family Archive/Melanie Hartlaub.

17. Viktor Lutze (photograph, July 1934). © Scherl/Süddeutsche Zeitung Photo. [# 14368]

18. SA party for children (photograph, 1935). © Scherl/Süddeutsche Zeitung Photo. [# 362978]

19. SA antisemitic propaganda in Recklinghausen, 18 August 1935. © United States Holocaust Memorial Museum, courtesy of Warren A. Gorrell. [# 80821]

20. SA men jumping off their horses (photograph). © AKG images. [AKG127254]

21. The wedding of an SA man (group photograph). © Staatsarchiv Sigmaringen. [N 1/68 Nr. 935]

22. Recording the noise of the SA boots (photograph, 15 August 1937). © Scherl/Süddeutsche Zeitung Photo. [# 365580]

23. *Reichswettkämpfe der SA* in Berlin (photograph, 17 July 1938). © Scherl/Süddeutsche Zeitung Photo. [# 362944]

24. SA men marching in the 'liberated' Sudetenland (photograph, 1938). © Bundesarchiv-Bildarchiv. [Bild 116-116-050]

25. *SA Staffellauf mit Luftschutzmaske* in Berlin (photograph, 2 April 1939). © Scherl/Süddeutsche Zeitung Photo. [# 362935]

26. 'This company is driving for the SA settlement free of charge' (photograph, c. 1937–8). © Stadtarchiv Rosenheim.

27. 'Postcard Bad Salzgitter' (c. 1940). Private collection.

28. Recruits of Feldherrnhalle units (photograph, 1941). © bpk. [# 50074765]

29. The SA general and diplomat Siegfried Kasche meets Istvan van Perceviv (photograph, 1941). © Bayerische Staatsbibliothek München/Bildarchiv. [Fotoarchiv Hoffmann. P6, no. Hoff-36272]

30. 'Melde Dich freiwillig zum Wehrdienst in der Panzer-Grenadierdivision Feldherrnhalle' (poster by Werner von Axster-Heudtlaß, 1944). © Bundesarchiv-Bildarchiv. [Plak 003-025-003]

31. Wilhelm Schepmann inspecting volunteers for the SA-unit 'Feldherrnhalle', February 1945. © AKG images. [00040702]

32. Election Poster of Hans Gmelin, 1954. © Alfred Göhner/Stadtarchiv Tübingen.

33. A caricature by Leo Haas of 'SA man Schröder' from 1957. © AKG images. [AKG1887603]

ACKNOWLEDGEMENTS

Although one individual author name appears on the cover of this book, it would never have been completed without the generous help and support from many colleagues, institutions, and friends. Work on this project started with an email I received on 18 April 2012 from Heather McCallum, back then publisher for trade books at Yale University Press. At that time, I was the DAAD Francis L. Carsten Lecturer for Modern German History at University College London's School of Slavonic and East European Studies (UCL-SSEES). Heather invited me to write a 'new authoritative history' of the SA in the English language, but it initially fell on deaf ears. 'The Brownshirts? Not again!' was my spontaneous reaction. However, after a period of consideration, I warmed to the idea, and soon after found myself immersed in archival documents and old newspapers. Looking for a particular book on the many shelves dedicated to the history of National Socialism became my surrogate sport.

During the past five years, I was fortunate enough to work at two excellent universities, University College London and Bielefeld University, which both provided ideal opportunities for intellectual debate and individual research. I am particularly grateful to Simon Dixon, Axel Körner, Michael Berkowitz, and Andreas Gestrich for their support in London and, later, back in Germany, to the members of my *Habilitationskommission* – Thomas Welskopp, Ingrid Gilcher-Holtey, Michael Wildt, Willibald Steinmetz, and Peter Schuster – who, in 2016, read and accepted an earlier version of this book as a habilitation dissertation. Thomas Welskopp, in particular, has been incredibly supportive over the past years, a brilliant historian and a true friend. For the opportunity to discuss aspects of this project at various universities, conferences, and workshops between 2013 and 2016, I am thankful to Arnd Bauerkämper, Frank Bösch, Hubertus Buchstein, Norbert Frei, Ulrike von Hirschhausen, Sylvia Kesper-Biermann, Gabriele Metzler, Markus M. Payk, Kim C. Priemel, Hedwig Richter, Martin Sabrow, Désirée Schauz, Dirk Schumann, Sybille Steinbacher, Nikolaus Wachsmann, Annette Weinke, Richard F. Wetzell, Michael Wildt, and Gerhard Wolf.

University College London, Bielefeld University, the Fritz-Thyssen-Stiftung, the Stiftung Mercator, and the North Rhine-Westphalian Academy of Sciences, Humanities and the Arts generously supported archival research for this project. I am very grateful to fellow historians Sebastian Panwitz and Jenny Fichmann for their expertise, time, and support in organizing rarely looked-at primary sources in Russia and the United States. Hauke Janssen and his team from the documentation department of the Spiegel publishing house in Hamburg provided an excellent working environment for some crucial days at the beginning of this project. At a later stage, a fellowship from Ludwig Maximilian University's Center for Advanced Studies, under the managing director Annette Meyer, allowed for detailed research in the archives and libraries of the Munich era.

Some of my ideas in this book have appeared in print elsewhere. Parts of chapter 10 are based on my article 'Writing the History of the SA at the International Military Tribunal: Legal Strategies and Long-Term Historiographical Consequences', which was published in the *Journal of Modern European History* in 2016. A slightly different version of chapter 7 has been accepted for publication in the *Journal of Genocide Research* in 2017. I am grateful to both journals for their permission to use these texts in modified form for my book.

It is impossible to name all friends, colleagues, and family members of former SA men who shared their knowledge and ideas on the Nazi period or helped in a multitude of ways in the completion of this book. I would like to thank Gleb Albert, Bojan Aleksov, Jörg Baberowski, Rüdiger Bergien, Robert Bierschneider, Stephanie Bird, Kirsten Bönker, Christina Brauner, Richard Butterwick-Pawlikowski, Bruce Campbell, Jan Daniluk, Herta Däubler-Gmelin, Stefan Dölling, Siglind Ehinger, Christiane Eisenberg, Ivona Fabris, Juan Luis Fernandez, Andreas Freitäger, Geraldine von Frijtag Drabbe Künzel, Mariola Fuerst, Vito Gironda, Michael Graupner, Barbara

Hachmann, Wolfgang Hardtwig, Melanie Hartlaub, Elisabeth Harvey, Daniel Hedinger, Susanne Heim, Lara Hensch, Benjamin C. Hett, Tom Hill, Stefan Hördler, Jochen Hung, Goran Hutinec, Melvyn Ingleby, Henning von Jagow, Mathilde Jamin, Volker Kasche, John Keyne, Egbert Klautke, Jonas Kleinhaus, Niklas Krahwinkel, Alexander Kranz, Christoph Kreutzmüller, Anja Kruke, Stefan Laffin, Stephan Lehnstaedt, Malte Ludin, Christoph Luther, Karl Lutze, Stephan Malinowski, Caroline Mezger, Dirk A. Moses, Yves Müller, Sönke Neitzel, Eduard Nižňanský, Armin Nolzen, Rainer Orth, Rudolf Paksa, Winfried Pätzold, Zuzana Pincikova, Jan-Philipp Pomplun, Sven Reichardt, Jana Remy, Thomas Reuß, Christiane Rothländer, Christian Schemmert, Markus Schmalzl, Mike Schmeitzner, Sabine Schroyen, Eckhard Steinmetz, Jens Thiel, Jutta Wiegmann, Tobias Winstel, Andreas Wirsching, Alexandre Zaljonov, and Benjamin Ziemann.

At Yale University Press in London, Heather McCallum, Melissa Bond, and Marika Lysandrou navigated this project with great enthusiasm through the stages of its *Buchwerdung*. Two anonymous reviewers provided careful and encouraging feedback that helped me shape crucial arguments made in the book. I am likewise extremely grateful to Sarah Vogelsong and Richard Mason, who, at different moments, carefully edited my manuscript and safeguarded its author from the linguistic traps a non-native speaker is prone to walking into. Finally, Marcel Krueger did not shy away from improving my translations of SA songs, despite their horrific lyrics. All remaining faults are, of course, my own.

Last but not least, this book benefited more than anything else from aspects of life that had nothing to do with history. Seeing my children taking their first steps and growing into personalities of their own kept me going, too. Jan, Emilia, and also Magdalena – my partner in crime – have witnessed the making of this book from close range. Despite my many hours of absence from home, they have remained cheerful and supportive throughout. I owe you more than I can possibly say.

Daniel Siemens
Bielefeld, January 2017

INTRODUCTION
A Night of Violence

*Countless images of the saints creep out of the bedroom's darkness; become
living caricatures and close in on him: half hostile, half preposterous.*
— August Scholtis, 1931[1]

In the East German province of Upper Silesia, 9 August 1932 was a cool
summer day, and the following night was unusually fresh. These were to
be the last hours of Konrad Pietrzuch,[2] an unemployed thirty-five-year-old
worker from Potempa, an obscure village in the Tost-Gleiwitz district that
boasted fewer than 1,000 residents and was located just three kilometres
from the Polish border. Here, Pietrzuch lived in a dilapidated hut that he
shared with his younger brother Alfons as well as their sixty-eight-year-old
mother, Maria. The walls of their home were decorated with holy pictures
but lacked any windows.[3]

All three were asleep when a group of men encircled the house in
the early hours of 10 August. These men came from the surrounding
villages and were members of the local branch of the National Socialist
Sturmabteilungen (SA), literally the 'storm detachments' or 'storm sections'
but better known as 'stormtroopers' or 'Brownshirts'. They stopped in front
of the Pietrzuch home, opened the unlocked door, and shouted: 'Get out of
bed, you cursed Polish Communists! Hands up!' Then the armed men
entered the house and, after pushing Maria out of the room, pulled Konrad
out of his bed and beat him savagely before one of them shot him in a

nearby cabin. Meanwhile, Alfons was forced to stand with his face to the wall and was beaten with equal severity, allegedly with a billiard cue or a truncheon. He suffered a serious head wound, which bled heavily, and lost consciousness for a time. According to his later testimony in court, the whole ordeal lasted half an hour. At nearly 2 a.m. the assailants finally drove away to the nearby village of Broslawitz, today's Zbrosławice in Poland. By that time, Konrad Pietrzuch was already dead.[4]

The autopsy report by forensic pathologist Dr Weimann revealed the brutality of the attack: the body of Konrad Pietrzuch, he found, was

all in all marked by 29 wounds, of which two were relatively unimportant. The corpse was extremely bruised around the neck. The outer carotid artery was completely shredded. The larynx displayed a large hole. Death resulted from suffocation as blood from the outer carotid artery poured through the larynx into the lungs. The deadly wound must have been inflicted to Pietrzuch while he was lying on the ground. In addition, the neck shows dermabrasion that is definitely the result of a kick. Apart from these wounds, Pietrzuch is battered all over his body. He has received heavy blows on his head with a dull-edged hatchet or a stick. Other wounds look like he was hit in the face with a billiard cue.[5]

Given the extent of these injuries, the authorities feared that Pietrzuch's maltreated body would immediately become an object of political interest. Consequently, after the crime became known, they confiscated his corpse in order to 'remove it from the eyes of the Communists' and prevent them from taking photographs of the body and using those for propaganda purposes.[6]

Although this crime was particularly savage, it was far from an isolated incident. In fact, a glance over the German newspapers from the summer of 1932 reveals daily lists of reports about Nazi attacks, largely on socialist and Communist workers, but also on Jews.[7] The liberal Jewish newspaper *CV-Zeitung* covered bomb and hand-grenade attacks in the Upper Silesian cities of Hindenburg (today's Zabrze), Gleiwitz (Gliwice), and Beuthen (Bytom) between 6 and 9 August 1932 alone.[8] Historians have described Nazi stormtroopers as engaging in a veritable 'terror campaign' through Silesia in the summer of 1932, following the Reichstag elections of 31 July that established the National Socialist German Workers' Party (NSDAP) as the nation's strongest party but did not lead to a Hitler-run government.[9]

The killing in Potempa quickly made nationwide headlines, thanks in large part to a new emergency decree 'against political terrorism' that had gone into effect at midnight on the night the attack was carried out.[10] Armed with this anti-terror legislation, and in a desperate attempt to stem the wave of everyday political violence that was rapidly becoming impossible to control, the government of Chancellor Franz von Papen requested the death penalty for the perpetrators of these politically motivated murders. Under the new law, those who committed political capital crimes were to be sentenced as soon as possible by newly established special courts. With this legislation, the already fragile German state attempted to insist on its monopoly on the use of force, but the message remained largely unheard and was the last attempt of its kind before the Weimar Republic finally collapsed a few months later.[11] Joseph Goebbels, since 1926 the leader (*Gauleiter*) of the regional branches of the NSDAP in Berlin and Brandenburg, rightly anticipated that this last effort would be in vain. On 10 August 1932, apparently not yet knowing about the Potempa murder, he wrote in his diary: 'Phone call from Berlin: new emergency decree with martial law ... But none of this will help anymore.'[12]

On 11 August, just one day after the murder was committed, the police arrested nine men on suspicion of murder: the miner and SA squad leader (*Scharführer*) August Gräupner (b. 1899); the pikeman and NSDAP member Rufin Wolnitza (b. 1907); the electrician Reinhold Kottisch (b. 1906); the SA troop leader and timekeeper (*Markenkontrolleur*) Helmuth-Josef Müller (b. 1898); a former police officer named Ludwig Nowak (b. 1891); and the miners Hippolit Hadamik (b. 1903) and Karl Czaja (b. 1894). They also arrested two innkeepers who had played a pivotal role in the crime: the SA man Paul Lachmann (b. 1893), who was also the municipal administrator (*Gemeindevorsteher*) of Potempa; and Georg Hoppe (b. 1889), who ran an SA tavern in the nearby village of Tworog.[13] Four other participants, including Paul Golombek, a local butcher and probably one of the main culprits, had already fled.[14] As these men's dates of birth and professions indicate, the attackers represented a fairly typical cross section of Upper Silesian men aged twenty-five to forty-three. According to historian Richard Bessel, a specialist on the Nazis' rise to importance in Silesia, the leaders of the attack at least 'had fairly solid middle-class occupations', indicating how 'naturally' the middle classes perceived, carried out, and justified violent attacks and even political murder in the region.[15]

All of those detained stood trial in front of the Beuthen special court between 19 and 22 August 1932. The historian Henning Grunwald has described the infighting at the Potempa trial between the National Socialist Lawyers' Association, which was under the control of Hans Frank, later the Governor General in Cracow, and the newly established 'legal advice bureau' (*Rechtsabteilung*) of the SA, which was headed by the top SA lawyer Walter Luetgebrune, as a 'veritable beauty contest'.[16] Given the prominence of the case, both Frank and Luetgebrune used all means available to prevail, including intimidating their rivals and local Nazi lawyers and bestowing gifts on the defendants to win their favour. This infighting was ultimately to the detriment of the accused, as the rivalry of the Nazi jurists 'made a smooth and effective provision of legal aid virtually impossible'.[17]

The judges established a version of the crime that was highly plausible, thanks to detailed testimonies of witnesses and the accused and the well-known political attitudes of the defendants. This chronology indicated that in the early hours of the evening of 9 August 1932, Nowak, the leader of SA-*Sturm* 26 in Broslawitz, had arranged for a group of SA men to carry out acts of political violence that would 'terrorize the region'.[18] This group then drove to Hoppe's tavern in nearby Tworog, another notorious Nazi meeting spot. Hoppe, *Sturmführer* of SA-*Sturm* 27 in Tworog, provided the men with additional weapons and instructed them to go to Potempa. There, the local innkeeper, Lachmann, served them large quantities of alcohol and cigarettes. Together with his friend, the butcher Golombek, Lachmann also apparently provided the names of four individuals to be attacked that night.[19] Pietrzuch was on the hit list. By sheer coincidence, the attack on him was the only one that proved fatal. In the course of the night, the heavily intoxicated Nazis approached two other houses as well, but they were unsuccessful in carrying out further attacks.

Lachmann later claimed that the murder expedition against the well-known but harmless troublemaker Pietrzuch was undertaken only partly because of 'political' reasons. Personal motives also came into play. Not only had Pietrzuch apparently insulted guests repeatedly at Lachmann's tavern, a local Nazi hangout, and supported Polish insurgents in previous years,[20] but the innkeeper also feared that Pietrzuch would publicly reveal his regular poaching trips to nearby forests.[21] A Communist pamphlet additionally claimed that Lachmann, in his role as municipal administrator, had denied the unemployed Pietrzuch brothers social benefits.[22] In this situation, 'political ' and 'personal' motives were inextricably linked, as was the case with so many violent incidents in the late Weimar Republic.

On 22 August 1932 the Beuthen special court sentenced five of the attackers to death: Lachmann because of 'incitement for political homicide' (*Anstiftung zum politischen Totschlag*) and Kottisch, Wolnitza, Gräupner, and Müller for 'homicide committed out of political motives'. Hoppe received a prison sentence of two years for 'abetment to dangerous bodily injury'. The remaining three culprits (Hadamik, Czaja, and Nowak) were acquitted.[23] The defendants reacted with shouts of '*Heil Hitler!*' and 'Down with the justice system!'[24] During the trial they had shown a surprisingly 'nonchalant and almost lively humour' in the courtroom, as press reports emphasized. They had greeted several Nazi officials who attended the trial, among them the notorious Silesian SA leader Edmund Heines, with Fascist salutes, and they did not seem overly bothered by the threat of capital punishment. A local Nazi newspaper expressed support for such behaviour by claiming that if the court 'should dare pass a single death sentence', a storm of protest would be raised throughout the nation.[25] This prediction proved true, at least on a local level and within particular segments of society: the verdict provoked fierce protests and some local acts of rebellion among the National Socialist supporters who had gathered in the streets around the courthouse in order to put pressure on the judges. The correspondent of the London *Times* covering the case reported that 'the disturbances around the Court became so serious that police wearing steel helmets and armed with carbines and automatic pistols were called out'. With the support of SA units that had arrived from the Silesian capital of Breslau, the Nazis, at least on that particular day, dominated the streets in Beuthen – not only in the vicinity of the court, but also in more remote areas of the town, where the windows of several shops and of a Socialist newspaper building were smashed. Jewish shopkeepers closed down their businesses and put up their shutters.[26]

After the verdict, the Silesian SA leader Heines, who since September 1930 had also served as a member of the Reichstag for the NSDAP, loudly predicted that 'the German people will soon render other sentences'. The Beuthen judgement, he added, would become a beacon of hope for the German awakening.[27] Several hours later he repeated this message from the balcony of a nearby café to a crowd of followers.[28] Heines felt at ease in his self-declared role of judge. Twelve years earlier, in 1920, when he had been a member of the *Arbeitsgemeinschaft Roßbach*, an infamous *Freikorps* unit fighting in West Prussia and the Baltic countries, he had 'judged' and executed an alleged traitor. Although the German courts ultimately sentenced him to a prison term of five years for this crime in May 1929, Heines – who had quickly regained his liberty after providing a bail of 5,000 reichsmark – soon afterwards proudly identified himself at an NSDAP party rally at the Berlin Sports Palace as a '*Feme* judge', or a 'judge' in a kangaroo court.[29]

After the national election of 31 July 1932, the NSDAP became the largest political party in the German Reichstag. Its leader, Adolf Hitler, turned the local events in Upper Silesia into a political attack on the national government. Several hours after the verdict in Beuthen became known, Hitler sent a telegram in which he declared his 'unreserved loyalty' to the attackers and condemned the death sentences as a 'most outrageous blood verdict'. Officially addressing the five men sentenced to death, he aimed to reach out to Nazi followers more broadly when he sharply criticized von Papen's conservative government and declared a revision of the verdict a national necessity: 'From now on, your freedom is a question of honour for all of us, and to fight against the Government which has rendered possible such a verdict is our duty.'[30] Hermann Göring likewise sent a telegram of encouragement to the condemned men and provided 1,000 reichsmark to their families. The SA Chief of Staff Ernst Röhm even travelled to Beuthen and visited the SA men in prison.[31]

The Nazi leaders' open defence of the Potempa murderers, although their crime caused widespread indignation and outrage in Germany as well as in the international press, becomes more intelligible by looking at the extensive 'proclamation' Hitler had printed in his name in the official Nazi paper *Der Völkische Beobachter* on 24 August 1932. With even more than his usual exaggeration, he claimed:

More than 300 massacred – one could literally say, butchered – party comrades number among our dead martyrs. Tens of thousands and even more tens of thousands have been injured . . . Only when the cup began to run over and the terror of the red bands of organized murderers and criminals became unbearable did von Papen's 'National Government' rouse itself to take action . . . Whoever of you harbours sentiments to fight for the honour and freedom of the nation will understand why I refuse to join this bourgeois Government . . . We shall liberate the word 'national' from the grip of an objectivity whose real innermost essence is inflamed by the judgement passed in Beuthen against national Germany. Herr von Papen has thus engraved his name in German history with the blood of national fighters.[32]

Joseph Goebbels, already notorious for his defamatory attacks on the political opponents, added another characteristic note to the Nazi propaganda in the Potempa case: antisemitism. In a leading article for *Der Angriff*, the capital's Nazi newspaper that he himself had founded in 1927 and edited thereafter, Goebbels printed in bold letters: 'The Jews are guilty.'[33] He repeated this slogan over and over again but did not establish any logical connection between the crime and his charge. Goebbels's strategy was as simple as it was effective among Nazi followers: he deflected their feelings of anger and frustration with the verdict, as well as with the political and economic situation more broadly, onto the usual scapegoat, the Jews. Goebbels went so far as to threaten them with violence: 'The hour will come when the Executive of the State will have other duties to fulfil than to protect from the wrath of the people those who have betrayed the people.'[34] In reaction to such slander and calls for pogrom, the authorities suspended the publication of *Der Angriff* for a week, but with no lasting effect.

By twisting the facts and using them to form an explicit political threat, Hitler and his entourage reached out to millions of his followers, and in particular the SA, who in the summer of 1932 expected an immediate seizure of power, not further sitting on the fence. Under such a weight of expectation, the Nazi leadership speculated that, in a political climate marked by fundamental ideological conflict and mutual hatred, not too many people would care about the fate of a simple worker, especially one who was supposedly a former Polish insurgent.[35] Hitler could count on his stormtroopers to perpetrate new bloody run-ins every day.[36] Under the circumstances, the details of the Potempa murder would be quickly forgotten and only their political interpretations would survive. The Nazi Party and its press made every effort to shift the blame for the Potempa murder onto the victim, the Communist movement, or the 'Judeo-Marxist system' more generally.[37] The following poem, allegedly written by an ordinary member of the SA and printed in a Silesian Nazi paper in early September 1932, illustrates the interchange of roles perfectly:

Beuthen!

Beuthen! It stands there on the horizon.
Still gleaming red and fresh.
Beuthen! Five comrades accuse
And what's lurking behind them is death.

Germany! Don't you hear their threats?
Not the millions' shout?
It sounds through the streets, it roars through the land:
We want our comrades out!

An army is marching for their freedom,
Bound together by blood.
One leader, one faith and one banner,
Sustained by fealty and pluck.

The faith in people and fatherland.
The loyalty for the leader, our stand.
The bravery of the fighting brown dead,
Falling in towns and throughout the land.[38]

It is hard to imagine a more complete conversion: the real victim of the crime, the murdered Pietrzuch, was eliminated for a second time, now rhetorically, whereas the five murderers sentenced to death were elevated to heroes, extolled as brave men who were faithful to the Nazi cause and allegedly were supported by millions of fellow countrymen. The excuses put forth for this reaction by leading Nazis are telling of what the British journalist F. A. Voigt in 1932 called the 'terrible barbarisation of German political life'.[39] According to one article in the Nazi press, the murdered Pietrzuch was a 'Polish rogue' and a 'sub-human' who had 'long ago forfeited the right to live on German soil'.[40] In similar terms, the writer and Nazi ideologue Alfred Rosenberg, known to the wider public as the author of the book *The Myth of the 20th Century*, published in Germany in 1930, justified the killing of Pietrzuch as an act of lynching – a practice he decribed as the 'only possible corrective to an unnatural law'. In the United States, Rosenberg explained, there is 'formal equality between the white man and the negro, but in practice there is a differential treatment'. The Nordic German was called upon to make similar and potentially lethal distinctions between 'Aryans', Slavs, and Jews.[41]

Nevertheless, the leadership of the Nazi Party was in serious trouble in the autumn of 1932. If the SA men sentenced to death were executed, the situation would become 'unbearable', Goebbels wrote in his diary.[42] In that event, he feared that the pressure from the impatient Nazi following would become so strong that an open confrontation with the authorities, termed by Hitler the 'guillotine Government', might become inescapable.[43] Regardless of the outcome of such a confrontation, this would have ended the alleged legal character of the Nazis' rise to power. Luckily for them, the Prussian *Staatsministerium*, which after the coup of 20 July 1932 (*Preußenschlag*) had fallen into the hands of the Catholic reactionary von Papen, gave in to pressure from various nationalist groups and altered the death sentences to lifelong imprisonment beginning on 2 September 1932.[44] The Nazi Party was thus able to maintain the pretence of being devoted to the rule of law.

Borderland Mentalities

The Potempa murder was a rather typical case for the period in that it linked the hardships of the immediate post-First World War period to the SA violence of the early 1930s. In many respects, these earlier grievances shaped the later patterns of violence within the nationalist faction in Germany as well as in some other central and eastern European states.[45] With regard to the actual crime, the close collaboration between the SA and other nationalist organizations in the region was key. The two youngest attackers sentenced to death, Reinhold Kottisch and Rufin Wolnitza, were in fact not yet officially SA men, but members of the Upper Silesian Self-Defence force (*Oberschlesischer Selbstschutz*). Both organizations overlapped heavily in the early 1930s, as can be seen from the fact that at least Wolnitza was also a member of the NSDAP.[46] Up to the time of their imprisonment, both men had lived in the 'SA home' in Broslawitz, where they engaged in paramilitary training that focused on the occupation of streets and forest edges, preparing for shooting battles, and the build-up of attacks by shock troops.[47]

The Upper Silesian Self-Defence force was an officially tolerated paramilitary organization created after the First World War to fight against the

Poles in this highly contested borderland region between the German Reich and the re-established Polish state.[48] In the autumn of 1918, the Poles had initially demanded that the whole area of Upper Silesia, a region developed since the nineteenth century into one of the German Reich's industrial centres because of its rich natural coal reserves, be integrated into the new Polish state. Leading politicians as well as the public in Germany bitterly opposed this idea, insisting on national self-determination and putting forward the argument that the area was, regardless of a strong Polish ethnic element, predominantly German. They further claimed that these territories were indispensable for their national economy, which had been badly hit as a result of the recent military defeat.[49] Three Polish uprisings between 1919 and 1921, inspired by the strong missionary zeal to 're-Polonize' the diverse population of the region, did not help to calm the passions running high in the towns and villages of Upper Silesia.[50]

The activities of German *Freikorps* militia, commanded by men like Peter von Heydebreck, Hermann Ehrhardt, Wilfried von Loewenfeld, and Horst von Petersdorff, further increased hostilities. These militias not only engaged in fighting with the Poles but also persecuted alleged German traitors, thus demonstrating that not only linguistic and ethnic but also political boundaries were highly contested.[51] The founder of the so-called 'special police' of the Upper Silesian Self-Defence force, Heinz Oskar Hauenstein, who later became one of the first members of the Berlin SA, claimed in a 1928 trial that his organization had been responsible for more than 200 '*Feme* murders'. The term *Feme*, alluding to a medieval Germanic practice of penalization, was used in interwar Germany to designate the political murder of a 'traitor' by perpetrators from the extreme right.[52] German *Freikorps* also summarily executed numerous alleged Polish spies.[53] One former *Freikorps* man later declared cynically, 'We actually spared the bullets when killing this riffraff.'[54] However, in a 1922 bill of indictment against members of the *Freikorps* Ehrhardt Brigade, even the Reich prosecutor in Leipzig described the anti-Polish efforts of the German militia sympathetically as acts of legitimate self-defence. He regarded them as necessary to fight off Polish attacks that were intended to 'smash the state and economic order in Germany' and were carried out 'with the help of foreign powers'. In these statements, the Reich prosecutor alluded to decisions made by the Inter-Allied Control Commission, which was widely accused of pro-Polish sympathies in Germany after the First World War.[55]

These currents of the immediate post-war years still reverberated in the nationalist and strongly anti-Polish sentiments of the Upper Silesian SA in the early 1930s. The group's firm anti-democratic convictions tied in with older, well-established political beliefs in the region. Many ethnic Germans shared widespread frustration with the supposedly lenient stance of the Weimar governments on questions of national security and in particular with regard to the defence of the German border to the east.[56] To a certain extent, the Upper Silesian SA was successful in passing itself off as a legitimate successor to the former *Freikorps* units.[57] Its rhetoric drew heavily on such comparisons, and was propagated by leading men of the extreme right like Manfred von Killinger, a former *Freikorps* leader who later joined the SA.[58] In particular, in regions close to the German frontier, the SA units presented themselves as veritable border guards, called to defend national unity against the Czechs and Poles in the east and the French in the west (Plate 6).[59] The effects of such a borderland mentality were not confined to the SA alone, as the following example illustrates. After the Nazis took power, the National Socialist Teachers' League (*Nationalsozialistischer Lehrerbund*) in Silesia repeatedly organized 'training camps' for its members. These two-week-long courses were designed to raise the 'border-consciousness' of German teachers, which was defined as the racial and historical awareness of Silesia's particular role within the 'pan-German East'.[60] Since the early 1920s, many teachers had been profoundly hostile to Poland and its protecting power, France. Now, they proudly boasted of their alleged 'German frontier perspective' and passed these attitudes and ideas onto their disciples.[61]

This mental orientation, which has not yet received enough attention in the existing research on the SA,[62] was indeed one of the most important ideological drivers that guaranteed the SA's identity up to 1945. In particular, in light of the German expansionist policies since the mid-1930s that chronologically coincided with the profound crisis of the SA following the 'Night of the Long Knives' (30 June–2 July 1934), the self-image of the SA as an organization that promoted 'Germanness' – through paramilitary training, physical exercise, ideological education, and later active fighting in the Second World War – became key. Starting in the late 1930s, at the latest, this held true well beyond the boundaries of the Reich. The high numbers of ethnic Germans who joined the SA in the Sudetenland and the Memel region between 1937 and 1939 testifies to the SA's lasting appeal, at least in regions that were to be integrated into the Reich.[63]

The history of the SA after the Nazi takeover of power in late January 1933 remained one of violence, hatred, and fighting. With regard to the Potempa case, already on 23 March, as the first political prisoners filled the newly erected concentration camps in Oranienburg, Dachau, and elsewhere, Hitler had the condemned SA murderers released from prison.[64] These former inmates were now 'acclaimed jubilantly' by the Upper Silesian press, complained the Union of Poles in Upper Silesia in October 1933 in a petition to the League of Nations. Since murderers were now officially treated as heroes, the Union claimed, the Polish minority had lost all sense of security.[65] The following years would confirm and even exceed its most pessimistic fears. Reflecting on the history of violence and bloodshed in Upper Silesia, the writer August Scholtis – an Upper Silesian native from the village of Bolatiz, today's Czech Bolatice – wrote gloomily in his 1959 autobiography: 'In this region, Middle Europe still seems to be in the Middle Ages. From generation to generation, the individual human being is torn apart between the Prussian and the Polish state borders here. People are interchangeably deprived of their free will by both sides; they are bullied, hunted down, looted or simply slaughtered along the roadsides.'[66]

The two decades following the Potempa murder of 1932 were no exception to this pattern. On the contrary, the Nazi takeover of power and the party's policy of enforced conformity through coercion were carried out with an extreme level of violence, not least in Lower and Upper Silesia. Several years later, the German-Polish borderlands and the territories farther east became lands of mass murder and genocide, the 'bloodlands' of the Second World War.[67] The SA, as will be demonstrated in this book, was among the organizations responsible for this radicalization of ethnic and political hatred. Taking up Ian Kershaw's dictum that in Nazi Germany violence was 'built into the system',[68] one might equally say that violence was built into the SA – not only as a means of actual behaviour, but also as a core element of its propaganda, the socialization of its members, and, finally, the establishment of a National Socialist identity.

Ruffians, Killers, Political Hooligans

Although excessive, the Potempa murder was just one of hundreds of politically motivated crimes that shocked Germany between 1927 and 1932, a foretaste of the systematic persecution of political opponents and other alleged enemies that would follow in the wake of the establishment of the Third Reich in 1933–4. Every one of these crimes helped unsettle the public's faith in the capability of the Weimar Republic to fight successfully against the increasing wave of political terror. The Republic was a fragile democracy but by no means doomed to fail from its inception in 1919.[69] Although the Nazi SA was not the only paramilitary organization to engage in violent clashes with opponents, its contribution to the rise of political violence was significant, both in quantitative and in qualitative terms.[70] On the eve of the national elections of 31 July 1932, tensions escalated. In June and July 1932 alone, politically linked street riots, shootings, brawls, and assassinations in Germany caused the deaths of more than 300 people and injured more than 1,000.[71] Within a political climate verging on civil war, the Potempa murder would probably not have made more than local headlines had it not been the first political felony to occur after President Hindenburg's emergency decree on political terrorism came into effect.

The Potempa murder case contains many of the elements on which I will elaborate in the following chapters: the forms and motives of the SA's political violence, the reaction of the democratic state vis-à-vis the increasing threat from the National Socialists, and their exploitation of border disputes between Germans and their neighbours that stretched back to the nineteenth century. After the National Socialists took power in 1933, the SA remained the party's Praetorian Guard and, at least according to the official propaganda, the embodiment of its values, attitudes, and readiness for combat. The individual SA man was expected to represent the 'most ideal National Socialist type'[72] and as such was propagated as a role model for (male) German youth, building in part on the *Freikorps* myth but also incorporating newer trends commonly associated with muscular Christianity and the 'conservative revolution' in Germany around 1930.[73] However, the murder of SA Chief of Staff Ernst Röhm and several dozen of his followers between 30 June and 2 July 1934 in the infamous 'Night of the Long Knives' considerably hampered the SA's ambitions to shape the politics of the Third Reich. According to the historiographical consensus, these events reduced the stormtroopers to a 'second-line propaganda group within the movement' for the remaining eleven years of the Third Reich.[74]

Against this well-known background, a new study on the SA does not necessarily need justification, but certainly an explanation of its intention, scope, and methodological approach appears to be necessary. This book will demonstrate not only that the narrative of the SA's rise and fall as outlined above is incomplete, but that it obscures the Brownshirts' deep and long-term effect on large numbers of Germans living in the Third Reich, an effect that lasted even longer than Nazi rule. The SA was, in the words of American sociologist Lewis A. Coser, a 'greedy institution', an organization characterized by 'omnivorous' demands on its members yet based on volun-tary compliance, loyalty, and commitment. Such organizations attempt to 'encompass within their circle the whole personality'.[75] The SA throughout the Third Reich remained an important organization for forming German men according to the regime's needs and wishes, but it also allowed the rank-and-file stormtrooper to participate in the Nazi project.[76] In this sense, the SA was highly relevant politically until 1945 – a contention that runs counter to the mainstream historiography on the SA, which emphasizes its fundamental loss of power and influence after the 'Night of the Long Knives' in 1934 and considers the SA in its later years an organization that was numerically still considerable, but politically irrelevant. To take up Hans Mommsen's famous interpretation of the course of Nazi politics as a 'cumulative radicalisation', particularly regarding its attitude toward the extermination of the Jews,[77] the existing literature of the later SA may be summarized as suggesting a cumulative banalization.

This assessment is misleading as it conveys the impression that the SA after 1934 was solely geared toward promoting a kind of nostalgic drinking companionship – an argument initially put forward by many SA activists after the war. Such a view ignores important activities that the SA performed in the pre-war years of the Third Reich, including its antisemitic violence, which peaked in the summer of 1935 and again in June and November 1938; its contributions to the Second World War; and its role in stabilizing the Nazi regime within Germany and the occupied territories well into the last weeks of Nazi rule. The following study therefore covers the entire period from 1921, when Nazi *Sturmabteilungen* were organized in Munich for the first time, until 1945, when they ceased to operate in the context of the ultimate collapse of the German war effort.[78] Furthermore, the situation of transitional justice in the German zones of occupation, as well as within the jurisdiction of the two German states founded in 1949, will be explored inasmuch as it deals with the SA and its crimes. I will argue that the courts decisively influenced the way in which the history of the stormtroopers was written during the first decades after the Second World War.

Finally, the SA's importance within a comprehensive social history, or *Gesellschaftsgeschichte*, of National Socialism will be reassessed.

Given the myriad studies that exist on the history of National Socialism, the Third Reich, the Second World War, and the Holocaust – fields that no individual researcher can claim to know in all their detail any longer[79] – the number of works that concentrate on the SA is surprisingly limited. With the exception of the controversy surrounding the SA's social appeal and the composition of its membership – as predominantly working class or middle class – the existing studies are quite uniform when it comes to interpreting the organization.[80] They overwhelmingly concentrate on the years from the mid-1920s to 1934, with a clear focus on the forms and consequences of SA activism.[81] An early and characteristic if unusually lively example of historical judgement is Ernst Niekisch's assessment of the stormtroopers in his book *Reich of the Menial Demons* (*Das Reich der niederen Dämonen*), published in the Federal Republic of Germany in 1953. As Niekisch wrote:

> The SA was a counter-elite; it attracted all those characters who were rotten and frail from within. In the SA, all criminal inclinations were let loose. The SA barracks were dens of vice; there were work-shy individuals, drunkards, losers [*Lebensbankrotteure*], homosexuals, ruffians and killers who hatched their sinister attacks by which Germany should be 'awakened'. The human quality of this brown heap, in which the sons of the German bourgeoisie were trained in gangland methods, illustrated the desolate human decline of the German middle classes.[82]

The former 'National Bolshevik' Niekisch, whom the Nazis had imprisoned in 1937, was later appointed a professor of sociology at East Berlin's Humboldt University. His personal anger at and hatred of the Nazis coincided with contemporary political doctrines, at least with regard to the stormtroopers. Both the educated West Germans and the Socialist establishment in the east regarded the SA men's violence and lack of morality as a cornerstone of Fascist rule, albeit for somewhat different reasons. In the Federal Republic, SA violence was often used to delegitimize National Socialism as a perverted political ideology and the 'rule of the mob'. The undertone of this claim was clearly apologist, as this image contrasted negatively with the alleged attempts of the middle classes to 'soften' the Nazi excesses. One might say that the stormtroopers were portrayed as 'fanatical Nazis' against whom even

supporters of the regime and regular party members could be compared positively. At best, the members of the latter group could now perceive themselves
to be 'tactical' or 'upright' Nazis. In the Communist East, the situation was
more ambivalent: in the immediate post-war years, SA violence that had been
committed in the early 1930s was severely persecuted, at times in show trials,
particularly when it had been directed against Communists. However,
attempts to win over the mass of former Brownshirts for the benefit of the
new socialist state prevailed, beginning in the early 1950s, and criminal persecution diminished accordingly. In both parts of Germany, disdain dominated,
at least until the 1970s. For the influential journalist and author Joachim Fest,
to quote a respected conservative intellectual in the West, the SA was a barely
disguised criminal mob, a 'racket with a political slant' (*Ringverein mit poli-
tischem Akzent*).[83] The historian Hans Buchheim in 1965 similarly regarded
the 'SA rowdies' as the 'most reprobated form of a perverted soldierly tradition' (*verkommenste Form einer abartigen soldatischen Tradition*),[84] and the
American historian William L. Shirer even claimed that many of the SA
leaders were 'notorious homosexual perverts'.[85]

However, such damning assessments tell us more about the preferences
of post-war historiography than about social realities in the SA. In sharp
contrast to these judgements, a 1931 internal police memorandum 'on the
fighting principles of radical organisations' emphasized that there was
'undoubtedly a lot of valuable *Menschmaterial*' among the stormtroopers,
who were led by 'highly qualified leaders'.[86] Karl Otto Paetel, a 'national
revolutionary' during the late Weimar years who survived the Third Reich
in exile and later introduced the West Germans to American beatnik poets,
formulated an intermediary position. He rightly emphasized as early as
1965 that the difficulty in writing about the stormtroopers would be to not
content oneself with a reconstruction of the SA's 'administrative schemes'
and orders. Instead, Paetel thought it paramount to convincingly explain
how, under such an 'administrative heap', two types of SA men could come
into existence and coexist: the 'idealists' and those he described as possessing
the 'jungle mentality of sadist hooligans'.[87] This is still a difficult task for
the historian, particularly because in the SA 'idealists' and 'sadists' – to stick
to Paetel's terminology for the moment – were hard to distinguish and
sometimes not identifiable at all.

Since the 1970s, several important studies on the SA that took up
this challenge have appeared in print. Whereas the aforementioned earlier

literature usually emphasized the 'criminal character' of the SA – admittedly, an important task of popular pedagogy in Germany, given the fact that until the late 1950s many Germans still regarded National Socialism as a good idea that had unfortunately gone wrong[88] – the authors of these new studies took a closer look at the social composition, mentalities, and political organization of the SA. Pioneering works – by Peter Merkl on the self-images of the stormtroopers, by Mathilde Jamin on the SA leadership corps and its problems after the so-called 'Röhm purge', and by Richard Bessel on the rise and the political violence of the SA in Silesia prior to 1933 – became cornerstones upon which recent research still builds. Peter Longerich's seminal political history of the SA, published in 1989, marks the provisional end point of this renewed interest during the 1970s and 1980s.[89]

From the 1990s onward, three different types of research on the SA have emerged. First, there have been a range of works that combine social historical approaches with more recent attempts to write histories of violence, often from a praxeological and micro-historical perspective, and at times even with a deliberate comparative design. These investigations stress that the SA units constituted 'communities of violence' (*Gewaltgemeinschaften*) that preached a particular 'way of life' in which excess and discipline complemented each other.[90] Sven Reichardt's imposing dissertation from 2002 comparing the German SA with the Italian *Squadristi* stands out as a particularly influential work of this school of thought.[91] Second, important aspects of the SA's history have also been analysed in the many regional and local studies dealing with the Nazi takeover of power, as well as in historical studies on the German police, the judiciary, and the early concentration camps.[92] In addition, books have appeared in which family members explore the past of those relatives with an 'SA career'. Largely based on ego-documents, these books often contain relevant information about the motives that individuals had for their commitment to the stormtroopers – information that is rarely documented in state archives.[93] Third, there have been increasing numbers of studies that are informed by the new cultural history. The authors of these studies take a vivid interest in the 'body images' of the men in the SA and SS, and analyse National Socialist rituals and symbols, particularly the death cult that has been so characteristic of Fascist ideologies.[94] Others explore the gendered dimension of interwar paramilitarism, scrutinize the cliché of the 'gay Nazi', or re-examine the relations between Nazi activists and the various Churches.[95]

New Perspectives

Although the SA can hardly be characterized as an understudied subject, no comprehensive account of its history and development has been attempted so far. This book attempts to fill this lacuna, not only by weaving the numerous loose ends together, but also through its presentation of information drawn from archival research in more than a dozen state, regional, and local archives in several countries, producing a more multi-dimensional and balanced view than has hitherto been presented.[96] This investigation aims to provide the first comprehensive history of the stormtroopers that combines extensive archival research with a thorough analysis of existing studies in order to reassess the SA's importance in the history of the Third Reich and Western modernity more generally.

Several points underline the importance of this study. First, as mentioned above, the history of the SA has been thoroughly researched only for the period up to the summer of 1934. Despite Bruce Campbell's pioneering article urging scholars not to overlook the later SA that was published more than twenty years ago, only a few historians have followed his call.[97] This has had consequences. I will argue that the historians' concentration on the SA's violence in the second half of the Weimar Republic – the *Systemzeit*, as the Nazis derogatorily called it – helped obscure two issues: (1) the fact that the SA not only survived the 'Night of the Long Knives' but even managed to have a partial comeback in the late 1930s; and (2) the extent to which this organization helped the Nazis to permeate German society. In 1939 the SA still comprised more than 1.3 million men – roughly three times as many as in 1932.[98] Violent mobilization and disciplinary integration into the SA were features of the Nazi *Volksgemeinschaft*, or 'people's community', until 1945. Over the past decade, historians of modern Germany have vigorously debated the appropriateness of this term and the nature of the society it designated, agreeing at least that the *Volksgemeinschaft* was a highly popular political promise, but never a social reality. However, the participants in this debate have not paid much attention to the stormtroopers. Against this background, the present study is not only an empirical contribution to this debate but also a critical comment on its mode of discussion and preliminary results.[99]

Second, then, this comprehensive view, which encompasses the SA's history in the Weimar Republic *and* in the Third Reich, enables us to see the SA more clearly than has hitherto been possible in a comparative and transnational context.[100] Not only the early years of the SA's existence have to be seen against the background of the White Terror in large parts of post-First World War central Europe and Mussolini's successful takeover of power in Italy in 1922. Beyond this, the increasingly transnational dimension of the SA in the 1930s – including the appearance of the so-called 'Austrian Legion', a branch of the SA that consisted of Austrian Nazis who had taken shelter in the Reich prior to the *Anschluss* of 1938,[101] and the geographical extension of the SA from the late 1930s onward into the territories annexed to the Nazi Empire – must also be acknowledged. By 1942, SA units existed not only in the territory of the former Czechoslovakian state, but also in Alsace, Slovenia, the Warthegau and the General Government in occupied Poland. The history of the SA in these regions is virtually unknown and allows us to gain important insights into the problems of 'Germanization', defined as the transformation of individuals from these regions into 'proper' Germans – as deemed by the Nazis' cultural and racial standards. My analysis thus also adds to an excellent body of studies that have focused on the SS, the Foreign Office, and the several agencies concerned with German settlement questions.[102] With regard to the 'SA diplomats', the German envoys from the highest ranks of the SA who were appointed to posts in southeastern European vassal states in the early 1940s, this book demonstrates that SA generals even had influence over Germany's foreign policy. They were experts in violence who were directly concerned with the implementation of the Holocaust.

Third, although the level of physical violence in which the SA was involved was certainly high, particularly in the excessive year of 1933, it does not stand out on an international scale – at least in comparison to the different cases of extreme mass violence in the twentieth century.[103] The SA is, however, a particularly useful example in scrutinizing what made and what makes the use of violence so attractive to young men in particular environments and times. Not only is violence a fact of human life, but its exercise also comes with considerable advantages and is thus often employed in a manner that is 'purposively rational'.[104] In the face of a capitalist modernity that not only produces economic winners and losers but also largely prevents the individual from experiencing feelings of excitement and belonging, the use of violence can provide key benefits, as the German philosopher and literary scholar Jan Philipp Reemtsma has recently argued.[105] It is a kind of exit strategy, in that middle-class considerations based on careful planning and subordination to an allegedly universally binding morality are replaced by feelings of liberation (to destroy), individual empowerment, and momentous gains, both material and spiritual. Violence therefore allows for a specific form of pleasure that is particularly attractive at times when alternatives become, or seem to become, less likely to materialize in the foreseeable future.[106] Consequently, political thinkers like Karl Marx and Friedrich Engels who did not believe in the reform of capitalism embraced revolutionary violence as the 'midwife of history' and as a legitimate 'tool' for new social movements in their attempts to destroy ossified political forms.[107] One can generalize from this point: if the temporary empowerment of individuals through violence can be justified as a way of serving higher ends – such as by rendering service to a nation or by doing God's will (or, ideally, both) – the actors of such barely restrained but self-legitimized violence will also profit from a relatively stable alternative group identity that is not necessarily weaker than the more established moral order they are fighting.[108]

Two Sides of Violence

As this book will demonstrate, the stormtroopers' use of violence was in many ways such a purposively rational and self-empowering choice. However, the possession of dangerous weapons that not only scare opponents but also serve to elevate their users into an identity constructed in sharp contrast to the mainstream society and its values, and an elaborate and highly skilful system of propaganda that encourages the violent individual to perceive himself or herself as a modern crusader for the nation and God, empowered to legitimately fight unbelievers, or even on behalf of mankind – all this was not exclusive to SA men of the 1920s and 1930s. Obviously, this is a history book on a particular organization and its members within the framework of a distinct period, and as such it cannot be considered a long-term study that systematically compares forms and regimes of violence until the present day. Yet, despite this reservation, the history of the SA is in many respects paradigmatic of the way politics, media coverage, violence, and grassroots activism were interwoven in the twentieth century.

Such a broad focus requires methodological rigour, and thus some additional methodological explanations are needed here. The focus of my book is on violence and its personal, strategic, and cultural implications, but it also concerns the integrating power that an organization like the SA was able to wield. I will pay particular attention to processes of violent mobilization and disciplinary integration. With regard to the stormtroopers, both phenomena were inextricably linked. The Nazi movement not only used violence as a means to mobilize its supporters and to fight its enemies, but also used it to discipline the population at large and its activists in particular. Whereas the first use of violence dominated up to the years 1933–4, in later years of the Third Reich the second usage prevailed. Yet even then, processes of disciplinary integration through violence always contained elements of mobilization – and, vice versa, the earlier mobilization had at the same time disciplinary effects on the rank and file of the SA.[109]

The history of violence is a field of study that has expanded considerably over the last twenty years.[110] The period 1914–45, at times described as a 'European civil war', has received particular attention from historians with an interest in the study of violence – not only because of the two world wars and their extremely high levels of destruction and death, but also because of the two opposing ideologies of Communism and Fascism that challenged democratic rule based on ideas of political liberalism.[111] National Socialism, as the German variant of Fascism or, more precisely, of 'authoritarian rightism', has been firmly embedded in a broad field of transnational and comparative studies on authoritarian, Fascist, or extreme nationalist movements and regimes in interwar Europe that replace older notions of totalitarianism.[112] The forms of political violence that these movements exercised have increasingly come under comparative and transnational scrutiny.[113] In effect, the history of National Socialism, or at least its early phase, is now increasingly analysed as a variant of a European phenomenon and less prominently interpreted as the keystone of the *Sonderweg*, the special path of modern German history that can be compared negatively with the imagined progressive course of modern Western history that unfolded elsewhere, a framework adopted in particular by the influential Bielefeld School of social history.[114] Nevertheless, to stress similarities does not mean to neglect differences. National Socialism became excessively violent with the establishment of the Third Reich and then again radicalized during the Second World War, when it implemented a programme of destruction and mass murder on an unprecedented scale, enslaving and killing millions of people whom the regime deemed 'undesirable', most notably the European Jewry.[115]

The present study follows this transnational historiographical trend without losing sight of the SA's national specificity. It analyses the changing patterns of stormtrooper violence and its effects, from the organization's early years as a genuine paramilitary *Wehrverband* to its heyday as a violent social movement, to the Nazi regime years when the SA was transformed into a mass organization with auxiliary police responsibilities but decreasing influence on the central government.[116] For the sake of clarity, I sometimes refer to these different stages as the first (1920/1–1923), second (1925/6–1933/4), and third SA (1933/4–1945). In order to adequately cover these different periods, with their changing forms of political activism, I rely on praxeological analyses of violent action, following the pioneering work of Sven Reichardt, who using the example of interwar Fascism has successfully demonstrated that praxeology as a method of studying social interaction allows for the reconciliation of structure and action, ideology and daily practices. By analysing the physical routines of the Nazi militants, their collectively shared worldviews, and their 'subjective attribution' of sense (to the acts they committed), it is possible to reconstruct the particular modes of *Vergemeinschaftung* in the SA.[117] However, I will also re-evaluate Reichardt's principal argument that in the SA, committing violence and feeling a sense of community were inextricably linked.[118] This is all the more important as his analysis predominantly concentrated on the narrow period of time between the late 1920s and the early 1930s. I will ask to what extent Reichardt's observations match the realities of the third SA and thereby attempt to clarify whether rupture or continuity prevailed in the history of the stormtroopers.

In scrutinizing the violence employed, I analyse the physical, psychological, cultural, and structural elements that such violence contains.[119] Whereas the first two forms are rather self-explanatory – physical violence is a direct assault on someone else's body, while psychological violence is a conscious attempt to compromise someone else's well-being – cultural and structural forms of violence, as well as forms of symbolic violence, are much harder to define and even more difficult to assess in retrospect. Apart from possible harmful intentions on the interpersonal level, such violence is here (also) the result of larger social and political processes.[120] The latter forms of violence thus blur the boundaries between the perpetrator and the victim, as they ultimately exert force on both of them. Responsibility is thus more difficult to attribute.

Regardless of such practical problems, two quick examples will make plain why a broad understanding of violence is needed for this study. First, a public SA march through a working-class neighbourhood around 1930 was meant by its participants and perceived by its political opponents as a violent provocation, even if no one was actually injured. Second, some years later, after the Nazi dictatorship was established, the sheer presence of a group of uniformed stormtroopers sufficed to scare potential dissidents and bystanders alike.[121] This was more than an aesthetic occupation of the public space. Everyone knew how quickly even a seemingly peaceful SA cohort could resort to physical violence, and many likewise knew that to ask for help from the police or the judiciary was often useless, if not a direct invitation to trouble.[122] The present study argues that this structural element of SA violence, its men's *Aktionsmacht*, or 'power of action',[123] remained in force throughout the Third Reich. Following Thomas Kühne, who has recently emphasized that in the Third Reich even seemingly harmless concepts as 'comradeship' contained a highly aggressive and ultimately genocidal tendency,[124] the present study likewise not only covers the SA's tangible violence, as documented in the press, court files, and memoirs, but also pays attention to the less spectacular forms of SA sociability and community and inquires into the extent to which they contributed to a social climate in which belonging and exclusion complemented each other and which ultimately made central Europe a *Gewaltraum*, a 'territory of violence' where forms of security that had structured human interaction in peacetime were no longer valid.[125] Whereas actual outbursts of SA physical violence remained relatively limited after the Nazi takeover of power was completed in 1934 – although, for the reasons just mentioned, we can assume that violent incidents involving stormtroopers were in fact more frequent than court and police records of the Third Reich suggest – it was the permanent menace posed by the Brownshirts' psychological and cultural violence in combination with other Nazi institutions that explains their lasting power and social impact.

To concentrate the historical analysis on the perpetrators and the structural framework in which they were operating would still be incomplete, however. A book on the stormtroopers is *ipso facto* also about those who were on the receiving end of their violence. Although in what follows I explore the intentions, actions, and mindsets of the men in the SA, I also hope to do justice to all those who directly experienced SA violence between the early 1920s and 1945. To analyse historical violence is not to excuse it, but it inevitably leads to a kind of rapprochement – a fact I tried to keep in mind while researching and writing this book.[126]

The Line of Argumentation

The following eleven chapters are arranged according to both chronology and topic and are divided into four parts. The first part, encompassing chapters 1 to 3, provides an overview of the early SA, from its inception in Munich in 1920–1 to its transformation into a kind of controlled social movement ten years later. I thus analyse the organizational and political history of the SA in light of the increasingly antagonistic and hostile political culture of the Weimar Republic. Without the experience of the First World War and the culture of paramilitary leagues in the 1920s, the phenomenal rise of the SA by the late 1920s would not have been possible, but this environment alone is not sufficient to explain its 'success story' between 1926 and 1933. The book therefore takes up the task of integrating the SA's institutional and political history into a study of everyday violence, of the palpable as well as the rhetorical kind. Both forms of violence were closely intertwined. My study scrutinizes more closely some of the (political) clashes that occurred in ever growing numbers starting in the late 1920s in order to demonstrate the mechanisms of a political strategy that was, to a large extent, built on the communicative aspects of violence and terror. I likewise re-evaluate the SA's crucial importance for the Nazis' growing success at the polls and – against this background – account for the growing dissatisfaction within the SA caused by the pretended 'legalistic course' of the NSDAP. Finally, this part of the book will explore the political motifs and the self-understanding of the oppositional groups within the SA, commonly identified with the brothers Gregor and Otto Strasser as well as Walther Stennes, the SA commander in Berlin until his expulsion in 1931. I will demonstrate that a closer look at the history of the SA does not attest to a straightforward 'march to power', as the party propaganda attempted to portray, but reveals an often complicated path of development, full of conflicts and internal quarrels.

The second part of this study, encompassing chapters 4 and 5, examines the SA's crucial role at the beginning of the Third Reich. In the first two years of the regime, until the summer of 1934, the SA was the most important

organization responsible for the incarceration and murder of political opponents. Although a considerable number of local and regional studies on SA
terror have been written in the last thirty years, we still lack an expert overview that goes beyond the mere retelling of particular crimes and biographies
to synthesize the forms and aims of the SA's para-police violence.[127] This
book thus analyses in depth how SA violence was embedded in the political
transformation of Germany from a democratic to a dictatorial state.
Exemplary case studies show how the SA interacted with the Nazi Party
leadership, the police, and the judiciary, illuminating larger trends. It will be
demonstrated that the SA's violence in this crucial period was hard to control
and even threatened the same people who had contributed to the rise of a
violent political culture in the preceding years. Furthermore, I explore in what
ways the individual SA man 'made sense' of these violent acts (for himself and
his peers), and how this meaning-making fits into the broader National
Socialist understanding of the times. By taking a closer look at individual
perspectives as well as the more systematic effects of SA violence, this book
provides not only a fuller picture of the SA but also a better understanding of
the establishment of the Nazi dictatorship. The second part concludes with a
chapter on the murder of Röhm, several dozen high-ranking SA leaders, and
other reputed enemies of National Socialism, in an event today known as the
'Night of the Long Knives', in early July 1934. I will re-evaluate the latest
literature on these thoroughly examined events with a particular focus on
their mid- and long-term effects.

The third part of the book, comprising chapters 6 to 9, analyses the
extent to which the SA not only survived the murder of considerable parts
of its leadership corps but also contributed to the militarization of society
in the following years and engaged in preparations for the Second World
War. Up to now, not much has been written about the SA in this period,
with the exception of its antisemitic violence in Germany and, later, also in
Austria. In order to paint a comprehensive picture of the stormtroopers'
relevance between 1934 and 1939, I will argue in chapter 6 that one should
not only focus on such high-profile outbursts of violence but also take into
account the structural aspects of the SA's transformation into a mass organization that penetrated German society on several levels. Beginning in the
mid-1930s, the Brownshirts were increasingly concerned with paramilitary
tasks related to the annexation of Austria and the Memelland and the
dismantling of Czechoslovakia. Chapter 7 will demonstrate that the SA

leadership even made settlement plans for eastern Europe, a task that it was ultimately forced to hand over to the rival SS. During the war years, analysed in chapter 8, the SA suffered from the drafting of the majority of its members into the Wehrmacht. Some fighting units, however – in particular, the SA-*Standarte* Feldherrnhalle – were composed exclusively of SA men. The earlier National Socialist concept of the 'political soldier' appeared during this period in an updated form: he was fighting Bolshevism now not in the German streets but on the Russian plains. Chapter 9 will for the first time ever provide a thorough analysis of the tasks and actions of those high-ranking SA generals who were sent as German envoys into the countries of southeastern Europe. I will argue that their appointment not only was an attempt to further bring the German diplomatic service under party control but also was intended to entrust diplomatic preparations for the murder of local Jews in these states to men who had been proven loyal NSDAP activists and fanatical antisemites. Even if the SA was no longer one of the dominant Nazi organizations in Germany, these examples demonstrate that it remained highly relevant as a network of 'committed' Nazi activists who contributed to the war and the Holocaust.

Finally, the fourth and last part, consisting of chapter 10 and the conclusion, is concerned with the legacy of the SA after 1945. I will demonstrate, first, that understandings of the third SA as utterly unimportant in the Third Reich were popularized in the immediate post-war years as a means of juridical defence and met with considerable success. Second, I will show that such partisan views were quickly taken up by the early historiography on the SA and have influenced our understanding of the stormtroopers until today. Against this background I will finally reassess the role of the SA in a comprehensive history of National Socialism, with the aim of providing a stimulus for further research that transcends narrow temporal and spatial boundaries.

This outline makes it clear that I take seriously the 'cultural politics of emotion' of the Nazis and the self-images that guided its activists.[128] I thereby aim to demonstrate how powerful the SA actually was – not only as a militia that targeted Communists, Social Democrats, and Jews in the German streets until 1934, but also as an organization active in the later years of the Nazi regime. The stormtroopers regarded themselves as a visible embodiment of the National Socialists' promise and as guardians of a racially structured 'people's community'. That the majority of highbrow intellectuals despised the Brownshirts for all kinds of good reasons does not diminish the force of this belief. Against the background of the popular idea of an egalitarian society, defined as a society in which every individual shares the same basic social obligations, the importance of the brown uniform as a social unifier should not be downplayed. Egalitarianism had a strong appeal in Germany throughout the twentieth century and was reinforced by the First World War and the social promises of the Weimar Republic, which raised expectations to a new level. The National Socialist ideology played into these expectations but sharply distinguished between those whom it considered to have legitimate social rights and those whom it excluded for fundamental ideological, racial, or social reasons. The party's idea of *Volksgemeinschaft* thus built on the discourse of national unity and inter-class solidarity that was also dear to the democratic parties, but it perverted this idea by making it conditional along racial and ideological lines while simultaneously fostering autocratic rule and a messianic leadership cult that contrasted sharply with the idea of democratic participation.[129]

The National Socialists' combination of a charismatic yet ultimately autocratic rule and popular demands for national belonging proved attractive not only to the marginalized, but even to men of the aristocracy. When, from the late 1920s, the last Kaiser's son, Crown Prince August Wilhelm of Prussia, nicknamed 'Auwi', wore the SA uniform on public occasions and even gave stump speeches on behalf of the NSDAP, many perceived him as a fool. For others, however, such symbolic gestures seemed to confirm that the Nazis were on their way to achieving something of considerable value: a true and not just imagined community that could unite patriotic Germans, from the ordinary man in the street to those born into the highest levels of the aristocracy and living in castles. This ideal of a *union sacrée* among the political leadership, the monarch, and the people had been established as a powerful political myth in the early nineteenth century with the alleged 'wars of liberation' against French troops led by Napoleon Bonaparte, and the Nazis successfully capitalized on it. However, the NSDAP was a modern political party and as such did not advocate for a monarchy based on the fortune of noble birth, but for a *Führerstaat* based on individual merits.[130] That Hitler regularly wore the SA uniform at party rallies and on the occasion of public speeches seemed to confirm the Nazi promise: in their state, every German, regardless of his social background, should be able to make it to the top on condition that he possessed the necessary leadership qualities and the right ideological convictions – and even then, he would remain the first among his peers.[131]

After the Second World War was lost and Germany lay in ruins, the Nazi promises of racially structured equality were not forgotten, as demonstrated by the case of Wehrmacht soldiers who openly defended the SA even when they were in American captivity. A certain Helmut Richter, a former lieutenant colonel, said that he still believed in the 'idea' of National Socialism, characterizing himself as an 'outright supporter' of Nazi organizations like the Hitler Youth and the SA, and declaring that he regarded the latter as a cornerstone of the people's community: 'Within the SA, a factory director counts as much as a worker, and the troop leader is even above the factory director, if the latter is no troop leader . . . It is simply the affinity to the people that is required; this is just the new thing.'[132] That a former Wehrmacht soldier could utter such a statement, even when he must have known that it would not be to his advantage, is a strong indicator that the SA had remained in the German mindset during the war, regardless of its limited direct political influence. To staunch National Socialists the SA even in 1945 remained a core element of Nazi ideology and rule, an organization that – despite all its limitations – stood for the central promises of Nazi ideology: social participation and national belonging for 'racially' pure Germans.[133]

PART I

TURMOIL IN POST-WAR GERMANY AND THE ORIGINS OF THE NAZI SA

Guns and hand grenades are not allowed in the theatres.
— Order of Munich's Municipal Command, 8 May 1919[1]

The Nazi stormtroopers were a typical product of the 'transnational zone of paramilitary violence' that emerged in central Europe after the First World War, and it is therefore apt to start this study by analysing the milieu that gave birth to this and several other right-wing paramilitary leagues.[2] The regional focus of this chapter is on Bavaria and, to a lesser degree, its neighbouring states Württemberg and Austria, as it was here that the SA was founded and operated until the mid-1920s. With regard to Fascism more generally, the impact of the Great War is hard to overestimate. The war contributed decisively to a new mentality that came to shape the political and social conflicts of the following two decades.[3] Prussian military reformers had conceptualized the army as the school of the nation as early as the beginning of the nineteenth century. During the war years their view proved correct, but the military's influence on society operated in a different, more comprehensive way: instead of instilling honourable virtues and soldierly discipline into the minds of the nation's aristocratic youth, the Great War, with its mass-scale killings at the front lines and its severe food shortages within Germany, ultimately destroyed the old order upon which such virtues were based and contributed to the emancipation of all those previously excluded from politics and the military leadership, particularly working-class men and women in general.[4] As historian Jörn Leonhard has recently pointed out, the First World War was also a 'revolution of rising expectations' that fundamentally shaped Europeans' perceptions of politics and society. In the United Kingdom, France, and Germany alike, ordinary servicemen beginning in 1916 increasingly mocked the established political and military authorities, inventing a new antagonistic vocabulary and a new language of belonging and exclusion.[5] What during the war was manifested as a particular form of (bitter) wartime irony, to be found in soldiers' newspapers, letters, and diaries, was transformed after the armistice into a more violent and confrontational political language that contributed to the sharply antagonistic political climate of the interwar period.[6]

Fighting for Order

In the years following the revolution of November 1918, which resulted in the abdication of the Kaiser and paved the way for the transformation of the German Reich into a parliamentary democracy, a myriad of new paramilitary organizations came to play an important part in German politics, testifying not only to the erosion of the state's monopoly on the legitimate use of force, but also to the fact that hundreds of thousands of ordinary men now felt called upon to take politics into their own hands. A provisional Reichswehr was established during the spring and summer of 1919, but because of the restrictions set by the Versailles peace treaty it remained limited to 100,000 men and 6,000 officers, at least officially.[7] This meant that the majority of the soldiers who had fought in the Imperial army were now superfluous. Although many of them returned home, a relatively important minority joined new paramilitary groups that complemented the new Reichswehr units but were only partly loyal to the young democracy, despite being politically and financially dependent on it. By 1921 approximately 400,000 men had enrolled in paramilitary activities in Germany. Estimates of the number of *Freikorps* units and other semi-official 'government forces' existing at the time range from 70 up to 400.[8] Whereas some of these units were recruited entirely from the Imperial army, others were short-lived hodgepodge militias comprising fewer than 500 men. These semi-legal troops initially helped to secure the borders of the Reich, particularly in the east and southeast. After their return to the

German heartlands, however, they were to a considerable extent responsible for the growing level of political violence that marked the early years of the Republic.[9] Yet they were not direct forerunners of the SA; according to new research on the German *Freikorps*, only between 1 and 5 per cent of these paramilitary members later joined the SA.[10]

The situation was most extreme in Bavaria, where the political turmoil of 1919 – which saw the establishment of the Munich Soviet Republic and its subsequent liquidation by a joint cooperative effort of Reichswehr forces and state-recognized paramilitary groups like the Ehrhardt Brigade,[11] the *Freikorps Epp*,[12] and the *Freikorps Oberland*[13] – laid the ground for what became known as the *Ordnungszelle Bayern*, literally the 'Bavarian Order Cell' (Plate 1). This was a regional development that can be characterized by its very careful acceptance of the new democratic order in the Reich and its growing willingness to support all kinds of nationalist groups, both politically, legally, and financially.[14] A key element of Bavarian politics in the early years of the Republic was the *Einwohnerwehren*, or 'Civil Guards': a patriotic self-defence organization headed by Georg Escherich. In the eyes of the authorities, the *Einwohnerwehren* were meant to back the government's attempt to impose law and order, but they ultimately contributed to the radicalization of conservative politics and helped form a lasting alliance between moderately patriotic and ultra-nationalist circles. Although the Reich government established so-called *Wehrkommissare*, a network of Reichswehr army officers supposed to watch over the *Einwohnerwehr* movement, Escherich and his deputy Rudolph Kanzler, backed by the Bavarian government, insisted on their organizational autonomy and steered a political course that helped to transform Bavaria and its capital city Munich into the 'headquarters of a massive counter-revolutionary conglomerate'.[15]

At the height of its influence, in the spring of 1920, the *Einwohnerwehren* comprised some 350,000 men. While many of their members were politically moderate in the sense that they intended to defend the heritage of the Bavarian monarchy, God, and fatherland against the 'sins of the revolution' and the political influence of the much-hated 'Prussians', the movement also provided a home for those soldiers and *Freikorps* members who had not been integrated into regular Reichswehr units. Under the protection of the *Einwohnerwehren*, extreme nationalist activists who 'had nothing but contempt for the latter's old fashioned parochialism' and their 'Lederhosen militarism' often joined mobile brigades called *Landfahnen* or *Reichfahnen*, which could be up to 30,000 men strong. Here, the extreme nationalists formed lasting networks, established official and secret contacts with representatives of the Bavarian government and the military, received training and weapons, and – above all – earned public recognition for activities that increasingly did not help to stabilize the democratic order but were aimed at overcoming it when the next suitable moment arrived.[16]

These developments, tolerated and even fostered by the Bavarian governments led initially by Johannes Hoffmann from the Social Democratic Party (SPD) and later, starting in 1920, by Gustav Ritter von Kahr, the unaffiliated candidate of the conservative Bavarian People's Party (BVP), soon aroused the suspicion of the Allies, who repeatedly demanded the dissolution of the German paramilitary units. However, it was not until June 1921 when von Kahr, meanwhile the 'strongman' of Bavaria, agreed despite personal reservations to disband the Bavarian *Einwohnerwehren* as well as their counterpart in the Reich, the Organisation Escherich – for short, the *Orgesch*.[17] Although these steps had stabilizing effects on the regional level within Bavaria in the years 1919 to 1921, at the same time they contributed to a growing antagonism between Bavaria and the Reich, dominated by its largest state, Prussia, which itself remained firmly in the hands of the Social Democrats until 1932 and turned out to be an 'unlikely rock of democracy'.[18] Throughout the Reich, however, many Germans still contested the legitimacy of the new political order, and even those who over the course of the 1920s made their peace with it, remained open to alternatives.

The rise and fall of the Bavarian *Einwohnerwehr* movement constituted the background against which the establishment of the National Socialist stormtroopers has to be viewed, particularly with regard to three factors. First, the formation of the paramilitary wing of the newly established NSDAP (which until 24 February 1920 had been called the DAP, the 'German Workers' Party') happened at a time when a political turn to the right was in full swing in Bavaria. Yet, at least initially, the Nazi movement was deemed insignificant by the Reich compared to the hundreds of thousands of men who organized in the *Einwohnerwehr* units and in several other patriotic *Verbände*, or groups. Second, with the *Einwohnerwehr* movement, clandestinely financed and armed paramilitary groups that did not shy away from political murder became a widely tolerated element of politics in Bavaria.[19] Third, the *Einwohnerwehren* cultivated the idea that political participation in Germany following the First World War required personal commitment both as a man and as a soldier. Consequently, even the most radical groups – the Nazi SA soon among them – were able in public to pass for legitimate defenders of law and order.

Establishing the Stormtroopers

The historiography of the National Socialists claimed that the party's *Turn- und Sportabteilung* (literally the 'Gymnastics and Sports Unit'), as the SA was originally called, had been founded under the leadership of the watchmaker Emil Maurice on 12 November of 1920.[20] On this day, a group of National Socialist stewards defended a party reunion being held in the Munich Hofbräuhaus against protesters from the *Republikanischer Schutzbund*, the 'Republican Self-Protection League'.[21] However, although this somewhat randomly selected date provides a powerful founding myth, it condenses a longer process. In reality, the organization of the SA was a gradual development that, beginning in 1919–20 and parallel to the political formation of the NSDAP/DAP and the growing *Einwohnerwehr* movement, ultimately culminated with the solidification of clearly defined units of political- paramilitary character in 1921–2.[22] Technically speaking, the SA and its mother party, the NSDAP, were a registered society bearing the name of *Nationalsozialistischer Deutscher Arbeiterverein e. V.* With the one exception of the period after the Hitler Putsch in November 1923, when both the NSDAP and the SA were outlawed, this legal status remained valid until 1935, when the Nazi Party finally became a public body.[23]

The practice of supporting party work by creating specialized protection forces was not unique to the *völkisch* right, however. The National Socialists could not even claim originality for the name and later 'brand' of the SA, as already in 1919 the Bavarian Social Democrat Erhard Auer had started to form protection forces for himself and Social Democratic meet- ings and party rallies, forces that were initially known as the 'Auer Guard' or 'Pitzer Guard', after its first commander Franz Xaver Pitzer.[24] The formation of these guards was a direct reaction to the assassination on 21 February 1919 of Kurt Eisner, the leader of the Independent Social Democrats (USPD) in post-war Bavaria and its premier until his death, by the extreme nationalist Anton Graf von Arco auf Valley.[25] From 10 November 1920 onward, the Bavarian SPD also officially organized *Saalschutz* guards, or stewards. In the following months these units were often referred to as 'SA',

understood as *Sturmabteilung* or *Saalschutzabteilung*. Lieutenant in Reserve
Wilhelm Buisson[26] led the socialist SA headquartered in Munich that,
according to the police, comprised between 2,000 and 5,000 men, including
those in units in the nearby cities of Freising, Ingolstadt, and Rosenheim.[27]
Several months after the Bavarian authorities banned Socialist paramilitary
organizations in October 1923, the leftist *Sturmabteilung* was integrated into
the new *Reichsbanner Schwarz-Rot-Gold, Bund Deutscher Kriegsteilnehmer
und Republikaner*, the nationwide paramilitary defence organization of the
Social Democrats founded in Magdeburg on 22 February 1924.[28]

The initial Nazi SA, which analogous to the Auer Guard was known as
the 'Hitler Guard',[29] was therefore – strictly speaking – if not a copy, then at
least deeply influenced by the Social Democratic attempts to create party-
controlled self-protection forces. It did not take long, however, before
important differences between these two organizations began to emerge.
Whereas the Social Democratic SA justified its existence on the basis of the
state's reluctance to adequately protect SPD meetings and the authorities'
proven inability to guarantee the physical integrity of leading politicians on
the left, the NSDAP's Gymnastics and Sports Unit could hardly claim a
purely defensive character. As early as 1920, the Nazis had formed *Stoßtrupps*,
or shock troops, which insulted and injured political opponents in the streets
of Bavarian cities without having been previously attacked.[30] Party mobs
also interrupted religious meetings, shouted antisemitic slogans, and attacked
audience members at a theatre performance based on the murdered Kurt
Eisner.[31] They also molested representatives of the Entente Commissions in
their Munich hotels and invaded the restaurant in the Munich House of
Artists, insulting those present as 'debauchees' (*Schlemmer*).[32] The self-
proclaimed goal of the stormtroopers was to 'blow up' all political meetings
in which Jews were allowed to address the crowd.[33] Among the authorities,
there were severe differences of opinion on how to react to this challenge.
Whereas the Bavarian Minister of the Interior expressed his 'serious disapproval' (*ernstliche Mißbilligung*) of the Bavarian police's lenient stance
towards the National Socialists in an urgent letter to the police president as
early as February 1921,[34] the latter regarded the Nazi stormtroopers as a
minor problem compared to their Socialist counterparts, at least until the
year 1923.[35]

Historians usually consider 11 August 1921 as the official founding
date of the National Socialist SA.[36] On this day, the party paper *Der*

Völkische Beobachter published a proclamation urging the 'German Youth' to join the new *Turn- und Sportabteilung* for the necessary 'heavy fight' against the Jews. This 'foreign race', the Nazis claimed, would continue to prevent the German people from recognizing their bitter reality, shaped by national shame and foreign domination. The proclamation contained some of the ingredients that over the next years were to be relentlessly repeated in the Nazi propaganda. The goal of this new subdivision of the NSDAP was to 'unite the younger party members' in order to provide the party with a 'battering ram'. With regard to its ideological function, the ambition was to create an organization that would keep alive the idea of national defence (*Wehrgedanken*) among the German people. Remarkably, the dual character of the SA as a party protection squad and an instrument for ideological-educational purposes, which throughout its existence confused friends and foes alike, was already ingrained in its first manifesto. The party rhetoric contrasted sharply with the very modest beginnings of these units, addressing the prospective stormtroopers directly as an elite group that had been called upon to shape Germany's destiny: 'Your services will be needed in the future!'[37]

Two weeks prior to this public summons, on 29 July 1921, background talks had been held between Hitler and Captain Hermann Ehrhardt, a leading figure of post-war Germany's extreme right who had just taken headquarters in Munich. Ehrhardt delegated the former marine lieutenant Julius Hans Ulrich Klintzsch – the twenty-two-year-old son of a Protestant senior pastor Johannes Paul Klintzsch and his wife Johanna Dorothea, from Lübbenau in Lower Lusatia, and a former member of the *Freikorps* Ehrhardt Brigade – to organize the NSDAP's 'self-protection' forces.[38] Previously an active participant in the Kapp Putsch, Klintzsch had moved to Munich in the early summer of 1921. A few weeks after his arrival, Ehrhardt entrusted him with the task of 'infiltrating' competing organizations of the extreme right. The NSDAP's self-protection forces were Klintzsch's first target in the Bavarian capital.[39]

Those involved in the deal between Hitler and Ehrhardt perceived it as a win-win situation: Hitler would gain further access to the web of military and conservative political leaders in Bavaria, and his young self-defence units would benefit from the military expertise of individuals like Klintzsch. On the other side, Ehrhardt, nicknamed 'the boss' by friends and admirers, hoped to gain in Hitler a public voice and in the NSDAP a new party that would be at his disposal.[40] Along with former Quartermaster General Erich Ludendorff, called by opponents the 'big spider in the Swastika' (*große Hakenkreuzspinne*) – so central was his role in the web of nationalist groups during the early 1920s[41] – Ehrhardt was a key figure of the extreme right who enjoyed an almost mythical reputation among young activists of this persuasion throughout Germany. A resident of the Bavarian capital for political reasons, he developed close bonds with like-minded extreme nationalists and Fascists in Austria, Hungary, and Italy.[42] He made use of well-trained soldiers-turned-terrorists by organizing them into a secret terror network, called the O. C. (Organisation Consul). Finally, he provided the early SA not only with logistical but also considerable financial support.[43] In contrast, Hitler was at this time merely a promising and regionally well-known political orator who still remained dependent on the goodwill of those with better access to weapons and Bavarian high society.[44]

Consequently, the early SA initially observed Ehrhardt's military command (via Klintzsch) and was said to have been only at the 'political disposal' of Hitler.[45] At this time the stormtroopers in the Bavarian capital consisted of at least 241 men and boys who were organized into twenty-one groups and, according to a membership list that made it into the hands of the authorities, predominantly aged between seventeen and twenty-four.[46] The choice of the twenty-three-year-old Klintzsch as commander seems therefore logical. In addition to his credentials as a soldier, he was just about an adult man – the legal age was then twenty-one – and thereby embodied the claim that 'youth is led by youth', an important element of the German youth movement.[47] Klintzsch's command was cut short, however, as he was taken into custody on 14 September 1921, suspected of having been involved in the murder of the former Reich Finance Minister, Matthias Erzberger, during the previous month.[48] Dietrich von Jagow supposedly represented Klintzsch in the following months until the latter was acquitted and released from detention in early December 1921 and returned to active duty as leader of the SA, a position he held until Hermann Göring superseded him in March 1923.[49] This short list of early SA leaders already demonstrates a consistent feature of the stormtroopers in the years to come: whereas the majority of the rank and file were made up of young men without practical military experience, their leaders were selected from the much smaller band of National Socialists who had occupied leading positions in the German military during the First World War.[50]

A Public Nuisance

The Nazi activists in the earliest days mostly originated from the lower-middle and working classes, but soon former military leaders of noble descent also took up important positions.[51] Those individual rank-and-file stormtroopers whose names have survived in press clippings and police files allow for a tentative picture of the early SA's social composition, particularly in light of the nonexistence of more reliable statistics. Professions like baker, locksmith, and merchant frequently appear, but there were also students, a farmer, a lieutenant, a chimney-sweeper, and at least two police officers.[52] These young men were not necessarily deeply politicized, but they had experienced the political instability and the social hardship of the post-war period as well as the excessive violence by revolutionaries and paramilitary forces alike from close range. Having grown up during the war years, with their glorification of German might and the idea of cultural superiority, these teenage boys and young men had not been 'brutalized' (as has been argued in parts of the historiography),[53] but they certainly lacked any personal pre-war experience that might have guided them through the post-war turmoil.

By all standards the initial months of these first SA units were very modest. Instead of fighting political enemies or parading the streets, the SA group leaders were above all busy organizing their groups, which usually comprised no more than ten men. On 26 August 1921, just two weeks after the publication of the call to join the SA, unit leaders noted a 'lack of discipline', and two months later they stressed that 'punctuality' should be considered a prime virtue and a basic prerequisite for joining the necessarily 'tight organization' – thus indicating the existence of fluctuations in commitment to the political cause among these first stormtroopers.[54] As undercover police reports on the 'control evenings' that were held weekly by the SA in Munich 1921 and 1922 make plain, it was not rare for only 50 per cent of the men ordered to report for duty to show up, despite the fact that Hitler often attended these meetings. They initially took place in inns like the Sterneckerbräu, located close to the Isartor, which had previously also hosted the first NSDAP office, or the Högerbräu, just a stone's throw away from the centrally located Marienplatz. The police described the atmosphere of such meetings as 'lively', 'humorous', and 'cheerful', with piano playing and much dancing, singing, and bouncing around.[55] Hitler usually arrived late. His addresses, however, 'energized' the young Nazi followers. To judge from the police reports, the dullest and most routine get-together of stormtroopers could be transformed by Hitler's speeches into a successful evening that usually ended with loud cheers and drunken young men stumbling home.

Hitler's talks lasted up to two and a half hours. At times he told autobiographic stories from his time in the List regiment during the First World War, but usually his speeches revolved around the 'Jewish question' and the future rise of the NSDAP.[56] 'We want to stir up hatred against everything and everyone,' Hitler exclaimed in a meeting on 6 April 1922, referring, of all things, to the historic example of the Reformation in the sixteenth century. He argued that faith was the prerequisite of a people's strong will, and that this would be the prerequisite of any deed. Just as Martin Luther had exploited the passions of his time to spur the Reformation, so the National Socialists should propagate and exploit the anti-Jewish sentiments of the day.[57] If critics would denounce his party as a 'coarse and brutal mob that would stop at nothing', he would be more than delighted, Hitler exclaimed: harsh criticism of that sort could only benefit his party, making it both feared and more widely known.[58]

How can we account for the phenomenon of hundreds of workers, students, and salesmen in Munich feeling uplifted by such political dema-goguery? With no stable or adequate replacement for the old order, easy answers became increasingly popular in post-war Bavaria. 'Bolshevism primarily means criminal tyranny, organized and led by the Jews,' one defamatory pamphlet in Munich claimed as early as 1919.[59] Such procla-mations set the tone for the following years, in which the nationalist right, building on the sharp rise in antisemitism that had occurred during the war years, increasingly identified 'Jews' and 'Bolsheviks' as national traitors, blaming all kinds of shortcomings and economic and social problems on the alleged influence of a Judeo-Marxist conspiracy.[60] Although the Nazis' propaganda of hate repelled many adherents even of the radical right, its underlying rationale was widely embraced. The Bavarian consensus that emerged during the 1920s was to a considerable degree built on clear friend-foe distinctions (Bavaria versus the Reich, good patriotic Christian Germans versus internationally oriented Jews and Bolshevists). Whatever the Nazi stormtroopers did, they often benefited from the fact that many Germans in Bavaria attributed patriotic and therefore honourable motives to them.[61] At a time when legal experts as well as the wider public regarded high rates of juvenile criminality as alarming signs of cultural change and social decline,[62] the political activism of the young Nazis, excessive as it was, could be viewed as a vague promise for a better future that would be won by determined and fearless political fighters. Important parts of the judiciary, the police, and the influential upper-middle classes interpreted the stormtroopers' radicalism and violence merely as defensive actions, a legitimate response to the alleged 'crimes' of the 'November criminals' and a consequence of the perceived social disorder. Considerable parts of the German public explained the rise to power of the Italian Fascists in 1922 in similar terms. The conservative *Bayerische Staatszeitung* commented: 'First and last, the fascists soak up force and power from the disappointments that the post-war period caused to large segments of the population, instead of bringing them prosperity and happiness, as promised. Furthermore, they profit from the opposition between the *völkisch* and national consciousness on the one hand and the international flattening (*Verflachung*) and the community of fate (*Schicksalsgemeinschaft*) on the other.'[63]

The first test of the National Socialist SA occurred on 4 November 1921, when Hitler spoke at a party rally held in Munich's Hofbräuhaus. That night, in a fight that lasted up to twenty minutes, forty-six stormtroopers were supposedly able to beat out of the hall 'nearly 400 soldiers of the Judeo-Marxist hit squad' (*Sprengsoldaten des Judenmarxismus*, in Hitler's words). In later accounts this number was increased to '800 Marxists'.[64] These figures were certainly an overstatement, but the story became a powerful second founding myth that set the tone for the SA's self-glorification in the following years: again and again, filigreed accounts of brave SA units successfully defeating a much stronger opposition appeared in Nazi papers and books, testifying to the supposed superiority of the party's ideas, ideas that enabled their activists to demonstrate superhuman strength and extraordinary courage, which, in turn, legitimized the ideas.[65]

What the Nazis exalted as the spearhead of the movement to liberate Germany from alleged Jewish 'stock-exchange terror' was in the eyes of the Social Democrats simply 'mentally immature rowdiness [*geistig unreifes Rowdytum*]'.[66] The political left early on identified the Nazis as an imminent political threat, not least because of the close relations among and between parts of the Bavarian police, the Reichswehr, and the SA. As became quickly known, the Reichswehr provided the stormtroopers with privileged access to weapons, and the police and public prosecutors frequently dealt sympathetically with the crimes committed by these militants.[67] However, it would be misleading to regard this early SA as a regularly armed, highly disciplined, and hard-hitting organization. It possessed weapons, but these were basically the weapons of the street: truncheons (nicknamed 'rubbers'), knuckledusters, knives, sticks, and whips. Some members owned small firearms (called 'lighters'), but such weapons were rarely used.[68] In Munich it was rumoured that the National Socialists had distributed hand grenades to individual stormtroopers on at least one occasion, but the truth of such statements is doubtful.[69] In any case, real fighting by these early SA units was rare – and if such events did occur, they generally showed the usual characteristics of beer-hall brawls, with little more destruction than flying beer mugs and broken chair legs. Among the numerous patriotic *Verbände* in Bavaria, the comparatively young and inexperienced boys and young men from the SA were a local nuisance, but hardly a relevant political factor – at least not until the spring of 1923.

Furthermore, its first units did not impress the public as possessing a coherent character or determination. They even lacked a proper uniform, as the brown shirt was not introduced until 1924 and was not made mandatory until late 1926.[70] Initially, the stormtroopers attended their meetings in casual clothes, marked only by red armbands emblazoned with the swastika. In November 1922 the NSDAP introduced the group's first uniform, consisting of grey riding trousers, windbreakers with the red armbands, and ski caps.[71] Slightly earlier, in July or August of the same year, the party had organized an 'SA bicycle troop' (*Radfahrerabteilung*),[72] the first step toward what ten years later had been transformed into a highly complex web of SA sub-groups; among them the Motor-SA (in 1934 transferred to the NSKK, the *Nationalsozialistisches Kraftfahrkorps*), the Marine-SA, the Reiter-SA ('Equestrian-SA'), and the Pioneer- and Messenger-SA were some of the most important.[73] In the early years, however, most of these sub-units existed only on paper. As late as the summer of 1923, the NSDAP possessed no more than two motorcars and two lorries suitable for the transport of men, and their drivers (among them Emil Maurice) regularly failed to report for duty.[74]

A police report on an outing of the SA bicycle troop to Bad Tölz, a spa town some fifty kilometres south of the Bavarian capital, sheds light on the character of the early SA's activities. Around noon on Sunday, 15 August 1922, a group of eighteen members of the NSDAP, all in their twenties and led by Klintzsch, arrived in Bad Tölz. The cyclists stopped at the Zum Oswaldbräu inn located in the city centre and symbolically occupied it by hanging a red banner with a large swastika on the front of the tavern. This provocation caused the local constable to be called to the scene. Anticipating violence, he warned the stormtroopers not to molest anyone but did not interfere otherwise. At about 1 p.m., and presumably after some pints of beer, the SA bicycle troop lined up behind the Nazi flag and started parading through the streets of the city singing 'national songs'. They marched across the Isar River and ended at the upscale Park Hotel, located near the city's spa park. This hotel was owned by Julius Hellmann, one of the few Jewish residents of Bad Tölz and a popular figure among upper-middle-class Jewry – a fact also known to the Nazis. As they paraded in front of the hotel, the young men sang the notorious Ehrhardt song that ended with the refrain 'Out with the Jews!' As was intended, some of the Jewish hotel guests came out and confronted the molesters, calling them 'rascals' and hitting them with the then popular walking sticks. At this point the local police intervened and had most of the Nazis identify themselves. Their leader, Klintzsch, requested that those guests who had violently confronted the stormtroopers also be identified, but – according to the police – that attempt failed when both the hotel guests and its owner refused to betray their compatriots. Finally, the local police sent the Nazis home and handed over the dossier on the incident to their colleagues in Munich. It is not known whether the attackers were punished for their actions in any way. Regardless, they did not fear punishment. Klintzsch in his interrogation even dared to threaten the policemen: 'We'll be back, you will see, things will change. We have been frequently at the police, we are not afraid of it [punishment]. It will not better us; instead, we will become ever more fanatical.'[75]

According to Klintzsch, the SA bicycle troop in the summer of 1922 undertook such trips nearly every Sunday and on public holidays, travelling to different places in the vicinity of Munich. We can therefore assume that the incident at Bad Tölz was somewhat typical, and not only with regard to the strong antisemitism that was voiced.[76] The SA's actions in Bad Tölz also contain several characteristics of what sociological research calls the 'expressive acting of violence' (*expressives Gewalthandeln*), defined as violence that is seen as an end in itself. For sure, the politics of the extreme nationalist right was not totally absent on this occasion, but it served largely as a means to provoke violent confrontation. The day trip started with several hours of physical exercise (such as cycling), continued with the symbolic occupation of a central public place in the city (the inn) and the performance of rites of male sociability there, and reached its climax with the successful provocation of the hotel's affluent Jewish guests. The trip thereby provided key benefits popular among male youth: an intensified appreciation of the body and its physical strength, the opportunity to feel manly by the demonstration of power and energy, and, last but not least, a means to enjoy collectively experienced 'fun'.[77]

Despite such hooliganism, which was legally an offence for disturbing the public order, the Bavarian police failed to change its view that the actions of the SA did not differ from the activities performed by other patriotic leagues. Although the police confiscated the large antisemitic posters that the Nazis publicly displayed to celebrate the stormtroopers' first year of existence in Munich in August 1922 – posters apparently containing such strong antisemitic rhetoric that Jewish organizations referred to them as a veritable 'call for a pogrom'[78] – they usually described the National Socialist field exercises as 'outings' that expressed a continuation of the pre-war German youth movement, with its joint cooking, athletic, and gymnastic activities. If the authorities recognized a 'military element' to the NSDAP's activities at all, official documents emphasized the 'always unarmed' nature of the units involved.[79] Even if one takes into account the Bavarian police's deliberate downplaying of the danger of the SA to the public order, there is no denying that the 'fighting value' of the Nazi militants was indeed limited. Ernst Röhm, who in the first half of the 1920s was an influential intermediary between the Reichswehr and several paramilitary leagues of the extreme right, in his memoirs from 1928 frankly wrote about the early SA: 'Doubtless it had hundreds of well-trained men who would address the task with enthusiasm and with a will, and were loyal to Hitler's person. Their training was naturally difficult, and they could not rise to the level of full military value. They would be no match in battle for trained troops.'[80]

The Crucial Year of 1923

In spite of their limited military power and often improvised public appearances, the stormtroopers – along with a few high-profile public speakers such as Hitler or the journalist Hermann Esser from the *Völkischer Beobachter*, who enjoyed Bavarian-wide publicity – progressively came to stand for the National Socialists in the eyes of the public, particularly as the NSDAP was not represented in either the Reichstag or any of the regional parliaments.[81] At this time, the party did not take part in elections because Hitler argued that although 'principled opposition' from within the parliament was theoretically conceivable, it could not be undertaken in practice. Conceding that the Nazis lacked a forceful press, he claimed that the party thus could not expect to reach the wider electorate, making successful campaigning impossible. Furthermore, Hitler openly admitted that his party had only a handful of qualified public speakers at its disposal, with most cadres producing little more than 'theoretic and fantastic reveries' (*theoretisch-phantastische Schwärmereien*).[82] Against this background the deployment of stormtroopers was a more reliable option for distributing the party's antisemitic propaganda, particularly because in such circumstances orderly conduct and brute physical strength counted for more than rhetorical talent.

Between late 1922 and November 1923, the Weimar Republic's second 'year of crisis' after its rocky start in 1919, the Nazi activists became involved in a growing number of clashes with political opponents that slowly but surely aroused the suspicion of the authorities. At the same time these incidents consolidated the Nazis' reputation within the nationalist camp as an organization of particularly determined young men. Mussolini's 'March on Rome', the successful Fascist takeover of power in Italy in late October 1922, further encouraged the National Socialists to come out into the open.[83] As the early SA was still more of a traditional *Wehrverband* than a party army, plans to stage a paramilitary coup in Bavaria with the ultimate aim of overthrowing the government of the Reich became highly popular, both among the military leaders of the SA and the young men who increasingly filled the ranks of its *Hundertschaften* (groups of a hundred). The street violence that characterized the group's activities in Bavaria prior to November 1923 therefore not only testifies to the early stormtroopers' high level of aggression but also proves to have been of strategic use to the NSDAP in the sense that, by destabilizing the public order step by step, the party's ultimate aim was to provoke a situation in which an attempt by the extreme nationalists to take power could be justified as a rescue of the fatherland.

Newspaper clippings from the time testify to the increasing SA violence in both Bavaria and neighbouring Austria, where SA units had existed at least since 1922, initially led by Hans Lechner. On 19 June 1922 there was a 'big brawl' in Vienna, where the National Socialist SA and up to 400 Communists clashed after a speech delivered by Hitler. Several people were injured, and fifteen participants were taken into custody.[84] Whereas on this occasion the stormtroopers were at least provoked by Communist hecklers, incidents like the following clearly demonstrate that in most cases they actively laid the foundation of the violence. On 29 August 1922 the Munich shopkeeper David Heß and his nineteen-year-old son Ludwig were about to remove an antisemitic pamphlet from their shop window when they were attacked and severely beaten by a group of stormtroopers who had been waiting nearby for their victims to come out. Although the local police arrested several SA men on the spot, only one of them was later indicted and sentenced to the mild penalty of a one-week prison term.[85] In September 1922, following a mass gathering prohibited by the authorities, the streets of Munich reverberated with shouts of 'Down with the Jews!' for the first time.[86] Several weeks later, on 14 and 15 October 1922, the National Socialists took part in a *völkisch* 'German day' in the Franconian city of Coburg, located in the north of Bavaria. The majority of the storm-troopers present, approximately 500 men, had come from Munich by train. Beginning immediately on their arrival, they repeatedly clashed with their political opponents in the streets and beer halls of the city. However, they also attended prayers in the prestigious Protestant Ehrenburg Palace Church, a symbolic gesture that was well received among Coburg's middle classes.[87] In contrast to publications that drew on such actions to present SA men as religiously devoted national fighters, newspapers sympathetic to the political left reported 'the barest street terror' (*nacktester Straßenterror*) and the 'most brutal tyranny' (*brutalste Gewaltherrschaft*) in Coburg. It was clear to contemporaries that the violence in the streets had not broken out spontaneously but was prearranged, as many of the Nazi attacks started with the blast of a whistle, whereupon seconds later the stormtroopers would strike out at opponents and ordinary passers-by, who were often caught by surprise.[88]

Just days after their return from Coburg between thirty and forty Nazi militants raided the café of the German Theatre in the Bavarian capital, allegedly after a Jewish guest had arrived. They threw beer bottles and smashed at least ten windows, but they also encountered resistance, as guests in the café hit back and injured at least one of the attackers.[89] And on 21 December 1922 ten stormtroopers armed with rubber truncheons entered a Jewish-operated communal kitchen in Munich's Klenzestraße 4, where they addressed the waitresses with the words 'Are you a Jewish wench [*Judenmensch*]?', attempted to steal a collection box for the Jewish National Fund, and repeatedly shouted: 'When do the Jewish gobblers arrive?' (*Wann kommen die Juden zum Fressen?*) By the time the police arrived, the troublemakers had long left.[90] In these weeks and months such SA provocations in front of shops, in cafés, and in restaurants, with the aim of prompting first verbal protests and then physical violence, became a regular, albeit unwelcome feature of Bavarian public life.[91]

This increase in antisemitic violence ran in parallel with the further expansion of the stormtroopers, who in the spring of 1923 acquired a leading role within the Bavarian *Arbeitsgemeinschaft der Vaterländischen Kampfverbände*, generally translated as the 'Joined Forces of the Patriotic Leagues' or the 'Working Community of Patriotic Fighting Organizations'. These forces comprised about 30,000 men in the capital city of Munich alone. Internal leadership changes in the SA at this time reveal that the group was undergoing a shift in character from an aggressive but limited network of 'defence units' to a small paramilitary army, a genuine *Wehrverband* with considerable access to weapons and the aim of interfering in Bavarian state politics. As a consequence Hermann Göring in March 1923 replaced Klintzsch as leader of the SA. The latter had increasingly struggled to organize the quickly growing numbers of stormtroopers, but the main reason for this leadership change was the growing estrangement between Hitler and Ehrhardt. Klintzsch from then on acted as Göring's Chief of Staff, but resigned only two months later.[92] By this time the SA in the Bavarian capital comprised three subdivisions, each of which was 300 men strong. Every subdivision was itself organized into three *Hundertschaften*, or 'battalions', that themselves contained four *Sturmtrupps* with up to twenty-five men.[93] Senior Lieutenant in Reserve Wilhelm Brückner, who in the 1930s would be promoted to SA-*Obergruppenführer* and Hitler's chief adjutant, from the beginning of 1923 oversaw three *Sturmtrupp* battalions in Munich, commanded respectively by Karl Beggel, Rudolf Hess, and Joseph Berchtold, the latter of whom was soon to be appointed leader of the newly formed *Stoßtrupp* Adolf Hitler, the nucleus of the later SS.[94] Within Bavaria as a whole the number of stormtroopers now amounted to approximately 3,000, organized into forty *Hundertschaften*. About two-thirds of these *Hundertschaften* were situated in and around Munich, not only because of the SA's rising recruitment figures, but also because entire formations like the *Arbeitsgemeinschaft Roßbach* and a certain *Frontsoldatengruppe W* had been converted to the NSDAP. In addition to this core SA, in early 1923 units also existed in the neighbouring states of Württemberg and Thuringia, as well as in Saxony, the Ruhr region, and the cities of Hamburg, Hanover, and Göttingen. Furthermore, there were several thousand SA men in Austria, ready to cross the border if need be.[95]

Public rallies, the recruitment of new party members, and the dissemination of propaganda were not always well received by the local population, as demonstrated by the so-called 'Battle at the Whale Cellar' in the Württemberg town of Göppingen on 11 December 1922. Here, the small local branch of the NSDAP had planned a public convention under the slogan 'National Socialism, Germany's future', but the local authorities prohibited the meeting at short notice, referencing Nazi violence in the previous days in nearby Stuttgart and Geislingen. Nevertheless, in the evening hours of 11 December, sixty to ninety armed stormtroopers arrived in Göppingen from Munich by train, accompanied by the infamous 'nurse Pia' (Eleonore Baur) and led by Ernst von Westernhagen, a former lieutenant and fighter in the *Freikorps Oberland*.[96] Hitler had personally instructed his Munich followers to make the meeting happen at any cost. However, from the time of their arrival, his men encountered severe resistance from local workers. As the Nazis sang their 'patriotic' songs in the streets of the town, several hundred workers intoned the 'Worker's Marseillaise' and denounced their opponents as 'Rathenau murderers' – referring to the fatal attack on the German Reich's Foreign Minister Walther Rathenau, launched by right-wing terrorists on 24 June 1922. At some point the confrontation escalated. Dozens of shots were fired, injuring four or five people on each side. The local police finally managed to escort the Munich stormtroopers back to the train station, from which they departed. Later in the night, infuriated Göppingen workers severely injured about twenty students from Tübingen who had arrived late for the Nazi meeting.[97]

Despite this rather unsuccessful outing – which was nevertheless elevated to a party legend in Nazi propaganda – Bavaria remained the main field of activity for the SA. Consequently, it was there that on 1 May 1923, the traditional holiday of the working-class movement, the National

Socialists made their first attempt to destabilize the public order to such a degree that the establishment of an authoritarian military dictatorship could be justified as a necessary act of self-defence. The SA furnished roughly half of the 2,000–2,500 men from the Patriotic Leagues, determined to disrupt the Socialist festival procession in the city under the guise of trying to save Bavaria from a Communist coup.[98] Most of the storm-troopers were Munich locals, but some arrived from the nearby cities of Landshut, Freising, and Bad Tölz, ordered into action by a barely disguised telegram sent from the SA Command with the words 'Send off all caps immediately!' (*Sämtliche Mützen sofort losschicken!*)[99] As the Munich police reported in a government communication on 3 May, in contrast to their public statements, which regularly stressed these forces' importance for the paramilitary training of German youth and their role in preventing a Communist putsch, the leading figures of these forces were clearly driving their rank and file into the camp of 'extreme right-wing nationalism' (*ausgesprochener Rechtsradikalismus*).[100] This had now become a political problem, the president of the Bavarian police admitted, as 'for years, the police had cooperated closely with these groups in order to prevent riots from the political left'. Furthermore, the groups in question increasingly carried arms, including artillery guns and mortars, which had partly been obtained from sympathetic soldiers from nearby Reichswehr barracks.[101] Despite the obvious risks of such cooperation, the police president was nevertheless convinced that any attempt to secure public order in the capital against the leagues of the extreme right would be impossible – an indirect confession that the authority's course of tolerance toward and clandestine cooperation with the extreme right in the previous years had failed. It had not increased political stability, but undermined it.[102]

In sharp contrast to the police's view, the Social Democratic newspaper *Münchener Post* described the events of 1 May 1923 as revealing the true character of the National Socialist SA as a 'purely military fighting league' (*rein militärische Kampftruppe*). According to this usually well-informed source, the 'SA officers' had expressed a determined fighting spirit and repeatedly stated that in the case of a major clash with the left, the Reichswehr would fight on their side. The paper also provided graphic details of the SA's armaments:

Every single man of the *Sturmtrupps* had a modern infantry rifle as well as a bullet pouch and a woven belt. The hand-grenade detachments disposed of entire boxes of their murder weapons; every man carried three grenades on his belt and was furthermore armed with a Browning pistol [...] A battery of lightweight 12cm field guns was stationed behind a cluster of trees, pointing in the direction of the workers on Theresienfeld [...] Captain Gehring [sic] who swaggered around showing his 'Pour le Mérite' [medal] was in military command.[103]

The Reichswehr commander in Munich, General Otto von Lossow, who was noticeably sympathetic to the NSDAP,[104] later denied that the Reichswehr had provided cannons to the SA, but confirmed the distribution of smaller weapons. However, he insisted that the Patriotic Leagues had returned all of these weapons on the afternoon of 1 May and furthermore complained that sensational press reports on the subject would only help the French authorities to locate hidden arms depots.[105]

Among the rank-and-file stormtroopers who gathered on the Oberwiesenfeld parade ground on 1 May were many youths. Rumours spread that even pupils from higher secondary-education schools in Munich had participated, which is less surprising if one notes that since the revolutionary year of 1919, university and high-school students had frequently joined the regular armed forces as 'temporary volunteers'.[106] Playing civil war was more interesting than learning from books in school, or so it seems. This development testifies to the increasingly popular perception that politics not only mattered to one's life, but required one's own physical commitment. Such views were by no means restricted to Germany. A leader of the *Avanguardie studentesche fasciste*, the Italian 'Fascist Student Avant-Guarde', explained this pragmatic logic with unusual clarity: 'The fist is a synthesis of many things [...] Since it interacts directly upon the body of the adversary in a manner which is short and sharp, it cannot be ignored.'[107] Similarly, a German boxing magazine in 1923 coined a rhyming motto for this particular attitude: 'You can't defend yourself with thoughts, you have to grab the boxing glove.'[108]

In reality, most stormtroopers seemed to rely more on weapons than on their fists, and they usually attacked single opponents from within a larger group. As Franz Schweyer, the conservative but Nazi-critical Bavarian Minister of the Interior from the Bavarian People's Party (BVP), said in the Bavarian *Landtag* on 8 June 1923, it was a well-known National

Socialist tactic to provoke attacks from the political left by sending two to three uniformed men, followed by fifty or sixty comrades in civilian clothes, through the working-class districts of Munich. If the few uniformed stormtroopers were attacked, their comrades would then 'retaliate'. Those involved in such incidents were overwhelmingly 'immature striplings' (*halbwüchsige Bürschchen*), the minister stated, assuring the public that the police had already taken effective measures against the growing violence among the capital's youth.[109]

Schweyer's observation is in tune with the more recent findings of the sociologist Randall Collins, who, in his widely acknowledged theories on the micro-sociology of violence, has emphasized that even those people we imagine as particularly violent – the early stormtroopers being the case at hand – react violently only in specific situations that allow for particular 'emotional dynamics'.[110] The task of the SA's leaders was to create these situations, which were so vital for the bonding between individual SA men and the political movement, in a way that at the same time prevented the actual violence from escalating. Against this background, Schweyer's optimistic claim of the forces' immaturity was only superficially correct. He rightly stressed that the boys and young men of the SA posed no substantial threat to the state as long as the armed forces were loyal to the government, but he did not grasp the dual role of the police as an instrument of the state and as a force that guaranteed shielded spaces in which repeated acts of highly ceremonial SA violence could occur in a controlled manner.

The previously described incident of SA violence in Bad Tölz illustrates this dual character of the police: whereas the constable's report stressed that his behaviour had prevented the political violence from escalating into a severe physical confrontation, he was blind to the fact that the securing of a public space allowed the National Socialists at least two hours to disseminate their propaganda (first in the inn, then in the streets), not to mention the ability to capitalize, at low risk, on the 'thrill' of a symbolic confrontation with the police, contributing to the stormtroopers' growing attraction for those young men prone to violence. Other examples even point to the police's direct complicity: in the evening hours of 19 October 1921 several dozen members of the SA spontaneously decided to march to the Munich main railway station, determined to 'batter every Jew who comes our way'. Despite the police's presence, they beat up at least one man in the station

hall until a constable escorted the victim of early Nazi violence out of
the aggressors' reach. The stormtroopers remained unmolested as they
intimidated the public and shouted antisemitic songs like the following,
a variation on the well-known Borkum song: 'The Jew with his flat feet,
and his crooked nose, and his frizzy hair, is not supposed to enjoy
the German lands: throw him out! Throw him out!'[111] The formerly
mentioned example of Göppingen, however, points to the limits of the
Nazi strategy. The NSDAP virtually required the police's protection for
its provocations to be successful. Without it, open violence could erupt
that might go either way.

After the National Socialist mobilization for a government overthrow
came to nothing in May 1923, the party and its SA suffered some loss of
prestige, both within the wider milieu of Bavarian nationalists and within
its own ranks. Angry stormtroopers requested the removal of unqualified
personnel in the SA military leadership, lamented the damage done to
weapons, complained about the henhouse (*Weiberwirtschaft*) in the party's
headquarters, and urged that proper bookkeeping be conducted.[112] As
undercover informers reported to the Bavarian authorities, the NSDAP
and its SA also underwent a serious financial crisis in the early summer of
1923, caused partly by the split between Hitler and Ehrhardt, and partly by
skyrocketing inflation. When party funds permitted, SA leaders at this
time preferred to receive their salaries in foreign currency. According to
Konrad Heiden, one of the first historians of the NSDAP, officers received
respectable sums of eighty to ninety Swiss francs per month.[113] The financial crisis of the party and its stormtroopers only came to a provisional halt
after Hitler toured throughout Germany and received a considerable donation from former navy lieutenant and NSDAP party member Hellmuth
von Mücke worth US$500, which in this time of hyperinflation amounted
to roughly 400 million *Papiermark*.[114]

It was this climate of semi-clandestine cooperation between the political realm and the military that allowed for some of the most remarkable
careers of 1920s Germany. Among them was that of Ernst Röhm, formerly
a professional soldier in the Bavarian army who in the troubled days of
1919 first served in the *Freikorps* Epp and then from May onward was
charged with the reorganization of Munich's security forces. In this role he
helped 'cleanse' the police of liberal and left-leaning officials and in turn
allowed for a rapprochement of paramilitary leagues including the SA, the

Reichswehr, and the police.[115] Until the end of his life Röhm's beliefs and ideas were not only shaped by National Socialist ideology but also remained deeply affected by his experiences as an officer in the First World War. His contemporary Konrad Heiden characterized him as 'a passionate politician who as passionately fails to understand politics'.[116]

The often-glorified background of 'wartime experience' served as a common denominator for very different individuals, not only in Germany but in interwar Europe more generally. To give one example, the biographer Nigel Jones characterized Röhm's contemporary, the British Fascist leader and well-to-do playboy Oswald Mosley, in a way that also fitted Röhm – regardless of the fundamental national, social, and educational differences between these two men. Both shared a 'contempt for democracy and civilian life; impatience with muddle and delay; desire for action and efficiency at almost every price; enjoyment of violence and the military life'.[117] Similar to other leading interwar figures of the European extreme right, like Miklós Horthy in Hungary or the charismatic leader of the Romanian Legionary movement Corneliu Codreanu, Röhm – and with him many of the early SA leaders – idealized and intended to create a militarized society in which unreserved loyalty to leaders and martyrdom for the nation ranked among the highest virtues. Historians usually portray Röhm as a 'military desperado', but in addition to being an uprooted professional soldier he remained a Bavarian nationalist with a profound nostalgia for the Wittelsbach monarchy (Plate 2).[118]

Despite a considerable literature on Röhm, in particular Eleanor Hancock's detailed 2008 biography, his influence on the Nazi stormtroopers prior to the Beer Hall Putsch of 1923 is difficult to assess. It is undisputed that he played an important role in Bavaria between 1919 and 1923 that was vital for the rapprochement of the middle classes and the extreme nationalist organizations that more and more became an unofficial element of what can be called the state of Bavaria's joint anti-Marxist forces. However, Hancock's view that Röhm was the 'party's patron' and that he played a decisive role 'in all important events of the National Socialist Party up to 1 May 1923' seems exaggerated.[119] Most of the information on Röhm provided in the secondary literature is taken from his autobiography, published in 1928 under the self-confident title *Geschichte eines Hochverräters*, the 'History of a Traitor'.[120] Its author, who shortly afterward left Germany to take up a job as a military advisor in Bolivia, would not have envisaged his rather surprising comeback in late 1930, which catapulted him into the leadership of the SA, but he clearly had no interest in making his debut as an investigative journalist either. In the years before his book came out, Röhm generally operated below the radar of the public's attention and only rarely made it into the files of the authorities and into newspaper columns. He was certainly more of a powerbroker than a visible politicized military, who focused on using his proven organizational skills and good connections to Reichswehr and *Freikorps* personnel to traffick weapons to the paramilitary right (and hide them from both the Reich government and the Allies).

By 1923, Röhm, sometimes called the 'machine-gun king of Bavaria' because of his abilities to procure and hide weapons,[121] had made himself into an important figure in Bavarian politics and the military. As the self-styled 'father' of the Patriotic Leagues, he was indeed one of the most important actors on the counter-revolutionary right in the weeks and months prior to the November Putsch.[122] Other works have traced in detail the political developments of this period, driven by quickly rising inflation rates and an ever stronger political polarization.[123] As has been analysed before, the stormtroopers were ready for action as early as April 1923, but they were too insignificant to directly influence the course of political change over the next months. When Hitler finally decided to attempt a putsch, he was encouraged to act by the public outcry that followed the collapse of the German resistance to the French in the occupied Ruhr district as well as by the development of similar plans by the Bavarian quasi-dictator Gustav von Kahr, who threatened to bypass him.[124] Hitler at this time relied on the SA in two ways. First, they were supposed to act as his 'Praetorian Guard', enforcing his orders through physical power against his political rivals. Second, they were to act as a symbolic manifestation of the new leader's might in the streets of Munich, similar to the role played there by the *Freikorps* units in May 1919. Whereas the stormtroopers succeeded in the first role, particularly when Hitler had the leaders of the Bavarian government arrested in the evening hours of 8 November 1923, they failed to secure a leading position in the state's security forces. In the morning hours of 9 November it became clear that neither the Bavarian police nor Munich's Reichswehr units had joined in the putsch. When the party activists undertook a rather desperate attempt to save their 'revolution' by confronting the much better-armed and better-trained government troops in the streets of Munich, they were quickly defeated.

After a short exchange of bullets within sight of the Feldherrnhalle, fourteen 'insurgents' lay dead, among them a waiter from a nearby café. Four policemen were also killed.[125] Hitler, injured in one shoulder, escaped but was apprehended a few days later in nearby Uffing in the country house of a confidant, the businessman Ernst 'Putzi' Hanfstaengel, put on trial for high treason, and sentenced to two years' imprisonment on 1 April 1924 in Landsberg Prison.[126]

More important than the stormtroopers' factual involvement in the treasonable activities of the November Putsch was their later veneration of those 'martyrs' shot dead on 9 November 1923, as well as those who died in the following days because of their injuries.[127] The Nazis remembered these sixteen men every year in a central party ceremony in Munich, to be complemented from 1930 onwards with the idolization of Horst Wessel, a charismatic Berlin SA-*Führer* killed by a Communist squad. His veneration allowed for a more memorable personification.[128] Beginning with the Party Congress that was held in Weimar in May 1926, Hitler swore in his followers in the presence of a new party relic, the so-called 'Flag of Blood' that had been carried past the Feldherrnhalle in 1923. The symbol of defeat was now turned into a banner of glory. The 'holy sacrifice' made by the SA in 1923 and on numerous other occasions in the following years served, in the eyes of the faithful, to legitimize their claims to national leadership and social participation.[129]

The Aftermath of the Putsch

When the Reich authorities on 23 November 1923 banned the NSDAP and other organizations that had taken part in that month's putsch, the SA officially dissolved. Although many of its rank and file provisionally lost touch with the now rather static 'movement', the leading figures of the party never considered letting the organizational build-up of the previous years peter out. While still in Landsberg Prison, Hitler in April 1924 'entrusted' Röhm with the 'rebuilding' of the SA, or so the latter claimed in his autobiography. Röhm likewise maintained that he held secret talks with Göring in his Innsbruck exile and with Gerhard Roßbach, the former *Freikorps* leader who had participated in the putsch and was now hiding from the German authorities in Salzburg. As a result, Göring is said to have 'appointed' Röhm – who, unlike him, could move freely on German soil – as his deputy with 'unlimited authority' over the SA.[130]

A first conference on the fate of the banned SA, held in Salzburg on 17 and 18 May 1924, brought together under Röhm's auspices Nazis from the Reich and Austria, but apparently without Göring who was suffering from the after-effects of a bullet he had received on 9 November 1923 that might have prevented him from returning to the SA leadership. It showed 'much disunity, discord, disagreement and uncertainty,' Röhm later remembered.[131] Although he might have drawn a deliberately negative picture of this situation in order to showcase his subsequent organizational work in more gleaming colours, the following months – until the first split between Röhm and Hitler in April 1925 – allowed only for a modest revival of the stormtroopers, who were slow to recover from the blow of November 1923. One factor that prevented a quick renaissance of the SA, at least in its prior form, was obvious: Hitler, the whip and tribune of the *völkisch* right in Bavaria, was not available – initially because of his confinement in Landsberg and then, after his release from prison shortly before the Christmas holidays in December 1924, because of a ban that prohibited him from giving public speeches. As we have already seen, as early as 1921 Hitler had risen to become a charismatic leader of the extreme right in Bavaria whose influence might not have yet reached the masses outside Munich, but whose regular beer-hall speeches in the capital worked as an instrument of bonding for the SA.

Röhm could not follow in these footsteps, and it is unlikely that he aspired to do so. Instead, he stuck to what he was more experienced in: organizing a new umbrella organization, the *Frontbann*, that would unite the remains of the Patriotic League, including the banned SA.[132] Unlike the stormtroopers prior to the November Putsch, the *Frontbann* partly succeeded in operating on a nationwide level. Its original name, *Völkischer Frontkampfbund Frontbann*, testifies to the broad appeal to which this new organization aspired, in sharp contrast to the Bavarian state-sponsored *Notbann*, a short-lived attempt to unite and control the moderate *Wehrverbände* as a special police reserve force.[133] Despite its ultimate failure, the *Frontbann* brought together northern and southern German political activists of the extreme right for the first time and thus proved an important stage in the establishment of a nationwide National Socialist network. Officially, this new organization, which comprised at most 30,000 men, was supposed to 'prepare young men for military service through physical exercise and by accustoming them to obedience', as Röhm explained to the Bavarian authorities in the summer of 1924.[134] The latter, sceptical after their experience with such groups in the previous year, remained hesitant to officially recognize this new organization – regardless of the fact that Röhm had been elected a member of the Reichstag for the *Nationalsozialistische Freiheitspartei*, the 'National Socialist Freedom Party', on 4 May 1924. Even the strong support he enjoyed from Ludendorff, who was still a man of great renown in Germany, did not help him now.[135] Yet more problematic for Röhm than the scepticism of the Bavarian government was Hitler's lack of approval for his ambitious new organization. Both men met on several occasions in Landsberg Prison between May and the autumn of 1924 but could not reach an accord on a joint strategy.

Despite Hitler's lasting opposition, Röhm pursued his plans until early 1925, assuming that Hitler could be won over once the *Frontbann* had risen to become a powerful organization in the hands of the National Socialists. The dissent between the two men persisted, however, because they had mutually exclusive ideas about the future of the National Socialist movement: whereas Röhm's plans were basically a more sophisticated way to unite the paramilitary forces on the extreme right with the ultimate aim of overthrowing the Weimar Republic through violent means, Hitler had come to the conclusion that every umbrella organization of this kind was hard to bring into line, as each group usually insisted on its autonomy. The fact that competing organizations such as the *Bund Wiking*, the *Bund Bayern und Reich*, and the *Blücherbund* had all attempted to lure storm-troopers into their own ranks after the failed November 1923 putsch, did not increase Hitler's confidence in these organizations.[136] Furthermore, he had learned the lesson of the failed putsch: that a genuine paramilitary coup was unlikely to succeed as long as Reichswehr and police forces remained loyal to the legitimate government, regardless of the sympathies many of their members quite openly expressed for the goals of the extreme nationalists.[137]

After Hitler was released from Landsberg Prison on 20 December 1924, as part of a general amnesty for political prisoners, he gave up all short-term attempts to gain power through an immediate act of violence against the state and instead proclaimed a strictly legal course. Observers from the beginning suspected this approach was purely tactical

– particularly after Hitler on 26 February 1925 publicly called for a refounding of not only the NSDAP but also the SA.[138] This new SA, he now claimed, should no longer carry weapons, but should operate on strictly legal terms, serving as a propaganda tool for the NSDAP and as a training school for the party youth.[139] Its members should wear uniforms in public in order to be recognizable to everyone in the streets. The Storm Detachment must not be allowed to sink to the level of a mere defence organization (*Wehrverband*), or secret society, Hitler wrote in *Mein Kampf*, not least because 'real soldiers cannot be made by training of one or two hours per week'.[140] There were also strategic reasons behind his decision, as it would be impossible to carry out a programme of voluntary military training for large masses of men unless one could be assured of absolute power of command.[141] Competing paramilitary leaders would have made Hitler's 'absolute power of command' impossible, or so he believed.

Initially, even National Socialists had a hard time understanding the new tasks and character of this reconditioned SA, as Hitler conceived it. To many of his followers, it was counterintuitive to refuse to strike with physical force at a time when their political opponents seemed to be organizing themselves along similar lines. In early 1924 the *Reichsbanner* – closely associated with the SPD – had been founded in Magdeburg, followed by the Communist Red Front Fighters League a few months later.[142] Hitler finally gave up trying to persuade all of his followers and, on 28 September 1926, simply forbade the 'entire National Socialist press' from reporting on the reason for the SA's existence and its tasks, basic principles, and subdivision.[143] A rather desperate move, this was more a sign of temporary frustration than a clever strategy to keep the prerogative of interpretation within the National Socialist camp. In any case, Hitler's order went largely unheard – particularly as newspapers and magazines on the political right became increasingly busy defending the SA against investigative reporting by their Socialist and liberal opponents.

The general public regarded the stormtroopers in the mid-1920s predominantly as a remnant of Germany's troubled post-war years, but hardly as an organization powerful enough to challenge the public order. In contrast to this view, however, the designated Supreme SA Leader Franz Pfeffer von Salomon in October 1926 praised the group, who at that time were still a fractured web of local National Socialist militias with not more than 40,000 members throughout the Reich, as the backbone of National Socialism. Even if it was common for Fascist leaders to boisterously stress the historic mission of their 'movement', directly or indirectly referring to it as a kind of religious crusade,[144] Pfeffer's predictions of the SA's future role are worth quoting in full as they set the tone for the self-perception of many stormtroopers in the future:

Only a [political] movement of immense inner strength is able to create such an organization as our SA. Unquestionably, it is first and foremost the SA that sets us apart from the ordinary parties in parliament. The SA will guarantee our victory once the parliamentary system and its 'means' collapse. I regard the SA as the crown of our organization and of our political efforts.[145]

STORMTROOPER STREET POLITICS
Mobilization in Times of Crisis

Propaganda is violence committed against the soul. Propaganda is not a substitute for violence, but one of its aspects. The two have the identical purposes of making men amenable to control from above.
— Franz Neumann, *Behemoth*[1]

The years 1925–6 marked the starting point of the 'second SA', which – unlike its predecessor analysed in the previous chapter – quickly transformed into a highly centralized, nationwide organization that ultimately challenged the state's monopoly on violence. The SA groups that survived the failed 1923 putsch or were founded afterward in many parts of Germany in 1925 and 1926 – often operating under cover names as sports groups – initially enjoyed considerable regional autonomy.[2] Like the Munich SA between 1921 and 1923, they frequently served as a kind of private militia, commanded by the NSDAP's regional bosses, the *Gauleiter*, who used the SA's strength to hold off potential party rivals. During this period, while in Landsberg Prison and in the year after his release, Hitler had only limited control over the SA. At this time the reorganization of the NSDAP throughout the Reich was his clear priority. Once this was achieved in the summer of 1926, however, he turned his attention to the stormtroopers, installing the *Oberste SA-Führung*, or 'Supreme SA leadership office', under the command of a 'Supreme SA leader' (OSAF), whose assignment took effect starting on 1 November 1926.[3]

Early Reforms

To head this centralized SA leadership office, Hitler chose Franz Pfeffer von Salomon, a former soldier who usually referred to himself as Franz von Pfeffer – omitting the Jewish-sounding 'Salomon'.[4] Born in 1888 as the oldest of seven children from a noble family of the Lower Rhine, Pfeffer von Salomon had studied law before opting for a career as a professional soldier. Promoted to the rank of captain during the First World War, after the armistice he became an active paramilitary, commanding his own *Freikorps* in the Baltic countries and in Upper Silesia between 1919 and 1921. He quickly gained a reputation for being an excellent organizer, a ruthless and violent leader, and an extremely self-conscious personality. During the French occupation of the Ruhr area that began in January 1923 and provoked strong passive resistance by the Germans, he committed acts of sabotage and was sentenced to death in absentia by the French authorities. In March 1925 Pfeffer von Salomon set himself up as the leader of the NSDAP's *Gau* Westphalia and its SA group, becoming one of the regional bosses of the 1920s discussed in chapter 1.[5] Hitler's choice of Pfeffer von Salomon to be the first nationwide SA leader was aimed at strengthening his position in the important northwestern regions of the Reich while simultaneously containing the aspirations of ambitious party rivals like Gregor Strasser and Karl Kaufmann; at this time Kaufmann was the *Gauleiter* for Rheinland-Nord and was soon to become the *Gauleiter* and *Reichsstatthalter* for Hamburg, positions that he held for many years.[6] It was a clear signal that the SA was now to play a leading role in all parts of the Reich.

Pfeffer von Salomon proved to be a decisive figure for the growth and success of the SA. In close cooperation with Hitler – who, as we have seen, published his ideas on the reorganization of the SA in the second volume of *Mein Kampf* in February 1927[7] – the ambitious Pfeffer von Salomon started his new job by issuing a series of orders that aimed both to consolidate his central role and to create a uniform and highly hierarchically structured SA force. With the goal of reducing the regional powers of the formerly quite independent party bosses who directly commanded 'their' own SAs, he introduced a top-down chain of command. Final authority over the stormtroopers was transferred to the OSAF in Munich, which was also given oversight of the *Schutzstaffeln* (SS) and the Hitler Youth (HJ),

founded at a party rally held by the NSDAP in Weimar in July 1926.[8]
These arrangements made Pfeffer von Salomon a key figure among the
National Socialist leadership until his resignation in August 1930. His
reforms shaped the SA for years to come – even if many of his guidelines
and orders were subject to revision by Ernst Röhm, who would succeed
him as head of the SA on 1 January 1931, claiming the new title of *Stabschef*,
or 'Chief of Staff'. It needs to be emphasized that the subsequent independence and rise of the SS to become the Third Reich's most notorious
and paradigmatic terror organization should not overshadow the historical
reality that until 1934 it was the SA that dominated the SS, and not the
other way round. Characteristic of the uneven distribution of men and
influence between these two sister organizations in their early years is
the order of Röhm in early 1931 that SS membership should number only
10 per cent of that of the SA. In reality, by then the SS only comprised
4,000 men nationwide, in comparison with 88,000 stormtroopers. With
regard to their activities, the second SA and the SS operated in a largely
similar fashion during the Weimar years, although internal conflicts about
strategy, competencies, and the distribution of manpower came to light
early on.[9]

Pfeffer von Salomon's new structure of the SA was modelled on the
German army. The smallest group of an SA unit became the *Gruppe*, or
'group', comprising six to twelve men.[10] Five to six groups formed a *Trupp*,
or 'troop', in place of the former *Kompagnie*. Three to five *Truppe* made up
a *Sturm*, literally 'storm', and three to five *Stürme* were united to form a
Standarte, previously known as a *Regiment*. Finally, several *Standarten* from
the same region formed a *Gausturm*. By late 1927 there existed eighteen
Gaustürme, which in 1931 were rearranged into *Gruppen* and *Untergruppen*.[11]
Alluding to the German military tradition, SA *Sturm* units were often
given the same numbers that had previously identified their respective
region's regiments in the Imperial army.[12] To further increase the SA's simi-
larity with a regular military body like the Reichswehr, Pfeffer von Salomon
also made gorget patches mandatory. The colours of each gorget patch
indicated a stormtrooper's regional affiliation, while its numbers offered
information about his *Standarte* and *Sturm*. The rank of every trooper was
indicated by braids, stars, and oak leaves, with the latter reserved for the
highest ranks, beginning with *Standartenführer*, or colonel.[13] In writing,
leadership positions were often given in abbreviated form: apart from the

OSAF (the supreme SA leadership), there were *Gaustufs, Stafs, Stufs, Trufs,* and *Grufs* – the abbreviations for *Gaustumführer, Standartenführer, Sturmführer, Truppführer,* and *Gruppenführer,* respectively.[14] With Pfeffer von Salomon's reforms, the SA also gained relative financial autonomy. For the first time it was now in a position to administer its own membership fees and thus was no longer entirely dependent on party contributions. However, money remained sparse throughout the next years, forcing the SA to explore other ways to increase funds, including such tactics as centralizing the sales of uniforms and equipment, introducing their own cigarette brand, and approaching sympathizers in German industry.[15]

However, by late 1926, when Pfeffer von Salomon installed his supreme leadership command, these reforms were not so much a reaction to a rising number of stormtroopers, as one might assume in light of the SA's rapid growth in the following years, as they were a statement of the growing professionalism of the SA. Pfeffer von Salomon did not want his organization to be regarded as just another *Wehrverband,* a controversial stepchild of the Reichswehr that ultimately depended on the goodwill of the authorities and their weapons. His aim was to create a people's militia that would be firmly in the hands of the NSDAP and its charismatic leader and would be used first and foremost for propaganda, but would not seek out military confrontation with the legal forces. The new structure responded further to the extended geographical space in which the SA was meanwhile operating. Between 1925 and 1930 local and regional cells of the NSDAP and its SA emerged all over the Reich to complement the party's former strongholds in the south and west. Although party functionaries stressed that the reorganized SA would no longer engage in paramilitary violence, the introduction of SA insurance schemes, in which monthly contributions of 20 pfennig per person became mandatory for all stormtroopers in late 1928, tells another story. Leading National Socialists were fully aware that their policy of aggressively provoking public confrontations with their opponents would inevitably escalate into physical violence, causing injuries and, in extreme cases, death to party members. In the last three months of 1928 alone, the office overseeing SA insurance policies had to deal with 163 cases of Nazi activists injured 'on duty' and paid out more than 9,000 reichsmark[16] – numbers that increased significantly in the following years, with 881 reports of such injuries in 1929; 2,506 in 1930; 6,307 in 1931; and 14,005 in 1932.[17]

From Splinter Group to Mass Movement

In what follows I will analyse and discuss the reasons for the remarkable growth of the SA between 1925 and 1932. The internal structural changes outlined in the previous section facilitated this development, but they were just one factor among many others that a thorough historical analysis needs to take into account. To begin with I will concentrate on exemplary midsize and large cities where the SA, in joint cooperation with other paramilitary groups, contributed crucially to the militarization of public and private life, or, in other words, to the 'politicization of the everyday'.[18] The situation in Berlin and Hamburg, the two largest German cities, will be analysed in some detail, not only because there now exist a substantial amount of studies on the rise of National Socialism and the role of the SA on which I can rely, but also because these cities housed strong working-class movements.[19] The stormtroopers regarded these big cities as dangerous and hostile zones of combat, and they described them using military jargon, transforming streets and neighbourhoods into trenches and battlefields.[20] Consequently, the Nazis attempted to showcase in these cities what they could achieve in a modern metropolis where large parts of the town were (allegedly) in the hands of the political left.[21] Alongside an outline of this spatial expansion, the forms of stormtrooper activism and their daily practices will be scrutinized in detail. What made life in the SA of the early 1930s so attractive that more than 300,000 men not only joined its ranks but also displayed unusual forms of commitment to and activism within it? Rising recruitment figures notwithstanding, the SA throughout these years remained a highly volatile organization, repeatedly shaken by scandals and leadership struggles that all too often contradicted the party rhetoric of unity and moral superiority, and negatively influenced the stormtroopers' public image. By September 1930, when the NSDAP celebrated a massive victory in the nationwide elections, the educated public widely perceived the SA as the embodiment of party-sponsored hooliganism and violence, and an indicator of an increasingly 'brutalized' society.[22] However, despite their more than ambivalent reputation, the Brownshirts not only experienced exceptional growth in urban milieus but also penetrated large parts of Germany's rural areas. This 'Nazification' of the countryside happened later, but more rapidly and more completely than in the big cities, where the population proved more resistant, if not to the extent that the historiography previously claimed. This Nazi success in the provinces was all the more important because nearly three-quarters of the German electorate resided in cities with fewer than 100,000 inhabitants, the majority of them living in villages and small towns that housed fewer than 10,000 people. 'Small and middle-sized communities were crucial to Nazi success,' noted the historian Rudy Koshar, aptly summarizing the results of historical psephology for Weimar Germany.[23] Given the extensive body of regional studies meanwhile available on this subject, the aim of this chapter is not to add even more details to an already vast field, but to synthesize its findings with regard to the SA and to provide some material for future consideration.[24]

So, to begin with, what did the SA's situation between 1925 and 1930 look like from a national perspective? Thanks to the moderate success of the *völkisch* bloc in the two Reichstag elections of 1924, the National Socialists did not totally vanish from sight after the November Putsch, but for the time being their brown-shirted activists remained a marginal phenomenon. Apart from their stronghold of Munich, the stormtroopers' membership numbers for local branches did not exceed low three-digit numbers, even in Berlin and Hamburg.[25] And even in the Bavarian capital, membership stagnated in the middle of the 1920s and, as in the autumn of 1927, even temporarily decreased in response to local party crises.[26] In many smaller cities early Nazi sympathizers until the mid-1920s did little more than meet in local taverns, where they organized various kinds of political reading clubs.[27] Overall, SA membership statistics for the whole of Germany are not available for the years prior to 1930 – but given the fact that only 6,000 stormtroopers participated in the NSDAP's party rally in Weimar in July 1926, we can estimate that their number in 1928–9 was certainly less than 30,000.[28] In any case, it did not exceed 60,000 before the end of 1930, when the spectacular gains of the NSDAP in the previous months increased interest and membership in the party considerably.[29]

Some examples illustrate that the marginal presence of the SA in many regions and towns until the late 1920s significantly restricted its activist potential to openly confront its rivals: according to an early party activist, the number of Brownshirts in the free Imperial city of Frankfurt am Main, with its roughly half a million inhabitants, amounted to fifty men in 1925. Two years later that figure had only increased three- or fourfold, and the authorities reported that the Frankfurt stormtroopers were in part composed of 'the most disreputable mob'.[30] Despite all propaganda maintaining otherwise, not before 1929 could they dare to confront their rivals in 'open battle'.[31] Similarly, in the entire territory of the Saar Basin, which had a population of more than 750,000, the total number of SA militants in 1929 amounted to a mere thirty men.[32] At the same time there existed only a few hundred storm-troopers for the whole of the densely populated Ruhr area and around 600 such men in Württemberg.[33] Finally, in several small cities and administrative districts of the Reich, local SA units were either absent or remained limited to only a handful of activists who did hardly more than organize regular informal gatherings prior to the Nazi takeover of power in 1933.[34] Even where the SA was present, its parades and other forms of activism suggest 'a limited use of violence, since massive use would have proved counterproductive to the image the organization sought to present as well as to its legal survival'.[35]

Although it is impossible to outline a general pattern of the SA's expansion, there is no denying that on the whole the SA grew slowly but steadily between 1925 and 1929, not least because it was able to integrate substantial numbers of members from competing paramilitary organizations like Ehrhardt's *Bund Wiking* and Röhm's *Frontbann*.[36] In Hamburg the SA more than doubled its size after a splinter group from the *Wehrverband Hindenburg*, a former *Freikorps*, joined in 1927, but as late as April 1929 it still had fewer than 300 members.[37] In Berlin many of the SA activists who joined the organization in these years had previously belonged to the paramilitary *völkisch* sports club Olympia e.V., which after the First World War became a reservoir for the recruitment of right-wing extremists and was outlawed by the Prussian authorities on 12 May 1926.[38]

In the German capital, where Joseph Goebbels was appointed the new district party leader, violent clashes involving National Socialists became a common feature of the city's street politics as early as November 1926. Goebbels advocated an aggressive strategy that would prove highly successful and was adopted by the entire party in the 1930s. This approach acknowledged the SA's initial weakness but speculated that precisely because of it the stormtroopers must seek a confrontation with their rivals, ideally on the latter's own territory.[39] Clashes should happen in the streets of the capital in plain daylight, mainly for three reasons: first, pure and simple, the National Socialists had to increase their visibility in a modern metropolis of more than four million inhabitants where time was limited and Hitler, the tribune of the Bavarian plebs, was a distant and somehow obscure figure. Against this background, a public march that could potentially escalate into violence was a reliable and cheap means to attract attention, a way to provoke a 'sensation' in the neighbourhood.[40] 'Disturbance is the main thing – never mind how it arises,' noted the *Kreisleiter* of the city of Hameln in 1931, testifying to the successful expansion of the Berlin SA's tactic.[41] Second, Goebbels cleverly exploited the necessary presence of police forces on such occasions. Against their will, the police, who by law had to prevent street violence from getting out of control, was thereby transformed into a protecting power for National Socialists during their propaganda marches.[42] Third, such seemingly audacious acts of provocation which – it is important to repeat the point – in reality took place precisely because the risk of escalation was contained, elated those who participated in them and thereby attracted new followers. Just two weeks after his move to Berlin, Goebbels's diary entries go into raptures over the SA 'community spirit' built on the foundation of violence: 'Today I attended the general mustering of the SA. All in shape. We can set ourselves to the great work now. Assault is followed by assault. Blood pours. Binder for the new community! I think revolution.'[43] The Berlin stormtroopers, who at this time were overwhelmingly young men in their late teens and early twenties, venerated Goebbels precisely because of his focus on violence. The twenty-one-year-old *Sturmführer* Horst Wessel, who after his death in 1930 was elevated to the position of a Nazi icon, noted enthusiastically in his autobiography from the summer of 1929: 'Never did he hold back, but always allowed the entirety of our accumulated energy to discharge explosively. The SA was indebted to him for this, in particular.'[44] In similar terms Nazi militants in Hamburg emphasized the existence of a 'generational gap', claiming that after having lost confidence in their fathers they now understood the need to take their fate into their own hands. 'Fighting had become our life purpose and goal,' one of them boasted.[45]

Despite such martial rhetoric, it is important to keep in mind that SA activism between 1925 and 1929 was not yet a mass phenomenon. In all of the larger cities the stormtroopers remained a tiny minority compared to the much larger *Wehrverbände* of the right as well as the paramilitary organizations of the left. Consequently, the SA was in the first place concerned with defending its own limited territory, which often did not exceed several bars, the local party headquarters, and their immediate surroundings.[46] To make those bars that served as Nazi hangouts identifiable, innkeepers could buy 11 inch by 11 inch enamel signs bearing the SA insignia from the SA-*Reichszeugmeisterei*. It is telling that the Nazis as late as 1930 emphasized the relatively neutral design of these signs, claiming that they were only recognizable to insiders and that their destruction by political opponents was not to be expected – a promise that, of course, could not be upheld.[47] Once their strongholds were secured, the SA could then venture to explore and temporarily occupy other parts of the city, calling attention to the NSDAP and its paramilitary wing. This strategy of infiltration and expansion had important effects on the mentality of the stormtroopers: as they perceived their surroundings as hostile, confidence in each other became a vital prerequisite for their motivation to endure and achieve success in political terms. At the same time, differences in class and fortune were of limited use in the SA's semi-legal activities and thus did not matter much. The heart of the SA's 'German socialism' in fact lay in the necessity of closing ranks and operating jointly, rather than in any programmatic statement of Hitler or other party leaders concerning the party's economic policies, even if the internal schooling of Nazi activists increased considerably from 1927 onward and over the next years contributed to the transformation of the NSDAP into a 'truly modern activist party'.[48]

Against this background, it is significant that Pfeffer von Salomon's reforms maintained a central element from the earliest days of the SA: the organization of the group into 'cells' that comprised only a handful of activists. The men within such small SA groups knew each other personally and over time developed close bonds, united by a shared ideology and the joint experience of party service. Goebbels freely acknowledged that the Nazis copied this system of small 'cells' composed of political activists from their Communist rivals, but this organizational feature of the SA can be traced back to its earliest days in Munich. It is therefore plausible to assume that both the National Socialists and the Communists were ultimately inspired by military units that fought in the Great War and, in particular, by the 'comradeship' that existed within the platoons of the post-war *Freikorps*. The radical left could also build on the long socialist tradition of organized and at times violent industrial action going back to the nineteenth century.[49] In any case, the National Socialists were successful in adapting this cell framework to the new realities of the SA, with these small groups forming 'local communities of violence' – communities that, particularly in larger cities, often acted as gangs, claiming contested territories for themselves.[50]

This approach proved increasingly beneficial for the SA, particularly during the years of economic misery. Many SA *Stürme* in larger cities now operated like street gangs – understand here less as a violent and often criminal youth organization, than as a 'specific form of social arrangements' that provided its members with basic needs including a network of more or less reliable comrades, food and shelter, and a sense of belonging.[51] As is made plain by the young Ernst Haffner's 'reality novel' *Jugend auf der Landstraße Berlin*, which became a literary sensation in Germany in 1932, the increasing phenomenon of violent youth gangs in the late Weimar Republic was a direct consequence of the miserable living conditions that prevailed in the working-class districts of German cities. Unable to find even badly paid jobs as day labourers, and often originating from dysfunctional families that did not possess the means to support them, such youths organized themselves into 'cliques', forms of solidarity communities. These groups were usually structured hierarchically (headed by the *Cliquenbullen*, or 'clique bull') and served as surrogate families for their members.[52] The SA stormtrooper units, ideally organized around a charismatic local SA leader, resembled such local gangs not only in their organizational layout, but they also fulfilled – or at least promised to fulfil – similar tasks. With the sociological jargon of the 1970s, the SA increasingly functioned as a 'spontaneous mass organization': in its basic structure hierarchically organized and applying a strict leadership principle, but built on small units that operated surprisingly autonomously.[53]

The Nazi Uniform and the Authorities

Regardless of the moderate numbers of these local groups of stormtroopers in those early years, their uniforms alone indicated to the public that they belonged to a larger body of some relevance. The brown shirts were introduced nationwide in 1926 and soon became the most notorious National Socialist symbol of recognition after the swastika. Plainly visible to friends and foes alike and easily identifiable by the police, they demonstrated the courage and determination of those who dared to wear them, particularly during times when the uniform was officially prohibited. Although the psychological effects of military uniforms had been publicized roughly twenty years earlier by Wilhelm Voigt, better known as the 'Captain of Köpenick', and some years later were brilliantly ridiculed in Heinrich's

Mann best-selling novel *Der Untertan*, published in English for the first time in 1921 as *The Patrioteer*, uniforms remained highly popular in interwar Germany.[54] Prior to 1914 a symbol that represented above all the authority of the state, over the 1920s uniforms were 'democratized' as more and more groups introduced their own versions. Such clothing now became the expression of a voluntary decision and demonstrated not only belonging and conviction, but also an individual's willingness to submit to certain restrictions of individual freedom. In the case of the SA, the uniform was thus also a tool in the service of what I defined earlier as disciplinary integration. Furthermore, it became a deliberate means of provocation, not least because the law-and-order image usually associated with the police and the military was so often and so openly contradicted by the stormtroopers' public presence. The uniform, finally, also acted as an element of community formation, empowering the individual wearer by reassuring him that he was part of a larger movement and introducing clear-cut boundaries between insiders and outsiders. Ultimately, it provided the SA men with a sense of agency.[55]

A stormtrooper is on duty every time he puts his uniform on, Hitler claimed in a letter to Pfeffer von Salomon in late 1926, and he requested that neither the consumption of alcohol nor smoking be permitted on these occasions. In public, the marching SA was prohibited from cheering and booing, and even the distribution of party pamphlets was disallowed. 'Politics is exclusively made by the party,' Hitler insisted, reducing individual militants to silent recipients of his orders and stripping them of all creative power.[56] After Röhm was appointed SA Chief of Staff in January 1931, these rules were further tightened. From now on, all SA men, including their leaders – with the exception of members of the Reichstag and those fulfilling special party functions – were prohibited from taking part in public discussions, talking to journalists, or publishing on political questions.[57] The Brownshirts were expected to make a lasting visual impression in the German streets, but not to explain party politics. This strategy proved beneficial in two ways: it spared the ordinary trooper from defending his political views – a task with which many would not have coped well, as even many Nazis admitted – and it also provided surplus meaning to the utterances of the few chosen Nazi leaders permitted to speak publicly.

The Nazis were by no means the only political party or association to clothe their faithful activists in uniforms, and consequently this alone would not have set them apart at the time. Members of the veterans' association *Der Stahlhelm, Bund der Frontsoldaten*, literally 'Steel Helmet, League of Frontline Soldiers', which comprised more than 250,000 members in 1925 and thus far surpassed the SA, dressed in grey uniforms, the colour of the official army.[58] The republican *Reichsbanner* marched in green shirts and blue caps, and even the Communist *Der Rote Frontkämpferbund*, or 'Red Front Fighters League', wore a kind of proletarian uniform that combined the traditional workman's cap with military insignias.[59] These four paramilitary 'armies', however, did not fight a civil war.[60] They marched in the streets and held mass meetings with increasing frequency, but they rarely clashed with other groups or people directly, largely because of the presence of the police. Their public demonstrations nevertheless provided opportunities for violent attacks, which usually occurred before or after the political events proper. These incidents were in fact a vital element of Weimar Germany's paramilitarism, and at least the Nazis and the Communists factored such violence into their strategies. 'Beat the Fascists, wherever you find them!' the Communist functionary Heinz Neumann wrote in the party organ *Die Rote Fahne* in early 1930, and the Nazis for their part called for nothing less than the complete annihilation of the 'Communist-Bolshevik *Untermenschen*'.[61] In contrast to such calls for direct and potentially murderous action, the *Reichsbanner* and the *Stahlhelm* largely contented themselves with acting within the symbolic dimension of public marches and rallies.[62] However, over time, these two organizations likewise radicalized, if more in speech than in action, so that the American journalist Hubert R. Knickerbocker compared Germany in 1931–2 to a 'town with four fire departments, each ready at the gong to leap down the brass pole and race for the goal. It is a village with four gangs, each ready at the drop of the hat to sally forth and slaughter the others.' Similarly, the young French author Jacques Decour, who worked as a temporary teacher for a Magdeburg gymnasium in the autumn of 1930, noticed 'revolts of ideas [*Ideenaufstände*] on every corner. These are the heroic times of the Republic. Everywhere faith, fanaticism.'[63]

Not surprisingly, the German authorities attempted to contain the escalation of violence in the streets. The strategies they adopted differed from region to region as well as in timing, intensity, and intention. Whereas Bavaria by and large remained an area of retreat for the National Socialists, the Prussian government in the hands of the Social Democrats repeatedly pushed for action against the party, particularly after the murder of Reich Foreign Minister Walther Rathenau on 24 June 1922 and the November 1923 putsch. Contrary to what has often been stated, they were not unsuccessful, as the following example demonstrates. In 1928 the Berlin police president forbade the holding of a funeral parade for the SA man Hans-Georg Kütemeyer. Official reports stated that Kütemeyer, whose body was found in the *Landwehrkanal*, the city canal, on the morning of 17 November 1928, had been involved in a brawl with construction workers the night before and had fallen and drowned in the canal in a state of acute intoxication.[64] The Nazis, by contrast, claimed that political opponents had murdered him, elevating Kütemeyer to one of the earliest *Blutzeugen*, or 'blood witnesses', of their movement in Berlin and Brandenburg.[65] As would soon become a regular habit, the National Socialists intended to honour an alleged party martyr with a lavish funeral parade. Such funerals were not only political demonstrations but also testified to the all-encompassing ambitions of the Nazi ideology, which provided, or at least heavily contributed to, fundamental services like marriage and death rites. The Prussian police clearly understood the political character of the upcoming procession. They claimed that the Nazi Party had irresponsibly enhanced the level of political emotions among its followers and therefore they feared for public security if these emotions were set free during the parade. The police also declared that they would not respond to Goebbels's official letter of protest 'because of its insolent and indecent form' – and that they would refuse to do so in the future as well.[66] Such details indicate that the authorities were all but helpless against early Nazi attempts to decide the 'rules of the game' – if there was strong political will to fight them and a basic understanding of how symbolic politics worked in an age of mass media and antagonistic ideological worldviews.

The authorities banned the second SA several times. In Prussia it was prohibited twice, first in the capital city of Berlin from 6 April 1927 to 5 April 1928.[67] This ban certainly made Nazi recruitment in the largest German state more difficult and thus contributed to the slow growth of the stormtroopers in this area between 1925 and 1928. However, this ban had no effect on other parts of the Reich and certainly did not strike at the heart of the SA in Munich.[68] A few years later, in 1932, the SA was prohibited again, this time on a nationwide level. The ban came into effect on 13 April, but the new chancellor, Franz von Papen, lifted it as early as 14 June.

A Bavarian initiative to extend the ban at least in its own territory failed two weeks later.[69] Overall, the effects of these temporary interdictions on the SA remained limited. When the Nazis were not allowed to wear their brown uniforms, they simply turned up to events in civilian clothing. A marching and singing SA troop operating under a fantastic cover name and with members dressed in white shirts or other surrogate 'uniforms' still remained highly recognizable. At times these events boasted up to 1,000 participants, even in midsize cities.[70] The Nazis' cat-and-mouse game with the authorities during these 'white shirt times' (Weißhemden-Zeit)[71] in the end more than contributed to the atmosphere of excitement and fun surrounding the SA than prevented men from joining the stormtroopers, not to mention the fact that it further undermined the authority of the legitimate governments. Instructive in this respect is the verdict from 13 March 1931 of the Kammergericht in Berlin entitled 'On the Prohibition of the Public Display of NSDAP Party Uniforms', which also applied to the well-known 'substitute' uniforms. The judges declared this prohibition invalid because, among other things, members of the public could not be expected to understand the Nazi dress code and therefore ran the risk of coming into the firing line of the police.[72]

Over the years the German states' pressure on the NSDAP and the SA was furthermore hampered by the growing sympathies for the Nazi movement among parts of the judiciary and the police. Both groups felt closer to right-wing nationalists, who claimed to fight for law, order, and the nation, than to their counterparts on the radical left, who favoured revolution, a profound change in the social and public order.[73] A closer look at the different political strategies of the extremist parties is instructive: whereas Nazi propaganda positively reached out to police officers by highlighting their unique grievances – their alleged abuse at the hands of the government, which forced them to clean up the mess the democratic parties were said to be responsible for – the Communists vituperated against the officers as henchmen of the 'system', dupes of the capitalist establishment, and traitors to their own class.[74] In the Free State of Saxony, where the NSDAP was present with ever more local groups since the mid-1920s and was particularly successful in those industrial regions with high unemployment,[75] the Nazis claimed to have infiltrated the regular police forces to the extent that, by their own statistics, 40 per cent of all officers were members of the NSDAP in 1932. In the working-class city of Chemnitz the number of 'Nazi policemen' amounted to more than 90 per cent, boasted a Nazi deputy in the Saxon *Landtag*, the regional parliament.[76] Such figures were certainly overstated, but are still indicative of the trend that even in those states and regions where the authorities promoted tough police action against SA violence, police officials did not necessarily share this view.[77] Social Democrats in Saxony repeatedly complained that the police were too lenient: they neither sufficiently engaged in the prevention of political criminality nor demonstrated zeal and commitment in redressing concrete crimes. As a result, workers in cities like Chemnitz found themselves no longer safe against the 'terror of Fascist mobs, not even in their own flats'.[78]

Laughing at the Stormtroopers

By 1930 the SA had become a regular and highly visible, but also very controversial, element in the German streets. When local communities showed a determination to prevent the Nazis from gaining a foothold – as was the case in the small city of Michelstadt in the Forest of Odes – several hundred stormtroopers from the region 'retaliated'. On 6 April 1930 they drove into the city, where they indiscriminately threw stones through windows and at local pedestrians, injuring many adults and at least one child.[79] Yet not only did the SA provoke the strong emotions of fear, admiration, and repudiation, but it also became the target of satire and ridicule. In December 1930 the weekly *Ulk*, a supplement of the highly respected liberal *Berliner Tageblatt*, ironically informed its readers of the unlikely event that 'recently three SA men had caused a stir at [Berlin's centrally located] Leipziger Straße by walking along silently and lost in thought'.[80] Describing the normal operation of Fascist mobs in singing and marching in the streets and committing acts of violence by the wayside, the journalist and writer Siegfried Kracauer laconically stated that events 'went the National Socialist way' (*nationalistisch zugegangen*) – thereby downplaying the political danger posed by the quickly growing number of such incidents.[81] The SA was also mocked in Erich Kästner's 1931 novel *Fabian: The Story of a Moralist*, albeit alongside his Communist counterpart. In one chapter Kästner describes a fictional shooting between a Nazi and a Communist that results in mutual injuries. When both of them arrive at the local hospital, the doctor on duty comments on the scene:

'You've brought me two politicians?' he said, with a smile. 'Altogether, we've had nine cases brought in tonight, one with a serious bullet wound in the stomach. All workmen and clerks. Have you ever noticed that these fellows come from the suburbs, and generally know each other? These political brawls are indistinguishable from the dance-hall scraps. In both cases they represent a perversion of German social life. It looks as if they are trying to reduce the unemployment figures by potting each other off. A queer kind of self-help.'[82]

Such forms of irony barely concealed the moral despair and political frustration that were widespread within the left-liberal intelligentsia of Germany in the early 1930s, particularly after the Reichstag elections of 14 September 1930 in which the NSDAP won 18.3 per cent of the votes (Plate 8). With a sixfold increase in support compared to 1928, it now represented the second strongest party in the new parliament. There was no denying that the Nazis had become a considerable political force, to the extent that just over one year later, in December 1931, a report from a secret meeting of KPD (*Kommunistische Partei Deutschlands*) propagandists in Berlin complained that the Communists had utterly underestimated the National Socialist danger: 'By now everyone accepts that sooner or later Hitler will come to power and reconciles himself to the idea that our time will come after the Nazis' failure [*Abwirtschaft*].'[83] Whether National Socialism became attractive because of the brown-shirted activists so prone to violence is still a matter of debate.[84] In addressing this question, one needs to take into account local varieties of the party as well as the general consequences of the fragmentation of the public sphere in Weimar Germany. As historian Stephan Malinowski has argued, an 'increasing dichotomisation of awareness' became a dominant feature of these years. He defined this 'dichotomisation' not only as the tendency to distinguish sharply between 'us' and 'them', but also as a basic operation that structured one's perceptions even before reflection could set in.[85] National Socialists and Communists were both successful in creating distinct public spheres that were tangible and compelling for their followers, but inaccessible to those who did not share their basic ideological assumptions. Both movements encouraged their adherents to block out unwelcome facts and worldviews, to the benefit of an idealized version of the party's own, allegedly 'proper', understanding of social and political realities.[86] The former SA-*Brigade* Leader, Franz Bock, summarized this attitude when interrogated at the International Military Tribunal in 1946: 'Every desire for self-preservation demands a struggle. The realization of National Socialistic ideas, with the aim to assume power in the State, required political struggles and fighting. Our weapons, however, were spiritual ones – propaganda, the spoken word, and mass demonstrations.'[87] While the latter part of this statement downplays the SA's central use of physical violence for tactical reasons, it testifies to the fundamental perception in 1920s Germany that politics was above all a matter of antagonistic and mutually exclusive worldviews.

The political theorist and legal scholar Carl Schmitt, who in 1932 justified the *Preußenschlag*, the unlawful removal of the SPD-led Prussian government, and soon afterward became the Third Reich's crown jurist, elevated this foe–friend distinction into a political philosophy. Within the SA, Schmitt's sophisticated academic reasoning clearly was less relevant than more concrete arguments, won through fists and fights. However, a similar trend of overstating political differences as fundamental ideological confrontations of utmost importance characterized both ends of the intellectual spectrum. Nazi propaganda constantly reminded the rank-and-file stormtrooper that he was part of a bigger picture, an eyewitness to a crucial period in history that he could actually and personally shape. Such optimistic determination was by no means exclusive to Germany; it was a common feature of all Fascist movements in interwar Europe, as Roger Griffin in particular has forcefully argued: extreme nationalists unanimously believed 'that Western history was itself at a turning point from which it could collapse into terminal barbarism and anarchy amidst social breakdown and war, or give birth to a new type of society beyond the current age of chaos and decadence'.[88] A random survey of several editions of the capital's two Nazi dailies, Goebbels's *Der Angriff* and Strasser's *Berliner Arbeiterzeitung*, confirm this ultimately eschatological view. In both papers, journalists aimed not at factual accuracy, but at creating an alternative public sphere in which extreme partisan views could find expression and their activists achieve recognition and salvation. For the uninitiated, the Nazi headlines at least provided 'sensation', a welcome stimulation for those Berliners who tolerated everything except boredom, speculated Goebbels, who was, as always, of two minds about the 'city of the intelligence and the asphalt'.[89] The public reaction to the stormtroopers' presence and actions can thus not be evaluated from a higher, 'objective', outlook but must be embedded in a careful reconstruction of the different situational contexts without glossing over the strong partisan views expressed in the historical documents.

What holds true for the SA is likewise relevant for the analysis of political violence in the late Weimar Republic more generally. Even those official – and by and large reliable – statistics at our disposal, which indicate a strong rise in political crimes between 1928 and 1932, do not tell us about the perspective of contemporaries.[90] All organizations involved in this violence regarded their own men as 'firefighters' and those of the other groups as members of criminal 'gangs' – to revert for a moment to Hubert Knickerbocker's colourful metaphors. Stormtroopers interpreted the risk of being personally attacked in the streets as just another indicator of this grave national danger. And this risk was indeed high, particularly in those working-class districts that the SA was determined to 'conquer'. As Anthony McElligott has demonstrated for the city of Altona, which in 1938 became a part of Hamburg, not only were early Nazi activists prior to 1933 greeted in the streets with shouts of 'Perish Nazi!' (*Nazi verrecke!*) or 'Heil Moskau!', but several were forced to move home after their flats were broken into and ravaged. Communist and *Reichsbanner* men repeatedly attacked individual Nazis when the latter left well-known Nazi hangouts, were recognizable by their uniforms, or were personally known to their assailants. Such attacks at times resembled genuine hunts. They were often carried out by a large group of armed attackers against a single man or a very few victims, who were hit in the faces and on the heads with nailed fencing stakes, stabbed, beaten, or trampled until they were severely injured or dead.[91] If one compares the actual acts of violence that occurred in the early 1930s, there were few practical differences between the street crimes of Nazi, Communist, *Reichsbanner*, and *Stahlhelm* perpetrators. Situational factors mattered more than ideological ones, which served above all as ex post-facto legitimization.

The Escalation of Violence

Official nationwide statistics for the year 1931 counted 8,248 people who had been injured or killed as a result of political violence. National Socialists represented the largest group of victims (4,699), followed by members of the *Reichsbanner* (1,696), Communists (1,228), and *Stahlhelmers* (625).[92]

Regional figures overall confirm this pattern: official statistics for the Hanover administrative district in 1931 note injuries to seventy-one Nazis, forty-seven members of the *Reichsbanner*, seven Communists, and six *Stahlhelmers*. In addition, one *Reichsbanner* man was killed in the region.[93] In Saxony 683 people were injured and fourteen died as a consequence of political violence in the same year. Among the dead were six National Socialists, two Communists, and four 'adherents of other parties'.[94] In Leipzig, of the six people killed for political reasons between 1929 and March 1933, three were National Socialists, one was a Communist, and one was a *Reichsbanner* man.[95] However, another statistic for the Reich, published by the left-liberal weekly *Die Welt am Morgen*, reported 155 deaths and 426 people injured as a result of political activities between 1929 and July 1931, with the majority of casualties belonging to the political left (108) and only thirty-one members of nationalist organizations being killed.[96] According to the Nazis' own data, 143 SA men were killed between 1930 and 1932 nationwide, with eighty-four deaths in 1932 alone.[97] Judging from these statistics, National Socialists seem to have been the group that was most often attacked and injured, whereas Communist and Social Democratic activists, while exposed to a significant risk of being killed, were attacked less frequently. If one considers, furthermore, that between 1929 and 1931 the number of stormtroopers and Communist paramilitaries was significantly smaller than the number of *Reichsbanner* and *Stahlhelm* men, it is safe to deduce that the activists of the two former organizations behaved in a considerably more violent manner than those of the latter.

To justify and at the same time further increase the hostilities, Nazi propaganda claimed that the collective national body and the individual stormtrooper's body were intrinsically linked, and consequently the personal risk of and harm inflicted on the latter was thus to be regarded as a direct assault on the nation. The establishment of such parallels between individual experience and the nation's fate – ultimately a grandiose gesture of self-empowerment – was a key element in the expansion of the Brownshirts' appeal in these crucial years. Another element was the SA's militancy. Although the group's leaders repeated, mantra-like, in public speeches that stormtroopers were not allowed to carry arms and would resort to physical violence only for legitimate self-defence, it was an open secret that the truth was often quite different. Even if the many SA men serving in border protection units who had been officially trained by the Reichswehr by and large did not (yet) engage in violent confrontation, this claim certainly did not hold for the SA 'gangs' in the larger German cities, where the possession of a gun was tantamount to an elevation in status. Admittedly, the early days of the Munich SA, when whole units could walk into a Reichswehr barrack to pick out heavy artillery and machine guns for their paramilitary exercises, were over. But the sheer amount of smaller firearms circulating in Germany more than made up for the loss of access to military equipment, particularly as these arms were now used more frequently, for training purposes as well as for attacks. During these years the police regularly confiscated from members of the SA such weapons as knuckledusters and rubber truncheons, but increasingly also pistols, daggers, guns, and explosives.[98] If one believes the memoirs of the former Prussian Minister of the Interior and Berlin police president Albert Grzesinski, the Berlin police in early 1932 even confiscated two 'life-size effigies' of the Prussian Minister of the Interior Carl Severing and himself, 'the heads of which were neatly punctured by bullet holes'. Both men had 'proven a convenient target for the young soldiers of the Third Reich,' Grzesinski remarked dryly.[99]

Finally, in 1931 and 1932 the authorities uncovered National Socialist plans to overthrow the legitimate government by force and to establish a dictatorship. In the autumn of 1931 they published the 'Boxheim documents', which contained detailed plans for a Nazi takeover of power in reaction to a possible Communist putsch. Drafted most notably by the twenty-eight-year-old probationary judge Werner Best of Darmstadt in Hesse – who later became SS-*Obergruppenführer*, chief of Section 1 of the Reich Security Main Office (RSHA), head of the civil administration of German-occupied northern France, and finally, in 1942, Reich plenipotentiary in Denmark – this strategy paper described how a state of emergency would be put in place and then upheld by the SA and other right-wing paramilitary 'defence' groups. Everyone who attempted to interfere in the Fascist takeover of power was to be executed on the spot.[100] Half a year later, in March 1932, the police in the Palatinate discovered that a series of bomb attacks that had started in the region the previous summer were perpetrated not by Communists, as had been assumed initially, but by the National Socialists. The leading figure behind these terror attacks was the regional SS leader Theodor Eicke, who in the summer of 1933 was to become commander of the Dachau concentration camp. In the early 1930s he had been in charge of plant security for I. G. Farben Ludwigsburg, a position in which he was well placed to procure explosives for approximately eighty bombs.[101]

In both cases Hitler and other leaders of the NSDAP hastened to persuade the authorities that such incidents had to be seen as excessive but ultimately legitimate reactions to the imminent Communist threat. Overambitious regional Nazi functionaries had drafted the plans and prepared the bombings against explicit orders from party headquarters, they claimed. At the same time the Nazi leadership exploited the mounting pressure on the government that resulted from such threats: public order in Germany, they argued, could now only be maintained with the help of the NSDAP and the SA, and not by turning against them. Reich Chancellor Heinrich Brüning personally requested the *Oberreichsanwalt* (attorney general) to handle the Boxheim scandal with care and to avoid drastic judicial action – not least in order to calm down the liberal and Socialist press that was determined to expose the Nazi doublespeak. It hardly came as a surprise that Best was acquitted of charges of high treason in October 1932.[102]

Starting in 1930, the boundaries between political criminality, 'organized' criminality, and petty criminality became more fluid than ever. In these times of widespread poverty and even starvation, a simple theft of food could be turned without further ado into a political act – justified, for example, as Communist self-help against capitalist exploitation.[103] In Berlin the (officially banned) Communist Red Front Fighters as well as the National Socialist stormtroopers occasionally formed political gangs that developed close ties with the underworld.[104] That many SA men combined their political and criminal activities was so obvious that, in the vernacular, *Sturm* 25, which operated in the working-class district of Berlin-Neukölln, was referred to as *Ludensturm*, the 'storm of pimps' – a characterization that the SA's historiography several years later bragged about as a kind of honorary title.[105] The notorious *Sturm* 33, based in the western city district of Berlin-Charlottenburg, was locally known as 'murder storm' because its members were repeatedly involved in fatal shootings.[106] Such criminal activities not only shook public opinion of the SA, but at times also diminished its assets: in 1931 police reports stated that penniless stormtroopers had repeatedly staged political raids in order to claim SA insurance benefits, a topic that anti-Fascist publications eagerly exploited.[107]

Propaganda marches increasingly began to escalate into violence, with Berlin's *Blutmai*, or 'Blood May', of 1929 and the Altona 'Bloody Sunday' of 1932 being the most fatal encounters. Most victims on these occasions were killed by police bullets, fired in an attempt to restore order. The Berlin *Blutmai*, provoked by the Communists, claimed thirty-one lives, while its Nazi-provoked Altona counterpart took seventeen lives. In both cases more than 100 people were injured.[108] Apart from those spectacular incidents, party meetings that ended in fisticuffs, direct assaults, and shootings involving members of competing political organizations mushroomed in ever more German cities. The 'pseudopacification' of these urban 'communities of violence' that had characterized the previous years was over.[109] Grzesinski described this change in retrospect: 'Ordinary brawls had given way to numerous attacks. Knives, blackjacks and revolvers had replaced political argument. Terror was rampant.'[110] Goebbels characterized the situation in similar terms as a 'bloody conflict with chair legs and revolvers' that, in his eyes, would be 'ever more necessary'.[111]

Whereas this phenomenon of intensified violence was initially largely confined to disadvantaged working-class neighbourhoods, it soon burst through the unofficial social boundaries, as the following example from Cologne demonstrates: on the evening of Friday, 6 March 1931, the local chapter of the Catholic Centre Party in Cologne-Braunsfeld met for an evening of discussion on the fashionable topic of 'Soviet Star and Swastika'. About seventy people were present in the room, among them a considerable number of uninvited local Nazis who had arrived on bicycles and motorbikes. They left the engines of the latter running, in case a quick exit would prove necessary. In the hall the Nazis initially listened quietly to the main speaker of the evening, a certain Dr Hertz, but soon began to heckle and insult him. Finally, Toni Winkelnkemper, a twenty-five-year-old student of law at the University of Cologne who had already risen to become NSDAP *Gau* office leader (*Gauamtsleiter*) for the Rhineland, and at least for this night was acting as the leader of the SA *Sturm* present, called the speaker a 'coward'. This seems to have been a prearranged code word, as the Nazis immediately started to throw chairs in the direction of the table where the organizers sat. The prosecutor later described the following minutes vividly:

> The defendant Winkelnkemper tossed a heavy ashtray in the direction of the pastor Dr Frings [...] At the same time, another person, who could not be identified, struck at the speaker Dr Hertz. The participants

of the meeting who belonged to the Centre Party confined themselves to protecting the women who were present and to parrying off those ashtrays and chair legs that were used as missiles. The whole process lasted about five minutes. During this period, 58 chairs were partly damaged, partly completely smashed; some other fittings of the room (glass door, lustre, panelling) were also spoiled. The damage amounts to 400 marks.[112]

Several men from the Centre Party were injured and needed medical care. The forehead wounds suffered by Pastor Frings – he would be elected Archbishop of Cologne in 1942 and elevated to the cardinalate after the Second World War – had to be stitched up.[113] Winkelnkemper was initially sentenced to a prison term of six months, but was granted a reprieve on his appeal.[114] Free to move in public, he continued to assault political opponents.[115] After the Nazis came to power, Winkelnkemper carved out a remarkable career: in 1933 Goebbels appointed him regional director for the Rhineland (*Landesstellenleiter Rheinland*) in the newly established Ministry of Public Enlightenment and Propaganda, and he also became a member of the Prussian parliament and of the (largely defunct) Reichstag. In 1937 the now Dr Winkelnkemper became director of the Reich radio station Cologne and later director of the *Reichsradiogesellschaft*. In 1939 he was promoted to SS-*Standartenführer*. His brother Peter became mayor of Cologne in 1941, occupying a position held some years earlier by Konrad Adenauer, the future first chancellor of the Federal Republic of Germany.

This short episode demonstrates not only how violent 'politics of the streets', criminal behaviour, and SA student activism were increasingly interrelated, but also that such acts were not restricted to young men with a wannabe 'gangster' attitude or to disadvantaged youth beyond party control. Instead, such incidents were a vital element of the officially sanctioned NSDAP street politics of the early 1930s. Those who 'rule[d] the street' would sooner or later also come to political power, as leading Nazis repeatedly argued.[116] In turn, this political strategy meant that every kind of public violence could now be elevated to a political act and praised as a further contribution to the final goal of abolishing the Republic. A characteristic, if extreme, example is the so-called Kurfürstendamm riots of 12 September 1931. On this day – Rosh Hashanah, the Jewish New Year holiday – hundreds of stormtroopers walked the famous Kurfürstendamm boulevard in Berlin,[117] shouting antisemitic slogans and savagely beating passers-by whom they believed to be Jewish. What was meant to look like a spontaneous eruption of violence was in fact a well-prepared attack arranged by Goebbels and the Berlin SA leader Wolf-Heinrich von Helldorff. With the stormtroopers strategically dispersed in small groups, the police, who were caught by surprise, had a hard time establishing order. In the end, more than thirty attackers were identified, prosecuted, and sentenced to prison terms and monetary penalties.[118] Many of the Nazi activists in Berlin felt betrayed by their party, which on the occasion of the trial denied that the SA had acted on previous orders. Thus, by the end of 1931 up to 400 discontented stormtroopers from the capital had formed the Comradeship Social Help group (*Kameradschaft soziale Hilfe*), a self-help group that advocated for a split from the Hitler movement and was – allegedly – even willing to support the *Reichsbanner* in case of an intensification of political violence in the capital.[119] Despite this internal dissatisfaction and the comparatively harsh sentences handed down in the Kurfürstendamm trial, from the perspective of the NSDAP leadership the riots were a symbolic success: the SA had demonstrated that its antisemitism and anti-democratic hate were no longer confined to beer halls and other venues of limited respectability, but that the party was strong enough to 'rule' even the most respectable streets in the nation's capital – if only for an hour. In the eyes of the party faithful, the storm-troopers had thus served the role dictated by propaganda of an ideologi-cally driven attack force, always ready for action.

Unemployment and Social Unrest in the SA

However, it would be misleading to take the claims of party leaders at face value. In 1931 and 1932, when the number of unemployed in Germany rose to over six million, men joined the SA for practical reasons as much as for ideological commitment.[120] In these years more than one out of two stormtroopers was temporarily or even permanently out of work, with unemployment figures in particular *Stürme* as high as 80 per cent. In Berlin between 60 and 80 per cent of all Nazi militants were underemployed in 1931.[121] The situation was similar in Hamburg, where 2,600 of 4,500 SA men – or slightly more than 56 per cent – were without a job in 1932.[122] With monthly membership turnover rates at times higher than 20 per cent, many who aligned themselves with the SA did not remain in it for more than a few weeks or months. What is more, hundreds of thousands of these newcomers only joined the SA, but not the Nazi Party, although membership in the party was officially compulsory starting in 1927.[123] Financial considerations certainly played a role in these decisions, a view supported by the fact that even those who held membership cards did not necessarily pay their dues. Participation in the SA's social life and paramilitary exercises, which now more than ever 'provided [an] alternative full-time activity to work' for German men, ultimately did not depend on such formalities, at least as long as the superiors deemed someone's active service to the movement as satisfactory.[124]

Group dynamics, the prospect of professional advancement, or simply the need for subsistence in these years, often constituted a more persuasive inducement for joining the SA than did ideological affiliation. Case studies point in the same direction. In Osterode, a small industrial city on the verge of the Harz Mountains with 9,000 inhabitants, only forty-eight of the seventy-one men who had joined the SA prior to 1933 had also become members of the Nazi Party.[125] And in one particular impoverished part of East Prussia there existed in 1931 a local SA *Sturm* of whose 118 men not one was a regular party member.[126] It is therefore safe to generalize that, throughout Germany, many of those who joined the stormtroopers in the last two to three years of the Weimar Republic were workers who were looking for protection against looming job cuts or, if already unemployed, speculated that the growing Nazi network in the region might provide a possibility of re-entering the job market.[127] In the meantime an increasing number of unemployed men spent their days and evenings in so-called *Sturm* taverns, bars that targeted a party-affiliated audience in the hope of economically surviving the sharp decrease in alcohol consumption that had begun in Germany in the late 1920s.[128] At the peak of the economic crisis, the SA established its own job agencies, trying to persuade party members to employ fellow stormtroopers. The SA even created 'work storms' (*Arbeitsstürme*) in which otherwise jobless and penniless militants offered their labour on the private job market.[129] The General Association of Christian Trade Unions in 1932 emphasized the close connection between the increasing political radicalism of German youth and the devastating economic situation: 'A social and economic system that fails to provide the youth both with a task and any hope for earning a living pushes them into the role of adventurers who have nothing to lose but all to gain from an overthrow. The political elections of 1931 demonstrate with utmost clarity that all those who are uprooted [. . .] run after those whom they sense to be engaging in deliberate action, even if this action is purely negative and destructive.'[130]

In light of these economic and political problems, the SA became increasingly difficult to run, despite its broad appeal and social activities. Nevertheless, its membership increased in ever-growing figures between late 1930 and the summer of 1932 – from 77,000 in January 1931 to 221,000 in November of the same year and 445,000 in August 1932.[131] As became characteristic within the Third Reich more generally several years later, networks and personal loyalties among leading National Socialists were often more important than instructions written on paper. Internal quarrels and personal rivalries, particularly among party functionaries and regional SA leaders who now commanded thousands or even tens of thousands of men, were common and at times even disgusted Nazi sympathizers. The former lieutenant and early NSDAP supporter Hellmuth von Mücke bluntly stated as early as August 1929: 'The party is totally rotten and corrupt, both when it comes to organization as well as in the domains of strategy and ideology. *The dominant aspect of the party is publicity* [. . .] In short, it is a pigsty.'[132]

There were, however, not only personal, but also substantial ideological differences that threatened the cohesion of the SA as well as the National Socialists' image as a unified and strong movement more generally. Particularly in the industrial centres of northern Germany, many stormtroopers became associated with the 'socialist' left wing of the NSDAP, which in the late 1920s was led by the brothers Otto and Gregor Strasser, Goebbels, and the Berlin SA-*Führer* Walther Stennes.[133] These men regarded national renewal and a social revolution as two sides of the same coin, if only sometimes for tactical reasons, and aimed at winning over in particular the young proletariat and parts of the impoverished middle classes. Whereas the NSDAP usually encapsulated its social promises in popular slogans like 'Breaking interest slavery' or 'Work and Bread', the 'Nazis of the Left' asked for more sweeping changes, like the nationalization of the big banks, the 'persecution of the profiteers', the introduction of a capital tax, and, of course, an immediate end to reparation payments according to the Young Plan, which was finally adopted in May 1930.[134]

Although these demands were hardly more than a popular and left-leaning sampling of the *völkisch* repertory embellished with anti-capitalist rhetoric that complemented the constant Nazi hammering of the Jews, some of these positions demonstrate a remarkable overlap with Communist views. Unlike the Hitler faction of the Nazis, the followers of Stennes advocated a close alliance with the Soviet Union (largely for tactical reasons that focused on opposing the Western Allies and in particular England) and championed the national independence movements in India and Egypt. They argued against German federalism (and for a strong centralized Germany), against the Catholic Church (using basically the same arguments that were put forward in the *Kulturkampf* of the late nineteenth century), and against the inviolability of private property.[135]

In this factional struggle ideological leanings and practical concerns were closely intertwined: with the SA growing into a veritable mass organization since 1930, its northern leaders impatiently requested greater financial contributions from the party for their institution, claiming that it was the SA, and not the party bureaucracy, that did most of the work in furthering the NSDAP's aims. Furthermore, many of them still favoured a violent putsch over the current strategy of a legal takeover of power – a slow and uncertain tactic that attracted voters and new party members but otherwise did not change much. This basic conflict not only led to the resignation of Pfeffer von Salomon as OSAF on 29 August 1930, to be replaced by the reactivated Ernst Röhm in January 1931,[136] but also lay at the heart of a series of violent clashes within the Nazi movement, most notably the two 'Stennes revolts' that occurred in late August 1930 and late March 1931.

After frustrated Berlin stormtroopers led by Stennes attacked the capital's local NSDAP headquarters on 30 August 1930, Hitler intervened and personally rushed to the capital, where he agreed 'in tears' to several of the SA's demands, promising the left wing of the party better pay and more influence. With the important Reichstag election only two weeks away on 14 September, internal quarrels had to be avoided at all costs.[137] However, Hitler and the NSDAP party leaders in Munich from this point on became determined to curb the influence of Stennes and his followers, whose constant agitation for revolutionary action threatened to derail the party's 'legal' course. The opportunity to strike came on 28 March 1931 when the Reich president passed an emergency decree to prevent political riots and requested that the NSDAP control its stormtroopers tightly or else run the risk of being outlawed. In reaction, Hitler deposed Stennes and his right-hand man, the *Stabsleiter* Walter Jahn, from office. Technically, this dismissal was achieved through a decree from the new SA Chief of Staff Röhm on 31 March 1931.[138] In return, Stennes and his followers opted to begin a new mutiny and on the next day once again occupied the Berlin party headquarters and the editorial offices of Goebbels's 80,000-circulation *Der Angriff*.[139] This time they found their internal party adversaries well prepared, however. To take the wind out of the opposition's sails, Röhm promised that as of 1 May 1931 all SA-*Gruppen* would be allocated fixed budgets. Most Berlin stormtroopers quickly pledged allegiance to the Führer, ensnared and partly also directly bought by Hitler who in the capital could rely on Kurt Daluege, Göring, and Goebbels. The agile *Gauleiter* not for the last time in his life had switched sides just in time. The fate of Stennes was sealed.[140]

Nevertheless, about 500 stormtroopers – roughly one-third of all Berlin's SA men at the time – went along with Stennes, creating the *Kampfgruppe Revolutionärer Nationalsozialisten*, or 'Fighting Group of Revolutionary National Socialists', which on 3 June 1931 merged with the *Nationalsozialistische Kampfbewegung Deutschlands*, the 'National Socialist Fighting Movement of Germany', founded in the summer of the previous year.[141] In contrast to the regular SA men, who – according to their critics – received basic paramilitary training but remained politically uneducated, 'fobbed off with catchphrases', these dissidents regarded themselves as true 'revolutionary fighters'. They claimed to represent National Socialism in its 'original form', as a *Kampfbewegung* – in contrast to the 'bourgeois' character of the current iteration of the party, dominated by 'office hunters', 'philistines', and ordinary party functionaries.[142] The new revolutionary fighters still referred to each other as 'SA men', with Stennes even claiming the title of *Oberster SA-Führer*, or the 'anti-Hitler', and his former adjutant Walter Jahn referring to himself as Chief of Staff, copying the position held by Röhm.[143] These alternative stormtroopers no longer dressed in brown, but in black shirts and blue caps – often after having redyed their original SA uniforms.[144]

Stennes initially claimed to have considerable support for his 'Black Front' and his alternative SA (also referred to as 'Black Guards') from dissatisfied Nazi activists throughout the Reich. Besides his strongholds in northeastern Germany, there were also dissident groups in Leipzig,

Cologne, Düsseldorf, Hanover, and several other cities. However, the vigour of this left wing of the Nazi movement quickly grew weak. As early as September 1931 the leaders of this alternative SA met with Hermann Ehrhardt in Berlin to explore the option of a potential alliance. This looked like a rather desperate attempt, given Ehrhardt's bad reputation among the stormtroopers after he had joined the *Stahlhelm* in the spring of 1926.[145] In the remaining months prior to Hitler's appointment as chancellor, the Stennes-led alternative SA, soon renamed as the 'revolutionary fighter movement' and in 1932 as the *Kampf-Staffel*, or 'Fighting Team', remained marginal. After the Hitler-led Nazis took power in January 1933, the leaders of the *Nationalsozialistische Kampfgemeinschaft* found their lives in danger. Gregor Strasser was murdered in the course of the 'Night of the Long Knives' in 1934; his brother Otto as well as Walther Stennes fled into exile. The latter subsequently served as a military advisor to the Kuomintang nationalists and as chief of Chiang Kai-shek's bodyguards in China where he remained until 1949.[146]

Similar but less prominent conflicts also broke out in many industrial cities of northern Germany between 1930 and 1932. In the blue-collar town of Bremerhaven, for example, the local SA in August 1931 interrupted a meeting convened by the NSDAP *Gauleiter* for the Weser-Ems district. After the instigators were expelled from the ranks of the party and the SA, they published an open letter to Hitler in which they accused him of exploiting for his personal and strategic ends the political 'sacrifices' made by the rank-and-file stormtroopers in recent years; they claimed that he had built 'a million-mark palace in Munich' (a reference to the new party headquarters, the Brown House), precisely at a time when unemployment among the SA had reached a catastrophic peak. Furthermore, they wrote, the party leadership was concerned only with its own political ambitions and repeatedly let the stormtroopers down. These Nazi dissidents concluded that 'only through revolutionary action' (meaning the SA) and not through a 'parliamentary party' could Germany be saved.[147]

Such reproaches were usually couched in a populist rhetoric that demanded a thorough clean-up of the current mess and an end to corruption and social injustices.[148] The divergences between the different factions in these conflicts were not so much about political goals as they were about the method of achieving them, laying bare fundamental differences between theory and practice, agitation and negotiation, boisterousness and deliberation.[149] The prevailing tensions in fact continued to strain the relation between the NSDAP and parts of its semi-independent SA until the violent submission of the latter following the murderous 'Night of the Long Knives'. Even if attempts to establish competing factions ultimately failed, discontent within the SA remained high. As the NSDAP successfully moved toward a legal takeover of power by making compromises with Heinrich Brüning and other leaders of the conservative right and by establishing close bonds with parts of German industry, many activists in the SA – particularly those affected by the economic misery – slowly but surely lost faith in the party and its promises. As we have already seen in the case of the Potempa murder, this situation became particularly problematic in the summer and autumn of 1932, when large parts of the SA were suffering from '[economic] depression', as Goebbels realized.[150] The Munich police in a detailed report from 20 October 1932 likewise noticed a 'massive despondency' in the SA and predicted a substantial exodus of stormtroopers if the party did not find a way to at least participate in the next government.[151] For the first time in years membership in the SA dropped.[152] By and large, however, Hitler not only managed to contain the popular unrest in the SA, but also succeeded in channelling his followers' dissatisfaction into aggressive and increasingly violent attacks on his political adversaries.

Brownshirts in the Countryside

Most of the examples provided in this chapter so far have been concerned with the growth of the SA and its activities in the German cities. Although this reflects the prevailing focus of most studies, it would be severely misleading to regard the stormtroopers as an exclusively urban phenomenon. At least as important for explaining the spectacular gains of the NSDAP at the polls starting in the late 1920s, and for a comprehensive analysis of SA activism, was the group's appearance in rural Germany. Surviving membership lists from several German provinces suggest that beginning in 1930 the SA recruited members more successfully in the countryside than in the cities. According to exemplary studies by Detlef Mühlberger, nearly 70 per cent of all stormtroopers in the early 1930s lived in small communities with no more than 5,000 inhabitants, whereas only 17.6 per cent came from cities with a population larger than 100,000.[153] In contrast to the big cities, where the official eight-hour day allowed young men, particularly those without family obligations, to reconcile work and party duties, recruitment for the SA in the countryside was more difficult. Here, people were generally more involved in family life, and traditional authority had not eroded as quickly as in urban areas.[154]

Falling prices for agricultural products were one of the most severe problems faced in many rural parts of the country, especially when they coincided with increases in taxes. As a consequence, Germany saw new waves of *Landflucht*, or 'rural flight', and a more radicalized peasantry, particularly among the young. In rural Brandenburg young peasants – notably those without the prospect of taking over their parents' farm – constituted in many places the absolute majority of their respective *Stürme*.[155] In Schleswig-Holstein the rise in discontent led to the development of a significant protest movement by 1928, the so-called *Landvolkbewegung*. Although this movement was not officially bound to a particular programme or party, the National Socialists successfully exploited the high level of popular discontent it tapped into, taking up the peasants' revolutionary slogans and presenting themselves as the alternative needed. The violent protests of the peasants' revolts as well as their widespread anti-capitalist and antisemitic sentiments provided fertile ground for the agitation of both Communists and Nazis, and the latter soon exploited the uprisings in many rural regions throughout northern Germany. By contrast, the Nazis' excessive nationalism appealed less to the established farmers, who were first and foremost concerned with their rather narrow *Lebenswelt* and its practical problems rather than abstract notions of fatherland and international politics.[156] Yet, with the economic situation deteriorating, they likewise became more susceptible to Nazi slogans and in particular to their highly symbolic actions. For example, in Western Pomerania in 1930, stormtroopers headed by the young and charismatic lawyer Wilhelm Karpenstein intervened at a compulsory auction of a county estate and gave the first bidder a stick, thus presenting themselves as defenders of the traditional local order against an alleged cold-blooded materialism.[157]

The central figure for the growth of the SA in Schleswig-Holstein was the agricultural labourer and later shop owner Heinrich Schoene, who joined the NSDAP in August 1925. Initially the local party, SA, and HJ leader for the Nazi *Ortsgruppe* in Lockstedter Lager, Schoene was appointed leader of the SA-*Gruppe* Nordmark in June 1929.[158] A few weeks prior to this appointment, he had summarized his experiences as a Nazi agitator as follows: 'The German peasant on his free soil is much more susceptible to National Socialism than the Marxist-infested townsman.'[159] The early Nazis' agitation concentrated initially on those areas of western Schleswig-Holstein where the *Landvolk* movement was particularly strong. In May 1929, for example, Schoene ordered his storm-troopers to carry out propaganda *Stürme* on bicycles during the Pentecost holidays, focusing on areas where the NSDAP was still in its infancy.[160] By the time the *Landvolk* movement began to decline, in the early 1930s, the NSDAP had established itself as the leading rural party in the region, replacing the previously strong conservative parties as well as splinter parties like the *Christlich-Nationale Bauern und Landvolkpartei*, the 'Christian National Peasants and Landvolk Party', an offshoot of the German National People's Party (DNVP).[161] Here, as well as in several other Protestant-dominated rural areas of Germany such as East Prussia, Western Pomerania, or the predominantly agrarian parts of Württemberg or Northern Hesse, the NSDAP developed into a milieu party proper, with a position similar to the pre-eminence of the Centre Party in most Catholic provinces.[162]

The *Landvolk* movement in Schleswig-Holstein had already radicalized the peasants to such an extent that they had engaged in civil disobedience, attacked courthouses, and even fired off bombs. Against this background, the methods of stormtrooper violence did not need special justification. Elsewhere, however, the situation differed markedly. A less antagonistic style of propaganda than was used in the big cities, one that positively emphasized the benefits the future Third Reich would have for the peas-antry, often proved beneficial to the NSDAP.[163] In most parts of the coun-tryside, life in the SA was dominated not by frequent physical clashes with competing paramilitary organizations, but by a constant campaign of pene-tration of the rural milieu, with its associations, loyalties, and habits.[164] In order to establish themselves, despite their limited personal and financial means, the Nazis tried to win over those powerbrokers who traditionally set the agenda in rural Germany – the primary-school teacher, the pastor, the big farmer, and, in the provinces east of the Elbe, the local aristocrat – and use them as 'milieu openers'.[165] Consequently, the SA in these regions recruited less from the lower classes than among young farmers and arti-sans who were well-respected and well-integrated members of their communities.[166] The party presented itself as a 'conservative peasants' and middle-class party'[167] that stood for traditional German values but that was – due to the circumstances of the troubled Weimar years – required to take a tougher stance than the organizations that had hitherto dominated the rural regions.

In areas where local news was transmitted from mouth to mouth rather than through newspapers, a strong visual and physical presence on the ground was vital for any party or organization to succeed in winning followers. As historian Wolfram Pyta has convincingly demonstrated, in the small communities of rural Germany the Nazi promises of implementing a 'people's community' mattered less than practical support or prospective personal gains. One way the party provided such support was to hire out groups of stormtroopers from the nearby cities as seasonal workers, usually paid in kind or with very small sums. Not surprisingly, farmers who were pleased with such mutually beneficial activism were more likely to react favourably to demands for food and other forms of party support (Plate 4). Their willingness to help impoverished Nazi militants was, however, severely put to the test as cases of SA leaders selling food they had received for free became more and more frequent. Farmers busy in their fields also wondered about the excursions of uniformed SA units on workdays, reflecting the widespread belief that active politics should be confined to weekends and not interfere in everyday community life.[168] Finally, in 1932, when unemployment figures for the Reich peaked, entire stormtrooper units swept over the countryside like a murder of crows, begging and stealing in such aggressive ways that even regional Nazi party leaders referred to their behaviour as '*landsknecht* manners'.[169]

Because SA membership in many places was initially not strong, its activities in small communities were often confined to particular days and events. On these occasions it used cars, lorries, motorbikes, and bicycles to transport stormtroopers from one place to another, thus creating the impression that the regional SA units were much stronger than was actually the case (Plate 5). Two new organizations greatly aided this propaganda. Since the late 1920s, the SA had formed subsections that pooled militants who possessed motorcycles and private cars. Beginning on 1 April 1930, these subsections were referred to as the Motor-SA. Their main task was to transport SA leaders to party and election meetings, but their members were also called to assist in the training of stormtroopers to drive a car or ride a motorbike, thus allowing them to later pass the official driving tests without paying for expensive driving-school lessons. Besides the Motor-SA, there also existed the *Nationalsozialistisches Automobil-Korps* (NSAK), which in April 1931 was renamed the *Nationalsozialistisches Kraftfahr-korps* (NSKK), a reservoir of motorized party sympathizers who were willing to take on occasional jobs for the 'movement'. Formal membership in the NSDAP and its sub-organizations was not required for membership in this group. Rather, as the Nazi propaganda rejoiced, it was the 'SA spirit' that 'bound together men and motor to a vital unity and transformed the motor vehicle into a weapon for the political fight'.[170] The Motor-SA grew rapidly, in line with the general SA, expanding from 100 *Sturm* units in October 1931 to 680 in August 1932, with the latter comprising 26,105 individuals. Similarly, membership in the NSKK mushroomed to 10,000 men in December 1931, after only 300 at the end of the previous year. Both organizations not only fulfilled important logistical tasks for the party but also contributed decisively to the 'modern' image of the NSDAP in the early 1930s; furthermore, they allowed middle-class sympathizers to serve the SA without taking part in long marches or paramilitary exercises.[171]

Between 1930 and 1932 the Nazi Party's voter support multiplied, particularly in villages and rural communities with a predominantly Protestant population.[172] As usually everyone knew everyone else's political preferences in such places, the growing number of ballots cast for the NSDAP should be seen less as a mass phenomenon driven by individuals than as a process of 'entire communities converting their loyalty'.[173] It was the result of a combined effort, one enhanced by the visual, yet infrequent, presence of SA and Motor-SA units touring the countryside who engaged in demonstrations that played on traditional feelings of national honour and relied on the influence of local leaders. It needs to be understood, however, that the Nazis' intense electoral campaigns were not only directed outward, aiming to win over voters and impress or scare opponents. They were also directed inward, and in two ways. First, the intensified activities that characterized the pre-election weeks provided a range of efforts to which the individual SA man could personally contribute and thus prove himself a 'political fighter'. Second, these campaigns also served as a means to control and discipline the rapidly growing number of stormtroopers who – as we have seen – were recruited in the early 1930s not only from those parts of the population committed to *völkisch* nationalism, but also from many German men suffering from economic hardship but lacking any firm political commitment.[174]

The regulations on so-called 'propaganda storms' for the April 1932 election campaign in Upper Silesia, drafted under the command of the notorious SA group leader Edmund Heines, provide a good example of this two-edged strategy. The guidelines requested the formation of five units, each ninety men strong and equipped with bicycles and a marching band. Between 3 and 10 April 1932, the week prior to the elections, each of these propaganda units was ordered to travel between thirty and forty kilometres a day, visiting at least six villages. In every village they would stop, distribute propaganda leaflets, and give a little concert in which traditional patriotic songs were given preference over Nazi fighting songs. In between these songs a local Nazi functionary would deliver a short speech.

However, most of the regulations for this rural propaganda campaign dealt with matters of internal discipline. Prior to their deployment, each propaganda *Sturm* was to be schooled for four days 'under the strictest control' of the SA-*Standartenführer* Hanns Günther von Obernitz, who in 1933 became police president of Nuremberg-Fürth.[175] After the units were deployed every *Sturm* was to be reviewed at least once a day by von Obernitz and other SA-*Standartenführer* who were touring the country by car. Night quarters were to be established exclusively on the estates of Silesian noblemen who were sympathetic to the Nazis but these quarters were to be anything but luxurious: eight to ten men were expected to sleep on mulched floors in farmhouses and barns.[176] Overnight stops in local inns were explicitly prohibited, as was the consumption of alcohol. A curfew had already been set for 9 p.m., to 'prevent the vagabonding of SA men with or without female company'. The regional SA leadership even prohibited the singing of 'provocative songs'.[177]

It seems unlikely that the actual behaviour of the propaganda *Stürme* would have followed such strict guidelines. However, the Prussian authorities were quick to ban these propaganda cycling tours, and when the Nazis started them nevertheless, the authorities stopped them immediately. In the following days at least 110 SA men from the propaganda *Stürme* were sentenced to fines and short prison terms following accelerated legal procedures.[178] Despite the actual failure of this Nazi propaganda effort, the plans as such make plain that the SA leadership subjected its rank and file to strict subordination and discipline. Concerns about the aesthetics and, in particular, the sounds made by the travelling SA men were prioritized over considerations around actual political discourse. As ordered by Pfeffer von Salomon and later Röhm, the young men were expected to impress the public by their discipline and determination, acting as *Wiedergänger* of a glorious past and at the same time as the embodiment of national regeneration, but they were urged to remain at a distance from the local population. The stormtroopers' wives and children were prohibited from joining their husbands and fathers on marches, so that any form of intimacy or possible conflict over the men's loyalties was restricted.[179] They were to be 'party soldiers' whose own biographies and views would become irrelevant once they dressed in the brown shirt. This worldview is mirrored in the highly conventional character of the Nazi autobiographies that have survived in the Abel collection at the Hoover Institution in Stanford, California. As embodiments of the Nazi vision, as walking and cycling Nazi advertisement pillars, the rank-and-file stormtroopers had to put aside their individuality.[180]

In other words, marching Nazi militants were now first and foremost a 'mass ornament', identified by the sociologist and journalist Siegfried Kracauer as the primary characteristic of modern life in the capitalist societies of the interwar years. This trend was indeed common in interwar central Europe, as it was precisely the 'masses as such – fluid, mobile, and mutable' that 'were the very media in which all central political questions were posed'.[181] For Kracauer, these 'mass ornaments' were ultimately empty forms of the cult of rationality and as such testified to the extent to which the capitalist way of doing business had penetrated the realms of human interaction more generally. However, he claimed that human emancipation from this tight framework was possible, not by shaping one's body to the detriment of individual expression, like his example of the Tiller girls, an internationally popular troupe of female revue dancers famous for their machine-like precision in moving their bodies simultaneously, but by the intellectual endeavour of realizing the correlation between such attempts at standardization and the demands of capitalism.[182]

Kracauer's original analysis did not include a discussion of the forms of political mass ornaments. Nevertheless, the similarities between his descriptions of the Tiller girls and the sight of Nazi stormtroopers parading in the German streets are obvious. The boots of the activists marching in step corresponded no less to the 'hands in the factory' than did the legs of the Tiller girls, at least from an aesthetic perspective. The 'sexless bodies' in uniform, to paraphrase Kracauer again, thus gained importance only inasmuch as they could form a mass ornament, becoming interchangeable and reduced in, if not devoid of, individuality.[183] Some fifty years later, Klaus Theweleit's interpretations of the Fascist psyche came to a somewhat different conclusion. For him, the bodies of the marching SA men with their stern faces were not 'sexless' but rather were embodiments of a particular type of masculinity. Their *Körperpanzer*, or 'body armour', corresponded to violent male fantasies of domination, fighting, and the pleasure of sexual assault, Theweleit claimed.[184] Regardless of such differences, both authors suggest that Nazi body politics was based on the repression of both natural instincts and middle-class ideas of intimacy.[185]

The SA internal educational material from 1929 supports this view: the stormtrooper, such materials claimed, was requested to live on a level above that inhabited by men who only sought sensual pleasure from women. Instead, he was called to respect and 'honour' German women and girls, their parents, and even the Churches. Individual attraction between the sexes was ultimately subordinated to formal criteria: 'No SA man is allowed to socialize with a girl who wears un-German clothes', one regulation noted, most likely referring to the urban chic of the 1920s 'new woman', who wore trousers and close-fitting dresses.[186] Such formal guidelines on interpersonal relations, of course, describe an ideal and not a social reality. They testify, however, to the SA leadership's attempt to control all spheres of the lives of the rank and file, including their sex lives. Observations made by foreign observers like the journalist Ferdinand Tuohy, who travelled to the nascent Third Reich in 1933, indeed suggest that there was an element of restraint in the relations between stormtroopers and women, at least in public: 'There seemed but one element missing, the feminine. Only one uniformed Nazi did I see with his girl and he looked betrothed many times over, judging by the stiff angle of his proffered arm. This movement is a very male one, please note, and pure to austerity at that.'[187]

The tightly disciplined SA troop in formation, seemingly unaffected by or at least sufficiently isolated from female temptations along the way, was an ideal 'mass ornament' in the sense outlined above, but it would be premature to end the analysis here. As Kracauer noticed, sardonically ridiculing the popular life-reform movement more generally and rhythmic gymnastics in particular, many of his contemporaries were attempting to free themselves from the demands of modern life, giving up rationality in favour of a regained unity between nature and soul.[188] Individual stormtroopers likewise did not regard themselves as a mere decoration of Fascist politics. They certainly took pleasure and pride in the formations they jointly created in their marches and parades, but they did not see them as reducing human agency. From their perspective, it was Fascist mass mobilization that allowed the individual to participate in the collective national will. Only because of and through the nation, they believed, could modern individuality stand up against the demands of capitalist modernity, a modernity that stormtroopers came to associate with economic exploitation and social marginalization. Fascist aesthetics therefore not only attempted to take advantage of the new kinds of mass formation, but also claimed to provide a solution for the individual in an increasingly anonymous and competitive society. At a time when individuality was widely perceived to be at risk, National Socialism promised to reconcile the evanescent modern self with the allegedly 'eternal' nation that represented the human achievements of the past embodied in folk traditions and racial origin, as well as to provide a link from that past into a bright future. This was ultimately a romantic ideology that appealed to those who shared the perception of living in an interim period, but it was neither anti-modern nor technophobic. It was Goebbels who most clearly expressed this amalgam of romantic longing and belief in technological progress and social engineering, proclaiming in early 1939: 'We live in an age that is both organic and steel-like, that has not lost its depth of feeling. On the contrary, it has discovered a new romanticism in the results of modern inventions and technology.'[189] As late as 1943 he held onto this idea and publicly assured his listeners that even the war years were a time of particular romanticism – a romanticism in the face of deprivation, harder and crueller than in previous periods, but one that 'remains romantic. The steely romanticism of our time manifests itself in actions and deeds in service to a great national goal, in a feeling of duty raised to the level of an unbreachable principle. We are all more or less romantics in a new German mood.'[190]

The Danger of Stormtrooper Violence

However, all of these aspects of the SA – the propaganda marches in the cities and the acute agitation in the villages – do not fully explain the party's overall success. National Socialism around 1930 appealed to a considerable proportion of Germans, but the Nazis could never have come to power without a substantial amount of people who, while not necessarily sharing their views, likewise failed to defend the Republic when it was on the brink of collapse. In fact, educated middle- and upper-class opposition to the NSDAP and its political style diminished considerably in the face of the rapidly degrading economic situation and a national parliament that had not yet been abolished but was constantly bypassed by Chancellor Brüning and his successors starting in 1930. In these days of existential crisis for millions, the popular German proverb *Der Ton macht die Musik* ('It's not what you say, but how you say it') did not mean much. Politics was no longer a matter of taste and careful deliberation, but a matter of 'street credibility', boldness, and immediate effect. As a consequence, even the Nazis' excessive antisemitism was now regularly downplayed.[191] A telling example is the lecturer Margarete Adam, who held a doctorate in philosophy from Hamburg University and was a disciple of the renowned philosopher Ernst Cassirer. Adam, a self-declared 'philosemite', claimed in late 1930 that 'the interests and hopes of 99 per cent of all those who had voted for the NSDAP on 14 September 1930' – including herself – were not connected to the 'party's excessive antisemitic agenda'. She regarded the Nazis' antisemitism as a natural consequence of the Weimar Republic's failures but did not perceive any real danger emerging from it – not even for the Jews. Every party programme is more radical than can be practically implemented, and that of the NSDAP was no exception, Adam reasoned. Consequently, she thought that Jewish life and property would be safe even under a National Socialist government.[192]

Business leaders who had been initially sceptical of the NSDAP now came to regard the party with sympathy, particularly after its symbolic reunion with the conservative right in the so-called 'Harzburg Front', a joint rally of rightist groups held in the spa town of Bad Harzburg on 11 October 1931.[193] The following extract from a private letter of Ernst Brandi, the chairman of Bergbau-Verein, an influential lobby group for the Ruhr's mining industries, sheds light on the calculations typical of the leaders of German heavy industry. Writing to one of his sons living in New York in early March 1932, a few months after the Harzburg rally and a few days before the first round of the German presidential elections in which Hindenburg, Hitler, and the Communist leader Ernst Thälmann ran for office, Brandi characterized National Socialism as:

> a movement of utmost importance. It is foremost the expression of a
> general and conscious dissatisfaction with the political development

since the middle of the war, the war's end and the revolution until the present day. It is a movement that is determined to bring to bear the good old qualities of the Germans, their proficiency, their sense of duty and their moral cleanliness, all this on a purely national basis, because they [the Nazis] rightly [...] see the category of the nation, of the fatherland, as the strongest moral driving force.[194]

By this time, Brandi and several of his colleagues were already supporting the NSDAP and its regional bosses, most importantly the *Gauleiter* of Essen, Josef Terboven, with considerable donations.[195] Many of them hoped to gain in the SA a 'protecting guard against the working-class parties' that would free them from granting concessions to the left and would generally allow them to act independently of volatile parliamentary majorities.[196] The Brownshirts in turn did not fail to demonstrate their determination and might. Just one week after the rally in Bad Harzburg, a large meeting of SA units from central Germany (*mitteldeutsches SA-Treffen*) took place in nearby Braunschweig, a residential city of slightly less than 150,000 inhabitants. On this occasion about 60,000 SA men literally occupied the town and – apart from holding a six-hour-long parade in the presence of Hitler – also engaged in violent 'punitive raids' in its working-class districts.[197] For Brandi, the position of the NSDAP also fitted with his own elitist concept of the German economy. The National Socialist movement would not only 'foster the feelings of German honour, but also the national militaristic traditions [*Waffenehre*],' he explained to his son. 'It is poised to destroy real Marxism root and branch and bent on replacing it with a system of the highest welfare for the whole of the people, based on private business, discipline and elite leadership selection [*Führertum durch Auslese*].'[198]

Short-sighted as it was, this assessment of the political and economic situation in the spring of 1932 makes it clear that the temporary alliance between the NSDAP and considerable parts of German big business was more than tactical in nature.[199] The Nazis were surprisingly successful at presenting themselves as a political alternative with an ambitious programme of moral and social renewal. Even in a private letter, which is unlikely to have been coloured by tactical considerations, Brandi did not have a critical word to say about the Nazis' antisemitic propaganda. He seems to have accepted the Nazi violence in the streets as a legitimate, or at least welcome, means of weakening and ideally destroying the German Socialist and Communist parties. Obviously, this letter reflects Brandi's personal views, but in the context of this study, they take on greater significance. With the constant threat of a political crisis, Brandi, Adam, and many other educated Germans gave up their initial reservations about the NSDAP and its SA. The storm-troopers' ugly propaganda slogans and aggressive violence did not disappear from the streets, but the Germans got used to it. It is telling that, by 1932, Hamburg schoolchildren had invented a new game: re-enacting clashes between Communists and Nazi stormtroopers using sticks and stones. At least in one case a police intervention was the only way to stop a game that was at risk of running out of control.[200] Many German elites regarded the high level of street violence as a deplorable feature of an antagonistic polit-ical climate, or even as an indicator of 'political degeneracy',[201] but at the same time they also saw it as nothing more than hot air, a temporary symptom of the economic crisis that would have no lasting impact or simply a crude children's game for demoralized grown-ups.

By contrast, NSDAP leaders described the stormtrooper activism of these years in genuine military terms. According to the SA intellectual Ernst Julek von Engelbrechten, the *Herbstoffensive*, or 'fall campaign', of 1929 pre-dated the *Durchbruchsschlacht* ('breakthrough battle') of 1930 that was in turn followed by the *Vormarsch*, or 'advance', in 1931.[202] Despite such militaristic rhetoric, several scholars have warned against the conflation of political discourse and historical fact. Germany in 1932, they claim, was far from descending into chaos and civil war. The historian Friedrich Lenger, referring to earlier studies by Richard Bessel, Dirk Schumann, and Bernhard Fulda, recently summarized this view in his masterful book on European metropolises in modern times by relying on three arguments. First, he claims that even in 1932 the German states' monopoly on violence was not seriously threatened. Second, he argues that the level of political violence was lower in the early 1930s than it was in the immediate post-war years – tacitly implying that, as the Republic did not succumb back then, there was no need for its ultimate failure in 1933 either. Third, he maintains that in comparison with other European cities, the level of violence in the German capital was not excessively high.[203]

However, on closer examination, none of these three points supports Lenger's principal argument. On the first point, regional studies on the Weimar period, the police, the military, and the liberal German-Jewish milieu have convincingly demonstrated that the years 1930–2 were a period of erosion from within that rendered the state's claims of a successful defence of its monopoly on violence to be shallow.[204] The more one moves away from Prussia and its capital in the early 1930s, the more it becomes obvious that any move by the government to toughen its stance toward political extremists, particularly by crushing their demonstrations using police and military forces, was increasingly in danger of producing the opposite effect. This was one of the main reasons for the absence of any systematic democratic resistance, either to the unlawful *Preußenschlag* of 1932 or to the establishment of the Third Reich in the following year.[205] With regard to Lenger's second argument, the extent to which the political and economic context of the years 1930–2 fundamentally differed from that of 1919–23 needs to be emphasized. There is no absolute threshold of violence that determines the stability of a political system – rather, a given level of political and criminal violence is just one factor that needs to be analysed in conjunction with several others. At a time when the national government, relying on emergency decrees, seemed unable to cope with massive unemployment and unprecedented pauperization, riots in the streets and political attacks gained much stronger significance than they had had in the early 1920s – particularly as they came to be exploited by a massive, well-organized Nazi grassroots movement.[206] Finally, with regard to Lenger's third argument, a closer analysis that compares Berlin with other European capitals is certainly instructive but does not suffice to base claims on a national level. Goebbels's 'Fight for Berlin' was symbolically of high importance for the National Socialists, but in real terms it was just one event in their nationwide takeover of power. The Republic did not collapse because of the capital, even if it was carried to its grave there.

Weimar Germany's leftists and liberals, highly aware of the risks present in the immediate post-war period just a few years back, understood the dangers of even such highly symbolic threats as those made by the SA in the early 1930s much better than did some later historians. The latter – in hindsight – have wondered at the alleged 'massive media panic, a press-induced over-reaction with politically disastrous effects' that occurred, blaming in particular the 'excessive partisan press coverage' that created a false impression of 'uncontrollable violence' and thus implicitly suggesting that a more restrained handling of the political violence in these years could have prevented events from escalating.[207] To a certain extent such views carry on the tradition of blaming the social and political elites of the

Weimar Republic for its ultimate failure, a line of argument prevalent in the first decades of post-war historiography.[208] However, it seems worth remembering that the increasingly strident warnings of contemporaries ranging from the revolutionary right to the Communist left were not proven wrong by the course of history, and many of those who perceived the political situation between 1930 and 1933 as a latent or incipient civil war were soon incarcerated, tortured, forced into exile, or murdered.

The stormtroopers' self-declared fight against the much-hated Republic came to an end on 30 January 1933, when Hindenburg appointed Hitler the new Reich chancellor. The Nazi Party had survived its serious internal crisis of the preceding months, but it had lost some of its most sworn supporters along the way. The party leaders knew that they were now under serious pressure to deliver, and they did not wait a single day to use the capital's splendid Unter den Linden boulevard – the formal parade ground for the Kaiser and his royal household – to stage a demonstration of their political ambitions. In the evening hours of 30 January up to 15,000 Brownshirts marched through the Brandenburg Gate, saluting Hitler, who greeted them from a window of the nearby Reich Chancellery.[209] As this parade had to be organized on the spur of the moment on a grey and cold winter day, the surviving images of this event were less spectacular than expected – which prompted the Nazis to repeat the parade several weeks later. Genuine supporters undoubtedly cheered the appearance of the new chancellor, but an attentive Berliner also witnessed stormtroopers forcing curious city dwellers with a thump on the back to give the Hitler salute.[210] Listeners on the radio, however, had no chance to perceive the ambivalent character of the original Nazi victory parade, as a surviving spoken text from Reich Radio Station Cologne's broadcast of the evening of 30 January 1933 makes plain. The voice of the radio reporter, who sounded like an activist of the first hour himself, intoned: 'A procession of 100,000 torches was brandished from Wilhelmstraße ... They have marched through the Brandenburg Gate, the brown columns of the SA – victors in a long, loss-making battle. Their banners blaze in blood red, with the swastika on white background – symbol of the rising sun! A marvellous, a glorious sight!'[211] The official tone for the upcoming months was set.

THE BROWN CULT OF YOUTH AND VIOLENCE IN THE WEIMAR REPUBLIC

Fascism wants man to be active and to engage in action with all his energies.

— Benito Mussolini and Giovanni Gentile,
The Doctrine of Fascism (1932)[1]

'The extent to which Hitler has young people on his side should not be underrated. We should not underestimate our opponent but realize what is a psychological force for so many and inspires them.' The German-Jewish philosopher Ernst Bloch, as much a fierce critic of National Socialism as a careful observer of his times, published this warning in the highbrow weekly *Das Tage-Buch* as early as April 1924.[2] Having witnessed the political and social turmoil in Munich after the First World War at close quarters, Bloch was familiar with the early Nazi Party, its propaganda, and its increasing appeal. This particular critical comment was an immediate reaction to the verdict in the so-called Hitler trial delivered on 1 April 1924, in which Bloch warned his readers not to regard the story of the local tribune of the Bavarian radical nationalists as over. Irony and disgust alone would not suffice to combat National Socialism, Bloch argued, as 'separate from the hideous gawpers and accomplices, new youth glows at the core, a very vigorous generation. Seventeen-year-olds are burning to respond to Hitler. Beery students of old, dreary, revelling in the happiness of the crease in their trousers, are no longer recognizable, their hearts are pounding.'[3]

Bloch's observations get to the heart of one of the fundamental problems with which every history of the early Nazi movement has to deal: the
fundamental emotional attraction of a form of politics that used violence as
a central element of community formation, establishing clear-cut boundaries between insiders and outsiders of the Nazis' 'people's community'. As
has already been demonstrated, the use of violence – physically as well as
symbolically – was from the early 1920s onward a core element of aggressive Nazi politics, despite all the practical limitations on its deployment. In
this chapter I will argue that a broad perspective which integrates some of
the most recent findings of a theoretically informed history of violence can
contribute to a fuller picture of this period of history. My perspective does
not focus exclusively on the Nazi movement but takes into account the
effects of what I call the SA 'cult of youth and violence' on the political
culture of the interwar years.

The wartime experience – individually lived through, remembered by
diverse war veterans' associations, and culturally elevated in literature and
film – shaped the outlook of two generations of European males.[4] Besides
those who had actually fought in the First World War, those who were
slightly younger were also deeply affected by the fate and the stories of their
older brothers and fathers. Germany was no different in this respect from
Italy, where an increasing number of adolescents embraced Fascist squad-
rism in emulation of their elders. Their pressing 'desire for action' was
'accompanied by a profound crisis of family bonds' and of adult authority,
particularly male authority.[5] The increasing significance of the stormtroopers was as much a consequence as it was a prerequisite of the growing
militarization of German politics. This process had several dimensions,
many of which went beyond the reach of the Nazi Party and even tran-
scended national boundaries.[6] In other words, this chapter aims to elucidate
the increasing appeal of the SA, a development that differed markedly from
the destiny of the hundreds of competing paramilitary nationalist organizations that usually existed only for a few years and could claim only limited
political influence. In addition to several well-established factors that
contributed to the increasing popularity of National Socialism in Germany,
I will argue that it was precisely the cult of youth and violence – not invented
but successfully institutionalized by the stormtroopers – which contributed
to the group's success starting in the late 1920s.[7] Between 1928 and 1932
the SA developed into an organization that shared the characteristics of a

social movement. Next to its aesthetic attraction, these characteristics were a main element of its public appeal.[8] Both elements contributed to the 'youthful image' of the Nazi movement as a whole. During these years the SA also grew into a possible partner for the Reichswehr in their joint efforts to overcome the limitations of the Versailles Treaty. The violent activism of the Brownshirts even provided role models for young Christians attempting to fight back against the 'evils' of the present times – identified with such catchwords as 'individualism', 'consumerism', 'pacifism', and 'internationalism'.

Every biographer is supposed to be aware of the dangers of involuntarily taking his or her subject as the point of reference from which all other social phenomena are to be interpreted. The same risk applies to histories of collective bodies and is particularly apt in a case such as the stormtroopers, whose worldviews were extremely self-referential. Consequently, this chapter gives room to the Nazis' internal perspectives but carefully aims to distinguish between ideas and emotions on the one hand and the party's often relatively limited impact on the 'factual' political developments of the day on the other hand. Furthermore, wherever possible I integrate comparative perspectives, contrasting the Nazi militants with other paramilitary party organizations. Although it is well established that this 'new activist style of politics' so characteristic of but not limited to Fascist movements was a frequent phenomenon in interwar Europe,[9] comparatively little research has investigated what made the German SA unique from a transnational perspective. The multifaceted approach chosen here will help to identify the reasons for the 'success' of the stormtroopers – a success that not only promoted a new political style which made the personal effort, the 'deed', a central element of political legitimacy, but also paved the way for the establishment of the Third Reich in 1933.

Militant Masculinity

Although from 1926 onward the highest leadership positions in the NSDAP's army were given to former military officers – that is, veterans of the First World War and one-time professional soldiers of the German Army – the SA proved most attractive to young men who were too young to have fought in the war.[10] This age bracket, often referred to as the 'war youth generation', was made up of young men born between 1900 and

1910. The term was originally popularized by the right-wing intellectual Ernst Günter Gründel in his 1932 book *Die Sendung der jungen Generation* (*The Mission of the Young Generation*) but was later converted from a political combat term into a category of historical analysis, although the problematic nature of this transfer and the gender bias it contains are rarely acknowledged.[11] The men of this age group had been exposed to the ubiquitous and often ferocious German war propaganda as pupils and were deeply influenced by stories of German heroism and sacrifice on the battle-field.[12] Only some of them later became activists of the SA. Yet, given the multitude of paramilitary and right-wing youth groups in Weimar Germany, it is safe to say that a considerable segment of male adolescents at the time regarded the diverse *Freikorps* units and nationalist leagues of the 1920s as a welcome opportunity to 'live their violent fantasies of a romanticized warrior existence' or simply to fulfil their duty to fight for the national cause.[13] Many of these young hotheads believed that they were being called to take up where their fathers had left off in 1918, when they were allegedly 'stabbed in the back' by disloyal Germans on the home front and subsequently disarmed by the Allied forces. Determined to prevent further national humiliation or, even worse, a Communist takeover of power, these young nationalists formed 'subcultures of ultra-militant masculinities'[14] and fuelled the drive of the SA up to 1934.

The case of Munich is once again instructive: as demonstrated in chapter 2, the political instability of Bavaria during the years 1919–20 combined with severe economic problems created a situation in which nationalists as well as Bavarian particularists turned their anger and shame at the military defeat and the subsequent national 'humiliation' against perceived internal enemies. Deep-seated resentments against 'Bolsheviks', Prussians, Bavarian Social Democrats, and Jews formed the background against which the violent activism of young men could be interpreted as defence of the fatherland. This view was established as early as 1919, when the new Reichswehr in Bavaria declared Munich's students indispensable to the task of upholding public order. So-called *Studentenkompanien*, military units formed of students that existed in Munich, Würzburg, and Erlangen, were regarded as being particularly loyal to the ideas and values of the lost empire. In the summer of 1919 such student battalions comprised approximately 50,000 men nationwide.[15] In the eyes of the military, these youths were still free of the alleged 'corrupting influence' of civilian morality and yet had been disenchanted by the horrors and the suffering of real combat experiences. Their idealism could thus easily be turned against an internal enemy. This strategy seemed all the more promising after an assembly of Munich students greeted the news of the assassination of the Bavarian premier Kurt Eisner on 21 February 1919 with cheers of joy, demonstrating that even political murder was not perceived as downright illegitimate.[16]

Paramilitary activism was a key element of student life in Munich during the first years of the Republic, as it was in other major cities of central Europe, most notably in the Hungarian capital of Budapest.[17] But even in the politically more stable Third Republic of France, the *camelots du roi*, the radical youth organization of the para-Fascist *Action Française*, recruited heavily among students in Paris's Latin Quarter during the 1920s.[18] The extreme nationalist propaganda of the First World War continued to reverberate among central European youths long after the armistice. Many of them perceived life, on an individual as well as a collective basis, to consist of a constant state of fighting. It posed risks, but it also contained the possibility of personal elevation and – eventually – fulfilment. In Germany public institutions supported this particular form of post-war youthful idealism. In Munich the University Directorate in May 1919 officially declared that service to one's country was the first and most noble duty of every student. The studies proper ranked only second in importance. The opening of the summer term in 1919 was postponed out of respect for the military obligations of a considerable part of the student body. After consultations with the Reichswehr, the University Directorate agreed that classes would only be taught between Monday and Thursday morning, so that students could devote the following three and a half days to military training and exercises.[19] Even those male students who had not received military training during the war years now acquired an intimate knowledge of the mental world of the military and learned basic fighting skills.

The universities thus proved fertile ground for the formation of the first National Socialist *Sturmabteilungen* in Munich between 1920 and 1923. For some of its earliest members, the activism of the first SA units was merely a prolongation of their paramilitary student experience of 1919. With the slow 'normalization' of social interactions in Germany and the absorption by the Bavarian home guard movement of important parts of the former paramilitary groups, such a militarized lifestyle soon survived only among the most extreme political parties like the DAP, soon to become the NSDAP.[20] Of course, students remained a minority in the early SA, but they formed an important part of the SA membership whose influence exceeded their statistical proportion. An early SA register intercepted by the police included 144 names for which a professional affiliation was listed. Of these, eleven were registered as 'students' (born between 1897 and 1905) and several others as 'pupils'.[21] In Franconia it was Gustav Steinbeck, a twenty-four-year-old student and former petty officer (*Fähnrich zur See*), who led the first local SA units.[22] The eleventh *Hundertschaft* of the Munich SA, until 1923 led by Rudolf Hess, who later was to become Hitler's deputy, is said to have been entirely composed of students.[23]

However, a closer look urges caution in drawing conclusions from such examples. At least in the case of the intercepted list, 'student' seems to have been a self-imposed title that was more closely related to an individual's social and educational background than his actual occupation.[24] Interrogated by the authorities in Baden in September 1921, just weeks after being appointed head of the SA, the 'law student' Klintzsch explained that after his resignation from active navy duty, ostensibly on 2 June 1921, he had spent the holidays on the East Frisian island of Borkum prior to beginning his studies. Situated in the extreme northwest of the German Reich, the island since the nineteenth century had taken pride in its reputation as an antisemitic beach resort[25] – a fact Klintzsch knew well. What he did not tell the authorities, however, was that he, as a naval lieutenant, had previously attempted to prevent the raising of the revolutionary red flag over the officers' mess on the very same island in November 1918, and that it was for this reason that he had not been accepted into the navy of the new Reichswehr later. In early 1919 he instead had returned to the *Joachimsthalsches Gymnasium*, a prestigious Protestant gymnasium in the city of Templin, north of Berlin. There, Klintzsch attended the so-called 'warrior's class', which prepared former soldiers for the *Notabitur*, a school-leaving examination that could be completed in a less formal and strict way. Klintzsch continued his pattern of reactionary agitation in the school and was one of the driving forces for the organization of an unofficial 'Kaiser's birthday party' that was celebrated there on 26 January 1919.[26]

According to his testimony from September 1921, Klintzsch had moved to Munich some months earlier with the aim of studying law and public policy (*Staatswissenschaften*). However, the new semester did not start until October. Over the summer months Klintzsch attended meetings of the NSDAP, an activity that he presented as a kind of alternative course of study: 'The ideas championed there mesmerized me to an extent that I have virtually limited my studies to the learning of the matters covered there. I very much devoted myself to questions dealing with the Jews and the Freemasons.'[27] Klintzsch enrolled at Munich's Technical University only for the winter term of 1921/1922 and for the summer term of 1922; he left without graduating.[28] His main activity in these years was working as a full-time instructor of the NSDAP's youth and as a paramilitary conspirator.

For other early SA leaders who matriculated at various universities, the seriousness of their studies can likewise be questioned. Dietrich von Jagow, who stepped in for Klintzsch as provisional head of the SA in the autumn of 1921, moved to Tübingen in late January 1922. Soon afterward he registered as a guest lecturer at Eberhard Karls University. By February 1922 von Jagow had also become a trainee at the city's long-standing Osiander bookshop, which was now in the hands of two ex-marine officers who had likewise been former members of the Ehrhardt Brigade.[29] Yet von Jagow's main activities were political, not bibliophilic. Hitler had sent him to Tübingen as SA Chief of Staff for Württemberg (*Inspekteur der SA für Württemberg*) in order to help develop and at the same time monitor the nascent stormtrooper units in this region. In April 1923 the Nazis in Tübingen operated under the cover name 'Wanderverein Schönbuch', which suggested an apolitical hiking club.[30]

The traditional university town of Tübingen proved to be a favourable place for the growth of the Nazi movement in Württemberg. The Social Democrat Hermann Schützinger, an ex-soldier promoted to head of the police in Saxony and later a leading member of the *Reichsbanner*, remarked as early as 1926 that in Tübingen 'stubborn small-town professors' were training the sons of the German middle classes in *völkisch* nationalism. The windows of the local bookshops displayed the memoirs of Ludendorff and Hitler's *Mein Kampf* 'next to all kinds of antisemitic Germanic kitsch spat out by the metropolis', Schützinger complained.[31] It is indicative of the ascendant nationalist mentalities in Tübingen that as early as 1925 university students clashed with the *Reichsbanner* when the latter attempted to protect a meeting with the lecturer Emil Julius Gumbel, a well-known statistician studying Weimar's political violence and a pacifist.[32] A local cell of the National Socialist Student League was set up at Eberhard Karls University as early as 1926; a genuine SA student *Sturm* followed there in 1929.[33]

A considerable number of the NSDAP and SA leaders who belonged to the 'war youth generation' during the 1920s oscillated between party work and lecture halls.[34] They not only contributed to the political radicalization of the student body in ever more German universities but also transferred the traditional student claim to leadership to their SA units, which comprised a broad spectrum of the German male population. Juvenile middle-class SA leaders such as Klintzsch as well as those with aristocratic backgrounds like von Jagow regarded themselves as forerunners of the people's community to come. They considered themselves a true elite, who did not believe in parliamentary rule but in the leadership of the 'most able men originating from the midst of the people', and they claimed that they already enjoyed the support of the (still silent) majority of the populace.[35] These beliefs legitimized their perceived role as educators of male German youth, whom they sought to keep away from 'taverns, card games, drinking alcohol, the dangers of the street and the immorality of the new, un-German literature and art'.[36] Although such programmatic statements contrasted sharply with the social realities of many SA *Stürme*, the SA ideology built on the positions of the pre-1914 youth movement. Both stressed 'purity' as a prerequisite for human and social progress, but pursued radically different goals: the German youth movement, in line with the ideal of the German *Bildungsbürgertum*, thought progress could be achieved by allowing young men and women to grow into physically and physiologically 'healthy' individuals.[37] By contrast, the stormtroopers regarded such things first and foremost as prerequisites for the successful remilitarization of male German youth. The physical training of young men in boxing and jiu-jitsu; their schooling in military discipline, fighting techniques, and the handling of weapons; and the Nazis' efforts to deepen their 'feelings of love' for *Heimat* and the German nature all served one central purpose: instilling revanchist ideas into the minds and hearts of a new generation of Germans.[38] The Nazis hoped that one day in the not too distant future, a new generation under the leadership of the SA would take the national destiny into its own hands and 'fight back' against internal and external enemies, above all the 'Marxists' and the Jews, the French and the British.[39]

Both this self-proclaimed war youth generation and the pre-1914 youth movement furthermore shared the belief that the dislocations of modern capitalism had to be overcome by a new 'spirit', a new 'idealism'. This idea, which was common among the radical right, resonated even with young Social Democrats.[40] Around 1930 it became a cross-party belief among politicized youth that the time of political liberalism and parliamentary rule as pillars of democracy was over. 'An epoch came to an end, and we have to liquidate it mentally as well,' exclaimed emphatically the young SPD Reichstag deputy Carl[o] Mierendorff in 1932.[41] Real democracy, a democracy that represented the true will of the people and not antagonistic class interests, was to be achieved by different means. The solution that Mierendorff and like-minded politicians and political writers proposed was a kind of 'authoritarian democracy' that received its legitimacy not from formal procedures but from the imagined organic bond between 'genuine political leaders' and their followers.[42] 'Today, nobody and certainly not the young are willing to climb the barricades for the parliamentary system,' argued Mierendorff's fellow party member August Rathmann, stressing somewhat paradoxically that democracy could only be saved 'by a different system of representation and government'.[43]

Within the late Weimar Republic, the popular battle cry 'Make Way, You Old Men!' thus gained a new, strongly political connotation. The Nazis 'exacerbated the existing generational tensions' that had been prevalent in Germany since the turn of the century, modifying them to their own ends. They effectively transformed political longings for youthful revolt that were initially ideologically diverse first into a vehicle for party propaganda and then, beginning in 1933, into alleged signs of youth support for the Third Reich.[44] A comprehensive booklet on the organization and values of the SA from late 1929 even claimed that it would be the SA leaders' task to provide their men with a higher sense of life, based on the ideas of National Socialism.[45] All those who subscribed to these ideas in practice were called to perceive themselves as members of a new German elite united by conviction and belonging, not by social homogeneity. Consequently, the SA leadership from its early days in Munich demanded that its stormtroopers 'regard each other as brothers and true comrades, irrespective of one's social status, profession, wealth or poverty'.[46]

Female Nazi Activism

To what extent such brotherly love should embrace women was very much a matter of debate among the stormtroopers. Andrew Wackerfuss has recently emphasized that women 'played a large but overlooked role in the SA', keeping the men 'dressed and fed' and comforting them when sick. Yet he also notes that women could only earn a 'limited place' within the movement, as they were prevented from experiencing 'combat' and thus could not request treatment equal to that received by their male counterparts.[47] Although women were not formally excluded from the SA until the late 1920s, it was clearly an institution made by men and for men. The duties of the 'SA woman', defined in paragraph 6 of the statute of the NSDAP's *Sturmabteilung*, which came into effect on 17 September 1926 and was slightly modified on 31 May 1927, limited female Nazi activists to practical aspects of support for the stormtroopers and to the maintenance of their social welfare more generally. Helping impoverished party members, catering to the needs of travelling fellow Nazis, and handing out presents at Christmas were listed as exemplary duties, next to the making of flags, shirts, hats, and party badges.[48] In contrast to the nationalist *Stahlhelm* which in 1931 categorically stated that 'our women shall not actively devote themselves to politics',[49] the National Socialists simply declared traditional forms of female tasks to be political. The NSDAP was aware that it had to reach out to women in order to maximize its support among the population, but its intellectual founders did not in the early days have a clue as to what proper female National Socialist activism might look like (Plate 3).[50]

The popular appeal to women of these 'female' tasks was limited, not only in comparison to the more active demands placed on their male counterparts, but also when contrasted with the party's otherwise immoderate rhetoric. As some of the fervent National Socialist women's autobiographies collected in 1934 by the sociologist Theodore Abel indicate, their writers actually shared similar values with their male counterparts and took pride in fulfilling tasks that resembled theirs.[51] Nazi women did not object to what the party officially requested from them and willingly contributed to the 'movement' by engaging in welfare activities and providing logistical support to their male comrades, but it was their execution of 'manly' activities that they described with the strongest emotional zeal. A certain Hilde Boehm-Stoltz from Berlin, for example, described herself as a 'fighter for

the true and pure soul of the race' (*Kämpfer um die echte artreine Rassenseele*).
No longer did she have any spare time, Boehm-Stoltz claimed, yet she felt
more than rewarded to be included among the ranks of the 'soldiers' of
National Socialism, a political movement that, according to her, was 'totally
based on idealism'.[52] The widowed Hertha von Reuß likewise emphasized
the moments of happiness she experienced when she was 'fighting' as a
member of early Nazi groups in the Bavarian provinces in the early 1920s.
Writing some years later, she noted that she had grown lonely because of a
'lack of understanding' from her 'politically right-wing family members'.
Having moved to Berlin, von Reuß remembered with fondness her nights
out in such illustrious Nazi hangouts as 'Ameise' (Ant), 'Wespe' (Wasp),
and 'Bärenhöhle' (Bear's Den). There, she had prepared and distributed
propaganda leaflets to spread the Nazi gospel face to face.[53] Finally, the
much younger Marlene Heder, a girl from the village of Kleinenglis in
Northern Hesse who came into contact with the Nazi movement in 1929
at the age of fifteen, described in similar terms the moments of 'danger'
that had resulted from her Nazi activities. Despite lasting incomprehension
from friends and family, she claimed to have not only remained faithful to
the Nazi cause, but to have even attended a dangerous 'red meeting' in the
city of Kassel (a meeting that was in fact organized by the *Deutsche
Friedensgesellschaft*, the 'German Society for Peace'!). As a well-known Nazi
supporter, Heder boasted that she was 'never safe' in her village, a victim of
nightly persecutions by opponents following her on bicycles. She also
claimed that she had been at risk of being hit by logs of wood thrown at her
from the neighbours' windows.[54]

Despite the questionable accuracy of these statements, which were
produced to provide exemplary accounts of National Socialist commitment
and were therefore shot through with propaganda clichés,[55] all of these
autobiographies indicate that although female Nazi activists fulfilled the
subaltern roles the party allotted to them, they emotionally responded most
strongly to those activities and experiences they shared with their male
counterparts, such as being exposed to physical harm, beatings, and spitting. This assessment does not contradict the dominant historiographical
view that Nazi street politics was first and foremost a male affair and that
women were confined to auxiliary roles. Yet it does modify long-held beliefs
about the alleged passivity of women in street politics, a belief that has been
successfully challenged with regard to the Communist Party, but less so for

the National Socialists.[56] Female Nazi activists aspired to take part in all aspects of the political fight, yet in ways that suited their identities as women.[57] 'We experience the "SA spirit" in our partnerships and for ourselves,' asserted Lore Snyckers, wife of the stormtrooper propagandist Hans Snyckers, in 1940.[58] In some cases the close bonds between 'SA mothers', a Nazi term of endearment for those usually mature women who particularly in the early 1930s cared for the much younger boys of the SA, and their charges were supposed to last beyond death. In Magdeburg a cenotaph erected in honour of the city's 'Old Fighters' expressed the expectation that Bertha Weinhöbel, an 'SA mother' who in 1931 celebrated her 60th birthday, would be laid to eternal rest next to her 'boys'.[59]

Regardless of their political preferences, women in the Weimar Republic, particularly those from the middle classes, overwhelmingly shared the view that the 'hypocrite bourgeois morality' of the nineteenth century that had confined women to the domestic sphere was not a realistic option for their future lives – at least not when they were forced into such a role. This does not mean that there were no longer any women who regarded a 'return' to the role of guardian of the family and motherhood as attractive. This holds true in particular for members of the lower middle classes, who were most strongly exposed to the effects of downward social mobility in the late Weimar years, when class affiliation determined the conception of female and male roles more than any other factor. Yet, by the early 1930s, such a 'return' had only become acceptable to women if they perceived it as a consequence of their own choices. The significant rise in the number of female students that occurred beginning in the late 1930s is just one indicator that the popular conception of the Third Reich as a regime that forced women back into the home is incomplete. Such a picture underestimates the *Eigensinn*, or 'self-will', of young women as well as the ambivalent character of the Nazi regime regarding gender in general.[60]

Satisfying Emotional Needs

Naturally, the remarkably bold self-perception of SA leaders provoked scorn and aversion from political opponents as well as the intelligentsia. The Nazi campaign of terror against all those they perceived as dissidents, Franz Schweyer wrote dryly in 1925, caused widespread disgust – all the more as the 'enforcer[s] of the new guidelines of public sentiments for the most part were of an age that seems a priori not to be called for such a task'.[61] It should be noted, however, that an excessive belief in the capacities of male youth to alter fundamentally the society in which they were living was by no means limited to Nazi ideologists. The aforementioned Social Democrat, Hermann Schützinger, likewise in 1925 emphatically described German youth as a 'new race', 'formed by the World War in iron blocks, aglow with the spirit of revolution and moulded into men by the touch of our new state'. The idealism and energies of these individuals, as 'shock troops' in the fight for the new state, should not be left to the extreme nationalists but channelled into a democratic renewal, Schützinger insisted. He imagined this renewal as occurring not through reform, but through revolution and war, a belief he expressed in slogans that were at times hard to distinguish from the Nazi rhetoric: 'Let us get ready for the fight of the state!'[62]

The stormtroopers during the 1920s were initially just one of the many groups that participated in this 'fight'. They benefited from the fundamental opposition of the early Nazi movement to the Weimar Republic, as they did not need to compromise for tactical reasons, unlike many of the other political youth organizations of the time.[63] The internal reforms of Pfeffer von Salomon and later Röhm had created a tightly disciplined paramilitary organization that gained from the exploitation of grassroots mobilization. Historians – particularly those concerned with the relatively recent research into a proper 'history of emotions'[64] – have pointed to 'emotion', 'charisma', and 'confidence' as key terms for the analysis of mass politics. Such analytical perspectives are indeed helpful for better understanding the motives behind the second SA's attraction to a considerable number of young German males in the interwar years, in particular when coupled with a path of research that since the 1970s began to analyse Fascism in general and National Socialism in particular as social movements.[65] Such studies argue that it was not ideology but participation and excitement that accounted for the attraction of interwar Fascism.

The twenty-four-year-old Richard F. Behrendt in 1932 was one of the first academics to advocate such views. After receiving his PhD from the University of Basel the year before, Behrendt returned to Berlin, where he had grown up and was now able to witness the last convulsions of Weimar democracy at close quarters.[66] The result was an original book on the forms and causes of the era's political activism, analysed from a sociological and psychological point of view.[67] Influenced by thinkers as diverse as Robert Michels, Hermann Schmalenbach, and Sigmund Freud, Behrendt forcefully argued that the crisis of the modern (German) state was a result of the inability of its institutions to satisfy the emotional needs of its people. As a consequence, he claimed, the political realm had grown, and would continue to grow, in importance. In Freudian terms, politics would even come to serve as an 'object of fixation', Behrendt argued. Only engagement in politics would allow the otherwise transcendentally homeless individual to prevent the development of 'acute neurosis'.[68] Collective (political) action could absorb the individual's 'free-floating libido' and thus satisfy him or her. As long as modern society did not allow the individual to establish bonds with a whole, or an imagined whole, particular groups defined and held together by collective activities would engage in mutually antagonistic struggles.[69]

Permitting such groups to carry out aggressive behaviour would allow for the 'emotional fulfilment' of their members, regardless of the ideology employed by their activists, Behrendt argued.[70] He regarded the latter as hardly more than a strategic political justification or, on the individual level, as an ex post facto rationalization. The ideal framework to organize bonding through collective violence would be the *Bund*, or 'league', commanded by a charismatic leader. Such a *Bund*, however, could necessarily exist for only a limited amount of time: it would always be a transitional form between (intimate) community and (anonymous) society.[71] For this reason, members of a *Bund*, who would inevitably perceive themselves as members of an 'avant garde' or 'elite', would set themselves apart from the existing social and political order, glorifying the establishment of a future order. They would necessarily long for conflicts, as personal success and fulfilment could only be achieved through action. However, Behrendt claimed that it would not be necessary for the political 'deed' to be translated into political 'success', as measured by traditional standards. In his view the political violence in Weimar Germany – the brawls and riots in the streets, taverns, and halls – was ultimately an end in itself. It was the field of politics that permitted the expression of the strongest emotions, similar to the 'sport frenzy' sparked by mass sporting events of the time. According to Behrendt, the military forces in the interwar years approached politics in a manner similar to hooligans who exploited the emotions of popular sporting competitions for their own personal ends: to test their physical strength as a means of excitement, empowerment, and ultimately self-elevation.[72]

It is instructive to analyse the activities of the Nazi stormtroopers in such a way, as long as one remains aware that this perspective sheds light on some, but not all, forms of SA sociability. Largely missing from Behrendt's book is, for example, any reflection on how these forms of 'political' activism influenced and helped shape the political organizations of the time. The most important advantage of his methodological approach is that it relieves scholars from having to explain how the crude Nazi ideology around 1930 became highly attractive for hundreds of thousands of German men virtually overnight. Even the vigilant liberal Jewish weekly *CV-Zeitung* noted that the spectacular Nazi gains in the September 1930 elections should not be interpreted as widespread support for the party's antisemitic creed, but as a sign of the 'deepest despair' of millions of voters.[73] Long-time National Socialist leaders certainly embraced the fundamental aspects of Nazi ideology, including its fervent antisemitism, but for many in the SA's rank and file the role the 'movement' played in allowing for the formation of 'emotional communities' was more important. Such communities enabled the expression of emotions such as despair and hate and encouraged the use of violence.[74] As the economic situation worsened, this form of community building became increasingly important for 'ordinary' German men and women, as already analysed in the previous chapter.

Behrendt's book appeared in print in late 1932, only weeks before the Nazis came to power. It has been completely forgotten today. More recent studies that adopt a similar model of explanation stress that the SA during the late 1920s and early 1930s was transformed into a social movement proper; it thus serves as a paradigmatic example of this kind of grassroots activism. However, such categorization is problematic. The influential sociologist Joachim Raschke in the 1980s defined a 'social movement' as 'a mobilizing collective actor which, based on high symbolic integration and only low role specification, pursues the goal of fundamental social change [. . .] by applying flexible forms of organization and action'.[75] It is obvious that the SA, at least until 1934, meets the majority of these criteria. First, as an organization particularly between 1929 and 1934 it was very successful in mobilizing mass support for the Nazi movement. Second, notwithstanding constant internal restructuring and leadership changes as well as short periods of illegality, it operated continuously. Finally, the SA was clearly an organization that promoted fundamental societal change. The SA's main goal was not only to destroy the democratic order of the Weimar

Republic and to replace it with an authoritarian form of government that would supposedly cope better with the internal and external problems of Germany, but also to instigate social change that would lead to the development of a true, socially inclusive 'people's community' which would blur existing class differences.

The problematic element of the SA when measured against that definition is the criterion of 'low role specificity', or the existence of only vaguely defined roles within a social movement. In the SA, which was organized like the NSDAP according to the *Führer* principle, the different positions were anything but flexible. Obviously, some stormtroopers built considerable careers over short periods of time, whereas others dropped out after a few weeks. However, it was the SA as a hierarchical organization that defined the different roles available – with no discretion for the rank and file to modify these rules. Even mid-level SA leaders, who were supposed to act as exemplary role models for their men and certainly wielded authority within the SA when fulfilling this role, ultimately had very limited power to transform the SA's hierarchy and organization. They had to lead and to obey at the same time, but they were explicitly not invited to engage in the process of shaping the SA as an organization. This is why Raschke struggled to decide whether the SA was a typical social movement or not. At times he described the SA as a 'totalitarian movement', which he regarded as a special kind of social movement in which the spontaneous activities of violent masses are embedded in a stable organizational framework.[76]

The historian Sven Reichardt later took up Raschke's definition. He had no problem with defining the SA as a social movement and highlighted in particular four elements that social and Fascist movements share: first, a loosely formalized but still effective organizational structure; second, an intrinsic dynamic; third, a certain 'closeness' of the political community; and fourth, an aggressive stance toward the prevalent political system.[77] Although Reichardt also informed his readers that not all parts of Raschke's definition fit the case of the SA, he did not explicitly discuss this problem, nor did he provide a solution to it. Instead, he repeated Raschke's claim that 'social movements do not possess an ordinary membership structure nor do they provide institutional solutions in order to solve internal problems', even though these two criteria did not fit the SA, as it had regular membership lists and arbitral jurisdiction.[78] Certainly, the NSDAP and the higher SA command at times had difficulties in keeping their men in check, particularly in 1931 and 1932, but this does not allow us to disregard the decisive influence exerted by the OSAF, or 'Supreme SA leader', and the party headquarters in Munich.

It is at this point that a rereading of Behrendt's 1932 book proves most beneficial, as he dealt extensively with the problem of leadership in social movements. Fusing his ideas with the findings of more recent sociological literature, I suggest defining the SA during the late Weimar years as a political organization that mobilized followers like a social movement but at the same time was hierarchically structured on a local and regional level as a *Bund*.[79] The mass of these *Bünde* on a national level were tightly dovetailed into a top-down paramilitary command that ensured the party's ultimate control but at the same time exploited the grassroots activism of the rank-and-file stormtrooper to its maximum degree.

The decisive figure ensuring the coherence of every *Bund* was its charismatic leader. Charisma as a concept has long been used to describe the influence and success of populist political leaders in the twentieth century, from Hitler and Mussolini on the right to Mao and Fidel Castro on the left.[80] However, charisma, understood as a 'purely emotional bond' between a leader and his followers, is by no means restricted to such iconic political leaders but encompasses the phenomenon of social movements that Behrendt defines as 'coalitions of charismatic communities'.[81] Although we are accustomed to viewing charisma (and 'charismatic rule', to use the original term coined by Max Weber) in modern times as an effect of propaganda and its dissemination through mass media, it is first and foremost a phenomenon that is necessarily 'rooted in the micro level of social interaction'.[82] In its daily operations the SA was – as Behrendt assumed early on – an organization that recruited its followers not so much through abstract political programmes and particular military aesthetics, but through the charismatic relationships that formed between the regional and local SA leaders and the rank and file in the particular stormtrooper units.

The charismatic SA-*Führer* was one of the key *personae* in the National Socialist movement, in action as well as in theory. The role is described early and in some detail in a document entitled 'Guidelines for the Formation of a Stormtrooper Unit' from 16 May 1922. The appointment by a local party leader (*Ortsgruppenvorsitzender*) of a particular SA leader was to be exclusively based on the latter's 'prowess and his military skills'.

Once appointed, however, even low-level SA leaders enjoyed considerable autonomy. They received general instructions and later also direct orders from the SA headquarters in Munich, but they were relatively free in putting these often quite technical rules into practical effect. Furthermore, according to the 1922 instructions, each SA leader was solely responsible for making sure that his men recognized his authority.[83] In other words, the larger SA organization attempted to ensure that only those SA men who were able to claim charismatic authority were appointed as leaders. Several years later, in 1931, when the SA had grown into a mass organization with more than 100,000 men, Röhm's Order no. 2 defined the *Sturmführer* as the most important role within the SA and explicitly held him responsible for the fate of his SA comrades, who, according to the new regulations, would number between 70 and 200. The *Sturm* leader was to be acquainted with the lives of all men under his command, sharing their daily sorrows and providing help if needed.[84] Needless to say, the social realities of this relationship were often different. In the small town of Frose in Anhalt in 1932, for example, a *Sturmführer* is reported to have attacked some of the men under his command with his fists and a knife in order to impose his will on them.[85]

The extensive system of responsibilities and mutual trust that was established ultimately proved beneficial to both the superior and his men. On the one hand, those ordinary and often very young men who success-fully commanded a group of like-minded followers could take pride in their own leadership qualities, while the rank-and-file stormtroopers at the same time benefited from the availability of a role model and a personal 'go-to guy'. The development of close personal bonds between a charis-matic leader and his men was also a way to mobilize mutual solidarity in the face of conflict,[86] increasing the fighting strength of these SA groups and at the same time contributing to their secretiveness, both ideologically and with regard to their day-to-day activities. Many personal documents written by stormtroopers during the Weimar years testify that the SA indeed provided emotional shelter against an outer world perceived by many as cold and hostile. Particularly for young men out of work, and those without a wife, children, or close relatives, the SA *Sturm* could become an *Ersatzfamilie*, or surrogate family. 'For the first time in my life I felt fully accepted as a human being,' a former stormtrooper later remembered.[87] When an SA man had to temporarily leave his 'family' due to his removal to a hospital or prison, his comrades were called to help him in every conceivable way: by paying him regular visits, by sending him 'entertaining and edifying' reading material, and by supporting his relatives emotionally and financially. Toward such ends, the Berlin NSDAP institutionalized an SA-*Gefangenen- und Verwundetenhilfe*, literally the 'SA Help for the Prisoners and the Wounded', in May 1930.[88] Initially, this aid organization was not financed by headquarters in Munich, but depended exclusively on donations from party members. Six months later the Berlin police noted that this institution was still relatively ineffective. Only a few stormtroopers remanded in custody had received small donations in kind. However, the police rightly predicted that the importance of this aid centre would soon grow.[89]

After Walther Stennes, the former SA-*Gruppenführer Ost*, was expelled from the party in April 1931, responsibility for wounded or imprisoned stormtroopers was transferred to the NS-*Notwehr* and the NSDAP's *Hilfskasse* in Munich.[90] Under their leadership, mandatory fees to the SA insurance schemes replaced the previous voluntary contributions; in 1931 these fees amounted to 30 pfennig monthly. Nevertheless, local initiatives remained of high importance in aiding individual SA members, as a proclamation from the NSDAP's Leipzig chapter (*Ortsgruppe*) makes plain. This order urged party members to provide fellow Nazis in need with all available material and moral support, including the procuration of legal and medical aid and the notification of close relatives and employers in cases of imprisonment. Furthermore, stormtroopers released from jail were to be given new employment and temporary accommodation in recreation homes run by the party or the SA.[91] Stormtroopers were also taken into well-to-do private families until their health was restored.[92] It was the 'honorary duty of every SA leader' to make sure that all incarcerated men were taken care of by their respective units in such a way that 'they d[id] not even for one minute experience the feeling of being let down', SA Chief of Staff Röhm solemnly declared, knowing well that immediate personal help was often more effective than payments from the Munich-based party insurance, with regard both to the needs of the individual stormtrooper and to the resulting propaganda effects.[93]

In sum, although the SA was a top-down paramilitary organization that relied on clear-cut hierarchies and the absolute power of its supreme leader, the secret of the Brownshirts' success was precisely that they encouraged the emergence of charismatic bonds on the local and regional levels, building on already existing networks of neighbours, work colleagues, and school friendships.[94] The SA paid its ordinary members not with financial compensation – in fact, its men had to spend a considerable amount of money on SA uniforms and other equipment – nor with jobs or social benefits, at least not in the short term. Instead, it rewarded its members with excitement, 'empowerment', and the feeling of being socially relevant and at the same time capable of forceful action within a political and social environment that most SA men perceived as hostile. Not only SA leaders experienced such feelings. Even the most modest individuals within the SA's 'community of action' (*Gemeinschaft der Tat*) – a telling term repeatedly used in SA publications during the 1920s – benefited from this experienced confraternity of German men who not only regarded themselves as a powerful group of loyal national 'fighters' but even imagined themselves as the vanguard of the people's community that the Nazi ideology proclaimed as its ultimate goal.

Critics of National Socialism acknowledged the force of this feeling of self-empowerment and correctly figured that the political consequences would be disastrous. Among them was the sociologist Theodor Geiger, who in 1932 prophetically warned that emotional excitement was no substitute for reason, noting: 'It is a horrible self-delusion of the NSDAP's best to believe that a new idealism is about to overcome the materialist spirit [*Materialismen*] of a corrupt era. On the contrary: a terrible and primitive naturalism based on the romanticism of the blood [*Blutsromantik*] has assaulted us and fundamentally threatens intellectual life as such.'[95]

Stormtrooper Merchandising

Being an SA man was more than a testament of political belief: it was also a lifestyle. As early as 1927 the leadership of the organization worked to generate additional income by building a veritable merchandising industry that soon not only provided party activists with the 'original' brown shirts, trousers, and caps, but also furnished them with propaganda books, all kinds of outdoor equipment, and cigarettes. To channel the money into the right coffers, the National Socialists founded a so-called *Reichszeugmeisterei*, a kind of centralized provider of Nazi goods that had been entirely transferred into the hands of the SA by late 1928.[96] From now on, stormtroopers were officially required to buy not only the official SA shirt but also the complementary fine cord breeches, a brown windbreaker jacket, puttees, the SA body belt as well as the corresponding waist belt, and the party badge, all exclusively from one of the regional departments of this provider. From 1929 onward a proper SA membership badge that could be used without the uniform was produced. It showed the two letters 'S' and 'A' in the form of a lightning bolt, alluding to the energy the movement claimed to have, and allowed its wearer to demonstrate his political leanings on all occasions. Previously used brown shirts, either handcrafted or bought in local stores, were from now on only to be used for hiking or at work, the SA Leadership Office decreed.[97]

Such orders, however, were easier given than put into practice. Because many stormtroopers were young and short of money, particularly after 1930, when the effects of the Great Depression set in and were later aggravated by Reich Chancellor Brüning's austerity policy, uniformity of the entire SA was almost impossible to achieve. In Danzig the local Hitler Youth deputy leader in the summer of 1929 even attempted to have his own brown shirts produced by a local factory – at least partly to avoid the heavy taxation, he claimed.[98] At the same time, precisely because the official SA shirt was expensive and at times beyond the means of members, it became an object of desire – similar to the modern-day 'official' football shirts sold so successfully around the globe. Once acquired, stormtroopers often wore 'their' brown shirt with particular pride – all the more as the repeated interdiction of the SA, which prohibited the public display of the party uniform, added to its symbolic value.[99] In line with the capitalist logic of the day, a mass article like the Nazi brown shirt became not only one of the NSDAP's cash cows in the years prior to 1933 but also a symbol of the individual man's affiliation and commitment, a commitment that no longer needed to be proven by individual action but could be bought.

The rapid growth of the NSDAP and the SA beginning in the late 1920s, which went hand in hand with an increasing demand for uniforms, saved one regional clothing manufacturer that has since turned into an international fashion company: Hugo Boss. In 1924 the thirty-nine-year-old Hugo F. Boss from the small Swabian town of Metzingen had converted the cloth shop he had inherited from his parents several years before into a little clothing factory. The small business that had fewer than thirty employees throughout the 1920s produced, among other things, uniforms for different organizations. After the war Boss claimed he had not initially known that these uniforms, among them the SA brown shirts, were intended as 'party uniforms'. The company came under serious economic pressure with the beginning of the Great Depression in 1929. Two years later, in 1931, it filed for bankruptcy but continued to operate. In this moment of existential crisis Boss joined the NSDAP[100] and – at about the same time – started to receive substantial orders from the party. From that point on, and continuously until 1945, Boss produced several types of uniform for the SA, SS, and Hitler Youth, and later, during the Second World War, also for the Wehrmacht and the Waffen-SS.[101] Other non-Jewish-owned German textile companies also profited from the rebounding of the economy in the mid-1930s, the increasing militarization of society that led to higher demand for uniforms, and the 'Aryanization' and shuttering of Jewish textile factories.[102] However, although 'Nazi Chic' garments[103] were produced in Metzingen, they were not designed there. Hugo Boss at that time only produced clothing and uniforms according to given patterns.

The example of Hugo Boss is typical insofar as it illustrates a more general tendency: after their takeover of power, the National Socialists gave preference to those companies that had supported them before 1933. In return, such companies exploited their close relationship with the party in their advertisements. Boss's company, for example, proudly informed its customers that the company had worked for the National Socialists since 1924.[104] Another example of this tendency was the leather company Breuninger in Schorndorf. Similar to Boss, Breuninger benefited from several big orders by the NSDAP and the Reichswehr in 1933. However, as the business historian Petra Bräutigam has demonstrated, it was not the quality of Breuninger's products that was responsible for these orders in the first place, but the close cooperation between the company and the National Socialists in the preceding years. When the workers of all Württemberg leather factories went on strike in November 1931, the Breuninger company called on the SA for help and, after twenty-eight National Socialists successfully acted as strike breakers, employed these men instead of the strikers.[105]

Such examples indicate that the anti-capitalist attitude widespread within certain SA units should not be taken as a general characteristic of the stormtroopers. Whether the rank-and-file SA man was encouraged to engage in economic and often antisemitic boycott actions or whether he was ordered to violently break strike actions for the benefit of local businessmen, who in return for such 'favours' financially supported the Nazi Party and its organizations, depended very much on the regional and local circumstances, as well as the local networks of National Socialism.

Smoking Politics

The cigarette industry provides another example of how capitalist logic and political identity successfully interacted during these years. The smoking of cigarettes became a mass phenomenon during the First World War. No longer associated exclusively with oriental luxury and the well to do, smoking nevertheless retained its function of marking differences – in regional provenance, in social class, and, starting in the mid-1920s, in political orientation.[106] In 1926 the cigarette pack, usually containing ten cigarettes, was successfully introduced in Germany. This innovation not only resulted in a boost in sales but also allowed for a new form of marketing, as the rectangular boxes proved to be ideal for graphic illustrations and thereby helped customers to identify specific cigarette brands.[107] As cigarettes were increasingly produced by machines and no longer exclusively by largely female workers, and as a consequence came to look almost identical, cigarette producers in Germany began to market hundreds of different brands of cigarettes, usually employing particular images. Many successful brands relied heavily on their capacity to demonstrate social status and used oriental images traditionally associated with the import of tobacco. However, even the marketing of well-established brands like the Reemtsma cigarettes 'Ova' and 'Ernte 23' soon reacted to changes in the political, social, and economic situation.[108] Between 1930 and 1932, as unemployment figures rose rapidly, advertisements for these two brands began using bold images of emergencies such as traffic accidents and shipwrecks. These images suggested that the smoker of these particular brands would react serenely and composedly in the face of such a situation – evoking the coolness desperately sought by millions of Germans confronted with personal economic ruin, often accompanied by family ruptures.[109]

The late 1920s were the 'Kampfzeit of the cigarette market' – a phrase that was not a direct allusion to Nazi terminology, but a contemporary wording used by marketers. Technological innovation and breakthroughs in modern marketing techniques in Weimar Germany forced the cigarette companies into fierce competition, leading to the creation of a diverse array of brands that allowed the individual smoker to express his 'personality' through the consumption of a mass product.[110] It was precisely in this period, in 1929, that a certain Arthur Dressler approached the NSDAP and its SA with his plans for a new cigarette factory in Dresden, which since the late nineteenth century had been one of the German centres of the cigarette industry and the Eastern tobacco trade.[111]

It was a remarkable time for a start-up enterprise to enter this largely saturated industry, all the more as Dressler lacked the considerable means necessary for such an investment. But Dressler, an NSDAP member, had an interesting idea: he suggested that the party produce a house-brand SA cigarette. If the SA would be willing to pressure its men into consuming his new brand exclusively, he promised the militia a reward of about 15 to 20 pfennig for every 1,000 cigarettes sold.[112] The SA leadership in Munich approved the plan.[113] With the help of Jacques Bettenhausen, a successful Dresden businessman who lent the very considerable sum of 500,000 reichsmark to the project, the *Cigarettenfabrik Dressler Kommanditgesellschaft*, better known under the name of its major brand, 'Sturm', was established.[114] No less a figure than Otto Wagener, who for several months in 1930 had acted as supreme SA leader, became a limited partner in the company in 1931.[115] This connection not only points to the very close and cordial relations between the Sturm Company and the SA, but also reveals that – contrary to the constant rhetoric maintaining that the 'poor' SA was operating just above the absolute minimum level – at least some high-level SA leaders benefited financially from the rapid growth of the organization in the early 1930s (Plate 9).

There was indeed money to be made from the stormtroopers' smoking habits. As early as 1930, Dressler was able to make monthly contributions to Röhm, the Dresden SA leaders Manfred von Killinger and Georg von Detten, and their Silesian counterpart, Edmund Heines.[116] And the success story continued in the following years, as the findings of Thomas Grosche, a young historian from Dresden, reveal with striking clarity: according to the balance sheets for 1932, the Sturm Company generated a profit of more than 36 million reichsmark. Most of the money was reinvested for the acquisition of new buildings and factories, and a considerable sum (128,325 reichsmark) was spent for publicity in magazines and newspapers, by the company-owned loudspeaker van, and even for hiring aeroplanes trailing advertisements. However, the owners as well as the SA made a considerable profit from the venture in 1932 and an even greater one in 1933. In that year the company's net profit peaked at 429,970 reichsmark. Of this, the SA enjoyed a handsome share. In 1932 the organization obtained 78,080 reichsmark from the Sturm Company, and the SA leadership was paid an additional 13,951 reichsmark. In the next year verified payments of about the same amount were made to the SA, with smaller sums for the SS and the NSKK (*Nationalsozialistisches Kraftfahrkorps*), the National Socialist Motor Corps. The fact that an additional reserve of 260,069 reichsmark was put aside to be paid later in the year to the SA and the SS clearly indicates that profits were much higher for 1933 than in the previous year.[117]

This financial success story was achieved not only because of a smart business model, but also – as was so often the case with the SA – due to violence, directed both against the regular SA men and business rivals. After the founding of the Sturm factory, not only did the Nazi media target stormtroopers with encouragements to buy only the new cigarettes, but SA leaders even formally forbade their men from buying different brands. To make sure their orders were obeyed, they engaged in bag searches and imposed fines for disobedience.[118] The Sturm Company, in an advertisement run in the *Völkischer Beobachter* in 1932, tried to convince the SA rank and file to buy its product with the following argument, which paraphrased official party rhetoric but obviously was not aware of the unintentional hilarity of the chosen wording: 'Only smoke your own brands. Do not spend money in other circles. To be a National Socialist means fighting and agitating until the last breath.' For men more inclined to practicality, the company enclosed vouchers for SA equipment in Sturm cigarette packs.[119] As several internal reports (*Stimmungsberichte*) from SA regional groups in the autumn of 1932 make clear, however, the ordinary SA man, that is, the consumer, could not even decide what to use these vouchers for. In Hesse, for example, SA men were ordered in September 1932 to turn in at least one voucher per day to the SA over a period of three weeks. The vouchers were to be used to finance an SA air show, intended as a major propaganda event in the region.

Regardless of such pressures, the Sturm cigarettes were popular in many parts of Germany in 1932. As regional SA leaders reported unanimously, SA men increasingly smoked the cigarette that 'in terms of quality, could compete with its rivals' and eagerly collected the vouchers and collector cards included in the packs. Every month the SA units received their share of the profits, which served, for example, to build regional SA leadership schools, pay for medical supplies, or benefit the SA stormtrooper units and their men directly.[120] Several reports from the time indicate that these commissions financed local SA activities to an 'important degree', and that for some units they were the only reliable source of income.[121] The Sturm Company was also popular among the National Socialists because it predominantly employed SA leaders as travelling salesmen, who in some cases could make a living from this activity.[122] In East Prussia all thirteen SA-*Standartenführer* were 'made mobile' in such a way in 1932.[123] The business model was so successful that it was quickly copied: the *Kameradschaft Zigaretten-Speditionsgesellschaft mbH*, literally the 'Comradeship Cigarette and Transportation Company', located in the city of Gera in Thuringia, soon also claimed to employ National Socialist party members exclusively and informed its distributors that its brands were to be marketed as 'other Nazi cigarettes'.[124] The SS and the National Socialist Factory Cell Organization (NSBO) allegedly supported this company.[125]

The only choice officially sanctioned by the SA, however, was among the different brands offered by the Sturm Company: the well-to-do stormtrooper could buy the relatively expensive 'Neue Front' (literally 'New Front') cigarettes for 6 pfennig each, or for 5 pfennig the cigarettes sold under the names of 'Sturm' or 'Stephansdom', the last named after Vienna's St Stephen's Cathedral. Most SA men, however, preferred the cheaper brands in the 'consumer price range' (*Konsumpreisklasse*): 'Alarm' and 'Balilla' for 4 pfennig, or 'Trommler' (literally 'drummer') for 3.5 pfennig. The latter brand was by far the most successful: in 1932, Trommler sales made up more than 80 per cent of the company's volume of sales, and in the following year 95 per cent.[126] These figures aptly parallel trends produced by the economic and social crisis in Germany.

Physical violence against competing companies and their distributors was another means employed by the Sturm Company. Dressler speculated that by agitating against his rivals, he would be able to drive down advertisement costs, which usually accounted for a large share of the cigarette industry's budget.[127] When the Nazis came to power in 1933, stormtroopers under the leadership of Alphons Michalke, an SA man and commercial director of the Sturm Company who in 1933 would become president of the Chamber of

Commerce in Dresden,[128] organized boycotts against the Dresden-based Bulgaria Compagny, another cigarette producer. This competitor was targeted as a 'Jew firm' because of its allegedly Jewish owner. On 31 March 1933 the SA blocked the entrances to the Bulgaria premises and carried out an illegal search of the house of Harry Carl Schnur, the director of the company. Schnur, however, had been warned beforehand by Philipp F. Reemstma, the head of Germany's biggest cigarette corporation, located in Hamburg.[129] Schnur was in fact Reemtsma's employee, as the latter had bought the Bulgaria Company from Salomon Krentner, a Jew, in 1928. This deal, however, had not been made public. Even if this particular boycott was therefore not intended to strike Reemtsma, other SA 'actions' clearly were. Stormtroopers repeatedly attacked cigarette dealers who sold Reemtsma products, smashed their shop windows, and even physically attacked those who worked there, giving the term '*Kampfzeit* of the cigarette market' an even more literal meaning.

However, such violence quickly backfired. Reemtsma, regardless of his personal liberal-conservative sympathies, was not willing to let the Brownshirts ruin his business.[130] The fact that the Nazis had initiated proceedings against him because of alleged corruption furthermore demanded immediate action, although tensions lessened somehow after Reemtsma was granted a personal meeting with Hitler in 1932.[131] Between August 1933 and January 1934, Reemtsma repeatedly discussed his and his company's problems with Hermann Göring, who had been appointed Reich Minister for Aviation and, as Minister President of Prussia, was in an ideal situation to exercise power over the SA. Göring's 'goodwill' was available, albeit at a price: Reemtsma had to donate the very high amount of 3 million reichsmark to the state, officially for the preservation of German forests and their wildlife, as well as for the state theatres. In return, Göring made sure that the criminal investigations against Reemtsma, the anti-Reemtsma publicity in the Nazi press, and the SA boycotts stopped.[132]

A final agreement with the SA, however, was not reached before its leaders were executed in the summer of 1934. Röhm's successor, Viktor Lutze, struck a deal with Reemtsma that resembled the agreement with Göring: in exchange for protection, Reemtsma would pay an annual fee into the accounts of the SA, as well as a one-time 'temporary allowance' of 150,000 reichsmark. The latter was intended to cover the anticipated losses of the Sturm Company.[133] According to other sources, the Reemtsma's 'storm obolus', a one-time allowance, amounted to as much as 250,000 reichsmark. Even so, the money was well invested. After the OSAF's order that stormtroopers buy only Sturm cigarettes was lifted in the summer of 1934, Dressler's company quickly experienced financial problems and finally declared bankruptcy in 1935. In the following years Reemtsma continued to be the undisputed king of the cigarette industry in Nazi Germany. However, even after the end of the Dressler venture, references to National Socialism remained a common element of the cigarette industry, as demonstrated by brand names such as *Braunhemden* (Brownshirts) and *Arbeitsdienst* (Labour Service, probably referring to the National Socialist *Reichsarbeitsdienst*, the Reich Labour Service).[134]

Modern Crusaders

It might strike readers today as counterintuitive, but many early storm-troopers regarded their commitment to the Nazi cause as completely in line with their religious beliefs. Some of them even perceived themselves as Christian crusaders fighting against the 'godless' and pagan 'Jew Republic'. Protestant National Socialists in particular advanced such views. From their perspective the Weimar Republic had abolished the formerly close bonds between throne and altar. According to the influential pro-Prussian school of historiography, this alliance had been one of the main pillars of Germany's rise to become a world power in the nineteenth century, and consequently a revitalization of this bond was expected to lead to a national renewal. Not only did representatives of the Protestant Churches and National Socialist activists share a deep-seated contempt for democracy, but many of them also regarded a rapprochement between their two groups as promising – at least as long as the Nazi Party claimed to be interested in cooperation based on mutual respect. The upcoming 'Third Reich', such clergymen hoped, would be a powerful Christian empire, with the stormtroopers serving as the propagators of these ideals.[135]

A characteristic albeit extreme example of such beliefs was the case of Pastor Max Michalik from Altmark in the Stuhm district, which in the 1930s was part of the German province of East Prussia. According to the Prussian Ministry of the Interior, not only was this pastor the deputy party leader in the region, but he also 'engaged in every possible way' with the NSDAP. He is said to have regularly participated in SA evenings at the local inn, dressed in his brown shirt. He also commissioned an unemployed stormtrooper as a door-to-door salesman distributing propaganda books written by a fellow Nazi minister. Michalik offered accommodation to travelling Nazi speakers and took injured militants in as guests, transferring his parsonage into an SA recreational home. In 1930 the Altmark Brownshirts and their pastor celebrated the Holy Night under a Christmas tree decorated with swastika flags, singing National Socialist fighting songs.[136] Michalik himself considered his activism as little more than a drop in the bucket. In his eyes the region he was living in was dominated by a working alliance between German and Polish Catholics who would in every way possible prevent Protestants from exercising influence. Among German voters, he complained, the conservative DNVP and the Catholic Centre Party would dominate, whereas the Nazis even in 1932 would remain a splinter party.[137]

Only a minority of Protestant clergymen joined in such radical political activism for the NSDAP, but it is important to observe that most pastors, and particularly those from the influential 'national Protestant' wing of their churches, did not perceive SA violence as either unpatriotic or ungodly.[138] The stormtroopers' violence was at best seen as a practical, but not a fundamental, problem. Whereas Protestant church leaders regularly dismissed individual acts of rowdiness and political fanaticism committed in the frenzy of emotion, they tended to justify the strategically employed Nazi violence as a legitimate means of self-defence against the supposedly ever-intensifying Bolshevist threat. At a time when some believers perceived the political situation to be nothing less than a 'new religious war', the temporary ban on the SA in the spring of 1932 was tellingly compared to the persecution of Christians in late antiquity. Even Protestant youth groups were now called upon to take up the sword and at times even met for military sports in Reichswehr training areas, assembling under slogans such as 'Christianity means fire, holy drive [*heiliger Drang*], battle!'[139]

Consequently, many pastors were willing to tolerate the presence of uniformed stormtroopers during Sunday service or on the occasion of funerals, or they even deliberately invited them – in contrast to the majority of their Catholic counterparts.[140] Heinrich Rendtorff, the regional bishop of Mecklenburg, stated that 'today, many members of the Protestant Church devote their hearts and souls to the National Socialist movement'. He warned the Nazis not to elevate *Volk* and race to false gods, but praised their ideal of confraternity (*Brudergedanken*) and acknowledged their general will to promote a 'positive Christianity', as laid down in point 24 of the NSDAP's 1920 platform. Although the bishop did not express agreement with all aspects of National Socialism, he thought it paramount to respect their 'great effort' (*großes Wollen*), which he hoped would lead the people along a Christian path.[141] In the same year Theophil Wurm, the regional bishop of Württemberg, spoke of the obvious duty of a German Christian to at least morally support the 'German fight for freedom' – a deliberate use of Nazi vocabulary that contemporaries could not have failed to understand.[142]

Similar to Rendtorff and Wurm, a considerable portion of the Protestant clergy in the early 1930s saw the rise of the NSDAP as a chance for their churches to again come closer to the people, particularly in the big cities.[143] Kurt Hutten, a young theologian who worked as the executive director of the *Evangelischer Volksbund Württemberg* in 1932, compared National Socialism to a 'ploughed field waiting for the seed of the Gospel to be sowed'.[144] In the same year Pastor Gerhard Meyer from Lübeck, a member of the NSADP and its SA since 1929, called the stormtroopers modern martyrs who would follow in the footsteps of Jesus.[145] And the well-known Magdeburg Cathedral preacher Ernst Martin, who between 1924 and 1928 served as a Reichstag deputy for the DNVP, in October 1932 officiated at an exclusive church service for the local SA in the city's imposing cathedral, a Protestant *lieu de mémoire* ever since the sack of Magdeburg in 1631. According to the Nazis, this church service was symbolically of higher value to the 'movement' than a speech delivered by Hitler in the city's civic hall.[146] Such events characteristically illustrate the erosion of civic values. Although Martin had held annual church services for the *Stahlhelmers* throughout the 1920s, in the 1930s the SA, for him as well as for many other believers, took the place of the former as the primary group defending the nation against the sins of materialist culture and the threat of Bolshevism. It did not come as a surprise that, in March 1933, Martin joined the NSDAP and became a strong supporter of the German Christians, the pro-Nazi wing of the Protestant churches. However, as early as 1934, he publicly objected to attacks on synagogues and Jewish shops and soon lost faith in the NSDAP's willingness to make Christian values and the fear of God central elements of the Third Reich.[147]

Martin's colleague, the popular Lutheran pastor Franz Tügel from Hamburg, embraced the Nazis more enthusiastically and for a longer time, calling them in 1932 a 'genuine popular movement of divine providence' (*schicksalsmäßig heraufgeführte Volksbewegung*) that was shaped by a 'willingness to sacrifice, by manly discipline and by trust in imminent victory' (*Opferbereitschaft, Manneszucht und Siegesfreudigkeit*).[148] Tügel became the Hamburg SA's 'foremost spiritual advisor' and, after the Nazi takeover of power, even dressed in the brown shirt himself. He publicly rationalized the stormtroopers' street violence as a legitimate and necessary defence of the nation and of the Christian faith.[149]

In neighbouring Schleswig-Holstein, however, the administration of the Evangelical-Lutheran State Church was more sceptical toward the Nazi movement. In late 1931 it published detailed guidelines about the 'political activities of pastors', prohibiting them from holding special services in churches for political parties and groups, from consecrating such groups' flags and banners, from actively participating in political rallies, and from publicly wearing badges of a political party.[150] That the Church in ever more German regions felt it necessary to publish such guidelines indicates that pastors engaged in such activities frequently.[151] All over Germany political leanings and the practice of religion increasingly became difficult to separate.

The relationship between the stormtroopers and the Catholic Church was more complicated, due to the traditional support of the clergy for the Centre Party and their mental and programmatic reservations about National Socialism. Yet the increasing popularity of the NSDAP among Catholic voters by 1929–30 posed a serious problem in the upper levels of the Catholic clergy. How could they keep their distance from such a popular movement without alienating a considerable part of the loyal and devout churchgoers attracted to it?[152] In February 1931 the bishops attempted to clarify the relationship between the Catholic Church and the Nazis, publishing a statement that condemned 'leading representatives of National Socialism' for placing race over religion and formally prohibited the clergy from taking part in the Nazi movement, but they remained silent on the movement's antisemitism and its open hostility toward the Weimar Republic.[153] The most pressing question – whether or not a devout Catholic layman was allowed to participate in the NSDAP and its organizations – was left to the local priests to decide. In the years that followed, the majority of the Catholic clergy remained rather cold and distant toward the NSDAP. Nevertheless, party propaganda claiming that without the SA's defence 'church-murdering' Bolshevism would have swamped Germany long ago did not fail to impress many devout Catholics.[154] In addition, a small but active group of Catholic clergymen publicly voiced their support for the NSDAP in the late 1920s and early 1930s. They advocated for a 'revival of Catholic support for the NSDAP', building on the temporary rapprochement of the two that had occurred in the early 1920s.[155]

Public perception of the 'Christian respectability' of the Nazis was certainly helped by the presence of their uniformed stormtroopers at carefully selected Sunday services, a relatively frequent sight in Protestant parts of Germany starting in the late 1920s. In Catholic areas such practices became more common only in the early 1930s. On one highly symbolic occasion about 400 Brownshirts equipped with flags and banners attended high mass in the cathedral of Regensburg in May 1930, despite the uncertain relationship between the Catholic Church and the NSDAP.[156] Three years later such spectacles had been transformed from the extraordinary to the everyday. After a uniformed Munich SA unit formed a guard of honour in a 'ceremonious and well-attended' mass on Friday, 28 April 1933 in the Frauenkirche, celebrated by Munich Archbishop Michael von Faulhaber, men dressed in SA uniform became a familiar if still somewhat peculiar sight at Catholic masses in Bavaria.[157] Regulations outlined in the *Pflichtenlehre des Sturm-Abteilungsmannes (SA-Katechismus)*, a small brochure of SA tenets modelled after Luther's *Small Catechism* and edited by SA-*Obergruppenführer* Hans Georg Hofmann in 1934, explicitly stated that the Nazi movement was pledged to protect the two Christian confessions of faith, Protestants and Catholics.[158] A similar booklet, entitled *Der kleine Katechismus Dr. Martin Luthers für den braunen Mann*, edited by the Deutsche Evangelische Männerwerk in the same year, exclusively targeted Protestant stormtroopers. It claimed that 'we need men who are prepared to fight for their faith'. This fight was to be inspired by the 'greatest role model of a fighter and comrade': Jesus, the exceptional man (but not Christ).[159]

Against this background it seems more than a coincidence that some of the earliest and most active SA leaders had close links to the churches: Hans Ulrich Klintzsch in Munich and Horst Wessel in Berlin, for example, were both sons of Protestant pastors. Their fathers had died by the time the sons became heavily involved in the early Nazi movement.[160] After the Second World War, Klintzsch is said to have aspired to become a pastor himself. From 1949 to 1952 he worked as a catechist in Schorndorf near Stuttgart, introducing schoolchildren to the doctrines of the Protestant faith.[161] Even the watchmaker Emil Maurice – usually portrayed as a simple and violence-prone footman to Hitler – kept ties with the pastor of his hometown in Schleswig-Holstein. In a personal letter from 1924, Maurice offered a justification of himself and the high level of Nazi violence to this pastor, apparently longing for the approval of a man of God.[162] To understand men like Klintzsch, Maurice, and Wessel, it is necessary to grasp that they perceived the political struggle of the 1920s as an eschatological battle, and themselves as modern crusaders fighting for the nation, the German race, and – ultimately – God.[163] Hitler supported such views early on. At the NSDAP's Christmas party on 17 December 1922, held in a packed Bürgerbräukeller in Munich, he praised Jesus Christ – of all people – as an exemplary model for the National Socialists. Of modest birth, Jesus was a man of high ideals who despised worldly goods and fame, and it was precisely because of this that the Jews later crucified him, Hitler claimed.[164] Implicitly, he modelled his own autobiography according to his version of the Jesus story – with himself as the new 'idealist' and his followers as the disciples, threatened by the Jews and by the foreign occupying powers, who assumed the role of the new Romans. The police agent present at this Nazi gathering did not mention this flagrant case of blasphemy in his report but noted enthusiastically that the occasion was, 'in a word, a pleasant and august celebration'.[165] Several years later, when the SA was on the brink of becoming a mass social movement, its activists still referred to their political mission in religiously tinged language. For example, Joseph Berchtold, the first leader of the SS who in 1928 returned to the SA, prophesied the upcoming victory of the National Socialist movement by claiming that the Brownshirts were 'the heralds of the German spring, of resurrection'.[166]

It is conceivable, however, that this was mere rhetoric which only superficially resonated with the rank and file. Consequently, we need to take a second look at how and to what extent a religious upbringing and exposure to Christian values and ideas actually influenced the behaviour of members of the SA. As recent historical research has convincingly demonstrated, at least some of the young stormtroopers understood their commitment to the Nazi movement as being in line with their religious identity. In a time when liberals and socialists seemed to dominate the political arena in many parts of Germany and its largest state, Prussia, these men felt called to raise the Christian banner. The swastika was a cross, after all. This general assertion, however, needs further refinement. The SA (as well as the NSDAP) proved highly attractive to young men in predominantly Protestant areas of Germany in particular, and it was in these areas that a phenomenon which might be called 'Christian National Socialism' flourished.[167] Hitler himself is said to have been acutely aware of denominational differences among his followers, although his understanding of such differences was rather crude. In a 1930 conversation with Franz Pfeffer von Salomon and his Chief of Staff Otto Wagener, Hitler explained the uneven recruitment figures for the SA and the SS in the Reich with reference to a long-established cultural border, the *limes Germanicus*. This was the former frontier line, fortified in the second century AD, between the Roman Empire and the lands of the Teutonic tribes, which in the modern Reich divided Germany into a larger northern and a smaller southern part. North of this former border, Hitler stated, the majority of people were Protestants and were more inclined to join the SA, whereas in the predominantly Catholic German south, young men largely favoured the SS. For Hitler this difference was not a coincidence: 'The SA attracts the militant natures among the German breed, the men who think democratically, unified only by a common allegiance. Those who throng to the SS are men inclined to the authoritarian state, who wish to serve and obey, who respond less to an idea than to a man.'[168]

The historian Richard Steigmann-Gall interprets Hitler's differentiation as one between the 'ideological substance' of National Socialism that proved attractive to many SA men and the 'authoritarian style' favoured by the SS.[169] Hitler's peculiar historical explanation echoes an uncritical veneration of the 'manly' and strong-willed Germanic tribes, in contrast with the allegedly 'effeminate' and degenerate Romans – a popular historical myth since the nineteenth century that found expression in buildings like the gigantic Hermann Monument in the Teutoburg Forest, inaugurated in 1875 by Kaiser Wilhelm I.[170] Hitler's statement nevertheless contains elements that are worth exploring further, particularly regarding the question of the degree to which National Socialist ideology shared basic ideas with particular strands of evangelical Protestantism known as 'muscular Christianity'. The analysis provided here barely touches the surface of such interrelationships, which can only be explored fully through further detailed empirical investigations.[171]

That many leading stormtroopers imagined themselves as Christian warriors is less surprising if one compares and contrasts the SA with other Fascist movements in interwar Europe.[172] The close relationship between the Spanish and French Fascists and the Catholic Church has long been known.[173] Yet in southeastern Europe, most notably in Romania, Slovakia, and Croatia, regional ultra-nationalist or Fascist militias also understood their political activism as a crusade. The Romanian Iron Guard, the Slovakian Hlinka Guards, and the Croatian Ustaša were 'deeply mystical movements' that resorted to excessive violence not despite, but because of, their religious currents. As Rory Yeomans points out with regard to Croatia, 'Many Ustasha leaders had been educated at seminaries, and, since its establishment, the Movement had been especially influential amongst theological students and the lower clergy.'[174] For Corneliu Codreanu, the charismatic leader of the Romanian Fascists, it was the 'spiritual patrimony' that constituted the main element of his extreme nationalism, 'because it alone bears the seal of eternity'. His idea of Fascism was a transfiguration of Christian doctrine into the realm of politics. Codreanu believed in a resurrection not only of individual human beings but also of nations and claimed that his politics ultimately followed the will of God, who had provided the Romanians with their 'historical destiny'.[175] From a transnational perspective the sometimes close relationship between early SA activism and ideas of Christian renewal is therefore less surprising than previously thought. Without a transcendental *Überbau*, or superstructure, National Socialism would not have been able to unleash its ultimately deadly energies. The regulations of the *SA-Katechismus* put this correlation in simple terms: 'Not only is the National Socialist movement not an enemy of the religions, but on the contrary we believe that the nation as well as the individual imperatively requires religions in order to hold command over the spiritual forces necessary to prevail in the struggle of life [...] We are also convinced that our entire German culture for more than one thousand years has been linked to Christianity and that it cannot be imagined without it.'[176]

Two years later, in 1936, however, the relationship between the NSDAP and the churches had significantly deteriorated, to the extent that the party now prohibited the wearing of party uniforms at church services.[177]

Nevertheless, a series of woodcut images by the artist Richard Schwarzkopf, a member of the Academy of Arts in Düsseldorf, continued to give artistic expression to the fusion of National Socialism and Christianity.[178] Schwarzkopf's woodcuts show highly stylized scenes of Nazi street fighting against Bolshevist *Untermenschen*; in them, the Communists appear determined to kill and are stirred up by the figure of a skeleton riding a horse, a personification of Death. By contrast, the stormtroopers are depicted as quintessential husbands and fathers, defending the German soil and mourning a 'fallen' comrade in a scene modelled after the Lady of Pity.[179] The series was showcased in 1937 at the Great German Art Exhibition in Munich and used widely in SA propaganda. From an artistic point of view, it was among the best of 'SA art' on offer (Plates 10 and 11).

Schwarzkopf's six woodcuts were influenced by the long tradition of the *danse macabre*, an allegory of the all-conquering universal power of Death whose earliest pictorial representations date from the fifteenth century. His direct model was a cycle of six woodcuts made by the Romantic painter Alfred Rethel, who in early 1849 had depicted the social revolutionaries of his days as inveigled by a political ideology that would only bring death and destruction to the people.[180] Rethel's cycle was extremely successful after it appeared in print in May 1849, not least because conservative associations bought the prints and distributed them for free in schools and barracks. For decades to come, his woodcuts remained popular among the middle and upper classes.[181] Schwarzkopf transformed Rethel's revolutionaries of 1848 into supporters of interwar Communism, but at the same time presented a possible saviour: brown-shirted stormtroopers, the new knights in shining armour. For the first time in the history of German arts, the press in 1937 rejoiced, an artist had created a *danse macabre* in which not Death but Life remained victorious – an outcome heralded as a consequence of the allegedly fundamental shift toward the 'life-affirming worldview of our times'.[182] The SA's struggle was thus elevated to an eternal fight between good and evil, between an organic nation willing to defend itself and the barren and ultimately deadly doctrine of Bolshevism. *German Passion*, the title of the series, directly evokes Christ and his suffering.[183] The parallel to the Christian message is obvious: as Jesus Christ gave his life for the salvation of his believers, so the Nazi stormtroopers sacrificed their lives for the nation. Their 'victory of faith', as the title of the last woodcut proclaimed, ultimately prevailed.

Relations with the Reichswehr

The stark contrast between the self-images of these young 'crusaders' and the dismal realities of their actions have long inspired critical observers to dismiss the Nazi self-image as the fantasy of an initially small group of misguided men who were unfit for modern life. The German scholar Joachim C. Fest was among the first to speak of the National Socialists as a 'veritable lost generation'. In his view its members were lastingly shaped by their experiences in the *Freikorps* and other nationalistic paramilitary formations in which they 'expressed their inability to live in a civilized way' by practising a 'radically tempered adventurism' and committing outright criminal acts that were barely concealed behind a facade of patriotism.[184] Consequently, Fest identified the 'nihilism in rank and file' (*Nihilismus in Reih und Glied*) as one of the central features of the Nazi stormtrooper units. The profoundly disturbing personal and cultural experiences of the first modern war on European soil had nourished such nihilism, Fest argued. The SA had to be understood as a product of the dynamism of the war youth generation coupled with a 'purposeful revolutionary will' that made it 'almost irresistible', he admitted, and devoid of any sympathy for the SA.[185]

However, such statements easily overshadow the fact that by the late 1920s the 'adventurers' of the SA were increasingly attracting the interest of the regular armed forces. In particular, younger Reichswehr officers came to see the NSDAP's paramilitaries less as dangerous rivals than as potential allies. Against the background of rising tensions in Germany and the ever more apparent weakness of its democratic regime, the Reichswehr from 1929 onward began to explore political alternatives. As is well known, the alliance between the army and the SPD, being the strongest democratic party after the war, was from the start no permanent love match but a temporary liaison. Although the Social Democrats more than once relied on the Reichswehr to put down Communist uprisings, the army only proved willing to support democratic politics as long as this system was seen as the only viable one among worse outcomes – be they a foreign invasion or a successful Communist takeover of power. After the November revolution of 1918 the German military repeatedly complained about the erosion of authority that 'came with the defeat and collapse of the monarchy'.[186] The following statement by Horst von Metzsch, in the 1920s one of the most prolific military writers in all of Germany, was character-istic. He wrote that for generations the great military heroes of Germany's past had provided 'far better prophets, more selfless friends, and more visionary pedagogues for the German people' than had the democratic politicians of the day, whom he defamed as 'demagogues [...] of the masses'.[187]

It was precisely this perception of visionary pedagogy that led some young Reichswehr officers to make contact with the rising NSDAP in the late 1920s.[188] Although the relations between the Reichswehr leadership and the Nazis remained officially strained, the two groups were increasingly connected by their shared goal of intensifying the military education of German youth despite existing Allied restrictions. On 15 March 1929, Hitler in a public speech proposed transforming the existing Reichswehr into a proper people's army (*Volksheer*), an idea that was followed by similar statements in the months to come.[189] At about the same time Richard Scheringer, Hans Friedrich Wendt, and Hanns Elard Ludin, three young lieutenants from the Fifth Artillery Regiment based in Ulm, started to discuss possible solutions for what they perceived as the most urgent problem of the Reichswehr and a major moral conflict: the challenge of remaining loyal to a 'pacifist' government that prevented the necessary restoration of the Reichswehr to its former greatness and thereby threat-ened the security of the nation. Although many young career officers had already developed sympathies for the NSDAP, the three lieutenants were among the first to officially engage in talks with the SA, a move that legally qualified as high treason. All three were taken into custody in March 1930, indicted, and sentenced on 4 October by the Reichsgericht in Leipzig to one and a half years of detention.[190]

Today, the so-called 'Ulm Reichswehr Trial' is best remembered because it was on this occasion that Hitler, called to the witness box, publicly asserted that his party would attempt to gain power only by legal means and no longer through a violent overthrow of the government. The trial was, however, also an important event that contributed to a further rapprochement between revolutionary-minded officers and the Nazi movement precisely because those officers who sympathized with the National Socialists felt humiliated by the trial's outcome and the fact that they stood trial at all. The violent conduct of the SA did not deter this growing connection, as 'the military ethos' of the time likewise 'believed that the failure or the betrayal of politics could be repaired by the virtues of violence'.[191]

The trial ultimately radicalized its key figures, albeit in different ways. Richard Scheringer converted to Communism during this time, while Hanns Ludin after his release joined the NSDAP. Ludin, the son of a gymnasium headmaster in Freiburg, represented the party in the Reichstag from July 1932 onward and was appointed leader of the SA-*Gruppe* Südwest on 1 April 1933.[192] Both men, who remained friends for the rest of their lives despite their different political leanings, regarded themselves as members of an 'activist generation through and through'. They wanted to be seen as idealists who, faced with the difficult task of reconciling their oath as professional soldiers with the duties of a German patriot, had opted for the latter.[193] Ludin at the time appeared a well-mannered and aesthetically inclined young man who only later adapted to the rough manners of the SA, Ernst Niekisch remembered, basing his judgement on a personal meeting in 1932 and later rumours.[194] By contrast, the young radical historian Eckart Kehr in 1930 sharply but prophetically criticized the younger Reichswehr officers for their lack of courage: 'The Reichswehr officer corps always looks for the *Führer*, the great man; they desire to be ordered about as the Praetorian Guard, yet they don't want to inquire as to the reason for this command.'[195]

The public notoriety of lieutenants like Ludin added to the growing respectability of the SA among the middle and upper classes in Germany in the early 1930s and the public perception of them as figureheads for the successful merger of German military tradition, *Bildung*, patriotic pride, and the fighting spirit. Even members of the aristocracy, who certainly had no interest in levelling social differences, had complex views of the SA in the early 1930s, particularly when they were young.[196] The later leader of the German military resistance effort against Hitler, Claus Schenk Graf von Stauffenberg, born in 1907 and therefore – like Ludin and Scheringer – a member of the war youth generation, as a Reichswehr lieutenant during the last years of the Weimar Republic moved freely within the esoteric and highly elitist circle of young men who gathered around the famous poet Stefan George and met nightly in illegal training courses that Stauffenberg organized for the SA.[197] As his sympathetic biographer Peter Hoffmann notes, the idea of a militia-based army, included in paragraph 22 of the Nazi Party platform of 1920 and strongly advocated throughout the early

1930s by SA Chief of Staff Ernst Röhm in particular, enjoyed widespread sympathy among aspiring military leaders like Stauffenberg.[198] The Reichswehr in the early 1930s offered training courses for the SA in 'nearly all garrison towns', one former instructor later remembered.[199] The army hoped to win over and transform the SA into a kind of *Notpolizei*, or 'auxiliary police', which could be called on in times of domestic upheaval or foreign attack.[200] In turn, Röhm restructured the SA according to military needs in February 1931.[201]

From the perspective of many nationalist Germans, a political movement that could win over men like Stauffenberg and mobilize their fellow Germans across social classes was worth serious consideration. Regardless of the fact that the SA's practices were at least as violent and aggressive as those of its competitors, many contemporary observers from the middle and upper classes framed them differently. Whereas these groups perceived the political violence of the left as a serious threat to law and order, they excused Nazi violence as a regretful but necessary and therefore ultimately legitimate means of national self-defence. By early 1932 the NSDAP estimated that nine out of ten Reichswehr members were sympathetic or loyal to the party.[202] Although this figure seems excessively optimistic, it sheds light on the exuberant confidence felt among the National Socialist leadership corps. And, regardless of the questionable factual accuracy of these estimates, the following years would undoubtedly prove that the party was right in its assumption that no sustained resistance against the implementation of Nazi policies could be expected from the German military.

PART II

TERROR, EXCITEMENT, AND FRUSTRATION

'Calm and order' is the battle-cry of the pensioner, but ultimately one cannot run a state to suit the needs of just pensioners.

— Ernst Röhm, 1928[1]

On 1 February 1933, two days after Hitler was appointed Reich chancellor, the influential liberal Berlin newspaper *Vossische Zeitung* published a front-page editorial entitled 'The German Man', written by Erich Koch-Weser, the former leader of the liberal German Democratic Party (DDP) and Reich Minister of Justice from 1928 to 1929. The newspaper editors, under the spell of the victory parade of more than 10,000 SA men through the Brandenburg Gate, considered Koch-Weser's analysis of the present times (which was actually an extract from his forthcoming book *Und dennoch aufwärts*, literally 'Upwards, in spite of everything!') a relevant comment on the new government. Although in the first part of his article Koch-Weser lamented in a rather conventional style the negative effects of modern society, in the second part he dissected the recent successes of the Nazi movement in an instructive way. As former Reich Minister of Justice, he had first-hand knowledge of the crimes committed by the SA in previous years. The Nazi appeal, Koch-Weser stated, first and foremost had to be understood as an indicator of widespread frustration:

The German man, in realizing that he cannot push through his own agenda, suddenly bows down to an extrinsic and brutal will. Feeling his inner strife as well as the fragmentation of the people around him, he calls for the strongman and a powerful state, to whom he hands himself in blind obedience. He refuses to justify his allegiance, to himself as well as to others [. . .] If he is not deemed worth anything, at least the large crowd he belongs to should. He snaps out of debates he cannot cope with and instead proceeds to action. Politics of ideas are rejected in favour of the politics of things and men. National Socialism with its superficial fuss, its mass gatherings and its displays of military power is to be understood as such a protest, directed against ideas and against personality. Sure enough, by parading through the streets in proud uniforms, you still feel yourself a personality. Sure enough, by mixing the noble platitudes of the Imperial era with the popular socialist catchwords, you can still believe you are standing up for ideas. Sure enough, by running behind a 'Führer', you can think of yourself as actively pursuing a cult of personality. In reality, however, it is the might and the masses that attract people, and the primitiveness that tempts them.[2]

Certainly, a critical stance toward the masses had been fashionable among European intellectuals since Gustave Le Bon published his influential *Psychologie des foules* in 1895.[3] However, Koch-Weser's observations went beyond popular cultural pessimism. They struck at the heart of the Nazi psyche of 1933, giving a plausible reason for the sudden paradoxical feeling of resentment and aggression experienced by many SA men at the alleged moment of triumph.[4]

This chapter explores in a threefold way the widespread terror carried out by the SA – first and foremost against the political left and the Jews[5] – which was a central factor in the establishment of the Hitler dictatorship: first, as direct physical assaults that intimidated, hurt, and killed thousands of people all over Germany; second, as a message that communicated the new Nazi code of behaviour to everyone, friends and foes alike; and third, as an expression of the long-pent-up emotions felt by stormtroopers that in the previous years had contributed so decisively to the appeal of National Socialism. However, one should not overestimate the unifying power of these outbreaks. In contrast to Elias Canetti, who in his famous study *Crowds and Power* defined this 'discharge' of the crowd as the decisive moment when all who belonged to it could 'get rid of their differences and feel equal',[6] I aim to demonstrate that the convulsions of Nazi terror and violence in 1933, besides achieving strategic gains, created at best temporary relief and certainly did not bring about harmony within an increasingly amplified, but internally fractured National Socialist camp.

Mixed Feelings and New Opportunities

With Hitler's appointment as Reich chancellor, the widespread pessimism that had spread among the SA men in the autumn of 1932 gave way to a new period of excitement and hope. From the perspective of many activists, the vision of a Third Reich, imagined as a racial and social community of Germans in which the stormtroopers' political commitment would be symbolically and materially rewarded, now seemed a realistic possibility, just one final effort away. In February and March 1933 the Reich government and the governments of the federal states not only started to ban leftist organizations but also liquidated many of the nationalist paramilitary groups. The SPD-dominated *Reichsbanner* and the 'Iron Front' were prohibited on 10 March 1933 and were followed two weeks later by the right-wing *Jungdeutscher Orden* (Jungdo), the *Bund Oberland*, the *Bayernwacht*, and Stennes's Black Guards.[7] At about the same time overambitious stormtroopers, who were eager to provoke the Polish armed forces with the aim of resuming the clashes that had broken out after the conclusion of the First World War, were ordered to stay away from the borders.[8] To the frustration of many in the SA, the creation and then consolidation of the Third Reich took priority over territorial matters until the second half of the 1930s.

The conquest of the Weimar state and its transformation into a modern dictatorship went hand in hand not only with waves of terror against all those the Nazis deemed foes, but also with an outbreak of often contradictory feelings: revenge, hate, rage, and excitement. The forty-five-year-old Gerhard Ritter, a professor at the University of Freiburg and later an eminent historian of the early Federal Republic of Germany, in mid-February 1933 claimed that the new German mood reminded him of a 'National Socialist alcohol frenzy' (*national-sozialistischer Rauschtrank*).[9] Similarly, the psychiatrist Alexander Mitscherlich in his 1980 autobiography *Ein Leben für die Psycholanalyse* remembered the time as being dominated by a 'general consensus, a nationwide, indeed, an almost ecstatic, alignment [*rauschhaftes Einschwenken*]'. He had been aware of the early concentration camps in the spring of 1933, Mitscherlich added, but had perceived them only as a somewhat 'latent threat'.[10] Franz Göll, an ordinary Berliner who chronicled his life meticulously, never forgot the 'rejoicing of the masses' and described his own feeling in 1933 of having 'fallen into a delirium' – a feeling that did not last long, however.[11]

Whether from excitement or as a matter of caution, the majority of Germans trimmed their sails to the new wind. Membership in the SA now became more attractive than ever. Entire shooting associations and gymnastic clubs requested acceptance into the SA, ideally as *Sonderformationen*, or special units.[12] Party members seized these opportunities so eagerly that long-time National Socialists expressed fears that the gold-rush mood within the party would bring self-seeking motives to the fore. Elfriede Conti, the wife of Leonardo Conti, an SA member who since 1928 had been the preferred physician of the NSDAP in the Berlin-Brandenburg *Gau* and was later promoted to *Reichsgesundheitsführer* and State Secretary in the Interior Ministry, as early as 3 March 1933 noted: 'Unselfish people seem to have become nearly extinct in Germany! My experience with the hunt for office, in the dark or in plain daylight, by the powerful and by the powerless, first and foremost taught me a lesson of contempt for mankind.'[13] In the spring of 1933 the term *Märzgefallene* – meaning 'March windfalls' or, literally, 'March Fallen' – made an unexpected comeback. Originally used to designate those who had been killed during the early days of the 1848 revolution, it was now sardonically adopted to refer to the 1.7 million Germans who joined the Nazi Party between January and late April of 1933 (Plate 15).

The stormtroopers were among those who benefited from the new opportunities. In the words of Karl Ernst, the leader of the SA-*Gruppe* Berlin-Brandenburg: 'It is a matter of course that the fighters of the SA must not be excluded from the manifold advantages that the new state is able and obliged to provide them.'[14] The provision of employment for Nazi partisans, a task that the official language of the regime glorified as the 'battle for work' (*Arbeitsschlacht*), ranked particularly high on the party's agenda. As early as June 1933 the German employers' associations, the employment agencies of the Reich, and representatives of the SA and the *Stahlhelm* agreed to a set of principles for a 'special action' (*Sonderaktion*) that would provide members of the SA, the SS, and the *Stahlhelm* with privileged access to jobs – on condition that the men in question had joined these organizations prior to 30 January 1933 and thus qualified as 'Old

Fighters'.[15] In order to make sure that municipal jobs and public contracts would be given preferentially to true members of the SA, and not to their recently discovered 'friends' and 'cousins', so-called SA-*Verbindungsführer*, or SA liaison officers, were established at several levels of the municipal and state bureaucracies. In some places such liaison officers did hardly more than collect the papers of unemployed stormtroopers and pass them on to regular employment agencies. In other places, such as the city of Detmold in Lippe, the SA successfully took control of the job market. In this town it formed a powerful executive committee within the local job agency that was composed of newly hired stormtroopers who ruthlessly pushed their interests through.[16]

By the autumn of 1933 the SA's influence had been extended to the semi-private and private sectors. In the capital, the SA-*Brigade* Berlin-Mitte appointed a 'consultant for the provision of employment' (*Arbeitsbeschaffungsreferent*), who forced local companies to hire substantial numbers of unemployed militants under threat of being excluded from public contracts or accused of sabotage.[17] Previously unemployed SA men also found 'shelter' in the Association of Local Health Insurance (AOK) and private insurance companies and banks, in which low-paid jobs were filled and at times newly created for this group.[18] For employers, such recruitment seemed the order of the day, a suitable way to demonstrate national responsibility and political compliance. For ordinary people, and particularly the Jews, such behaviour contributed to the surprisingly quick Nazification of the German public sphere, which, in turn, fostered a retreat into the intimacy of the family wherever possible.[19] Precise figures on how many German men benefited from the National Socialist 'battle for work' in 1933 are not available, but in light of the significant decline in numbers of unemployed stormtroopers between 1933 and 1935, it is safe to assume that the majority of them in one way or another profited from SA aid, whether outside legal bounds or through the official job placement programmes.[20]

Yet despite such preferential treatment, not all stormtroopers could be successfully provided with jobs – and not only because the remaining few consisted largely of ex-convicts, handicapped persons, and persons over sixty, as the Nuremberg job centre in July 1934 sardonically noted.[21] Certainly, in the days following the 'Night of the Long Knives', widespread public frustration with the autocratic SA found expression in such dismissive characterizations. Yet there was unquestionably a lasting mismatch between the self-image of many 'Old Fighters' and their professional qualifications that often did not allow them to occupy even the most basic positions. Furthermore, many of the stormtroopers did not like the jobs available, which were usually in construction work or farm labour, preferring 'clean' office jobs. In the latter domain, however, the *Alte Kämpfer* were forced to compete with better-educated men who had joined the NSDAP and its organizations only recently.

As a consequence, early Nazi activists of lower rank and modest educational background soon began to express contempt for those Germans who had not previously been involved in the Nazi movement. From the SA's perspective it was scandalous that the experienced 'streetfighters' who had allegedly risked their health and lives for the Nazi cause could not reap the fruits of their previous labour, but had to struggle against a quickly growing number of opportunists.[22] Across the nation, the more than sixty SA-*Hilfswerklager*, or 'welfare camps', that housed up to 20,000 men in 1933 and 1934 developed into centres of local unrest and dissatisfaction, despite the fact that the salaries paid to SA leaders in these camps were more than generous compared to the economic misery most Germans were suffering at the time.[23] In contrast to their superiors, however, the barracked rank-and-file stormtroopers received only very modest weekly allowances. Not surprisingly, small-scale benefits granted by city administrations to the SA, such as reduced entrance rates for public swimming pools, the allocation of city buildings for SA purposes, and exempted taxes for SA messenger dogs, did not pacify party activists.[24] Violent clashes with the local population in bars and taverns made the SA's *Hilfswerklager* fairly unpopular among the public. These incidents were often provoked by intoxicated Nazis from the camps who committed acts of vandalism, threatened local dignitaries with arrest, or used their guns to go trout 'fishing'.[25]

This economic and social background must be taken into account when assessing the stormtrooper violence of the early years of the Third Reich. It hardly needs mentioning that, first and foremost, such violence was directed against the Nazis' real and perceived political and ideological opponents: Communists, Socialists, unionists, and Jews. In addition, however, this violence more and more became a message to those within the Nazi camp that demanded respect for the SA's ambitions and a fulfilment of the social promises made to them. That several SA leaders quickly rose to positions of power and considerable income did not do much to calm the unrest within the party. It gave these leaders the financial and sometimes also the social capital to support their subordinates, but it also quickly widened the gap between the party establishment and its followers.

An incident from the city of Koblenz illustrates the growing expectations of the SA leadership as well as popular dissatisfaction with their ever more autocratic habits. On 17 April 1934 a 'higher SA leader' who was house-hunting ran an advertisement in a local newspaper looking for a 'modern apartment with 5–6 rooms, with all modern conveniences', preferably located close to the River Rhine, a good address.[26] Although it was and still is common in Germany to use one's professional status to convince landlords of one's respectability, this ad aroused criticism. An alleged 'old Party member' complained about it in an anonymous letter to Rudolf Hess, who in 1933 was appointed Deputy Führer to Adolf Hitler. The writer argued that the wording of the ad had created negative feelings among the people of the town. Everyone would agree, he added, that a high-ranking SA official who would make such demands clearly 'lacked National Socialist spirit and conviction'.[27] The social divide between the upper SA leadership and the foot soldiers, characteristic of the SA since the days of Pfeffer von Salomon, was never overcome, despite all party propaganda to the contrary.[28]

Hunting and Humiliating the Enemy

With Hitler appointed Reich chancellor of the new nationalist government, the Communist Party (KPD) expected to be formally banned and prepared to become illegal. The Nazis, however, opted to engage in barely disguised terrorism instead of respecting legal procedures. The burning of the Reichstag building on the night of 27–28 February 1933 was used by the Nazis both as a highly symbolic event and as a pretext for the systematic persecution of their political enemies. The parliament building was still in flames when police forces, supported by the SA and the SS, started to raid the KPD offices and the homes of their activists and supporters, arresting them using previously compiled blacklists. Not least because of this temporal coincidence, many contemporaries assumed that the Nazis had been directly involved in the arson. In contrast, the post-1945 historiography largely embraced the so-called 'single-perpetrator thesis', identifying the Dutch anarchist Marinus van der Lubbe as the only culprit, acting as a lone wolf.[29] Recent research by historian Benjamin Hett and others, however, has successfully challenged this long-held view. Hett has convincingly argued that it is indeed most likely that a special group of stormtroopers with detailed knowledge of explosives set fire to the building on the orders of Karl Ernst and Göring.[30]

While the causes of this event are still a matter of debate, there is no disagreement about its consequences. The emergency 'Decree of the Reich President for the Protection of People and State', signed by Hindenburg on the afternoon of 28 February 1933, suspended key civil rights guaranteed by the Weimar constitution. In the weeks following, the Nazis used this decree as justification for their ruthless campaign to track down all those who stood in their way. In Berlin alone 1,500 Communists, ranging from the rank and file to high party functionaries and even members of parliament, a clear breach of the latter's immunity, were incarcerated in immediate reaction to the Reichstag fire. Ultimately, the Nazi raids effectively destroyed most of the party structures that existed on the local and regional levels. In Leipzig the Nazis took 476 people into 'protective custody' in March 1933. By April, SA and regular police forces in the Ruhr and the Rhineland had arrested as many as 8,000 Communist Party functionaries. In Bavaria the number of arrests amounted to 3,000, while in the district of Halle, it was as high as 1,400, and in Baden in the southwest as high as 900.[31] A second large group of victims was, of course, the Jews. Ideological prejudices and economic interests coalesced in this wave of persecution. The best illustration can be found in the Nazi boycott actions of March and April 1933. In these months stormtroopers not only stood guard in front of Jewish shops and painted antisemitic slogans on their walls, but also abused Jewish tradesmen and their families, often to the gratification of the victims' business competitors (Plate 12).[32]

It is impossible to determine the precise number of Nazi victims during this period. The New York *Evening Sun* reported on 8 April 1933 that Hitler himself had estimated the 'rebirth of Germany' had cost 330 lives, with an additional 40,000 wounded and 100,000 driven from commercial life.[33] Hitler, however, in giving these figures, had in mind the Nazi 'victims' of the previous 'years of struggle', not those Germans whom his followers had hunted down, incarcerated, and murdered in the weeks after his accession to the chancellorship. From today's perspective, even a conservative estimate has to assume that the Nazis interned more than 80,000 people over the course of 1933. More than 500 people, and maybe even twice as many, were killed directly by the Nazis or died later as a result of beatings and torture.[34]

In the first weeks of the Nazi takeover of power, most of the captives were brought to the illegal SA prisons that mushroomed in the larger German cities. Cellars of SA taverns, sports facilities, youth hostels, barracks, and deserted factory buildings were all used as provisional prisons. These locations often only existed for days or weeks before they were replaced by a string of larger concentration camps that were run either by the German states or by the SS and the SA.[35] In Berlin alone the latest historical research has identified the existence of as many as 240 places where National Socialist torture was carried out and eleven early concentration camps. In 1933 these centres were located all over the city and were operated relatively autonomously by SA units from the neighbourhoods.[36] The centralized location of many of these provisional prisons and torture chambers made this early SA terror a highly visible and at times also audible element of Nazi rule. Terrified Berliners who lived near such prisons could hear the screaming of inmates as they were heavily beaten by their guards. Doctors in the city's hospitals were confronted with several cases of tortured and barely recognizable men, many of whom were in a state beyond help or already dead.[37]

The stormtrooper violence of this period was above all physical in nature, but it was often coupled with a strong symbolic dimension. Its ultimate goal was the humiliation and breakdown of its opponents, which at times resulted in the victims committing suicide during detainment or after release.[38] In many cases those interned were subjected to a myriad of degrading practices. Severe beatings that often lasted for hours and threats of execution were common. In Berlin a member of the *Reichsbanner* was forced to polish the boots of his SA guards, to drink their urine, and even to lick one stormtrooper's behind.[39] In Erfurt inmates of an early camp were forced to shout antisemitic slogans while being beaten with iron rods, shoulder straps, and rubber truncheons.[40] Prisoners of the early concentration camps were repeatedly required to carry out monotonous and degrading manual labour, like brushing off the ground with a toothbrush or cleaning the camp toilets with their bare hands. The so-called 'sports exercises' that the prisoners, enfeebled and often bruised, were forced to perform before the eyes of sneering SA guards, served a similar purpose (Plate 13).[41] In an SA prison in Cologne-Porz the personnel gave inmates 'swimming lessons' by draping a rope around a prisoner's neck and then lifting him up to a height at which the victim could barely stand on his toes and desperately started to flail about.[42] Drastic methods of physical and psychological torture were combined in the case of Hermann Liebmann, the former SPD Minister of the Interior in Saxony. As a prisoner of the SA in the Hohnstein concentration camp, Liebmann was forced to repeat the political speeches he had delivered in the Saxon *Landtag* in the previous years before he was stabbed with knives. Liebmann lost one eye and died of the after-effects of his wounds in 1935.[43]

These practices of SA violence in 1933 clearly had a gendered dimension. This violence, carried out by men and directed overwhelmingly against other men, not only strengthened the hyper-masculine identity of those who were finally able to exert power over others after years of economic hardship and social marginalization, but also feminized or 'demasculinized' the male victims of SA violence.[44] In Leipzig the SA arrested male Communists in plain daylight and forced them into 'cleaning squads' that were ordered to wash off anti-Nazi slogans.[45] Furthermore, the sexualized dimension of many of the SA's torture practices speaks volumes. This element of terror should not only be attributed to the personal shortfalls of the alleged SA sadists, but needs to be analysed in light of its political and social function. The Nazi terror of 1933 aimed at destroying the political organizations of the left, but it also attempted to ensure that its political activists would not dare return to politics. The forms of abuse therefore directly targeted their victims' honour as men.[46] Even after political prisoners were released from 'protective custody', they were effectively prevented from seeking justice, not only by the lack of state institutions willing to get involved, but also by the psychological barrier they would have to overcome to lodge a complaint. These barriers were high and therefore very effective, as can be seen from the fact that reports from former inmates circulated widely among German exiles but had only limited effect within Germany. To be morally in the right did not help many German men who saw their own powerlessness to defend themselves against abuse as a dishonouring stain on their masculinity.[47]

Notorious places of SA terror in 1933 were the barracks of the SA Field Police in Berlin-Schöneberg and the Oranienburg concentration camp, located a short drive north of the capital in a former brewery building. Starting on 21 March 1933 the local SA-*Standarte* 208 here interned more than 2,000 prisoners over the next twelve months. Among the most prominent inmates of Oranienburg were Ernst Heilmann, the leader of the SPD parliamentary group in the Prussian *Landtag*; the well-known writers Kurt Hiller and Erich Mühsam; the Reichstag deputies Friedrich Ebert Jr. and Gerhart Seger; and the popular radio journalist Alfred Braun. Alongside many such high-profile politicians and intellectuals of the left, forty teenagers from a Jewish welfare home and training school in Wolzig in Brandenburg were also imprisoned in the camp. The youngest of them was only thirteen years of age. This mix of inmates, together with the particularly bad treatment of the Jewish detainees, underlines the firmly established conclusion of historical research that the Nazi terror from the beginning to the end was not only politically but also racially motivated.[48]

Seger managed to escape from Oranienburg in December 1933. He went into exile in Czechoslovakia and in 1934 published the first detailed report of the situation in the German concentration camps.[49] Of particular interest to this study is a chapter in his report entitled 'The SA in the Camp'. Here Seger provided the reader with a short analysis of the stormtroopers' group mentality, which was, given his background and personal experience, surprisingly balanced. The large majority of the 80 to 100 men serving as SA guards in the camp at any given time, Seger noted, had only enjoyed a very moderate education, particularly compared to the overall level of education of the Socialist Youth movement. Contrary to what his readers in 1934 might have assumed, Seger emphasized that 'it would be completely misleading to believe that the average SA man had even the slightest political understanding'. The guards would discuss the upcoming Reichstag elections on 12 November as if they were a Max Schmeling boxing fight or an important football match – a level of political ignorance that Seger found hard to believe: 'Before they came in contact with us political prisoners, how many SA men had not the faintest idea that there existed other worlds than rifle 98, Army revolver 08, truncheon, cards, beer and sex!'[50]

Yet, despite their ignorance, not all SA guards actively engaged in sadist practices, Seger explained. Some of them not only stood aside during such instances but even showed generosity toward the prisoners when possible. Both the inmates and the SA guards were put under constant pressure,

Seger realized.[51] Similarly, the young Jew Peter Blachstein, a member of the Socialist Workers' Party (SAP) who between early 1934 and August of that year was a prisoner in the Saxon SA concentration camp in Hohnstein Castle, remembered his captors exhibiting both extreme brutality and temporary restraint, with the latter occurring in particular when the SA guards realized that they could exploit the professional skills of the prisoners for their own ends (Plate 14).[52] Yet both eyewitnesses set the proportions of this behaviour straight: 'Among the stormtroopers, brutality is much more widespread than brotherliness.'[53] At least sixteen of the 3,000 Oranienburg prisoners died; in Hohnstein the ratio of deaths was formally forty out of 5,600 prisoners, with an estimated number of unregistered deaths as high as 140.[54] Compared with the number of inmates and the length of time these camps had existed, some of the short-lived early concentration camps had an even higher death rate than Oranienburg and Hohnstein. In the SA-run concentration camp in Börnicke near Berlin, which existed only between May and July 1933, ten prisoners are reported to have been murdered. Inmates of this camp were forced to carry pieces of railway track for days without sufficient rest. They had to sleep on the bare floor and were given only the most sparing food rations of poor quality.[55]

The terror campaign of the new regime served not only as a means of destroying opposing organizations, networks, and individuals, but also as a way of intimidating undecided bystanders. Extreme physical violence was just one method of achieving this. Naming and shaming fulfilled a similar purpose, as the following examples demonstrate. At the University of Heidelberg three students dressed in their SA uniforms interrupted a lecture being given by Georg Blessing, a professor of medicine, and led him away to the police. The stormtroopers claimed that Blessing, a member of the Catholic Centre Party, had embezzled money from the university clinic and approached female students in indecent ways.[56] Similarly, in Rostock, a mob of SA students in May 1933 'escorted' to the police station the former university rector Rudolf Helm, whom they accused of embezzlement of public funds and of having a Jewish wife. Helm remembered the circumstances of his detainment as more humiliating than the fact that he was taken into protective custody. The university not only did nothing to restore the honour of its former rector but abstained from any form of punishment of the students involved.[57] Even more extreme were cases of 'racial defilement', such as one that occurred in Cuxhaven in July 1933.

Here, members of the local Marine-SA forced a German-Jewish couple to run the gauntlet through the streets of the town. The male victim was forced to wear a defamatory banner saying 'As a Jew-boy, I only take German girls up to my room!', and the woman was forced to carry a sign bearing the slogan 'I am the biggest swine in town and only go with Jews!' A trumpeter who accompanied the procession through the streets drew additional attention to the spectacle. The regional newspaper *Hamburger Tageblatt* interpreted this event as a 'return to a healthy *völkisch* sensitivity'.[58] SA units repeatedly performed such acts over the following years.[59]

Yet not all violence in 1933 was carried out in concentration camps or in broad daylight in the German streets. Many incidents of violence took place in private or in the semi-private sphere and never made it into the public record, as the following example illustrates. Julie Braun-Vogelstein, a fifty-year-old highly educated German-Jewish woman and a widow, lived in a villa located in Klein-Machnow near Berlin. During the 1920s she had made a modest name for herself as editor of the writings of the Social Democratic activists Lily and Heinrich Braun as well as their son Otto. A number of servants took care of Braun-Vogelstein's house and garden while she delved into her studies on the ancient Greeks and their arts. One long-time servant joined the stormtroopers in 1933 and started to blackmail his employer. After she refused to pay him protection money, hordes of men from the local SA repeatedly invaded the garden after twilight, destroying the flowers and intimidating her. Braun-Vogelstein left Germany in 1935 and ultimately emigrated to the United States two years later.[60] It is ironic that in molesting Braun-Vogelstein, the Nazis were attacking a proponent of a heroic form of German nationalism who had invested considerable time and energy in glorifying Otto Braun, killed in 1918 on the western front at the age of twenty, as a national leader who was untimely eliminated.[61] This example, however, illustrates the social dynamic of the Nazi takeover of power. Even if the stormtroopers' ambitious desire to establish themselves as members of a new elite did not materialize, the political transformation in which they participated encouraged them to pull down traditional social hierarchies and to exploit the new political situation, often for personal benefit. In this particular example, class and race were both factors that the aggressors saw as justification for their actions.

In cases like these the German judiciary was not much help. Courageous German-Jewish lawyers, like Hans Litten in Berlin and Walter Kronheim, legal counsellor for the *Reichsbanner* and president of the community of synagogues in Wanne-Eickel in the Ruhr district, as well as, to a lesser extent, prosecutors and judges, soon became the target of National Socialist intimidation, physical attack, and incarceration.[62] In early March 1933, just days after the Reichstag Fire Decree went into effect, setting off the Nazis' hunt of their political opponents, SA troops began to invade German court-houses and 'cleanse' them of Jewish lawyers and judges. One of their victims was the German-Jewish lawyer Ludwig Foerder, who since the early 1920s had been a committed activist with the liberal Central Union of German Citizens of Jewish Faith (CV-Verein) and an outspoken critic of antisemi-tism within the German judiciary.[63] Foerder later remembered that the SA's attack in Breslau started with a 'roaring, as if from wild animals'. A moment later two dozen SA men appeared, yelling 'Jews, get out!' When Foerder did not comply, one of them hit him on the head with a metal weapon.[64] Similar incidents occurred in many other German cities. Although at times non-Jewish judges and lawyers protested against the SA's attacks on their Jewish colleagues, by and large the protests were tame and in any case had no influ-ence. In addition to the strong symbolic dimension of the Nazis' nationwide boycott of Jewish shops and tradesmen in late March and early April 1933, the exclusion of Jewish jurists contributed to what the Nazis called the 'Germanization', or racial purification, of the German legal system.[65]

The pressure exerted by the SA on the German judiciary not only disturbed the course of justice but directly benefited the stormtroopers, who for political, financial, or personal reasons committed thousands of crimes during the years 1933 and 1934. To make things worse, the top positions in the German police forces were reorganized and filled with either National Socialists or conservatives willing to execute the will of the new strongmen. In Hamburg an 'Old Fighter', the SA-*Standartenführer* Alfred Richter, was appointed to the position of Senator of the Interior and chief of the Hamburg police forces in early March 1933.[66] Over the following weeks Richter systematically 'cleansed' the local administration of Social Democrats, Communists, Jews, unionists, and all those whom the Nazis deemed undesirable for 'racial reasons'.[67] A similar situation could be found in many other German cities and states. In Munich, Heinrich Himmler became commissarial police president on 9 March 1933, and in the Thuringian capital of Erfurt, SA-*Gruppenführer* Werner von Fichte was installed as deputy police president a few weeks later.[68] In Prussia in

February 1933, Göring, as Minister of the Interior, discharged fourteen police chiefs in major towns and replaced them predominantly with conservative candidates of the nationalist right.[69]

Such tactical moves barely disguised the National Socialists' real aims in the spring of 1933, and in some areas they made no attempt to cloak their ambitions. In Schleswig-Holstein, Bavaria, Hesse, and Württemberg, for example, the NSDAP promoted long-standing and loyal party members, particularly SA leaders who had already proven their 'readiness for action', to key positions in the local and regional administrations. Such Nazi *Führungspersönlichkeiten* (leadership personalities) often lacked the formal qualifications that up until then had been considered necessary for these positions. In Neumünster, a midsized town located halfway between Hamburg and Kiel, a former sales agent and unemployed chemist named Friedrich-Georg Brinkmann, who served as SA-*Standartenführer* for the area, took control of the police forces on 1 April 1933.[70] His counterpart in Wuppertal was SA-*Oberführer* Willi Veller, a notorious ruffian with no fewer than fourteen previous convictions.[71] And in Potsdam the bankrupt aristocrat Wolf-Heinrich von Helldorff, who had played a leading role in the infamous 1931 'Kurfürstendamm riots', was appointed police president in March 1933, largely as a result of Göring's influence. On 18 July 1935 Helldorff was chosen for the same position in nearby Berlin, where he became one of the driving forces in the antisemitic assaults of 1938.[72]

These weeks saw not only the redistribution of leadership positions in the police forces, but also the establishment of a new category of officers. In Prussia, Göring recruited and armed 50,000 men from the SA, SS, and *Stahlhelm* as 'auxiliary police'.[73] In doing so, he followed in the footsteps of the National Socialist minister president Carl Röver, who in the Freistaat Oldenburg in the summer of 1932 had enlisted between 230 and 250 stormtroopers to cope with the rise of political violence in a way that was favourable to the Nazis.[74] What had in 1932 been a disturbing sign of regional importance became official Nazi policy one year later, with far-reaching consequences. Now, the German police forces comprised both long-term officers and local gangsters, who patrolled side by side. Göring made it clear that the Prussian state would treat the excessive use of force by these police officers with the utmost benevolence. In order to quash the political left, all means were ostensibly justified – 'if necessary by resort to the unconditional use of weapons'.[75]

Auxiliary police from the ranks of the SA, SS, and *Stahlhelm* were also recruited in many other states and soon made up between 40 and 100 per cent of the regular police forces, effectively doubling their power. In the larger cities of the Ruhr, such as Dortmund and Bochum, this meant that the local auxiliary police forces, which were armed with regular police weapons, quickly comprised more than 1,000 men.[76] Wherever possible, the comradeships established within the SA units were kept intact. Whole SA *Stürme* were thus transformed into police units.[77] In the spring and early summer of 1933 these new police forces were involved in the detention of those the Nazis considered political enemies; in May 1933 in particular, regular SA and auxiliary police helped smash the independent unions by occupying their buildings, confiscating their assets, shutting down their presses, and seizing their functionaries.[78] Local business leaders in return sponsored the auxiliary police.[79] The State of Bavaria, according to a calculation by its Ministry of Finance, in 1933 spent at least 1 million reichsmark on the auxiliary police and 'protective custody' costs, which were largely related to the concentration camp in Dachau.[80] By the late summer of 1933, however, the auxiliary police were becoming less necessary. The organizations and parties of the left had been dissolved, and their possible reconstruction prohibited by law. Potential new opponents had been effectively intimidated. Thus, beginning in August 1933, the German states began to disband their auxiliary police forces, a process that lasted for months.[81] The last German state to abolish its SA auxiliary police was Bavaria, which passed the measure on 21 December 1933. However, throughout Germany, newly recruited police forces could be seen dressed in SA uniforms as late as the autumn of 1934.[82]

Despite these close entanglements between the regular police forces and the NSDAP's paramilitary wing, relations between them remained tense. In fact, throughout 1933 the SA operated largely outside the control of and often in competition with the police. For many 'Old Fighters' in the SA, police officers who had served under the Weimar governments before 'converting' to National Socialism remained enemies.[83] Furthermore, SA leaders like the Nuremberg-based special commissioner and SA-*Untergruppenführer* Hanns Günther von Obernitz regarded the regular police, despite the forces' overall willingness to obey the party, primarily as a nuisance. He preferred to settle the Nazis' scores with their enemies with the help of his stormtroopers, who cared little about legal norms and restrictions. In a letter to the Bavarian Ministry of the Interior from 20 July 1933 von Obernitz noted that he was 'fully aware' that he had exceeded his legal bounds when he ordered the Franconian SA and SS units to search Jewish properties for allegedly incriminating anti-Nazi propaganda, passports, exit visas, and money.[84] On this occasion stormtroopers detained about 100 Jews and brought them to a local sports field, where they were later handed over to the regular police forces in Nuremberg. In reaction, Dr Benno Martin, the chief of the Nuremberg police and later a general in the Waffen-SS,[85] complained of the SA's high-handedness in a letter to the Bavarian prime minister. Long-term initiatives of the Franconian police concerning Jews, he argued, had been made impossible by the SA's arbitrary operation. Martin added that some SA men had even threatened to arrest the regular police officers should they dare to interfere.[86]

This was not an isolated incident. Stormtrooopers repeatedly used violence against police officers, particularly those who were known to have been loyal to the Republic.[87] In Goslar, for example, the local SA *Sturm* in June 1933 sent a threatening letter to a policeman, informing him that they could no longer guarantee his 'life and well-being' if he continued to report for duty. Several weeks later, stormtroopers in the same city burst into an official interrogation of the former chief of the constabulary (*uniformierte Polizei*), the Social Democrat Friedrich Ostheeren. Although Ostheeren had been suspended from active duty on 8 April 1933, infuriated Nazi activists pushed him down the stairs of the town hall, punched him in the face, and kicked him severely. He died several months later. On 31 August 1934 the public prosecutor nevertheless closed proceedings that had been opened against the SA men in question, arguing that the crime had been committed by the perpetrators' 'over-eagerness in the fight for the National Socialist idea' and therefore fell under the amnesty of 7 August (*Gesetz über die Gewährung von Straffreiheit*).[88] In these years the citizens of Goslar privately referred to the core group of local stromtroopers as the 'pirate gang' – expressing both fascination for and moral indignation at such violent conduct outside of the law.[89]

The barely restricted SA violence of 1933 was so extreme that even the new regime which benefited from it finally felt obliged to interfere. In order to control marauding and undisciplined stormtroopers while at the same time protecting them from formal prosecution by the regular police forces and the judiciary, the SA-*Feldpolizei*, or field police, was established in

Prussia by decree of Röhm in August 1933.[90] Two months later, on 7 October 1933, this special police unit, which was led by SA-*Standartenführer* Walter Fritsch, was given the name of *Feldjäger-Korps*.[91] Only the most reliable and imposing men were recruited for this new unit, which by the nature of its task would unavoidably encounter trouble. The roughly 200 men serving in the *Feldjäger-Korps* operated under the direct command of the OSAF. In this way Röhm aimed at a further centralization of power that at the same time would reduce the ambitions of local and regional SA leaders.[92] In Bavaria a similar SA police unit, called *Feldjägerkorps in Bayern*, and placed under the command of SA-*Obergruppenführer* Johann Baptist Fuchs, was established on 27 February 1934.[93] However, after the initial waves of heavy persecution of political opponents lessened considerably by that summer, the SA field police lost much of their former importance. In Hamburg in March 1935, for example, the field police were charged with such unimportant tasks as arresting drunken stormtroopers who stumbled home after midnight, the official curfew time.[94]

Only a few weeks later, on 1 April 1935, the Prussian Minister of the Interior officially dissolved the SA field police. Suitable officers from the SA were now to be integrated into the regular Prussian uniformed police, an institution that more and more came under the influence of Himmler and his SS. Yet, as the new Chief of Staff Viktor Lutze ordered in May 1935, the rank-and-file stormtroopers were still expected to engage in regular SA patrolling duty. Tellingly, Lutze justified the necessity for such service not on the basis of political instability, the justification used in 1933 and 1934, but by deeming such patrols vital for the 'preservation of the inner service of the SA units (*Aufrechterhaltung des inneren Dienstes der SA-Einheiten*)'.[95] This demonstrates that the mechanisms of SA sociability established during the years of the Weimar Republic did not change fundamentally in the Third Reich, despite the seizure of power by the NSDAP. The SA needed enemies that it could violently oppose, even if those enemies were fictitious. After the summer of 1934, SA violence – a fundamental element of the groups' public appeal and internal cohesion – lacked political meaning and purpose. It was to a good degree autotelic. Between 1935 and 1938, when the Nazi ambition to create a Greater German Reich allowed for a partial comeback of the SA, the stormtroopers' antisemitic assaults provided them with one of the rare opportunities available to experience power and create a genuine feeling of belonging among themselves.

Reactions

The intensity of the SA terror intimidated and shocked many Germans, but it did not provoke massive resistance. In early 1933 the Social Democrats did not call for a general strike, a political weapon that had proved successful against the extreme nationalists in the 1920 Kapp Putsch but was now perceived as unlikely to succeed. Communist calls for mass resistance also remained largely unanswered. There were many reasons for this passivity. First, from the perspective of many Germans, the established parties of the Weimar Republic had been discredited by their failure to resolve the problem of soaring unemployment. Second, these parties and their para-military organizations had proved too weak to prevent the National Socialists from coming to power. The inability of the parties of the left to defend their followers against the SA's violent raids even in their own working-class strongholds was a symbolic humiliation of the first order and contributed massively to their loss of prestige.[96] How likely were they to develop a successful defence strategy now? Third, Communist resentment of Social Democrats, and vice versa, effectively prevented the working-class parties from fully mobilizing their still considerable power. As Joachim Häberlen has demonstrated for Leipzig, the penetration of politics into everyday life beginning in the 1920s did not have the effect of uniting the different working-class movements, but on the contrary deepened the divisions among them. In 1933 mutual distrust and hate were common among party activists and their supporters alike. Such feelings did not provide a basis for cooperation and joint action.[97] Fourth, the political left regarded the willing cooperation of large parts of the conservative establishment with the Nazis as the springboard for their own political comeback in a not too distant future. Convinced that the Hitler government would not be able to deliver on its promises, would the left not sooner or later emerge victorious?[98] Similar thoughts had also inspired von Papen and his neo-conservative followers in their efforts to bring the Nazis to power. Like many non-Nazi members of the German middle classes, these groups did not approve of the extreme violence of the National Socialists, but they sympathized with the goal to once and for all destroy the 'Bolshevik danger' in Germany. Von Papen and his advisors even assumed that once the 'plebeian' Nazis had burned themselves out, the old elites would be the ultimate winners, called upon to build an authoritarian regime that would be firmly in the hands of the traditional establishment.[99]

Others did not share such political daydreams but attempted to moderate the Nazi violence from within. A telling example is the case of Albrecht Böhme, who in 1933 was the chief of the criminal investigation office (*Kriminalamtschef*) in Chemnitz, a working-class city of 350,000 inhabitants in Saxony where political passions had risen sharply in parallel to the increase in social problems since the 1920s.[100] Böhme was a politically conservative jurist who had made a considerable career for himself during the years of the Republic. He nevertheless sympathized with the National Socialists and particularly with their crime-prevention programme, a field of applied politics that also interested Böhme from a scientific point of view.[101] In the first half of 1933, however, Böhme became increasingly appalled and disgusted by the SA terror that unfolded in his city. On 18 February stormtroopers stabbed a Communist functionary to death. The next day a *Reichsbanner* man was slain. On 31 March a Jewish businessman allegedly committed suicide when the Chemnitz SA threatened to detain him. Finally, less than two weeks later, the corpse of the well-known Jewish lawyer Arthur Weiner was found in a sandpit on the outskirts of town.[102] According to Böhme's post-war testimony, Weiner had been executed on the orders of SA-*Oberführer* Kurt Lasch. His son Eberhard was said to have been one of the murderers.[103] The *Brown Book of the Hitler Terror*, published in London in September 1933, recorded no fewer than ten instances of murder by the Nazis in Chemnitz and its immediate surrounding areas for the period 3 March to 1 August 1933.[104]

Investigating these and other crimes, Böhme described the extent of the stormtroopers' brutality and sadism in detail. In a report to the Saxon Ministry of the Interior submitted on 16 July 1933, he advocated a 'resolute crackdown' on what he called illegal 'single actions' (*Einzelaktionen*) of party organizations. The original excitement over the National Socialists' coming to power had quickly given way to an 'extremely tense situation' in Chemnitz, Böhme reported. The main culprits of this terror he identified as the local SA-*Sturm* 2/104, under the leadership of the electrician Max Schuldt, whom he accused of having established a 'true terror regime' in the town. In some cases the victims of the SA had been 'tied up, undressed and beaten up until they passed out'. SA torturers had pricked their prisoners with red-hot iron sticks and forced some of them to spend a night rolled up in a box, 'like a snake'. The maltreatment was at times so extreme that 'no spots of unhurt skin could be found on the victims' bodies'.[105] These crimes were unacceptable, and those responsible for them had to be detained, Böhme argued, stressing that the 'national rising' (*nationale Erhebung*) must not be compromised: 'The new time must not tolerate systematic, sadist atrocities of defenceless prisoners [. . .] it must not touch on the noble goal of the people's community by covering up crimes, it must not allow for any exceptions from the Führer's will.'[106] It is hard to determine whether Böhme used such reasoning for tactical purposes or whether it reflects his honest convictions. In 1938 he was appointed police president of Munich, and on 1 December 1940 he was promoted to SS-*Obersturmbannführer*; nevertheless, he remained an officer with *Eigensinn*, strong opinions and stubbornness until the end of his life.[107]

Böhme's determined effort to stop the SA's excesses in 1933 and 1934 'from within' the bureaucracy remained an exception to the rule. Most members of the German educated middle classes in private condemned the excesses of Nazi violence but made no public commitment to stop it. More common was a deliberate averting of the eyes and an attempt to not personally cross into the firing line. Yet widespread fear was only one element that allowed Nazi terror to continue its reign. There was also an element of approval for such violence among the public – the view that Nazi violence was an excessive yet necessary transition period in overcoming the problems of the previous years. Characteristic of such reasoning is a statement made by Pastor Friedrich von Bodelschwingh Jr., who since 1910 had served as president of the Protestant Bethel Charitable Foundations in Bielefeld, which enjoyed an international reputation for its work with disabled patients. In a private letter to a Jewish physician who had enquired about a job with the foundation, von Bodelschwingh defended the Nazi violence of the spring of 1933 by blaming the victims, particularly the Jews: 'Judging from the amount of dirt, degradation and mendacity originating from a degenerate Jewish spirit that have polluted public life over the last twenty years, in particular in the big cities, one surely understands that a strong and tough reaction against it was historically unavoidable. And in revolutionary times, riots can never be fully repressed.'[108]

Bodelschwingh's comment was in line with the common reaction of German Protestants to the Nazi 'revolution'.[109] In official publications the churches praised the 'iron energy' and 'determined will' of the new government as necessary instruments for the political restructuring that they glorified as the product of the 'robust heroic times'. Easter cards from the spring of 1933 that compared Hitler's appointment to the chancellorship with Jesus's resurrection were certainly extreme expressions of such feelings.[110] Yet there is no denying that many Protestant spokespeople downplayed the excesses of violence as 'labour pains of a new era' and justified the Nazis' antisemitic brutishness as 'drastic cures against the Jews'.[111] The majority of Germans in 1933 were impressed by the determination and skilful symbolic policymaking of the new government, even if they worried about the extremely violent settling of scores, enforced political conformity, and abolition of civil rights by the Enabling Act, passed by the Reichstag on 23 March 1933.[112]

Foreign observers likewise often approvingly commented on what they perceived as the 'dynamic force and will-power of the movement'.[113] Yet some were also alarmed by the rapid growth in might of the SA and SS in 1933. In September the military attaché to the British Embassy in Berlin, Colonel Andrew Thorne, reported that these 'semi-military associations' were clearly attempting to be 'part and parcel of the German defence forces'. Even if their actual military training lagged behind their ambitions, Thorne insisted that in 'keenness and discipline' these units were already superior to the British Territorial Army.[114] Several British officers in the summer of 1933 toured Germany to study the development of the SA and the *Stahlhelm*, taking note of troops engaging in military exercises.[115] At this time SA units armed with shoulder rifles and machine guns were a common sight in southern Bavaria.[116]

Nazi officials starting in the summer of 1933 became noticeably less enthusiastic about the SA's capacities and military skills. Commenting on the possible integration of former Communist functionaries into the SA, a functionary of the SA-*Gruppe* Berlin-Brandenburg in October 1933 declared that the former KPD activists would be 'exemplary able political soldiers' who would stand head and shoulders above the average stormtrooper when it came to political skills and ideological firmness. Nevertheless, he declared, even when former Communists came with the best intentions, 'demoralizing elements who are unfortunately common in the SA' would not allow for a successful integration.[117] From an organizational perspective the SA's massive expansion and the terror that its members could provoke represented at once an opportunity and a burden. Röhm's ambition to expand the SA at any cost in order to further consolidate its preeminent importance in the nascent Third Reich threatened the organization's already fragile ideological coherence as well as its controllability from above.

Above the Law

Nothing more forcefully illustrates that the SA in 1933 perceived itself as an extra-legal institution that was no longer bound by the German penal code than Ernst Röhm's secret 'disciplinary decree' of 31 July 1933. For every stormtrooper killed by political opponents, Röhm authorized the regional SA leader in charge to execute up to twelve members of the enemy organization that had carried out the attack.[118] This order reveals the degree to which the logic of civil war determined the thinking of the SA leadership, and that the notorious *Feme* tradition of the immediate post-First World War years was still alive. Several of the political murders committed by the regime between January 1933 and June 1934 targeted National Socialist 'traitors' who had allegedly disclosed internal secrets or simply happened to have powerful and ruthless enemies within the Nazi camp. According to Röhm's decree of 31 July, such executions were justified as a kind of 'atonement' as long as a proper SA jurisdiction (*SA-Gerichtsbarkeit*) had not yet been established.[119]

Without a doubt the pending uncertainties about the legal handling of the crimes committed by members of the Nazi organizations, which lasted well into 1934, further encouraged the stormtroopers to commit such acts. Sentences for most crimes that they had committed prior to the Nazi takeover of power had already been suspended due to the amnesty of 20 December 1932, with the exception of prison terms longer than five years.[120] Röhm and the OSAF in Munich insisted that incidents involving SA men be handled in special SA disciplinary courts, not the regular courts. In order to achieve this aim the SA pushed for a 'disciplinary law' that would provide the statutory basis for what would have amounted to a nearly complete exemption of SA and SS members from punishment by the regular criminal courts.[121] Röhm regarded the establishment of an SA 'military justice system' as an important step in his ambition to transform the SA into a people's militia. Despite the fact that the NSDAP, its member organizations, the ministries of justice, and the civil authorities were never able to agree on the terms of such a 'disciplinary law', regional SA leaders until June 1934 repeatedly threatened public prosecutors who dared to open proceedings against individual stormtroopers. One of these regional leaders was Heinrich Schoene, the SA-*Führer* in the 'Nordmark'.[122] Over the summer months of 1933 he fought an intense battle with the civil and legal authorities in Schleswig-Holstein over whether some SA men from the region who had organized so-called *Prangerfahrten*, or 'pillory processions', had to stand trial for breaching the peace, assault (*Nötigung*), and unlawful detention.[123] After a meeting with the Schleswig-Holstein district president ended in disagreement, Schoene wrote two letters on 10 July: one to the president of the *Oberlandesgericht* in Kiel, and the other to Hanns Kerrl, the Prussian Minister of Justice. As long as the new disciplinary law was not passed, he would simply prohibit the SA men under his command from appearing in court, Schoene stated. He would not accept any kind of penalty for his men, as 'even if the courts are formally in the right, it was ultimately the SA who had successfully achieved the national revolution and even if misdoings had been committed during and after this period, such acts needed to be pardoned'.[124] In the letter to Kerrl he even stated: 'If we proceed according to the letter of the law, then this will lead to a sentimental humanitarianism [*Humanitätsduselei*] that might have the gravest consequences.' In Schoene's view, any legal restrictions on the stormtroopers would ultimately be frail and therefore dispensable: 'A swine [*Schweinehund*] or a rascal is best served and educated by a sound flogging.'[125]

Even if, for obvious reasons, the SA attempted to impose its will on the German judiciary in a particularly forceful manner, this effort was only one element of a larger project that aimed at nothing less than the total control of the national and state bureaucracies. In order to achieve this aim, Röhm appointed so-called special representatives who were to 'take immediate and urgent corrective action against friction that occurs' during the Nazi takeover of power.[126] SA leaders were encouraged to oversee virtually all aspects of the political and social transformation of the public administration, a clear example of Röhm's attempt to consolidate the SA's preeminent role in the process of *Machtergreifung* (takeover of power). Röhm's claims were as clear as they were presumptuous, blatantly dismissing legalistic concerns: 'The special representatives need to push their interests through ruthlessly. I demand of them an energetic and target-oriented presence.'[127]

Such special representatives were appointed in most German states, including Prussia, Bavaria, and Württemberg. In some parts of Germany their power did not last longer than a few months, as the regular state administration quickly became embarrassed by their energetic but unbureaucratic new masters. In Württemberg, for example, the special representatives' term of office came to an end as early as May 1933.[128] In Prussia and Bavaria, however, the SA's special representatives (*Sonderbevollmächtigte* as well as *Sonderbeauftragte*) remained in office until the days following Röhm's death on 1 July 1934.[129] Special representatives were even installed at universities, but the civil authorities soon realized that their way of 'doing business' had a damaging effect on the institutions' academic reputations and thus soon stopped this unhappy liaison between politics and science.[130] However, as late as 9 March 1934, Röhm was still declaring that the civil administrations and the SA's special representatives were both called to work for the common goal of the 'build-up of the state in the interest of the National Socialist movement and its revolution'. In particular, he urged all ministries to contact the special representatives prior to making decisions that concerned the SA. This request was less ambitious than those made one year previously and indicated the regained strength of the traditional state bureaucracy, which as a rule despised the often rough and seldom properly qualified stormtroopers. Yet, had Röhm's demands been satisfied, this would have resulted in the SA continuing to exercise a kind of political control over the state administrations and the elevation of Röhm into a second ruler in Bavaria, next to *Reichskommissar* Franz von Epp.[131]

In reality, Röhm never ascended to such heights. A closer look at the special representatives in Bavaria nevertheless demonstrates to what extent they helped him secure power and influence. In Bavaria between 12 March and September 1933 the OSAF appointed 133 special representatives (*Sonderbeauftragte*) and special agents (*Sonderbevollmächtigte*), who each earned between 125 and 300 reichsmark per month (starting on 1 October, their pay rose to 200 and 400 reichsmark, respectively).[132] When combined with related expenses, this resulted in costs to the state of at least 371,520 reichsmark for the year 1933, according to the Bavarian Finance Ministry. However, the real costs were considerably higher, as the SA leadership also demanded at least an extra 100,000 reichsmark from the Bavarian state, to be spent at its discretion. The authorities in the autumn of 1933 did not fail to remark that all payments for the SA's special representatives had been disbursed illegally, as a legal basis for such payments did not exist.[133]

However, in a meeting on 20 October 1933 between Röhm and the Bavarian Prime Minister, Ludwig Siebert, the latter agreed to pay Röhm 25,000 reichsmark per month, including retroactive payments as far back as 1 September, to be used primarily for the special representatives.[134] This provided Röhm with the financial means to sustain his autocratic rule over the Bavarian SA in the following months. After Röhm's execution on 1 July 1934, his bank informed the authorities that besides a private bank account containing nearly 40,000 reichsmark, he had also maintained a checking account entitled *SA-Spendenfonds des Stabschefs Ernst Röhm, München* worth 56,000 reichsmark.[135]

The Integration of the Stahlhelmers

In the first twelve months after Hitler was appointed chancellor, the SA grew dramatically. While there had been fewer than 430,000 stormtroopers in Germany by late 1932, their number rose to four million by April 1934.[136] A decisive factor in this spectacular growth was Röhm's successful attempt to integrate the majority of the members of previously competing organizations into the SA. Most prominent among those groups was the *Stahlhelm*, the nationalist paramilitary organization popular among the German middle class and the aristocracy, which in 1932 still boasted about 500,000 members and thus surpassed the SA by several 10,000 men.[137]

Up to 1933 the relationship between the SA and the *Stahlhelm* was marked by a general consensus on the rejection of liberal democracy, despite obvious differences in the class affiliation of the groups' bases and their fighting tactics. Between 1923 and 1933 the *Stahlhelm* had been transformed from a genuine veterans' organization to a kind of 'surrogate Reichswehr'.[138] Against this background the rise of the paramilitary SA constituted a thorn in the flesh of the *Stahlhelm*, even if both organizations on the local level continued to cooperate in joint 'patriotic' rallies and protests against political rivals.[139] Yet the youthful activism of the stormtroopers starting in the mid-1920s contributed to a deepening rift with the *Stahlhelm*, whose members continued to regard the *Fronterlebnis* in the First World War as the central criterion for leadership. Consequently, *Stahlhelmers* too young to have fought in the war were required to accept a subordinate role in the organization, regardless of the level of their everyday commitment. Not surprisingly, ever more *Jungstahlhelmers* therefore began to see the Nazi SA as a model to follow, a young organization that not only allowed but forcefully encouraged its members to prove themselves in battle against an ideological enemy who was depicted as at least as dangerous as the Allies of the Great War, even if these battles were for the time being only fought in the German streets.[140]

In reaction to this tendency the leaders of the *Stahlhelm* increasingly distanced themselves from the 'plebeian' yet 'pretentious' SA. Typical of the confrontational style of the leaders of both organizations was a statement of Gottlob Berger, later a general in the SS. In 1932, when he was still a member of the SA-*Untergruppe* Württemberg, Berger described the situation in his region as follows: 'We fight each other. The spoiled sons of the aristocracy [*Herrensöhnchen*] and the calcified active officers set the tone in the *Stahlhelm*. In the countryside we now start to organize riders' storms [*Reiterstürme*] and thereby do the best possible harm to the *Stahlhelm*.'[141] On the other side, Theodor Duesterberg, with Franz Seldte one of the two national leaders of the *Stahlhelm*, made no attempt to hide his contempt for the SA. In a speech delivered to *Stahlhelmers* in the capital in early February 1933 he expressed embarrassment that 'fully fledged shirkers and juveniles who during World War I were still in their swaddling clothes or went to school' now dared to openly accuse the *Stahlhelmers* of a lack of patriotism.[142]

Duesterberg, who had run for president in April 1932 and won more than two and a half million votes, insisted in the spring of 1933 on the *Stahlhelm*'s independence from the Nazi movement. Seldte, however, adapted more flexibly to the political changes and quickly outmanoeuvred his co-leader. Since 30 January 1933 he had served as Reich Minister for Labour and as such had a seat in the Cabinet. He joined the NSDAP on 27 April 1933 and in the following weeks and months negotiated what turned out to become a step-by-step integration of the *Stahlhelm* into the SA.[143] The concerns of sceptical *Stahlhelmers* who feared that their organization would be turned into a 'second-class SA' were pushed aside.[144] As early as June 1933 *Jungstahlhelmers* were transferred into the SA, while the members of the *Scharnhorst Bund*, the youth organization of the *Stahlhelm*, were integrated into the HJ.[145] In the following month a separation was established between the *Wehrstahlhelm*, which comprised all *Stahlhelmers* up to the age of thirty-five, and the *Stahlhelm*. The leader of the *Wehrstahlhelm*, Elhard von Moroczowicz, became a member of the OSAF and was charged with the task of 'bring[ing] the *Wehrstahlhelm* into the SA'.[146] On 6 November 1933, Röhm finally implemented a new structure for the considerably enlarged SA. There now existed three different sub-groups. First, there was the 'active' SA, which comprised all regular SA and SS men between eighteen and thirty-five years of age, including the more than 300,000 former *Wehrstahlhelmers* who had been integrated into the organization the previous July. Second, there was the 'SA-Reserve I' (SA-R I), in which all former *Stahlhelm* members between thirty-six and forty-five were organized.[147] Third, an 'SA-Reserve II' (SA-R II) consisting of men over the age of forty-five (i.e. members of the *Kyffhäuserbund*, other veterans' organizations, and colonial lobby groups) was established and placed under the control of Röhm and his SA.[148] As of 28 March 1934 the remains of the *Stahlhelm* were referred to as *Nationalsozialistischer Deutscher Frontkämpferbund* (NSDFB). Already the new name indicated that the days of the independent *Stahlhelm* had passed.[149]

The Nazification of German Academia

By the end of 1933 the Nazis had acquired complete political and symbolic control over Germany. The journeyman Patrick Leigh Fermor's first impression of the small city of Goch, situated at the Lower Rhine close to the border with the Netherlands, can be taken as fairly representative. The then eighteen-year-old noted that 'the town was hung with National Socialist flags and the window of an outfitter's shop next door held a display of Party equipment: swastika arm-bands, daggers for the Hitler Youth, blouses for Hitler Maidens and brown shirts for grown-up S.A. men; swastika button-holes were arranged in a pattern which read *Heil Hitler* and an androgynous wax-dummy with a pearly smile was dressed up in the full uniform of a *Sturmabteilungsmann*.'[150] In the memoirs of his journey on foot to Constantinople in 1933 and 1934 that would make him famous decades later, Leigh Fermor recalled several encounters with SA men while hiking through the hibernal western and northern parts of Germany. Writing with hindsight, he remarked on a certain mismatch that existed between his actual memories and his historical knowledge. In the same city of Goch the young Leigh Fermor encountered a bunch of SA men in a local tavern who 'looked less fierce without their horrible caps. One or two, wearing spectacles, might have been clerks or students.'[151] These SA men started singing popular folk songs. Leigh Fermor remembered the situation as 'charming' and stated that 'the charm made it impossible, at that moment, to connect the singers with organized bullying and the smashing of Jewish shop windows and nocturnal bonfires of books'.[152]

This observation reminds us of the complexities of the SA's appearance in the first one and a half years of the Third Reich. Not all stormtroopers of the time engaged in physical violence, burned books, or guarded and tortured inmates of the early concentration camps. The short-lived episode of the SA-*Hochschulamt* (literally, the SA University Office) and its regional branches demonstrates this diversity.[153] On 9 September 1933, Hitler ordered the establishment of the SA-*Hochschulamt*, which was located at Berlin's Wilhelmstraße and headed by SA-*Brigade* General Heinrich Bennecke, an early Nazi activist and a trained historian who held a PhD from Leipzig University.[154] The task of the SA University Office was to educate every student at a German university physically and mentally 'in the spirit of the forerunners of the German revolution', which meant heavy ideological indoctrination as well as constant physical exercises.[155] This new orientation was an important aspect of the *Gleichschaltung*, the forcible coordination, of the German universities. Intellectual training and contemplation from this time on mattered far less than physical boldness and mental determination, for the National Socialists first and foremost understood leadership as the toughness to push one's will through, regardless of the quality of the arguments employed. It was the personality and charisma of the new generation of academic leaders that counted, not their reasoning. Adolf Hitler had expressed such views as early as 1922, when he urged the male youth of Munich to join the nascent SA: 'The boy who does not find the way to where the destiny of his people is campaigned for in a good way now, who at this crucial moment prefers to study philosophy and sits behinds his books or is a stay-at-home, such a boy is not a German boy!'[156]

Whereas Hitler's anti-intellectual statement in 1922 expressed the opinion of a radical minority in Germany, for a short time in 1933 and 1934 such views were highly popular. At Rostock University, for example, as many as 71 per cent of all students enrolled in 1933 were members of the SA.[157] Yet even in light of the inclination of substantial parts of the male student youth population to embrace the ideas of National Socialism since the second half of the 1920s, the initial plans of the newly founded SA-*Hochschulämter* were extremely ambitious, as the example of Munich illustrates. There, the adjutant leader of the city's regional branch of the SA University Office, the twenty-three-year-old law student Karl Gengenbach, in a letter to State Minister Hermann Esser from 24 January 1934 outlined a set of plans that in practice would have resulted in a complete transformation of German student life.[158] He urged that male students be educated and trained during their first three semesters with the ultimate aim of winning every student over to the SA. While freshmen during their first semester would only be subjected to political indoctrination, male student life during the following two semesters would be largely devoted to the SA. Besides weekly three-hour 'theory lessons', students would be required to take part in four hours of practical training that comprised shooting exercises, marching, and the vaguely defined 'political education according to the standards of the SA'. In addition, weeks of practical military training and field exercises in nearby SA camps would occupy most weeks of the student holidays. However, the SA University Office in Munich lacked the necessary facilities to train the approximately 2,000 second- and third-semester students who were enrolled in the city's universities every year. Gengenbach therefore made plans to build a large SA training and sports camp that could accommodate up to 800 students in Oberstdorf, a popular tourist spot in the Allgäu Alps. As the SA-*Hochschulämter* were shut down shortly after the 'Röhm Putsch', it is unlikely that these plans ever materialized, but from Gengenbach's surviving correspondence with the Bavarian authorities, it seems that large parts of the 250,000 reichsmark necessary for the construction of the school were secured, then promised by the Bavarian Ministry of Culture and the municipality of Oberstdorf, which saw the plan as a great opportunity to increase tourism in the region.[159]

At another prestigious German university, in Heidelberg, SA paramilitary training courses were in full swing by 1934. As in Munich, starting in the summer semester of 1934, male students in their first and second years were obliged to participate in SA field exercises. One of the participants in the spring of 1934 was the twenty-one-year-old Felix Hartlaub, who was then studying Romance philology and history and would become one of Germany's most talented young writers of the 1930s and early 1940s.[160] In a letter to his father, the museum director Gustav Friedrich Hartlaub, young Felix in 1934 described the atmosphere of such SA training exercises at some length. Having participated in them for several weeks, his impressions were mixed. On the one hand, he was critical of most of his fellow students, who did not behave in a comradely fashion but were overambitious and selfish, without any 'proper soldierly ethos'. Their methods of socializing were dominated by the 'heavy drinking intimacy' (*Bierinnigkeit*) of corps students. Among them, no traces of the new 'manly community spirit' could be found (Plate 16). On the other hand, Hartlaub was impressed by the SA leadership corps who organized these training courses, many of whom he perceived to be 'great fellows' (*großartige Typen*). None of them were of the 'unpleasant type of non-commissioned officers', Hartlaub wrote, alluding to the bad reputation that lower-ranked military leaders had had since the First World War. Instead, the young student praised the combination of the military and the ideological beliefs and skills of the party's most dedicated activists and supporters (*weltanschauliches Parteijüngertum*) as 'very decent'.[161]

Hartlaub's description contradicts the majority of later judgements of such SA training courses, which usually emphasize their dull and uninspiring character.[162] His view is certainly not representative, but it indicates that the specific combination of ideological training and physical exercise could prove attractive for well-educated middle-class youth who embraced the SA's 'modern' attitude. Other students and lecturers, however, were clearly appalled by this political element of university life in 1933–4, particularly when confronted with its most extreme forms. In this respect the lyrics of a 'blood song' performed by SA students in the spring of 1934, and the controversy that originated from them, are instructive:

Whet the long knives
On the curbstone!
And then let them slip
Into the Jew's bone!

Blood must flow, a whole lot of it,
And we shit on the freedom of the Jew Republic.
Come the hour of revenge
We are ready for every type of slaughter.

Up the Hohenzollern
High up the lamppost!
Let the dogs swing
Until the heads come loose!

Blood must flow, a whole lot of it,
And we shit on the freedom of the Jew Republic . . .

In the synagogue
Hang up a black pig,
Into the parliaments
Throw a grenade on a stick!

Blood must flow, a whole lot of it,
And we shit on the freedom of the Jew Republic . . .

Pull the concubine
Out of the prince's bed,
And grease the guillotine
With the Jews' fat.

Blood must flow, a whole lot of it,
And we shit on the freedom of the Jew Republic . . .[163]

This was a parody of the original 'Song of the Persecuted' or 'Absalon Song', which had become highly popular as the 'Hecker song' during the 1848 revolution. It had remained popular in the German lands throughout the second half of the nineteenth century and, with the addition of more militarist lyrics, turned into a commercium (academic) song around the turn of the century. The original version praised the indefatigable longing for a German democracy using an intelligent play on the verb 'to hang' that contrasted its meaning of to hang somebody versus that of hanging on to the dream of the German republic. The extremely violent lyrics of the Nazi version, by contrast, took linguistic bits and pieces of the original as well as its anti-royalist elements but gave them a very opposite meaning. By adding elements of the well-known anti-parliamentarian clichés of the extreme right from the 1920s, anti-Catholic insults ('black pig'), and above all threats toward the Jews, the stormtroopers produced one of the most extreme hate songs ever to be heard in German streets.[164]

After SA student groups from Munich and nearby Weihenstephan repeatedly performed this song in the towns of Memmingen, Freising, and their vicinity in May 1934, the general vicar of the Archdiocese of Munich and Freising jointly with the directorate of Ludwig Maximilians University lodged a formal complaint with the Bavarian Ministry of Education and Culture. The vicar not only urged the authorities to stop the singing of this 'coarse, bloodthirsty and filthy song' but also noted that many residents of Memmingen and even members of the town's SA group had been annoyed by it. This complaint indicates that the instructors may have actually forced many of their students to sing the song against their own moral and political convictions.[165] Nor was this incident an isolated case. As early as 1929 a leader of the SA in Wandsbek near Hamburg complained to his superior about 'offensive swine songs' being sung by the stormtroopers in his city. Such songs, intoned by badly dressed and ill-behaved SA men, would not only scare away the wider public, but would also discourage the participation of right-minded Nazi activists, this SA leader claimed, adding that he had forbidden the men under his command to sing them.[166] The Munich SA University Office in 1934 likewise banned the singing of the 'blood song' for the future but justified its earlier singing on the grounds that it was among the most popular at the Reich leadership school and 'was not unsuited to teach the young students in the revolutionary spirit of the old SA guards'. In another letter of 19 June 1934 to the Bavarian Ministry of Education and Culture, the SA justified its formal interdiction on performing this song not with regard to its content, but because 'the inner morale [*innere Haltung*] of the students to be educated does not yet meet the revolutionary spirit of the established SA guards'.[167]

Less than two weeks later, Röhm and many of the high-ranking SA leaders were shot or imprisoned and – as a consequence – the realization of the highly ambitious plans of the SA University Offices became very improbable. Hence, in another letter dealing with the singing of the 'blood song', written at the end of August 1934, the previously self-assured tone of the University Office's correspondence had largely vanished. The SA functionaries in Munich now admitted that the song had been performed in other cities like Bamberg and Speyer as well, but that they had had nothing to do with its performance. Only forty of the 2,200 students registered by the SA-*Hochschulamt* Munich had ever sung the 'blood song', they now claimed, and in any case the whole affair had to be seen as a deliberate attempt by the Catholic Church to discredit National Socialism, in an attack reminiscent of the 'most vicious press polemics of yesterday'.[168]

Despite the shutdown of the SA University Offices, students and lecturers dressed in brown shirts remained a common spectacle in German universities.[169] The National Socialist *Wissenschaftspolitik* (science policy) clearly benefited a younger generation of scholars with ideological ties to the Nazi movement, many of whom were often only too willing to replace those who had been forced to resign.[170] By contrast, established professors soon started to complain about the imposition of politics into the academic world. The Freiburg-based historian Gerhard Ritter lamented in April 1934 that the university authorities would only admit 'SA student types' [*S.A. Naturen*] as freshmen – precisely those individuals who were 'the least interested in science'.[171] Others were more optimistic. Emanuel Hirsch, a well-respected professor of Protestant theology at the University of Göttingen, also acknowledged that the 'SA students' of 1934 were less mature and profound than the previous generation, which had been shaped by their experience of the trenches in the First World War. However, Hirsch enthusiastically praised the new era as a most welcome opportunity to reconcile Protestant theology and nationalist politics. He was willing to bow to the new atmosphere in the German universities: 'Our students are rightly aware that only the band of fighters [*Kämpferschar*] to which they belong protected and still protects us teachers with our intellectual work and our influence from the threat of Bolshevism. As is the case with the German *Volkstum* generally, the German mind today exists and has relevance only within the new collective volition established and guaranteed by the *Führer* and his SA.'[172]

Hirsch was by no means an exception. In many universities the SA initially enjoyed considerable support from German lecturers and students, particularly among the faculties of Protestant theology. In Rostock students of theology joined the SA to a considerably higher degree than did students of law and medicine, and in Greifswald two professors of Protestant theology actively contributed to the formation of a *Kirchliche Kampfschar Pommern*, a student activist group that engaged in the *Kirchenkampf* by resorting to SA methods.[173] In Münster not only many students but also several lecturers and professors of Protestant theology between 1932 and 1934 joined the Brownshirts, if not necessarily the party. In 1946 one of these individuals explained that 'it was in the interest of the *Volksgemeinschaft* that confident and active Christians were in the SA', a statement that echoed the hopes that many younger Protestant theologians from the early 1930s had placed in a genuine renewal of Christian faith through a close alliance with the Nazi movement, which would serve as a starting signal for a new 'popular mission' (*Volksmission*).[174]

A few years later such hopes had proven a chimaera. But even in early 1937, when the influence of the stormtroopers had considerably decreased and many faculties in Münster were using the opportunity to withdraw their students from the SA, the faculty of Protestant theology did not.[175] For ideologically committed theology students the formal ban issued by the regime only a few months later, which declared the study of theology incompatible with membership in the SA and the Hitler Youth, came as a bitter shock, particularly as it did not distinguish between the different factions within the Protestant churches, that is, between the Nazi-friendly German Christians and the more sceptical adherents of the Confessing Church.[176] As clergymen and theology students were explicitly banned from joining the party in September 1937, when the NSDAP again began to accept new members, this combination of regulations constituted a total barrier.[177]

By 1938 the importance of the SA at German universities was a far cry from what it had been only a few years earlier, partly because those young men with military ambitions could now enter the Wehrmacht directly. Students at German universities who were still members of the SA had to arrange to carry out their SA duties.[178] At the University of Cologne, for example, the majority of students registered with the stormtroopers no longer joined the SA group at the university but preferred to stay within their original units – and often did not show up for duty in either place. As the surviving correspondence in the University of Cologne's archive makes clear, the SA representatives at the university reacted to this decline in registration with a twofold strategy: first, they regularly granted leaves of absence to those students who were preparing their final exams; and second, they compelled first- and second-year students to attend SA meetings.[179] These meetings, however, took place only rarely and in no way demanded the extensive physical presence required of the students in 1933 and 1934.[180] Politically and career-driven students were now advised to enter the ranks of the SS, on the grounds that the SA provided little more than an official stamp of one's political loyalty to the regime.

Sacking the State

The years 1933 and 1934 not only fundamentally changed the SA's relationship to the state and its police forces, but also considerably improved its financial situation. Prior to 1933 money was usually short, to the extent that political activism for the rank-and-file stormtrooper often went hand in hand with painful financial sacrifices. The Nazis' successful takeover of the state granted the SA access to Germany's financial resources and in addition allowed members to benefit from illegal extortion schemes that at times developed into proper protection rackets. Beginning on 21 June 1933, for example, an 'SA Self-Help Working Group' (*Selbsthilfe-Arbeitsgemeinschaft der SA*) in Berlin-Brandenburg sold signposts stamped with the words 'German Business' to 'Aryan' enterprises for an annual subscription fee.[181] In Wuppertal racketeers from the SA even handed out receipts for the 'protection money' they received, which amounted to substantial sums for those small-scale grocers who were most affected.[182]

Yet the sums generated by such practices were 'peanuts' in comparison to the money the Brownshirts now received from the German Reich. Starting on 19 May 1933 the High SA Command received regular payments from the Ministry of the Interior, at times as often as twice per month. While the first instalment of 100,000 reichsmark was comparatively moderate, the payments quickly multiplied and reached up to 8 million reichsmark in January and again in March 1934. All in all the German taxpayer supported the Brownshirts with slightly less than 45 million reichsmark between May 1933 and April 1934, of which more than 42 million reichsmark were immediately spent. The Ministry transferred all of these payments to the Ingolstadt branch of the *Bayerische Hypotheken- and Wechselbank* in which the OSAF had no fewer than seven different bank accounts. Only two of these accounts were used for deposits from the Reich, one for the above-mentioned payments from the Ministry of the Interior and one for payments from the Ministry of Finance, which provided the OSAF with another 28 million reichsmark.[183] The total state budget for the SA of more than 72 million reichsmark for the financial year 1933–4 neither included payments from membership dues or voluntary contributions by the relatively small group of well-to-do stormtroopers nor from big business.[184]

The SA used this money to modernize its equipment, to support the SA training camps (*Hilfswerklager*) that were now established all over Germany, and to fund the regular budget of its groups and sub-groups. Personnel expenses of more than 33 million reichsmark represented the lion's share of expenditures. The training camps ranked second in spending, using up slightly less than 5 million reichsmark, followed by one-time investments such as the acquisition of uniforms, boots, and underpants for 150,000 'stormtroopers in need'. The Reich Court of Auditors in a detailed report from 8 June 1934 stated that the SA had expressed the intent to use the money in an 'economical' fashion, but that a detailed tracing of most expenses was not possible. A transparent picture could only be provided if the finances of the SA groups in the different provinces could be scrutinized in detail.[185]

The NSDAP in the summer of 1934 had no interest in state control of its financial conduct, particularly as regional investigations of its activities by the Court of Auditors had revealed illegal practices. The SA-*Gruppe* Berlin-Brandenburg, for example, in 1933 had labelled all regular salaries as 'expense allowances', with the result that neither the SA as an organization nor the individual stormtroopers had paid income tax or social security contributions for the whole year. The group had also paid salary advances to some of its members without asking for a payback. Finally, the SA in the capital had spent more than 10,000 reichsmark for 'political purposes' in April 1933 alone. What precisely was financed by this sum is unclear.[186] The Reich's support of the SA-*Gruppe* Österreich, an organization that the Austrian government had made illegal with its ban on the NSDAP on 19 June 1933, amounted to a subsidy of 1,326,000 reichsmark for the group's personal expenses and nearly 3 million reichsmark for its winter clothes in 1933–4.[187]

The 'Night of the Long Knives' served as a welcome opportunity for the NSDAP to once and for all solve its problem with the Reich Court of Auditors. In a letter from 23 July 1934, NSDAP Reich Treasurer Franz Xaver Schwarz, who had recently been appointed SS-*Obergruppenführer*, informed the president of the Court of Auditors that all financial affairs of the SA would from then on be the sole responsibility of the NSDAP. As Hitler's plenipotentiary, Schwarz would personally oversee all further payments from the Reich to the SA.[188] Two weeks later Schwarz informed the Reich Ministry of Finance that all state funding for the SA was with immediate effect to be transferred to the party's OSAF bank account at the Bayerische Staatsbank in Munich. More important, all further financial oversight was to be handled not by the Reich Court of Auditors, but by the NSDAP itself.[189] This new system effectively blocked state attempts to control and oversee the SA's budget in the years to come. Further letters from the Reich Court of Auditors to the Nazi Party, with the last written on 21 June 1935, went unanswered. The NSDAP meanwhile declared itself a 'public body' and became an integral part of the state, with unlimited access to the Reich Treasury.

Because of the lack of independent financial reviews of the SA after 1934, attempts to provide exact figures for its total budget in the following years have proven futile. Most of the money used by the stormtroopers continued to come from the state via the NSDAP, which, with its oversight of financial matters established, came to effectively control the formerly semi-autonomous SA. Within this framework the SA Chief of Staff continued to enjoy a relative autonomy that he seems to have exploited in a manner similar to that seen in the pre-purge SA. On 4 November 1938, for example, SA Chief of Staff Lutze ordered that all leaders of the SA-*Gruppen* and at the OSAF be granted an expense allowance of 200 reichsmark per month in addition to their regular income as full-time SA leaders as long as they did have another source to generate an extra income.[190] Lutze himself, like many other Nazi luminaries, became a very rich man during the nine years he served as SA Chief of Staff.[191] According to information that he provided to the Berlin-Mitte tax office in 1932, he possessed no assets in 1931 and only earned a modest 12,194 reichsmark in 1932.[192] After his death on 2 May 1943, however, his testamentary executor discovered that Lutze had accumulated a fortune of more than 200,000 reichsmark, in addition to a considerable amount of outstanding money from a Hanover-based company, two country residences, and a stud farm.[193] The overall value of his estate amounted to 396,000 reichsmark. Lutze's sources of income had been diverse: next to his monthly salary as SA Chief of Staff and several expense allowances related to his official functions, Lutze had also benefited from the provision by his hometown of Bevergern of a vacant tract of ten acres, on which he built a splendid manor house, the Saltenhof, in 1936–7. He also received at least one donation from Hitler, who, on Lutze's fiftieth birthday on 28 December 1940, personally wrote him a cheque for 100,000 reichsmark.[194] Despite his considerable assets, Lutze paid no taxes at all between 1939 and 1943, passing off Hitler's endowment as a debt that the Reich Chancellor could reclaim at any moment. However, as Hitler did not wish formal inquiries for tax evasion to be opened, Lutze's wife and sons held most of the money and assets until after the Second World War. A post-war British-inflicted 'blockade of finances' (*Vermögenssperre*) was finally lifted in 1956. After the death in August 1957 of Lutze's last remaining son, Adolf, who at the age of twenty-one died, like his father, in an accident with his Porsche sports car, the community of heirs sold the Saltenhof for 280,000 deutschmark in 1958. Even divided by the twelve parties to benefit, these proceeds were still a considerable amount of money in the early years of the Federal Republic of Germany.[195] The promises of SA propaganda on social equality within a national community never materialized, but at least for some of the group's propagandists and their families it had paid very real dividends.

Consolidation and Discontent

Over the course of 1933 dissatisfaction among the stormtroopers grew prarallel to the stabilization of Hitler's leadership and the consolidation of the NSDAP as the only remaining legal political party. Although Röhm in a speech in Frankfurt an der Oder on 18 June 1933 continued to praise his SA as the 'trailblazers of the new Reich' and requested that his men 'be active in the same spirit as before', Hitler, his Minister of the Interior Wilhelm Frick, and other leading National Socialists around the same time announced the end of the National Socialist 'revolution'.[196] The excessive violence of the previous months committed to a very considerable extent by the SA could no longer be 'justified' on the basis of an imminent danger posed by determined and powerful political opponents. Consequently, the position of the SA weakened, despite the fact that it continued to grow by incorporating previous rivals into its ranks and improved its financial situation to the degree that it could preserve at least a relative independence from the NSDAP. Many SA men felt increasingly left out of or even betrayed by the party, as the eagerly awaited elevation of their social status, including material 'compensation' for their political activism, only materialized for a minority of them – largely, the more high-ranking SA leaders. Among the rank and file calls for a 'second revolution', or at least for the next step in establishing the *Volksgemeinschaft*, thus became popular. These stormtroopers expected that the proponents of this new 'revolution' would not compromise with the establishment but would fulfil the promises of a fundamentally new social order in which the SA would sit at the top of the hierarchy. Such inner-party opposition was dangerous for Hitler, particularly as it was a grassroots phenomenon, fuelled by the dissatisfaction of those who were only too keen to (re)gain a middle-class respectability and stability through a permanent 'civil' job. Because of this sharp contrast between rhetorical radicalism and longings for social stability, some historians have lampooned SA men as 'desperadoes in search of a pension' (*Desperados mit Pensionserwartungen*).[197] Such intellectually well-placed criticism nevertheless neglected the very real pressure that most SA men felt at a time of persistent hardship, frozen wages, and record unemployment, and that rather obscured some of the motives behind the ever-growing alienation of the party establishment from its paramilitary rank and file.

THE 'RÖHM PURGE' AND THE MYTH OF THE HOMOSEXUAL NAZI

It is possible and seems likely that the masses of the petite bourgeoisie fall again into a morality tailored for them on the basis of a dirty psychology; and that they see Hitler as the saviour once more.
— Thomas Mann, journal entry, 4 July 1934[1]

Although the first wave of Nazi violence against real and imagined opponents of the dictatorship lessened toward the end of 1933, the early months of 1934 saw increasing tensions in Germany. This growing conflict was largely internal and pitted those who insisted on completing the 'revolution' by pushing for a fundamental transformation of German society in line with National Socialist ideology against those who favoured compromise with traditional elitist groups in order to further consolidate the NSDAP's newly acquired position of power. These two positions, commonly associated with Röhm on the one side and Hitler, Göring, and Himmler on the other, were not only about ideological differences but also fundamental discrepancies in life experience and social status. This chapter will first trace the lines of this important conflict and re-examine the political ambitions of the SA in the first half of 1934. It will then analyse the events that unfolded between 30 June and 2 July in some detail and discuss their immediate political consequences. Finally, it will put the 'Night of the Long Knives' into the wider context of the legal and political development of the Third Reich, touching as well on the origin of the cliché of the homosexual stormtrooper.[2]

Showdown

Despite the Nazi takeover of power and regardless of the stormtroopers' elevated social status and improved chances on the job market, as outlined in the previous chapter, dissatisfaction among them had grown steadily since the summer of 1933. A considerable number of the better educated but relatively new members of the Nazi Party had already been able to embark on new careers thanks to their new political affiliation. In common parlance, these individuals were the so-called *Märzgefallene*, the 'March windfalls' or 'March victims', an allusion to the more than 200 revolutionaries who had died in Berlin and Vienna in March 1848. By contrast, many of the long-time activists still suffered economic hardship, persistent unemployment, and generally poor career prospects. These men were quick to blame the usual suspects, Jews and the 'fat cats' of industry and politics, but increasingly they also questioned the party leadership's ambition and ability to fulfil the far-reaching promises made in previous years.

Furthermore, the thousands of Communists and Social Democrats who now dressed in the brown shirt contributed to the growing dissatisfaction that in particular troubled the long-time rank-and-file stormtroopers. The extent to which these former competitors infiltrated the SA has been a matter of debate since the early 1930s.[3] Even prior to the Nazi takeover of power, the KPD claimed that it had successfully penetrated the SA. By its own account, by late 1932, it had no fewer than 164 'confidants' in Berlin, and in Saxony had established eighteen in Zwickau, and forty-two in Chemnitz.[4] In the following two years it is clear that many more Communists and Social Democrats joined the SA, at times voluntarily, at times by summary integration. The notoriously unreliable Rudolf Diels, the first chief of the *Geheimes Staatspolizeiamt*, or Gestapa, later claimed that about 70 per cent of all new members of the SA in the capital in 1933 had been former Communists.[5] Such figures are certainly excessive. It should also be noted that some of these 'beefsteaks' (so named because they were brown on the outside, but red within) only joined the Nazi paramilitaries for tactical reasons and not out of enthusiasm or political 'awakening'. At a time when SA terror was almost unrestricted, many reasonably believed it advisable to join the ranks of the stormtroopers, particularly if one had a background in a rival organization. Those Social Democrats and Communists who in the spring and summer of 1933 joined the *Stahlhelm*, the only remaining legal non-Nazi paramilitary group, for tactical reasons quickly found themselves integrated into the expanding SA. The degree of loyalty that existed within the ranks was therefore extremely unclear, all the more if one recalls that paramilitary affiliations prior to 1933 were in many cases not stable, with the parties involved regularly struggling to determine whether conversions were 'genuine' or 'formal'. Yet contemporary observers and later historians agree that the number of individuals who joined the SA for tactical reasons was significant, and that they were partly responsible for the intensified anti-capitalist and anti-reactionary currents among the stormtroopers in the early stages of the Third Reich.[6]

In December 1933, Hitler appointed Röhm and Hess as Reich ministers without portfolio. The ambitious Röhm took this as an endorsement of his far-reaching goal to secure a lasting and important role for the SA in the Third Reich in general and in military matters in particular. To achieve this, the SA was to be elevated to the most important armour-bearer in the Reich, ideally absorbing the comparatively small Reichswehr and its 'reactionary' generals. The 'grey rock' of the Reichswehr had to sink in the 'brown flood', Röhm allegedly once said.[7] It is, however, highly doubtful that Röhm intended to push through such plans at any cost. For his biographer Eleanor Hancock, it is more likely that he would have backed down if he had been unable to win Hitler's favour for his plan, as he had done in 1925.[8]

At the beginning of 1934 the SA numbered more than three million men, whereas the Reichswehr remained officially limited to 100,000 professional soldiers. In the following months the rivalry between the SA and the Reichswehr escalated into a veritable beauty contest for the favour of the Führer. Initially, Hitler refrained from taking sides. Even if he was early on more inclined to favour the Reichswehr for military reasons, he sought to benefit from the SA's pressure on the regular army, which he believed would make its leaders more willing to accept the political prerogatives of the regime. However, in a keynote speech delivered to military leaders on 28 February 1934, Hitler for the first time publicly rejected Röhm's plans to turn the SA into a people's militia and instead confirmed that the Reichswehr would remain the regular armed force of the German Reich. For practical reasons he urged close collaboration between the Reichswehr and the SA in the areas of border protection and pre-military training of German youth for the time being, but he left no doubt that in the longer run the SA was to abstain from acting as a military force.[9] In doing so, Hitler renewed his commitment to a position that he had taken ever since the reorganization of the SA in 1925–6. Yet Röhm also remained loyal to his ideas from the mid-1920s. In this way the earlier conflict between Röhm's *Frontbann* politics and Hitler's idea of a party-controlled SA now clashed for a second time. In 1934, however, this conflict was no longer confined to the fringes of an obscure splinter party and its paramilitary wing, but took centre stage in national politics. Consequently, more actors were involved, and all of them were playing for high stakes.[10]

Röhm had been a controversial figure in the NSDAP ever since he had returned from Bolivia in late 1930, and his position had not been helped by the ex-Nazi Helmuth Klotz's publication in March 1932 of Röhm's private letters to the physician Karl-Guenter Heimsoth, a psychologist who shared the SA supreme leader's military passion and had himself a strong interest in male homosexuality.[11] Highly intimate in nature, these letters left no doubt about Röhm's homosexuality. Not least for this reason, Röhm developed more and more enemies within the NSDAP and even became the target of a murderous conspiracy that failed.[12] In the spring of 1934 he faced not only hostility from several Nazi leaders, including Göring and Himmler, but also pressure from Werner von Blomberg and his loyal assistant Walter von Reichenau. Dubbed a 'rubber lion' by the military staff for his well-known allegiance to Hitler, Blomberg in the months prior to 30 June 1934 deliberately played up the risks posed by the SA and presented the Reichswehr as the only reliable defence the regime had. Some historians, most notably John Wheeler-Bennett, have claimed that Blomberg successfully compelled Hitler to initiate a violent crackdown on the SA. The available evidence does not validate such accusations.[13] Yet there is no denying that Blomberg and his confidants intended to defeat the rival SA and were willing to pay a high price for that success.[14]

In the spring of 1934 another group in German politics attempted to strike at the SA and in this way target the Nazi regime more generally. This was the opposition from within the government. The core of this group consisted of men who worked for Vice-Chancellor Franz von Papen. Led by the Bavarian lawyer and political writer Edgar J. Jung and von Papen's chief press officer Herbert von Bose, these individuals belonged to the so-called *Jungkonservativen*, or 'neoconservatives', who had initially advocated for an authoritarian state to overcome the problems of the Weimar

Republic but were quickly repelled by the Nazi regime's contempt for human rights and civil liberties. They were disgusted by the SA's radical rhetoric, seeing a Nazi 'social' revolution as the ultimate victory of the 'rule of the inferior', and thereby of terror, brutality, and lawlessness.[15] Unlike von Papen, who constantly talked about higher values and morale but in the end would accept even the political murder of his closest collaborators, the members of this circle demonstrated genuine courage and determination. They prepared to overthrow the Nazi regime and ideally replace it with a new government of the conservative right supported by Reich President Paul von Hindenburg and the Reichswehr.[16]

As a starting signal of their campaign the members of this group carefully drafted a damning speech for von Papen to deliver in Marburg in Middle Hesse on 17 June 1934, with the hope that such harsh criticism of the Nazi regime would spark a political sea change. This criticism was both substantial and cutting, and represented a frontal attack on the character of the NSDAP's rule as well as its ideology: 'No nation can afford a constant revolt from below if it wants to pass the test of history,' von Papen lectured. 'The movement must come to a standstill some day; at some time a stable social structure must emerge, maintained by an impartial judiciary and by an undisputed state authority.' Not surprisingly, the speech did not dismiss the 'national revolution' of 1933 and its 'achievements' of the last one and a half years, but it clearly deplored the 'excesses' that had occurred. The conspirators' conclusion was nothing less than a verbal declaration of war: 'The time of emancipation of the lowest social orders against the higher orders is past.'[17] When von Papen spoke these words, much to the delight of the majority of his audience, two local SA leaders in uniform are reported to have left the hall.[18]

The location of the speech, the old auditorium of one of Germany's most respected universities, was well chosen for an attack on the arrivistes of the Third Reich. The decorous academic atmosphere contrasted sharply with the bloody realities of the streets. However, it also demonstrated the isolation of the conspirators. While the Nazi Party could easily bring together thousands of followers in market squares and sport stadiums, the former had chosen a respectable but in many respects limited location for their damning words. These limitations were aggravated by the fact that Goebbels's Ministry of Propaganda just hours after the speech prohibited the newspapers from reporting on it and also prevented it from being broadcast on the radio. Nevertheless, the speech became widely known in Germany and abroad, as the conspirators, in anticipation of Nazi censorship, had distributed hundreds of copies of it to friends and foreign journalists, who in turn made it into an international media event. Yet the intended political wake-up call turned out to be a failure, as the Reichswehr as well as the aged Reich President Hindenburg did nothing. The speech did not cause a change of government; instead, it accelerated the arrival of the long-built-up clash within the Nazi camp.

On 19 June 1934, just two days after von Papen's Marburg speech, the governors of the German provinces met at the Ministry of the Interior in Berlin. In his opening speech at this confidential meeting Wilhelm Frick, the Reich Minister of the Interior, not only announced a further centralization of powers, but also lamented the increasing internal frictions that were undermining the authority of the state. In addition, he reported, in what was perhaps a direct reference to the von Papen speech, acts of sabotage had increased over the last few days. The euphoria of the spring of 1933 could not be expected to last very long, Frick said, claiming that it was all the more necessary to take a tough stance against 'defeatists' of all kinds. Following this speech, several governors offered reports of widespread criticism of the Nazi Party and its representatives in their respective regions. They pointed out that many 'character deficiencies' among local and regional Nazi leaders had become a serious problem for the public image of the party. The German population could not understand the comparatively high salaries of higher functionaries of the Nazi Party and its organizations, the *Oberpräsident* Ferdinand von Lüninck from Koblenz claimed, particularly as several of these leaders now boasted openly of their new titles and wealth. His colleague from Düsseldorf, Carl Christian Schmidt, referred directly to the SA as one of the sources of local discontent in his province and asked for more support from the SA field police to deal with marauding stormtroopers, who were otherwise nearly exempt from prosecution.[19]

The immediate results of this meeting are not known. Yet the topics addressed, as well as the relatively frank debate that occurred, indicate that the von Papen speech had encouraged conservative critics of the NSDAP and its policies to come out into the open. In line with this shift, the U.S. ambassador to Germany, William E. Dodd, reported on 20 June 1934 about the tensions existing within the German government. There were rumours, he said, 'that the Reichswehr, which has already increased its force with new recruits, will, in conjunction with the SS troops, of which the SA are jealous and which are supposed to be composed of conservative elements and also perhaps with the Prussian police, compel the Chancellor to dismiss his radical advisers and also the SA troops, and to govern conservatively. Some seem confident that this consummation will be reached fairly soon.' However, the ambassador continued, a 'revolution to the right' was unlikely to happen, as Hitler, not least because of his 'unwillingness to sever connections with his old followers', would not 'lend himself to any such movement'.[20]

Dodd's report testifies to the extent to which observers expected a violent clash between the 'revolutionary' SA and the comparatively 'conservative' forces of the Reichswehr and the increasingly powerful SS in the early summer of 1934. Although the ambassador clearly overemphasized Hitler's loyalty to Röhm and other 'Old Fighters', he was right about the timing of this confrontation, in that it took only several days for these political tensions to erupt into a veritable political coup within the Nazi Party. Ever since the deadly events of early July 1934, political observers have speculated on the background of the killings and those who orchestrated them.[21] Many who were directly involved in politics during this time reported that Hitler was not the central figure in the events, as he seemed quite reluctant to press for tough decisions until late in June 1934. However, as we will see later in this chapter, it was Hitler who made the final decision to strike and, once he had made up his mind, pushed it through without mercy or remorse.

It is meanwhile well established that the driving individuals in the fatal attack on Röhm and the OSAF in the months prior to 30 June 1934 were Göring; Himmler; Himmler's adjutant Reinhard Heydrich, the head of the SD or *Sicherheitsdienst*, the SS intelligence agency; and the Reichswehr generals Werner von Blomberg, in 1934 the Minister of Defence, and Walter von Reichenau, at this time head of the *Wehramt* under Blomberg's control. In the view of the historian Kurt Gossweiler and the materialist historiography advocated within the German Democratic Republic, 'big business' was another, if not the most important, factor in the liquidation of Röhm's SA, as the latter allegedly aimed at the 'abolition of the preeminent position of the heavy industries' and big farmers (*Großagrarier*).[22] Goebbels switched sides in this clash just in time to remain in office, yet most commentators of the time noticed that his position after the purge seemed considerably weakened. By contrast, post-war statements that asserted the existence of an elaborate 'SA plot' to overthrow the government in order to violently fulfil the Nazi 'revolution' and kill lists 'issued by the OSAF' should be treated with extreme care.[23] Dissenting voices and the dissatisfaction of many SA leaders should not be confused with a sustainable political strategy. A proper plan for violent action against Hitler, the increasingly powerful SS, and the Reichswehr simply did not exist.[24]

'Reich Murder Week'

There is no lack of colourful accounts of the course of action that unfolded between 30 June and 2 July 1934.[25] Instead of providing yet another detailed narrative, the aim of the following section is to single out those aspects that shed light on the ways the SA reacted during and immediately after this deadly blow. The best documents for investigating this aspect of the events are the detailed notes of Viktor Lutze, appointed by Hitler as Röhm's successor on 1 July 1934 (Plate 17). A few weeks after his appointment, Lutze began to regularly record his political thoughts in writing, a habit he continued until his death in a car accident on 2 May 1943. His 312-page-long 'political diary' remains unpublished to this day, with the exception of his notes on the 'Röhm purge', which were printed in a series of three articles that appeared in the liberal *Frankfurter Rundschau* between 14 and 16 May 1957. Similar to the diaries of Joseph Goebbels, Lutze's notes were written both for himself and for posterity. After the 'Röhm purge' the new SA Chief of Staff felt a particular need to defend himself against the accusation that he had betrayed his comrades in the SA, as he was one of the very few SA leaders who personally benefited from the murderous events. This desire for justification was an important reason for starting his diary in the first place. In later years, particularly between 1941 and 1943, the activity of writing in his notebook also took on a therapeutic character, as Lutze found it increasingly difficult to find a political audience, let alone influence the course of politics, which left him frustrated and ultimately depressed.[26]

Despite Lutze's long and successful career within the Nazi movement, including his service as governor of the Prussian province of Hanover between 1933 and 1941, he has never attracted strong interest among historians on Nazi Germany.[27] In most cases Lutze is presented as a submissive man without character,[28] a 'pale vassal of Hitler',[29] one of his 'featureless creatures' (*nichtssagende Kreatur*).[30] Such harsh characterizations partly reflect the stereotypes of the post-1934 SA, but they also point to the perception that he was unimportant, at least compared to his predecessor. However, it was Lutze who oversaw the complicated mutations of the SA, which remained one of the largest National Socialist mass organizations, for the next nine years, until May 1943.

Lutze was born on 28 December 1890 in Bevergern in Tecklenburg. A professional soldier during the First World War and, starting in 1922, an early member of the NSDAP and the SA, he became the leader of the SA 'Gausturm Ruhr' in 1926 and two years later was promoted to SA-Oberführer Ruhr. After the September 1930 elections he represented the NSDAP in the Reichstag. Despite his important role in the Nazi movement prior to 1 July 1934, his appointment as head of the SA came as a surprise. It is indicative of his low public profile that his name was not mentioned even once in the nationally distributed illustrated weekly Der SA-Mann between January 1932 and June 1934.[31] From the perspective of Röhm's adversaries, the promotion of Lutze to SA Chief of Staff was intended to permanently diminish the influence of the Brownshirts. As Lutze could not (yet) rely on a stable power base within the SA, he was entirely dependent on Hitler's goodwill. As his diary notes make plain, he uncritically venerated the Führer and exempted him from all criticism. Even more than other SA generals, Lutze was willing to execute his master's will and careful not to overstep his own authority.

In his diary Lutze noted that he had first learned of the plans to remove Röhm from the leadership of the SA on 22 June 1934 from Hitler himself. On that day the chancellor had requested that Lutze come to Berlin and in a face-to-face conversation presented him with the alleged 'Putsch' plans supposedly contrived by Röhm.[32] When Lutze replied that he had never heard of such ideas, Hitler referred to evidence provided by the Gestapo and commanded Lutze to no longer accept orders from the OSAF in Munich.[33] If we believe Lutze's version to be 'true' – in the sense that he himself believed what he wrote – then he was not offered Röhm's position prior to 1 July. Yet, from 22 June 1934 onward, he was aware that an upper leadership change within the SA was imminent. We can also reasonably assume that Lutze expected to be on the winning side of this conflict.[34]

Lutze pretended not to have been involved in this matter until 28 June 1934, when he attended the wedding of Gauleiter Josef Terboven in Essen, at which both Hitler and Göring were groomsmen. As the dinner was being served, Hitler quickly left the wedding table to receive several phone calls from the Gestapo and the Minister of State in the Prussian State Ministry, Paul Körner, Göring's right-hand man. 'I got the impression that certain people had an interest in exacerbating the situation precisely at a moment when the Führer was not in Berlin and could not be informed in writing, but saw and heard everything only on the phone,' Lutze commented later. He maintained the view that Röhm had never planned a putsch against Hitler on 30 June 1934. If anything, Lutze credited Röhm with formulating plans to limit or abolish the 'reactionary and un-socialist military [sic!]'.[35]

Hitler left Terboven's wedding party early and spent the rest of the night in the nearby Hotel Kaiserhof with Göring and Lutze. During the evening hours Körner arrived from Berlin with news that – according to Lutze's report – provoked Hitler to exclaim: 'I am fed up, I will make an example!' Hitler then called Röhm and summoned a meeting with him and the other SA leaders in the Hanselbauer Pension located in the spa town of Bad Wiessee in Upper Bavaria, a short drive south from Munich. This meeting was to take place at 10 a.m. on 30 June, the first day of the SA's national holiday month. At about 1 a.m. on 29 June, Göring left Essen for Berlin, charged with carrying out the events planned for the capital.[36] Berlin was to become the second centre of the murderers' action, after Bavaria.

Hitler and Lutze spent Thursday, 29 June, in Bad Godesberg near Bonn. Goebbels arrived later that day. Lutze described the atmosphere as relaxed until shortly after midnight, when Hitler received another call from Berlin and ordered that he, Goebbels, and Lutze be driven to the nearby Hangelar Airport. Their plane departed at about 1.45 a.m. Lutze remembered a 'magnificent, clear sky' and the shining lights of Frankfurt. The men on board did not speak much. Lutze claimed to have approached Hitler and to have asked him to 'alter the way of the impending arrests', but supposedly did not receive an answer. Their plane finally landed at the Oberwiesenfeld Airfield at sunrise. SS men immediately surrounded Hitler and passed on the latest news to him, which led to a new outburst of rage and excitement. Hitler then had the two local SA leaders, the SA-*Obergruppenführer* August Schneidhuber and the SA-*Gruppenführer* Wilhelm Schmid, woken up and summoned to the airfield. When they arrived he called them 'traitors' and snatched off their epaulets, declaring: 'You are arrested and will be shot!' SS units then swarmed into town with blacklists containing the names of those to be taken into custody. Next, Hitler, Goebbels, and Lutze, accompanied by

Hitler's adjutants Julius Schaub and Wilhelm Brückner and several SS men and police, drove southbound.[37] In Bad Wiessee they had Röhm and several other SA leaders present arrested and brought to Munich's Stadelheim Prison. There, they were shot either in the early evening hours of the same day or, in the case of Röhm, the following day.[38]

At about 11.30 a.m. on 30 June, still prior to the first executions in Munich, a meeting of leading National Socialists including Hitler, Goebbels, Hess, and other party luminaries took place in the city's 'Brown House'. Several SA-*Obergruppenführer* were present as well, among them Lutze, his later successor Max Jüttner, and SA-*Gruppenführer* Karl Schreyer. The latter in 1949 remembered that Hitler dashed into the hall 'like a madman, with foam at the mouth'. He accused Röhm of high treason and called the alleged putsch the greatest betrayal the world had ever seen.[39] Hitler then appointed Lutze as Röhm's successor. 'For a moment, I would have preferred to refuse,' Lutze noted, before explaining at length how over the following days he had consolidated and attempted to help his fellow SA leaders but had not been able to prevent the pre-planned executions from taking place.[40] The situation was so tense that even the new SA Chief of Staff did not dare go to the OSAF headquarters but instead took a room in Munich's *Vier Jahreszeiten*, a luxury hotel, where he claimed to have installed a kind of provisional bureau.[41]

In Berlin, Göring, Himmler, and Heydrich acted with similar ruthlessness. They were well prepared for their task, having previously asked the Gestapo and the SD to compile lists of the names of those to be arrested.[42] At about 10 a.m. on 30 June 1934, Goebbels called Göring in Berlin. When the prearranged code word 'Kolibri' was exchanged, Göring knew what to do. In close cooperation with Himmler and Heydrich, he ordered the arrests and executions of several high-ranking SA leaders, as well as the former chancellor Kurt von Schleicher and other influential Nazi critics and internal rivals. Members of the SS-*Leibstandarte* Adolf Hitler carried out at least sixteen summary executions in Berlin-Lichterfelde between 30 June and 2 July. Nine other people were shot in their homes or offices, in the cellars of the Gestapo headquarters, or 'taken for a ride'.[43]

To publicly justify the executions and arrests, the regime claimed that Röhm and his conspirators in the SA had planned a violent overthrow, and that Hitler had therefore carried out a pre-emptive strike. Because of the imminent danger a less violent option had not been available. In the late afternoon hours of 30 June, Göring in a public speech called the operation 'a process of purification' and promised that its ultimate goal would be a 'cleaner, more consolidated state'.[44] A detailed decree from Hitler to Lutze, published on the same day, adopted the same rhetoric. Containing twelve points, it ordered the SA leaders 'to help maintain and to strengthen the SA as a clean and tidy organization'. Hitler asked all stormtroopers for nothing less than 'blind submission' and 'absolute discipline' – in other words, unrestricted obedience. The days of splendid parties with alcohol flowing were over, once and for all, Hitler decreed. Most humiliating for the SA was a paragraph that characterized the organization as shot through with morally depraved homosexuals. From now on, Hitler declared, 'SA men should be leaders, not abominable apes!'[45] Whereas Hitler's tone was crude, Werner von Blomberg's order to the army of 1 July 1932 was a plainly cynical move. He not only assured the Nazi authorities of the army's gratitude for the party's 'self-sacrifice and loyalty', but also pretended to be on friendly terms with the now 'purified' SA: 'The good relationship towards the new SA, demanded by the Führer, will be fostered with plea-sure by the Army, conscious of their common ideals.'[46] Two days later, on 3 July, the murderers granted themselves absolution with the 'Law on State Self-Defence Measures', which exempted all crimes committed by the regime between 30 June and 2 July from criminal prosecution.[47]

Despite the high level of uncertainty and violence of these days, the German public reacted to the news calmly and with composure. Nowhere did the SA try to fight back once the news of the arrests and Röhm's removal were confirmed. The disarming of individual men and complete SA units proceeded without impediment, even if Lutze in his diary complained bitterly about the arrogant and humiliating methods employed by the SS.[48] The U.S. military attaché, Jacob Wuest, reported from Berlin on 2 July 1934: 'The trouble was over within a few hours and by Saturday evening all was again quiet, the people of the streets hardly realizing that anything had happened. The lack of excitement on the streets both during the raids and subsequent thereto was remarkable.' He also observed that as the raids unfolded, 'practically all brown uniforms disappeared from the streets', although he admitted that this was probably not simply an imme-diate reaction to the violence, but also a consequence of the beginning of the stormtroopers' long-planned July vacation.[49] The Bavarian authorities likewise reported that all Bavarian cities had remained calm, with the exception of Munich, where some people had been arrested during the night of 1–2 July because they had been spreading 'inappropriate' rumours about the recent events.[50]

Such rumours continued to circulate in the following weeks, particularly as hundreds of people had disappeared and their relatives and friends remained without the slightest idea of their whereabouts. At times the news of someone's execution reached the victim's family only weeks or months later, as in the case of Kurt Mosert, the leader of the SA-*Standarte* in Torgau. His parents learned only in October 1934 that their son had been shot while 'trying to escape' from KZ Lichtenburg three months earlier.[51] In the meantime some of those who had been directly involved in the killings bragged about their participation. According to post-war testimonies, Max Müller, a groundsman at the Munich Sports Club, and his son of the same name were two such figures. In the summer of 1934 both men were members of the SS and were said to have publicly shown acquaintances the badges of those SA leaders who had been executed.[52]

Behind the scenes, the regime tried to strike compromises with the relatives of the victims, particularly when they had been influential or prominent. On 5 July, four days after the murder of Röhm, the Bavarian Minister President Ludwig Siebert claimed that Hitler had given orders that Röhm's mother Sofia Emilie should inherit her son's private estate, and that her apartment should from now on be spared further raids. According to Siebert, the seventy-six-year-old woman had unsuccessfully attempted to kill herself after she learned of her son's execution.[53] Several families of those who had been murdered between 30 June and 2 July 1934 were later offered compensatory monthly payments. According to Viktor Lutze, at least one of the widows turned her back on the proposal in disgust, claiming that a state that pretended to operate on an 'idealist' (*ideell*) basis but resorted to financial compensation exemplified the 'rule of mammon'. 'Where has the decent National Socialist gone?' she asked.[54] The regime prohibited the publication of obituary notices and never cleared the names of those it had executed.

The overall number of victims between 30 June and 2 July was close to 100. Rainer Orth, as much a knowledgeable historian as a scrupulous detective, has so far identified ninety of the murdered people by name.[55] Even if regional studies suggest that some additional killings were so successfully hidden from later scrutiny that the belated identification of these victims is impossible, the number of these 'unsolved' cases can prob-ably be counted on the fingers of one hand.[56] The latest figure of 100 is surprisingly close to that reported in official statistics from the summer of 1934. An early alphabetical 'dead list', provided by the police and approved by Hitler, contained the names of eighty-three people, as well as the places and dates of their executions. As this list makes clear, the cities of Munich, Berlin, and Breslau were the centres of the executions, with twenty-four, twenty-two, and nine victims respectively. Murders also took place in Dresden, Stettin, and near the Lichtenburg concentration camp, as well as in the cities of Stuttgart, Plauen, Glogau, Tilsit, Landshut, and a few other places.[57]

Apart from Berlin and Munich, the geographical distribution of the murders reveals a regional focus on Lower Silesia and Saxony, areas in which the SA had been particularly 'unruly' in the previous years.[58] Yet the SA leaders executed – among them the Berlin SA leader Karl Ernst, his Silesian counterpart Edmund Heines, and the head of the SA's special representatives in Prussia, Georg von Detten – were just one group of victims among many. Well-informed observers like the writer Thomas Mann speculated that several of the killings were in fact cover-up execu-tions that targeted those who were directly involved in or knew too much about the Reichstag fire.[59] Still other victims had been outspoken oppo-nents of the regime and were killed for this reason alone. Such was the case in the murders of Kurt von Schleicher, Edgar Jung, and Herbert von Bose. A fourth and final group consisted of those unfortunate individuals who were executed by mistake, among them the music critic Wilhelm Schmid, who had been confused with the SA-*Gruppenführer* of the same name.[60]

In the months and years following the purge, anti-Nazi authors often speculated that the murder rate had been much higher. Excessive numbers like Kurt Lüdecke's figure of 'over five hundred SA men murdered'[61] were at times the result of deliberate exaggerations, but they can also be attrib-uted to the uncertainty and widespread fear that followed the 'Reich murder week' (*Reichsmordwoche*).[62] In early July 1934 more than 1,000 people were arrested, and many more went temporarily into hiding. Two anonymous reports from imprisoned Berlin SA leaders testify to the bad treatment such detainees faced during their internment, first in the noto-rious Columbiahaus Prison in Berlin-Tempelhof, and then later in the Lichtenburg concentration camp. Explanations for their arrests were initially not provided, and none of the more than sixty SA leaders held in confinement in Lichtenburg was ever arraigned.[63] A similar situation unfolded in other parts of the Reich. SA leaders who were not shot were kept in limbo for days and sometimes weeks, with the authorities not even pretending to investigate the alleged preparations for a violent putsch planned by Röhm and his followers. According to official German press communications from August 1934, the regime took no fewer than 1,124 people into 'protective custody' on the occasion of the 'Röhm revolt'. While the regime claimed to have released 1,079 of them by mid-August, the other forty-five remained in prison 'for further inquiries'. Despite these pending arrests a governmental statement issued in August declared that the 'action of 30 June 1934' was over.[64] For many high-ranking storm-troopers this declaration was premature. Apart from those interned by the Gestapo and the SS, many more were temporarily suspended or even permanently expelled from the SA. On 2 August 1934, Lutze, in collaboration with Walter Buch, the chairman of the NSDAP's Supreme Party Court, established an SA disciplinary court consisting of two to three SA leaders and Buch himself that started the internal cleansing of the SA leadership corps, as requested by Hitler on 1 July.[65]

A list compiled by the Silesian SA of those regional SA leaders who were temporarily removed from the ranks in late July 1934 contains detailed information on the accusations later advanced in this court. Some of these charges were juridical in nature, concerning participation in excessive violence, defalcation, or male homosexuality. Other charges were highly subjective and, in a stricter sense, hardly more than moral judgements based on personal observations or rumours. One SA leader, for example, was accused of 'having been in nearly all political parties' prior to joining the SA in 1932, while another was accused of being married to a Czechoslovakian wife who was now regarded as a spy. Still other SA leaders were criticized for their 'totally improper private lives', for being a 'bumbler', or for being 'too young, arrogant, and with an unclear comportment' during the Röhm revolt.[66] As these examples demonstrate, the accusations partly reflected criticisms previously levied by Hitler, but they also point to the interpersonal character of the 'cleansings'. Even those character traits that had previously been considered positive qualities for an SA leader during the *Kampfzeit* – such as boldness and the readiness to violently push one's interests through – could now be turned against those caught in the crosshairs.[67]

This 'transvaluation of values' constituted a severe problem for many convicted stormtroopers long after the immediate crackdown on the SA had come to an end, as even those who remained in the organization and even climbed the SA's hierarchy were unable to forget the humiliation of the summer of 1934. The scars from these events remained, even after Hitler in his infamous justification for the killings delivered on 13 July 1934 reached out to the SA, predicting that 'in a few weeks' time, the brown shirt will once again dominate the German streets'.[68] Lutze remained a sworn enemy of Himmler for the rest of his life, in private accusing the *Reichsführer*-SS of murder and hypocrisy.[69] Even if the SA leaders managed to push aside these painful memories in carrying out their daily routines, a grain of insecurity remained. A good example of these lingering effects is the case of Siegfried Kasche, who, as leader of the SA-*Gruppe* Ostmark in Frankfurt an der Oder, only narrowly escaped the hangman in July 1934. Seven years later, in November 1941, while serving as German envoy to Croatia, he met with Himmler in Hitler's New Reich Chancellery in Berlin on the occasion of Croatia, Romania, Slovakia, Bulgaria, Denmark, and Finland joining the Anti-Comintern Pact. When the men disagreed about the SS's influence in eastern Europe, Himmler maliciously told Kasche that 'he had apparently not yet forgotten the 30 June'. 'I understood the warning his words implied,' Kasche wrote in his personal notebook. He was apparently so troubled by this clash with the *Reichsführer*-SS that he noted this incident twice – the only repetition in his otherwise short and apho-ristic notes.[70]

The Myth of the Homosexual Nazi Activist

'Daddy, what does homosexual mean?' Hitlerjunge Knax asks his begetter.

'That is what you become as soon as you are a traitor,' his father snarled.[71]

This joke, printed in the Social Democratic *Neuer Vorwärts* in Czechoslovakia on 15 July 1934, in a nutshell sarcastically summarizes how the murderers in the wake of the 'Röhm purge' exploited the stigma of male homosexuality to legitimize their politically motivated killings. The paradigmatic image that was produced to help justify such actions appeared in a summary of the events of 30 June 1934 provided by the Reich Press Office on the same day: 'The enforcement of the detention [of Röhm and the other SA leaders in Bad Wiessee, D.S.] revealed images morally so sad that the slightest grain of sympathy had to vanish. A number of the SA leaders present had taken toy boys along, and one even had to be awoken and arrested in the most despicable situation. The Führer ordered the uncompromising extermination of this pestilential bubo.'[72]

Colourful accounts of Hitler breaking into the Pension Hanselbauer in the morning hours of 30 June 1934 and finding SA leaders in bed with other men are part of many accounts of the 'Night of the Long Knives'.[73] From a careful historian's point of view, it is impossible to verify such testimonies, given the political context and the partisan stance of those numerically few witnesses who were later able to provide first-hand accounts of the arrests. Even if one assumes that such statements were based on facts, their morally self-righteous tone was plainly hypocritical, as the homosexuality of some high-ranking SA leaders, most notably Röhm and Heines, had become an open secret within Germany prior to June 1934.[74] Hitler had early on taken notice of it but until the 'Night of the Long Knives' had come to Röhm's defence, claiming that the SA was 'not a school to educate the daughters of the upper classes, but a formation of rough fighters'.[75] Moralization was for a long time second to mobilization. As party leader, Hitler had also tolerated the presence of other known homosexuals in the upper ranks of the SA, much to the distaste of many in his party.

The *Münchener Post* had attacked Röhm and with him the SA for homosexual activities as early as June 1931. Yet it was the publication of Röhm's private letters in March 1932 that proved most influential in triggering debates on 'morality'. These letters had been confiscated by the Berlin police in 1931 and were then leaked to the journalist Helmuth Klotz, a former Nazi activist who had switched sides. Since 1929, Klotz had worked closely with the SPD and edited several anti-Nazi brochures on its behalf.[76] Some 300,000 copies of Röhm's letters were published and a few weeks later provoked a violent incident in the national parliament.[77] On 12 May 1932, Heines recognized Klotz in the Reichstag café and, with several other Nazi deputies, beat him bloody on the spot. The attack made nationwide headlines and helped establish a connection between National Socialism and male homosexuality. Derisive nicknames such as 'Rent boys' and 'Paragraph 175 Guard' – referring to the paragraph of the German penal code that illegalized male homosexuality – became common. Nazi opponents publicly greeted stormtroopers with shouts of 'Hot Röhm!' (*Geil Röhm!*) or 'Gay Heil!' (*Schwul Heil!*).[78]

However, it would be wrong to assume that in the early 1930s those opposing the Nazis widely exploited such accusations for their own ends. Apart from the tone emanating from the Communist and Socialist left, a restrained atttitude dominated the discourse.[79] Characteristic of the efforts to not misuse intimate private information to influence national politics was an article by Kurt Tucholsky in the left-liberal *Die Weltbühne* in April 1932. The well-known writer and journalist had no problem revealing the hypocrisy of the National Socialists, who publicly attacked the allegedly sinful republic while at the same time tolerating homosexuals within their leadership. Yet a personal attack on Röhm's homosexuality, which he carefully tried to keep private, could not be justified – not for the purpose of preserving his dignity, but for preserving our own, Tucholsky explained: 'One should not go to see one's opponent in bed.'[80] Even if the perception that parts of the SA leadership were gay gained ground in the two years following the 'Röhm scandal', it was ultimately the National Socialists themselves who contributed to its lasting effect. The previous rumours and disclosures had set the stage for the regime's 1934 accusations that the SA was a bunch of homosexual 'perverts', and the idea immediately caught on, to the extent that the cliché of the 'gay Nazi' is still firmly embedded in the cultural imaginary of the Nazi movement.

Yet, as Laurie Marhoefer, Alexander Zinn, Jörn Meve, and Andreas Pretzel have rightly emphasized, the 'myth of legions of gay Nazis has no historical basis'; rather, it was a 'propaganda tool created by the German Left' that survived well into the post-war decades.[81] This is not to say that homosexual stormtroopers did not exist, but rather that we have no historical record to assume that the percentage of homosexual men in the SA was higher than their proportion in the general male population.[82] This assertion holds true despite the companionship and mutual affection among men in local units, as Andrew Wackerfuss has recently demonstrated with regard to the Hamburg SA in the *Kampfzeit*.[83] In fact, it would have been highly surprising if homosexual men had deliberately chosen the SA as an environment in which to live out their sexuality. The official Nazi discourse was distinctly homophobic, putting forward 'biological' and 'social' arguments against the orientation. Official party doctrine declared that in order to guarantee the future of the German people, all attempts to legalize and promote male homosexuality had to be blocked. As early as February 1933 the new government under Hitler started to close down places of homosexual encounters, such as gay bars and bathhouses. This was only the beginning of a violent crackdown on male homosexuals that in the following years led to the condemnation and imprisonment of several 10,000 men, including hundreds of cases of forced castration.[84]

Among National Socialists the conception of a homosexual 'fighter' as a particularly masculine identity – in the tradition of Hans Blüher's *Männerbund* ideal – remained a minority opinion.[85] Unlike Röhm, most of its militants did not believe in the image of the 'homosexual warrior-activist' and instead conventionally associated male homosexuality with 'femaleness' and weakness, characteristics with which they carefully contrasted their own self-images.[86] For a stormtrooper to 'come out' by free choice was thus extremely difficult, if not impossible. The fact that homosexuals in the SA leadership at times established networks that protected or actively promoted fellow homosexuals, such as those created in the Silesian SA under Heines and within the SA leadership under Karl Ernst, was ultimately a consequence of the party's homophobia – and not the other way round.[87] Yet, after 1945, the popular myth of the gay stormtrooper featured even in the serious historical scholarship on the SA. When it came to sexual politics, there was no zero hour; instead, a homophobic continuity prevailed, stretching from the self-declared moral crusades of the SS to later mainstream historiography. Homophobic attitudes now coalesced with anti-Fascist convictions, an unfortunate liaison that for decades contributed to the belittlement of the persecution of homosexual men in the Third Reich.[88]

Consequences

Mindful observers understood the fundamental consequences of the events that took place in the summer of 1934. An American diplomat called the occurrences of 30 June 1934 'without parallel in the history of civilized Europe'.[89] Ten years later, when news of the failed assassination of Hitler on 20 July 1944 emerged, the 'Night of the Long Knives' still served as a point of reference in Germany. A critical observer remarked that the 'butchery of 1934' would be nothing compared to the crackdown on conspirators that he expected to follow.[90] And even long after the Second

World War had come to an end, the liberal daily *Frankfurter Rundschau* in 1957 referred to the summer of 1934 as 'one of the most atrocious chapters in the history of our people'.[91]

In contrast to these later judgements, the opinion in Germany in the days and weeks after those deadly days was divided. After the arrests became known, Social Democrats observed that the first reactions in the streets of the capital on the afternoon of 30 June 1934 were often smiles and expressions of *Schadenfreude*. Others noted disbelief and apathy, particularly from rank-and-file stormtroopers.[92] Because several SA leaders had the reputation of being corrupt and indecent, many Germans credited Hitler for what they regarded as his determined intervention. Some even saw the days of a 'moral renewal' drawing near.[93]

On 13 July 1934, Hitler attempted to justify his line of action in the previous weeks in a long speech at the Kroll Opera House, the provisional parliamentary building. The speech was broadcast live and eagerly awaited by many, yet the reactions to it were very mixed. One critical listener described Hitler as having been 'in a state of highest excitement and near-pathological depression'. Hitler had even exclaimed that he would put a bullet through his own head if the state and the party organizations did not remain united.[94] Thomas Mann noted in his diary that Hitler had delivered a 'barking speech' in which he elevated the murders into an act of salvation, interrupted by frequent applause. The writer's comment was short: 'Nightmarish'.[95] Yet, by and large, Hitler's unusually emotional address did not fail to impress the public. For example, the conservative but independent mayor of the city of Celle in Lower Saxony, in a public speech on the occasion of the annual marksmen's festival, said that he had been deeply moved by Hitler's confession (*Selbstbekenntnis*) and even exclaimed: 'From a human point of view alone he merits our profound sympathy and honest adoration.'[96] Such a grotesque, but not atypical, reaction transformed this cold-blooded killer into a sensitive and responsible political leader. Hitler's (staged) suffering paid direct political dividends – and it seemed to contrast him favourably with the allegedly simple-minded and brutal 'hotheads' of the SA. Within the Reichswehr, the events of 30 June 1934 confirmed the army's role as the nation's only armour-bearer and were celebrated as nothing less than a decisive 'victory over the SA and the party' – regardless of the blood-soaked nature of this political success that made the regular military command accomplices in crime.[97]

Whereas the Celle mayor's appreciation was derived from his taking Hitler's emotional theatre at face value, Carl Schmitt, the leading jurist of the early Third Reich, justified the political murders as a form of higher justice. On 1 August 1934, Schmitt published an article entitled 'Der Führer schützt das Recht' ('The Führer Protects the Law') in which he not only justified the killings but even elevated the 'Führer's action' into an act of 'true jurisdiction'. Taking up Hitler's remarks on the alleged Socialist betrayal during the First World War, Schmitt insisted that a true political leader would thereby also serve as the nation's highest judge, and as such would 'defend the law from the most fatal abuse if, at a moment of danger, he creates unmediated justice'.[98] In so arguing, Schmitt not only abandoned the established principle of the separation of powers but even compared the new state of lawlessness favourably to the alleged liberal 'positive web of compulsory legal norms'.[99] This was a remarkable position even for Schmitt, who less than five months earlier had insisted on the ability of German jurists to distinguish between a politically motivated 'empty dictum' (*leerer Machtspruch*) and a 'legal dictum' (*Rechtsspruch*).[100] National Socialist ideology was to be applied in those cases where sweeping clauses were at hand, but in all other cases the legal norms had to be respected, Schmitt had argued. Yet even in this earlier text, Schmitt accepted the pre-eminence of formal laws only conditionally. It was ultimately the political sovereign who enjoyed the discretion to alter the legal framework at any given moment, Schmitt argued, as he was restricted only by a higher righteousness that was beyond human judgement. Consequently, Schmitt reduced the state in its entirety to a 'body at the disposition of the leader of the [Nazi] movement'.[101]

With his highly political legal writings Schmitt contributed to what Ernst Fraenkel in 1940 described as the parallel existence of the 'prerogative state' and the 'normative state'. Although the German judiciary applied legal norms in a formal way throughout the Third Reich, the government was permitted to 'exercise unlimited arbitrariness and violence', Fraenkel observed.[102] In this respect the 'Night of the Long Knives' was a key event, not only putting an end to the far-reaching ambitions of the social-revolutionary wing of the Nazi movement but also indicating that from now on Nazi leaders could justify even the most serious capital crimes as long as they were deemed necessary to prevent an imminent danger to the nation's development and expansion. Based on such reasoning, even Hitler's

'Commissar Order' of June 1941, which requested the summary execution of alleged Bolshevists behind the eastern front lines, or the Nazi policies of ethnic cleansing and mass murder in eastern Europe, could be technically 'justified'. The 'Night of the Long Knives' thus contributed decisively to the development of a Nazi morality that did not accept uncircumventable limits.

The immediate consequence of these developments was that 'power shifted decisively upwards', as the economic historian Adam Tooze has put it. Unlike the political situation of the early 1920s, not only was the independent labour movement destroyed, but the 'autonomous paramilitary potential of the right' was also strictly contained.[103] The SA special representatives were officially recalled on 10 July 1934, indicating the end of the short-lived era of ambitious and somehow 'autonomous' SA politics.[104] At about the same time, the infamous SA-run concentration camp in Oranienburg near Berlin closed. On 19 July 1934, Adolf Wagner, the Munich *Gauleiter* and Bavarian Minister of the Interior, decreed that from now on the civil administrations alone would be charged with maintaining public order and security.[105] In the years to come, the Nazi Party kept the SA on a short leash, allowing only brief outbursts of violence. Most of the time the stormtroopers were assigned tasks that were considerably more 'civilian' in nature, testifying to the transformation of the SA into a regular feature of German society. Young men who received professional training in one of the SA's northern schools, for example, served their local communities by furnishing a marching band at a children's fair, organizing an SA artist group, staging amateur theatre performances, fighting against environmental problems, and organizing midsummer festivals (Plate 18).[106]

However uncertain the political consequences of 30 June 1934 appeared to be in the immediate aftermath of the killings, it was obvious to all observers that the SA would 'doubtless be lessened in size' and perhaps reduced in status to an 'unarmed political organization'.[107] Yet the political murders not only marked an end point in the sense that they concluded the period of the Nazi takeover and consolidation of power.[108] They also indicated the beginning of five relatively stable years that witnessed Germans' growing approval of Hitler's domestic and foreign policy. The reincorporation of the Saarland after the plebiscite of 13 January 1935, the remilitarization of the Rhineland in 1936, and the *Anschluss* of Austria in 1938 all contributed to the restoration of German hegemony in central Europe and added to Hitler's ever-growing popularity in the Reich.

For the SA, however, these five years were anything but stable. The organization underwent a radical transformation, both internally and with regard to its political goals. The days of relative independence from the NSDAP were irrevocably over, as were the times of political brawls with ideological opponents in the streets of the German Reich. The new role of the SA was comparatively unadventurous: they were supposed to educate the male German youth in Nazi ideology and to prepare them for military service in the Wehrmacht. At first glance this mission was a far cry from the organization's far-reaching ambitions of the previous years. A closer examination will prove, however, that this new role had a lasting effect on the political situation in Germany and the mentalities of its people.

PART III

PART III

THE TRANSFORMATION OF THE SA BETWEEN 1934 AND 1939

We are under the impression that within the SA one still finds the most upright Nazis and that many of them are heavily radicalized.
— Report of a Bavarian Social Democrat, 1935[1]

The deadly crackdown on the SA leadership in the summer of 1934 shocked many of the organization's rank and file, who up to then had believed the constant trumpeting of the SA's central place in the Third Reich. All of a sudden the SA's 'achievements' of the previous years, as well as its members' far-reaching goals for the future, faced a serious challenge. A November 1934 letter from forty-one-year-old SA-*Obersturmbannführer* Wilhelm Blessing to his superior illustrates widespread fear and uncertainty among SA men in these troubled times. Although Blessing initially stated that he avoided thinking about the general aspects of the SA, as these thoughts bothered him to such an extent that they could not be dealt with in writing, several lines later he linked his personal material and emotional problems with a lack of respect for the SA and its achievements. Full of sarcasm and helpless anger, Blessing wrote:

Please do not believe that I have joined the camp of the materialists, only because I look at my future from that perspective. Nowadays, one is forced to act according to that viewpoint. And one certainly has family obligations that one can't ignore. My first marriage broke down because I did not care enough for it – I am not inclined to let this happen again with my second marriage. That's simply how it is: who nowadays is skilled at pushing to the fore or at licking the boots of one's superior makes progress and is soon free of financial worries. Whoever doesn't fit this mould will croak.

Whereas the majority of Germans had supposedly managed to obtain secure positions in the Third Reich, the SA leader, said Blessing, was 'in limbo and doesn't know what will become of him tomorrow. Nobody is mindful of the fact that it was us who participated in the takeover of power a little bit.'[2]

This statement reveals a contradictory tendency. On the one hand, Blessing's grievance testifies to a *Verbürgerlichung*, or growing middle-class sentiment, within the SA. In contrast with the 'time of struggle', when stormtroopers took pride in the fact that they needed neither material nor social comfort, Blessing in the autumn of 1934 emphasized that his private life did indeed matter, both with regard to his new marriage and in view of his (still limited) ability to free himself from pressing financial worries (Plate 21). On the other hand, his complaint is couched in the language of a 'Nazi morality' which started from the premise that personal effort and dedication to the political cause rather than qualifications or professional networks should determine one's success in the 'people's community'.[3]

The liquidation of several dozen SA leaders in the summer of 1934 cast serious doubt on such high expectations. Many militants reacted to the 'Night of the Long Knives' with initial disbelief and showed signs of apathy in the following months. According to Gestapo reports from the second half of 1934 and 1935, feelings of despair were widespread within the ranks. In the autumn of 1934 many stormtroopers stayed away from duty. Those who showed up declared that they were no 'sports students', but soldiers who required military training with real weapons.[4] A report from May 1935 plainly stated that 'the ordinary SA man does not know at all why he is taking part in SA activities'.[5] And the Gestapo observed that a specifically designed programme of 'SA employment therapy', which consisted of frequent but mostly tame duties and sporting events like the SA Reich Sport Contest (*Reichswettkampf der SA*), kept the men busy but barely concealed the Brownshirts' lack of perspective and 'firm purpose'.[6] Accordingly, the Social Democratic Party in exile came to the conclusion that the SA units more and more resembled a 'container' for 'primitive forms of comradeship'. The SA's ideology would be like dust on the surface of that container – unable to penetrate the minds and hearts of the storm-troopers.[7]

There was a degree of wishful thinking in such assessments, yet even so, all empirical evidence suggests that the SA's mobilizing power declined sharply in the wake of the 'Night of the Long Knives' and that its members suffered from feelings of uncertainty and vulnerability. As late as April 1936, Alfred Rosenberg, on the occasion of a speech he had given in front of several thousand Brownshirts, noted in his diary that his listeners had been extremely thankful for his encouragement, an encouragement that was 'unfortunately still needed'.[8] A report on the future of the SA produced at the end of 1934 from the American Embassy in Berlin analysed the situation aptly by outlining two possible developments: 'It remains to be seen whether the educational work set forth by Hitler can afford a satisfactory substitute for the excitements and hopes of the past. If the morale and prestige of the organisation cannot be maintained, it will either decline in importance or become a focus of growing discontent in the party.'[9]

Searching for New Tasks

In the three years following the 'Night of the Long Knives' the SA went through a period of decline, uncertainty, and reorientation. It lost its financial autonomy and came to be dependent on the NSDAP and its Reich Treasurer, Franz Xaver Schwarz.[10] The regional SA-*Gruppen* were granted the authority to expel all rank-and-file stormtroopers whom they deemed unsuitable for ideological or personal reasons, and the SA leadership corps (defined as the rank of *Sturmführer* and above) was subjected to thorough investigation by a newly created SA court, the *Sondergericht der Obersten SA-Führung*.[11] It is not without irony that the fulfilment of Röhm's aspiration to establish a special SA court did not lead to the protection of his men against criminal charges from the authorities, but to the impeachment and instigation of disciplinary actions against them. Between 1934 and 1939 more than 15 per cent of all high-ranking SA leaders – or 1,900 men – received disciplinary penalties, mainly for alcoholism, embezzlement of funds, or illegal violent acts.[12]

The high number of punishments handed out as well as the public humiliation of the SA that accompanied them combined to make it appear less a Nazi elite formation and more a bunch of conceited fools. This development provoked very different reactions among the organization's men. As the declining membership numbers between the summer of 1934 and April 1938 indicate, one out of two stormtroopers during this period left the SA for good, with the majority departing voluntarily.[13] Yet the decline in membership was actually surprisingly moderate, given the SA's traditionally high turnover rates, falling unemployment in Germany from 1935 onward, and the mismatch between the rather bleak present and the official new narrative that extended the SA's 'mission' of the *Kampfzeit* into the circumstances of the consolidated Third Reich. Whereas Viktor Lutze and the OSAF propaganda glorified the SA as the 'birthplace of the German *Volksgemeinschaft*' and the individual SA man as someone who had transformed from a pioneer of Nazism into a guardian of the new state, the stormtroopers' everyday activities in the mid-1930s not only lacked a sense of purpose but were sometimes as 'unheroic' as the uprooting of trees in the local communal forest or the provision of help after a car accident.[14] At a time when Communists with daggers drawn were no longer to be found in the smoky taverns of the German cities, the evils of nature, poverty, and self-righteous individualism were presented as the new adversaries. Getting up early to participate in an SA activity was sufficient grounds to be elevated into a model of sacrifice for the *Volksgemeinschaft*. Consequently, the contribution of Silesian stormtroopers building new settlement houses was praised as a 'symbol of the comradeship of our times'. At least in propaganda, the militants' duty of ensuring the cohesion of and solidarity among the 'Aryan' Germans now replaced their previous task of street-fighting against political rivals. The militarized language of this propaganda nevertheless remained the same. The SA's fundraising efforts for Winter Aid were characterized as a 'peaceful expedition', and on the occasion of the annual Christmas celebrations the SA was to be found 'at the very front'.[15] Such formulations contribute to the unintentionally hilarious impression such texts have on today's readers, and even at the time of their publication, in the late 1930s, they had only a limited popular appeal. Yet, despite all these shortcomings, the SA of 1938 was still three times as big as it had been in the worst period of economic depression in 1932.

Many longstanding stormtroopers remained in the humiliated and 'cleansed' SA because they lacked alternatives and feared the professional disadvantages that might result from leaving. Although high expectations for the SA's central role in the new societal order of the Third Reich were clearly unrealistic after the summer of 1934, a relatively stable position in the organization proved for many their only advantage in competing for jobs and influence against their many more qualified, younger, better-born, or simply more ambitious rivals.[16] Furthermore, those stormtroopers who had joined the ranks of the SA in the 1920s had been taking a radical step that had frequently caused ruptures with old friends and pre-existing social networks. In return, the new 'SA family' provided them with bonds and emotional shelter, but it also made them dependent on the organization. The writings of these men often reveal a fragile self-esteem; in the words of historian Peter Merkl, they even display a pattern of 'psychological marginality'.[17] This insecurity was barely concealed by rough manners and was reinforced by the uncertainty of the political situation and the persistent financial problems many activists continued to face. All of these factors produced a situation that discouraged members from making independent, let alone brave decisions.

There were also those who remained committed to the Nazi ideology and for precisely that reason remained loyal to the SA. One of them, the Austrian stormtrooper Herman Stühlinger, co-founder in 1930 of the National Socialist German Doctors' League, claimed as late as July 1938: 'There is only one formation that represents the people's community, only one that passes on the idealism and the willingness to sacrifice, and that is precisely the SA!'[18] Regardless of the degree of wishful thinking such a statement expressed, it should not be dismissed as unimportant, as it points to a striking continuity in the self-understanding of the SA, which persisted in seeing itself as the guardian of core Nazi values and as the organization that guaranteed social cohesion in the Third Reich. High-ranking SA generals assured each other as late as 1940 that 'the SA not only possessed an educational mission on its own terms, but is rather responsible for the National Socialist political education per se'.[19] If anything, well into the Second World War, Germany remained not an 'SS State', as Eugen Kogon famously put it in 1946, but an SA state.[20] During the war years, the SS dominated in the occupied territories and abroad, but within the Old Reich men in SA uniforms prevailed.

Particularly among the 'Old Fighters', widespread disappointment at the lukewarm 'social revolution' that had accompanied the Nazi takeover of power and the humiliation and trauma caused by the 'Röhm purge' prevailed and led to an intensification of their aggressive attitude. The first stanza of the song *Achtung SA!*, popular in northern Germany in 1935, is a particularly characteristic expression of this mood:

> The Reds are defeated,
> The whole bigwig pack is overcome.
> And yet the cheeky fat bourgeois arises,
> Who never bled and had no fighting done.
>
> All you bourgeois and bigwigs, on guard we stand!
> We are our old selves, even today.
> We bled, fought and earthworks we manned,
> For Germany, but never for you.
>
> So forward, forward, clear the streets!
> Bourgeois, beat it!
> Bourgeois, beat it!
> We'll break all your bones like treats,
> And smoke out your temples while at it![21]

In light of such aggressive songs it is no surprise that for many Germans the brown shirt signalled danger, before and long after 1934. The German Jew and later historian Fritz Stern of Breslau remembered that he saw his first SA man at a North Sea resort in the summer of 1931, at the age of five. At the time, the young boy could not have been fully aware of the violence the SA was capable of performing, but in the historian's recollection this seemingly unimportant detail is portrayed as the first direct contact with an organization that turned out to be a deadly enemy.[22] Among the oldest memories of the political activist Reinhard Strecker is the noise of SA units on the evening of 9 November 1938 as they stormed the apartment house in Berlin-Charlottenburg where the then eight-year-old boy lived with his family. 'The trampling of hobnailed boots, rushing up the stairways, is for me the sound of the Third Reich,' Strecker remembered (Plate 22).[23] People throughout the 1930s knew that a stormtrooper propaganda march could easily turn into a violent brawl. For the young mother Helene Fußhoeller from Cologne, the characteristic sound of a group of SA men tramping through the streets was even more frightful than the howling of aerial mines during the Second World War.[24]

These examples underline the extent to which the 'brown army of millions' characterized the outer appearance of the Third Reich to a considerable degree. This impression was no longer achieved by the provocative marches and brawls of the late Weimar years, but by the sheer presence of hundreds of thousands of SA men who were continuously encouraged to create and to defend the 'people's community' even within the most remote corners of society. One of these remote corners was the little village of Weildorf located near the market town of Teisendorf in the Alpine foothills and not known as a stronghold of anti-Nazi activities. Yet in the winter of 1936–7 a violent incident occurred there that was in many ways typical of the problems and the agitation caused by the SA in traditional rural milieus. Although the origins of this incident remain obscure, Weildorf in 1936 was the site of a kind of local revolution after its honorary mayor, a local peasant named Johann Helminger, was forced to step down for political reasons. After some months of interim, he was finally succeeded in November of the same year by a farmer from neighbouring Hörfing, the twenty-five-year-old Johann Traxl. As one of his first actions in office, this young Nazi mayor launched a kind of 'punitive expedition' with the goal of strengthening his authority and disciplining the peasants. To this end, he ordered between thirty and forty stormtroopers to come to Weildorf on Sunday, 6 December 1936. Upon their arrival the SA men disturbed the regular Catholic afternoon mass by marching and singing around the church. Soon afterward they entered the local inn, where they mingled with the farmers and announced, among other things, that a showcase of Julius Streicher's notorious antisemitic weekly *Der Stürmer* would be installed next to the local classrooms. These provocations of a devout Catholic population had an instant effect, as several of the peasants objected to the public display of *Der Stürmer* propaganda. Interestingly, one of them argued that he had once regularly read this publication and now thought it irresponsible to confront schoolchildren with such graphic detail of the 'moral misdoings of the Jews'. Although this statement hardly indicated fundamental opposition to the Nazi regime, the SA leader present used such tame criticism as an opportunity to have the peasant arrested for several days. Another farmer from Weildorf explained that although he would in principle not object to participating in a paramilitary exercise he was ordered to attend, for the time being he was needed more at home to run his farm and take care of his large family. For this statement alone he was insulted, beaten severely, and finally taken into 'protective custody'. The Brownshirts furthermore called several guests in the inn 'bastards' (*Schweinehunde*), 'buggers' (*Misthackl*), and 'traitors of the fatherland'. An official report concluded that the peaceful, modest, and hardworking peasants of Weildorf had not deserved such treatment by the SA. 'This is not the way to win someone over, but to make the well-meaning stubborn.'[25] Nevertheless, the young Nazi mayor responsible for the violence remained in office until the end of the Third Reich, a fact that points to the limits of local resistance – understood here as a more restrained form of discontent than outright political opposition.[26]

As incidents like this one in Weildorf make obvious, the role of stormtroopers after 1934 cannot simply be reduced to that of 'collecting box rattlers' (*Sammelbüchsenrassler*), block leaders, or air-raid wardens.[27] They also served as a kind of semi-official party police that intimidated, molested, and often arrested those the regime deemed in need of punishment, be it for racial, political, or – as in Weildorf – religious and at times very personal reasons. Variations notwithstanding, the SA therefore remained a relevant and violent organization, particularly on the local and regional levels. On the national and international levels, stormtroopers were ordered to fulfil more directly political tasks that were closely related to the SA's paramilitary origins. In what follows, I will analyse three fields of action that demonstrate to what extent the SA still heavily influenced the lives of millions of Germans in the years between 1934 and 1939. This influence was exerted, first, by its repeated antisemitic boycott actions, riots in the streets, and outright acts of unprovoked physical violence; second, by its successful takeover of the leadership of Germany's shooting associations and riding clubs; and third, by its renaissance as a paramilitary strike force in the context of the *Anschluss* of Austria, the reintegration of the Memelland, and the destabilization and dismembering of Czechoslovakia in 1938–9.

Defining the Limits of *Volksgemeinschaft*: Antisemitic Violence

One of the fields of action for which the Brownshirts are best known was their antisemitic agitation against and physical attacks on Jews, which intensified with the NSDAP's rise to power and culminated on 9 and 10 November 1938 in *Kristallnacht*, or the 'Night of Broken Glass'. As historian Alan E. Steinweis noted, although this was 'the single instance of large-scale, public, and organized physical violence against Jews inside

Germany before the Second World War', it built on a series of previous attacks on Jews that in many cases were carried out by stormtroopers.[28] It was precisely the SA's record of long years of antisemitic activity that – in conjunction with its ideology – made the outburst of 9 November possible. Furthermore, in order to understand the behaviour of ordinary Germans during this time who often not only took no action to stop the violence or plundering of Jewish property but in many cases joined in, an analysis of the appeal and reach of the SA's anti-Jewish violence between 1933 and 1938 is key.[29] That physical assaults on Jews were a major factor in the establishment of the Nazi terror regime in 1933–4 has already been explained in chapter 4. Therefore, in what follows, the focus is on the period beginning in the second half of 1934 and lasting until the spring of 1939.

The 'Röhm purge' did not constitute a halt of the SA's anti-Jewish attacks. On the contrary, precisely because the militants from 1934 onward often lacked the opportunity to engage in the physical violence that during the 'years of struggle' had so successfully served as a means of bonding for SA units, they welcomed opportunities to attack Jews. Engagement in interpersonal violence steadied the shaken confidence of those storm-troopers who participated in such actions, particularly as the SA man's self-image was to a substantial degree based on his ability to impose himself on others physically. The widespread frustration among the SA rank and file after the executions of the summer of 1934 therefore more than once translated into attacks on Jews, the regime's scapegoats; this violence both acted as a valve for the Brownshirts' pent-up aggression and was a consequence of their ideological convictions.

When the authorities ordered the SA to abstain from antisemitic 'pillory actions' (*Prangeraktionen*) in the city of Breslau in June 1935, the storm-troopers formally requested permission to continue such violence in plain clothes. Nazi mobs composed of young men and women, with many Brownshirts among them, assaulted Jewish and 'Jewish-looking' passers-by during the following weeks in the streets of the Lower Silesian capital. They hit, spat on, and insulted even children. A Jewish café was attacked with the purpose of 'dragging out' and beating up its guests. When police officers called to help arrived at the scene, they were greeted with insults such as *Judenknechte!* or 'servants of the Jews', and accused of defending the regime's enemies.[30]

Besides such barely disguised SA attacks were incidents that were indeed spontaneous, the outcome of a dangerous combination of ideology, personal frustration, and alcohol. Late on the night of 10 October 1935, for example, a drunken stormtrooper dressed in his uniform rang the bell of a Jewish Berliner, Alice Meyer, and threatened to invade her apartment and to 'crush the small of her back'.[31] The multitude of similar incidents that occurred throughout the Reich made it clear to the German population that, despite the regime's repeated calls for moderation, the Brownshirts continued to pose a significant risk to whoever happened to come into their firing line. It is significant that the perpetrator of the above-mentioned attack in Berlin was released from police custody the same night, and that the victim did not press charges. As in Breslau, the capital's uniformed police complained about repeated verbal and physical attacks on its officers, particularly on occasions when the latter attempted to stop 'anti-Jewish demonstrations' in the area of the Kurfürstendamm.[32]

Such anti-Jewish attacks also had another, more political dimension. Whereas the Nazi regime from 1933 onward systematically marginalized Jews by legal means, stormtroopers made such racial exclusion highly visible (Plate 19). Their violence in the years 1933 to 1938 regularly took place in public, in front of the eyes of the local and regional communities. Insulting, spitting at, and beating Jews not only humiliated and terrified the victims of such assaults but also illustrated the new, highly unequal balance of power in German society. This was a 'lesson' that many non-Jewish as well as Jewish Germans learned quickly. They could either join in such actions or, in case of disagreement, at least they understood it was best not to oppose it. The Brownshirts' belief in the SA as the educator of the German masses could thus be upheld. From this perspective SA anti-Jewish violence was a key strategy in the regime's attempt to create a politically loyal 'people's community'. It not only served to intimidate those deemed 'outsiders' but also clarified the extent to which the criteria for processes of integration and exclusion were racially grounded.[33] By early 1936 this process had advanced to the point that SA Chief of Staff Lutze, in an official address to the diplomatic corps in the Reich's capital, referred to the German Jews as 'unwelcome guests' who had committed 'countless crimes against the German people' and would now face the stormtroopers' legitimate punishment.[34]

Such official statements made it clear to the German Jews that in the years to follow they could not expect anything good from the SA. The territorial expansion of the Reich in the second half of the 1930s only made things worse. In particular, the *Anschluss* of Austria in March 1938 was a decisive watershed for the Jews, both in Austria and in the Old Reich.[35] Social relations in what now became the Reich's *Ostmark* literally changed overnight. Even seventy-five years later the last remaining eyewitnesses of this time remember particular incidents that shed light on this transformation. According to the Jewish Viennese pensioner Vilma Neuwirth, the local SA became particularly insolent after this event. The daughter of a local hairdresser, aged ten in 1938, remembered a steady customer visiting her father on the day following the *Anschluss*. This man requested his regular haircut but now sported a tailored SA uniform and shining boots. From now on he would rule the roost, this long-time customer declared boldly. Instead of paying for the haircut, he simply walked away once it was done – but not before he had spat on the ground in front of the hairdresser to humiliate him and illustrate the new power relations in the city.[36] In the weeks and months to follow, many Austrian Jews had similar experiences. As a consequence, half of the 190,000 Jews living in Austria had left their home country by the spring of 1939 – including several thousand who were illegally deported by the SS and the SA.[37]

In the Old Reich, the same situation could be seen, with the months following the *Anschluss* witnessing a dramatic rise in antisemitic violence everywhere in Germany. This violence aimed to exclude the Jews, factually and symbolically, from their local communities and force them to emigrate. Starting on 13 June 1938, police forces arrested thousands of male Jews on an order from the *Reichskriminalpolizeiamt*, signed by Heydrich. Every police headquarters had to take at least 200 male Jews who were 'fit for work' into 'preventive custody'. On the same occasion all male Jews who had previously been sentenced to a prison term of at least one month's length were to be arrested also.[38] In the following weeks, the authorities seized about 12,000 Jewish men and sent the vast majority of them to concentration camps.[39]

Such raids and imprisonments were not only carried out by regular police forces. According to the authorities, local groups of SA and HJ jointly arrested about 1,000 Jews in the capital city of Berlin between 17 and 21 June 1938 alone.[40] In the predominantly middle-class neighbourhood of Berlin-Schöneberg nearly all Jewish shop windows were 'decorated' with antisemitic graffiti, French newspapers reported. In the eastern parts of town, which were generally more working class, SA troops went from shop to shop, bowing to 'Aryan' customers and abusing Jewish tradesmen.[41] Stormtroopers even cordoned off cinemas and arrested their Jewish viewers, ordering the cinema operators not to let any Jews watch movies in the future.[42] The lawyer Hans Reichmann, a long-time board member of the liberal *CV-Verein*, remembered in his memoirs that in the days following these arrests, German Jews were frightened by persistent rumours that 100,000 militants had been ordered to seize all Jewish homes in Germany.[43] Even though these rumours turned out to be false, they strongly suggest that the German Jews had come to fear the stormtroopers no less than the political police or the SS.

On the occasion of this increase in what the Nazis referred to as *Judenaktionen*, or 'Actions against Jews', the acting Bavarian Minister of the Interior, Adolf Wagner, informed the five Bavarian *Gauleiter* – Fritz Wächtler, Julius Streicher, Otto Hellmuth, Karl Wahl, and Josef Bürckel – on 31 October 1938 that such attacks were harmful to the reputation of both the NSDAP and the state. However, his reasoning makes it clear that his criticism did not stem from any disagreement with the goals of these acts:

> We no longer have to resort to violent acts in order to reach our objectives, in particular with regard to the Jews, as our state and its institutions are not only strong enough, but also absolutely determined to do everything that is necessary to reach our goals and to preserve public calm and order. Should it happen that a Jew commits a serious offence, that he is tedious or that his removal becomes necessary, then the police are at any moment in the position to operate properly and lawfully, to take the Jew into protective custody or to remove him in some other way. Not under any circumstances can we tolerate violent measures being taken.[44]

This statement indicates the defencelessness of the Jews in Germany in 1938 – if not in the legal, then certainly in the political sense. The report was not worth the paper it was written on.

Only ten days later, on the night of 9–10 November 1938, thousands of Jewish citizens throughout the Reich were violently attacked, imprisoned, injured, or killed, their businesses destroyed, and their synagogues burnt down. Today's estimates of the total number of Jewish men arrested on this night vary between 30,000 and 60,000. Whereas Nazi leaders on

12 November 1938 stated that the number of synagogues destroyed was slightly higher than 100, the Social Democratic Party in exile provided the more reasonable figure of 520. At least ninety-one Jews were killed.[45] Contemporaries immediately understood the symbolic dimension of 'Crystal Night'. The Nazi regime did not need to put its message into words: it was clear that it wanted centuries of Jewish life in Germany to come to a violent end, once and for all. The social composition of the mobs that participated in *Kristallnacht* differed from town to town, from region to region. Most perpetrators were adult men, but women and even children also took part, often to a considerable degree.[46] Despite variations, the large majority of accounts agree that the stormtroopers were the most active group carrying out the crimes, although not all eyewitnesses might have realized this immediately, as the SA men were officially prohibited from dressing in their uniforms during that night.

Few accounts explain the SA's role in and overall character of this pogrom better than a report provided by the SA-*Gruppe* Nordmark in early December 1938, four weeks after the events had taken place. Written by the group's leader, SA-*Obergruppenführer* Joachim Meyer-Quade, this four-page-long report reveals with rare clarity the chain of command and actions taken in the city of Kiel. On the evening of 9 November, Meyer-Quade had been in Munich at the Hotel Schottenhammel on the occasion of the annual NSDAP celebrations of the failed Hitler Putsch fifteen years previously. At about ten in the evening, Goebbels informed the party leaders present that in retaliation for the murder of the German diplomat Ernst vom Rath in Paris by the Jew Herschel Grünspan, a concerted operation against German Jewry was necessary. Meyer-Quade immediately offered the services of his men to Hinrich Lohse, the *Gauleiter* of the Nordmark. At about twenty minutes past eleven, Meyer-Quade telephoned his Chief of Staff in Kiel and ordered the destruction of Jewish businesses and assembly rooms in the larger cities of the *Gau*. According to his report, he explicitly prohibited any mistreatment of Jews. Yet other orders he gave over the course of the night – 'foreign Jews must not be touched' and 'in case of resistance weapons are to be used' – reveal that physical violence, at least against German Jews, was not only tolerated but strongly encouraged.

By midnight the regional police president as well as the state police had been informed about the upcoming pogroms. Over the following three hours, the SA leaders of Kiel met with other leading representatives of the

SS and the NSDAP in the Nordmark at the city's 'brown house' to discuss the imminent operation. The Kiel police delivered to them lists of Jewish homes and businesses in the city, lists that were to provide the basis for the destruction carried out by the SA mobs. According to Meyer-Quade's report, all Nazi leaders present agreed that the Jews of Kiel had to be taken into custody and should be transported to the city's police headquarters. They likewise agreed that 'blood should be paid by blood', and that 'at least two Jews', chosen from a blacklist of the 'politically most dangerous Jews', were to be executed. The Nazis even arranged the organization of two veritable execution squads comprising a member of the SA and the SS and an officer from the state police.

The attacks were set to start at 3.45 a.m. Shortly before that time the stormtroopers met at the Adolf-Hitler-Platz at the heart of the city. Many had spent the evening hours in bars and pubs, celebrating the Hitler Putsch jubilee. Those who were still dressed in their brown shirts at this time received civilian clothing from the nearby town hall. From there, they then started their campaign of demolitions and arrests, accompanied by police officers who stood guard outside the places of destruction. Under their eyes the organized mob vandalized the local synagogue and at least eleven Jewish shops, as well as an unknown number of private homes. Fifty-eight Jews in Kiel were imprisoned. However, the 'execution squads' were only partly successful, as the two Jews targeted – the middle-class shop owners Paul Leven and Gustav Lask – were shot and severely wounded but survived the assaults and later emigrated to the United States.[47]

Similar scenes occurred in many other German cities.[48] An eyewitness described the events that unfolded in the city of Bocholt on the Lower Rhine as follows: 'SA men with torches. *Völkisch* songs. Roaring. Devastation of Jewish shops and flats. Men beaten and jeered at. Attack on the synagogue, the sexton and his wife.'[49] In Niedermarsberg, a small city in southern Westphalia, the SA *Sturm* that was most active during the pogroms consisted of men who were employed by the town's psychiatric clinic as physicians and carers. Nursing personnel helped destroy the local synagogue, attacked Jewish citizens, and vandalized their homes.[50] In the spa town of Bad Harzburg, the Nazi mob arrested at least seven men and several women. They were brought to the local town hall, and the men were later transported to the state prison in nearby Wolfenbüttel. Two of the city's Jews were so heavily beaten that they died shortly afterward. However, when the widow of one of them requested that the local Protestant church inter the urn of her deceased husband in its cemetery, the parish refused to do so – alarmed by the city mayor who claimed that he could not guarantee that the SA and the SS would not dig up the grave and have the remains removed.[51] Viktor Lutze in his otherwise detailed personal records noted the events of the night in very terse fashion, without a word of remorse or a sign of empathy for the victims: 'Retaliation for the murder of v. Rath in Paris – Jewish businesses shut down, synagogues put down.'[52]

These examples, taken from one larger city and several provincial towns, not only testify to the preeminent role that SA units all over Germany played in these events but also make clear the extent to which the storm-troopers' antisemitic violence had become official state policy. The SA provided the Nazi state with shock troops that were quick to mobilize and experienced in carrying out violence. Yet, unlike the SA of 1933–5, the SA in 1938 was a disciplined organization under the control of the NSDAP that respected the limits of its operations set by the regime. In turn, the Nazi leadership made sure that the activists' longings for personal benefits were satisfied. The confiscation of Jewish properties in Vienna in the pogrom allowed 2,200 flats to be provided to party members, claimed the *Gauleiter* Odilo Globocnik. The NSDAP's local *Untere Donausstraße* chapter in the Austrian capital used the opportunity to provide its party office with new furniture and typewriters, stolen from an allegedly Jewish stockbroker. In Upper Silesia schoolchildren in the days after the pogrom boasted of the new valuables their fathers had brought home from their raids. And in the small Franconian town of Markt Berolzheim near Weißenburg, a stormtrooper on the afternoon of 10 November 1938 even organized an auction of the private belongings of Jewish families and the Jewish community.[53]

It would be wrong to assume, however, that the mass participation in these antisemitic attacks indicated unanimous agreement – in other words, that the ideology and practices of the SA had so deeply penetrated the minds and hearts of the majority of Germans that pogroms like *Kristallnacht* were widely embraced. 'Are we upright Germans or just a mob [*Pöbelhaufen*]?' an exasperated German woman asked rhetorically in her diary.[54] And the historian Gerhard Ritter, writing to his mother two weeks after the events, expressed what many thought, but rarely said openly: 'What we have expe-rienced throughout Germany in the last two weeks are the most disgraceful and dreadful events to have happened for a long time. How did we come to this?! One of the many consequences is [. . .], for the first time now, general shame and indignation.'[55] Yet the moral indignation expressed here – even if sincerely felt – makes one wonder how Ritter had interpreted the many acts of antisemitic violence that had taken place in the months and years before. From today's perspective, it is obvious that *Kristallnacht* was the most excessive incident of its kind, yet in many ways not a singular event. Its scale and dimension were unique, but the perpetrators' rationale and the forms of violence to which they resorted were not. In defence of Ritter and his fellow Germans, however, it should not be overlooked that even many SA men did not necessarily associate their organization with attacks on the Jews. Although the stormtroopers spread the regime's obsessive antisemitic ideology and propaganda, not all of them translated that ideology into practical action, as personal notes and diaries of SA men from this period will demonstrate.

Penetrating German Society

One stormtrooper whose personal comments on the SA in the mid- and late 1930s have survived was Wilhelm Hosenfeld, a village teacher and later army officer who became known to the wider public in recent years as the man who helped the Polish-Jewish musician and composer Władysław Szpilman, immortalized in Roman Polanski's 2002 film *The Pianist*. While Hosenfeld's help for Jewish and Polish civilians in occupied Warsaw during his time with the Wehrmacht earned him the title of 'Righteous among the Nations' from Yad Vashem, in the context of this book his earlier remarks as an SA-*Truppführer*, a position comparable to a technical sergeant, are of particular interest.

Hosenfeld, an observant Catholic, joined the SA on 15 April 1933. Throughout the 1930s he lived in the small village of Thalau in Hesse, near the city of Fulda. This region was very pious, rural, and poor – a far cry from the big cities with their predominantly proletarian SA-*Stürme* that historians have often taken as representative of the whole organization. Hosenfeld – attracted by the SA's comradeship and paramilitary sports culture, which reminded him of his youth in the *Wandervogel* movement – was soon promoted to lead the small SA-*Sturm* in Thalau.[56] 'In the uniform of the SA man one is no longer a free agent. One represents the larger community,'

Hosenfeld noted enthusiastically on 19 January 1936.[57] According to his diary entries and notes from the time, he initially shared the national exhilaration that spread throughout Germany in the wake of the National Socialist 'revolution' and seemed to enjoy his activities as SA-*Truppführer*, at least until 1936, when more and more sceptical comments start to prevail in his diaries. The murder of Ernst Röhm and its impact on the SA do not appear in his writings – nor do the antisemitic activities of the SA, even in 1938.[58] Instead, what Hosenfeld mentions repeatedly are the stormtroopers' athletic competitions,[59] propaganda marches in the region and on the occasion of the *Reichsparteitage* in Nuremberg – Hosenfeld participated in 1936 and 1938 – and social evenings with his comrades.[60]

This selective choice of events is remarkable particularly because Hosenfeld otherwise appears an alert observer of the social transformations of the early years of the Third Reich. His comments demonstrate that one should be careful not to dismiss the sporting and social activities of the SA in these years as peripheral. For Hosenfeld, a happily married father of five, 'SA community' in the countryside was not based on bloody clashes with political opponents or attacks on Jews. Nor did he take an interest in the SA as a tool for professional advancement, using it like an 'old boys' network', as Blessing did. Rather, the SA provided Hosenfeld with a new and welcome form of manly sociability, building on older ideas of a nation in arms as well as the rather modern idea of the necessity of physically training one's body. In the same way that it had appealed to the Christian deacons who joined the SA in large numbers in the early 1930s,[61] the SA proved attractive to the village teacher Hosenfeld for three reasons. It gave him the opportunity to exercise power and develop his leadership skills, it provided him with social recognition, and it allowed him to actively but safely participate in the Nazi project of a 'German awakening'.

These attractions were not specific to Hosenfeld, as an analysis of the SA's influence on the German associations, particularly those in small cities and villages, makes clear. Two fields of activity that were highly popular in small-town and rural Germany in the 1930s and increasingly fell under the control of the stormtroopers demonstrate this influence: shooting associations and riding clubs. Unlike the research on other European Fascist or para-Fascist regimes like in Spain, for which Dylan Riley has recently demonstrated the extent to which Fascist rule relied on its penetration of traditional associations, such a perspective has been largely absent from studies on the early years of the Third Reich.[62] Yet it is highly instructive for a history of the SA. As has been demonstrated above, the SA's 'conquest' of Germany's rural areas had already been successful in the years prior to the Nazi takeover of power. Building on this strategy, the SA in the early years of the Third Reich continued and even intensified its attempts to establish itself as an indispensable organization that combined political ambitions with small-town sociability.

The first field of activity in which the SA's strategy was most successful was the assimilation of the German shooting associations. For a long time the domain of the influential and the powerful, shooting clubs began to mushroom in the early days of the Weimar Republic, expanding to the middle and lower-middle classes. Small-scale calibre shooting, introduced in 1920, quickly achieved such popularity that only five years later, in 1925, it had become the third most popular sport in Germany, with about 500,000 participants organized in diverse clubs and leagues.[63] Even prior to the NSDAP's rise to prominence and later power, participation in such shooting clubs was not an innocent hobby divorced from politics. As their members' identity was based on a particular form of masculinity that regarded the ability to defend oneself, one's family, and one's homeland as a core value, shooting associations, in line with the even more popular *Kriegervereine*, or 'veterans' associations', tended to favour national or even nationalist sentiments.[64] The organizers of marksmanship festivals in the German provinces openly espoused an intimate connection between the shooting skills to be acquired in the clubs and the larger national mission to enable the German people to break free from the 'chains' of Versailles and to overcome the national humiliation they had suffered. Many understood membership in shooting associations to be an alternative form of military service.[65]

Such an ideological predisposition facilitated increasing collaboration between the German shooting associations and the SA from the mid-1930s onward, even if former *Stahlhelmers*, who had represented large portions of the membership of diverse middle-class associations since the 1920s, were anything but amused by any new attempt to drag them into a National Socialist organization. Yet, by and large, the new political situation in the Reich that followed the Nazi takeover intensified the 'mutual rapprochement' that already existed between the NSDAP and the millions of Germans who actively enjoyed the associations and clubs of middle-class sociability.[66]

Unlike the German sports clubs, which since 1933 had lost a considerable portion of their six million members to National Socialist organizations like the SA, the SS, and the HJ, the shooting associations maintained a position of relative independence and strength until the second half of the 1930s.[67] In 1937, however, the *Deutscher Schützenverband*, the umbrella organization for the shooting associations, began to formally integrate into its membership representatives from the *Reichskriegsministerium*, or 'Reich Ministry of War', the OSAF, and the German Labour Front (DAF). In line with the broader militarization of (male) civil life in Germany, the publications issued by the shooting associations began increasingly to highlight their contributions to the ultimate goal of a general German *Wehrhaftmachung*, or the transformation of a civil society into one able to engage in (defensive) battles and military conflicts.[68] The rhetoric was basically identical to that used by the stormtroopers.

It should therefore come as no surprise that the SA, once its organizational power and reputation were sufficiently consolidated, made an attempt to impose itself on the dense web of German associations that shared its basic ideological values and engaged in similar practices. By 1938 the SA had achieved a monopoly over the 'physical training and promotion of the *Wehrkraft*'. In contrast to the *Deutscher Reichsbund für Leibesübungen*, which was specifically concerned with first-class sports, the SA oversaw mass sports and organized events like the *NS-Kampfspiele* (first staged in 1937), the National Socialist Fighting Games (Plate 23). These occasions encouraged not top accomplishments by a very few elite sportsmen and sportswomen, but solid performances by teams engaging in sports and paramilitary exercises such as the throwing of hand grenades. The good general fitness of Germany's male population and its versatility in the use of arms were the first priorities.[69] Consequently, beginning in 1938, the *Deutscher Schützenverband* was formally headed by SA-*Obergruppenführer* Max Jüttner, with the former president demoted to the position of deputy. As a kind of welcome gift, and in anticipation of criticism from the shooting associations, the OSAF stressed that it would devote considerable energy and money to the expansion of the shooting sports.[70] Over the following months, protests from dissatisfied club members remained rare; and critical remarks referring to the SA taking control of the clubs as an act of piracy date from the post-1945 period and are thus not reliable.[71] Already at the end of 1938 the German shooting associations celebrated New Year's Day with the motto 'We fight and shoot for Adolf Hitler and his Greater Germany!'[72]

Similar developments could be observed within the German riding clubs. Horse-riding had an even more elite status in German society than membership in shooting associations. Yet, even prior to the Nazi takeover of power, the SA had established regional SA-*Reiterstürme*, or 'rider storms', initially as an attempt to win over local dignitaries and influential peasants in rural Germany as well as parts of the urban establishment.[73] With the regime firmly in the saddle, however, the SA started to popularize horseback riding as a social activity that would help train German men for war. To quote a typical example of the SA rhetoric: 'Riding is constant fighting, a constant affirmation of one's militant desire for success' (Plate 20).[74] As the historian Nele Fahnenbruck has recently demonstrated in a pioneering study, the SA expanded its 'rider storms' over the 1930s to such an extent that in 1938 there existed no fewer than 101 SA-*Reiterstandarten* in Germany. The stormtroopers praised riding as 'perfect *Wehrsport*', an ideal opportunity to train men's physical abilities and character.[75]

The SA's attempt to win over a considerable portion of German riders competed with similar strategies employed by the SS and the Wehrmacht. Yet, the stormtroopers ultimately had the most wide-reaching appeal and organizational clout.[76] After the establishment of the *Nationalsozialistisches Reiterkorps* (NSRK), the equivalent of the *Deutscher Schützenverband*, in March 1936, the SA formally oversaw the training of all aspiring riders and – according to its own statements – '80 per cent of the entire German riding population'.[77] Similar to other sports, riding in the SA did not focus on excellent performances by a few elite riders, but was meant to show real 'SA spirit' at work. Consequently, team competitions were more highly valued than those for individual riders. The SA understood its riding competitions as a way of advertising itself by exploiting the interest of village youth in riding and at the same time serving as a symbol for a *Volksgemeinschaft* that overcame class boundaries through common effort, ideological firmness, and social awareness.[78]

By late 1938 the cooperation between the SA and the shooting associations, riding clubs, and general sports clubs had been formally established. High-ranking SA generals controlled all three areas: the sports umbrella organization *Reichsbund für Leibesübungen* was headed by SA-*Obergruppenführer* Hans von Tschammer und Osten (who in the OSAF presided over the *Hauptamt Kampfspiele*); the NS-*Reiterkorps* was led by SA-*Obergruppenführer* Karl Litzmann (who in the OSAF was *Chef des Hauptamtes Reit- und Fahrausbildung*); and the German Shooting Association was presided over by SA-*Obergruppenführer* Max Jüttner (who in the OSAF was the *Chef des Führungshauptamtes*).[79] This overlap demonstrates that the SA had successfully integrated itself into those branches of German civil life that were related to its new task of overseeing the paramilitary training of German males. The process that led to this result was not a unilateral one of forced coordination but is more adequately described as the solidification of a mutual rapprochement between the NSDAP and the existing middle-class networks and associations. Without a considerable degree of self-mobilization, the process of political subordination could not have unfolded as smoothly as it did.[80]

The SA's political oversight and social infiltration of important branches of German middle-class social life had a lasting effect, even if, on the surface, the regional and local events of the German provinces continued to take place in a traditional way. The most obvious change was that some of the local dignitaries now dressed in Nazi uniforms, but they otherwise did not directly interfere in the proceedings, apart from delivering some welcoming speeches that were hardly ever popular. Yet such an assessment would underestimate the importance of the political shift that had taken place, as well as the lasting clout of NSDAP formations like the SA, whose members – in the blink of an eye – could turn from jovial club mates into watchdogs for the regime with considerable police powers.[81] What is more, the SA's quest for suzerainty would soon facilitate the use of the dense network of associations and clubs it had infiltrated for the prosecution of war.[82]

However, not all stormtroopers approved of this new course of action. For many, the long-term rationale behind the SA's new role was no substitute for the former activities that had powerfully combined political violence against ideological opponents with popular forms of male sociability. These men still wanted to be political activists, not self-satisfied Babbitts.[83] Correspondingly, in 1937 and 1938, Wilhelm Hosenfeld's comments on the SA became less enthusiastic. 'SA duty: again only few men participated. Most of them had sent excuses, but some others should have shown up. They lack the proper understanding of the SA's significance, and that will only sink in when real tasks need to be solved,' he noted in his diary on 15 April 1937.[84] Yet satisfying tasks remained few and far between. Instead, the local SA leaders met in September 1938 to discuss the exciting activity of 'collection of scrap metal'.[85] Hosenfeld himself became increasingly unsure about the SA's mission. In May 1938 he wrote disappointedly that he had just participated in an 'SA sports day' in the nearby city of Fulda, but that he had found it off-putting once again: 'More and more I realize the pointlessness [of the SA].'[86] Yet Hosenfeld remained on active SA duty until he was drafted into the Wehrmacht in 1939. For other soldiers with an SA background, active duty with the organization likewise became less important with the beginning of the war. The jurist Fritz Otto Böhmig on 6 June 1940 wrote to his wife how he imagined a weekend à deux: 'Of course, there must not be SA duty on Sunday morning [. . .] I don't want to experience how you would react if, on the first Sunday after my return, I got up at six in the morning and went to the SA!!'[87] Böhmig's words imply that he regularly participated in SA duties on weekends prior to the war. In his letter he did not exclude that his wife thought he would continue this former habit once given the opportunity. More than a year later, on 24 August 1941, Böhmig indeed wrote to her that he was preparing a letter to be sent to his former SA-*Sturm*.[88] As the war continued, Hosenfeld and Böhmig both became increasingly estranged from the SA and its ideas. The few remarks Hosenfeld made on the stormtroopers in occupied Warsaw during the war years were mostly negative. For him, this organization was now 'them', not 'us'. He also repeatedly commented on violent acts committed by SA men.[89] On the occasion of an 'SA sports competition' in Warsaw in September 1943, he informed his wife dryly: 'A lot of mumbo-jumbo, but few accomplishments. Propaganda is the main thing. It rained the whole day.'[90]

Hosenfeld's attitude was typical for many of those who had initially welcomed the SA's propaganda only to become frustrated with its development in the years after 1934. Yet there were also others for whom the SA did not decline but increased in importance in the second half of the 1930s. The stormtroopers of the latter category were often those born outside the German Reich's borders. For them, membership in the SA provided both financial and political advantages that would be realized once the German expansionist policy was implemented. In what follows I will take a closer look at the men in the so-called Austrian Legion and then turn to the newly arranged SA formations in the Sudetenland and the Memelland.

The Austrian Legion

Since the formation of the NSDAP and its SA in the early 1920s, close connections between German and Austrian National Socialists had been established and maintained.[91] Whereas in the 1920s it had usually been the stormtroopers from the Reich who had benefited from the assistance of their Austrian brothers in ideology and arms – especially after the failed Hitler Putsch of 1923, when many high-ranking National Socialists found cover and shelter in Austria – ten years later this relationship had been reversed. Now it was the SA in the German Reich that was in a position to help its Austrian comrades, particularly after the authorities in Vienna banned all National Socialist organizations, including the SA, on 19 June 1933. The Austro-Fascist regime under Engelbert Dollfuß and his successor Kurt Schuschnigg actively persecuted those National Socialists who sought an end to the Austrian nation state and a union of Austria with the Third Reich, particularly after the Austrian Hitlerists attempted to violently overthrow the national government in July 1934.[92] Despite the Austrian SA's considerable organizational weaknesses, the teacher Hermann Reschny, since 1926 the leader of the Austrian SA (*Hitlerbewegung*), made plans to march on Vienna with stormtroopers from Styria and the Reich. In June 1934 the SA leadership in Austria even decided on two hitmen for the assassination of Dollfuß, yet it was the SS man Otto Planetta who in the end carried out the actual murder.[93]

Ever since the National Socialists had taken control in Germany, the authorities in Austria had feared an SA-led military invasion by the Third Reich.[94] Concern focused in particular on the more than 14,000 Austrian political refugees in the Reich who referred to themselves as 'legionaries' or members of the Austrian Legion, which was officially part of SA-*Obergruppe* VIII (Austria).[95] According to the Austrian government, the legion possessed 1,500 motorcars and was thus able to reach the German-Austrian border within 24 hours.[96] These Austrian stormtroopers in German exile were initially concentrated in several barracks located in different places in Bavaria (Lechfeld, Bad Aibling, Reichersbeuern, Egmating, Wöllershof, and others). Later, operating under the cover name *Hilfswerk Nordwest*, they were transferred to several locations further north (among them Bocholt, Dorsten, and Lippstadt), far from the German-Austrian border. These men carried out construction work and received paramilitary training from the Reich's SA as well as from the Bavarian police and the Reichswehr. They also organized the smuggling of arms, explosives, and propaganda material into Austria, contributing to the destabilization of the political order there. As long as the SA in the Reich under Röhm continued to fight for its status as a people's militia, the Austrian Legion constituted a serious threat to Austria's sovereignty.[97]

From the perspective of the Third Reich, its considerable financial and political support for the Austrian Legion, which amounted to approximately 24 million reichsmark in 1935, had mixed success.[98] The legionaries more than once attracted negative attention from the German population because of their lack of discipline and education. In particular, their brutal anti-Catholic agitation in areas where the German population was traditionally deeply religious provoked a strong dislike. In Bad Aibling in August 1935, for example, Austrian legionaries drove through the streets of the town in lorries displaying a poster that depicted a Jesuit priest and the biblical verse 'Suffer the little children to come unto me!' The poster also contained the phrase '§ 175' in yellow type, alluding to the cliché of the homosexual child abuser in the robe of a man of God.[99] On the diplomatic level, the well-known financial support of the Reich for what was internationally perceived as state-sponsored terrorism provoked tensions with both Austria and Mussolini's Italy. Yet despite its organizational and military shortcomings, the Austrian Legion remained a political weapon for the Nazi regime up to 1938.[100]

After the SA's loss of influence following the 'Night of the Long Knives', the legionaries were ordered to deliver their weapons – more than 10,300 rifles and 340 machine guns – to the Reichswehr.[101] In Austria concern lessened to the extent that the authorities became more willing to interpret the flight of thousands of Austrian stormtroopers to the Reich not as conscious terrorist acts, but as 'pardonable sins of their youth'. From intercepted letters and other confiscated documents, the Schuschnigg administration knew only too well that the Austrian legionaries were less dangerous than initially feared, and that their military fighting power was limited at best. The authorities furthermore interpreted the substantial numbers of Nazi militants returning to Austria (more than 2,500 between July 1936 and November 1937) as a sign that many had left the country not only for reasons of political 'entrapment' (*Verhetzung*), but also out of 'youthful ignorance and a thirst for adventure'.[102] Although the Austrian Nazis increasingly benefited from sympathizers within the ranks of the Austrian bureaucracy, a certain degree of conspiracy remained necessary to organize its illegal political activities. One of the measures the stormtroopers took was to encode all phone calls that dealt with party affairs. This code relied on a simple language that named SA units according to male family roles: 'Son'was the code word for an SA-*Schar*, an 'uncle'designated an SA-*Sturm*, and 'father' meant an SA-*Standarte*. The numbers of the SA units were replaced with the names of their respective city districts. If the Nazis spoke about a 'father from Hietzing', for example, they were actually referring to the *Standarte* 4 of the SA-*Gruppe* Vienna. The SA as a whole was, interestingly, referred to as female and called 'sister'.[103]

However, when the *Anschluss*, the incorporation of Austria into the German Reich, actually took place in March 1938, the Austrian Legion did not play an important role. The decisive steps had been taken in negotiations and through diplomacy behind closed doors. The German military invasion of more than 50,000 soldiers and policemen on 12 March 1938 confirmed on the ground what had previously been achieved at the table. When the Austrian legionaries finally returned home between 30 March and 2 April 1938, they did not come as triumphant liberators but as uninvited conquerors. Their popularity in Austria in the following months was fairly limited, to say the least. Many Austrian state institutions and even bodies of the NSDAP only very reluctantly accepted the former 'legionaries' into their ranks, as the latter quickly earned a reputation for being lazy and arrogant.[104] Even the Austrian Nazis early on feared that the presence of up to 9,000 legionaries in the country would become problematic, as they might freely vent the rage they had built up over the preceding years.[105] Many of them did indeed take part in antisemitic assaults. Furthermore, ever since 1933, promises of future professional advancement, particularly in the Austrian bureaucracy, had motivated the legionaries to remain loyal to the party cause.[106] Now, in 1938, they asked and received 'compensation' to a remarkable extent, benefiting from the many 'Aryanizations' that occurred in the *Ostmark* and successfully pressuring leaders for employment. Among the tangible benefits recouped were a middle-class car (a Steyr XII), a set of furniture, and even a complete dental practice.[107] The aid rendered to former legionaries in the Austrian SA in 1938 and 1939 was so extreme that even long-time members were repelled by the ubiquitous *Freunderlwirtschaft*, the Austrian term for cronyism. Just weeks after the *Anschluss*, these members started to romanticize their previous years of illegality, with their allegedly genuine comradeship, in a process similar to that described for the Reich in 1933.[108]

The Austrian Legion officially ceased to exist on 31 October 1938, half a year after the *Anschluss*. By then, most of its former members had benefited extensively from the political sea change. Others whose demands for 'compensation' and professional advancement were not met in the following year made new attempts to capitalize on the 'Aryanization' of Jewish firms and property or to go on the prowl in the protectorate of Bohemia-Moravia.[109] Yet, in at least one respect these 'Old Fighters' ultimately had to concede defeat. In 1941 the Nazi authorities definitively refused to accept former duties in the Austrian Legion between 1933 and 1938 as an alternative form of military service.[110] The Austrian Legion had served its purpose in the days before the *Anschluss*, but the active role of the SA in the German expansion into central and eastern Europe was just about to begin.

Activities in the Sudeten and Memel Territories

The successful *Anschluss* of Austria sounded the bell for the annexation of those territories bordering the Reich where a considerable ethnic German population lived. After the internal consolidation of the Third Reich in the first years of the regime was achieved, the NSDAP attempted to fulfil a central ambition of German nationalism that went back to the mid-nineteenth century: to enlarge the Reich until all Germans living in cohesive settlements in neighbouring states could enjoy the benefits of German citizenship. Yet, unlike the vision of the nationalists of the 1848–9 revolutions, in which a democratic Germany would be so attractive that many people in central and eastern Europe would voluntarily opt to become Germans, by the mid-1930s it had become clear that such attempts would provoke fierce opposition in the neighbouring states, particularly as many of them were newcomers on the political scene that had been established in the wake of the First World War. As the decades progressed, German nationalists more and more shared the view that the *Volkstumskampf* in these regions would have to be carried out by arms more than by promises and persuasion.[111]

The Sudetenland was historically a part of Bohemia and Moravia that after the dissolution of the Habsburg monarchy in 1918 became the heartland of the newly created Czechoslovak Republic. Here, the National Socialist movement was initially closely intertwined with the diverse leagues and organizations of the German youth movement.[112] In both rhetoric and action the NSDAP paid particular attention to this densely populated border region of the Reich. From neighbouring Saxony its functionaries attempted to establish SA cells in Czechoslovakia as early as the late 1920s. German Nazi activists in the Sudetenland initially understood the HJ and the SA to be National Socialist youth organizations and compared their political activities in the region to the *bündisch* youth's *Grenzlandfahrten*, which during the years of the Weimar Republic had been organized with the aim of raising the consciousness of the Reich's youth regarding the alleged German civilizational mission in central and eastern Europe. Because Germany after the First World War was confined to 'narrow borders', these activists argued, it was the proper time to instil the nation's best with a deeply rooted feeling of obligation for the fate of ethnic German minorities in eastern Europe and to prepare them for a leading role in the pending *Volkstumskampf*.[113] A key figure in such attempts was Rudolf Schmidt, the leader of the HJ's *Grenzlandamt*, or 'Borderland Office', who frequently organized *politische Bildungsreisen*, that is, politicized educational trips, for the Sudeten German youth. The participants on such trips, which extended as far as Poland, the Baltic States, Hungary, Austria, and Romania, regularly dressed in the Nazi brown shirt or at least carried Nazi gear in their rucksacks.[114]

With the Nazi takeover of power in the Reich, the relationship between Czechs and Germans in the region became even more complicated. Despite official restraint, Nazi propaganda as well as the Reich's clandestine financial support for nationalist German organizations like Konrad Henlein's *Sudetendeutscher Heimatbund*, the predecessor of the Sudeten German Party, promoted the public expression of patriotic sentiments on both sides.[115] In 1933 and 1934 German stormtroopers from neighbouring Saxony more than once felt called upon to arrange illegal border patrol units that regularly advanced into Czechoslovakian territory, claiming that the local authorities there were trying to suppress the German 'liberation movement'. In turn, German men dressed in SA or SS uniforms increasingly ran the risk of being arrested by the Czechoslovakian police in the border regions.[116] Yet, despite passions running high on both sides, the official German policy toward the German minority in Czechoslovakia in the first years of the Third Reich was marked by prudence and restraint – at times in sharp contrast to the regional German nationalism promoted in particular by the increasingly chauvinist *Deutscher Turnverband* (German Gymnastics Association) and, from May 1938 onward, the Sudeten German *Freiwilliger Schutzdienst* (FS; literally Voluntary Protective Service), a kind of unofficial SA that was 15,000 men strong.[117]

After the successful *Anschluss* of Austria, the German nationalist community in the Sudetenland actively expected and prepared for an analogous development. The Reich's public calls for moderation contradicted its actual policies, which aimed at aggravating the ethnic conflicts in the region to the extent that a German military intervention could finally be justified. In early September 1938, German nationalists in the region engaged in a series of assaults and bomb attacks.[118] The Czechoslovakian authorities responded using the police and the judiciary. After the successful suppression of a violent Sudeten German putsch in the first half of September, tens of thousands of German nationalists fled across the border into the Reich.[119] In the Free State of Saxony alone, there existed at least nineteen different camps for Sudeten German political refugees.

On 18 September, in direct reaction to these developments, the Sudeten German Party published a proclamation that requested the formation of a Sudeten German Free Corps (*Sudetendeutsches Freikorps*), or SFK.[120] At about the same time the Saxon SA immediately launched a recruitment programme among the refugees that offered them ideological and paramilitary training in the hope of subsequently integrating them into the regular SA. On 19 September an internal report from the Saxon SA claimed that it had already registered about 5,000 Sudeten German refugees and provided them with swastika armbands and badges, insignias of the NSDAP that many men in the camps wore with 'nothing less than a touching pride'. A few days later the total number of Sudeten Germans won over to the SA had doubled. These men were to form the core of the future Sudeten SA and were divided according to their regional provenance. Yet the report warned that they were not to be used for an immediate military operation, as their equipment and weapons were 'totally insufficient'.[121] The Munich agreement of 29–30 September 1938 at least temporarily exchanged peace for land and provided the Reich with the long sought-after Sudetenland. In its wake the previously illegal paramilitary activities of the German nationalists now became state-sponsored politics. In the four weeks of its existence the Sudeten German Free Corps, with a total strength of 40,000 men, killed more than 110 people, deported about 2,000 Czechoslovakian citizens to Reich territory, and caused about 200,000 Czechs, Germans, and Jews to leave the region.[122]

After the German occupation of the Sudetenland in the first days of October 1938, regular SA formations were quickly established in the region, building on the preparatory work of the previous months (Plate 24). Many members of the FS and the Sudeten German Free Corps, which were officially dissolved on 9 October, were eager to join National Socialist organizations like the SA and the SS, to such an extent that the new SA-*Standarte* Aussig as early as December 1938 had to impose a temporary ban on new members 'for organizational reasons'.[123] To cope with the demand the OSAF sent no fewer than 600 SA leaders from the Old Reich into the region. These individuals mostly occupied central administrative positions, whereas the leadership of the SA-*Stürme* and *Standarten* was placed in the hands of stormtroopers from the Sudetenland.[124] The latter were in many cases identical to the former leaders of the *Deutscher Turnverband*.[125] During the pogrom of 9 November the newly formed SA units in the Sudetenland played roles similar to those assumed by their counterparts in other parts of the Reich, with the exception that here not only local Jews but also non-Jewish Czechoslovakians and ethnic Germans critical of the Nazis were attacked. 'First the Jews and then the Czechs!' was the SA's battle cry in the region.[126]

The leader of the Sudeten SA was the charismatic Franz May, a Catholic peasant from Warnsdorf, a rural district near to the Czechoslovakian-Saxon border. When he was appointed SA-*Gruppenführer* on 15 October 1938, May could look back at several years of political activities in support of the German 'liberation'. He had also been the leader of Group 4 of the Sudeten German Free Corps in the weeks prior to his official appointment in the SA.[127] 'May is familiar with the questions of the borderland struggle [*Grenzlandkampf*], he knows how to adequately confront upcoming dangers with his well-known energy and his clear ambitions,' Henlein stated. May would be 'one of the most reliable and genuinely popular' German leaders in his *Gau*, Henlein added in a letter to SA Chief of Staff Lutze, attempting to secure a deferment from military service for his former campaigner in November 1941.[128]

The SA's practice of imposing itself on established, traditional structures worked well in the context of Germany's territorial expansion. The continued support of the SA for nationalist Sudeten Germans over the previous years made the organization genuinely popular among the German population of the former Czechoslovakia at a time when the SA in the Old Reich was still struggling to define its future role. In January 1940 the SA-*Gruppe* Sudeten comprised slightly fewer than 129,000 men. This amounted to 4.4 per cent of the overall population of the *Gau* Sudetenland, compared to the roughly 1 per cent of the Reich population who at the same time served in the SA. This made the Sudeten SA the strongest of all SA-*Gruppen* of the time.[129]

A similar development on a much smaller scale took place in the Memelland (in Lithuanian, the *Klaipėdos kraštas*, or Klaipėda region), a small strip of land north of the German province of East Prussia. Inhabited by predominantly ethnic Germans, this province had been separated from the Reich in 1919 as part of the post-war rearrangements of central and eastern Europe.[130] In the immediate post-war years administered by the French on an interim basis, Memelland became an autonomous region of Lithuania in 1923. In the following years local political initiatives and media that advocated close cooperation with Germany were regularly suppressed.[131] With the increasingly aggressive German foreign policy between 1935 and 1938, the fate of the ethnic Germans in this border region became again an ever more pressing item on the political agenda. The Lithuanian government carefully observed the growing ambitions of the Third Reich and the intensification of calls for a 'return' of the Memelland. They feared that their region might follow the example set by the Saar region, which had been incorporated into the Reich after a referendum was held on 13 January 1935.[132] Caught between much larger and more powerful states and in particular confronted with both German and Polish territorial claims, the Lithuanian government finally agreed to back-door negotiations with Berlin. With the Munich agreement signed and the subsequent German annexation of the Sudetenland, the Lithuanian government put one and one together and introduced their own appeasement policy in order to avoid a similar fate. On 1 November 1938, Lithuania lifted the state of emergency in the Memelland and thereby allowed German nationalist organizations to again operate legally in the region.[133] Just over a month later, on 11 December, a Unified German list of candidates (*Memeldeutsche Liste*) won the provincial elections with a landslide victory of 87 per cent of the votes.[134] Six days later Hitler secretly told the leader of the German nationalists in the Memelland, Ernst Neumann, that he intended to annex the territory in the spring of 1939.[135]

Neumann, born in 1888, played a similar role in this region to that assumed by Konrad Henlein in the Sudetenland. A former *Freikorps* fighter in the Baltic area in 1919 and a veterinary surgeon by profession, Neumann had founded the Memelland Socialist People's Party (SOVOG, *Sozialistische Volksgemeinschaft des Memelgebietes e.V.*) in 1933. It was the second National Socialist party to form in a region that had hosted a secret cell of the NSDAP as early as the late 1920s.[136] These first National Socialist activists had formed the core of the Christian Socialist Party of Memelland (CSA, *Christliche Sozialistische Arbeitsgemeinschaft des Memelgebiets e.V.*), formally established in May 1933 under the leadership of a Protestant clergyman, the pastor Theodor Freiherr von Saß. However, the NSDAP in the Reich quickly came to the conclusion that a National Socialist alternative to the CSA was needed because of its members' 'pseudo-revolutionary' manners and 'overt dilettantism'.[137] Therefore, the government in Berlin backed Neumann and his counter-organization, the SOVOG. In the following years Neumann became a 'flame of hope for all who longed for an end of foreign rule', as a German expellee magazine published in the Federal Republic of Germany in 1955 put it with patriotic zeal, echoing the rhetoric of the Memelland's 'time of struggle'.[138] Such glorification built on the broad support that Neumann managed to attract among the Memel Germans in the 1930s, but it obscured other aspects of the story that proved less welcome after the war: both parties, the CSA as well as the SOVOG, were overtly antisemitic and had very close ties to the NSDAP in Germany.[139] Both quickly formed paramilitary groups consisting of young men between the ages of eighteen and twenty-six, called *Sturmkolonnen* (SK) in the case of the CSA or *Sturmabteilungen* in the case of the SOVOG. The historian Martin Broszat characterized these groups as 'something between the Hitler Youth and the SA'.[140] According to the Lithuanian authorities, both paramilitary organizations were in close contact with the SA in Germany and particularly with SA units from the neighbouring East Prussia. The SA-*Gruppe* there, SA-*Obergruppe* I, or Ostland, was estimated to comprise no fewer than eight brigades with a total of 170,000 men by the end of 1934. These brigades were financed by the Reich and armed, among other weapons, with heavy machine guns, allegedly in preparation for a German military occupation of the Memelland in the near future.[141] Based on these accusations, which were backed by a large number of police documents, the Lithuanian High Court Martial in Kowno convicted both Neumann and von Saß, together with more than 100 German nationalists, of high treason and sentenced them to lengthy prison terms in 1935.[142] As part of the above-mentioned policy of détente, Neumann was pardoned in 1938 and immediately returned to his former political activities.

Although Hitler had advised Neumann not to provoke any kind of diplomatic crisis, the latter once again started to build up SA units in late 1938. These units now officially carried the name of *Sicherheitsabteilungen*, or 'security units'. In late January 1939 they allegedly comprised twelve units consisting of a total of 2,500 men.[143] Other sources, however, claim they comprised only 500 individuals.[144] Neumann expected every Memel German over eighteen years old to join these new formations, which he defined as 'corps permeated by National Socialist spirit' and made up of active fighters for *Volk* and homeland.[145] In its final state, he proclaimed, the Memelland SA should comprise roughly 20,000 men aged between eighteen and fifty – a very high expectation, given that the region had fewer than 200,000 inhabitants.[146]

The new SA complemented the existing Memel German Security Service (*Ordnungsdienst*) that Neumann had reorganized several weeks earlier to 'protect' the integrity of the December elections. Whereas the Security Service, which was at Neumann's personal disposition, was intended as a kind of elite formation, consisting of men under thirty years of age and, according to a contemporary source, 'strictly organized in a National Socialist way', the Memel SA was apparently a less exclusive movement.[147] In the first place, its members were charged with spreading the Nazi ideology in the region.[148] Similar to the strategy adopted in 1933–4, both organizations were expected to be on hand to support Wehrmacht units in case of a military confrontation with the Lithuanian army. Erich Koch, the *Gauleiter* of East Prussia and a local rival of Neumann, even prepared to 'liberate' the Memelland with the help of these SA forces.[149] Such fights did not take place, however. On 22 March 1939, Hitler incorporated the Memel area into the German Reich after reaching a formal agreement with Lithuania. In Article 4 of this agreement both states declared that they would neither attack each other nor support a third party that attacked one of them.[150] Neumann and Koch oversaw the short

1. This photograph depicts a street in the centre of Munich in 1919, with the towers of the Frauenkirche in the background. On the left-hand side are heavily armed soldiers in a car decorated with a skull and crossbones. The original inscription on the upper left-hand side translates as 'Crushing of a pocket of Spartakists by governmental troops with machine gun.' However, looking more closely, the viewer realizes that a large female figure, the companion of the soldier on the extreme right, has been made invisible. The same has happened to a figure walking in front of her. Thus, the actual street scene photographed here was rather peaceful. The retouching served the purpose to dramatize the political situation in post-war Bavaria and justify the – at times extreme – violence employed against the far left.

2. This portrait of Ernst Röhm depicts him as a man of several worlds. It was taken in his temporary Bolivian home between 1928 and 1930. Röhm is wearing the full dress uniform of the Bolivian army, yet he also has on the medals he had received in the First World War. Behind him, one can see the flag of Bolivia and, above, the German Imperial War Flag. The framed photograph on the table to the left is probably a portrait of Rupprecht, Crown Prince of Bavaria.

3. A group photograph of 'Trupp Bötzow', later to become Berlin SA-*Sturm 2*, taken in Weimar's central market square on the occasion of the NSDAP party rally on 3–4 July 1926. The Swastika banner in front of the well-known Neptune fountain symbolizes the Nazi occupation of the city centre. Particularly noteworthy are the five girls in the first two rows. At least three of them are dressed in the brown shirt and also exhibit the party badge. Such images are extremely rare yet important. Although in their writings young male Nazi activists rarely mentioned closer contacts with girls and young women, travelling the country in the company of fellow Brownshirts was a way of making contact with the opposite sex. The young man in the third row, fourth from the left, is Horst Wessel, the later Nazi martyr; his brother Werner is in the same row, second from the left.

4. This group photograph from 1928 shows uniformed members of the SA on a farm in the surroundings of Prenzlau in Brandenburg, located some 100 kilometres north of Berlin. Some people, standing on the left, are in civilian clothing, among them a young woman. The stormtroopers are holding brooms, barrows and pitchforks in their hands, suggesting that they are helping out on the farm. However, cleanliness also mattered to them, as demonstrated by the water bowl and two towels that feature prominently in the foreground. Two uniformed Brownshirts are posing on horses. 'Work trips' to the countryside, usually on weekends, contributed to the SA's popularity in rural areas of Germany, yet they also served other purposes such as paramilitary training and propaganda marches. Especially in the eastern provinces of Germany some owners of large estates voluntarily invited SA units in on a temporary basis.

5. This photograph depicts members of the Berlin SA-*Sturm* 1 standing in front of a fruit plantation in the vicinity of the small town of Ketzin near Potsdam on 27 January 1929. According to the original caption in the photo album from which this image was reproduced, the purpose of the trip was *Landpropaganda* – 'propaganda in the countryside'. The banner on the car translates as 'Away with Dawes' (referring to the reparation regulations of the 1924 Dawes Plan), 'First bread, then reparation', and 'Read the *Angriff* [Goebbels's Berlin Nazi newspaper]'. The young boy standing on the far right is holding copies of the *Angriff* in his hands. The man in the grey coat is Horst Wessel. The poses of the young Nazi activists show determination and pride in their own propaganda 'achievements', in sharp contrast with the idyllic snow-covered and empty landscape around them.

6. Poster by Leo von Malotki from Danzig-Langfuhr (today's Polish Gdansk), printed by the publishing house A. W. Kafemann GmbH in Danzig around 1933. A multi-headed snake marked with two Stars of David, as well as the abbreviations 'SPD' (Social Democratic Party), 'KPD' (Communist Party of Germany), and 'RF' (Red Front), attacks a stormtrooper marching on the right-hand side. In the background, across the harbour basin, one sees the city of Danzig and, above, effectively a shadow of the stormtrooper, a white figure of Saint George, venerated as a 'Christian soldier'. Contemporary viewers, familiar with the idea of a German *Volkstumskampf* in eastern Europe, could not fail to get the message: the Nazis were fighting a religious and ideological war against the evils of the present, similar to the Teutonic Knights who had 'Christianized' large parts of Pomerania, Prussia and the Baltic region since the thirteenth century.

Deutschlands Autarkie

7. A propaganda image of an SA-*Sturm* marching through the streets of Berlin-Spandau in 1932. Two officers of the Prussian police guard this political demonstration. Parades and processions were common spectacles in the German capital at this time, and, consequently, only some of the many people in the streets took a closer look at the marching Brownshirts.

8. This cartoon by Erich Schilling, 'Germany's autarky', first published in the satirical weekly *Simplicissimus* in August 1932, was a sarcastic comment on the increasing hostilities and bloody run-ins on German streets at the end of the Weimar Republic. The cartoon depicts two armed Reichsbanner men on the left and two armed Brownshirts on the right, each pair ready to confront the other. The subtitle translates as 'What progress since 1914! When it comes to warfare, the Germans finally made themselves completely independent from abroad.'

9. This 1932 poster advertises the cigarette brand Trommler (Drummer), a product from the Dresden-based Sturm company that reached out to the rapidly growing number of Brownshirts as consumers. A share of the company's profits was handed over to the SA; in return, the organization requested their men smoke cigarettes made by Sturm exclusively. In doing so, the poster claimed, they were acting *Gegen Trust und Konzern* – 'Against Trust and Big Business'.

10 and 11. These two woodcuts by the Düsseldorf-based artist Richard Schwarzkopf from 1936 were part of a series of six, entitled 'The Fight of the SA: The German Passion'. The woodcuts depict the fight of the SA in the form of a *danse macabre*. Next to traditional motifs of marching Brownshirts in the woodcut 'The Victory of Faith', 'The Red Devil Rages' features the stormtrooper as a farmer and a father, alluding to the changing purpose of the SA after 1934.

12. Members of the SA block the entrance to the Ehape department store on Cologne's Bahnhofstrasse on 1 April 1933. The Ehape Einheitpreis-Handelsgesellschaft mbH was part of the department house consortium Leonhard Tietz AG that, from July 1933 onwards (and after the Tietz family was pressured to sell their shares), became known as Westdeutsche Kaufhof AG. The photograph shows at least three different reactions to the boycott. While the women pass by the SA men rather quickly, ostensibly not paying attention, two men are pictured in conversation with the Brownshirts. The man with the bicycle seems to be having a relaxed chat with the SA leader present, while the body language of the man with the hat suggests he is more critically minded.

13. This photograph depicts prisoners of the SA-run concentration camp at Oranienburg who are forced to engage in physical exercises, so-called SA sports. One SA man in the middle gives commands and demonstrates what to do, while other Brownshirts standing behind the prisoners are overseeing the correct execution of the exercises. The photograph was probably taken on behalf of the camp management in the spring or summer of 1933 as part of a series used for publications inside Germany and distributed to foreign press agencies to counter reports of torture in the early camps. Such Nazi propaganda often focused on the bodies of prisoners that were to be 'educated' and 'disciplined' through sports and hard labour, so that, ideally, the prisoners could one day return to the Nazi 'people's community' as valuable members. Propaganda images of this kind took care to present the prisoners in good health. The clearly visible SA man with the Red Cross on his armband suggests that the prisoners were well taken care of. The photograph also demonstrates that the concentration camp was located in direct proximity to family houses.

14. This photograph depicts SA guards and their prisoners from the early concentration camp at Hohnstein Castle in Saxony. This staged scene was presumably made on behalf of the stormtroopers, as a kind of trophy. The carefully written board translates as 'Labour battalion of the Preventive Detention Camp Hohnstein Castle 28 April 1933'. Two prisoners were later highlighted on the photograph with the numbers '1' and '2', yet they could not be identified.

15. After the Nazi takeover of power in 1933, many German producers attempted to benefit from the political sea change by launching products that targeted driven National Socialist consumers. This photograph from December 1933 shows a young saleswoman working for a puppet factory in Schönhauser Straße, located in central Berlin, presenting a puppet in SA uniform giving a Hitler salute. The picture suggests that a wide variety of similar figures, in SA and BDM uniforms, was available to German boys and girls for Christmas.

16. A drawing by the German student and writer Felix Hartlaub on the occasion of his time as a participant in an SA paramilitary student camp in Heidelberg during the spring of 1934. The banner in the background reads *Schlachtfest* ('Country feast with freshly slaughtered meat'). The Latin toast *Amico pectus, hosti frontem* translates as 'Friends stretch forth your heart and enemies your forehead', alluding to the traditions of German student fraternities, here intermingled with the new soldierly but equally 'wet' habits of the SA.

17. The new SA Chief of Staff, Viktor Lutze, leaves the SA offices in Berlin, Wilhelmstraße 6, on 24 July 1934, and is greeted with the Hitler salute. At the time, more than a thousand men incarcerated in the alleged Röhm purge were still held in prisons and concentration camps. Lutze repeatedly tried to restore the organization's reputation after 1934, leading the SA until his death in a car accident in 1943.

18. This photograph from 1935, made for propaganda purposes, was taken on the occasion of the second anniversary of the 'Day of Potsdam' (21 March 1933), the symbolic reunion of the National Socialist government with proponents of the conservative elites. Men of the 'SA motor unit' (SA-*Motorstaffel*) M 28 serve hot chocolate and cakes to children in the Tivoli, a club house and cinema in the working-class neighbourhood of Berlin-Moabit.

19. Members of the SA stand on lorries in preparation for a propaganda tour through the streets of Recklinghausen in the Ruhr district on Sunday, 18 August 1935. The banners translate as: 'He who knows the Jews knows the devil!' and 'The bourgeois: . . . "The economy is everything."' The poster in the middle depicts a stormtrooper using a swastika to strike two heads caricatured as Jews, who have aggressive-looking snakes emerging from them. The Jews are associated with the dangers of Communism, as the hammer and sickle next to the snakes makes plain. Such violent propaganda slogans, which blended together anti-Communist, anti-Jewish, anti-capitalist and, at times, anti-Church sentiments, were typical of the SA in the 1930s.

20. In the 1930s, the SA promoted riding as a particularly 'manly' sport that would train German men for future military operations. This photograph depicts three Brownshirts jumping off their horses at Alt-Möderitz in Mecklenburg, an exercise that was part of the obligatory 'riding test'.

21. A group photograph at a wedding in front of the restaurant Zum Erbprinzen in Inzighofen near Sigmaringen in the southern part of the Swabian Alps, taken between 1933 and 1938. The bridal couple is standing behind a flower-adorned portrait of Hitler. The groom is wearing an SA uniform, as are many of the middle-aged guests, whereas members of the older generation are in their traditional Sunday best. The young boys sitting in front are dressed in children's SA uniforms. This photograph demonstrates the Brownshirts' pride in their uniform as well as their integration within local communities.

22. A journalist bows down to capture the noise of a marching SA unit on his microphone. The photograph was taken at an SA festive parade on 15 August 1937 in Berlin. By this time, the trampling of SA boots was a well-known and recognizable symbol of the regime – deliberately recorded for use in mass media, yet feared by many ordinary Germans as a symbol of Nazi violence.

23. Photograph from the *Reichswettkämpfe der SA*, the 'SA National Sports Competitions', in the well-filled Olympiastadium Berlin on 17 July 1938. Pairs of SA men from the SA-*Gruppe* Nordsee are holding hands, balancing on the backs of their comrades. This exercise symbolized the aim of SA sports in general. It was not about individual record performances, but about collective efforts that could foster the bonds among the participants.

24. A group of SA men marching through the city of Eger, today's Cheb, in the Sudetenland, greeted by the local population with the Hitler salute. This photograph from early October 1938 was taken at the 'liberation festivities' that occurred when German troops, including SA units, took occupation of the area. In the following months, young men from the local German population flocked to the newly established SA-*Gruppe* Sudeten in high numbers.

25. In preparation for future military confrontations, SA men in full gear and wearing gas masks run through a middle-class neighbourhood in Berlin on Sunday, 2 April 1939, accompanied by an SA man on his bicycle. A few passers-by in their Sunday best are watching the scene. The numbers fixed to the men's trousers, referring to their respective SA unit, suggest that this was a kind of competition between different SA units in the capital.

26. The SA settlement scheme was limited in scale, yet rewarding for Nazi propaganda. This photograph, taken in Rosenheim-Kastenau in 1937 or 1938, depicts workers unloading a wagon of excavated soil onto a dump truck, instructed by a stormtrooper in uniform. A teenage boy is watching the scene. The banner translates as 'This company is driving gratuitously for the SA settlement'.

27. This postcard, distributed around 1940 by the Hanover-based company Graphischer Kunstverlag H. Lukow, consists of nine photographs celebrating the Nazi settlement initiatives in the city of Bad Salzgitter near the Harz Mountains. With the founding of the *Reichswerke AG für Erzbergbau und Eisenhütten 'Hermann Göring'* in 1937, the area developed into a highly industrialized part of the German Reich. The streets in the 'SA settlement' were named after 'martyrs' of the Nazi movement (Dietrich Eckart, Horst Wessel), and streets in the nearby *Fliegersiedlung* carried the name of First World War fighter pilots, such as Ernst Udet and Oswald Boelke.

28. A photograph of recruits of the SA-*Standarte* 'Feldherrnhalle', sworn in on 3 May 1941 at an unknown location.

29. On the occasion of taking office as the new Germany envoy to Croatia, SA-*Obergruppenführer* Siegfried Kasche (right, in uniform) greets the Croatian general Ivan Perčević (left, in civilian clothes) on the airfield in Agram, today's Zagreb, in April 1941.

30. During the Second World War, SA propaganda attempted to win over young men for its Feldherrnhalle division. The war transformed marching stormtroopers into a powerful tank crew, and boys into men – as suggested by this recruitment poster by Werner von Axter-Heudtlaß from October 1944.

31. Until the very end of the Second World War, the leaders of the SA not only issued morale-boosting slogans but also engaged in the practical training of the *Volkssturm* and the Hitler Youth. This photograph depicts the last Chief of Staff of the SA, Wilhelm Schepmann (far right), and the General Labour Leader, Wilhelm Decker (second from the left), inspecting an RAD (Reich Labour Service) training department for young volunteers who registered for the 'Feldherrnhalle'.

32. The mayoral election poster of the former SA-*Standartenführer* and diplomat Hans Gmelin in his home town of Tübingen in 1954. While the official slogan translates as 'Hans Gmelin the right man for Tübingen', protesters have added the note: 'When he's finally mayor / Then he can properly flaunt / With the "steel helmet" on his head / Confront all storms! Tandarady!' After a controversial yet ultimately successful campaign, Gmelin became the uncontested strongman in local politics, remaining in office for twenty years.

33. This 1957 caricature by Leo Haas, a cartoonist living in the GDR, depicts the Minister of the Interior of the Federal Republic of Germany, Gerhard Schröder, in SA uniform, 'securing the election path for the CDU', the conservative party of Chancellor Konrad Adenauer. In 1933, Schröder – then a junior lawyer in Bonn – had applied for membership in the SA. In the caricature he secures a narrow path by placing signposts next to the abysses saying 'Interdiction of democratic organizations', 'Interdiction of DFD [the East German Democratic Women's League of Germany, prohibited in the Federal Republic in 1957]', and 'Interdiction of KPD [the Communist Party of Germany, banned in West Germany in 1956]'. The caricature illustrates the popular accusation of East Germany's Socialist Unity Party (SED) that the democratic governments in the West were essentially former Nazis in disguise.

transformation period before the laws of the Reich came into effect in the Memelland on 1 May 1939. At that time the former *Sicherheitsabteilungen* were immediately incorporated into the regular SA-*Gruppe* Ostland, while the SS took over the former Security Service.[151]

The Rise of the Periphery

This chapter has demonstrated that the SA between 1934 and the beginning of the Second World War underwent a difficult and often painful process of internal reform and search for new meaning. As previous studies have rightly emphasized, more than 50 per cent of all members of the SA in early 1934 left its ranks in the following years. These decisions to drop out reflected the decline in status and importance of the SA that occurred once its political adversaries had been defeated, but they were also a consequence of the fall in unemployment figures and the improvement in young men's chances to marry and have a family. Yet this development was only one side of the coin. Even at a time when the SA in the Old Reich was struggling to keep its men involved, more than one million German men remained loyal to the SA and its political programme. Throughout the 1930s antisemitic assaults were a regular field of SA activity. Such attacks allowed for community formation through jointly committed violence and as such continued a practice of association well established during the *Kampfzeit*. At the same time, the decreasing legal protections for the Jews in Germany and later also in the Greater German Reich allowed the stormtroopers to line their own pockets with pilfered spoils. In this respect the SA men were indeed forerunners, pioneering what during the deportations and murder of the European Jewry became a common practice in Germany and beyond.[152]

By 1937–8 the internal disciplinary procedures came to an end and the SA's reorganization had largely been completed.[153] It now successfully started to penetrate many realms of German civil life, as this chapter has demonstrated with regard to the German shooting associations and riding clubs. The party functionary who dressed in his brown shirt only one or two days a week while pursuing a regular profession and acting as a family man more and more replaced the activist *Gewaltmensch* devoid of competing group affiliations that was so characteristic of the rank and file of the SA until 1934. Yet even these more respectable stormtroopers remained men with

Aktionsmacht, self-empowered guardians of Nazi values who temporarily exercised auxiliary police roles. By the late 1930s observers had perceived a new level of discipline and commitment within the SA.[154] What boosted the OSAF's morale most decisively was the success of its renewed paramilitary activities in the border regions of the Reich and, later, in the incorporated territories. In both the Sudetenland and the Memelland – regions with considerable German populations administered by Czechoslovakia and Lithuania, respectively – regional nationalist paramilitary organizations of ethnic Germans were successfully integrated into the SA once the political situation allowed. In contrast to the situation in the German heartlands, where the prestige and strike capacity of the SA had suffered after 1934, the new SA units proved attractive to many, not least because they provided a relatively uncomplicated way of proving one's loyalty to the new state without giving up one's integration into existing social networks. As in central Europe after the First World War more generally, the borderlands proved a fruitful recruiting ground for paramilitary organizations with a nationalist agenda. What is more, in these regions the regime valued the paramilitary tasks the SA was still able to perform.

In the following years, the OSAF more and more capitalized on its experiences of 1938–9. It continued to establish new SA units in central and eastern Europe that recruited heavily from among the *Volksdeutsche* and that fulfilled ever more military and police functions. In addition, it also developed far-reaching plans for the time that German domination in Europe would be established and secured by military force. The leadership of the SA realized that not only the future of the Reich but also the future of the Brownshirts was to be decided in the east.

STREETFIGHTERS INTO FARMERS?

The SA and the 'Germanization' of the European East

No domain is by nature better suited to turn into a stomping ground for romantic fantasies than the settlement.

— Report of the Social Democratic Party in exile, 1935[1]

Important research on the *Generalplan Ost*, literally the 'General Settlement Plan East', has been undertaken in the last decades. Likewise, the German expansionist policies in central and eastern Europe in the late nineteenth and early twentieth centuries, as well as their academic and intellectual forerunners, have been analysed in detail.[2] The stormtroopers, however, have seldom been examined in this context, although the SA in the years following the 'Röhm purge' not only helped stabilize the Nazi regime within the boundaries of the Reich but also contributed importantly to the furtherance of German expansionist policies from 1935 onward. During these years it was the general goal of the NSDAP to win over those Germans living abroad and, after the incorporation and annexation of the borderland territories they partly inhabited, to make them a genuine part of the nation. In this respect the semantic shift is telling. Whereas Germans abroad were until the early twentieth century called *Auslandsdeutsche*, literally 'Germans living in foreign countries', the Nazis during the 1930s began to refer to them as *Volksdeutsche*, or 'ethnic Germans'.[3] The SA felt called to actively engage in this process of 'Germanization', not least because it afforded an opportunity to regain lost power within the patchwork of competing National Socialist organizations. The stormtroopers thus put forward their own ideas for the 'Germanization' of the European east, including stimulating the settlement of SA men from the Old Reich in the newly occupied and annexed territories, particularly the Warthegau and the General Government, and establishing new SA units there that predominantly comprised 'ethnic Germans'.

The following chapter is divided into four parts. In the first part, I will take a closer look at the SA's contributions to the settlement movement of the 1930s, which was originally concerned with the construction of new villages and city districts for the party faithful and the transfer of the population of the German Reich within its existing borders to stimulate agriculture and the economy in disadvantaged regions, particularly those of the northern and eastern provinces.[4] In the second part, I will concentrate on the work of the so-called *Beauftragter des Stabschefs für Neubauernsiedlung und Volkstumsfragen*, literally the 'Commissioner of the (SA) Chief of Staff for the Placement of New Farmers and for Matters of Ethnicity', between 1938 and 1943. The results of these efforts and the SA's ultimate failure will be critically assessed in the third section. In the final part, I will discuss my findings with reference to the current state of research on the German settlement policies shortly before and during the Second World War. Although the SA's initial ambitions for its 'Germanization' policies failed, largely because of the power of Himmler's SS and the shortage of qualified SA men, it nevertheless contributed in important ways to the ideological and pragmatic formation of a *Volksgemeinschaft* at war.

Early Settlement Initiatives

It was no coincidence that the SA's interest in the German settlement movement intensified in the mid-1930s, shortly after the 'Night of the Long Knives'. In its attempts to open up new fields of action that would keep the stormtroopers busy and help its leadership corps claim important positions in the consolidated Third Reich, the SA started to get involved in the settlement movement. As early as June 1933 the Nazi government had declared resettlement a national priority in its 'Law on the New Formation of German Peasantry'.[5] Already in the late 1920s the NSDAP and its auxiliary organizations – most prominently the SA – had systematically reached out to the people of rural Germany in an attempt to exploit this population's high level of discontent related to the 'agrarian crisis' that had increased migration to the cities. The NSDAP in many parts of Germany successfully exploited this high level of discontent and presented itself as the political party determined to preserve the habits and values of the German provinces, which they glorified as the 'bloodspring of the German people' (*Blutquelle des deutschen Volkes*).[6]

Initially, the involvement of the SA in the settlement movement was limited to attempts at population transfer within the German Reich. For example, it encouraged rank-and-file stormtroopers from Lower Saxony to move as so-called 'West-East settlers' to more thinly populated areas in Mecklenburg and Pomerania.[7] However, it did not take long for the SA to expand the scope of its efforts and to develop settlement plans for the soon-to-be occupied and incorporated territories beyond the actual borders.[8] Beginning in 1937 at least one large SA settlement project was initiated in every territory in which the organization was present. Financed in part by the so-called *Dankopfer der Nation*, an annual national collection organized by the SA on the occasion of Hitler's birthday, such settlements were designed to help deserving SA men, disabled ex-servicemen, and large families live on their 'own soil'.[9] The Supreme SA Command (OSAF) supported these SA settlements with the relatively meagre amount of 225,000 reichsmark.

Widely varying in size, these settlements were located in Osterholz near Bremen, in the Pfalzdorf swamp, and in nearby Petkum, close to the East Frisian city of Aurich. Other SA settlements were built in the north of Braunschweig, in Wittstock/Neumark, in the Bavarian city of Rosenheim (Plate 26), in Jena in Thuringia, and in the Upper-Silesian Eichenkamp near Gleiwitz, today's Gliwice.[10] The latter settlement, later re-baptized the *SA-Dankopfersiedlung Glaubenstatt*, or 'Place of Faith', became the SA's model settlement, built partly for the purpose of creating a '*völkisch* dam' to hold back the 'Polish appetite for expansionism', at least symbolically. Although the outbreak of the Second World War prevented the original plans from being fully realized, most buildings of this settlement, which was to provide a home for up to 2,000 people, could be completed.

Glaubenstatt had two centres: the stadium with a tower that was to serve as a youth hostel, and a market square that was surrounded by an assembly hall, a school building, and a home for the Hitler Youth. Yet there was also a shooting range and an air-raid shelter. A track-and-field arena for paramilitary sports was planned, but never completed.[11] The conception of the Glaubenstatt complex exemplarily demonstrates that the SA's 'Germanization' policies have to be seen in the context of its pre-military training of German males, to be carried out in close cooperation with the Wehrmacht and the Hitler Youth. This paramilitary education comprised both practical exercises with physical training and shooting lessons, but also 'political education' (*politische Erziehungsarbeit*).[12] It did not only target men in the Old Reich, whom Nazi propaganda continuously exposed to the idea that racially homogeneous settlements had to be regarded as 'prerequisite for the fulfilment of the regime's economical, domestic and racial objectives',[13] but would later also reach out to ethnic Germans organized within the SA in the occupied territories.

Regional plans from 1937 aimed at the construction of no more than 2,500 settlement plots nationwide, most of which were intended to contain small single-family homes.[14] Every house was expected to comprise three or four rooms, covering at least 60 square metres, to be complemented by a garden of 1,000–1,500 square metres intended mainly for the cultivation of vegetables and the breeding of small domestic animals. Unlike Glaubensstatt, which was built on former woodland, most of these modest settlements were so-called *Stadtrandsiedlungen*, or 'suburban settlements', located close to existing developments. Their parcels of land were much too small to allow for self-dependent agriculture.[15]

According to a regulation from 1934, only male candidates who were either married or engaged and possessed the 'necessary good hereditary factors' were to be considered for such settlement colonies. When the authorities realized that the comparatively small size of the houses did not correspond with the regime's emphasis on sexual reproduction, it slightly increased the housing space so that families with many children could also be accommodated.[16] Overall, the authorities imagined society in these settlements as competitive, racially pure, and devoted to the Nazi project. However, contrary to the loud rhetoric of 'building a people's community', they deliberately fostered social inequalities, granting settlers different amounts of land. The rationale for this unequal treatment was that it would intensify the competition among the new settlers and would help develop political and economic leadership.[17] The NSDAP pointed to its settlement projects as proof that the party kept its social promises. In reality, however, the number of 2,500 SA settlement holdings was small compared to the overall 22,000 holdings established between 1933 and 1939, and even more so compared to the 57,457 holdings created during the years of the Weimar Republic, of which 7,500 lay east of the River Elbe.[18]

Despite the limited extent of the Nazis' 'internal colonization' efforts, they quickly became viewed as a preliminary stage for much more ambitious colonization projects abroad.[19] In contrast to the social realities of life in the Third Reich, particularly the widening gap between the incomes of farmers and industrial workers and the subsequent decline in the popularity of agricultural labour,[20] the official discourse on settlements was one of blood and soil. According to Nazi propaganda, it was the SA, together with the *Reichsnährstand*, the statutory corporation of farmers in the Third Reich, that would stop rural flight and preserve the peasantry. Because of their willingness, ideological training, and combat strength, the SA men were supposedly ideally suited to serve as 'innovators of the German peasantry'. Already early in the Third Reich the regime regarded the population transfer of loyal party Activists as one tool to achieve a politically coherent national community. Even if this population transfer was initially limited to Germans in the Old Reich and only put into practice on a modest scale, it demonstrated that the ideology of creating and reorganizing existing *Lebensraum*, or 'space to live', long before the beginning of the Second World War, informed the course of Nazi politics. What Nazi propagandists usually did not openly address was that German agriculture suffered from severe lack of a workforce in the late 1930s. The often poorly qualified SA men were therefore talked into farming jobs also for purely practical reasons.[21] Instead, high-ranking Nazi officials like the Reich Minister of Food and Agriculture, Richard Walther Darré, emphasized in a guest article for the magazine *Der SA-Führer* in 1938 that the peasantry and (political) soldiers were expected to join hands in the 'Germanic-Teutonic people's struggle for survival'.[22]

Such statements did not only constitute a remarkable departure from the common image of the SA man as urban street fighter, an image still omnipresent in the Nazi propaganda during these years. Whereas the quintessential stormtrooper of the *Kampfzeit* had been an aggressive and determined young man and 'comrade',[23] disciplined at the party's command but more than willing to react with his fists at all provocations when let loose, the 'SA peasant' was presented as a man in his prime, still physically strong, but in the first place a responsible family man and as such a defender of the German race. The former hotheads of the urban jungle had matured into hardworking and self-reliant individuals, exemplary German men who valued and cultivated the German soil, held firm to the regime's values and ideas, and were at the same time actively involved in fighting what the Nazis perceived as white-collar effeminacy.

This new rhetoric also built on the idea that fascinated at least parts of the Supreme SA High Command from 1936: reintroducing the SA back into the political game by promoting the settlement of individual SA men as farmers and agricultural labourers in the European east, perceived as *Lebensraum* for battle-tested National Socialists. Historical research so far has stressed that the internal colonization movement in Nazi Germany lost its importance with the establishment of the Wehrmacht in 1935, which called not farmers but soldiers to protect the German borders.[24] However, I will demonstrate that these early National Socialist settlement plans remained politically important throughout the second half of the 1930s as a preliminary stage in the redevelopment of the soon-to-be captured *Lebensraum*. A closer look at the plans of the Commissioner of the SA Chief of Staff for the Placement of New Farmers and his successors between 1938 and 1943 will make this plain.

Siegfried Kasche and the SA's Intensified Settlement Plans

The man of central importance to the SA's 'Germanization' plans during this period was SA-*Obergruppenführer* Siegfried Kasche.[25] Born on 18 June 1903, he belonged to the so-called 'war youth generation', like so many committed Nazi activists. He received his training at the prestigious cadet school in Berlin-Lichterfelde during the First World War and while still a very young man fought with *Freikorps* units in Berlin and the Baltic region. In the early 1920s, Kasche joined a 'Joint Work Service' (*Arbeitsgemeinschaftsdienst*) in Pomerania and later also worked in the banking sector, the glass industry, and the textile trade. He became a member of the NSDAP in 1926 and began what was to be a stellar career in the SA. In 1928, at the age of only twenty-five, he was appointed to the position of deputy *Gauleiter* of the Ostmark, based in Frankfurt/Oder. Two years later he won a seat in the Reichstag. Kasche narrowly survived the 'Night of the Long Knives' in 1934 and was promoted to SA-*Gruppenführer* in Lower Saxony on 9 November 1936. One year later, SA Chief of Staff Victor Lutze appointed him leader of the SA-*Gruppe* Hansa, headquartered in Hamburg. Finally, as SA-*Obergruppenführer*, Kasche became the first German envoy to Agram/Zagreb in Croatia on 17 April 1941.[26]

According to his own account, Kasche and Darré began talks about possible farming settlements as early as 1936. Two years later, in September 1938, an agreement between the SA, the *Reichsernährungsministerium*, and the *Reichsnährstand* was reached,[27] and Lutze officially appointed Kasche to the position of 'Commissioner of the SA Chief of Staff for the Placement of New Farmers and for Matters of Ethnicity'. In this role Kasche replaced SA-*Gruppenführer* Georg Mappes, who as SA-*Reichskassenverwalter*, or SA Reich Treasurer, had been responsible for the organization's settlement affairs.[28] The new commissioner took his new task very seriously, as several lengthy and detailed guidelines and reports penned by Kasche make clear. The first of these important documents was the 'Guidelines for the SA's Participation in the New Formation of the German Peasantry' from 8 September 1938. This document specified that farmers selected for the new settlements in the Third Reich, to be located largely in Silesia, Pomerania, and in the eastern parts of Prussia, should be chosen according to both their qualifications and their 'hereditary value' (*blutsmäßigem Wert*). It is important to emphasize, however, that these guidelines were still intended to apply exclusively to settlements within the existing borders of the Reich. The SA was expected to furnish up to 30 per cent of all new peasant settlers in order to guarantee the 'political-ideological firmness' of the new rural communities. Kasche requested that the sixteen existing SA groups in the Reich maintain close contact with the 'settlement agencies' (*Siedlungsunternehmen*) operating in their respective regions and identify potential settlers from within their ranks. The groups were asked to keep lists in special 'red books' of all those interested in the settlement project.[29] However, only those SA men who possessed the *Neubauernschein*, a certificate from the *Reichsnährstand* attesting to the potential settler's (and his family's) racial, mental, and physiological qualities, could be considered for participation in the settlements. Only men who were at least twenty-five years of age, married, and of 'Aryan descent' were permitted to apply.[30] Once these criteria had been met, the SA-*Standarten* in charge were ordered to provide a judgement on the applicant based on his service in the SA, his personal and professional circumstances, and his physical fitness, character, and intellectual capacities and accomplishments. In the end, an overall mark was attributed to each candidate, ranging from grade one ('very well suited for placement') to grade four ('poorly qualified').[31] Surviving lists of applicants from the year 1941 show that only rarely was a very good mark given. Most applicants were ranked as group two ('well suited') or three ('suited'). For the acquisition of a new farm, Kasche estimated that an SA settler would need about 9,000 reichsmark, with more than half of that money financed by the *Dankopfer der Nation*.[32]

In the tradition of the modern Prussian borderland settlements established since the beginning of the second half of the nineteenth century, such settlements were planned as German bulwarks against the neighbouring Slavic peoples, whom many German *Grenzland* ideologues perceived as being at a lower level of cultural development.[33] Shortly before the German attack on Poland in 1939, SA-*Oberführer* Udo von Alvensleben, who dealt with settlement questions for the OSAF on Kasche's behalf, claimed that a 'peasantry on guard' (*wehrhaftes Bauerntum*) had been responsible for securing German influence over eastern Europe ever since the military conquests of the Teutonic Knights in the Middle Ages. Accordingly, he concluded: 'What we have won by the sword needs to be defended and secured by the plough.'[34] Such arguments were by no means an invention of the National Socialists. As the historian Christoph Dieckmann has demonstrated, expansionist German plans developed during the First World War had called for the expulsion of the Polish, Russian, and Jewish populations from Lithuania and demanded the establishment of German *Wehrbauern*, groups of peasants who would serve as a defensive bulwark, throughout the Baltic states.[35] For German experts in spatial planning, eastern Europe during the First World War served as an experimental arena in which they could test their increasingly radical settlement plans and colonial fantasies. Two decades later, National Socialist politicians and experts happily built on such exploratory work.[36]

However, the SA settlement plans from 1938 also contained a disciplinary component that was supposed to have an internal effect on the local populations in these new settlements. The high proportion of SA men among the new settlers was intended to ensure political homogeneity and guarantee the preeminence of the NSDAP and its ideology within these new settlements. The active recruitment of stormtroopers to settle in the border regions of the Reich began with a number of talks that Kasche and his contributors delivered to SA leaders in March 1939. These efforts culminated in a four-day-long work session in Berlin and Frankfurt/Oder and a field trip to the Upper Silesian village of Schlochau in early May. In addition to representatives of the SA High Command, participants included the regional representatives of the 'peasantry settlements' (*Neubauernsiedlung*) of every SA group.[37]

The SA settlement initiatives enjoyed a new lease of life with the Wehrmacht's military victory over Poland in the autumn of 1939, even if the recruitment of settlers suffered from the fact that many of the previous SA recruiters had been drafted into the military. Despite such practical difficulties, Kasche regarded the war as an opportunity to expand the SA settlement plans eastward. As early as 8 November 1938 he informed Lutze and SA leaders in a confidential letter that the placement of new SA farmers had gained greater importance because of the newly acquired territories. In defiance of the appointment of Heinrich Himmler as 'Reich Commissioner for the Strengthening of Germandom' on 7 October 1939,[38] Kasche insisted that an 'extensive involvement' by the SA in the 'Germanization' project continued to be highly desirable. Therefore, he urged his fellow SA leaders to identify even more potential farmers from the ranks of the SA with the aim of placing them in these new territories, despite 'all possible inhibitions and ties to their homelands'.[39]

A circular from 8 December 1939 specified the next steps in the settlement initiative, indicating that the new SA settlements should initially be concentrated in those areas of Upper Silesia that had been integrated into the German *Gau* Silesia. In cooperation with the governor of Silesia and the *Schlesische Landgesellschaft* based in Breslau, farmland in the annexed parts of Upper Silesia was released for 'immediate settlement'.[40] Previously Polish-owned farms, usually about 20 acres in size, were to be expropriated. Several of these small Polish estates could then be merged to create between 3,000 and 4,000 larger farms of at least 80 acres. If these figures were correct, this means that the number of farms in the previously Polish parts of Upper Silesia that the Germans seized after their military victory was approximately 15,000. In contrast to the course taken in 1938, the SA leadership now informed potential settlers that personal capital was no longer needed for the move eastward: 'The farms will be handed over with inventory.' However, a two-year-long probationary period during which the new German peasant had to demonstrate his ability to run such a farm was to precede the final transfer of ownership.[41] As the majority of stormtroopers had by this time been drafted into the Wehrmacht, the SA leadership repeatedly stressed that the men who had taken up arms would in no way suffer a disadvantage in the settlement process because of their inability to obtain a placement immediately. The Polish settlement area, they reminded the men, was large enough to host all aspirants, during and after the war.[42]

Despite such assurances, isolated farmers from the ranks of the SA at the beginning of the war began to contact the *Reichsnährstand* directly to be considered as administrators of former Polish estates. That these individuals initially bypassed the SA frustrated Kasche, and he warned his fellow stormtroopers that this had to be taken as proof of the SA's organizational weakness.[43] Nevertheless, such problems continued. Two years later, in 1941, Kasche claimed to have contacted the *Hauptamt Volksdeutsche Mittelstelle*, literally the 'Main Welfare Office for Ethnic Germans', to ensure that the approximately 700 SA men working for this organization were being cared for. In the previous two years the OSAF had no direct influence on these stormtroopers.[44] Despite these shortcomings, the surviving archival documents demonstrate that the SA persistently tried to secure a decisive influence over settlement matters, not least to create a reliable power base for the organization's future growth.[45] This became all the more important as the build-up of regular SA units in the newly occupied territories beginning in the autumn of 1939 took place in a limited way. The new SA units were initially not incorporated into the Reich SA; furthermore, the OSAF did not supply those SA groups bordering these new regions, in other words the SA-*Gruppen* Ostmark, Ostland, Silesia, and Sudeten, with additional financial means in order to expand their areas of operation.[46]

In practical terms, the SA intended that at least 5,000 new SA settlers would be ready to move into the settlements at the end of the war. The candidates were to be selected according to political and racial criteria established by a joint effort of the SA with Darré's *Reichsnährstand*, and they were to be educated in three specially designed SA settlement schools (*Siedlerschulen*) located on SA estates that were to be established within the 'incorporated Eastern territories'.[47] In 1941, Kasche claimed that he had met with Himmler and his representatives several times to discuss the necessary transfer of ownership of suitable estates. He also asserted that he had held talks with the office of the *Generalverwalter für die öffentliche Landbewirtschaftung in den eingegliederten Ostgebieten*, literally the 'General Authority for Public Land Management within the Incorporated Eastern Territories', located in Litzmannstadt (*Łódź*).[48] The provisional outcome of these talks, Kasche noted, was an agreement that the SA would receive a fifteen-year lease on the 'Estate Krośniewice' at the end of the war. *Gauleiter*

Arthur Greiser had made this decision by the summer of 1940 or even earlier, but he had informed the SA that the final transfer of property into the hands of the NSDAP could only happen after the war, allegedly for legal reasons.[49] Located near the city of Kutno in the *Reichsgau* Wartheland, some 100 kilometres west of Warsaw, Krośniewice had previously been owned by a Polish noble family. With the transfer of the estate, the SA would also become the proprietor of Błonie Castle, built on its grounds.[50] Kasche at this time also demonstrated considerable interest in the *Gut Freihufen*, a county estate of considerable size in the rural district of Rawitsch/Rawicz.[51]

Plans for the new SA training schools to be established stated that the SA was to offer two-week-long courses for new settlers and SA leaders that aimed to 'prepare them for their particular ethnic tasks [*volkspolitische Aufgaben*]': 'To fight foreign and inferior influences, we have to inculcate every fellow German with the awareness of his hereditary value [*stolzes Blutbewußtsein*] [...] Even the individual man needs to know that this is not his private affair, but a matter that concerns the vital question of his people's survival. The SA is requested to attach absolute importance to the observation of such issues.' In this way the SA farmers in the new settlements were conceived not only as exemplary cultivators of land, but also as a kind of vice squad for the regime.[52]

Despite Kasche's repeated orders that the new SA peasants contribute to the historical task of 'making the regained territories German again for all time',[53] the actual number of men willing to leave the German heartland for newly acquired territory in the European east was most disappointing. In contrast to the estimated number of 50,000 SA men from the rank and file who had the practical experience necessary for farming, only a mere 1,045 men had signed up for the settlement project by the deadline of 20 June 1940.[54] Admittedly, this number had doubled to 2,150 by 30 April 1941, but this figure still remained far below the expectations of the SA leadership.[55] Kasche, however, attributed this low number exclusively to practical, war-related problems. In 1941 he was still claiming that the SA would easily furnish the 45,000 men needed for settlement – without drawing on the repatriated ethnic Germans, who had been moving to Reich territory in large numbers since the beginning of the war.[56] This remark was a swipe at Himmler, for whom Kasche had maintained a firm distaste ever since the 'Night of the Long Knives'. Himmler likewise disliked his rival. The two men's relationship remained poor even after Kasche was appointed German envoy to Croatia and left the field of 'applied' SA settlement policies.[57]

A closer examination of the geographical distribution of potential SA settlers, as determined from Kasche's report and several monthly registers from the second half of 1941, indicates that the vast majority of those interested in such a transfer lived in the north and east of the German Reich, in borderland regions where the idea of a 'defensive peasantry' built on a tradition going back to the nineteenth century and even further. The Pomeranian and Silesian SA groups had the most success with recruiting, producing more than 300 candidates for relocation each, followed by the SA *Gruppe* Nordmark (from Schleswig-Holstein), with 240 candidates. The SA groups from Hesse, Bayerische Ostmark, and Alpenland, by contrast, produced only twelve, seven, and three candidates respectively.[58] When faced with these numbers, it is hard not to qualify Kasche's assertive remarks as a calculated optimism that was out of touch with the realities of German society at war.

Despite the practical problems of recruitment and Kasche's over-emphasis on his own achievements, his reports demonstrate that the SA continued to pursue its own 'Germanization' policies. The SA Supreme Command intensified its settlement planning with the outbreak of the Second World War, despite Hitler's appointment of Himmler as 'Reich Commissioner for the Strengthening of Germandom' in October 1939. The Führer's decree explicitly stated that the new Reich Commissioner would be responsible for the 'configuration of new German settlement zones by relocation, in particular through the settlement of Germans and ethnic Germans returning home from abroad'.[59] Theoretically, the responsibility for carrying out the 'Germanization' policies was thus divided. While the SS was responsible for the settlement of Germans 'returning home',[60] the SA could claim that it was entitled to take care of the resettlement of German peasants originating from the Old Reich. As late as January 1941, Kasche insisted on this division of responsibilities between the SA and SS. He stated not only that stormtroopers would not be employed in settlements 'where the SS is providing the National Socialist core', but also pointed out that 'it needs to be emphasized that the safeguarding of the German east depends on the German peasant taking roots with the soil by the work of his own hands. A German master class [*Herrenschicht* – here Kasche critically alludes to the tradition of the influential Prussian *Junkers*] overseeing soil-rooted masses of foreign peoples would not accomplish the task.'[61] Such a distinction eluci-dates how in the SA older ideals of *Werkstolz* – the pride in work from one's own hands – were closely related to new geopolitical concepts of racial and cultural superiority. The new German master class was to be a class of nationally conscious (male) workers, Kasche postulated, and it would be characterized, as Ernst Jünger had written as early as 1932, by voluntary discipline, the contempt for pleasure, and a war-minded spirit.[62]

However, Himmler, who while studying plans for the creation of a Greater Germany in 1936 had taken a deep interest in questions of ethnicity and race, became with his appointment in 1939 a direct rival of Kasche and Darré.[63] The powers wielded by these men were extremely unevenly distrib-uted. By 1939, Himmler, as *Reichsführer*-SS and chief of the German police forces, had ascended to one of the most powerful positions in the Third Reich. His standing among the Nazi leaders had been further increased by the myriad crimes his SS had committed in the wake of the German attack on Poland.[64] Kasche, on the contrary, could only count on the considerably weaker SA, the *Reichsnährstand*, and a few supportive influential National Socialists like Reich Minister Alfred Rosenberg and Martin Luther of the Foreign Office.[65] Kasche certainly lacked the power to challenge Himmler when it came to the implementation of their competing political ideas. For example, when Himmler advocated the creation of larger farms and country estates in the occupied east for German families of particular racial value – a plan directly opposed to Kasche's more egalitarian vision – the only thing the SA-*Obergruppenführer* could do was to insist that some of these new large landowners be recruited from the ranks of the SA.[66] This is just one example of Himmler's successful marginalization of the SA in the field of 'Germanization' policies between late 1939 and early 1941. Besides the SA's internal problems of recruitment, this diminished role was another important reason why its settlement plans drafted in 1938 and during the early months of the war could not be carried out. Instead, the SA's planning concentrated more and more on the immediate post-war period, leaving questions about the actual distribution of powers open.[67]

After Kasche took over the position of German envoy to the Independent State of Croatia (NDH) in April 1941, Lutze did not appoint a formal successor for nearly a year, indirectly admitting defeat in the trial of strength with Himmler. Finally, in February 1942, SA-*Obergruppenführer* Max

Luyken was appointed *Inspekteur für Neubauerntum und Volkstumspflege in der SA und den SA-Wehrmannschaften*, literally the 'Chief of Staff for New Peasant Settlements and for Matters of Ethnicity in the SA and the SA-*Wehrmannschaften*'. Unlike the young and energetic Kasche, Luyken, who was aged fifty-six in early 1942, was an SA bureaucrat who felt no need to confront Himmler.[68] At this time the SA gave up any direct involvement in the settlement project besides keeping records of potential settlers from its ranks. In the spring of 1942, just weeks after Luyken's appointment, a propaganda article published in the monthly *SA in Feldgrau* informed readers interested in participating in the settlement project of the necessary qualifications and application procedure for the *Neubauernschein*. The regulations governing qualifications implemented under Kasche in 1938 remained in place, but the only institution from now on directly involved in the application procedure was the *Landesbauernschaft*, the regional dependence of the *Reichsnährstand*, which handled the paperwork, organized medical examinations of an applicant and his wife, checked their pedigree papers, and obtained information on them from local party chapters and the police. The *Landesbauernschaft* was even urged to undertake an unannounced visit to the applicant's home. The SA as an organization was not mentioned once in the outline of these procedures; its judgement on an applicant's political suitability and commitment to the regime was apparently no longer needed.[69]

Nevertheless, the SA continued its settlement propaganda and the registration of potential SA farmers until early 1943, with the number of candidates rising from 1,196 on 1 April 1942 to 2,555 on 1 January 1943. In the remaining archival documents no explanation is given for why Luyken's tenure started with slightly more than 1,000 enrollees, whereas Kasche had specified 2,150 as the overall number of applicants on 30 April 1941. It is likely that some of the original applicants were placed successfully in the interim, while others died on the battlefields between 1939 and 1942. Luyken's new number comprised all possible settlers, both those who were interested in a transfer within the boundaries of the Old Reich and those who longed to be placed in the new 'German east'. The latter group comprised 1,304 individuals, or 51 per cent of all those registered on 1 January 1943.[70]

These numbers, at least from Luyken's perspective, reflected the intensified propaganda campaigns that the SA organized in close collaboration with the *Reichsnährstand* during 1942 and that were intended to whet the

Germans' appetite for farming and rural life. Informational events were organized around topics such as 'SA settlers tell about their lives', 'SA comradeship in the settlements: help from the neighbours', and, adopting the vocabulary of the life-reform movement, 'The happiness of our children: breathing freely and growing up in close touch with nature.'[71] By this point a few settlers had already made their way from the ranks of the SA into an eastern European farmhouse. However, in August of the same year Lutze prohibited all future transfers of new farmers from the Old Reich into the 'German east'. Only war veterans and ethnic Germans from abroad were to be settled there for the remainder of the war years.[72]

According to an internal statistic from January 1943, the SA had transferred only a total of 422 registered applicants to the settlements. It is not clear whether this number designated all stormtroopers sent between 1939 and late 1942 or only those resettled since Luyken took office, and whether it comprised internal migration settlements or only those in the new German territories. But even with no reliable statistics at hand, it seems likely that the total number of SA peasants settled in the east did not exceed a number of three digits. Finally, on 16 February 1943, two weeks after Germany's defeat at the Battle of Stalingrad, Lutze eliminated Luyken's post without providing a substitute.[73]

Peasants and Ideologues

Despite all ideological and practical difficulties, the SA's relevance for the Nazi settlement policies was not peripheral, mainly for two reasons. First, even after Kasche had reported for duty as the envoy to Croatia, he was still Hitler's first choice for the new position of 'Reich Commissar for Moscovy', a position that was expected to be created after the (allegedly imminent) German victory over the Soviet Union.[74] Alfred Rosenberg, as Reich Minster for the Occupied Eastern Territories, requested an absolutely 'ruthless personality' for this job – and he recommended Kasche.[75] In this capacity Kasche's main task would initially have been to sharply suppress all possible forms of Communist resistance. Provided that the Wehrmacht had successfully defeated and occupied the Soviet Union, Kasche as the SA's expert on questions of settlements and ethnicity would then have played an active and influential role in carrying out the Reich's 'Germanization' policies in eastern Europe, and maybe even beyond.[76]

Kasche's ambitions, in any case, remained visionary. As late as June 1941 the Hamburg professor of education Gustaf Deuchler, a fanatical storm-trooper himself, produced at Kasche's request a draft report on the 'necessity and the tasks of an SA colonial storm, or '*K-Sturm*'.[77] According to Deuchler, the SA '*K-Sturm*' would bring together older Germans with colonial experience in Africa and a new generation of Brownshirts who aspired to 'go into the colonies'. The older members of the *K-Sturm* would provide these younger men with the 'spirit of German colonial policies', a political attitude that, according to Deuchler, would be required for 'proper judgement in colonial affairs' and the development of 'some basic skills in the treatment of the natives [*Eingeborene*]'.[78] This draft never achieved any political significance, not least because of Kasche's new position as German envoy to Croatia. Yet even as late as 1944, Kasche maintained that the SA was well prepared to furnish the necessary 'human material' (*Menschmaterial*) for the German settlements in the post-war period. He was convinced that the Third Reich's social and political order and, within it, the SA as an organization that could mobilize millions of men, would then serve as role models in post-war Europe as a whole.

Second, the SA's settlement plans and activities under Kasche also merit recognition because a comparison with the later SS settlement policies reveals some important continuities. Although the number of German settlements required increased substantially with the Nazis' territorial gains between 1939 and 1942, the SS's deliberations on the transfer of Germans from the Old Reich closely resembled the previous statements of the SA. Furthermore, the SS suffered from the same problems. In its preliminary work on the *Generalplan Ost* in the spring of 1941, the *Reichsführer*-SS's Main Planning Office in Berlin noted that roughly 200,000 families would be needed for the formation of a German peasantry in the newly occupied and annexed territories of eastern Europe.[79] In order to accomplish the goal of 35 per cent of the population in these areas working in agriculture, the planners calculated that a total of 1.46 million agricultural workers of German origin would be needed.[80] The new farmers were expected to provide 'the foundation of the entire ethnic German build-up' (*Volksaufbau*). Unlike many farmers of the Old Reich, whom the SS characterized as politically conservative and narrow-minded, these new farmers were supposed to represent a new kind of peasantry, one that was fully conscious of its national and racial tasks. The SS claimed that the German farmer in the newly conquered eastern territories had to regard himself as a true political fighter 'on the attack'.[81]

Such formulations did not reflect the realities of the German occupation, which was initially characterized by the largely uncoordinated settlement of ethnic Germans from Galicia, Volhynia, Bessarabia, and the Baltic region.[82] Germans who were living within the borders of the German Reich of 1937, however, did not show much enthusiasm for a permanent migration eastward. Himmler acknowledged that by June 1942 the SS had only received 4,500 settler applications from the German heartlands. Two-thirds of those applications had been submitted in the previous year, after the German attack on the Soviet Union that summer.[83] The attempt to increase the number of 'Germanic' *Wehrbauern* by tapping into the pool of farmers from the Netherlands, who had been targeted by German and Dutch propaganda since 1941 and whom Himmler had praised as 'racially incredibly valuable' (*blutsmäßig unerhört wertvoll*), was likewise at best an ephemeral success. Many of the 5,000 settlers from the Netherlands who moved to the 'German East' between 1941 and 1944 only remained there for a short while. A report from the Dutch *Commissie tot Uitzending van Landbouwers naar Oost-Europa*, literally the 'Commission for the Secondment of Farmers to Eastern Europe', in February 1942 lamented the regularly very low level of education of the Dutch peasants in the east and contemptuously called them a 'bunch of adventurers' with very little professional knowledge and insufficient leadership skills.[84]

Such numbers and remarks put the aforementioned failure of the SA's recruitment attempts within their own rank and file in perspective. It was apparently not only the SA's inadequate organization but a much more deeply rooted problem that was to blame for the relatively low numbers of applicants. Despite intense Nazi propaganda prior to and during the Second World War, only a few Germans living in the Old Reich warmed to the idea of leaving their home towns and villages for good in order to build a new existence as 'defensive peasants' in eastern Europe. As everyone with a grain of historical and political knowledge knew, control over these areas had been fervently contested by numerous national groups, and in the 1940s these regions were characterized by excessive violence. One might say that the relative failure of earlier 'internal colonization' attempts repeated itself in these areas on a larger scale. Theory and practice did not converge.

Undoubtedly, millions of German men and women, as soldiers, policemen, officials, teachers, nurses, and auxiliaries, participated in the racially motivated quest to conquer large parts of eastern Europe. They looted, robbed, and murdered.[85] However, this did not imply that they were committed to implementing the National Socialist vision of a post-war 'German East' with a will of their own and presumably far-reaching personal consequences. This holds true in particular for peasants, who were usually closely attached to their family's soil. Whereas many of those who actually moved east were young and unmarried, thus relatively open for change and excitement, the SA men targeted in the National Socialist propaganda were middle-aged husbands and family fathers, a group whose members in many cases had already decided on where to live, with whom, and how to sustain a living. For these men, the economic risk of possible failure loomed large, especially as many lacked the necessary financial and social capital to recover quickly in the event of losing their income and home.

This observation qualifies the assumption that the Nazi regime attempted to satisfy the expectations and demands of German peasants by the acquisition of new 'living space' and new settlements there.[86] The actual implementation of the far-reaching SS settlement plans that, in 1942, provided for the migration of up to 220,000 peasant families from the Old Reich, would have required massive state force.[87] Yet social and political protests on the 'home front', a persistent fear for First World War veterans like Hitler, were to be avoided at all costs. The contemporary catchword *Ostrausch*, meaning 'a frenzy for the east', thus described a phenomenon that was largely confined to a small number of people, particularly planning experts and young unmarried 'adventurers' who wished to contribute to the 'German mission' in the east. Peasants from the Old Reich, by contrast, who were wearied by the *Erzeugungsschlacht*, the 'battle of agricultural production', and suffered from a shortage of available labour, reacted far less enthusiastically. Against this backdrop the regular assurances of SA and SS leaders that 'no German soldier fighting at the front' would return too late to benefit from the new settlement projects had little significance in practice.[88]

Contributing to the Formation of a 'People's Community' in Eastern Europe

Farming in the occupied east proved attractive only to a minority of Germans. In consequence, resettlement experts like SS brigade leader

Herbert Backe acknowledged as early as July 1942 that the 'new formation of German peasantry in occupied Europe' should be seen as a long-term project that would probably not be completed until after the war.[89] This outlook was consistent with SA propaganda, which continued to assert that after the war the stormtroopers, as 'exemplary fighters' for the Greater German Reich, would also become peacemakers in the 'greatest and most durable settlement initiative of all time'.[90]

The SA's 'Germanization' policies were far more than an obscure foot-note in the history of National Socialism for three reasons. First, the SA's plans constituted – temporally as well as in terms of content – the connecting link between the *Reichsnährstand*'s earlier 'internal colonization' projects and the later, more radical, 'Germanization' projects of the SS. The plans and steps taken to implement them thus contributed to the 'racial mobili-zation'[91] of the Third Reich by increasing the individual SA man's 'racial consciousness' (*Blutsbewusstsein*) and by strengthening his (imagined) 'bonds to the soil' (*Bodenverbundenheit*).[92] In this way, they merged the traditional discourse of the German 'defensive settlements' (*Wehrsiedlungen*) with the National Socialists' new racial categories.

Second, the SA's 'Germanization' plans remained important for the organization's activities in the final years of the war. Despite the fact that the original plans were never put to a broad practical test, their principles continued to have an effect on the SA's conception of itself. The settlement plans therefore serve as a paradigmatic example of the construction of the late SA's initiatives and activities around the two poles of discipline and inte-gration with the aim of contributing to the formation of the *Volksgemeinschaft* along racial lines. Consequently, Kasche ranked the bringing into line and the 'steering' (*Führung*) of his fellow Germans as among the most important aspects of the SA's settlement initiative.[93] The concrete plans for the resettle-ment of SA men in conquered eastern Europe, developed as early as 1938, were an important element of the larger process of transforming the *Erwartungsraum*, or 'space of expectations', for a racially and politically homogeneous 'people's community' into an *Erfahrungsraum*, or 'space of experience', in the near future.[94] That the SA possessed barely any practical experience in ethnic settlement issues (*Volkstumsarbeit*), as Kasche himself freely acknowledged in 1941,[95] paradoxically contributed to the ability of the organization to maintain its expectations for the future, despite being, to all intents and purposes, ousted by Himmler and the SS.

Third, the SA's 'Germanization' policies have to be seen in the context of the pre-military training of the German people, carried out in close cooperation with the Wehrmacht and the Hitler Youth. The SA's paramilitary education comprised both practical exercises, such as physical training and shooting lessons, and *politische Erziehungsarbeit*, or 'political education'.[96] This multifaceted programme not only targeted stormtroopers living in the Old Reich, insisting that racially based settlements were a 'prerequisite for the fulfilment of the regime's economic, domestic and racial objectives',[97] but also represented an important contribution to the German colonization attempts in eastern Europe.[98] In this context more research is needed to determine the importance of *Volksdeutsche* within the SA, and in the General Government in particular. The following chapter will analyse more fully the SA formations of the General Government that were created from April 1942 onward, partly by incorporating the previously established 'defensive border guards' (*Wehrschützenbereitschaften*).[99] Within the history of the stormtroopers, one can therefore draw a line from the 1920s to the 1940s. Already in the early years after the First World War, the idea that the nascent SA, in line with other *Wehrverbände*, had been called to defend the legitimate interests of the German people living in the borderlands of the German Reich was prevalent.[100] Ten years later, this idea became more radical with the rise of the German settlement movement, which attempted to intensify the existing German 'internal colonization' project along racial and political lines. By the 1940s, the emphasis had shifted from internal to external colonization, looking toward the conquest of new German territories in the European east. The *Volksgemeinschaft* came to be understood as a *Wehrgemeinschaft*, with the implementation of the settlement initiatives postponed until peacetime.[101] Nevertheless, the idea of racial superiority and the SA's alleged settlement mission continued to inspire its 'defensive activities' against increasing 'partisan attacks' until the last phase of the Second World War. Although the actual settlement of stormtroopers in eastern Europe failed, the movement's concepts of race, discipline, and self-defence contributed to the radicalization of the people's community in the occupied territories.

STORMTROOPERS IN THE SECOND WORLD WAR

As the Führer's most loyal followers, we, the stormtroopers, know only two things in our lives: faithfulness towards the Führer until the last breath and fanaticism in our everyday lives, and, if necessary, in battle.
— Wilhelm Schepmann, 1944[1]

The role of the SA during the Second World War has not been studied in detail.[2] Some historians, however, have long felt that the violence exercised by SA men in the preceding two decades must have had an impact on how the Wehrmacht, the SD-*Einsatzgruppen*, the auxiliary police forces, and the SS fought this war, not only because many SA men were now drafted into the Wehrmacht. It is evident that the Brownshirts, as a mass organization as well as a paramilitary force, did not play a major strategic role in the war, but the regular SA man, ideologically reliable and accustomed to physical violence, did. In line with this argument, Michael Mann has observed that although the SA as an organization was for a second time 'sidelined' after *Kristallnacht* in 1938, 'many of its hard-core members were transferred to other killing institutions'. Given the circumstances, going to war seemed a logical next step to those 'Old Fighters' who had built considerable careers in violence.[3] The propagandists of the OSAF recognized such a linkage early on. SA-*Hauptsturmführer* Wilhelm Rehm, a Protestant pastor, secondary schoolteacher, and leader of the *Deutsche Christen* (DC) in the mid-1930s, claimed in 1941 that 'the unique victories of the German Wehrmacht' were at least substantially due to the SA's readiness for action (*Einsatzbereitschaft*), willingness to sacrifice, comradeship, and community spirit.[4]

This chapter seeks to study how the individual conditioning in the SA, Nazi ideology, personal commitments, and strategic war efforts influenced and mutually reinforced each other. It also re-evaluates the importance of the SA within the framework of the National Socialist mass organizations during the war years. The SA was severely weakened by the drafting of the vast majority of its younger members into the Wehrmacht. Yet, contrary to what has often been believed, the SA did not sink into oblivion but attempted to seize the opportunities and initial territorial gains provided by the Second World War to expand its field of activities, both during the conflict and in the imagined post-war era. As late as March 1944, high-ranking SA leaders met for a three-day workshop in Posen in the Warthegau. As the official programme indicates, they not only discussed the problems of the day, but attended lectures on very general historical and political questions, including 'The form of rule in the Roman Empire', 'The reign of the Mongolians', 'The foundations of the British Empire, and 'The dollar imperialism'. Among the lecturers were two prominent SS officers, SS-*Oberführer* Franz Six, speaking on England, and SS-*Obergruppenführer* Gottlob Berger, lecturing on the German mission in the European east. SA Chief of Staff Wilhelm Schepmann, who had succeeded Viktor Lutze and the interim leader Max Jüttner in August 1943, gave a speech on 'The idea of the Reich as a political mandate'.[5] The climax of the meeting was a mustering of the SA leaders in the city and a public speech delivered by Alfred Rosenberg on 'The Empire of the Germans'.[6] Despite these triumphant themes, participants were advised to bring their food stamps and were warned not to frequent restaurants and bars apart from a few carefully selected and specially secured establishments.[7] The contrast between the wide-ranging lectures on the problems of imperial rule and the everyday security problems within the region is indicative of the discrepancy between the persistently grandiose ambitions of the Nazi leaders and the increasing improbability of their achievement. Grotesque as it may appear today, this widening gulf offers yet another strong indicator that the SA once again became a relevant political factor in the last stages of the Third Reich. The following chapter will demonstrate why.

The SA and the Wehrmacht

The relationship between the Wehrmacht and the SA improved considerably in the second half of the 1930s. For sure, mutual distrust and hostilities on both sides following the showdown of 1934 did not vanish overnight, but with the passage of time and the territorial expansion of the Third Reich between 1935 and 1939, at least a working relationship could be established. More and more, it became Himmler's SS that rivalled the Wehrmacht, not the 'tamed' SA. Bold self-confidence and far-reaching political ambitions no longer characterized the commanders of the SA; instead, deference to the will of both Hitler and the Wehrmacht prevailed. The moderate comeback of the SA as a paramilitary organization and its initially clandestine but later official operations in Austria and Czechoslovakia boosted its morale, yet this stimulus was achieved through actions that were completely in line with the aims of Hitler and the military and no longer reflected the 'social revolutionary' inclinations of the pre-1934 period.

With the expansion of the German Reich and its preparations for war, the profile of the SA rose at the end of the 1930s. The high point of this political rehabilitation was Hitler's decree of 19 January 1939 in which he assigned responsibility for the pre-military and ideological training of the German men to the SA (Plate 25). Every German man between eighteen and twenty-one who fulfilled the preconditions for regular armed service now had the 'moral obligation' to earn the SA-*Wehrabzeichen*, the new term for the SA Sports Badge, issued since 1933 but available to non-SA members only beginning in 1935.[8] Preparatory training to acquire this badge lay in the hands of the SA, which was ordered to establish so-called SA-*Wehrmannschaften*, literally 'SA Defence Teams'. The men in the *Wehrmannschaften* were to receive regular ideological and physical training from full-time SA instructors, a mission that provided the latter with a job guarantee.[9] According to plans from the summer of 1939, 20,000 permanent positions in the SA were needed to fulfil this task, which would have more than doubled the figure of 6,000 full-time SA leaders employed at that time.[10] The financial funds for the new jobs were to come from the army, which was to transfer 11.7 million reichsmark to the SA on a month-by-month basis.[11]

As a result of the beginning of the war, such a massive enlargement of personnel did not take place. Nevertheless, in the summer of 1940, the OSAF boasted that nearly 13,000 SA-*Stürme* were involved in the training of the *Wehrmannschaften*, which by then comprised some two million men.[12] This figure was probably too high for 1940, but it seems plausible that between 1939 and 1942 more than two million men overall successfully participated in the three-month SA training courses.[13] Through this programme the Nazi Party aimed at increasing the German men's fighting strength while also monitoring and disciplining them. 'Blood and soil, people and ground [*Erde*], folkdom [*Volkstum*] and national space [*Volksraum*]' were to be the leading points of the National Socialist military education (*Wehrerziehung*) in the SA-*Wehrmannschaften*, Max Luyken informed his fellow SA generals in a speech from the first half of 1939.[14] In such a way the NSDAP was able to get a firm grip on those German men who were too old for the Hitler Youth but too young for military service. Besides this group, the SA-*Wehrmannschaften* was also intended to comprise all reserves and those soldiers who had successfully fulfilled their military service.[15] This organizational framework, which combined comprehensive control with constant indoctrination, constituted yet another component of the Nazis' 'totalitarian' ambition never to let German men be free again, as Hitler stated in a speech in Reichenberg on 2 December 1938.[16]

Viktor Lutze's personal notes provide background information on the genesis of Hitler's important yet often underestimated decree of 19 January 1939, devolving responsibility for the education of German men to the SA. Lutze recorded that Hitler had summoned him to the Obersalzberg in the days after 9 November 1938 for a 'debate about *Feldherrnhalle*' and, in a personal conversation, had requested that Lutze discuss future regulations for pre- and post-military education (*Wehrerziehung*) with Walther von Brauchitsch, the chief of the Army High Command. Hitler asked Lutze and von Brauchitsch to create a report that could provide the basis for a new regulatory framework. Both sides were well aware that this decree would partially redefine their mutual relations. In the following weeks, Lutze claimed to have discussed matters extensively with von Brauchitsch, Franz Halder, Göring, and Erich Raeder, the leader of the Naval High Command.[17] He also credited his *Stabsführer* and SA-*Obergruppenführer* Otto Herzog with having had a decisive influence in these negotiations.[18] After an accord was reached and confirmed by Hitler, Lutze commented enthusiastically: 'After all these long years this is the first step from exclusively ideological party work to a great task that, if understood properly, to my mind forms one of the most fundamental prerequisites for Germany's future. In such a way the political soldier will form close bonds with the soldier in arms [*Waffensoldat*], the readiness for war [*Wehrbereitschaft*] will be closely intertwined with the military strength [*Wehrkraft*], the party will be connected to the Wehrmacht.'[19] However, after this cry of joy, Lutze conceded that competing National Socialist organizations, particularly the SS, the Hitler Youth, and the NSKK, had immediately attempted to block the revaluation of the SA after the decree of 19 January 1939.[20]

This decree and the subsequent regulations issued by Lutze in the following months highlight that this effort aimed at nothing less than the total political and ideological submission of the Wehrmacht to the NSDAP and its Führer. Consequently, the SA's attempt to organizationally cement its new power resulted in the establishment of an SA-*Wehrstab*, literally the 'SA Staff for military matters', on 1 June 1939, which was headed by Georg von Neufville, subsequently the commander of Infantry Regiment 195.[21] The SA in 1939 thus was given a new purpose that, had it been carried out, would have made it an important organization for a very substantial proportion of German men. The military historian Manfred Messerschmidt has rightly called this development a 'kind of recompense' for the SA's humiliation in 1934.[22]

Yet, the SA's feelings of satisfaction were short-lived. The outbreak of the Second World War just weeks after the SA-*Wehrstab* was established decisively changed the situation – and, once again, to the disadvantage of the stormtroopers. Some 467,000 men, or 32 per cent of all members, were drafted into the Wehrmacht in August and September 1939 alone. By late 1940 the figure had risen to 741,208, or 53 per cent of all able SA men.[23] As a result, regular SA service in the German Reich could not always be fulfilled. What is more, the moment a stormtrooper was drafted, the OSAF lost control of him, as his formal affiliation to the NSDAP and the SA was held in abeyance during his service.[24] Among those drafted from the ranks of the SA was Neufville himself, who was called to the front and died on 3 November 1941 following wounds sustained at the Battle of Moscow.[25] Nevertheless, Lutze and other high-ranking SA generals continued to view the January 1939 decree on the SA-*Wehrmannschaften* as a starting point for further growth.

A telling example of the uplifted spirit of the OSAF in these months can be found in a lengthy letter written by Max Jüttner in April 1941. Jüttner was at that time responsible for 'leadership education' (*Führerausbildung*) within the SA. In this letter he claimed that it was first and foremost thanks to the SA's educational efforts that a unique 'spiritual and emotional defence community' (*seelisch-geistige Wehrgemeinschaft*) had been established in recent years. This community could be found in the battle zones as well as on the home front, Jüttner asserted, and he consequently concluded that it would be the SA's future task to secure this 'defence community of German men' and to ensure its continuation by future generations. He repeatedly stressed that this community was to be exclusively male, stating that the current distribution of male and female roles in Nazi Germany would likely remain a permanent feature of German life in the foreseeable future.[26]

The OSAF's ultimate yet ever more utopian aim was to establish the stormtroopers as a major political and social force in a German-dominated post-war central Europe that would be based on allegedly male virtues such as readiness for action, paramilitary training, and ideological firmness. In line with such ambitions, the SA planned a propaganda offensive in Fascist Europe shortly after the outbreak of the war. Toward this end its *Aufklärungsdienst*, a kind of intelligence and propaganda service, had a brochure on 'The History of the SA' printed in Italian and Spanish in November 1939. According to the contract with the publisher, the astonishingly high number of 850,000 copies were to be produced and distributed. However, the brochure never reached its audience, as the Foreign Office's Language Service regarded the translations as extremely unsatisfactory, and, in the end, the Nazi regime blocked the publication's distribution.[27]

Such incidents were certainly disconcerting for Lutze and the OSAF, but they constituted only a small problem compared to the major obstacle that the organization faced during the war years: the constant loss of manpower. By early 1941 up to 70 per cent of all rank-and-file storm-troopers and more than 80 per cent of high-ranking officials in the SA had been sent to fight.[28] This drainage of members decisively weakened the SA in the Reich, but at the same time it impacted on the Wehrmacht. The armed forces did not simply swallow up the former stormtroopers and thereby render them invisible.[29] As the exemplary study of the Rhenish-Westphalian Infantry Division 253 by the historian Christoph Rass demonstrates, slightly more than one-third of all soldiers in this division were or had been members of one or more National Socialist organizations. A closer look reveals that the overwhelming majority (85.6 per cent) had been members of the Hitler Youth or the SA (or both), whereas the propor-tion of soldiers with affiliations to the SS and the NSDAP did not exceed 4.9 and 3.7 per cent respectively. Of all soldiers in this division, 13.7 per cent were SA men and 18.9 per cent were former members of the Hitler

Youth.[30] Rass also analysed the correlation between memberships and age brackets, distinguishing three groups: a cohort born before 1910, another cohort born between 1910 and 1915, and still another born after 1916. In the first cohort only 11.6 per cent of all soldiers were members of a Nazi organization. These 'Old Fighters' were, unsurprisingly, overwhelmingly members of the SA, SS, and NSDAP. In the second cohort the SA and the HJ began to dominate, with 38.6 per cent being members of one or more Nazi organizations. In the third cohort, consisting of the youngest soldiers, the Hitler Youth predominated, and 62 per cent were affiliated with one or more Nazi organizations.[31]

These statistics demonstrate that it was not the 'Old Fighters' with their previous ideological training who composed the majority of Wehrmacht soldiers, but a younger generation, born in the 1910s, who had generally joined the SA in 1933 or later, at around the age of eighteen. This 'post-war youth generation', politically socialized in the last years of the Weimar Republic and subsequently 'educated' under the Nazi regime, overwhelmingly lacked any personal experience with the political battle of the late 1920s and early 1930s that was so often glorified in Nazi propaganda. This 'second generation' of SA men, who numerically dominated among those Wehrmacht soldiers with National Socialist affiliation, were therefore less shaped by the 'glorious' years of the SA than by their own experience of the transformation of the SA into a hybrid of a pre-military training organization and a politically controlled social welfare institution.[32]

These findings are not representative of all units in a technical sense. However, Infantry Division 253 was in many ways a typical Wehrmacht unit, fighting on both the western and eastern fronts.[33] Based on Rass's evidence, it makes sense to distinguish two groups when speaking of former SA men-turned-soldiers in the Second World War: the minority of 'Old Fighters' and the considerably larger group of younger men whose adolescence had coincided with the establishment of the Third Reich. These latter SA men had been shaped by their education under the swastika, with its emphasis on paramilitary training and personal hardening and its diminution of intellectual engagement, as well as by the need to conform to a given order and to accept the prerogative of the NSDAP at all costs. A considerable number of these younger soldiers had already served in the Wehrmacht before the war as a result of the reintroduction of conscription in 1935.

The distinction between these two groups is crucial. It strongly indicates that a straight line cannot be drawn from the pre-1933 violence of the SA to the violence of the Second World War. There was certainly much continuity among the *Landsknechtnaturen* (mercenary types) of the older SA activists, but this continuity did not exist among their younger SA comrades. To understand the motives and actions of the latter, it will prove fruitful to examine how their education in the SA in the second half of the 1930s translated into military action during the war. I will discuss this point by analysing individuals' motives in joining the SA, the operations of the SA-*Standarte* Feldherrnhalle, and the effects of SA propaganda in the last years of the conflict.

The Beginning of the War

In the early stages of the Second World War, the SA longed for an intensified level of cooperation with the army under von Brauchitsch, chief of the Army High Command. This was a natural move, as the decree of 19 January 1939 that ordered German men to alternate between participation in the SA-*Wehrmannschaften* and regular military service automatically brought the Wehrmacht and the stormtroopers closer together. Irrespective of their mutual reservations, this new alliance would prove beneficial for both sides in the years to come.[34] The army profited from the SA's equipment, logistical help, and trained men, while the SA gained at least modest respect as the army's junior partner. The high recruitment figures of the SA in Memel, Austria, and the Sudetenland in 1937 and 1938 had already contributed to a rise in the organization's prestige, and many stormtroopers in 1939 saw the outbreak of war as a new opportunity to prove their worth. Consequently, in the first months of the military campaign, many militants longed to be assigned to active duty in the regular army units. A report from the SA-*Gruppe* Hamburg dated 15 September 1939, just two weeks after the German attack on Poland, stated that 35 per cent of its members had already been drafted into the military, and that many more were eagerly waiting to join the Wehrmacht as quickly as possible: 'All men are proudly following the news of the lightning combat actions in the East, but they are also afraid of coming too late. The leaders and sub-leaders of the SA in particular suffer from the painful certainty that, later, they will be standing in front of their units knowing that they will comprise men with *Fronterlebnis* (front-line experience).'[35]

To understand the prevalence of this perceived problem, a generational approach is useful. Unlike the stormtroopers who had taken up arms, many of the higher-ranking SA leaders belonged, as previously noted, to the 'war youth generation' – those who had been too young to fight in the First World War and had experienced their adolescence in the 1920s as a time of crisis. The same men now feared they were the wrong age again – this time, being considered too old to join the regular forces and therefore confined to the role of involuntary spectators in a war that many perceived as a decisive ideological battle of global importance.[36] Active participation in the war was the fulfilment of these men's political ambitions, the next step that 'naturally' followed a period of paramilitary training and uncertain career prospects that had lasted for many years.[37] Consequently, with the outbreak of the war the OSAF began to pressure the Wehrmacht for expanded career opportunities for full-time SA leaders from the rank of *Sturmführer* upward. It reminded the army that in the negotiations following the 19 January 1939 agreement, both sides had consented to particular officer courses for SA cadres. Even if the continuation of these courses was no longer viable with the beginning of the war, a preferential treatment of SA leaders in the German army was desired.[38]

On 29 January 1940 von Brauchitsch reacted positively to such demands. He decreed that higher-ranking SA leaders not yet drafted were to be mustered immediately. Those already serving in the army were to be placed in positions in which they could prove themselves fit for later promotions to officers' ranks. Furthermore, he explicitly declared that SA leaders should not be deployed in subaltern roles, such as typists, drivers, or telephone operators – a common practice in the first months of the war.[39] These tasks might have corresponded with the individual SA leader's skills, yet those assigned to these roles often perceived them as humiliating. The soldier Konrad Jarausch in his diary described a forty-year-old SA-*Standartenführer* from Magdeburg who had been drafted in reaction to these new orders. Jarausch noted that this officer candidate 'is one of these down-to-earth men that keep the party organizations running today. He is not lacking in knowledge, at least in some realms. He also has been around quite a bit. Yet he has hardly any connection to the cultural and intellectual traditions.'[40] It is not clear to what extent and how long the Wehrmacht observed orders to give SA leaders preferential treatment. The fact that many military service records of former stormtroopers did not contain any information on their paramilitary background suggests that the Wehrmacht did not think too highly of the training provided by the SA, despite all the rhetoric to the contrary.[41]

Immediately after the beginning of the war, the OSAF began to emphasize the SA's contribution to the German war effort in 1939 and early 1940. The 'liberation' of the free city of Danzig was a frequently cited example. Beginning in June 1939, the SA-*Standarten* 5, 14, and 128 of the Danzig SA-*Brigade* 6 furnished the men for 'enhanced border control units' (*Verstärkter Grenzaufsichtsdienst*, or VGAD) in this region who were officially charged with the mission of preventing Polish attacks. These units were armed with machine guns and hand grenades, weapons that were used in the following weeks in regional skirmishes that cost the lives of at least one Polish soldier and one SA man. Immediately prior to 1 September 1939, those men in the border control units who had detailed local knowledge were integrated into the Wehrmacht, and local *Sturmbanne* of the Danzig SA were transformed into complete Wehrmacht companies, which were later involved in an attack on the small town of Dirschau, today's Polish Tczew, located south of Danzig. The city's Marine-SA contributed to the capture of Westerplatte and Gdingen/Gdynia.[42] On 15 October the *Gruppe* Eberhardt, or Eberhardt Brigade, under the command of the professional soldier Friedrich-Georg Eberhardt and composed of men from the Danzig police, stormtroopers, the 'Heimwehr', and individual volunteers, became the 60th Infantry Division.[43] Although the National Socialist propaganda certainly played up the involvement of these organizations, it is highly likely that the pre-military training of the 3,000 militants from the city and its neighbouring areas used in the attack on Poland facilitated their integration into the regular army.[44]

Farther south a 1,600-man-strong SA unit of 'Old Fighters' and newly integrated ethnic Germans from nearby Poland was formed on 25 August 1939. From 1 September onward, these men penetrated Polish territory dressed in civilian clothes and are reported to have successfully prevented the destruction of important industries in the Upper Silesian industrial region. According to an unpublished OSAF paper, *Standarte* 22 from Gleiwitz, today's Polish Gliwice, and *Standarte* 62 from Ratibor, today's Racibórz, suffered heavy casualties in these missions.[45] In the first weeks of the war, SA men dressed in uniform started to establish 'homeland security units' of *Volksdeutsche* in several newly occupied Polish cities in an attempt to copy the successful model pioneered in the Sudetenland in 1938. In the future these units were expected to provide the basis for the formation of local NSDAP chapters.[46] A little later, a formal SA position called *Beauftragter für die Organisation der volksdeutschen Mannschaft*, literally, the 'Commissioner for the Organization of the Ethnic German Formations', was created and filled with a certain SA-*Obersturmbannführer* Schröder.[47] Very soon these ethnic German units became known as *Volksdeutscher Selbstschutz*, a paramilitary organization that was dominated by the SS but whose men semed to have provided the nucleus for later SA units in the area. In close cooperation with the *Einsatzgruppen* of the security police, its members killed more than 40,000 people in the former Polish territories in 1939 alone.[48]

SA units were also involved in the German attack on Poland's southern borders. In the autumn and winter of 1939 an SA unit from the Sudetenland led by Leo Bendak, a former leader of the Sudeten German gymnastics movement, was placed in charge of the procuration of weapons for the Wehrmacht, the safeguarding of munitions transports, and the 'cleansing and securing of the area' of action, a task that included the construction and oversight of prisoner-of-war camps.[49] Stormtroopers with a knowledge of foreign languages – and particularly those from multilingual border regions – interrogated prisoners and passed on relevant information to the army command. Such tasks were not confined to the early stages of the war. In 1941 the OSAF boasted that no fewer than eighteen SA-*Gruppen* were involved with the transport and guarding of prisoners in their respective territories.[50]

The illustrated book *Sudeten SA in Polen* published in February 1940, part of the OSAF's renewed attempts to present the SA in the proper light, provides additional information on the operations of stormtroopers in southern Poland – both on a factual level and on the mentality of the SA troops involved.[51] In his foreword to this book Franz May, leader of the Sudeten SA, tellingly wrote that the stormtroopers who in the autumn of 1939 crossed the Polish-Slovak border were overwhelmingly men who – due to the high level of volunteers – had not been accepted into the Wehrmacht. Within this context they were said to have been 'grateful' to be used for organizational and logistical functions.[52] One group, the *Grenzwachregiment Zirps*, operated for eight weeks as a 'battalion' at the request of the Armed Forces High Command (OKW), while another initially received training in the Austrian Alps. The book provides a flattering account of the SA's achievements in Poland, beginning with the securing of the border in a joint operation with Slovakian forces and ending with Lutze's late October 1939 visit to Spiš, or Zipser Land, a small strip in northern Slovakia that had been home to a relatively small group of ethnic Germans since the thirteenth century, usually referred to as Carpathian Germans.[53]

Most of the activities described in *Sudeten SA in Polen* indicate that the group followed the Wehrmacht troops but did not actually fight on the front lines. However, some entries clearly reveal the violent character of the SA's 'cleansing' of villages and small towns, stating that the SA was repeatedly involved in nightly clashes with 'Polish and Jewish snipers' who allegedly plundered the camps and murdered German soldiers under the screen of night. Unsurprisingly, the SA is said to have quickly located and 'neutralized' these enemies. On the very same page of the book, a photograph of a burning house is provided, graphically adding to the image of the SA as a dangerous and determined unit. The antisemitism of this work is striking, even by the standards of the Third Reich. The typical storm-trooper is portrayed as hands-on and clean, 'always ready to help', in sharp contrast to the 'dirty Jew'. A caption under two photographs allegedly showing two Jewish men suggestively reads: 'The SA's help, however, cannot heal the wounds that these Jewish exploiters have opened in the course of several generations.' Historical research has so far not analysed the extent to which SA units behind the front lines were involved in the mistreatment and killing of Jews in this particular region in the autumn of 1939. Yet the prominence of the alleged Jewish danger in this book of propaganda, as well as the previous terrorist attacks on Jews carried out by the Carpathian-German *Freiwilliger Selbstschutz* (FS) since early 1939, strongly suggest that its graphic examples reflected real operations.[54]

A simple Manichaean worldview also characterized the SA's attitude toward the non-Jewish Poles. In his political diary for the year 1940, SA Chief of Staff Lutze justified even excessive retaliation against Polish civilians as long as the approval of such violence was not to be interpreted as a licence to kill: 'It is ultimately for reasons of state, the political situation, the necessities of the future that determine whether one asks for 10 or 100 or 1,000 or even 10,000 Poles [to be executed] in retaliation for a German,' Lutze wrote. 'It is never, however, permissible to hand over the enemy or the defeated man as fair game to an individual, a group of men [*Menschen*], or to organizations. One cannot accept that a man, with a gun in his hand, becomes a "master of life and death" at any given moment that pleases him.'[55] In light of German brutalities and war crimes against Poles and Jews, which during this period caused the deaths of more than 10,000 civilians murdered behind the front lines,[56] Lutze in his personal writings advocated a more careful line of action. However, his attitude was more one of political caution than of categorical criticism. Lutze preferred the deportation of Poles from German-occupied territories to the illegal killing of them because 'a family cannot be exterminated completely without someone taking notice. Someone from the family, from the village, from the neighbourhood, from the kin [*Sippe*] always remains [. . .] and these people become much more dreadful accusers, much more wicked agitators and much more unforgiving, bloodthirsty avengers than could otherwise be the case.' Aside from all these reasons, Lutze added naively: 'I know for certain that the Führer never ever approves of it, simply because it is not the German way!'[57]

The SA-*Standarte* Feldherrnhalle

The SA also participated directly with combat units in the Second World War, albeit operating under the supreme command of the Wehrmacht. As early as October 1935 an elite SA unit was formed under the name of *Wachstandarte Stabschef*, intended as an SA equivalent to the SS-*Leibstandarte* Adolf Hitler.[58] The first recruits to the *Wachstandarte Stabschef* comprised members of the former SA-*Feldjägerkorps* who had not been incorporated into the regular police forces and stormtroopers who had been previously barracked in the SA 'welfare camps'.[59] According to recruitment guidelines from April 1936, only unmarried and unemployed (or poorly salaried) men aged eighteen to twenty-five who had a 'racially immaculate look' were to be accepted into the ranks. Those who wore glasses were to be excluded, as were those who did not possess an 'average command of orthography'.[60] The men of the *Wachstandarte* were used for official ceremonies and parades and as guards of symbolically important places such as Hitler's New Reich Chancellery in Berlin. At a party rally held in Nuremberg on 11 September 1936, Hitler bestowed the name SA-*Standarte* Feldherrnhalle on this unit, alluding to the central location of early Nazi martyrdom in Munich's city centre. By late 1936 the Feldherrnhalle consisted of six *Sturmbanne* based in Güterfelde near Berlin, Erding, Hattingen, Fichtenhain, Stettin, and Stuttgart. After the *Anschluss* in 1938 a seventh *Sturmbann* was installed in Vienna-Kaltenleutgeben, and in 1939, after the dismantling of Czechoslovakia, an eighth was established in Prague.[61]

Hermann Göring received the Feldherrnhalle's 'honorary command' on 12 January 1937 as a kind of present for his forty-fourth birthday.[62] This was another humiliation for Lutze, who knew only too well of Göring's central role in the 'Night of the Long Knives'.[63] Although the new unit comprised fewer than 2,000 men dispersed throughout the Reich and was thus only an extremely poor consolation for the stormtroopers' failed plan for a people's militia, the *Standarte* Feldherrnhalle became the SA's flagship group during the remaining years of the Third Reich. The men of this elite unit were the only German soldiers who were allowed to wear SA insignias to symbolize the fusion of 'SA spirit' and military skills. In the eyes of the OSAF, the Feldherrnhalle represented the successful transformation of the NSDAP's paramilitary organization of the Weimar years into a serious military formation that worked hand in hand with the regular armed forces to instil *Wehrwillen* in the hearts and minds of the German people. Service in the Feldherrnhalle was voluntary and, as of 27 October 1938, recognized as equivalent to regular military service. Men who now opted to join the SA instead of the Wehrmacht were required to bind themselves to the organization for at least three years. Service in the Feldherrnhalle was also attractive to many men because of the prospect it brought of full-time employment by the SA after the completion of active service.[64] It was thus a prestigious elite formation with the entitlement to lifelong service.

On 20 June 1938, Göring, in his function as Reich Minister of Aviation, formally assigned the Feldherrnhalle to the Luftwaffe, an assignment that remained in place until 31 March 1939. During this period the Feldherrnhalle was an independent airborne regiment that belonged to the 7th Air Division (*Fliegerdivision* 7), even though it was trained as an infantry regiment.[65] As such its participation in the occupation of the Sudetenland in October 1938 and in the dismantling of the rump of Czechoslovakia in March 1939 served as a kind of mock 'baptism by fire'. According to Viktor Lutze's personal notes, he himself piloted one of 160 Junkers 52s that departed from Breslau in October 1938 and flew south to penetrate the Czechoslovakian airspace. However, as the Munich agreement of 29–30 September had already fixed the line of demarcation between the two states, a violent encounter with the enemy did not take place, and the Feldherrnhalle's contribution to the 'liberation' of the Sudetenland thus remained more peaceful than anticipated. 'No casualties, just seven airplanes with some kind of damage to the landing gear,' recorded Lutze almost disappointedly.[66]

Over the course of 1939 the Feldherrnhalle split into several factions. This development put an end to the OSAF's hopes of having an armed corps completely at its disposal and left its commander, SA-*Gruppenführer* Erich Reimann, 'totally embittered and discouraged'.[67] Already in the first quarter of 1939 the majority of his men, about 1,200 stormtroopers, had been formally integrated into the regular air and paratrooper divisions of *Fliegerdivision* 7, removing them from the OSAF's control.[68] Nevertheless, these stormtroopers continued to be used as important role models in SA propaganda. Their contribution to their new units was indeed considerable. Of those German paratroopers deployed in 1940 in Belgium and the Netherlands, the OSAF claimed in 1941 that up to 90 per cent came from the SA.[69] Later, paratroopers with a Feldherrnhalle background fought in Greece and southern Italy.[70] It is therefore safe to deduce that the *esprit de corps* of the German *Fallschirmtruppe* was at least partly based on the 'SA mentality' and its particular values.[71]

A smaller fraction of the *Standarte* Feldherrnhalle throughout the war years served in their original function as guards in both the Reich and the German-occupied territories. Within the General Government, members of the Feldherrnhalle were also deployed for 'special purposes' alongside the SS and the police forces.[72] In the city of Warsaw from late 1940 onward, about fifty men from the Feldherrnhalle were charged with standing watch at Brühl Palace, the headquarters of the district chief for Warsaw in the General Government, as well as at other public buildings.[73] As self-declared representatives of the new *Herrenrasse* (master race), they acted as police forces, pressed civilians for money, and in at least one case even staged an attack on the palace as a pretext for killing a Polish man and raping two women. Their behaviour violated even the extremely racist standards of the German occupiers to such an extent that in May 1943, the Warsaw German *Sondergericht* (Special Court) sentenced thirteen Feldherrnhalle members to prison terms and even imposed the death penalty on one.[74] The judges increased the normal penalties because the crimes in question were committed while the men were in the uniform of an elite formation and before the eyes of the Polish population. However, the judges also found mitigating circumstances. They reasoned that all thirteen defendants were *Volksdeutsche* with allegedly lower moral standards than the (Reich) German norm and as such would simply need more time to adjust to the higher level of German morality.[75]

In the autumn of 1939 a third faction of the *Standarte* Feldherrnhalle formed the third battalion of the 271st Infantry Regiment, initially one of only two regiments that constituted the 93rd Infantry Division.[76] This motorized grenadier regiment was led by August Raben, a professional soldier.[77] Similar to the paratroopers, the men in this regiment were glorified in OSAF propaganda as the embodiment of SA values and as the representation of the successful merger of the SA's fighting spirit with the glorious tradition of the German army.[78] The 271st Regiment fought on the western front in 1940 as part of the First Army and contributed to the German breakthrough of the Maginot Line near Barst-Marienthal in northern Lorraine. After the victory against the French, the regiment was placed on leave from August 1940 until February 1941. Once reactivated, Herbert Böhme, one of relatively few German soldiers to be awarded the *Ritterkreuz*, then assumed command of the regiment. Böhme was an early Nazi activist who had joined the SA and the NSDAP in 1930 and later served as SA-*Oberführer* in the staff of the SA-*Gruppe* Schlesien prior to joining the Wehrmacht in 1937.[79]

With the German attack on the Soviet Union in the summer of 1941, the 271st Infantry Regiment was deployed to the northeastern front and participated in the siege of Leningrad.[80] The Nazi propaganda praised the regiment's military achievements as an example of 'SA spirit at the Eastern Front'. Ideology was a key part of this regiment's self-image, as can be seen from the bestowal of the honorary title of *Horst-Wessel-Kompagnie Leutnant M* on those soldiers killed at a battle on the River Volkov.[81] On 9 August 1942 the designation 'Feldherrnhalle', so far only used for the third battalion, was given to the entire regiment.[82] On 4 May 1943 the unit was finally incorporated into the 60th Infantry Division (motorized), which was in dire need of fresh blood after its very heavy losses in the battle of Stalingrad, and was from then on referred to as *Panzergrenadier-Division Feldherrnhalle*.[83]

Apart from personal memories that form the heart of Internet discussions among the few surviving soldiers as well as military enthusiasts, not much is known about the foot soldiers of the Feldherrnhalle, whom SA propaganda during the war glorified as the paradigmatic stormtroopers of the Wehrmacht. The remaining personnel files and troop lists of the former German army are held at the *Deutsche Dienststelle* in Berlin, but this state-run institution would only grant access to the remaining personnel files of the former members of the third battalion of the 271st Regiment on condition that the soldiers' names are made anonymous. Unfortunately, only a very small number of their personal papers have survived. The material is nevertheless sufficient to allow at least some tentative conclusions as to the group's social composition and the motivation of its members to join the Feldherrnhalle. My research focused on the group's staff and Companies 9 and 10. In November 1939 these two companies each consisted of between 165 and 180 men strong, while the staff comprised 91 soldiers.

According to the surviving membership lists, most soldiers of the third battalion of the 271st Regiment were young men, overwhelmingly born after 1914. Information is rarely provided on their dates of enrolment in the SA, but it is evident that those men who would have referred to themselves as 'Old Fighters' (i.e. those with experience in the SA from 1933 and earlier) constituted only a small minority of the group. Instead, on average the soldiers of this regiment in late 1939 were between nineteen and twenty-three years of age, similar to the norm in other Wehrmacht units. The biography of Karl A., from the city of Walsum on the Lower Rhine, was in many ways typical of the men in the 271st Regiment. Born in 1920, this married storekeeper joined the SA in early 1938, around his eighteenth birthday.[84] After serving as a regular member of the Luftwaffe between 20 June 1938 and 31 March 1939, Karl A. served in the SA-*Standarte* Feldherrnhalle until he was transferred to the 271st Regiment on 9 September 1939. In the following years he participated in the regiment's battles in France and then, from the summer of 1941 onward, in the Soviet Union. Highly decorated, with the Infantry Assault Badge, the Iron Cross (II. Category), and the East Front Winter Campaign Medal to his name, he joined the Grenadier Regiment Feldherrnhalle on 1 November 1942 and was promoted to non-commissioned officer on 1 September 1943. On New Year's Eve in 1943, Karl A. was severely wounded but seems to have quickly returned to the front. He went missing in the area of Mogilew near Minsk 'between 24 June and 7 July 1944', at a time when the Wehrmacht had stopped providing the exact location and date of individual soldiers' deaths in the east.[85]

Herbert M. from Dortmund, a floor tiler by training, was born in December 1920 and also joined the SA at a very young age, several weeks before his eighteenth birthday. Initially a member of the Feldherrnhalle's *Sturmbann* I and later its *Sturmbann* V based in Prague, he was transferred to the 9th Company of the 271st Regiment's third battalion in the autumn of 1939. Herbert M. participated in the military campaigns against France and the Soviet Union and was wounded by shellfire on 19 April 1942 near Spasskaja-Polist on the eastern front. Probably because of his lasting injuries, Herbert M. was exempted from further front-line duties and sent back to the Feldherrnhalle's Vienna *Sturmbann* in March 1943. Information about his life in the next twelve months is not available. On 26 April 1944, Herbert M. died in the military hospital for reserves in Prag-Reuth (Prague, Krč district). At the request of his wife, his remains were transferred to Düsseldorf and buried there.[86]

Kurt M., to provide a final example, was among the youngest members of the Feldherrnhalle when he joined in 1938. Born in Munich in May 1921 into a lower-middle-class family, he attended a gymnasium for four years before transferring to a commercial school (*Handelsschule*), where he remained for another three years. He joined the Hitler Youth in 1935 and then entered the ranks of the SA in 1938. Kurt M. volunteered for the Feldherrnhalle because of the prestige of Göring's Luftwaffe and was integrated into the fourth *Sturmbann*, based in Erding near Munich, on 20 June 1938. However, he was unable to become a paratrooper 'because of an illness' and instead joined the 271st Regiment on 9 September 1939. Despite mixed evaluations from his superiors, Kurt M. advanced quickly and was recommended to participate in an officer-training course in August 1941.[87] A letter of recommendation written by one of his superiors in 1941 portrays the young man as the paradigmatic SA fighter: 'Intellectually average, sparsely yet clearly thinking, tall and slim, thoroughly fit and tough [...] In combat M. reveals himself as a cool-blooded daredevil, who by his personal example had led his group even in situations of extreme enemy action and never lost control of his leadership.' Despite such qualities, Kurt M., later promoted to the rank of staff sergeant (*Oberfeldwebel*), was still alive in April 1944.[88]

These three case studies are certainly not representative of the 271st Regiment's membership in a technical sense, but the existing data strongly suggest that their biographies are typical of the average men in the regiment.

Among the soldiers of the Feldherrnhalle, working-class professions heavily dominated. Several of these young men joined this elite formation as early as 1938, attracted by the prestige of the Luftwaffe under Göring and the prospect of avoiding regular military duty and building a stable career in the military branch of the SA. In particular, young men of low educational background saw the Feldherrnhalle as an available path to modest upward mobility that was in line with their ideological preferences (Plate 30).[89]

Yet, at least until they joined the Feldherrnhalle, these young men's personal experience with the SA was limited. For them, the typical SA narratives of the *Kampfzeit* were stories from and for another generation. Compared to their forerunners, this new generation of SA men had grown up in a political climate in which National Socialist values were already the norm; consequently, they did not represent the opposition, but the new mainstream. Many of them seem to have regarded service in the Feldherrnhalle as a regular career path within the Nazi regime – a conclusion supported by the substantial number of stormtroopers in this unit who were already married, despite their young age and their often incomplete vocational training. Finally, the men in the Feldherrnhalle were not drawn from any particular region but came from all parts of the Greater German Reich, including the annexed territories. At least in this respect, they represented a cross section of the German male population.

Communist Propaganda

In an immediate reaction to the German attack on the Soviet Union in the summer of 1941, the propagandists of the Communist International in Moscow decided to launch additional German-language radio programmes to reach out to particular audiences. The programme *Sturmadler*, literally 'Storm Eagle', was meant to appeal to German youth, while *SA-Mann Hans Weber* was designed to influence the rank-and-file National Socialist. In 1942 both programmes became part of the *Deutscher Volkssender*, the umbrella radio station in the Soviet Union that served as the unofficial voice of the German Communist Party in exile.[90] The journalist Fritz Erpenbeck, who later in the war became the deputy director of the radio programme *Freies Deutschland*, took the role of renegade stormtrooper Hans Weber. It is impossible to assess the impact of these twenty-minute-long daily broadcasts, which could be heard in many parts of the Reich. The creators of the programme nonetheless believed in its efficacy, as they quickly added a companion for Weber, a fellow SA man called Max Schröder, voiced by the journalist Max Keilson. This anti-Nazi comedy show built on the German Communist tactic of the 1930s of infiltrating the SA through *Zersetzungsschriften*, subversive 'SA journals'. Written in simple popular language, at times in the form of fictitious dialogues, these works had attempted to draw dissatisfied 'Old Fighters' over to the other side by emphasizing the mismatch between the SA's rhetoric of social revolution and the 'selling out' of the party establishment.[91] The new radio programme was also influenced by the clandestine British radio station *Gustav Siegfried Eins*, or GS1, which had started up some months earlier, in May 1941. On this station an anonymous 'boss' uttered verbal slanders against both Nazis and Communists. In contrast to the British broadcast, the German Communist programme was intended to be 'less vulgar and obscene', Erpenbeck remembered after the war, not least because of initial Soviet censorship.[92] In light of what we know about Nazi humour today, this was a wise decision, as the Germans at the time preferred rather innocent and tame jokes to outright, aggressive abuse that directly pointed the finger at what was perceived as ridiculous or scandalous.[93]

The key mission of *SA-Mann Hans Weber* was to reach out to the everyday Nazi using the colloquial language of the heavily industrialized and densely populated Ruhr, a dialect complemented later by the popular Berlin idiom. Both SA characters, modelled after the familiar type of the committed but limited Nazi, demonstrated the imperfections of the Third Reich by commenting on the affairs and endemic corruption of Nazi functionaries. Again and again they emphasized the discrepancies between the party propaganda and the social realities in Germany.[94] Particularly memorable episodes that were allegedly based on accounts from intercepted German letters included a 'thick description' of party officials from a Westphalian town who had taken part in sexual saturnalia with a teenage girl, and a request from a German mother to her husband in the Waffen-SS to 'send children's clothing' with the addendum, 'I don't mind if it is bloody, I'll wash it out.'[95] As such examples make clear, accusations of sexual abnormalities were still a regular feature of anti-Fascist propaganda. The Communists portrayed the National Socialists as sadistic perverts, in sharp contrast to the regime's own morally saturated propaganda.

In the context of this study, it is remarkable that the surviving German Communists in Soviet exile – whose ranks had been heavily decimated by the Stalinist terror of the previous years – still believed in the potential to turn those working-class men whom the Communist movement had lost to the Nazis in high numbers between 1928 and 1934 back toward Communism.[96] As the German Communists had done during the first years of the Third Reich, provoking confusion and discontentment within the ranks still appeared to be a reasonable strategy. Despite the fact that most stormtroopers had been drafted into the military, they still mattered. The German Communists not only identified them as a vital group for maintaining order in the Nazi state, but also deemed them re-educable. A few years later the Communist policy in the Soviet Zone of Occupation, from 1949 onward the GDR, would prove consistent with this policy. Whereas the judiciary continued to take a harsh stance toward the SA, at least in the first years after the war, it also worked toward the conversion of petty Nazis into good Socialists.[97]

Auxiliary Police in the General Government, the Protectorate, and in Slovenia

The German military victory in 1939 was the prerequisite for the subsequent break-up of the former Polish state. Its western parts were annexed and incorporated into the Greater German Reich, while its eastern parts became Soviet territory. The Polish heartlands, however, with the capital cities of Warsaw and Cracow, were transformed into a German zone of occupation called the General Government. Although the jurist and SA-*Obergruppenführer* Hans Frank ruled over this part of occupied Poland, the stormtroopers did not initially play a role in the region. Unlike the earlier cases of Austria, the Sudetenland, and the Memelland, the National Socialist regime in the General Government had no significant ethnic German population to mobilize as part of the newly established stormtrooper units. Whereas in the earlier cases the SA had helped pave the way for a later German occupation of the respective territories, in the case of the General Government it was the other way around. The military occupation had established a status quo that the stormtroopers in the following years attempted to uphold.

On 30 October 1939 the first instructions issued by SA-*Obergruppenführer* Max Jüttner on the 'set-up of the SA in the German territories of the former Polish state' made the SA-*Gruppen* Ostland, Ostmark, Silesia, and Sudeten jointly responsible for creating SA 'cells' in the adjoining regions. However, no regular SA structures beyond the most basic levels of *Scharen*, *Trupps*, and *Stürme* were to be created. Uniforms and money would follow but could not be provided for the time being.[98] A few weeks later, with the district borders of German-occupied Poland redrawn, responsibility for the build-up of the SA in this area was redistributed among the SA-*Gruppen* Ostland and Silesia, which each became responsible for the *Gaue* of the same name. In addition, the SA-*Gruppen* 'Weichsel', headquartered in Danzig (responsible for Danzig-Westpreußen), and 'Warthe' (for the Warthegau), based in Posen, were established.[99] As early as November 1939 the SA started to recruit in cities like Łódź and Bielitz, 'with excellent results'.[100] On 22 January 1940 the SA-*Obergruppenführer* Heinrich Hacker was promoted to the leadership of the SA-*Gruppe* Warthe, which, according to SA statistics, comprised more than 10,000 men by March 1940 and more than 25,000 by the summer of 1941.[101] Most of these men were so-called *Volksdeutsche* who had either lived in the region prior to the outbreak of the war or had moved into the area from regions farther east, such as Volhynia, Galicia, and Bessarabia.[102] The leaders of these new SA units, which initially often came from the Old Reich, but also consisted of many Baltic Germans, quickly realized that a considerable proportion of the 'robust men [*kernige Menschen*] with a German look' under their command did not speak German.[103] They therefore organized German language and history lessons for the stormtroopers in the Warthegau – a fact that demonstrates the extent to which the SA literally 'made' German men.[104]

A fanatical anitisemite, Hacker cooperated closely with *Gauleiter* Arthur Greiser in the years that followed.[105] However, Hacker was extremely ambitious and in September 1941 requested to be transferred farther east, preferably to the Caucasus. His motivation for this transfer was that 'the fight of the SA would be quite naturally completed by ruling over Russia. The triumph of the SA spirit over Bolshevism calls first of all the storm-trooper to take the lead in the East.'[106] This reasoning elucidates the extent to which the proponents of such 'escapism for fanatics' grounded their ambitions in a language that invoked early Nazi stereotypes of the enemy as much as colonial fantasies.[107]

In February 1940 the first SA leadership training course for ethnic Germans living in the territories of these new SA groups was held at the SA Reich School in Dresden. 'Better than I thought ... also racially and physically,' Viktor Lutze wrote in his diary.[108] One year later, in early February 1941, the SA-*Gruppe* Warthe comprised two brigades based in

Posen and Litzmannstadt, whereas the SA-*Gruppe* Weichsel had four brigades headquartered in Danzig, Elbing, Bromberg, and Thorn.[109] At the same time, dispersed SA units were also established in the Protectorate, the occupied but unannexed parts of the former Czechoslovakian state. According to the Nazi press, SA-*Stürme* or even *Standarten* existed in Königinhof (Dvůr Králové nad Labem), Königgrätz (Hradec Králové), Pilsen (Plzeň), Brünn (Brno), and Prague. Reliable information about these units is sparse, but they seem to have overwhelmingly comprised ethnic Germans from the respective regions. They were at least partly led by professional SA leaders from the Reich and, in addition, received training from the Wehrmacht. Here, as in other German-occupied parts of central and eastern Europe, the SA fostered a sense of 'Germanness' among its members, who often performed auxiliary police duties.[110]

The situation was different in the General Government. In this region, regular SA units were not established until the spring of 1942, although SA leaders were mustered as part of the official festivities held to celebrate the General Government's first year of existence on 26 October 1940.[111] However, at this time all SA leaders in the General Government were citizens of the Reich who had been sent to the east to carry out administrative and military functions. On official occasions they dressed in their SA uniforms, with the symbols of their respective home regions, but they had not been organized into new local units. The first attempt to change this state of affairs occurred in the autumn of 1941, when the NSDAP allowed the formation of an honorary SA storm (*Ehrensturm*) in Cracow to be used for parades and ceremonies.[112] In the following months, however, the situation changed dramatically in response to the increasing 'security problems' in the region, which were largely a consequence of the ever more repressive and inhumane German colonial rule. German authorities executed no fewer than 17,386 alleged 'bandits' in the General Government in 1942 alone.[113] With the conditions of life for Poles and Jews becoming more and more unbearable, armed resistance driven by despair multiplied.[114] In order to uphold their rule, Hans Frank and Himmler, usually vying for supremacy in the General Government, tried to come to terms to establish the so-called *Wehrschützenbereitschaften*, a mixture of an ethnic German militia, a neighbourhood watch group, and an auxiliary police force that was to be trained by SS officers and in some ways was a new version of the SA-*Wehrmannschaften* established in 1939.[115] When these negotiations did not lead to an agreement, Frank, well aware that Lutze and the OSAF were eagerly waiting for an opportunity to increase their importance and influence, called for the SA to take the place of the SS in the region. In late October 1941, SA-*Standartenführer* Kurt Peltz, who had previously been employed by the SA Reich Leadership School in Munich, arrived in Cracow to organize the *Wehrschützenbereitschaften*.[116] With effect from 17 December, all German men in the General Government aged seventeen or older were registered in such units.[117]

As was to be expected, Himmler and the SS were furious. They feared that the SA would use its influence on these new *Wehrschützenbereitschaften* to establish proper SA units that would be at the disposal of the autocratic Frank. On 3 February 1942, Himmler thus decreed the formation of a new rival unit, the SS-*Sondersturmbann* Ost.[118] Several weeks later, on 20 March, Lutze responded by mandating the establishment of a proper SA-*Gruppe* in the General Government to lead the *Wehrschützenbereitschaften*. Peltz estimated that 'after some initial difficulties' the SA in the General Government could comprise up to 50,000 men, a number he later reduced to 22,000.[119] Frank on 16 April finally decreed the formation of a new SA unit for the General Government, the SA-*Einheit Generalgouvernement*.[120] The SA was to take responsibility for the 'registration, training, and leadership' of the former SA-*Wehrschützenbereitschaften*, which from now on would be referred to as the SA-*Wehrbereitschaften*. Frank, who had previously been an honorary SA-*Obergruppenführer*, would himself formally command the SA in the General Government.[121]

As internal documents make clear, the OSAF was convinced that this step 'would by far' accomplish more than the organization of a paramilitary defence force. As every German man in the region – with 'German' defined in terms of both nationality and ethnicity – who was not an active member of another National Socialist organization was required to serve in these new units, they hoped that a thorough programme of 'political education that is of invaluable benefit for the colonization in the East' could be instituted.[122] As early as 19 June 1942 the SA-*Wehrbereitschaften* comprised 8,000 men in Warsaw and 12,000 men in Radom.[123] Three months later there were eleven SA-*Standarten* with more than 200 *Stürme* in the General Government.[124] Detailed membership lists do not seem to have survived, but a very conservative estimate should assume that at least 30,000–40,000 'ethnic Germans' were organized in these SA-*Wehrbereitschaften* by late 1942.

To the OSAF's disappointment, the SA was only allowed to organize and train these men, whereas the decision to call them to action resided with the SS and the regular police forces.[125] As the security situation in the General Government further deteriorated, however, the SS's attempts to minimize the military clout of the SA in the region lessened considerably.[126] In the spring of 1943 the new SA-*Gruppe* already participated in the 'inspection' (*Überprüfungsaktion*) of ethnic German settlers in the General Government.[127] Hans Frank at the same time complained that with a mere 11,000 policemen to oversee the 16.5 million people living in the General Government, he could only secure the public order in Cracow, Warsaw, and some of the smaller cities.[128] In this context, stormtroopers recruited from among the *Volksdeutsche* became indispensable, and the SA came to 'very largely dominate the political life in the General Government', as one of its leaders in December 1943 boasted.[129] By this time, entire groups of 'completely armed' stormtroopers were carrying out regular police duties.[130]

The regional SA leader, Peltz, had meanwhile fully adapted to the local habits of the German occupiers. Previously, in 1938, his SA superiors had deemed him a 'very reliable SA leader', but had noted a certain 'softness' and reticence in his character. In 1944, by contrast, one of his subordinates complained to the OSAF about Peltz's luxurious lifestyle in Cracow. Peltz, he declared, would request additional food ration coupons for his wife and himself and would send his men to buy rare goods at the city's black market. Peltz defended himself against these charges rather half-heartedly, insisting that the additional food was needed to live up to the standards of a German bureaucrat with social obligations.[131] Accusations that high-ranking SA leaders were ravaging the occupied territories in fact went back to the beginning of the war. Erich Reimann, for example, preparing for a trip home from Poland in December 1939, filled his car with parcels for his wife and the spouses of his SA and Wehrmacht comrades.[132] Even the OSAF in Munich had benefited from the booty, receiving 20,000 metres of Polish uniform cloth.[133]

With the SA's increasing participation in the German 'policing actions' in the General Government, stormtroopers more and more came within the crosshairs of Polish resistance fighters. SA-*Oberführer* Peltz was the target of a failed bomb attack in 1943, and on 15 July of the same year a squad of the Polish resistance group *Gwardia Ludowa* threw a hand grenade at a marching SA column in Warsaw, severely wounding several men. The

German authorities executed about 130 Poles in retaliation.[134] A year later, when the Warsaw Uprising broke out in August 1944, the city's storm-troopers actively participated in the counter-insurgency and suffered heavy losses.[135] By this time, Hans Frank's characterization of the SA in the General Government as the '*Sturm* fist of fighting Germandom' (*Sturmhand des kämpfenden Deutschtums*) was more than the usual Nazi rhetoric. Since 1943 the SA in the General Government had been heavily involved in the ever more violent attempts to control the population and uphold German rule through the recruitment of forced labourers for defence work, punitive expeditions, and an unknown number of acts of local violence that left few traces in the remaining documents.[136] These former latecomers (in comparison to those regular SA units established in the Warthegau, Alsace, and Lorraine) had been transformed into the spearhead of an ever more brutal German occupation regime.

This development was not unique to the General Government. Between 17 April and 15 May 1941 armed SA units comprising Austrian residents and refugees from the Bukovina region operated in Southern Styria and Carniola, areas that had been occupied by the German military in early April 1941.[137] As had occurred in western Poland in the first weeks of the war, undercover SA units from the SA-*Gruppe* Südmark, with a total strength of between 3,500 and 4,500 men, followed the Wehrmacht's advance in the Balkan campaign. As a euphemistic report written on behalf of the SA noted, the stormtroopers established order in the 'liberated areas of Southern Styria and Carniola'. They secured vital public utilities and 'cleansed the areas of roving hordes'. These tasks were completed quickly and rigorously, wrote the embedded journalist in the service of the SA.[138] This article, however, was never published – perhaps because of its very direct language, which made it clear that the SA in the border regions of the Reich had been transformed into an armed political police and fighting force that was deeply implicated in the war. In contrast to this official restraint, a publication of the SA-*Gruppe* Südmark in May 1941 openly boasted of the stormtroopers' 'special operation in the liberated lowland' in Styria and beyond. Whereas the majority of the men deployed there were used for the protection of industrial plants and for 'general security tasks', 600 of them were sent into the Pohorje Mountains to cleanse the area of 'franc-tireurs' and dispersed 'Serbian troops'. This operation was placed under the command of SA-*Gruppenführer* Walther Nibbe, the leader of the

SA-*Gruppe* Südmark, and was carried out by 'closed SA units' (*geschlossene SA-Einheiten*).[139]

From the early summer of 1941 onward such tasks were taken over by the newly formed SA-*Wehrmannschaften* under the command of the *Steirischer Heimatbund* and the *Kärntner Volksbund*, two organizations created to serve as regional NSDAP branches. One year later, in the summer of 1942, the Nazi weekly *Illustrierter Beobachter* printed a photo essay under the headline 'Border patrol against bandits' (*Grenzwacht gegen Banditen*), which stated that armed *Wehrmannschaften* under the leadership of the SA were successfully fighting 'Bolshevist rabble-rousers' and dispersed groups of soldiers from the former Yugoslav army in the new borderlands of Upper Carniola.[140] Similar to the development in the General Government, the SA-*Gruppe* Südmark thus played a vital role in the 'securing' of Southern Styria and Carniola, an effort that included the persecution of both alleged and real partisans. However, the official task of the SA-*Wehrmannschaften* was not to pacify Southern Styria and Carniola by fighting partisans, but to provide their members with a 'National Socialist education' that included paramilitary training, in line with the SA's general mission since 1939. Service in the SA-*Wehrmannschaften* was considered *the* main way to 'show its members the way back into Germandom [*Rückführung zum Deutschtum*]'.[141] As in other annexed or occupied parts of the Greater German Reich, regional policing went hand in hand with attempts to 'Germanize' those parts of the local populations deemed racially sufficient.[142]

Yet the activities of the *Steirischer Heimatbund* and the *Kärntner Volksbund* in conjunction with the SA-*Wehrmannschaften* did not have the intended effects. Instead, only one year of National Socialist rule produced a complete change of mood among the local population, largely because of the violence and corruption of the German organizations put in place.[143] The situation became so critical that the SA-*Wehrmannschaften* of the *Kärntner Volksbund* were dissolved in October 1942. In its place, a proper SA-*Standarte* Oberkrain was formed, but only slightly more than 1,000 men had joined its ranks by January 1943.[144] From that autumn onward, the continuing operations against 'partisans' were increasingly carried out, with an extreme level of violence, by the so-called SS-*Karstwehr* under the command of SS-*Standartenführer* Hans Brand.[145] Once more, the SS ultimately surpassed the SA.

On the Home Front

Not all SA men served in the Wehrmacht or in units within the occupied territories. In particular, those too old for active duty instead took on auxiliary roles on what the regime's propagandists referred to as the 'home front'. Such duties were diverse and started immediately with the beginning of the war. In Greater Hamburg, for example, the local SA was placed in charge of air-raid alert duties starting in September 1939, a task that kept nearly 500 SA men busy. Large numbers of stormtroopers were also ordered to support the work of the 'provision aid organization' (*Ernährungshilfswerk*) of Greater Hamburg (600 men) and to build air-raid protection trenches in the region (400 men).[146] These jobs were certainly less prestigious than front-line duty, but as the war progressed they became increasingly important for the maintenance of public order in the Third Reich.

A few years later, in July and August 1943, such preparatory work yielded fruit when massive Allied airstrikes on Hamburg in 'Operation Gomorrah' destroyed substantial parts of the city and killed about 37,000 people.[147] This was at least the perspective of Gustaf Deuchler, one of the most fanatical Nazi activists within German academia. A committed stormtrooper since 1934, Deuchler euphorically praised the emergency aid administered by the Brownshirts in the days of the bombings. At a time when centralized commands could not be given, the local SA units had demonstrated a remarkable level of self-organization, he claimed. He and his fellow comrades had to carry out the extraordinarily difficult tasks of providing for the hundreds of thousands who had been bombed out of their homes, helping the injured, and locating the dead. The SA also secured buildings at risk of collapse, organized the evacuation of those made homeless, and fought the fires that blazed all over the city. The fulfilment of these tasks was all the more remarkable as many of the stormtroopers had themselves lost their homes and relatives, Deuchler claimed. He even maintained that, at this time of crisis, the men of the SA had been the main ones providing help and consolation: 'Where an SA man appeared, he immediately drew the attention and had the respect of the *Volksgenossen* [. . .] The trust in the SA man was simply boundless. The SA man knows everything, can achieve anything, is capable of doing anything. That was the discernible conviction of the *Volksgenossen* vis-à-vis the SA.'[148]

This uncritical glorification of the SA by one of its members was of course exaggerated, yet it contained a grain of truth. Since the beginning of the war, the SA had been involved in a range of activities that had not always flattered the stormtroopers' self-esteem but had indeed contributed to what Nazi propaganda referred to as the 'securing of the home front'. Those SA men who were not drafted participated in an SA 'care service' for the families of their comrades in the military, were repeatedly called on to donate blood, and helped with the transport of wounded soldiers. By 1941 some SA groups also disbursed funds to pay for cigarettes, books, newspapers, and pocket money for injured comrades being treated in military hospitals.[149] SA units furthermore helped in the construction of anti-aircraft gun shelters and the Siegfried Line on the Reich's western border, aided German farmers during the harvest, helped in the resettlement of ethnic Germans 'returning home', attempted to prevent forest fires, and supported the regular border police as 'auxiliary policemen', as they had done in 1933–4.[150] Of particular importance was the policing of those foreign slave labourers who were being put to work in the factories and fields of the Reich in ever larger numbers. By August 1944 the number of foreigners in the Reich had risen to nearly eight million, with the vast majority of them being forced labourers. In order to keep these large numbers of foreigners under control, the regime relied on more than one million German men, who, as auxiliary policemen or *Land-* or *Stadtwachtmänner*, were responsible for preventing escapes and racially undesirable intimate encounters and upholding public morale in the wider sense.[151]

The *Landwacht* and *Stadtwacht* were under Himmler's control, and, in light of the SS's pressure on the SA since 1934, the OSAF understandably feared that the new bodies would recruit heavily from the ranks of the SA. In April 1942 the SA leadership therefore requested that at least its leaders be excluded from recruitment. Otherwise, the SA's 'mass work' (*Breitenarbeit*) risked coming to a complete standstill. The OSAF was not willing to hand over its last remaining cadres on the 'home front' to Himmler. At least this time it won the tug of war against the chief of the German police, who in June 1942 gave in to its demands.[152]

Later in the war, with the increased destruction of German cities, the stormtroopers were ordered to collect those remains of bombed-out flats that were still usable, such as stoves and bathtubs, and to make them available for those in need.[153] They also enforced the frequent lights-out orders and, in cooperation with the National Socialist People's Welfare (NSV) group, provided civilians in need with carbon during cold periods.[154] All these activities served the purpose of maintaining public order. In this capacity the stormtroopers also strictly disciplined both foreigners and the German population. Deuchler, in his above-mentioned report on Hamburg, did not fail to note that among the SA's tasks was the 'inconspicuous watch of dubious or suspicious people'[155] – a description that was applied to various foreign slave labourers as well as everyday German civilians.

Despite this multitude of tasks, many long-standing members of the SA complained about a lack of recognition for their contributions. For example, SA-*Sturmführer* Fritz Hancke, an employee of the SA archives in the Horst-Wessel-Haus and an 'operating air-raid warden' (*Betriebsluftschutzleiter*), expressed the belief that he, as a committed Nazi, was not being used in the right capacity: 'At least our fellow Germans can now see that we old rowdies are still of use during the war. Unfortunately, we are no longer welcome at the front, although it is precisely us who should have a right to participate in the final march against the Bolshevists, we the active fighters of the first hours. But unfortunately, we have to stay here and keep house [*einhüten*]!!!'[156] Similarly, Viktor Hölscher, a stormtrooper and the owner of the Munich-based H. Traut photography company, complained about his situation in an inflammatory six-page-long letter to the OSAF in June 1942. Many of the rank and file regarded active service in the SA during the war years as extremely unsatisfactory, Hölscher stated. The men under his command were mostly between twenty-eight and forty years of age, ideologically firm and experienced, and desperate to contribute actively to Germany's final victory – but instead, they were condemned to a *Stammtischgemeinschaft* that did little more than regularly meet at an inn for perfunctory and largely social gatherings. 'No activist can stand this week by week, month after month!' Hölscher exclaimed. In his view the SA had come to resemble a veterans' association more than a modern and strategically important party organization. Consequently, newcomers to the SA were now mostly candidates for the civil service (*Beamtenanwärter*), for whom membership in at least one party organization was required. Such people at best became formal 'members', but with no guarantee that they would be committed and activist-oriented 'real SA men'. All in all, there was no denying that the SA was the only important party organization that did not fulfil a strategic task, Hölscher concluded.[157]

Such criticism from committed SA activists struck a nerve within the organization. Still, it is important to distinguish between the SA's activities in the Old Reich and its tasks in the newly acquired or occupied territories. Whereas the numerically reduced SA units in Germany's heartlands in the first years of the war did indeed often lack purpose and motivation, this was less the case farther east and south, in those regions where SA units had only been established recently and early on became part of the German war effort. It is indicative of the SA's continuing relevance that Himmler continued to supervise the group's activities closely in these years and to monitor news about the efforts of Lutze and later Schepmann to enhance the stormtroopers' importance. Yet as the war intensified and bombings of German cities and industries multiplied, the SA was assigned an increasing number of tasks in the Old Reich as well. With the majority of younger men fighting on the front lines, the ability of the SA to gather, discipline, and employ both older and extremely young German men, as well as to keep an ever more anxious civilian population in check, became a vital element of the nation's war effort.

These new responsibilities also had a gendered dimension, as an example from Munich illustrates. A secret report from September 1942 written by Hans Sponholz, a moderately successful novelist who served as an SA propagandist in the OSAF, stated that women were talking about a recent Allied airstrike on the city in ways that alarmed the authorities. Specifically, they were openly speculating that the German Reich had attacked the Allies first and that thus moral outrage about the raids – as voiced in the official propaganda – was not justified. What is more, some of them even interpreted the high number of civilians killed or made homeless by the bombings as a 'judgement from above' for the fact that Germany 'had forced the Jews across the border and had engulfed them in misery'. In order to stop such discussion, Sponholz recommended sending some SA leaders in plainclothes into shops to 'nail down some individual cases'.[158] It might be a coincidence that he used in this instance a verb with sexual connotations in German, but even if it was, it is remarkable that he identified the problem as woman-related and suggested an explicitly male intervention as a solution. His message was clear: when women became weak in the face of terrifying airstrikes, strong-willed men had the right to punish them as an example to others.[159] In a society at war, the SA, as moral police and 'guardians of the people's community', not only targeted foreigners and those declared social outsiders, but also ordinary *Volksgenossen* in Nazi Germany.

To the Last Man

Ever since the economic crisis of the early 1930s, the SA had focused on finding jobs for its rank-and-file stormtroopers. Prior to 1933 the Nazis also attempted to penetrate the unions, which were then firmly in the hands of the SPD and the KPD, and even established their own kind of union, the *Nationalsozialistische Betriebszellen-Organisation* (NSBO). In practice, the relationship between the SA and the NSBO was not free of tensions, particularly when the NSBO had more success than the SA in providing jobs for its members.[160] As explained above, the SA then started to organize so-called *Hilfswerklager*, or 'welfare camps', provisional work camps in which unemployed stormtroopers were housed in barracks. The men in these camps constituted a cheap labour pool at the disposal of the party and the state and were employed mostly for infrastructure work such as the building of new roads. At the same time these *Hilfswerklager* were an attempt to control the population and channel the persistently high level of discontent and violence among ordinary militants in a more productive direction.[161]

As the economic situation recovered in the second half of the 1930s, most of these 'welfare camps' were closed down. Some of them, however, such as the camp in Lockstedter Lager, today's Hohenlockstedt in Schleswig-Holstein, were transformed into so-called SA-*Umschulungslager*, or 'occupational retraining camps', later re-baptized SA-*Berufsschule*, or 'SA professional schools'.[162] Here, stormtroopers who struggled to find regular employment were trained for one or two years for regular jobs in industry. The aim of the camps was to qualify as many men as available 'in the shortest time possible' to become *Facharbeiter*, or 'skilled labourers', an officially recognized professional status that entitled its bearers to higher pay than unskilled workers. These camps produced locksmiths, mechanical engineers, ship builders, precision mechanics, coppersmiths, galvanized steel workers (*Feinblechner*), and welders.[163] Local companies in return were asked to contribute the training equipment of the schools and help improve their facilities.[164]

The SA professional school in Lockstedter Lager was initially quite popular, welcoming more than 1,000 trainees in 1938.[165] At this time, one-quarter of all apprentices were aged thirty or above. In other words, as in the *Hilfswerklager* tradition, the 'professional school' was initially concerned with qualifying 'Old Fighters', but over the next years, it became more and more successful in attracting young German men who only knew of the 'time of struggle' by hearsay.[166] The majority of these candidates increasingly came from impoverished border areas of the Reich. In 1938, Lockstedter Lager welcomed its first unemployed stormtroopers from the Sudetenland, and in 1939 it accepted several hundred men from Upper Silesia.[167] During the war years it took in apprentices, at times as young as fifteen years old, from the previously Polish part of Upper Silesia, the Memelland, and occupied Lithuania.[168]

Similar SA professional schools built on this successful model. By 1941 there were four different SA professional schools that carried the names of their respective regions: the above-mentioned *Nordmark* in Lockstedter Lager; *Nordsee* in Westerstede near Oldenburg; *Ostland*, later renamed *Tannenberg*, located in Contienen near the East Prussian capital of Königsberg, today's Kaliningrad; and *Weichsel* in Schulitz, today's Polish Solec Kujawski, a small town in the vicinity of Bromberg, or Bydgoszcz.[169] During the war, the Marine High Command provided the financial support for the construction and development of these four schools.[170] From July 1941 onward they were run by the SA leadership in Munich in close cooperation with the Consortium for the SA Professional Schools (*Industriegemeinschaft für die SA-Berufsschulen*), a group of several northern and eastern German companies led by Heinrich Middendorff, a former submarine commander and chairman of the executive board of the *Deutsche Werke Kiel AG*.[171] The companies Middendorff represented were active in the shipbuilding business, which, while benefiting from an increase in demand for war cruisers and submarines, lacked qualified workers due to conscription.[172] Furthermore, the physically demanding shipbuilding business did not attract many workers with an educational background, so the industry targeted the extremely young as well as those 'older German men who for whatever kind of misfortune had failed to learn a trade'. In the face of this shortage, the industry cooperated with the SA, which it had (rightly) identified as a lobbyist for men with relatively low social status and education. However, Middendorff officially insisted that the goal of the companies he represented would not be 'to employ whatever people were available in the shortest time possible', but to train the best men, defined as those who were 'politically and personally qualified SA men'.[173]

In most cases the men who enrolled in these professional schools were sent there directly from the German job centres. Prior membership in the

SA was not a formal requirement for enrolment, but every aspirant had to signal willingness to join the SA later on.[174] Peasant labourers were explicitly prohibited from joining these schools for practical and ideological reasons.[175] First, these men were needed in the agricultural sector, particularly during the war years; and second, the Nazis did not want to contribute to further rural flight, especially as they regarded practical work on 'German soil' as physically healthy and morally important. The SA in fact had a hard time defending 'political education' as a vital part of the school curriculum.[176] It also struggled to fill the 5,500 places available in these schools, even though the education they offered was free of charge and the schools provided accommodation, work clothes, and a small salary.[177] Further compounding these difficulties was the fact that many of those admitted did not stay long but were quickly sent home by the school administration. The SA justified these decisions by claiming that no company would have an interest in employing workers who suffered from tuberculosis, cardiac problems, or feeble-mindedness – a defence that threw a glaring spotlight on the social composition of the men in these professional schools during the war years. According to the OSAF, the job centres were to blame for this problem, as they only sent to the camps a dubious selection of those few men available in Germany at the time.[178]

In the summer of 1942, the OSAF started to realize that Middendorff had only cooperated with the SA as long as the German industry was in dire need of workers. With the military campaign against the Soviet Union looking promising and new waves of Russian and Polish forced labourers becoming available, Middendorff's enthusiasm for the inclusion of SA ideological education in the professional training of unskilled labourers lessened considerably. In July 1942 he strongly urged the SA leadership in Munich to accept Russian 'civil workers' (*Zivilarbeiter*) into the school at Lockstedter Lager to maximize the number of workers who could be brought into the shipyards.[179] The SA, however, strongly opposed such plans, arguing that its activities were first and foremost meant to benefit German workers and the people's community, not necessarily wealthy industrialists. If the Russians were to be accepted at all, their barracks had to be separated from the other quarters by a fence three and a half metres high.[180] By now, Middendorff had proven an 'extremely ruthless manager' (*Betriebsführer*), complained SA-*Brigadeführer* Herbert Merker, the officer in charge of the school. When it came to matters of social concern,

Middendorff was 'as unaffected as a newborn child'. Such judgements not only attest to the bitterness of long-time SA activists once again confronted with the fact that industrial needs were deemed more important than ideological matters,[181] but also reveal the survival of certain elements of the NSDAP's 'socialist' ideology from the time prior to 1933. Most instructive in this regard is a statement from Siegfried Uiberreither, the *Reichsstatthalter* and *Gauleiter* of Styria. In a speech to the SA men of his region delivered in the spring of 1941, he declared that once the war was over, they should 'grab again the banner of the revolution' and transform Greater Germany into the 'greatest welfare state on earth'.[182]

As German stormtroopers in need of professional and ideological training became increasingly unavailable, Merker concluded that the existence of the SA professional schools (from November 1942 referred to as SA-*Werklager*, or 'SA work camps') could only be justified on the basis of the strategic necessities of a nation at war.[183] Although the *Werklager* Nordmark operated until the end of the war, the raison d'être for these schools/camps was shifted into the near future, in the context of the peacetime that was to follow the German military victory. At present, Germany's top priority was the formation of the 'best Wehrmacht possible', Merker admitted. However, after the war, the military soldier would be replaced by a new role model: the 'workman soldier' (*Soldat der Arbeit*). In Merker's view, the SA was called to shape this new type of German skilled labourer by helping him obtain a higher level of technical skill and training him both ideologically and physically. Once qualified, the German worker would ultimately be able to serve as 'defender of the newly acquired space' (*Verteidiger des neu erworbenen Raumes*).[184]

There are striking parallels between this conception and the idea of the SA *Wehrbauern*, or 'defensive peasants', from the new German east, as analysed in the previous chapter. While the activities of SA units in many regions of the Old Reich between 1940 and 1944 were severely diminished by a lack of available men and the absence of an overarching sense of purpose, the SA leadership compensated for its temporary unimportance by making ever more grandiose plans for the post-war period. In its imagination, the new German society would be one in which even traditional 'civil' professional activities, such as farming and industrial work, would be carried out with soldierly conviction. Peace, in its literal meaning of the absence of war and violent confrontation, was no longer viewed as feasible.

Just as the individual stormtrooper had in the earliest days of the Nazi 'movement' been in need of violent conflicts to prove his determination and social worth, so the German *Volksgemeinschaft* post-Second World War was imagined as a community constantly threatened by enemies living outside its boundaries. Consequently, the German man throughout his adult life was to have two closely intertwined professional identities, a civil identity and a military one. Put bluntly, all German men were in the future expected to be ideologically firm stormtroopers or SA-*Wehrmänner* throughout their entire adult lives, ready to be mobilized for war at any given moment.

Confronting Defeat

In contrast to such high-flying expectations, the situation of the SA between 1943 and 1945 was anything but promising. Its intensified activities did not make up for its overall lack of reputation, resources, and prospects. By the autumn of 1943 even the notoriously optimistic SA Chief of Staff Wilhelm Schepmann had to concede that the situation of the organization was critical. In a long speech at a meeting of the *Reichsleiter* and *Gauleiter* in Posen on 6 October 1943, he explained that his organization should be judged not by its immediate results (or lack thereof), but by its long-term impact. The general tone of his speech was defensive.[185] Schepmann repeatedly emphasized that the role of the SA was as an instrument of the party and of Hitler.[186] Consequently, he was eager to improve its relationship with other party organizations, particularly the Hitler Youth and the SS. In direct talks with Himmler, Schepmann seems to have unconditionally accepted the preeminent role of the SS and the Waffen-SS, at least during wartime. He explicitly stated that he would not pursue plans for a Waffen-SA, which would comprise exclusively SA men, even as he claimed that Himmler had previously agreed to establish such a group. Modelled along the lines of the *Standarte* Feldherrnhalle, but under the command of the Wehrmacht, the projected SA combat unit to complement the Waffen-SS was never established. It is highly unlikely that Himmler ever intended to form such a unit. He most likely made the promise merely to demonstrate goodwill toward the new SA Chief of Staff and ensure his obedience. An agreement between the SA and SS from the year 1944, allowing stormtroopers to volunteer for the 18th SS volunteer Panzergrenadier Division 'Horst Wessel', served the same purpose.[187]

Yet the dramatically deteriorating military situation from 1943 onward increased the relative importance of the SA against all odds. Until the end of the Third Reich, paramilitary activism became once again a regular feature of stormtrooper practice. As the front lines rapidly approached and then penetrated the territory of the German Reich, the remaining Brownshirts – about 500,000 in 1944[188] – were mobilized to organize and coordinate the national defence effort 'from within'. The enemies of the *Volksgemeinschaft* would now be confronted by the SA's 'revolutionary drive', the organization's propaganda exulted: 'We live again in the *Kampfzeit*.'[189] Consequently, the SA – alongside other National Socialist organizations like the Hitler Youth – resorted once more to street parades in 1944, aiming to publicly display an allegedly undaunted *Volksgemeinschaft*. One critical observer commented in his diary that such processions were understandably 'highly popular at this particular time', as they could 'provide a feeling of security when dreadful things announce themselves from out front [*wenn draußen Schreckliches sich ankündigt*]'.[190]

In 1944 and early 1945 the Nazi leadership ordered the stormtroopers to fight against both the military enemy and the rapidly deteriorating German morale, not only with rhetoric and demonstrations, but also with force. On 26 September 1944, SA Chief of Staff Schepmann was appointed Chief of Staff for the German *Volkssturm*'s Shooting Training (*Inspekteur der Schießausbildung im Deutschen Volkssturm*).[191] The unequal distribution of power between Himmler and Schepmann continued. Whereas Himmler, as Commander of the Reserve Army (*Befehlshaber des Ersatzheeres*), determined the *Volkssturm*'s operational missions, Schepmann was given responsibility only for the training and equipping of those considered too old or too young to fight in the regular Wehrmacht.[192] In addition to SA leaders serving as *Volkssturm* instructors or commanders, rank-and-file stormtroopers came to provide the nucleus of many *Volkssturm* units.[193] For example, the leader of the Austrian SA-*Brigade* 94 Oberdonau was given command of the formation of fighting units, which were to be recruited from the *Gauwehrmannschaften*, the Austrian civil-defence formation. The Nazi militants were ordered to organize and supervise this 'last draft' and were expected to provide these men 'with clear political attitude', 'soldierly expertise', and a grasp of military necessities.[194]

Under the circumstances, the training offered by the SA could not meet high standards, even if the propaganda of the Nazi regime naturally asserted the opposite.[195] Schepmann promised that the new *Volkssturm* units would be trained so effectively that they would be able to turn back any 'urgent danger' to the Reich territory. Many of the men now being drafted had been trained in the SA-*Wehrmannschaften* in previous years, he pointed out. Furthermore, the new training would be organized in a less formal way than had previously been seen. The main goal of the relatively short instructional courses would be 'to awaken' men's 'interest in shooting' in order to 'maximize firepower'.[196] Over the course of the next few months, power and weapons were transferred from the disintegrating SA to the regional *Volkssturm* units.[197] Despite organizational shortcomings, the SA continued to provide many of the fanatical 'believers' who attempted to defend the Third Reich and its social system until the last days of the regime (Plate 31).

The OSAF's instructions for the 'total war' effort, distributed by Schepmann to the SA leadership corps in early December 1944, allow some insight into the mentality and self-understanding of the late SA activists. The ultimate goal of this effort, Schepmann explained, was to 'fanaticize' the individual stormtrooper to a degree of 'unconditional commitment' to the *Volksgemeinschaft* and total resistance to the enemy. Therefore, SA men were encouraged to wear their uniform at the workplace and in the general public.[198] Drawing an audacious historical parallel, Schepmann compared the Reich's situation in late 1944 with the wars of liberation that had broken out across Europe in the early nineteenth century. As his predecessors more than 100 years prior had done, he regarded the racial and ideological unity of the nation as a prerequisite for Germany's liberation.[199] Schepmann declared that 'international Jewry in its quest for world domination' was responsible for the war. In a way his rhetoric echoed that employed in the early days of the NSDAP in Munich, with the addition of apocalyptic threats. The future of a defeated Reich was extremely bleak, if there was a future at all, Schepmann warned. Families would be torn apart and slave labour introduced. Millions would die of hunger. The Jewish *Untermenschentum* would destroy German culture and the German language.[200] In short, the Reich would suffer from what it had done to its eastern neighbours in the previous years – a logical connection that Schepmann of course did not make explicit, but of which he and many others were certainly aware.[201]

Such alarmist propaganda was not only a consequence of the current military situation. Ever since the Germans had launched 'Operation

Barbarossa', the attack on the Soviet Union, in July 1941, extreme anti-Bolshevism and antisemitism – combined in the term 'Jewish Bolshevism' – again became vital elements of the SA's ideology.[202] SA magazines began to repeatedly publish extracts from soldiers' letters that condemned the Soviet 'workers' paradise' as the greatest of lies. What they had seen with their own eyes, such writers declared, was far worse than they had expected. While the German *Volksgemeinschaft* would accept social differences only as long as they were based on commitment to the community and individual talent, Soviet society according to such statements was one of extreme social difference resulting from a Jewish-Bolshevist conspiracy, which aimed to mercilessly dominate the Russian people. The common people of Russia reminded the soldiers of animals, without prospects or hope and exploited by the Jews: 'Here, the Jew raged himself out. State and people rear his very own ugly head.'[203]

With the course of the war turning, such rhetoric was used less as a call to change the European east for the better than as a way to mobilize the remaining Germans in the Reich. To prevent the worst-case scenario of the Red Army winning the war, the stormtroopers were ordered to be extremely vigilant in their attempts to keep the nation safe. Hidden enemies could be anywhere. In particular, the Brownshirts were urged to keep a sharp eye out for all 'foreign races' (*Fremdvölkische*). The final battle would bring ultimate empowerment, or so Schepmann argued. Unrestricted by legal or moral concerns, he declared, 'the SA man has always to take a tough stance against all that can harm the spiritual warfare (rumours – defeatism). If necessary, he has to help himself as during the *Kampfzeit*. As at that time, we break resistance with our fists.'[204]

It is hard to measure the effectiveness of such calls. Yet, even if by late 1944 the majority of the German population was weary of war and only partly susceptible to such propaganda, the acts committed by many stormtroopers in the last months of the conflict suggest that at least they took such calls to heart.[205] As they had previously done in the General Government, local SA leaders now increasingly performed police service all over Germany. At times they even took the lead in spontaneous hate crimes, as in the industrial city of Rüsselsheim, where, after heavy Allied bombing, an angry mob of Germans tortured and killed several captured American airmen on 26 August 1944. After an initial wave of blows, Josef Hartgen, the local Nazi Party official and an SA leader, pulled out his revolver and shot at least four of the men. The next day Hartgen attended the funeral of the American soldiers dressed in his brown-shirted uniform, thus attempting to transform the mob violence and his own murderous actions into acts of legitimate self-defence.[206] Following a similar logic, stormtroopers in rural Germany continued to uphold the racial boundaries established by the regime. As in the mid-1930s, when they publicly humiliated German-Jewish couples for alleged racial defilement, these men now severely punished sexual relations between Germans and slave labourers, particularly if the latter were of Slavonic descent. SA propaganda from the time characterized Poles and members of other eastern European nations as 'cruel and insidious' and in need of supervision, particularly in the countryside, where the danger of 'blood mixing' was said to be very high.[207] Local SA searches for such couples regularly ended in beatings. In the most extreme cases it escalated into genuine acts of lynching, events that up to the present constitute some of the most vivid memories of those Germans old enough to have grown up in the countryside in the 1940s. In the rural district of the small city of Herford in Westphalia, for example, uniformed stormtroopers in cooperation with the SS hanged at least one male Polish slave labourer from a tree in a small grove. They also compelled several other forced labourers from the region to attend the execution, threatening them with a similar fate if they refused to obey.[208]

What had previously been glorified as the 'German fighting spirit' in the last weeks of the regime vanished as the local hierarchies of power disintegrated. Those who still wore their Nazi uniforms now noticed an increasing hostility from the general public.[209] Because of the heightened danger of Allied airstrikes, the SA headquarters in Munich were relocated to the training school run by the SA-*Gruppe* Hochland on the shores of the Schliersee in the Alpine upland, approximately fifty kilometres south of the Bavarian capital.[210] Used from 1938 onward for the schooling of the SA's regional leadership corps, the facilities from the spring of 1944 onward served as provisional SA headquarters.[211] Yet it was not until 1945 that Chief of Staff Schepmann and his family arrived here.[212] By that time there was effectively nothing left for him to do. Already in the weeks leading up to his arrival, the OSAF, in the absence of a functioning bureaucracy, proved incapable of effectively controlling the hundreds of thousands of SA men who still lived in Germany.

Instead, provisional groups consisting of committed National Socialists who claimed leadership on the local and regional levels mushroomed. Some stormtroopers still felt empowered to defend the people's community by violent means. Their activism was directed against Allied forces, Jewish concentration-camp prisoners, and German 'defeatists', but it predominantly harmed members of the two latter groups. According to the latest research by historian Patrick Wagner, fanatical National Socialists murdered several hundred German civilians during the last months of the war.[213] The number of Jewish and eastern European slave labourers killed during the final months of the regime was as high as 250,000.[214] Particularly well researched are the massacres of Hungarian-Jewish slave labourers sent to Mauthausen concentration camp in March and April 1945. Local *Volkssturm* units in Styria were called upon to oversee these 'death marches', and a 'police company' from the city of Eisenerz that consisted of 150 'reliable' SA men was ordered 'to kill as many Jews as possible'. These stormtroopers shot between 150 and 200 people on 7 April 1945 alone.[215] Some of the Nazi *Freikorps* units, hastily arranged in the last months of the war, proved more dangerous to German civilians than to Allied soldiers. A special 'hit squad' of the *Freikorps* Sauerland, headed by an SA man called Friedrich Jäger, hunted down deserters and dissenters and killed at least five people: two alleged deserters, a male civilian, a female civilian, and a mine manager who was held responsible for the flying of a white flag on the pithead of his mine in Weidenau near Siegen.[216] In southwestern Germany another group called the *Sturmabteilung Freikorps Adolf Hitler* was sent to Munich to crush an anti-Nazi movement in April 1945. Still another SA task force that operated in Bavaria and was led by the SA-*Brigadeführer* Hans Zöberlein, a writer and fanatical National Socialist, killed ten civilians on 28 and 29 April 1945 in the small working-class town of Penzberg, some fifty kilometres south of Munich, where the local mayor had been forced to step down to enable a peaceful surrender to the Americans.[217]

In most places, however, the slogan 'Fight until the last drop!' was replaced by 'Save yourself if you can!' virtually overnight. When local media spread the news that Allied troops had reached the area, local Nazi authorities usually went into hiding, and the rank-and-file National Socialists disposed of their insignias, banners, and party badges. People from the Schliersee region raided the last remaining headquarters of the SA on 5 May 1945 and, according to the testimony of the town's pastor, destroyed or stole up to 2,000 SA coats, several radios, clothes, and furniture, all 'of the highest quality', in a 'barbaric frenzy'. In one room the looting mob even discovered the bodies of a 'Nazi' and a woman who had jointly committed suicide, but no one attempted to bury them.[218] During this period *Mein Kampf* disappeared from the bookshelves in Germany and, together with other Nazi memorabilia, was hidden away until children and grandchildren cleared out the homes of their parents or grandparents, sometimes decades later. Highly visible signs of ideological commitment to the Nazis, such as the stormtroopers' brown shirts, were usually not part of such belated 'discoveries'. As one eyewitness from the city of Höxter remembered, dozens of SA uniforms could be seen floating in the nearby River Weser in April 1945.[219] In many cases these castoffs represented more than a simple changing of clothes, as the Nazi identity of their former owners seems to have been washed off as well. As will be analysed in the last chapters of this book, the transformation of the hearts and minds of the former stormtroopers was actually a more complicated process – and one that was in many respects the most ambiguous and long lasting.

Everyday Fanaticism

Between 1939 and 1945 the character of the National Socialist project of the *Volksgemeinschaft* changed. Reflecting its initial military and political gains, the regime up to 1941 made sure that the needs of the war machine were met while at the same time carefully paying attention to the material well-being and morale of Germans on the 'home front'. However, as the prospect of German hegemony over large parts of Europe became more and more obsolete, the regime's repressive character increased dramatically. The people's community was now imagined as a community fated to fight a heroic battle for survival on an unprecedented scale.[220] In line with this general development the importance of the 'greedy institution' of the SA increased precisely in those regions where this battle was to be fought. Between 1939 and 1942 the focus of this battle was predominantly viewed as the annexed and occupied territories, where the formation of new SA units offered a low-threshold opportunity for *Reichsdeutsche* and ethnic Germans to prove their loyalty to the regime. From 1942 onward these SA units became part of the broader German effort to uphold public order in these increasingly unstable areas.

As the front lines approached and ultimately crossed the borders of the Old Reich, the Nazi regime attempted to replicate these experiences from the occupied territories in the German heartlands. By then, however, the generation of German men who were in their late twenties and thirties –

those who had previously so decisively contributed to the Nazis' rise and consolidation of power – were already serving in the Wehrmacht and the Waffen-SS. The regime was forced to grasp at straws to organize civil defence and uphold its rule. Those local and regional leaders of the SA who had not been drafted, many of whom were 'Old Fighters', were the natural choice to organize the last defence – even if by 1944–5 the OSAF's former capacity to mobilize and discipline its men had been severely curtailed. Nevertheless, the ideological fervour and militancy of the local SA leaders to a certain extent made up for the group's organizational shortcomings in the last phase of the war. The disciplinary power of the individual storm-troopers in the villages and towns, and not the strength of the organization as a whole, turned out to be one key factor that prevented the regime from collapsing from within. In many places local activists still had the power to mobilize and intimidate a war-weary population. With their backs to the wall, the National Socialists resorted once again to extreme violence. 'Local liquidating communities' killed representatives of civil authorities who were willing to hand over power to the Allies and murdered former concentration-camp inmates on 'death marches'.[221] The training of the SA, ideologically as well as militarily, proved to have deadly repercussions.

SA DIPLOMATS AND THE HOLOCAUST IN SOUTHEASTERN EUROPE

Domination as service to those under our rule: is there a greater entitlement to our leadership claim imaginable than this attitude towards the fundamental questions of life between peoples and the German accomplishments tried at the forum of a thousand-year-long history?
— An SA-*Rottenführer*, summarizing Germany's 'mission' in eastern Europe, July 1941[1]

On the evening of 20 July 1941, SA-*Obergruppenführer* Adolf-Heinz Beckerle sat in his room in the prestigious Hotel Kaiserhof in the heart of Berlin and contemplated the events of the day.[2] He had just arrived from his home town of Frankfurt am Main, where he had served as police president, and was now making a stopover on his way to Sofia. Three days before, Beckerle had been appointed the new German envoy to Bulgaria, where he would spend the next three years. Unlike some Wehrmacht soldiers on their way to the eastern front to whom Beckerle had listened for a while during the train's stop at Magdeburg's central station that afternoon, the thirty-nine-year-old was full of optimism about the war. He noted on the hotel stationery: 'It is really annoying that most people are hardly aware of the importance of the times they are living in, as this is a time that guarantees the national future in such an astonishing and cheerful way.' However, his personal feelings were mixed. He felt exhausted and in need of a change: 'No fighter can cope with such high levels of intensity [*Raubwirtschaft*]!'[3]

Beckerle was one of five SA generals who served as ambassadors of the German Reich in southeastern Europe from 1940 onward. In line with older German geopolitical planning, the Nazi regime perceived the region as an *Ergänzungsraum*, a 'complementary space', that would provide natural resources, food, and men for the Greater German Reich's war effort. From the military point of view, a close alliance with the states of the region was advisable in order to avoid opening another front.[4] Besides Beckerle, the other men chosen to represent German interests in this economically and politically close 'informal empire' were Manfred von Killinger, Hanns Elard Ludin, Siegfried Kasche, and Dietrich von Jagow. Ludin, who had previously served as the leader of the SA-*Gruppe* South-West, was assigned to Preßburg/Bratislava, Slovakia, in December 1940. At the same time von Killinger, who had previously been in charge of the recruitment department at the Foreign Office and had also served for a few months as Ludin's predecessor in Bratislava, was sent to the Romanian capital of Bucharest. Both men reported for duty in January 1941. Several months later, and after an eight-week 'probationary period', the former SA settlement expert Kasche was assigned as envoy to the new German Embassy in Agram/Zagreb in Croatia. Finally, Dietrich von Jagow, who had previously led the SA-*Gruppe* Berlin-Brandenburg, took over as German ambassador in Hungary's capital of Budapest in July 1941, at about the same time that Beckerle assumed his new responsibilities in Bulgaria.[5]

This chapter aims to explain why these five SA generals were appointed to serve as German envoys to southeastern Europe at this particular historical moment and to what extent they championed a particular SA style of diplomacy. Their involvement in the murder of European Jewry will come under particular scrutiny. Although considerable effort has been made to study the Holocaust in all five of the countries examined here, the role of those German diplomats with SA backgrounds in this effort has hardly been touched upon. The following analysis will demonstrate that each SA general-diplomat was actively involved in shaping German foreign policy toward the Third Reich's allies in southeastern Europe. I will also discuss why the attempts of surviving family members to restore the public memory of these diplomats failed and explain why the SA diplomats retained a special status in the *Erinnerungspolitik* of the Foreign Office after 1945.[6]

Stormtroopers in the Foreign Office

All five men who entered the diplomatic service from the SA were highly decorated 'Old Fighters'. The 'Night of the Long Knives' in the summer of 1934 had left its scars on these SA generals – von Killinger, Kasche, Beckerle, and Ludin had only narrowly escaped the death squads – but had guaranteed their loyalty to the party and to Hitler, who could expect them to assert his interests on three fronts: against possible resistance from the professionally trained diplomats in the Foreign Office, whom the Führer (by and large needlessly) regarded with suspicion; against possible objections from the High Command of the Wehrmacht, for whom military needs were ultimately more important than ideological positions; and against the ever-growing influence of the SS.[7] However, the appointment of SA diplomats was not without risk. Although all of them shared a common belief in core National Socialist values, they lacked proper diplomatic training. They formed a distinct group within the Foreign Office, supported there by a few fellow stormtroopers and committed National Socialists like Undersecretary Martin Luther, the 'almighty man in the Foreign Office' until his fall from grace in 1943.[8] At least some career diplomats regarded their new colleagues from the SA with suspicion, as one of Beckerle's diary entries makes plain. Several days after he arrived in Sofia, one of his assistants told him that many members of the Foreign Office in Berlin were critical of the new SA diplomats and believed them to be 'brutal KZ-men' with a 'personal concentration camp' at their disposal.[9]

In sharp contrast to this perception, Beckerle – who had studied economics (*Volkswirtschaft*), philosophy, and law in the 1920s – regarded himself as a political leader, a *Führungspersönlichkeit* with cultural interests and taste, and an artist.[10] He used his spare time in Sofia to dry-point and to write short stories and poems.[11] The pseudonym he chose for his only published book, an autobiographical travel account that recounted his adventures in South America during the 1920s, is revealing: *Edelmann* – a person of noble rank. This pseudonym must also have pleased the woman Beckerle married in 1935: the actress Silke Edelmann.[12] Unlike Beckerle, who could only aspire to high social rank, von Jagow descended from the Prussian aristocracy and held its values in high esteem, blended together with Nazi ideology. In a letter to his son, written at the beginning of the Second World War, von Jagow reminded his five-year-old of the family's 'tradition of honour, loyalty, knightliness and bravery', while also urging the boy not to be a 'moral coward' (*Duckmäuser*) and to remain faithful to the 'National Socialist idea' unto death.[13]

This group of SA diplomats in southeastern Europe was headed by the significantly older Manfred von Killinger, a former Navy lieutenant, *Freikorps* leader, and a leading member of the extreme right-wing para-military *Bund Wiking* who had been involved in the murder of Matthias Erzberger, the former Reich Finance Minister, in 1921. Von Killinger entered the ranks of the SA in 1928, was appointed Minister President of Saxony in May 1933, and served as German consul in San Francisco from 1937 to 1939. In 1939 and again in 1940, Joachim von Ribbentrop, the German Foreign Minister, sent him on two extensive journeys through the Balkans to collect information on the activities of German institutions and organizations such as the embassies and the *Sicherheitsdienst*, or SD, the Security Service of the SS.[14] Von Killinger was thus already a kind of 'expert' on southeastern Europe by the time he was appointed German ambassador to Slovakia in July 1940.[15]

The five SA diplomats operating in the region knew each other from their paramilitary activities in the 1920s and later repeatedly met at Nazi Party rallies, SA meetings, and training courses. Together, they formed an old boys' network that was bound together by a common past in the *Kampfzeit*-era SA and an imagined bright future in a German-dominated Europe after the Second World War.[16] Their correspondence and personal papers reveal that they trusted their 'SA comrades' more than their profes-sionally trained colleagues in the diplomatic service. These bonds were so close that their families spent holidays together, a practice they continued even after 1945.[17] At least in the initial phase of their missions, Beckerle and Kasche – whose personal papers have survived – were anxious to learn about the perspectives and aspirations of their colleagues.[18] They all seemed to understand that their new positions were temporary ones, albeit further steps in their careers.

However, the level of satisfaction these men felt for their new tasks differed sharply. On 4 October 1941, Beckerle noted that Kasche had recently told him that rumours that he (Kasche) was going to be assigned to Moscow were true.[19] According to Beckerle, this assignment was a matter of friction within the party: the recently appointed *Reichsminister* for the occupied eastern territories, Alfred Rosenberg, was pressing for such a move, much to the distaste of von Ribbentrop.[20] Whereas Kasche – who, as we have seen, maintained a strong interest in the colonization and 'Germanization' of eastern Europe – seemed to enjoy his new position in Croatia, the majority of his colleagues had some problems adapting to a life filled with representational duties and social gatherings. Dietrich von Jagow was initially 'deeply unhappy' about being called to the diplomatic service and apparently complained about attending meetings and ceremonies while his comrades were fighting at the front.[21] Hanns Ludin in Bratislava was rumoured to join the German forces at the eastern front on his holidays, a rumour, however, that cannot be verified and seems unlikely to be true.[22]

Fighting behind the Scenes

There has been some speculation as to why these men from the 'uncompromising generation', who glorified the ideal of the strong German fighter and believed in the power of physical violence as well as rhetoric, were appointed to these diplomatic posts during the first years of the war.[23] While the existing documents indicate that the reasons for these appointments were primarily political, they contain few details about the key players in, or the overall strategy of, this decision. One reason for the promotion of high-ranking SA generals to ambassadorial posts was certainly to counter the influence of the increasingly powerful SS and SD. In a letter to Himmler from 17 April 1941, Gottlob Berger, the head of the SS main office, complained about a veritable 'fight against the SS' within the Foreign Office and identified Undersecretary Luther as the main adversary. By exclusively appointing SA-*Obergruppenführer* to posts in southeastern Europe, Berger claimed, Luther was attempting to 'prove his loyalty to the party' and 'assure himself of the powerful protection of the SA and thereby the Wehrmacht'.[24] According to information from a 'credible source', Berger claimed that von Jagow was slated for Budapest, Kasche for Agram/Zagreb, and Beckerle for Sofia. All these predictions proved correct. The only exception was Fritz von Twardowsky, who since 1939 had served as director of the Cultural Department (*Kulturabteilung*) in the Foreign Office. Von Twardowsky was originally slated for Belgrade but ended up as consul general in Istanbul in 1943.[25]

A second letter from Berger to Himmler nine days later, on 26 April 1941, contained additional information on the appointment of the SA generals. Berger reported that Hitler had recently conferred with SA Chief of Staff Lutze for over an hour, and that afterward Lutze and von Ribbentrop had spoken for ninety minutes.[26] In the course of this conversation Lutze allegedly offered his best men to von Ribbentrop, assuring him that the SA leadership would abstain from any direct interference with the Foreign Ministry once these appointments were made.[27] From Lutze's point of view, this was not an altruistic offer, but an attempt to bring the SA back into the front row of wartime politics, if only through the back door. Its motive was to reaffirm the important role of SA leaders in the colonization and 'Germanization' of eastern Europe, in competition with Himmler's SS.[28] This insertion of the SA in 'his' affairs infuriated the *Reichsführer*-SS. In early 1943 he lost his temper when the name Kasche was mentioned and insulted him as an 'enemy of the Reich' whom he would 'smash'.[29]

The documents also make clear that the appointments of SA generals to diplomatic posts must be seen against the background of the radicalization of German foreign policy during the Second World War and the implementation of the so-called *Generalplan Ost*. A memorandum of a meeting between Hitler, Rosenberg, Göring, and Field Marshal Wilhelm Keitel at the Führer's headquarters on 16 July 1941 provides some insight into the political motives as well as problems of these appointments.[30] Hitler explained that the approach toward eastern Europe was a matter 'of cutting up the giant cake according to our needs, in order to be able first, to dominate it; second, to administer it; and third, to exploit it.'[31] Detailed plans of which territories should be annexed to the Reich and who should govern those areas only temporarily occupied by the Wehrmacht were made. Rosenberg supported Lutze's idea of appointing high-ranking SA leaders as *Reichskommissare*, or governors. Apart from the names already mentioned, those present discussed the possible assignment of Wilhelm Schepmann to Kiev; Arno Manthey, Heinrich Bennecke, and Karl-Siegmund Litzmann to Estonia; and Otto-Heinrich Drechsler to Latvia.[32] Furthermore, Rosenberg informed Hitler that he had received a letter from von Ribbentrop asking for active participation of the Foreign Office in the territories under discussion. Rosenberg, however, took a different view, arguing that 'the internal organization of the newly acquired areas was no concern of the Foreign Ministry'. According to the memorandum, Hitler 'absolutely' shared this view and likewise voiced no objections to the employment of SA leaders in a diplomatic capacity.[33]

A short essay written in the autumn of 1941 by a certain Dr Otto from Budapest, and sent to the OSAF for publication, contains further information on the appointment of SA generals as diplomats. Entitled *SA-Obergruppenführer und Diplomat*, it set out to present the recent appointments of SA generals to the diplomatic service as the latest step in a policy that Otto von Bismarck had begun in the second half of the nineteenth century. Based on the assumption that 'the true National Socialists of all peoples' would respect each other 'as National Socialists', the appointment of the SA generals as diplomats was, Dr Otto argued, a clear sign of paradigmatic change. From now on, diplomats would no longer act on the interests of states, but would work to further the interests of peoples. Particularly in southeastern Europe, with its many German allies, Dr Otto argued, a process had begun in which Western role models would be replaced by a 'realistic understanding of life [*wirklichkeitsnahe Lebensauffassung*]', according to which the legitimate interests of peoples would be more important than legal claims for territory and state sovereignty: 'The reactionary tricky diplomacy [*Winkeldiplomatie*] of the cabinets is wiped out. The clear, honest and generous diplomacy of the peoples, of their delegated political soldiers, is at work, to serve the vital needs of the peoples and Europe's destiny as honest brokers faithful to Bismarck's legacy.'[34] Whether the governments of southeastern Europe would understand such reasoning as a promise or a threat is hard to determine. The Foreign Office in Berlin feared the latter and prevented the publication of the essay, arguing that although its reflections were essentially correct, a public discussion of the points raised would not be in the German interest 'for the time being', especially as its ally Italy might reap some unwelcome consequences.[35]

Within this context the role of the SA diplomats in southeastern Europe now begins to take shape. They are best understood not as envoys in the traditional sense, but as designated German governors or future *Reichskommissare*, who, for the time being and because of diplomatic considerations, officially acted as ambassadors.[36] Hitler made it clear that although it would be best at present to convey the impression of exercising a temporary mandate only, Germany would 'never withdraw' from the occupied areas of eastern Europe.[37] Against this background, one particular detail in the biographies of Beckerle, Ludin, von Killinger, and von Jagow merits closer attention: all had held leading positions in the police of the Third Reich. Beckerle had served as police president in Frankfurt an Main from September 1933 to 1939, and as temporary head of police in the Polish city of Łódź after the German occupation in the autumn of 1939; Ludin as acting police president of Karlsruhe in February and March 1933; and von Killinger and von Jagow as *Reichskommissare* in Saxony and Württemberg respectively.[38] In these roles they had actively contributed to the establishment of the Third Reich by intimidating and incarcerating political rivals of the NSDAP. They had also been complicit in the imprisonment and murder of alleged opponents of the Third Reich during these years, as well as the concealment of these crimes.[39]

In other words these SA generals might not have been the best diplomats available, but they were experienced and ideologically loyal activists, accustomed to the use of violence for political and personal means. Their big moment was yet to come, or so they thought. Once the war was over these men expected to rule over large parts of southeastern Europe and help establish German supremacy in the Balkans and Slovakia, Hungary, Romania, and Bulgaria. In the meantime, as the war continued, their principal task was to push through Hitler's agenda in close cooperation with the existing national governments and to ensure that the Wehrmacht's needs did not take precedence over the long-term political goals of the regime.

In everyday politics the influence of these SA diplomats was nevertheless limited, with notable exceptions. The most prominent and at the same time most controversial example of their influence is their contribution to the murder of European Jewry. Although SS, SD, police, and Wehrmacht units organized the deportations and committed the actual murders of the Jews, often in collaboration with local forces, the SA diplomats actively supported the Holocaust by pressuring the local governments to cooperate with Berlin. In Hitler's words, the envoys were 'experienced experts' of whom he expected support for National Socialist attempts to deal effectively with the 'Jewish question' in their respective regions.[40] The 'achievements' of these individuals, however, differed greatly as a result of their diverse local circumstances. The following section aims to elucidate the role of these SA diplomats in the implementation of the Holocaust in southeastern Europe, a topic that is usually passed over in the otherwise excellent and detailed literature on the murder of European Jewry in the region.[41]

Organizing the Holocaust in Slovakia

In Slovakia, where von Killinger served as envoy in the second half of 1940, followed by Ludin in January 1941, the task was comparatively easy.

Although recent studies have argued that Slovakia, after its declaration of national independence from the Czechs on 14 March 1939, pursued a more independent policy toward the Third Reich than was previously claimed,[42] it must be emphasized that the new Slovak Republic had extremely close ties to Germany and was dependent on the Third Reich militarily and economically. However, it is also important to note that Slovakia had implemented its own laws to marginalize its Jewish population politically, economically, and legally before von Killinger and Ludin were appointed to their posts.[43] The main task of the two envoys was therefore to exploit these 'home-grown antisemitic policies' for the benefit of the Nazi regime's ultimate goal.[44] As became clear to those involved in high-level bi-national talks over the course of 1941 and 1942, this was the notorious 'final solution', the murder of all European Jews.[45]

To understand Ludin's role in Bratislava, some background information on Slovakia's policies on the 'Jewish question' is needed here, particularly as the Germans initially cooperated closely with the Slovakian government. It was not until relatively late, beginning in the summer months of 1942, that the Slovakian government distanced itself from the Nazis' attempt to murder all the country's Jews, but by this time the vast majority had already been deported and killed, and their property confiscated by the state or simply looted. In his defence the former Slovakian head of state, the Catholic priest-turned-politician Jozef Tiso, reasoned after the war that the Slovakian government had 'tried to solve the Jewish question' in order to prevent a German occupation in the autumn of 1938.[46] In contrast to more radical Fascist attempts by the Foreign Minister, Vojtech Tuka, and by the Interior Minister and leader of the Hlinka guards, Alexander Mach, to incarcerate and deport thousands of (male) Slovakian Jews, Tiso claimed to have favoured a more 'conservative' solution that would have reduced the impact of the Jews on the Slovakian economy (down to 4 per cent of the overall economy, in line with their numbers in the overall population) but would not have completely removed them from public life.[47] After the Slovakian government issued anti-Jewish legislation targeting non-Slovakian Jews in February 1939, Tiso assured a Jewish telegraph agency reporter that the Slovakian government supported Jewish emigration to Palestine.[48]

With the beginning of the war, however, emigration was no longer a viable option, and the legal exclusion and deportation of Slovakian Jews, as well as the plundering of their property, increased dramatically, tolerated and in many cases even encouraged by the Tiso government. The situation resembled that which had occurred in Austria after the *Anschluss*: privately owned Jewish properties, bank accounts, and businesses were strictly regulated or taxed at high rates. After the establishment of the Central Economic Office (CEO) in August 1940, Jewish businesses were increasingly 'Slovakized', with the effect that by the end of 1941, 84 per cent of all Jewish businesses had been liquidated. The Jewish population, forced to wear the Star of David starting on 22 September 1941, quickly fell into poverty.[49] This process of political marginalization and social exclusion led to numerous attacks on Jews that ranged from blackmailing, looting, and beatings to outright murder. In one of these incidents, several elderly Jews were burned alive in 1940, after being forced to leave their Jewish retirement home in Bratislava and transported to barracks in the former Patrobka cartridge factory that was subsequently set on fire.[50]

Throughout 1941 diplomatic talks between Ludin and high-ranking representatives of the Slovakian government, particularly Tiso and Tuka, intensified. On 4 December, Ludin finally reported to Berlin that the Slovakian government 'agrees in principle with the deportation of Jews of Slovak citizenship from within the Reich to ghettos in the east'.[51] Soon after the notorious Wannsee Conference held in Berlin on 20 January 1942, the raids on and deportations of the Slovakian Jews began. In late February 1942 the Slovakian government agreed – although the details of the agreement are still not entirely clear – to start deportations of its Jews to German-occupied Poland, where they would allegedly be employed as forced labourers. These deportations were partly overseen by Hlinka guards, in cooperation with the Carpathian-German *Freiwilliger Selbstschutz* (FS), later known as the *Freiwillige Schutzstaffel*.[52] The Slovakian government agreed to pay the German Reich 5,000 crowns (500 reichsmark) per Jew for its 'professional retraining' of the population, and in return the Germans let the Slovaks freely ransack Jewish properties.[53] Germans and Slovaks worked hand in hand in these efforts, as a statement by Ludin from April 1942 illustrates: 'In the absence of any German pressure, the Slovak government has agreed to deport all Jews from Slovakia. Even the president has personally agreed to the deportation, in spite of an intervention by the Slovak episcopate.'[54]

Between April and October of 1942 at least 58,000 Slovakian Jews were deported and by far the majority of them killed in German-occupied Poland, either by mistreatment, starvation, excessive slave labour, or outright execution. Most of these deaths took place in the death camps of Auschwitz, Treblinka, and Majdanek.[55] Contrary to post-war testimonies, Ludin neither criticized these deportations nor was unaware of their ultimate purpose. On 26 June 1942 he reported to Berlin that while 'the deportations of the Jews from Slovakia' had come 'to a dead end', he recommended a '100 per cent solution to the Jewish question'.[56] Confronted with protests from the Vatican and growing unease within the Slovakian population, Tiso finally stopped the transports in late 1942. By this time rumours had already spread throughout Slovakia that those deported would be 'boiled to soap'.[57] A second wave of deportations started only with the German occupation of Slovakia in September 1944, this time organized and carried out by SS-*Hauptsturmführer* Alois Brunner, who had succeeded the 'Jew Councillor', SS-*Hauptsturmführer* Dieter Wisliceny, after the latter was transferred to German-occupied Hungary.[58] Ludin's involvement in the deportations of 1944 is clear from his personnel file at the Foreign Office. A cable from the Foreign Office alludes to a meeting arranged for late July or early August in Budapest between Ludin and SS Brigade General Edmund Veesenmayer, since March the Reich plenipotentiary in Hungary, to officially 'discuss the handling of the Jewish question [*Behandlung Judenfrage*]'.[59] Overall, current estimates of the total number of Jews deported from Slovakia are at least 70,000, with the number of those murdered estimated as 65,000 (or 110,000, if the Slovak-occupied territories of Hungary are included).[60]

An important 'connecting link' between the German officials and the Slovakian government was the engineer, journalist, and politician Franz Karmasin, nicknamed the 'Slovak Henlein', the founder and leader of the Carpathian German Party[61] and since 1935 also State Secretary for German Affairs in the Slovak regional government.[62] In the early 1940s, Karmasin called himself *Führer der Deutschen Volksgruppe in der Slowakei*, or Leader of the Ethnic Germans in Slovakia. He was also the commander of the FS, the successor of the Slovakian faction of the *Sudetendeutsches Freikorps*, which in 1938 had so decisively contributed to the dismantling of Czechoslovakia (see chapter 6). The FS was modelled after the German SA and SS, and only Slovakia's status as an independent state prevented this organization from being officially included in the SA, as its counterparts in the Protectorate of *Böhmen und Mähren* and the Memelland had been. However, in the propaganda book *Sudeten SA in Polen* both terms were used nearly interchangeably, and they seem to have operated along the same lines.[63] Karmasin was promoted to the honorary positions of SA-*Oberführer* on 17 May 1939, SA-*Brigadeführer* on 30 January 1941, and SA-*Gruppenführer* on 9 November 1944.[64] In short, he became an honorary SA general in an Axis state where – for political reasons – the stormtroopers only existed in the form of the FS.

On the German side, Wisliceny, Brunner, and Karmasin were the central figures urging Tiso to take ever more extreme action against the Jewish population.[65] The terror they encouraged, however, also targeted some ethnic Germans, as a letter from Karmasin to Himmler dated 29 July 1942 makes plain. In this letter, Karmasin thanked Himmler for his 'once again generous help by allowing us to resettle asocial elements'. This 'help' referred to the deportation of nearly 700 members of the German community – in Karmasin's words, 'drunkards' and 'imbeciles' – to nearby Austria, now called the *Ostmark* of the Greater German Reich. In the following days and weeks the large majority of these deportees were 'euthanized', that is, murdered. According to Karmasin, the Carpathian Germans praised this initiative as valuable 'social aid', and the German Embassy strongly supported it.[66] Envoy Ludin was on an intimate footing with Karmasin, and, according to the latter's post-war testimony, 'both men discussed all relevant political questions'. They seem to have established a kind of division of responsibilities: Karmasin, in line with the SS, put pressure on the leading figures within the Slovakian government, while Ludin's task was to urge Tiso on the diplomatic level to comply with Hitler's demands.[67] There is no evidence that the 'Jewish question' was handled any differently. A verbal note from Ludin to the Slovakian Ministry of the Interior from 1 May 1942 explicitly assured the Slovakian government that, as a matter of principle, the German Reich would not send back those Slovakian Jews that had so far been deported to German-occupied territory.[68] By that time both sides knew exactly what this meant in practice. Karmasin's driver, who had accompanied his boss on a visit to the Auschwitz concentration camp in July 1942, put it bluntly after the war: 'It was a matter of common knowledge that the people in Auschwitz were killed.'[69]

Deadly Varieties of a Pattern

The negotiations between the SA diplomats and the national governments of Croatia, Romania, Bulgaria, and Hungary proceeded in many ways along a path similar to that taken in Slovakia, but they resulted in quite different outcomes. Of lasting influence in these negotiations was the German envoy to the Independent State of Croatia (*Nezavisna Država Hrvatska*, or NDH), Siegfried Kasche (Plate 29). Backed by Hitler, who shared Kasche's sympathy for the Croatian nationalists, the German ambassador to Zagreb played an important role in Croatian politics between 1941 and 1945, both in influencing the Ustaša regime to fall in line with German war aims and in speeding up the imprisonment, deportation, and execution of the Croatian Jews. The historian Alexander Korb has characterized Kasche as an 'effective champion of German interests on difficult terrain'.[70] Kasche maintained close and personal contact with the leading figures of the Ustaša regime and proved to be a strong and lasting supporter of Croatian home rule, a position that between 1942 and 1944 proved ever more problematic and finally earned him the sarcastic nickname of the 'Don Quixote of German diplomacy in Zagreb'.[71]

The Ustaša regime, immediately after it assumed power, introduced antisemitic legislation and started a programme of internment of the Jewish population. Because of the devastating conditions in these camps, more than half of the Jewish population in Croatia died in the first twelve months of the NDH's existence, avoiding the direct intervention of the German ambassador or the SS 'Jew experts'.[72] The deportation and murder of the Jews of Croatia was part of a larger project of resettlement and ethnic cleansing that primarily targeted Serbs and Slovenians but also extended to the much smaller minorities of the Roma and the Jews.[73] German and Croatian authorities discussed the framework for this policy in a meeting held at the German Embassy in Zagreb on 4 June 1941, less than three months after Kasche had arrived.[74] Most deportations of Jews to Croatian concentration camps took place in the autumn of that year, after Croatian authorities had formally requested the permission to subsequently deport the country's Jews to the German Reich.[75] The Reich Security Main Office (RSHA), however, opposed this solution, either because the practical details of 'solving' the Jewish question in its entirety had not yet been fully decided or because the death toll in the Croatian camps had become so high that costly deportations were deemed unnecessary for the time being.[76]

The situation changed in 1942 when the Italians openly provided protection for 4,000 to 5,000 Jews who had fled to the cities of Mostar and Dubrovnik.[77] In response, Kasche, in close cooperation with the SS and the Foreign Office in Berlin, pushed for the deportation of Jews from Croatian territory in its entirety, regardless of possible conflicts with the Italians. Between August 1942 and May 1943, Germans and Croats in a joint undertaking deported thousands of Jews from Croatian territory to Auschwitz.[78] In October 1942 the Croats agreed to pay the Germans 30 reichsmark per deported Jew, a much cheaper rate than that granted to the Slovaks. The local authorities passed on at least part of the costs to the Jewish communities, while simultaneously profiting from the looting and robbing of their properties.[79] With the Italian capitulation in September 1943, those Jews in Croatia who had formerly been protected were included in the deportations. In April 1944, Kasche informed the Foreign Office that Croatia had been entirely 'cleansed' of Jews, with only a few exceptions.[80] According to current estimates, up to 30,000 Jews in Croatia fell victim to the Holocaust, half of whom were killed in Jasenovac, in other camps, or shot on the spot, and the other half in Auschwitz.[81]

In contrast to Ludin's and Kasche's impact on their respective countries, Beckerle's and von Killinger's influence on Bulgarian and Romanian politics respectively remained limited. Von Killinger arrived in Bucharest on 24 January 1941, with clear instructions from Hitler to prevent any further tensions between the Third Reich and Marshal Ion Antonescu's regime.[82] Just days earlier, Antonescu had violently cracked down on the highly antisemitic Legionary Movement, known as the 'Iron Guard', which had attempted to overthrow the government. Because the legionaries enjoyed the support of the SS and the SD, the new ambassador was from the start greeted with distrust and caution.[83] Von Killinger encountered a complicated political framework in Romania that he failed to navigate adequately in the following years, as both his Romanian counterparts and the German Foreign Office quickly realized. Personally, von Killinger never warmed to his new surroundings. He publicly called Romania a *Scheißland*, a 'fucking country', and in October 1941 complained that the best thing one could do for the Romanian capital, which was in his eyes an 'absolute shambles' (*einziger Saustall*), would be to set it on fire.[84] He preferred to escape to the Carpathian Mountains some 150 kilometres north of the capital, where he ranged the woods for days or even weeks at a time hunting brown bears, armed with his rifle and a bottle of cognac.[85] At least with regard to the Holocaust, however, it is doubtful whether a more qualified diplomat would have been able to meet a larger number of German demands. In Romania, as in the neighbouring southeastern European states allied with Germany, the handling of the 'Jewish question' was a complicated affair that involved foreign, internal, economic, and moral policies, as well as, above all, the course of the war.

In von Killinger's first year in Bucharest, things still went relatively smoothly – at least from his perspective. Unfamiliar with diplomatic habits and also unwilling to fully accept them, he took Antonescu's statements at face value until August 1944, when King Michael sacked the marshal and the new Romanian government changed sides to support the Allies.[86] One of von Killinger's main fields of activity was the 'Jewish question'. In June 1940 – several months before he was formerly appointed envoy – von Killinger visited Romania for the first time and met with General Mihail Moruzov, who was then head of the Romanian state security police force. The men discussed the 'Jewish problem', and von Killinger suggested that Moruzov invite qualified German experts to Romania to consult its leaders on the matter.[87] Half a year later, in April 1941, SS-*Hauptsturmführer* Gustav Richter, a legal expert from Himmler's Reich Security Main Office, arrived in Bucharest. In the following years Richter officially operated as 'counsellor for Jewish affairs at the Bucharest legation'. As had occurred in Slovakia, Richter negotiated with a 'government plenipotentiary for Jewish affairs', a position filled in Romania by Radu Lecca.[88] Von Killinger was regularly informed of the progress of these negotiations, as his reports to Berlin illustrate. On 13 November 1941 he wrote to the German Foreign Office that the Romanians had agreed to the deportation of Jews with Romanian citizenship who lived in Germany or German-occupied territory.[89]

Initially, the Romanian government was also willing to sacrifice those 'non-Romanian' Jews who were living in territories that had only recently become part of the state. In June 1940, Romania had annexed the northern Bukovina region, and a year later, in July 1941, it also retook Bessarabia with the support of German troops from the Soviet Union. The Romanian authorities regarded the Jews living in these two regions as national traitors who had sold out Romanian interests to the Soviets.[90] With the aim of creating an ethnically homogeneous 'Greater Romania', both Romanian and German official units and local militia either murdered the Jews in these areas on the spot or deported them to Transnistria, a small strip of land on the River Dniester in southern Ukraine. Between the summer of 1941 and March 1944, 130,000 to 150,000 Jews were deported to this region, the majority of whom were shot in mass killings, died of illnesses such as typhus, or starved to death.[91] By December 1943 only 50,000 of these Jews were still alive. Estimates of the total number of Jews killed in Romania and Transnistria during the Second World War range from 250,000 to 410,000.[92]

Over the course of 1942 the German authorities urged the Romanian government to agree to an extensive deportation programme for the country's Jews but were only partially successful. On 28 August 1942 von Killinger informed the Foreign Office that no definite agreement had yet been reached,[93] and the situation did not change in the following months. Antonescu was clearly playing for time – continuing the talks and assuring the Germans of his agreement with their position – but taking few concrete steps toward a general implementation of the Holocaust.[94] When in 1942–3 the Antonescu regime attempted to 'sell' up to 80,000 of its remaining Jews in Transnistria to Syria and Palestine, the German Foreign Office urged von Killinger to intervene, as these plans 'represented a partial resolution unacceptable within the framework of the fundamental lines followed by the German government for a European solution to the Jewish problem'[95] – in short, the 'Final Solution'.[96] However, Antonescu in the autumn of 1942 had decided 'not to carry out antisemitic reforms for the Germans and under the doctrine of Dr Rosenberg [. . .] We must make our antisemitic reform a creative reform, not a demagogic one.'[97] Because of Romania's strategic importance to the German war effort, putting more pressure on the Antonescu regime was not advisable, and consequently von Killinger's attempts to press for further deportations gradually halted over the course of 1943.[98]

Like von Killinger in Romania, Beckerle in Bulgaria also had only limited 'success' in his attempt to bring about a complete annihilation of the Jews, despite the fact that he portrayed himself as a strongman from the start of his diplomatic mission. In his diary he frankly admitted that his initial task when appointed was to 'end the national independence of Bulgaria'.[99] In a first private meeting on 26 July 1941 the 'new tough German ambassador' urged the Bulgarian king to take resolute action against Serbian partisans operating in Bulgaria. Such 'hordes' should be 'eliminated once and for all', claimed Beckerle.[100] Several weeks later the German envoy requested severe reprisals against the perpetrators of a partisan attack on a German guard in Bulgaria – specifically, the shooting of 100 Bulgarian Jews. This excessive demand caused widespread indignation among the Bulgarian authorities and was refused.[101]

With regard to the full implementation of the Holocaust, Beckerle's task was complicated by the fact that antisemitism had not been an important element in Bulgarian politics prior to the beginning of the Second World War. However, between 1940 and 1942 the Bulgarian government under Prime Minister Bogdan Filov increasingly made concessions to German demands in return for territorial gains and a close military and political alliance with the Axis powers.[102] In 1941, Bulgaria introduced anti-semitic legislation, including the imposition of forced labour for male Jews, and at the same time started confiscating Jewish assets.[103] Like the Slovakian government half a year earlier, the Bulgarian government finally agreed to the deportation of its Jews from Germany and German-occupied territory in July 1942.[104] Over the autumn of 1942 the German Foreign Office inten-sified its efforts to deport the 50,000 Jews living on Bulgarian soil, who amounted to roughly 1 per cent of the country's overall population. Beckerle received instructions on this matter from Undersecretary Luther in a three-hour meeting in Berlin on 9 October 1942. After his return to Sofia, Beckerle discussed the issue with Filov, who in principle agreed to the German initiative but argued that 10,000 Jewish forced labourers were needed for construction work in Bulgaria. He also informed Beckerle that his govern-ment considered the price the Germans had demanded for the deportations – 250 reichsmark per Jew – to be 'extremely high'.[105]

Despite pending questions the Germans in late 1942 thought that the ground had been prepared for mass deportations.[106] Consequently, in January 1943, SS-*Hauptsturmführer* Theodor Dannecker of the Reich Security Main Office arrived in Sofia with instructions from his superior, SS-*Obersturmbannführer* Adolf Eichmann, to deport as many Jews from Bulgaria as possible.[107] He succeeded in this effort only in part: the Bulgarians allowed the deportation of 11,343 Jews from Macedonia and Thrace (regions that since 1941 had been part of Bulgaria) between 2 and 29 March 1943,[108] but prevented the deportation of those Jews living in the Bulgarian heart-land.[109] The reason for this compromise was threefold. First, as in Slovakia and Romania, details of the Holocaust became widely known in Bulgaria beginning in 1942, alarming the government and drawing protests from the Bulgarian population. Second, the Bulgarian government rightly interpreted the ultimate German defeat in Stalingrad in early February 1943 as a turning point of the war. They therefore thought it advisable to consider other options and not compromise their position with a record of war crimes. The third reason was purely economic: the deportations would have ended all Bulgarian chances of further exploiting and robbing 'their' Jews.

Between April and the summer of 1943, Beckerle and Dannecker repeatedly discussed the best timing for further deportations.[110] In July, however, Beckerle realized that 'to insist on the deportation [of Jews from the Bulgarian heartland] at the present time makes no sense whatsoever'. He nevertheless expected the deportations to resume when Germany's military success became 'apparent', a possibility he still thought realistic in early 1944.[111] When interrogated by the Soviets after being captured in September of the same year, Beckerle took pride in the success he had achieved in deporting Jews from Macedonia and Thrace.[112] His extreme antisemitism is best illustrated by a brief report from Beckerle on his time in Litzmannstadt, the former Łódź. In it he compared the German reconstruction efforts after the occupation of Poland most favourably against the traditional life in the Jewish quarters of that city, for him 'the most dirty places of the most disgusting East European Jewry'. All antisemitic clichés were present. He was repelled by orthodox men with long beards, 'draped in dirty caftans', as well as by the 'insolent' Jewish women, and obsessed with the idea of Jewish dirt.[113]

Beckerle's diaries, today held in the German Foreign Office's Political Archive, also shed light on his self-image and his interpretation of his diplomatic mission. Although he still felt closely attached to his men in SA-*Gruppe* Hesse (and struggled with giving up its command in 1942), Beckerle the diplomat saw himself as someone who had to 'represent National Socialism in its entirety'.[114] He was not very popular in Bulgaria, even among the ethnic Germans. In his diaries he repeatedly expressed feelings of loneliness and, at times, revealed signs of a mid-life crisis.[115] He became sentimental and homesick when thinking of the SA in Germany but consoled himself with the fact that he was nevertheless better off than the German soldiers and civilians at home, who were increasingly suffering from the Allied bombings of German cities.[116] In Sofia, however, rumours spread that Beckerle's wife had greeted the first Allied bombings of the Bulgarian capital with the words: 'Thank God! Finally, there is some work for us, too' (*Gott sei Dank, nun kriegen wir auch mal Arbeit*).[117]

Last but not least, we now turn to the role of Dietrich von Jagow as German envoy in Hungary. Only four years the junior of von Killinger, von Jagow had also enjoyed a similar career as his colleague prior to joining the German Foreign Office in late June 1941. He fought in the First World War as a lieutenant and later senior lieutenant in the navy, and in 1919 joined the

Marine Brigade Ehrhardt and took part in the Kapp Putsch of 1920. At about the same time he became a member of the NSDAP and between 1921 and 1923 served as inspector of the nascent Württemberg SA. After the party re-emerged later in the decade, von Jagow rejoined and began a stellar career in the SA, leading the SA-*Gruppe* Berlin-Brandenburg between 1934 and 1939. With the onset of the Second World War he returned to the military, fighting for two years in the Wehrmacht, before being appointed a diplomat.[118]

However, like von Killinger, von Jagow struggled to meet the requirements of his new position. Prior to his appointment, Hungary and Hungarian politics were *terra incognita* to him, and his deep-rooted contempt for civilian life did not help him warm to his new job.[119] Von Jagow's main tasks as envoy were to recruit ethnic Germans from Hungary for the Waffen-SS, to monitor the military situation in the Balkans, particularly in light of a possible Allied invasion, and to deal with the 'Jewish question'.[120] However, Miklós Horthy, the regent of Hungary who had introduced antisemitic legislation as early as 1938, insisted that the latter task was a purely Hungarian affair. In contrast to the other states discussed previously, Hungary initially faced only relatively mild pressure on the 'Jewish question' from von Jagow and the Foreign Office. This was, however, a tactical decision, framed as giving the Hungarian side more time to 'prepare' the ground for the pending 'final solution'.[121] As early as August 1942 the Hungarian ambassador in Berlin noted that the Germans had made it very clear to him that the 'Jewish question' needed to be solved immediately. In the spring of 1943, German pressure further intensified with the first official visit to Hungary of SS Brigade General Edmund Veesenmayer, who later became plenipotentiary there.[122] In the meantime Hungarian Jews were compelled into forced labour but were not (yet) deported.[123] Consequently, in March 1944, 762,000 Jews still lived in Hungary, 150,000 of them in Budapest alone.[124]

Von Jagow's role in enforcing the German 'Jew policy' in Hungary is difficult to assess from the remaining documents. Compared to Ludin and Kasche, who are best characterized as diplomat-politicians with personal agendas, von Jagow remained in the background, more an observer than a man of diplomatic initiative. He conveyed the German demands for a 'radical solution' of the 'Jew question' to the Hungarian premier Miklós Kállay via Foreign Minister Jenő Ghyczy on 17 October 1942.[125] Therefore, it is certain that he knew the regime's ultimate goals, but it is unclear whether he had a strong personal commitment to the cause, as his official reports abstain from personal commentary. In any case, von Jagow reported to the Foreign Office in late October and again in mid-November that he did not expect the Hungarians to give in to the German demands.[126] Over the course of the following year the Foreign Office as well as the RSHA slowly but surely lost faith in von Jagow's ability to impose the German will on the Hungarians, whom they regarded as increasingly problematic after the German defeat at Stalingrad and the subsequent advance of the Red Army.

The situation of relative calm changed dramatically on 19 March 1944, when German troops occupied Hungary. As an official ambassador was no longer needed, von Jagow was relieved of his duties, and Veesenmayer took over as the plenipotentiary of the Greater German Reich in Hungary.[127] In the following months the new Szálasi regime, supported by the Arrow Cross militia and instructed by Eichmann and Veesenmayer, efficiently ghettoized, deported, and expropriated the holdings of the majority of Hungary's remaining Jews.[128] Between 16 May and 8 July alone 437,000 Jews were deported to Auschwitz, the vast majority of whom were killed immediately upon arrival there. Only 255,500 of the previously 762,000 Hungarian Jews survived the fall of Fascist Hungary.[129]

On 8 May 1944 von Jagow was officially recalled to Berlin, where he reported for duty on 1 June but was not given a new role in the Foreign Office. In September he returned to his proper realm, the world of the military, where he was placed in command of a *Volkssturm* battalion in Upper Silesia. His family moved to a mansion in Groß-Münche in the Warthegau, today's Polish Mnichy near Kwilcz.[130] In January 1945 von Jagow and his men shot down four Russian tanks by *panzerfaust*, a military achievement that earned him an honorary mention in the Wehrmacht report of 21 January 1945.[131] However, during the action, von Jagow was struck in the head by flying parts of the exploding tanks and lost one eye. After several weeks in hospitals in Dresden and Leipzig, he was reunited with his family for the last time in Constance in March 1945. Shortly afterward the Foreign Office sent him as a messenger to the Italian village of Fasano at Lake Garda, which was serving as the administrative centre for the German occupation of Italy in the last stage of the Second World War.[132] The instructions he was given for this trip are unknown. On his way von Jagow took up quarters in Merano in the house of the German plenipotentiary to the Italian Social Republic, Rudolf Rahn, where he shot himself shortly after his arrival on 26 April 1945.[133]

The Impact of the SA Diplomats

Overall, the trajectories of the different SA diplomats' activities in southeastern Europe between 1941 and 1944–5 reveal striking parallels. The commencement of these individuals' duties coincided with a radicalization of the 'handling' of the 'Jewish question' in their respective states, culminating in the decision in the summer of 1941 to move toward the 'final solution'.[134] The SA diplomats were not the driving forces behind this policy, but they often acted confidently and independently to carry it out. Apart from the Holocaust, their political influence was limited, particularly from 1943 onward. Certainly, they were newcomers to the diplomatic realm, did not speak the local languages, and were not well informed about the peculiarities of the regions to which they were sent. Scepticism about their suitability for their complicated missions was widespread, even among the German leadership. After the war Rudolf Rahn commented that he had always believed that it had not been a good idea to 'put politically naïve SA leaders in diplomat uniforms, in the belief that foreign policy could be done by party methods'.[135] And the Austrian general Edmund Glaise von Horstenau, when first informed about Kasche's appointment to Zagreb, commented bitterly that 'he should at least be able to find Croatia on a map'.[136] But even von Horstenau, a sworn enemy of the German envoy, acknowledged later that Kasche had been 'far better' than he had initially feared.[137]

A comparative analysis of the roles of the five SA diplomats in southeastern Europe indeed suggests that a balanced assessment is needed.[138] Personal shortcomings notwithstanding, their ultimate failures were as much grounded in their individual character traits as they were a consequence of their unusual positions. They were neither *Reichskommissare* with extensive authority nor conventional diplomats accustomed to dealing with autonomous governments. Given the fluidity of the political situation between 1941 and 1944 in southeastern Europe, one may be surprised to learn that at least Beckerle and Kasche extensively researched the peculiarities of their respective regions. As long-term stormtroopers, all five of these SA diplomats sympathized with the paramilitary organizations of the Fascist right in their host countries.[139] In the autumn of 1939, SA Chief of Staff Lutze paid the first official NSDAP visit to Tiso's Slovakia, where he met with Karmasin to lay a wreath at the grave of Andrej Hlinka, the namesake of the Slovak Fascist militia.[140] Both the Hlinka Guard and the SA shared strong antisemitic convictions, and later Ludin in his negotiations with his Slovakian counterparts would stress the natural bonds of the new Slovak state with the Brownshirts' Third Reich. Because of such sympathies, however, he failed to notice the growing scepticism and anti-German sentiment among the Ludaks, a failure for which he was sharply criticized by the German SD in 1943. For the *Sicherheitsdienst*, it was by then obvious that Tiso and his followers were playing a double game.[141] In Hungary von Jagow also advocated closer cooperation with the Fascist Arrow Cross movement but was restrained by the German Foreign Office. In consequence, he lacked recognition even among those who shared his ideological convictions.[142] In the Balkans, Kasche in late 1943 expressed more faith in the ideological power of National Socialism than in violent oppression. Drastic measures might be justified for the time being, he argued, but a lasting alliance with the Ustaša and other nationalists in the region could only be achieved through a cooperative policy that respected national traditions and the people's welfare.[143] Finally, the Bulgarian Prime Minister Bogdan Filov criticized Beckerle for being 'too friendly with right-wing extremists' in his country, as well as for being an 'extremely limited person'.[144]

The longer the SA diplomats remained in office, the more they came to the conclusion that the German policy in southeastern Europe was counterproductive; at least insofar as it alienated even those nationalist circles and groups that had initially supported the German advance. The diplomats advocated instead a policy that would grant at least partial autonomy to these groups, in the hope that such a division of power would ultimately strengthen the bonds between the Germans and the nationalist governments in the region. As the war progressed, this became an ever more naive position, as German foreign policy from 1943 onward was increasingly driven by the economic and human exploitation of its southeastern allies and ultimately concerned with its own survival.[145] After Martin Luther's arrest on 10 February 1943 for involvement in a failed putsch that aimed to remove von Ribbentrop from office,[146] the SA diplomats lost further support from Berlin. By 1944 they were fighting a losing battle, neglecting or simply ignoring the fundamental political changes that were unfolding in the region. A letter of complaint on Ludin's failures as a diplomat, written by an Austrian civil servant in Bratislava to the German Foreign Office on 27 October 1944, cut right to the heart of the matter, asking, with deadly irony: 'After the events in Romania, Bulgaria, Hungary – do you have more of such "experts" out there?'[147]

The Struggle for Reputation

By the autumn of 1944, German diplomacy was effectively over, and the SA envoys' vision of a German-led southeastern Europe had evaporated. Von Killinger and his embassy staff on 23 August 1944 became de facto Romanian prisoners in the German Embassy in Bucharest. One week later, on 31 August 1944, the Red Army reached the Romanian capital. On 2 September the German diplomats were transferred to the building of a school named after the Romanian national hero Mihai Viteazu. That same day von Killinger first shot his female secretary Helga Petersen, with whom he had had an affair, and then killed himself.[148] Von Jagow, as previously mentioned, committed suicide in Merano on 26 April 1945, only days before the end of the Second World War. Three weeks later the Americans took Ludin into custody and, after interning him in the Natternberg camp in Bavaria, handed him over to the Czechoslovakian authorities on 5 October 1946. Ludin faced trial in Bratislava, was sentenced to death, and was executed on 3 December 1947.[149] Nearly six months earlier, on 17 June 1947, Kasche had been sentenced to death by the Croatian State Court and was hanged the following day.[150] Only Beckerle, who had been caught at the Bulgarian-Turkish border and brought to Moscow by soldiers of the Red Army in late September 1944, survived the immediate post-war years.[151] He returned from Soviet detention to the Federal Republic of Germany in 1955, where the Frankfurt mayor greeted him with handshakes on the steps of the city's town hall. Beckerle is even said to have received compensatory damages of 6,000 deutschmark. However, the joy of his return was overshadowed by the news of the suicide of his wife in 1951 that coincided with the successful restitution of the previously 'Aryanized' villa she lived in. An attempt to hold the former police president accountable for his involvement in the persecution of members of the German opposition during the 1930s came to nothing, and the Frankfurt prosecutor's office closed the case in 1957. The general attorney Fritz Bauer then attempted to bring Beckerle to court on charges related to the murder of Bulgarian Jews. In September 1959, Beckerle was arrested, yet the main trial did not begin until November 1967.[152] The proceedings against him were closed in the summer of 1968 because of his 'ill health'. Beckerle died a free man on 3 April 1976.[153]

In post-war Germany the families of these SA diplomats struggled with the involvement of their husband, brother, or father in the Holocaust.[154]

Malte Ludin's acclaimed documentary film *2 oder 3 Dinge, die ich von ihm weiß* illustrates with empathy and exemplary clarity the long-lasting shadow that his father's life and death cast over his surviving family members.[155] Hanns Ludin had been a complex personality: he had been popular among the SA rank and file in southwestern Germany and a loving father, but he had also been personally involved in the deportation of tens of thousands of Jews whom he knew were destined to be killed. Unsurprisingly, his children struggled to balance the historical evidence with their private memories.[156] Ernst von Salomon's glorification of Hanns Ludin in the best-selling 1951 novel *Der Fragebogen* had a particularly deep impact on the family's memory. Von Salomon first met Ludin in the prisoner-of-war camp run by the Americans at Natternberg in 1945 and later glorified him as 'the best man in the camp' and as a model of decency. At one time Salomon even referred to him as a 'camp-Christ' (*Lager-Christus*) – half in jest, but also half in earnest.[157] Ludin's widow and several of his children only too willingly adopted Salomon's literary image as a realistic description of their husband and father's personality. Salomon's novel, Malte Ludin claimed, served as a 'moral *vade mecum*' and a 'consolation book'. It allowed them to remember Hanns Ludin as a morally superior individual who – despite his conviction and execution as a war criminal – served as a role model and martyr for the nation.[158] When asked today about his father's personality, Dietrich von Jagow's son Henning refers to private letters that characterize his father in very similar terms as a 'political idealist, naive and relatively stubborn with regard to political developments, but at the same time a decent man, guided by Christian-ethical principles, for whom morality and honour were impor- tant and who, in later years, surely had his doubts' about the evils of the Nazi regime.[159] In this light von Jagow's suicide in 1945 seems less a flight from political responsibility than a courageous act that was in line with his morality and aristocratic code of honour.

Whereas the Ludin family's controversial coming to terms with their past is well known to the German public, the parallel process within Kasche's family has remained a private affair. Files from the German Foreign Office hint at the difficulty that surviving family members had in accepting Kasche's criminal guilt, particularly as other former diplomats in many cases remained in office or, if sentenced to prison terms by the Allies, were quickly released and had their public honour restored.[160] Beginning in 1954, members of the Kasche family requested help from the West German authorities in proving that the Yugoslav authorities had sentenced the former diplomat to death against international law. One of Kasche's brothers, in a letter to the Ministry of Justice, claimed that the former envoy had been innocent and was only executed 'because of the well-known Serbian desire for revenge' for the war crimes committed by the Croatian Ustaša and tolerated or supported by the Germans during the Second World War.[161] An important motive behind such a request was the fact that the family of a war criminal could not claim a widow's or children's pension.[162] Although a Bavarian denazification court had initially ruled that Kasche belonged to the category of 'major offenders' – with the consequence that 50 per cent of his assets could be confiscated by the state and surviving family members could not claim state pensions – a subsequent appeal was successful, and monthly payments were made to the family from 1954 onward.[163] However, the Kasches made a second attempt to gain what they perceived as 'moral justice' in 1968, as the new Foreign Minister Willy Brandt was preparing an official visit to Tito's Yugoslavia. In a personal letter to Brandt one of Kasche's brothers urged the Foreign Minister to intervene on their behalf and threatened to sue the state of Yugoslavia in The Hague to receive compensation for this alleged injustice. Furthermore, he reminded Brandt of the Foreign Office's duty to care for its former members of staff and their families, adding pointedly that Chancellor Kurt Georg Kiesinger from the conservative Christian Democratic Union (CDU) had himself worked for the Foreign Office during the Third Reich and 'should therefore know my brother'.[164] Addressing Brandt directly, Kasche's brother stated that because 'now for the first time in a generation a member of the SPD is Foreign Minister', justice should finally prevail.[165] However, the matter was simply not important enough to risk offending Tito, a strategically important political partner at a time of 'détente', particularly as the former envoy Kasche belonged to that group of Nazi ambassadors from whom professional diplomats wished to distance themselves – by now not only for personal reasons but even more so for ideological ones.

PART IV

PART IV

'NOT GUILTY'

The Legacy of the SA in Germany after the Second World War

Many do not like to remember the Nazi past. A few others don't like to be reminded of it: these are the ones who remember it with pleasure!
— Radio and TV journalist Hans Rosenthal, 1983[1]

After the armistice of 8 May 1945 civilians only slowly returned to Berlin, now a city of ruins, its inhabitants beset by hunger and disease. From more than four million inhabitants in the early 1920s, the number of 'Berliners' had decreased to fewer than three million, many of them physically and morally wounded. One of the early returnees to the capital was the writer Rudolf Ditzen, better known under his pseudonym 'Hans Fallada'. He had survived the war years in a kind of 'inner exile' in a rural area of northern Germany, removed from the centre of political power. However, in 1945, Fallada returned to Berlin and, in a kind of frenzy, wrote his last novel within a few weeks during the autumn of 1946. Shortly afterwards he died at the age of fifty-three.[2]

This last novel, *Alone in Berlin* (*Jeder stirbt für sich allein*), reprinted in recent years and nowadays popular with an international audience, provides a literary panorama of German society between 1941 and the end of the Third Reich. Engagingly written, it testifies to the author's profound sadness and anger in response to the widespread destruction and despair, as he tells a gripping story based on fact that also charts the mentality of people in the immediate post-war period. It is by and large free of the distortions that would soon penetrate most accounts of life under National Socialism in the following decades.[3] The book reveals the degree to which the party uniforms of the SA, SS, and Hitler Youth dominated the streets of the German capital during these years. Far from being mere ornamentation for the Nazi state, SA leaders are portrayed as powerful and dangerous arch-Nazis, capable of intimidating 'ordinary' German workers in a factory meeting, sending people to concentration camps, and putting the police under serious pressure. Fallada in his novel used the 'signal effect' of the Nazi uniform and simultaneously employed the then popular strategy of excuse, summarily referring to 'Aryan' and 'non-Aryan' Germans as the first victims of the Third Reich. In his portrait of Berlin in the early 1940s most Germans and German Jews in particular live in a form of prison, kept under guard and tortured by Nazi Party officials, from the SA and SS. In this respect Fallada's interpretation is typical of the general tendency of people in post-war Germany to concentrate initially on their own suffering, emphasizing the character of the Nazi state as a 'terror regime', the German loss of lives during the war, and the expulsion of Germans between 1944 and 1948. In return, the fate of the Sinti and Roma, the non-German Jewry, the up to eight million forced labourers, and the millions of civilians murdered by Germans in Europe was by and large ignored, at least until the 1960s.[4]

In the years after Fallada's death many Germans shared his view that the SA had been the ugly face of National Socialism. It came to represent the brutal violence, fervent antisemitism, and complete lack of compassion for 'outsiders' beyond the 'people's community' that characterized National Socialism. However, many soon drew an important distinction that hinged on historical events. The SA, they claimed, had been a powerful and strong paramilitary group until the summer of 1934, but in the following years it became an organization strong in members but weak in political and social importance: a 'totally subsidiary organization of the party' or an 'insignificant union of beer drinkers' (*unbedeutender Bierverein*).[5] Such an understanding also predominated within the academic scholarship on the SA in the following decades.[6] To give one example: the four expert opinions written for the Frankfurt Auschwitz trial in 1964, intended to provide the judges with a trustworthy overview of the political and historical developments of the Nazis' rise to power and the Third Reich, were published in 1967 and entitled *Anatomie des SS-Staates* – 'Anatomy of the

SS State'.[7] In this work the SA is only mentioned in passing, and only with reference to its role in the terror campaigns prior to the Nazi takeover of power and the establishment of the Third Reich in 1933–4.[8]

In what follows, I will analyse how the image of the SA as a violent yet politically peripheral organization developed in post-1945 Germany. To begin with, I will argue not only that the International Military Tribunal (IMT) at Nuremberg in 1945–6 constitutes an exemplary test case for analysing the correlation between legal practices and historiography, but that its proceedings against the SA set the tone for subsequent assessments of the stormtroopers. I will then, in the second and third sections, discuss two exemplary case studies from the 1950s and 1960s that demonstrate how the diminution of the SA and its crimes allowed the post-war careers of the jurist and former SA-*Standartenführer* Hans Gmelin, from 1954 until 1975 mayor of Tübingen, and the historian and former Chief of the SA-*Hochschulamt* Heinrich Bennecke. In the fourth and final part I will explain how, beginning in the 1970s, the focus of both academic and non-academic research on Germany's Nazi past shifted from the political to the social, with mixed effects for the history of the SA. Although many local and regional studies underlined the sometimes extreme violence carried out by mid- and low-ranking stormtroopers, particularly in 1933, the SA as a mass organization with political ambitions and clout slowly but surely disappeared from sight. In twenty-first-century Germany, 'SA methods' is still used as a term of political combat, but it has become unstuck from its original historical context.

The SA at the International Military Tribunal in Nuremberg

Even if one does not agree with Robert Kempner's early assessment that the IMT was 'the greatest history seminar ever held', historical research over the last few decades has confirmed that the trial 'embraced a didactic purpose', aiming to provide a moral lesson that would stand independent of the sentencing of individual defendants.[9] The Nazi organizations that stood trial in Nuremberg were therefore of particular relevance, as the outcome of the IMT had the potential to profoundly affect the lives of the former members of those organizations, which in the case of the SA comprised several million men. As the IMT was the first legal authority to embrace an interpretation of the SA that distinguished sharply between its pre-1934 identity and that of later years, it set the course not only for subsequent criminal proceedings but also for the analysis of later historians. In this respect the Nuremberg judges indeed wrote history – with lasting effects.

Alongside leading politicians, military commanders, and business leaders of the Third Reich such as Hermann Göring, Rudolf Hess, Karl Dönitz, and Hjalmar Schacht – to name just a few of the twenty-four defendants – some of the most important repressive and terror-exercising organizations of the Nazi state, such as the SS, the Gestapo, and the SA, also faced trial at Nuremberg. These groups were declared 'criminal organizations' if they (1) had provided a framework in which their members had committed 'crimes against peace', (2) were responsible for the commission of 'war crimes', or (3) had participated in 'crimes against humanity'. Article 6 of the charter of the IMT defined 'crimes against peace' as the 'planning, preparation, initiation or waging of a war of aggression, or a war in violation of international treaties, agreements or assurances, or participation in a common plan or conspiracy for the accomplishment of any of the foregoing'. War crimes, the same article stated, included 'murder, ill-treatment or deportation to slave labor or for any other purpose of civilian population of or in occupied territory, murder or ill-treatment of prisoners of war or persons on the seas, killing of hostages, plunder of public or private property, wanton destruction of cities, towns or villages, or devastation not justified by military necessity'. This list was not intended to be exclusive, but rather was meant to set the tone for the proceedings to follow. Finally, 'crimes against humanity', a legal category used for the first time by the IMT and highly contested on the basis of its technical applicability, incorporated the murder, extermination, enslavement, or deportation of and other inhuman acts committed against any civilian population, regardless of whether or not these acts were committed in violation of the 'domestic law of the country where perpetrated'.[10]

The declaration of the SA as a 'criminal organization' would have had direct consequences for the judicial proceedings against Nazi criminals that would unfold in the years to come. In post-war Germany a finding by the IMT of membership in the SA would have constituted sufficient grounds for legal punishment, without the courts having to prove the individual guilt of a particular defendant. Understandably, such a verdict would have been a worst-case scenario for millions of former militants.[11] Some 10,000 wrote affidavits for the Nuremberg SA defence team which at best acknowledged that some individual SA men had not always behaved properly but exempted the SA as an organization from all charges.[12] This very high number not only demonstrates that the Nazi networks established during the Third Reich still operated effectively after the war, but also suggests that a broad condemnation of the SA would have provoked intense criticism from thousands of former stormtroopers and their families.

Characteristic of the usually apologetic tone of these documents is a detailed memorandum by SA-*Obergruppenführer* Max Jüttner, written while in American custody in Internment Camp 75 in Kornwestheim near Stuttgart in January 1946.[13] Jüttner was one of the two surviving individuals who had temporarily led the SA between 2 May and 8 August 1943. According to his memo, he read about the Nuremberg trial in the newspapers available at the camp and 'as the only SA representative within reach' immediately contacted the IMT in October 1945. As the court did not pay much attention to his initial correspondence, he set out to write a justification of the SA and himself with the encouragement of the defence lawyer Robert Servatius in January 1946.[14] Jüttner's nearly 100-page vindication is at times almost comical, particularly with regard to the SA's attitudes toward Jews and political adversaries. According to Jüttner, neither he nor Lutze had ever ordered the persecution of Jews. Only from the Allies had he learned about the torture and murder of members of these groups within the concentration camps. Any reasonable man who believed in justice would give the SA credit for its honourable motives, Jüttner wrote.[15]

The oral proceedings against the SA began on the afternoon of 18 December 1945, the twenty-second day of the trial. The main prosecutor of the SA was the American jurist Robert G. Storey, who, together with nine colleagues, coordinated the evidence and decided on the sequence of the proceedings.[16] Storey began the prosecution's accusations by defining the aim and scope of the SA, though not without difficulty. According to him, the SA

> was an agency adapted to many designs and purposes, and its role in the conspiracy changed from time to time – always corresponding with the progression of the conspiracy through its various phases towards the final objective: abrogation of the Versailles Treaty and acquisition of the territory of other peoples and nations. If we might consider this conspiracy as a pattern, with its various parts fitting together like the

pieces of a jigsaw puzzle, we would find that the piece representing the SA constituted a link in the pattern vitally necessary to the presentation and development of the entire picture.

The word 'conspiracy', as used here, referred to the Nazis' attempt to overthrow the democratic state of Weimar and to replace it with a Fascist dictatorship that aimed to transform Germany into a European empire by attacking and occupying other countries. The most distinct feature of the SA, Storey stated, was its members' 'fanatical adherence to the philosophies and ideologies conceived by the Nazi conspirators'.[17] This shared belief was easy to prove, but it was much harder to draw a link between such a vague assessment of the SA's general character and particular crimes punishable by law.

Storey claimed that between 1934 and 1939 'the SA developed from scattered bands of street ruffians to a well-knit, cohesive unit organized on a military basis with military training and military functions and, above all, with an aggressive, militaristic, and warlike spirit and philosophy'.[18] From 1934 onward, he added, up to 25,000 officers and non-commissioned officers were trained annually in the twenty-five SA troop schools and three SA *Reichsführer* schools.[19] However, somewhat contradictorily, Storey also claimed that the SA 'started a rapid decline in its importance' after the murder of Ernst Röhm in 1934.[20] Regardless of such inconsistencies, Storey's accusations against the late SA appear well grounded. As evidence that the SA 'had been used as a striking force in the first steps of the aggressive war', Storey pointed to the group's role in the *Anschluss* of Austria and the occupation of the Sudetenland.[21] In both cases, he argued, the SA provided not only logistical help, but also thousands of fighters forming the 'backbone' both of the Sudeten German Free Corps and the Austrian Legion.[22] In the last stages of the war, from 1944 onward, Storey noted, drawing on the testimony of SS-*Brigadeführer* Walter Schellenberg,[23] the SA took over several 'functions which had previously been entrusted only to the SS, the Sipo [*Sicherheitspolizei*], and Army', including the guarding of concentration camps and prisoner-of-war camps and the supervision of forced labourers in Germany and the occupied areas.[24] All this evidence proved, Storey concluded, that both individual members of the SA and the SA as an organization 'were in fact co-conspirators and participants in a conspiracy which contemplated and involved Crimes against the Peace and Crimes against Humanity and War Crimes'.[25]

On the other side, the SA's defence team in Nuremberg consisted of three parties: the lawyer Georg Boehm and his team as well as the two chosen barristers Dr Martin Löffler and Dr Theodor Klefisch.[26] The personal papers of Klefisch, who since the late Weimar years had been a respectable though only regionally known criminal defence lawyer from Cologne, were made available for historical research only recently.[27] These papers contain, among other things, documents related to his role as a lawyer before the IMT and allow a relatively detailed analysis of the strategy adopted by the defence team. Klefisch never spoke in court and only filed a single 'speech in writing' on 15 August 1946, a fact that was partly the result of tensions among the lawyers defending the SA.[28]

Klefisch's work concentrated on those SA men who had formerly been members of the *Stahlhelm, Bund der Frontsoldaten*. As outlined previously, the relationship between the *Stahlhelm* and the SA had been strained in its early days, not least because of generational differences, and it had remained complicated ever since. In simplified terms the SA appealed to young men, the *Stahlhelm* to their fathers.[29] In the final plea of the SA defence lawyers, delivered on 28 August 1946, Georg Boehm emphasized this divide, as well as the (alleged) strong ideological differences between the NSDAP and the *Stahlhelm*, concluding: 'A large number of the members of the *Stahlhelm* represented a body within the SA, united by common ideals, who regarded the events of the time with the greatest distrust.'[30] As this statement illustrates, the overall strategy of the defence team was to use to their own advantage the complexities of the SA's internal structure and the fact that its form had changed considerably at least twice between 1921 and 1945, arguing that it would be highly unfair and legally unsound to declare such a massive organization, with its up to 4.5 million former members, an outright 'criminal' group.[31] Löffler pointed out that such a declaration would further be incompatible with the denazification laws of the American Zone of Occupation, according to which all SA ranks up to the level of *Sturmführer* were not regarded as subject to automatic punishment. In fact, Löffler noted, some of the former members of this allegedly criminal organization had recently been elected community councillors.[32]

This defence strategy proved successful. On 28 February 1946 chief prosecutor Robert H. Jackson asked that all wearers of the SA sports badge who were not regular SA members, as well as members of the SA-controlled home guard units and the SA Reserve, be exempted from prosecution.[33]

He now requested that only the main body of the SA be considered for punishment. However, Löffler claimed in the following session on 1 March that criminal proceedings against the SA still affected everyone 'who ever belonged to the SA, even for a very short time, during the 24 years between its establishment in 1921 and its dissolution in 1945, that is to say, during a period of almost a quarter of a century'.[34] Not surprisingly, Löffler downplayed the SA's importance during the war years as best he could, stating:

> Crimes against the laws or customs of war are not charged to the SA. It is true that the Prosecution presented an affidavit saying that the SA also took part in guarding concentration camps and prisoner-of-war camps and in supervising forced labor; but, according to the presentation of the Prosecution, this did not occur until 1944 within the framework of the total war raging at that time, and it has not been charged that this activity of the SA involved any excesses or ill-treatment [. . .] The few offenses against humanity charged to the SA by the Prosecution and committed by individual members in the course of almost a quarter of a century can in no way be compared with the serious crimes against humanity of which we have heard here.[35]

Löffler went so far as to try to impress the court by presenting figures no one could actually verify, claiming that at most 2 per cent of all SA men had participated in punishable individual actions, whereas 98 per cent had 'kept their hands clean'. He even argued that the overwhelming majority of all former SA men would strongly deny that their leaders had ordered them to carry out criminal acts.[36] Without being explicitly mentioned, the intense and often resentful public debate about German 'collective guilt' lingered beneath such reasoning.[37]

The Nuremberg judges passed their verdict on 30 September 1946. Their findings distinguished between the SA that existed up to the summer of 1934 and the SA that existed thereafter. Regarding the SA of the first period, they determined that although the stormtroopers had committed crimes, these crimes were limited to German soil and did not meet the criteria for the categories of crime established by the tribunal. With regard to the SA of the latter period, the judges tried to reconcile the contradictory perspectives of the prosecution and the defence. 'Isolated units of the SA,' the judges ruled, had been 'involved in the steps leading up to aggressive war and in the commission of war crimes and crimes against humanity', thus confirming the argument of the prosecution. As evidence, the judges explicitly cited the occupation of Austria, the SA's contribution to the formation of the Sudeten German Free Corps, and the transport and guarding of prisoners of war by the SA-*Gruppe* Sudeten and SA units in Danzig, Poznań, Silesia, and the Baltic states.[38] The judges also noted the SA's active participation in the anti-Jewish pogroms of 9 November 1938 and the 'ill treatment' of Jews in the ghettos of Vilna and Kaunas.[39]

In contrast, however, the court agreed with the defence inasmuch as it accepted the proposition that 'the SA was reduced to the status of a group of unimportant Nazi hangers-on' after the 1934 purge. It was this conclusion that finally brought the judges to a verdict of not guilty: 'Although in specific instances some units of the SA were used for the commission of war crimes and crimes against humanity, it cannot be said that its members generally participated in or even knew of the criminal acts. For these reasons the Tribunal does not declare the SA to be a criminal organization within the meaning of Article 9 of the Charter.'[40] The same conclusion applied to the Reich Cabinet and the 'General Staff and High Command', whereas the SS, SD, Gestapo, and certain groups within the NSDAP leadership were found guilty. The silent majority of Germans, even if they contested the legitimacy of the court, approved of this verdict, not least because it fitted into the prevailing tendency of both small-scale and leading Nazis to downplay their (usually voluntary) participation in the Third Reich.[41]

Klefisch attributed the relative leniency of the Nuremberg judges toward the stormtroopers largely to his own defence strategy, which had painted a portrait of the SA as a highly complex but ultimately toothless bureaucratic institution to which many Germans had only involuntarily belonged for a brief period.[42] Shortly after the IMT's verdict, in a letter from 5 November 1946, Klefisch claimed that the integration of the former *Stahlhelmers* into the SA had more or less saved the whole organization from punishment: 'That the entire SA was not declared a criminal organization was to a good degree a consequence of the fact that it had incorporated a great deal of people from the *Stahlhelm* within its rank and file. The conduct of the latter had been proven to be without a flaw. It was simply not possible to label an entire organization as outright criminal if it contained such a great number of irreproachable members.'[43]

However self-congratulatory this statement may have been, it is hard to ignore that the Nuremberg acquittal set a precedent for the handling of trials of former stormtroopers over the following decades, at least in the Federal Republic of Germany. Convictions by West German courts of individual stormtroopers remained limited to those implicated in the SA's crimes during 1933, 1934, and *Kristallnacht*. The 'public', highly visible nature of attacks by the Brownshirts now backfired, as it often allowed for detailed reconstruction of these acts, even fifteen to twenty years later.[44] Unsurprisingly, in the Soviet Zone of Occupation, Soviet and later also East German authorities took a particularly vivid interest in the prosecution of SA crimes that had been directed against members of the Communist and Socialist parties.[45] Yet even in the Soviet Zone judicial attempts to punish Nazi crimes, initially intended to help legitimize the new political order, decreased dramatically once the GDR was firmly established in the early 1950s, demonstrating a remarkable parallel to the West German process of *Vergangenheitsbewältigung*, or 'overcoming history'.[46] By the mid-1950s even the long prison sentences imposed on SA guards from the former Hohnstein concentration camp could be suspended if the former stormtrooper agreed to spy for the newly established Ministry of State Security.[47] In 1950, after a visit to her homeland, Hannah Arendt remarked that many Germans had willingly sought refuge in the belief that they had been victims of the nation's 'culture of obedience' (*Gehorsamkeitskultur*).[48] Millions of former stormtroopers ceased to acknowledge their prior (usually voluntary) commitment to National Socialism as 'little guardians of the people's community'.[49] Furthermore, the West German *Straffreiheitsgesetz* of 31 December 1949, which granted an amnesty to those offenders sentenced to prison terms of less than six months, meant in practice that the majority of SA criminals were spared incarceration.[50]

From the mid-1950s onward even former high-ranking SA leaders were able to live unmolested, with a few notable, yet ultimately unsatisfactory exceptions, such as that of Adolf-Heinz Beckerle.[51] Across the board, convictions from the early post-1945 period were often suspended, and prison terms considerably shortened. The case of Wilhelm Schepmann, the last SA Chief of Staff, is instructive in this respect. In 1950 a Dortmund jury court had sentenced Schepmann to a modest prison term of nine months – not for his leadership role in the SA, but because of his involvement as Dortmund's police president in the violent Nazi takeover of power in 1933.[52] However, Schepmann, who had been successfully 'denazified' by a German court in Lüneburg in 1952, appealed the decision and was ultimately acquitted in 1954.[53] Two years later he was elected deputy mayor for the city of Gifhorn in Lower Saxony. He died in 1970.

The posthumous denazification of the former SA-*Obergruppenführer* and Nazi diplomat Dietrich von Jagow as a 'lesser offender' further illustrates the general tendency of post-war proceedings. The Freiburg *Spruchkammer*, the local denazification court, ruled on 13 February 1950 that von Jagow had not been involved in the production of propaganda for the Nazi cause and had held his offices – as SA-*Obergruppenführer*, Prussian state councillor, ambassador, and member of the *Reichstag* – 'in an idealistic and decent spirit'. Consequently, the court granted him extensive extenuating circumstances.[54] With von Jagow's wife and seven children living in cramped conditions, it appears that the judges' ruling was intended more to create the legal conditions that would permit his widow to receive a pension than to give a realistic portrayal of the deceased.

The continuing use of key terms from the Nazi regime's vocabulary long after 1945 testifies to the lasting effect of the National Socialist 'revolution' in morals and manners. In the words of the historian Bernhard Gotto, during the years following the ultimate defeat of the Nazi regime, its former leaders on the local, regional, and national levels actively and often successfully worked toward the 'invention of a "decent National Socialism"' – one purified of 'aberrations' such as the persecution of the Jews or the Third Reich's racial and exterminatory character. Instead, its proponents now emphasized the regime's social goals and achievements.[55] The 1949 attempt by Otto Strasser to re-establish his 'Black Front' under the cover name of *Liga für die Wiederauferstehung Deutschlands* (literally, the League for the Resurrection of Germany) fitted this pattern.[56] Other former Nazis clung to their aggressive rhetoric. Such was the case, for example, with Gustaf Deuchler, the former professor of pedagogy at Hamburg University and stormtrooper who had enjoyed giving lectures in his brown shirt and had glorified the stormtroopers' services on the home front. In 1952 he became one of the leading figures in the Hamburg branch of the *Verein der Entnazifizierungsgeschädigten* – literally, the Association of the Victims of Denazification. Deuchler characterized the denazification process in Hamburg as an effort of 'reckless brutality' and 'boundless hate', fuelled by an 'obsession with retaliation' that would never be extinguished.[57]

By the mid-1950s even prior convictions for active participation in pogroms against and deportation of Jews – actions often euphemistically labelled in official documents as *Aussiedlung*, or 'resettlement' – no longer prevented an individual from being fully integrated into German post-war society. Such formulations stood in remarkable continuity with the language of the Nazi regime a decade earlier and often betrayed the intention of their users, who urged the public to overcome the burdens of the past and close the prior chapter of German history. As the municipal council of the Bavarian city of Treuchtlingen in 1956 explained with rare clarity, a harsh stance toward former National Socialists could no longer be justified, as the former Nazis who had taken part in the 'anti-Jewish pogroms' (*Judenpogrome*) and had therefore lost their positions in the first years after the war had since, to a large degree, had their former rights reinstated.[58]

Stormtroopers as Misguided Idealists

A telling example of the general tendency to integrate previously committed National Socialists back into society was the remarkable post-war career of the jurist Hans Gmelin, who in 1954 was elected mayor of his home town of Tübingen in Württemberg. A former law student at Eberhard Karls University who descended from one of the city's respectable middle-class families, the ambitious Gmelin joined the *Stahlhelm* on 12 December 1931 and then was integrated into the SA in the autumn of 1933. In the years following he occupied several leading positions in the Württemberg branch of this organization while at the same time pursuing his professional goals. According to his own account from 1939, Gmelin served as the leader of four different SA *Stürme* (13/216, 56/125, 2/180, and 1/119) and was promoted to SA-*Sturmbannführer* on 9 November 1938. Gmelin had joined the NSDAP on 1 May 1937, after the entrance ban was lifted, and in the following year assumed leadership of the 'Hanns Ludin' company of the Sudeten German Free Corps, which was active from 19 September to 15 October 1938. Having passed this military litmus test, Hanns Ludin, at that time the leader of the SA-*Gruppe* Süd-West, offered Gmelin the position of a full-time SA-*Standartenführer*. Initially, the gifted young jurist preferred to enter the ranks of the Reich Ministry of Justice, but thanks to a compromise between the state judiciary and the SA he was appointed to the rank of *Landgerichtsrat* for life in May 1939, with the Reich Minister of Justice granting him a two-year leave to continue his career in the SA.[59] After serving in the Wehrmacht until the end of 1940, Gmelin followed his mentor and friend Ludin into the Foreign Office in January 1941. Both men arrived in Bratislava in April of the same year.[60]

In the Slovakian capital Gmelin's office was located next door to his boss and he was also a friend of Franz Karmasin, the infamous *Volksgruppenführer*. Gmelin's initials on several official documents from the German Embassy in Slovakia confirm his intimate knowledge of the deportation of the Slovakian Jews.[61] In a lecture delivered at a party leadership meeting in Vienna in January 1944, Gmelin freely acknowledged that the policy of 'Aryanization' had served the Reich's interests well. Even the fact that some Jews remained in Slovakia would help the Germans, he added, because as long as the Slovaks could still rob the Jews, it was unlikely that they would turn their backs on their protecting power, despite the Red Army's advance.[62] Later the same year, however, in November 1944, Himmler requested a complete overhaul of the German Embassy in Slovakia including the removal of Gmelin. After four years in office there, Gmelin would be on the way to turning into 'half a Slovak', Himmler argued.[63] The *Reichsführer*-SS feared that Ludin's and Gmelin's good relations with local Fascists had made them blind to the risks of the latter changing sides as the Red Army's advance became increasingly unstoppable.

After spending more than three years in American and French internment camps from 1945 to 1948, Gmelin was classified a 'lesser offender' (category III) in Tübingen in July 1948.[64] The court sentenced him to the minimum penalty for this category: a two-year probation period during which he was forbidden from becoming politically active. Despite this verdict the denazification panel stated that Gmelin had an 'impeccable, clean character'. He had been a committed National Socialist, the judges admitted, but 'he was no fanatic' and during the days of the Third Reich he had believed that by 'positive work' the NSDAP could return to 'moderate and reasonable positions'.[65] Six years later Gmelin attempted to demonstrate precisely that.

During his mayoral election address in Tübingen, printed verbatim in the regional newspaper *Schwäbisches Tagblatt* on 2 October 1954, Gmelin promised that he would deal openly with the Nazi past. In light of what the electorate in the city knew anyway, Gmelin opted for a kind of pre-emptive defence, addressing his time as SA-*Führer* and Nazi diplomat openly, but claiming that such functions within the Third Reich could not be taken as clear-cut indicators of one's standpoint or actual behaviour at the time. When he was a young man, there had simply been no political alternative to the Nazis, Gmelin said. Later, 'when the ship was sinking' (i.e. when Germany was about to lose the war), he and the vast majority of his fellow Germans did not have the option of leaving the country – a thinly veiled jab against those who had left Germany for political reasons between 1933 and 1945.[66] Gmelin asserted that he had suffered internal conflict during the war but insisted that, at a time when one could either obey orders or follow one's conscience, he had always helped those who were dear to him (*im eigenen Lebenskreis*) and who had asked him for assistance. Tolerance had always been the guiding star of his personal and official conduct, he assured his listeners (Plate 32).[67]

Even more characteristic of the zeitgeist of the mid-1950s was the controversy that followed Gmelin's election. It started with the publication in *Schwäbisches Tagblatt* of an open letter of protest from Gerhard Ebeling, a professor of Protestant theology at Tübingen University. Ebeling lamented that the election of Gmelin indicated that the majority of voters did not care about the new mayor's Nazi past – or, what was more likely, that they had voted for Gmelin precisely because of it. Calling the election an alarming sign of 're-Nazification', Ebeling argued that even the end of the war had not produced a true victory over National Socialist ideology.[68] In response, a storm of protest broke loose, filling the newspaper columns over the next few days. Most of the letters printed were written in favour of the new mayor. Several of them urged Christian clemency. Qualified men like Gmelin who had been successfully denazified should not be blamed for their youthful idealism until the end of their lives, these writers declared. A colleague of Ebeling, a certain Professor E. Hennig, even praised Gmelin's personality as a true leader who had been admired by most of the rank-and-file stormtroopers. Hennig ascribed a 'post-war psychosis' to those criticizing Gmelin for his Nazi past and demanded an urgent end to the 'collective verdicts of the *Spruchkammern*'.[69] Many other writers complained about Professor Ebeling's alleged arrogance, testifying to the endurance of the anti-intellectualism of the Nazi years, even in an old university town.

The SA repeatedly served as a point of reference in this debate. One writer noted that a speaker at a party rally had been prevented from continuing his speech after addressing the audience with the words 'My dear comrades from the old SA', while another writer assured Ebeling that 'a brown shirt soaked in blood' was no longer an item in demand in German society. According to this latter writer, he had dressed in such a shirt at the age of sixteen, but had since exchanged it for a prosthesis – an allusion to a war injury.[70] Whereas most writers in defence of Gmelin signed their letters with their full names, those who sided with Ebeling more often remained anonymous. One female writer felt so threatened by the heated atmosphere in Tübingen that she explicitly asked to be identified by her initials only, declaring: 'I have seen and heard the short-tempered and primitive supporters of Herr Gmelin!'[71]

The highly popular Gmelin remained in office for twenty years after being re-elected as the only candidate in 1962, with a landslide victory of more than 94 per cent of the vote (on a 51.7 per cent turnout). He became a towering figure in local politics, committed in particular to the Franco-German reconciliation process.[72] To his supporters, his post-war career symbolized West Germany's successful transformation from Nazi dictatorship to Western democracy.[73] According to his daughter, the SPD politician Herta Däubler-Gmelin (Germany's Minister of Justice from 1998 to 2002), after the war Hans Gmelin devoted himself fully to the reconstruction of a democratic Germany in order to atone for his Nazi past, even as he continued to meet with 'old comrades' and actively helped them when possible. 'This was one of the points that frequently led to heated arguments in our family,' Däubler-Gmelin remembers, yet she also stresses that her father, after his initial reluctance, finally faced up to such criticism from within his own family.[74] However, it is worth remembering that Hans Gmelin's post-war career was only possible because of a combination of three factors: first, his trivialization of his SA activities in the 1930s as participation in a kind of sports club; second, his whitewashing of his time as a German diplomat in Slovakia; and third, a political environment in Württemberg that throughout the 1950s and 1960s continued to hold the National Socialist vision of a 'people's community' in high esteem – perverted, or so it was argued, by the Nazi establishment once lured by the temptations of power.

Mutilated Stories

During the 1950s historians also started to contribute to the narrative of the SA's relative political impotence. Particularly relevant in this respect was Dr Heinrich Bennecke, leader of the SA University Offices in 1933–4.[75] This formerly high-ranking SA leader started to work in the late 1950s as an associate researcher with the prestigious Institute for Contemporary Research in Munich (IfZ), established in 1949 as the *Deutsches Institut für Geschichte der nationalsozialistischen Zeit*, literally the 'German Institute for the History of the National Socialist Time'.[76] The surviving correspondence between the IfZ and Bennecke begins in 1958 and ends in the late 1960s. Both parties benefited from their collaboration, exchanging documents, expertise, and money. Bennecke prepared notes and short exposés on the history of the SA for the institute's internal use, commented on manuscripts and books, and interviewed former National Socialist leaders, most often using a set of questions provided by the IfZ.[77] From time to time the institute paid him modest sums: initially, he received a kind of honorarium of between 50 and 200 marks,[78] but ultimately a contract was drawn up that guaranteed Bennecke a total of 3,600 marks for interviews to be held with former Nazis between 1 July and 31 December 1963.[79]

Bennecke's attempts to be employed by the IfZ on a regular basis failed.[80] Nevertheless, his collaboration with the institute not only provided him with the financial means to conduct interviews with fellow high-ranking Nazis, but also helped him become a respectable scholar on the SA in the 1960s. Based on his inside knowledge from twenty years as a leading stormtrooper, combined with his unique access to unpublished documents provided by the IfZ, Bennecke completed two monographs: *Hitler und die SA* (1962) and *Die Reichswehr und der 'Röhm-Putsch'* (1964).[81] Both books concentrated on the SA's history between the mid-1920s and the 'Röhm purge' and remained standard German-language books in the field until the 1980s. In early 1963 he also prepared a manuscript on the history of the SA between 1918 and 1923 that was bought by the IfZ but never appeared in print.[82] Another of his manuscripts, commissioned by the German Federal Archives, was published only in 2012.[83] Bennecke knew very well that these books only dealt with the middle period of the SA's existence, completely leaving out the post-1934 period.[84] Nevertheless, based on his reputation as a researcher, Bennecke was invited to teach various courses on the political history of the Weimar Republic at the *Hochschule für Politische Wissenschaften* in Munich (today's *Hochschule für Politik*) between 1967 and 1972.[85]

In his works, Bennecke took a traditional political history approach that focused on a close circle of Nazi leaders and belittled the level of violence exercised before and after 30 January 1933. Although his publisher claimed that the first book on the SA was not written 'with the intent of justification' but had been inspired by the author's 'love of truth', a critical reading demonstrates that Bennecke made every effort to distinguish between Hitler and the SA. Writing about the organization's early days in Munich, he described the SA as a *Wehrverband* by the grace of Ehrhardt and Röhm, diminishing the role played by the NSDAP and Hitler in its formation.[86] In this respect the title of the book should be translated as 'Hitler *and* the SA', not 'Hitler's SA'. Bennecke consistently downplayed the stormtroopers' notorious antisemitism and the Nazi terror campaign that unfolded in the summer of 1932, which for him was only a reaction to 'pre-election terror from the left'.[87] Discussing the Nazi leadership's strong support for the Potempa murders, which peaked with Hitler's telegram promising 'unreserved loyalty' to the perpetrators, Bennecke emphasized that these actions were above all intended as a declaration of war to von Papen. He even claimed that not only Hitler, but 'probably also many of the newspaper readers back then', had thought it embarrassing that the National Socialists involved in the Potempa murders had received much harsher sentences than had those members of the *Reichsbanner* who were standing trial at the same time in another Silesian city, Brieg, for their involvement in a political clash that had taken place in Ohlau on 10 July 1932. What Bennecke did not say was that the lighter punishments in the Ohlau case were partly attributable to the fact that the crimes had been committed in the weeks before the emergency decree against political terror came into effect.[88] The late Weimar logic of setting one crime in opposition to another still very much shaped Bennecke's political thinking in post-war Germany.[89]

Nevertheless, his studies were seen as important contributions to the field in the 1960s and 1970s, not only because of their intimate knowledge but also because of a lack of alternatives on the book market.[90] In hindsight, Bennecke's historical writings on the SA illustrate the general problem that dogged the early IfZ's efforts to write an 'objective' and purely 'factual' history of the recent past. As critics like historian Nicolas Berg have argued, the heavy emphasis on 'primary sources', which necessarily relied on official documents in which the Nazi perspective was encoded, involuntarily favoured a narrative that followed the paths chalked out by the regime – all the more so in cases such as Bennecke's, in which the interpreting historian was identical to the former historical agent.[91]

Politics of Remembrance

The most up-to-date historical scholarship inevitably has only limited power in resolving contemporary public debates, as the public perception and memory of the stormtroopers in Germany after the Second World War demonstrates.[92] Historians ranging from the academically trained Bennecke to the journalist Heinrich Höhne with his best-selling book *Mordsache Röhm* (1984),[93] also serialized in the influential weekly *Der Spiegel*, remained interested in the SA's role in politics in the 1920s and early 1930s. However, beginning in the 1970s, many Germans were more disposed to remember the Brownshirts' public appearances, marches, brawls, and terror alongside their standing in their local communities. Whereas most ordinary people had not had close personal contact with the SS, SD, or Gestapo, the Nazi organizations mainly responsible for the regime's crimes, the stormtroopers had been familiar figures – neighbours, colleagues from work, the ambitious schoolteacher, or, in more unfortunate circumstances, the notorious village underachiever, who, merely because of his uniform, was for once in his life given the opportunity to look down on and dominate others.

The vast majority of former Nazi activists were able to enjoy the fruits of the German *Wirtschaftswunder*, or 'Economic Miracle', after the war. The social and interpersonal networks of the pre-1945 period often survived the war, particularly in the countryside and in small cities. German shooting associations, riders clubs, and sports clubs – which in many cases had been integrated into or at least presided over by the SA in the 1930s – continued to operate, ignoring or passing over in eloquent silence the twelve years of the Third Reich. When German men told stories of the Nazi past, they usually spoke about the years of the Second World War, in which the majority of them had been conscripted. Fighting for the home-land and suffering as a soldier of the allegedly 'clean Wehrmacht' made a much better impression than insisting on one's voluntary contribution to the Nazi project as a brown-shirted stormtrooper.[94] Because of the modest educational background of many former rank-and-file SA men, detailed autobiographies recounting their youthful political activism remained extremely rare. Whereas the veterans of the Waffen-SS in post-war West Germany regularly met for 'comradely gatherings' that attracted up to several thousand people, no SA veterans' organizations were created.[95] Slowly but surely the SA as an organization that had not only contributed to the Nazi terror, but also shaped the lives of millions of German men and their families, vanished from public memory.

Against this background it is not surprising that some former SA leaders even became respected local dignitaries or had successful second careers as journalists, politicians, and environmental campaigners. Particularly noteworthy is the post-war career of the long-time SA propagandist and SA-*Obersturmbannführer* Hans Sponholz, whose books about the stormtroopers from the 1930s and early 1940s have been cited in previous chapters.[96] A journalist for the conservative Bavarian newspaper *Merkur* for many years, he also enjoyed a modest political career in the Bavaria Party. Sponholz became regionally famous as a highly regarded conservationist who initiated the Association for the Protection of the Ebersbach Forest (*Schutzgemeinschaft Ebersberger Forst*), an environmentalist group that decisively prevented the Bavarian State government from permitting the construction of CERN, the European Organization for Nuclear Research, in the extensive woodlands east of Munich. Sponholz's rhetoric in the environmental campaigns of the 1960s illustrates the degree to which the passage from *Volksgemeinschaft* to *Schutzgemeinschaft* was at times a short one: 'Nature conservancy must be ready for battle,' the former SA propagandist now urged.[97] For his commitment he was awarded the Bavarian Conservation Award (*Bayerischer Naturschutzpreis*) in 1973, together with the famous behaviourist and Nobel Prize winner Konrad Lorenz.[98] Sponholz also received the Order of Merit of the Federal Republic of Germany in 1980, and two streets in the region were named in his honour. However, his Wikipedia entry as of late 2015 provided no details of his post-1945 career and listed the date of his death as 'unknown'.[99]

Starting in the late 1970s, the history of the everyday gained prominence in the Federal Republic, inspired by the History Workshop movement in Britain and by the Swedish author Sven Lindquist, who memorably proclaimed, 'Dig where you stand!' Action groups now began to work on local and regional histories of the Third Reich, tracing the roots of former Nazi networks and identifying their main participants.[100] Members of these groups located former SA prisons and early concentration camps and recorded the biographies of those ordinary men and women who had fallen victim to the Nazi terror. After what were often long delays, some of these historic places of violence were transformed into museums, as with the prison of the SA Field Police in Berlin's General-Pape-Straße, which opened to the general public in 2013. Some thirty years passed after residents of the area had learned about the former use of their cellars before the commemoration of SA violence could be institutionalized in the form of this museum.[101] In the eastern part of the city, by contrast, 'Köpenick's week of bloodshed' in June 1933 was commemorated as early as 1945. In the decades to follow, the GDR made considerable efforts to remember the early Nazi terror, yet it also shaped this remembrance to fit its own anti-Fascist founding myth. As with the former SA prison in General-Pape-Straße, the district of Berlin-Köpenick today supports a small museum to commemorate the early Nazi terror.[102]

Contrary to Bennecke's attempts to portray the stormtroopers as misguided idealists, the increasingly dominant view saw them as little more than ruffians, dim-witted toughs, or uniformed philistines (Spießbürger), who under the influence of alcohol turned into part-time hooligans. In light of this development, it is not surprising that comparisons with the SA were used early on in both German states to denounce organizations and individuals for political purposes (Plate 33). Two examples demonstrate the tone and character of such comparisons. First, in the heated atmosphere of the Cold War, Heinrich von Brentano, Foreign Minister of the Federal Republic, in a parliamentary speech in 1957 defended the decision of his ministry not to financially support a guest performance in Paris by the Bochum municipal theatre of Bertolt Brecht's famous Dreigroschenoper (The Threepenny Opera), using the argument that the writer's 'late lyrics' could only be compared with the poems of the SA bard Horst Wessel. Such a comparison was utter nonsense, of course, at least from an artistic point of view. Brentano was taking deliberate aim at Brecht the politician, who after the war had accepted a call from East Berlin and, at least in the eyes of West Germany, was now providing the Communist rulers with support in return for personal privileges.[103] Brentano's comparison might also have been a clumsy attempt to counter the persistent revelations by the GDR, the self-declared 'Better Germany', of the Nazi past of several high functionaries within the Federal Republic.[104]

The second example dates back to the late 1960s. With emotions running high in the streets, lecture halls, and newspaper offices of West Berlin in the summer of 1968, the best-selling staunchly anti-Communist tabloid Bild, published by Springer Press, denounced the protesting students as being like new Brownshirts: 'They must see blood. They wave the red flag and believe the red flag. Here the fun ends [. . .] and democratic tolerance. We have something against SA methods.'[105] The Marxist philosopher Theodor W. Adorno joined in such criticism, yet on a very different intellectual and personal level. The former emigrant of German-Jewish descent was shocked when confronted with the tumultuous 'teach-ins' at West German universities in the late 1960s. He regarded the most radical students not as members of a new political avant-garde but as 'storm-troopers in jeans'.[106] Similarly, the political scientist Ernst Fraenkel, who in *The Dual State* (1941) had offered a pioneering analysis of National Socialism, warned members of the left-wing Socialist German Student League (*Sozialistischer Deutscher Studentenbund*, or SDS) to abstain from 'exactly the same methods as the raiding squads of the SA'.[107]

More recent scholarship has sometimes echoed such views when accusing the more radical protesters of 1968 of 'Nazi hooliganism', a charge referring in particular to these students' frequent shouting down of those professors who were not to their liking.[108] Students in the late 1960s in turn used similar metaphors to denounce the alleged 'pogrom journalism' of the Springer Press.[109] In their eyes the work of these journalists deliberately sought to provoke physical violence. The students regarded Springer as a cornerstone of the repressive 'capitalist system' that had allegedly been established in the Federal Republic. Both antagonistic views shared common ground in referring to the Nazi past to denigrate their political enemies. Remarkably, these political fights continued to carry echoes of the interwar period.

Over the last decade or so the number of people who could personally remember the SA has diminished for natural reasons. However, the Brownshirts have remained a point of reference in German public debate, particularly with regard to acts of political and criminal violence. This was most obvious in the early 1990s, immediately after reunification, when waves of xenophobic riots broke out across the country. The most notorious incidents were the assaults in Rostock-Lichtenhagen, a Plattenbau area in one of the largest cities of the former GDR, in August 1992, and the arson attacks in the West German cities of Mölln in November 1992 and Solingen in May 1993 during which, respectively, three and five people were killed. The liberal politician Cornelia Schmalz-Jacobsen of the Free Democratic Party, acting as federal commissioner for foreigners, commented at the time on these outbursts of violence in a way that illustrated the still-vivid memory of the Nazi years, at least among older Germans: 'Human beings are being hunted down as they were in the worst times of the SA.'[110] This comparison was obviously incorrect insofar as the xenophobic riots of the 1990s, unlike those of the Third Reich, were not sponsored by the government. The perpetrators rather understood their violence as a sign of their frustration with the political establishment, and their excessively nationalistic slogans were at least partly a sign of desperation in the face of a quickly changing political and economic environment.

New outbursts of political and racial violence have taken place in Germany since the autumn of 2015. However, despite this development, 'SA' as one of the most contested political catchwords of twentieth-century Germany has continued to lose its power. Attempts by right-wing extremists to re-establish the stormtroopers as exemplary role models of patriotic pride and political activism have failed and seem unlikely to achieve success in the near future.[111] The history of the SA meanwhile is a genuine historical topic, yet it amounts to more than an academic exercise. The defeat of National Socialism and the subsequent establishment of a capitalist democracy in Germany is rightly seen as a political, economic, and social success story, yet it will not be the end of history. Significant numbers of youths in search of a transcendental, national, or social vision that provides them with meaning and a place in the world continue to be attracted to physical violence. A society that glorifies the satisfaction of consumer and bodily desires through means that are beyond the reach of many of its younger citizens invites both criticism and violence, if only as a means to express frustration and helplessness. The history of the Nazi stormtroopers between 1921 and 1945 provides a poignant example of the forces that this mixture of youthful longing, political exploitation, militaristic predisposition, and social degeneration can unleash. Although this particular example is historically specific, its patterns are not unique to either a single time or a single place. Political regimes based on violent mobilization and disciplinary integration are still widespread; to overcome them by advocating more peaceful and humane ways for communities to coexist remains as important as it has ever been.

CONCLUSION
Stormtroopers and National Socialism

A s early as 1932 the stormtroopers had been deemed worthy objects of academic study, as revealed by a German PhD dissertation submitted to and accepted by Leipzig University's *Institut für Rassen- und Völkerkunde*. The author of this study was a twenty-five-year-old student and SA man, Peter Sachse, the son of a Protestant pastor from Dittersbach in the Erzgebirge. For his dissertation Sachse had photographed and anthropometrically measured 300 stormtroopers from the Leipzig SA-*Standarten* 106 and 107 between November 1932 and February 1933. His findings – that the average height of Leipzig's stormtroopers was 171 centimetres, their average weight was 64 kilograms, and their skulls were predominantly of the 'brachycephal type' – offer little more than an illustration of the curious state of a particular strand of German science in the 1930s, as they demonstrate only that Leipzig's stormtroopers were rather average men for their times.[1]

However, one should be careful not to dismiss such studies too easily. That they were planned, undertaken, and from 1933 onward financed with public money sheds a spotlight on the close nexus existing in the 1930s between ideological preferences, political activity, and 'scientific' claims of racial superiority. At least those exemplary mechanics, bookkeepers, and construction workers photographed naked and so portrayed in this study were pleased to figure as visual representations of a racially superior type of German manhood. Yet, more importantly, the mentality expressed here would ultimately have significant repercussions for the Nazi bureaucrats' settlement of stormtroopers in eastern Europe a few years later. Within the Third Reich race was a flexible concept and – despite its ideological pre-eminence – *not* the most important criterion when it came to questions of ethnicity, as the historian Gerhard Wolf has recently demonstrated with regard to the *Deutsche Volksliste* in German-occupied western Poland during the Second World War.[2] While the Nazis were certainly racist and shared an axiomatic belief in the genetic inferiority of Slavs and 'Semites', part of the movement's attraction for large segments of the German population was its apparent voluntarist character. Within the borders of a racially defined 'people's community', personal dedication and ideological conviction were taken as markers of alleged racial superiority. This understanding not only benefited Nazi leaders such as Hitler and Goebbels who hardly represented the ideal 'Aryan' man, but also elevated rank-and-file Brownshirts to the status of an alleged racial elite that was called to transform German society according to Nazi ideals and lead the nation to a bright future.[3]

The previous chapters have analysed the origins, growth, and decline of the SA between 1921 and 1945. The story that emerged in them is one full of contradictions: high hopes and lasting disappointments, individual empowerment and collective mobilization, pressure to conform and pressure to obey, selfishness and comradeship, extreme violence and boredom. Prior histories of the stormtroopers did not fully grasp these contradictions. Because they generally concentrated on only one period of the SA's existence and were primarily interested in the organization's contribution to the Nazi rise to power rather than the consolidation of that regime, the mainstream historiography on the Third Reich has tended to downplay the importance of the SA. Consequently, recent work on subjects such as the voluntarist and coercive elements in Nazi society or the centrality of the regime's colonial ambitions has frequently made no reference to the SA at all. To address this lacuna and suggest ways of overcoming it, I will here summarize the principal results of my analysis and discuss how they contribute to a new general history of National Socialism more broadly.

1. As the initial chapters of this book demonstrated in detail, the first National Socialist SA was established in Munich in 1920–1 and grew to considerable size and regional might up to 1923, when the Hitler Putsch took place. This early SA was a party-protection force typical of the early 1920s that embraced elements of both *Wehrverbände* and political terror

organizations. The social composition of this early and rather insignificant SA was less working class than is usually claimed. Instead, students and members of the middle classes constituted a considerable portion of its rank and file and certainly dominated its leadership ranks, alongside the small band of older professional ex-militaries. Although this first SA was firmly rooted in Bavaria, with a slowly developing web of cells in neighbouring states such as Württemberg and Thuringia, its prominent activists (e.g. Maurice, Heines, Klintzsch, and Göring) originated from the northern and eastern parts of Germany. Antisemitism was from its inception *the* key element of both the early SA's ideological convictions and its violent practices. Whereas the possibility of participating in antisemitic mob violence especially attracted young men in quest of excitement and purpose, many conservative politicians as well as the High Command of the Bavarian Reichswehr downplayed these youthful 'excesses', instead highlighting the importance of the SA as a bulwark against the Communist menace and pacifist tendencies within German society. The stormtroopers thus benefited from and at the same time contributed to the deepening rifts within German society following the First World War, but they remained too insignificant to challenge the existing order, let alone destabilize the state.

2. After the failed 1923 putsch, state authorities prohibited the SA. Despite the fact that many regional cells survived by adopting cover names and maintaining a loose connection to the *Frontbann*, Ernst Röhm's new umbrella organization, they lacked coordination and in many cases developed into private forces at the disposal of regional Nazi luminaries. Against this background the internal reforms initiated by SA Chief of Staff Franz Pfeffer von Salomon in 1926 can be seen as an attempt to centralize power. They provided the organizational basis for the subsequent growth and national breakthrough of the SA between 1928 and 1930. Pfeffer von Salomon modelled the Brownshirts on the German army, allowed the organization a degree of financial autonomy, and organized a system for providing care to wounded party soldiers. It was this organizational framework that allowed the SA to cope with the massive increase in membership that it experienced from the late 1920s. The reinvigorated SA promoted a new style of mass politics that demanded absolute loyalty and high levels of personal and financial commitment in return for political orientation, job opportunities, and diverse outlets for male sociability. These benefits proved all the more alluring during difficult economic times, when many men

found themselves unable to maintain a lifestyle that upheld the traditional ideas of respectable manhood. The habits promoted by the SA, with its own brands and rituals, was key to the group's appeal in these years. It was based not on an elaborate set of theoretical ideas, but on feelings of community and self-empowerment. This dynamic did not go unnoticed. An important strand within the Christian churches attempted to 'channel' this energy into a new *Volksmission*, or Christian renewal, while at the same time deploring the stormtroopers' excessive acts of violence. The Reichswehr likewise started to reach out to the SA in hopes of using it as a recruitment pool in the absence of compulsory military service. Cooperation between the two organizations was particularly intense in border areas.

3. The rise of the stormtroopers from scattered splinter groups into a powerful political organization, which mobilized followers like a social movement but operated on a tight hierarchical basis and attracted hundreds of thousands of men in the early 1930s, was as much a vital element as it was the result of the 'vibrant and violent cultures of interwar Germany and Austria'.[4] Although the SA was initially an urban phenomenon, by the early 1930s it had expanded into rural Germany, contributing to the 'Nazification' of the countryside, a fundamental step in the party's rise to power. The increasingly violent character of political clashes throughout the Reich in the early 1930s further contributed to the SA's popularity, and not only because it allowed the stormtroopers to prove themselves 'in battle'. It also undermined the general public's belief in the power of the state to enforce its monopoly on violence and in the eyes of the quickly growing number of sympathizers justified the embrace of Nazi 'self-help'. Despite circumstances to the contrary, the SA insisted on the purely defensive character of its actions, a view that an increasing number of judges and police officers came to accept. National Socialist victims of the political clashes of these years were indeed numerous, yet they were also a product of a deliberate party strategy that cynically sacrificed the lives of its rank and file in its drive to attain power.

Ultimately, the decisive appeal of the stormtroopers rested on the emotions and hopes they were able to evoke. The organizational principles of the SA encouraged the creation of strong bonds that provided leaders with self-esteem and influence and the rank and file with imagined social power. Whatever may be rightly said about the anxieties and fears of this period, with its social dislocations and leadership problems, it must be emphasized that the SA, in the eyes of its members, provided one forceful and seemingly persuasive answer to the omnipresent problem of (democratic) representation in interwar Germany. At a time when individual longing and national unity were increasingly seen as mutually exclusive, the SA 'community of action' created the impression of offering a solution to this fundamental problem of modern societies. It could be achieved, so the Nazi activists hoped, without giving up traditional liberal ideas of self-determination through education and economic independence in favour of a set of vague 'totalitarian' ideologies that eliminated the self by focusing on the collective, as previous historians have sometimes claimed. On the contrary, mass participation in paramilitary political movements such as the SA was – somewhat paradoxically – viewed as a way to reassert a male identity even in the absence of financial assets, family status, or particular professional and intellectual skills. Paramilitary participation was *not* seen as an exchange of individual identity for a new collective identity. The Fascist activists in mass organizations like the SA regarded themselves not as individuals, but as personalities. The SA's popularity among male students in the early days of the Third Reich makes it clear that the common image of the stormtroopers as 'losers' only covers one segment of the organization's followers, at least in the first half of the 1930s. The combination of an upbringing in times of material hardship and resentment, youthful idealism and bold self-esteem contributed to this unusual liaison of mind and muscle. True, the stormtroopers voluntarily subjugated themselves to the rule of a messianic Führer and his regional proxies, but they expected considerable rewards in return. Their commitment to the SA not only provided them with everyday guidance and a sense of spiritual salvation, but also empowered them to become leaders themselves, viewing their role as the guardians of the people's community and the visual embodiment of the sacralized nation.[5] It was not least this obscene pretentiousness that caused many contemporaries as well as later historians to avert their eyes from the SA and its violent ideology in disgust.

4. Somewhat counterintuitively, the year 1933 marked not only the heyday of the SA's influence but also the beginning of its decline. Social unrest and disappointment among the 'socialist' faction of the SA, which had its strongholds in the northern and eastern industrial cities of Germany, had become an ever more pressing problem for the organization since the early 1930s, yet the NSDAP addressed it only half-heartedly. Instead,

the constant assertion that Hitler's chancellorship would solve all problems had increased the expectations of many rank-and-file stormtroopers to an extreme level. Combined with the strong desire for revenge after years of uncertainty and danger, these expectations translated into extreme violence in the spring of 1933. Stormtroopers hunted down, incarcerated, and murdered their political and ideological adversaries. Besides overseeing provisional concentration camps that interned approximately 80,000 people over the course of 1933, the SA also engaged in highly symbolic acts of public humiliation in which their victims, who were overwhelmingly men, were 'feminized' and the Brownshirts' own (hyper-)masculine identities were reasserted. Jews in particular became the target of degrading practices, and even those who were not imprisoned and tortured suffered from the nationwide boycotts that took place in March and April of this year. That SA leaders were appointed police presidents in many German cities and regions at this time rendered the stormtroopers de facto immune from prosecution, even if some unsung heroes within the German justice system attempted (largely in vain) to punish at least the most outrageous crimes.

In return for carrying out the 'dirty work' of the National Socialist seizure of power, the SA men expected to receive material and symbolic rewards. Hundreds of thousands of stormtroopers did indeed benefit from special initiatives that aimed to provide previously unemployed SA men with work, or at least with shelter and a small pay cheque in one of the more than sixty SA 'auxiliary camps'. Particularly effective was the appointment of storm-troopers as auxiliary policemen, a solution that allowed political and employment strategies to converge. However, Röhm's attempt to irrevocably influence the course of politics during the Nazi 'revolution', by appointing SA 'special representatives' to control and influence the German bureau-cracy, quickly failed, for both ideological and practical reasons. He succeeded, however, in channelling millions of reichsmark to his organization and at least in Bavaria was able to become an influential figure who shaped regional politics through a dense web of allies. Nationwide, the SA received at least 72 million reichsmark from the governments in 1933–4, with most of the money trickling down to the local and regional levels.

5. In the years following the Nazi takeover of power, the party's appeal extended beyond the ideologically faithful. Social integration in National Socialist Germany must be analysed as a product of the interaction between 'staged' (i.e. party-orchestrated) community experiences and

everyday practices, a blend that provided individuals with a sense of emotional belonging and the possibility of pursuing their individual goals.[6] My account of the history of the SA has attempted to combine and examine the interaction of these different analytical angles in order to better explain the violent mobilization and individual attraction of National Socialism. Particularly during 1933 and 1934 the stormtroopers fulfilled a dual role. First, they provided millions of German men with the opportunity to join the Nazi camp and thereby benefit from the new pool of political and job opportunities. Second, they violently enforced the regime's segregationist policies and contributed to the implementation of an 'antisemitic *Konsensfiktion*', namely the phenomenon that – regardless of one's actual approval or disapproval of Nazi antisemitic policies – interpersonal communication in the Third Reich increasingly proceeded from the assumption that the majority of Germans took such consent for granted.[7]

Although the SA continued to exercise these roles well into the 1940s, hopes for personal advancement through service in the organization as well as far-reaching hopes of transforming the German economy and society according to 'German Socialist' principles came to an abrupt end in the summer of 1934 with the 'Night of the Long Knives'. After this event, disciplinary integration in and through the SA mattered more than political mass mobilization, particularly as the regime adopted other means of coercion. Belonging to the people's community was no longer guaranteed by membership in one of the many Nazi organizations but became a state of permanent uncertainty. The individual *Volksgenosse* had continually to prove his or her worthiness by performing social acts that demonstrated persistent commitment to the cause. This became difficult for many SA men once their political opponents had been defeated, as their previous ways of distinguishing themselves – by street-fighting, violent acts, or forms of 'manly' sociability such as heavy drinking and the symbolic occupation of public places – increasingly proved inadequate.

The murder of Röhm and his followers in 1934 combined with the liquidation of key anti-Nazi 'neoconservatives' fundamentally altered the history of the Third Reich. The regime now started to exploit the homophobic prejudices previously nurtured by the anti-Fascist left to discredit National Socialism in order to stigmatize the SA leadership corps as morally questionable. At the same time it actively sought to appeal to the desire of rank-and-file stormtroopers for order, 'cleanliness', and *völkisch* morality. To friends and foes alike, the Nazi dictatorship made it unmistakably clear that it would respect neither legal limits nor previous political norms.

6. The men who continued to engage in the SA after 1934 were a remarkably heterogeneous group, comprising people from different walks of life. Besides the predominantly working-class 'Old Fighters', who remained loyal to the SA out of a mixture of ideological conviction and a lack of professional and social alternatives, there were also middle-class men who regarded membership in the SA as a means of demonstrating loyalty to the regime without giving up their hobbies of shooting and riding, important areas of male middle-class sociability in interwar Germany. By contrast, young men from the lower-middle and working classes who entered the ranks of the elite Feldherrnhalle units in the late 1930s deliberately opted for a career in the military, embracing the group's ideological leanings. Finally, the *Volksdeutsche* who joined the new units established in the annexed and occupied territories after 1938 saw membership in the SA as a chance to participate in and benefit from the new political regime. However, as the war continued and the SA was more and more used for police tasks to help uphold public order, service in the SA and its *Wehrmannschaften* was transformed from a voluntary commitment to compulsory service.

7. The stormtroopers, despite being barred from involvement in upper-level decision-making since 1934, continued for the remaining years of the Nazi regime to be principal actors in the enforcement of the NSDAP's will in everyday life. They were 'coercive instruments of violence', 'protecting' the racial community of Germans against its alleged enemies to the bitter end,[8] but they were also involved in securing public order in the Nazi-occupied and annexed territories as well as on the home front in the Old Reich. Although the SA suffered severely from the drafting of the majority of its more than one million members into the Wehrmacht beginning in the autumn of 1939, the organization continued to provide a multitude of services to the regime until 1945. These services were not limited to the provision of paramilitary education and ideological training. They also comprised the transport and guarding of prisoners and concentration-camp inmates, the policing of forced labourers, the provision of paramilitary fighting units that operated undercover behind the front lines, and the carrying out of more 'civilian'-style tasks – the organization of clean-up operations after air raids on German cities and the provision of aid to wounded soldiers and their families. In order to preserve what they perceived as a

'spiritual and emotional defence community',[9] many stormtroopers continued to engage in deadly violence up until the last weeks of the Third Reich.

8. The aggressive Nazi foreign policy from the second half of the 1930s onward furthermore provided the SA with new opportunities to regain some of its former might and influence. The SA contributed to the militarization of male civilian life by expanding and coordinating its paramilitary activities with those of the German shooting associations and riding clubs, carrying out auxiliary duties for the Wehrmacht in the wake of the occupation of the Sudetenland and Memelland, and providing many of the leaders of the Sudeten German Free Corps. After the successful occupations it helped tie many of the regions' ethnic Germans to the NSDAP. Beginning in 1936 the OSAF even made plans to retrain its men as hereditarily valuable 'armed peasants' who would settle in the borderland regions of the Reich and the annexed or occupied territories and defend the German race there by cultivating land and having children. However, the appointment of Heinrich Himmler to the position of 'Reich Commissioner for the Strengthening of Germandom' in October 1939 severely hampered the SA's plans. Although the ambitious targets of its recruitment campaigns were never met and the entire programme was finally suspended in early 1943, exemplary 'peasantry settlements' were constructed, schools for the training of ethnic German SA men as settlers were established, and at least several hundred SA men were successfully placed in the German-occupied east.

9. Farther south, in the German-allied states of Slovakia, Romania, Hungary, Bulgaria, and Croatia, five high-ranking SA generals were appointed as German envoys in late 1940–1. For the remaining years of the war these diplomats attempted to push through the political, economic, and cultural interests of the Third Reich in their respective countries. Although these 'Old Fighters' did not demonstrate a distinctive style of SA diplomacy, their conditioning in and through the SA contributed to a belief in the desirability – and possibility – of a kind of 'fascist International of the multi-colored shirts' in the Balkans.[10] As the war progressed, this became an ever more naive position, particularly after the German defeat at Stalingrad, when the national governments in the region began to prepare for the time after the Third Reich's military domination. By 1944 at the latest, the SA general-diplomats were fighting a lost cause.

10. Previous histories of the SA that have proposed a narrative of decline and failure for the years after 1934 missed out on these important aspects

of the organization's history. As has been demonstrated in this study, one reason for this oversight is that such accounts have followed a line of argument that was developed as a legal defence strategy for the International Military Tribunal in Nuremberg and that over the following two decades helped former stormtroopers to downplay their earlier involvement in the SA. Even as historical research on all aspects of National Socialism has vastly expanded and improved, the post-war image of the SA has gone unquestioned. This book was written in an attempt to challenge this established narrative and in line with recent studies on the popular appeal of the Third Reich which stress that the Nazi people's community was widely perceived as a 'moral community' or a 'quasi-religious community of shared moral engagement and common interest'.[11] Attempting to recalibrate the place of the political activists of the Nazi movement within the larger framework of modern German history, this book has demonstrated that while the prevalent image of the stormtroopers as rowdies and political hooligans is not wrong, it covers only one side of the story and systematically neglects other factors that contributed to the appeal of the SA, particularly in the early 1930s. From the perspective of party activists as well as substantial segments of the German populace who did not necessarily embrace the regime's violence but cherished its social aims, the anticapitalist and – within its imagined racial boundaries – egalitarian SA empowered millions of ordinary German men to make politics their own. It allowed them to enrich themselves materially while at the same time claiming to fight class snobbery, and, most importantly, to consider themselves valuable members of the national community. These feelings of empowerment survived long after the summer of 1934 and have shaped many Germans' post-1945 memory of the Third Reich until today.

NOTES

A full bibliography is available for download at https://wwwhomes.uni-bielefeld.de/dsiemens/bibliography.pdf

1. Letter from Boris Pasternak to Warlam Schalamow, 9 July 1952, in Boris Pasternak, *Polnoe sobranie sochinenii s prilozheniiami*, vol. 9, ed. E. B. Pasternak and E. V. Pasternak (Moscow: Slovo, 2005), pp. 684–90, here p. 686.
2. Wolfgang Sofsky, *Traktat über die Gewalt* (Frankfurt am Main: Fischer, 2005 [1996]), p. 10.

Introduction

1. August Scholtis, *Ostwind: Ein schlesischer Schelmenroman* (Munich: dtv, 1986 [1931]), p. 275.
2. The spellings 'Pietczuch' or 'Pietzuch' can also be found in the documents related to this case.
3. Unless noted otherwise, the facts of the following account are drawn from APK (Archiwum Państwowe w Katowicach), akt nr 15/28 Starostwo Powiatowe w Gliwicach (Politische Angelegenheiten, 1928–1933), vol. 5, pp. 334–45: Bill of Indictment of the Senior Prosecutor in Beuthen, 14 August 1932; Richard Bessel, 'The Potempa Murder', in *Central European History* 10:3 (1977), pp. 241–54; Paul Kluke, 'Der Fall Potempa (Dokumentation)', in *Vierteljahrshefte für Zeitgeschichte* 5 (1957), pp. 279–97; Günther Schmerbach, *Der Kampf der Kommunistischen Partei Deutschlands gegen Faschismus und Kriegsgefahr im Bezirk Oberschlesien 1932/33*, diss., Friedrich-Schiller-Universität Jena, 1957, pp. 104–27; and newspaper coverage by the liberal *Vossische Zeitung* (Berlin).
4. For more details on the night of the murder, see also 'Raus aus dem Bett, Ihr verfluchten Kommunisten!', *Sozialistische Arbeiter-Zeitung* (hereafter *SAZ*) (Breslau), 12 August 1932; 'Nine Nazis on Trial', *The Times* (London), 22 August 1932, p. 9.
5. Quoted in 'So wurde Pietrzuch ermordet', *SAZ* (Breslau), 26 August 1932, http://library.fes.de/breslau/sozialistische-arbeiterzeitung/pdf/1932/1932-192.pdf. See also Kluke, 'Der Fall Potempa', p. 291.
6. APK, akt nr 15/28, vol. 5, pp. 333–4: 'Letter from the Landjägerhauptmann Seeliger to the Landrat in Gleiwitz', 15 August 1932; Bessel, 'The Potempa Murder', p. 248; Schmerbach, *Der Kampf der Kommunistischen Partei*, p. 109.
7. Naturally, all of the parties involved portrayed themselves as victims who only reacted to the violence of the other side. Instructive in this respect is a comparative reading of Nazi and Communist propaganda in the Potempa affair: Gerhard Pantel, *Potempa-Beuthen: Ein Signal für alle deutschen Deutschen* (Munich: Eher, 1932); Robert Venzlaff, *Der Schuldige ... Die Mordnacht von Potempa*, ed. Rote Hilfe (Berlin: Tribunal Verlag, 1932).

8. 'Rückblick auf eine Woche "Burgfrieden"', *CV-Zeitung*, 15 August 1932, pp. 1–2.
9. Bessel, 'The Potempa Murder', p. 243; Marjorie Lamberti, *The Politics of Education: Teachers and School Reform in Weimar Germany* (New York and Oxford: Berghahn, 2002), p. 228.
10. See *Reichsgesetzblatt* 1932, vol. 1, no. 54 (9 August 1932), pp. 403–4.
11. For the final stage of the Weimar Republic, see in particular Dirk Blasius, *Weimars Ende: Bürgerkrieg und Politik 1930–1933* (Göttingen: Vandenhoeck & Ruprecht, 2005); Richard J. Evans, *The Coming of the Third Reich* (London: Penguin Books, 2004), pp. 231–308; Detlev J. K. Peukert, *Die Weimarer Republik: Krisenjahre der klassischen Moderne* (Frankfurt am Main: Suhrkamp, 1987), pp. 243–65. With regard to the SA's violence in Upper Silesia, see Richard Bessel, *Political Violence and the Rise of Nazism: The Storm Troopers in Eastern Germany 1925–1934* (New Haven, CT: Yale University Press, 1984), pp. 75–96.
12. Joseph Goebbels, *Die Tagebücher von Joseph Goebbels, Teil I: Aufzeichnungen 1923–1941*, vol. 2/2 (Munich: K. G. Saur, 2004), p. 336.
13. APK, akt nr 15/28, vol. 5, pp. 334–45, here pp. 334–5: Bill of Indictment of the Senior Prosecutor in Beuthen, 14 August 1932.
14. Bessel, 'The Potempa Murder', p. 248.
15. Ibid., p. 249.
16. Henning Grunwald, *Courtroom to Revolutionary Stage: Performance and Ideology in Weimar Political Trials* (Oxford: Oxford University Press, 2012), p. 168.
17. Ibid., p. 169.
18. Bessel, 'The Potempa Murder', p. 246.
19. Kluke, 'Der Fall Potempa', p. 288.
20. Nazi propaganda and the arguments of SA lawyer Luetgebrune in court emphasized that Pietrzuch had repeatedly 'betrayed' the Germans of Upper Silesia in the years following the First World War through such actions as disclosing illegal arms depots to the French authorities and threatening those determined to vote for Germany in the plebiscite of March 1921. The radical left, in defence of the 'worker and communist' Pietrzuch, however, claimed that he had courageously supported the German minority in his home village of Potempa against Polish insurgents in that same crucial year. See Pantel, *Potempa-Beuthen*, pp. 9–13; Venzlaff, *Der Schuldige*, p. 4.
21. In 1936 Lachmann was sentenced to a seven-year prison term for fraud and perjury, and in 1940 an NSDAP *Gau* court sentenced him on two charges of poaching; Sopade (Sozialdemokratische Partei Deutschland in exile), *Deutschland-Berichte*, vol. 3 (1936), p. 239; Bessel, 'The Potempa Murder', pp. 245–6.
22. Venzlaff, *Der Schuldige*, p. 4.
23. Kluke, 'Der Fall Potempa', p. 287.
24. 'Fünf Todesurteile in Beuthen', *Vossische Zeitung*, 23 August 1932, p. 1.
25. 'Nine Nazis on Trial', p. 9. See also Goebbels's diary entry from 23 August 1932: 'In Beuthen 5 Todesurteile gegen unsere Leute. Das Ungeheuerlichste, das auszudenken ist. Die Regierung wird nicht wagen, sie zu vollstrecken'; Goebbels, *Die Tagebücher von Joseph Goebbels, Teil I: Aufzeichnungen 1923–1941*, vol. 2/2, p. 346.
26. 'Nazi Death Sentences', *The Times* (London), 23 August 1932, p. 10; 'Five Nazis to Die: Sentences at Trial', *The Manchester Guardian*, 23 August 1932, p. 9; 'Krawalle nach dem Urteilsspruch', *Vossische Zeitung*, 23 August 1932, p. 3.
27. As quoted in Max Domarus, *Hitler: Speeches and Proclamations 1932–1945. The Chronicle of a Dictatorship*, vol. 1: *The Years 1932–1934* (London: I. B. Tauris, 1990), p. 160.
28. 'Five Nazis to Die', p. 9.
29. BArch Berlin (Bundesarchiv Berlin), NS 26/2515: Letter from Landeskriminalpolizeiamt Berlin to the Police President Bielefeld, May 1931; BArch Berlin, NS 26/1348: 'Fememörder Heines als MdR', *Vorwärts*, 5 October 1930.
30. Adolf Hitler, telegram to August Gräupner, Reinhold Kottisch, Paul Lachmann, Helmuth-Josef Müller, and Rufin Wolnitza, in Adolf Hitler, *Reden, Schriften, Anordnungen: Februar 1925 bis Januar 1933*, vol. 5: *Von der Reichspräsidentenwahl bis zur Machtergreifung. April 1932–Januar 1933. Part 1: April 1932–September 1932*, ed. Klaus A. Lankheit (Munich: Saur, 1996), p. 317.
31. Kluke, 'Der Fall Potempa', p. 284; Bessel, 'The Potempa Murder', p. 251.
32. Adolf Hitler, 'Nationalisten! Deutsche!', *Völkischer Beobachter*, 24 August 1932, as quoted in Domarus, *Hitler: Speeches and Proclamations 1932–1945*, vol. 1, pp. 159–60. Hitler had

publicly justified immoral political deeds for the sake of the nation in similar terms as early as 1922; see BayHStA (Bayerisches Hauptstaatsarchiv München), MInn (Ministerium des Innern), no. 81594: 'Die Maischlacht Hitlers', *Bayerischer Kurier*, 3 May 1923.

33. With remarkable consistency, Goebbels used this wording again and again in the following years; for example, see his notorious article 'Mimicry', published in the highbrow Nazi newspaper *Das Reich* on 20 July 1941. See Saul Friedländer, *Nazi Germany and the Jews*, vol. 2: *The Years of Extermination* (London: Phoenix, 2008), p. 204.

34. Joseph Goebbels, 'Die Juden sind schuld!', *Der Angriff*, 24 August 1932, pp. 1–2.

35. Interestingly, there were cases in which Social Democrats likewise accused their Nazi opponents of being former Polish insurgents; see 'Der "Märytrer"', *Vossische Zeitung*, 4 November 1932, p. 6.

36. According to official statistics, political violence in 1932 caused 155 deaths in all of the provinces of Prussia. Of these casualties, 55 had been members of the NSDAP, 54 had belonged to the Communist Party, and twelve had been members of the Reichsbanner and/or the Social Democratic Party; see Dirk Schumann, 'Political Violence, Contested Public Space, and Reasserted Masculinity', in *Weimar Publics / Weimar Subjects*, ed. Kathleen Canning and Kerstin Barndt (New York: Berghahn Books, 2010), pp. 236–53, here p. 244.

37. For the most impudent distortions of this kind, see Pantel, *Potempa-Beuthen*.

38. IfZ Archive (Institut für Zeitgeschichte, Archiv, Munich), ED 414 (Herbert Frank), vol. 181: Joachim Leo, 'Beuthen!', *Schlesischer NS-Beobachter* (Breslau), 3 September 1932. I am grateful to Marcel Krueger, Berlin, for his help in translating this and other poems and songs in this book.

39. 'Five Nazis to Die', p. 9.

40. Such was the logic of the Nazi *Hamburger Abendblatt*, as quoted in 'Why Nazi Newspaper was Suppressed', *The Manchester Guardian*, 26 August 1932, p. 9.

41. Alfred Rosenberg in *Der Völkische Beobachter*, as quoted in 'Killing Not Murder', *The Manchester Guardian*, 27 August 1932, p. 15.

42. Goebbels, *Die Tagebücher von Joseph Goebbels, Teil I: Aufzeichnungen 1923–1941*, vol. 2/2 (Munich: K. G. Saur, 2004), pp. 346–7.

43. 'Defence of the Nazi Murderers', *The Manchester Guardian*, 24 August 1932.

44. Bessel, 'The Potempa Murder', p. 252.

45. For an overview, see Robert Gerwarth and John Horne, 'Vectors of Violence: Paramilitarism in Europe after the Great War, 1917–1923', *Journal of Modern History* 83:3 (2011), pp. 489–512.

46. Kluke, 'Der Fall Potempa', p. 292.

47. Ibid., p. 287; GSt PK (Geheimes Staatsarchiv Preußischer Kulturbesitz), I. HA, Rep. 77 titl. 4043, vol. 311, p. 325: Racliffe (Polizeimajor), 'Denkschrift über Kampfvorbereitung und Kampfgrundsätze radikaler Organisationen' [1931].

48. On the political context, see Enno Eimers, 'Oberschlesien während der Unruhen in den ersten Jahren der Weimarer Republik', in *Geschichte, Öffentlichkeit, Kommunikation: Festschrift für Bernd Sösemann zum 65. Geburtstag*, ed. Patrick Merziger (Stuttgart: Steiner, 2010), pp. 383–404; Dawid Smolorz, 'Die deutsch-polnische Grenze in Oberschlesien 1922–1939', in *Granica: Die deutsch-polnische Grenze vom 19. bis zum 21. Jahrhundert*, ed. Karoline Gil and Christian Pletzing (Munich: Meidenbauer, 2010), pp. 75–86; Bernard Sauer, '"Auf nach Oberschlesien". Die Kämpfe der deutschen Freikorps 1921 in Oberschlesien und den anderen ehemaligen deutschen Ostprovinzen', *Zeitschrift für Geschichtswissenschaft* 58 (2010), pp. 297–320; Kai Struve (ed.), *Oberschlesien nach dem Ersten Weltkrieg: Studien zu einem nationalen Konflikt und seiner Erinnerung* (Marburg: Herder-Institut, 2003); Karsten Eichner, *Briten, Franzosen und Italiener in Oberschlesien, 1920–1922: Die Interalliierte Regierungs- und Plebiszitkommission im Spiegel der britischen Akten* (St Katharinen: Winkel Stiftung, 2002); Ralph Schattkowsky, *Deutschland und Polen von 1918/19 bis 1925* (Frankfurt am Main: Lang, 1994); Günther Doose, *Die separatistische Bewegung in Oberschlesien nach dem Ersten Weltkrieg: 1918–1922* (Wiesbaden: Harrassowitz, 1987).

49. C. A. Macartney and A. W. Palmer, *Independent Eastern Europe: A History* (London: Macmillan, 1962), pp. 105–6.

50. The first uprising took place 16–24 August 1919; the second 19–28 August 1920; and the third 3 May 1921 and the early days of July 1921. For the Polish efforts to 're-Polonize', see Richard Blake, 'Interwar Poland and the Problem of Polish-Speaking Germans', in *The*

Germans and the East, ed. Charles W. Ingrao and Franz A. J. Szabo (West Lafayette, IN: Purdue University Press, 2008), pp. 262–3.

51. Sauer, '"Auf nach Oberschlesien"', pp. 302–3; Daniel Schmidt, 'Der SA-Führer Hans Ramshorn. Ein Leben zwischen Gewalt und Gemeinschaft (1892–1934)', *Vierteljahrshefte für Zeitgeschichte* 60:2 (2012), pp. 201–35, here p. 228. Many *Freikorps* leaders, in particular those from the gentry in these borderlands, later joined the SA; see Stephan Malinowski and Sven Reichardt, 'Die Reihen fest geschlossen? Adelige im Führungskorps der SA bis 1934', in *Adel und Moderne: Deutschland im europäischen Vergleich im 19. und 20. Jahrhundert*, ed. Eckart Conze and Monika Wienfort (Cologne: Böhlau, 2004), pp. 119–50, here pp. 126–8, 138–42. For an instructive case study, see Kai Langer, 'Der "Fall Flotow" – vom Aufstieg und Fall eines mecklenburgischen SA-Führers', *Zeitgeschichte regional: Mitteilungen aus Mecklenburg-Vorpommern* 7:2 (2003), pp. 5–13.

52. See Irmela Nagel, *Fememord und Fememordprozesse in der Weimarer Republik* (Cologne: Böhlau, 1991), with further references.

53. Sauer, '"Auf nach Oberschlesien"', pp. 308–9, 316.

54. Idem, '"Verräter waren bei uns in Mengen erschossen worden": Die Fememorde in Oberschlesien 1921', *Zeitschrift für Geschichtswissenschaft* 54:7/8 (2006), pp. 644–62, here p. 645.

55. Archive of *Der Spiegel*, Hamburg (hereafter HA-Spiegel), Personal Papers of Heinz Höhne, no. 124: Bill of indictment of the Reich Prosecutor against Alfred Hoffmann, Manfred von Killinger, and others, 16 May 1922.

56. For details, see Hagen Schulze, *Freikorps und Republik 1918–1920* (Boppard am Rhein: Harald Boldt Verlag, 1969), pp. 214–35. Recent research has emphasized that this widespread presumption did not match the 'realities'; see Rüdiger Bergien, *Die bellizistische Republik: Wehrkonsens und 'Wehrhaftmachung' in Deutschland 1918–1933* (Munich: Oldenbourg, 2012), esp. pp. 355–406.

57. On this point, see the excellent study by Matthias Sprenger, *Landsknechte auf dem Weg ins Dritte Reich? Zur Genese und Wandel des Freikorpsmythos* (Paderborn: Schöningh, 2008).

58. According to Killinger, in its desire to 'consolidate and strengthen' the German national character, the fight against the Poles in Upper Silesia directly foreshadowed the 'mission of Adolf Hitler' that by 1934 had become an indispensable element of 'our pan-German destiny'. See Manfred von Killinger, *Kampf um Oberschlesien 1921: Bisher unveröffentlichte Aufzeichnungen des Führers der 'Abteilung v. Killinger' genannt 'Sturmkompanie Koppe'* (Leipzig: K. F. Koehler, 1934), p. 124. See also Klaus Gundelach, 'Der Opferweg zum Sieg', in *Vom Kampf und Sieg der schlesischen SA: Ein Ehrenbuch*, ed. SA-Gruppe Schlesien (Breslau: Korn, 1933), pp. 11–15.

59. HA-Spiegel, Personal Papers of Heinz Höhne, no. 242: Report of the Oberster SA-Führer to the SA-Gruppenführer, Munich, 28 August 1931.

60. Lisa Pine, *Education in Nazi Germany* (Oxford and New York: Berg, 2010), p. 15.

61. Lamberti, *Politics of Education*, pp. 221–6.

62. Notable exceptions are Bessel, *Political Violence and the Rise of Nazism*; Stefan Dölling, 'Grenzüberschreitende Gewalttätigkeit – die SA und die "Sudetenkrise"', in *Bürgerkriegsarmee: Forschungen zur nationalsozialistischen Sturmabteilung (SA)*, ed. Yves Müller and Reiner Zilkenat (Frankfurt am Main: Lang, 2013), pp. 241–63; Bergien, *Die bellizistische Republik*; Schmidt, 'Der SA-Führer Hans Ramshorn', pp. 227–9.

63. For details, see chapter 6 of this book. On the importance of the German borderlands as 'hotbeds' of Nazi perpetrators, see also Michael Mann, *Die dunkle Seite der Demokratie: Eine Theorie der ethnischen Säuberung* (Hamburg: Hamburger Edition, 2007), pp. 329–36, 351.

64. Their release took place in the context of a general amnesty for the 'pioneers of the national revolution'. See Kluke, 'Der Fall Potempa', p. 286; Blasius, *Weimars Ende*, p. 95.

65. 'Making Murderers into Heroes', *The Manchester Guardian*, 13 October 1933, p. 9.

66. August Scholtis, *Ein Herr aus Bolatitz: Lebenserinnerungen* (Munich: List, 1959), p. 10.

67. Timothy D. Snyder, *Bloodlands: Europe between Hitler and Stalin* (New York: Basic Books, 2010).

68. Ian Kershaw, *The End: Hitler's Germany, 1944–45* (London: Penguin, 2011), p. 208.

69. Peter Fritzsche, 'Review: Did Weimar Fail?', *Journal of Modern History* 68:3 (1996), pp. 629–56; Moritz Föllmer and Rüdiger Graf (eds), *Die 'Krise' der Weimarer Republik* (Frankfurt am Main: Campus, 2005).

70. For a detailed discussion of political violence in the late Weimar Republic, see chapter 3.

71. Reinhard Sturm, 'Zerstörung der Demokratie 1930–1932', *Informationen zur politischen Bildung*, no. 261, http://www.bpb.de/geschichte/nationalsozialismus/dossier-nationalsozialismus/39537/zerstoerung-der-demokratie?p=all.

72. RGVA (Rossiiskii gosudarstvennyi voennyi arkhiv), Osobyi Archives, Fond 720, Opis 1, no. 47, pp. 140–2, here p. 141: Badisches Landespolizeiamt, 'Die SA und die SS der NSDAP', Karlsruhe, 15 May 1931.

73. These and other aspects of the SA are discussed in detail in the following chapters, where the relevant specialist literature is also noted. The annotations to this introduction are therefore limited to works that deal overwhelmingly, if not exclusively, with the history of the SA or with methodological issues.

74. See, for example, Peter Longerich, *Geschichte der SA* (Munich: Beck, 2003), pp. 284–5; Conan Fischer, *Stormtroopers: A Social, Economic and Ideological Analysis 1929–35* (London: Allen & Unwin, 1983), p. 225; Rudy Koshar, *German Travel Cultures* (Oxford and New York: Berg, 2000), p. 137; Dorothee Hochstetter, *Motorisierung und 'Volksgemeinschaft': Das nationalsozialistische Kraftfahrkorps (NSKK), 1931–1945* (Munich: Oldenbourg, 2006), p. 73.

75. Lewis A. Coser, *Greedy Institutions: Patterns of Undivided Commitment* (New York: The Free Press, 1974), pp. 4–6.

76. See Alfons Bora, '"Partizipation" als politische Inklusionsformel', in *Inklusion und Partizipation: Politische Kommunikation im historischen Wandel*, ed. Christoph Gusy and Heinz-Gerhard Haupt (Frankfurt am Main: Campus, 2005), pp. 15–34, esp. pp. 24–7, 33.

77. Hans Mommsen, 'Cumulative Radicalisation and Progressive Self-Destruction as Structural Determinants of the Nazi Dictatorship', in *Stalinism and Nazism: Dictatorships in Comparison*, ed. Ian Kershaw and Moshe Lewin (Cambridge: Cambridge University Press, 1997), pp. 75–87.

78. Sven Keller, *Volksgemeinschaft am Ende: Gesellschaft und Gewalt 1944/45* (Munich: Oldenbourg, 2013); Ian Buruma, *Year Zero: A History of 1945* (London: Atlantic Books, 2013); Cord Arendes, Edgar Wolfrum, and Jörg Zedler (eds), *Terror nach Innen: Verbrechen am Ende des Zweiten Weltkrieges* (Göttingen: Wallstein, 2006); Patrick Wagner, 'Die letzte Schlacht der "alten Kämpfer". Isolation, Vergemeinschaftung und Gewalt nationalsozialistischer Aktivisten in den letzten Kriegsmonaten 1945', *Mittelweg* 36:4 (2015), pp. 25–50.

79. The second edition of Michael Ruck's bibliography on the historiography of National Socialism, published in 2000, contained approximately 37,000 titles; Michael Ruck, *Bibliographie zum Nationalsozialismus*, 2 vols (Darmstadt: Wissenschaftliche Buchgesellschaft, 2000). In consequence, newer bibliographies usually cover only certain aspects of the subject in order to achieve at least a partial completeness. See Janosch Steuwer, 'Was meint und nützt das Sprechen von der "Volksgemeinschaft"? Neuere Literatur zur Gesellschaftsgeschichte des Nationalsozialismus', *Archiv für Sozialgeschichte* 53 (2013), pp. 487–534; Christoph Nonn, 'Nationalsozialismus als Geschichte: Neuere Literatur zum Umgang mit der NS-Vergangenheit in Deutschland', *Neue politische Literatur* 49:3 (2003), pp. 407–26; Birthe Kundrus, 'Widerstreitende Geschichte: Ein Literaturbericht zur Geschlechtergeschichte des Nationalsozialismus', *Neue politische Literatur* 45:1 (2000), pp. 67–92.

80. See Conan Fischer and Detlef Mühlberger, 'The Pattern of the SA's Social Appeal', in *The Rise of National Socialism and the Working Classes in Weimar Germany*, ed. Conan Fischer (New York: Berghahn, 1996), pp. 99–113; Detlef Mühlberger, *Hitler's Followers: Studies in the Sociology of the Nazi Movement* (London and New York: Routledge, 1991), pp. 159–80, 202–9; Peter Longerich, *Die braunen Bataillone: Geschichte der SA* (Munich: Beck, 1989), pp. 81–8; Michael H. Kater, *The Nazi Party: A Social Profile of Members and Leaders 1919–1945* (Cambridge, MA: Harvard University Press, 1983).

81. Paradigmatic in this respect are Claus-Christian W. Szejnmann, *Nazism in Central Germany: The Brownshirts in 'Red' Saxony* (New York: Berghahn, 1999); Otis C. Mitchell, *Hitler's Stormtroopers and the Attack on the German Republic, 1919–1933* (Jefferson, NC, and London: McFarland & Company, 2008); Thomas D. Grant, *Stormtroopers and Crisis in the Nazi*

Movement: Activism, Ideology and Dissolution (London and New York: Routledge, 2004); Fischer, *Stormtroopers*. The history of the SA provided by Wilfred von Oven, a former National Socialist, likewise ends in 1934, yet – unlike the books mentioned above – it is a disappointing read. Its value for academic scholarship consists above all in the fact that it expresses the perspective of an incorrigible lifelong Nazi; Eleanor Hancock (ed.), *Hitler's Storm Troopers: A History of the SA. The Memoirs of Wilfred von Oven* (London: Frontline, 2010).

82. Ernst Niekisch, *Das Reich der niederen Dämonen* (Hamburg: Rowohlt, 1953), p. 115.

83. Joachim C. Fest, 'Ernst Röhm und die verlorene Generation', in his *Das Gesicht des Dritten Reiches: Profile einer totalitären Herrschaft* (Munich and Zurich: Piper, 1993 [1963]), pp. 190–206, here p. 195.

84. Hans Buchheim, 'Befehl und Gehorsam', in *Anatomie des SS-Staates*, ed. Hans Buchheim, Martin Broszat, Hans-Adolf Jacobsen, and Helmut Krausnick (Munich: dtv, 1999 [1967]), pp. 213–320, here p. 220.

85. William L. Shirer, *The Rise and Fall of the Third Reich: A History of Nazi Germany, with a New Introduction by Ron Rosenbaum* (New York and London: Simon & Schuster, 2011), p. 120.

86. GSt PK, I. HA, Rep. 77 titl. 4043, vol. 311, p. 319: Racliffe (Polizeimajor), 'Denkschrift über Kampfvorbereitung und Kampfgrundsätze radikaler Organisationen' [1931].

87. Karl Otto Paetel, 'Die nationalsozialistischen "Sturmabteilungen"', *Politische Vierteljahresschrift* 6:1 (1965), pp. 103–5, here p. 104; Karl Otto Paetel (ed.), *Beat: Eine Anthologie* (Reinbek bei Hamburg: Rowohlt, 1962).

88. See the careful synopsis by Edgar Wolfrum, *Die geglückte Demokratie: Geschichte der Bundesrepublik Deutschland von ihren Anfängen bis zur Gegenwart* (Munich: Pantheon, 2007), pp. 169–86; Axel Schildt and Detlef Siegfried (eds), *Deutsche Kulturgeschichte: Die Bundesrepublik – 1945 bis zur Gegenwart* (Munich: Hanser, 2009), pp. 46–57, 130–52.

89. Peter Merkl, *The Making of a Stormtrooper* (Princeton, NJ: Princeton University Press, 1980); idem, *Political Violence under the Swastica: 581 Early Nazis* (Princeton, NJ: Princeton University Press, 1975); Mathilde Jamin, *Zwischen den Klassen: Zur Sozialstruktur der SA-Führerschaft* (Wuppertal: Peter Hammer, 1984); idem, 'Zur Rolle der SA im national-sozialistischen Herrschaftssystem', in *Der Führerstaat: Mythos und Realität. Studien zur Struktur und Politik des Dritten Reiches*, ed. Gerhard Hirschfeld and Lothar Kettenacker (Stuttgart: Klett-Cotta, 1981), pp. 329–60; Bessel, *Political Violence and the Rise of Nazism*; Longerich, *Die braunen Bataillone*.

90. On urban 'communities of violence', see Sharon Bäcker-Wilke, Florian Grafl, and Friedrich Lenger, 'Gewaltgemeinschaften im städtischen Raum. Barcelona, Berlin und Wien in der Zwischenkriegszeit', in *Gewaltgemeinschaften: Von der Spätantike bis ins 20. Jahrhundert*, ed. Winfried Speitkamp (Göttingen: V&R unipress, 2013), pp. 317–41.

91. Sven Reichardt, *Faschistische Kampfbünde: Gewalt und Gemeinschaft im italienischen Squadrismus und in der deutschen SA* (Cologne: Böhlau, 2009). See also Sven Reichardt, 'Praxeologie und Faschismus. Gewalt und Gemeinschaft als Elemente eines praxeologischen Faschismusbegriffs', in *Doing Culture: Neue Positionen zum Verhältnis von Kultur und Praxis*, ed. Karl H. Hörning and Julia Reuter (Bielefeld: transcript, 2004), pp. 129–53; idem, 'Zeithistorisches zur praxeologischen Geschichtswissenschaft' in Arndt Brendecke (ed.), *Praktiken der Frühen Neuzeit: Akteure – Handlungen – Artefakte* (Cologne: Böhlau, 2015), pp. 46–61; and the contributions in Stefan Hördler (ed.), *SA-Terror als Herrschaftssicherung: 'Köpenicker Blutwoche' und öffentliche Gewalt im Nationalsozialismus* (Berlin: Metropol, 2013). On praxeology as a historiographical method more generally, see the pioneering article by Thomas Welskopp, 'Der Mensch und die Verhältnisse: "Handeln" und "Struktur" bei Max Weber und Anthony Giddens', in *Geschichte zwischen Kultur und Gesellschaft: Beiträge zur Theoriedebatte*, ed. Thomas Welskopp and Thomas Mergel (Munich: Beck, 1997), pp. 39–70, and, more recently, Hilmar Schäfer, 'Einleitung: Grundlagen, Rezeption und Forschungsperspektiven der Praxistheorie', in his *Praxistheorie: Ein soziologisches Forschungsprogramm* (Bielefeld: Transcript, 2016), pp. 9–25; Dagmar Freist, 'Historische Praxeologie als Mikro-Historie', in Brendecke (ed.), *Praktiken der Frühen Neuzeit*, pp. 62–77.

92. Irene Mayer-von Götz, *Terror im Zentrum der Macht: Die frühen Konzentrationslager in Berlin* (Berlin: Metropol, 2008); Kim Wünschmann, *Before Auschwitz: Jewish Prisoners in the Prewar Concentration Camps* (Cambridge, MA: Harvard University Press, 2015); Benjamin C. Hett,

Crossing Hitler: The Man Who Put Hitler in the Witness Stand (New York: Oxford University Press, 2008); Daniel Siemens, *The Making of a Nazi Hero: The Murder and Myth of Horst Wessel* (London: I. B. Tauris, 2013). Regional studies that deal with or at least contain relevant information on the SA in 1933–4 are discussed in detail in chapter 4.

93. See Astrid Gehrig, *Im Dienste der nationalsozialistischen Volkstumspolitik in Lothringen: Auf den Spuren meines Großvaters* (Essen: Westfälisches Dampfboot, 2014); Dörte von Westernhagen, *Von der Herrschaft zur Gefolgschaft: Die von Westernhagens im 'Dritten Reich'* (Göttingen: V&R, 2012); Malte Ludin, 'Hanns Elard Ludin', in *Stuttgarter NS-Täter: Vom Mitläufer bis zum Massenmörder*, ed. Hermann G. Abmayr (Stuttgart: Abmayr, 2009), pp. 30–9.

94. Next to Klaus Theweleit's pioneering two-volume work *Male Fantasies* (Cambridge: Polity, 1987/8 [first published in German in 1977/8]), see also the studies by Paula Diehl, *Macht – Mythos – Utopie: Die Körperbilder der SS-Männer* (Berlin: Akademie, 2005); Sabine Behrenbeck, *Der Kult um die toten Helden: Nationalsozialistische Mythen, Riten und Symbole* (Vierow bei Greifswald: SH-Verlag, 1996); and the recent contributions to a special issue of *Central European History* 46 (2013): Timothy S. Brown, 'The SA in the Radical Imagination of the Long Weimar Republic', pp. 238–74; Bruce Campbell, 'New Perspectives on the Nazi Storm Troopers. Autobiographies of Violence: The SA in its Own Words', pp. 217–37; and Andrew Wackerfuss, 'The Myth of the Unknown Storm Trooper: Selling SA Stories in the Third Reich', pp. 298–324.

95. See the contributions in Müller and Zilkenat (eds), *Bürgerkriegsarmee*, as well as my review of this book in *German History* 32:1 (2014), pp. 153–4; and Szejnmann, *Nazism in Central Germany*. On the SA and the churches see Ernst Klee, *'Die SA Jesu Christi': Die Kirche im Banne Hitlers* (Frankfurt am Main: Fischer, 1989); Manfred Gailus, *Protestantismus und Nationalsozialismus: Studien zur nationalsozialistischen Durchdringung des protestantischen Sozialmilieus in Berlin* (Cologne: Böhlau, 2001); Richard Steigmann-Gall, *The Holy Reich: Nazi Conceptions of Christianity, 1919–1945* (Cambridge: Cambridge University Press, 2003); Doris L. Bergen, *Twisted Cross: The German Christian Movement in the Third Reich* (Chapel Hill, NC, and London: University of North Carolina Press, 1996); Derek Hastings, *Catholicism and the Roots of Nazism: Religious Identity and National Socialism* (Oxford: Oxford University Press, 2010); Manfred Gailus and Daniel Siemens (eds), *'Hass und Begeisterung bilden Spalier': Horst Wessels politische Autobiographie* (Berlin: be.bra, 2011). On the SA and homosexuality, see Andrew Wackerfuss, *Stormtrooper Families: Homosexuality and Community in the Early Nazi Movement* (New York: Harrington Park Press, 2015); Alexander Zinn, 'SA, Homosexualität und Faschismus. Zur Genese des Stereotyps vom schwulen Nazi', in *Bürgerkriegsarmee*, ed. Müller and Zilkenat, pp. 393–413; Hans Rudolf Wahl, '"National-Päderasten?" Zur Geschichte der (Berliner) SA-Führung 1925–1934', *Zeitschrift für Geschichtswissenschaft* 56:5 (2008), pp. 442–59; Hans Rudolf Wahl, 'Männerbünde, Homosexualitäten und politische Kultur im ersten Drittel des 20. Jahrhunderts. Überlegungen zur Historiographie der SA', *Zeitschrift für Geschichtswissenschaft* 52:3 (2004), pp. 218–37; Sven Reichardt, 'Homosexualität und SA-Führer: Plädoyer für eine Diskursanalyse', *Zeitschrift für Geschichtswissenschaft* 52:8 (2004), pp. 737–40.

96. The archives consulted were predominantly located in Germany, but some of the archival material is drawn from institutions as far away as Moscow, Zagreb, and Stanford in California. This was partly due to the course of history (for example, the Polish sociologist Theodore Abel, who collected an impressive list of Nazi autobiographies in 1933–4, emigrated to the United States, and large parts of the archival material of the Saxon SA were seized by the Russians in 1945 and are nowadays stored in Moscow); but it was also the consequence of the fact that the history of the SA after 1934 increasingly became an international affair, not only because of German expansionism in the second half of the 1930s, but also because the Nazis ruled over large parts of Central and Eastern Europe during the Second World War.

97. Bruce Campbell, 'The SA after the Röhm Purge', *Journal of Contemporary History* 28:4 (1993), pp. 659–74. Among the exceptions: Ives Müller, 'Wilhelm Schepmann – der letzte SA-Stabschef und die Rolle der SA im Zweiten Weltkrieg', *Zeitschrift für Geschichtswissenschaft* 63:6 (2015), pp. 513–32; Daniel Siemens, 'Dem SA-Mann auf der

Spur: Nationalsozialistische Erinnerungspolitik im Berlin der 1930er Jahre', in *SA-Terror als Herrschaftssicherung*, ed. Hördler, pp. 147–63.

98. Armin Nolzen, 'Die NSDAP, der Krieg und die deutsche Gesellschaft', in *Das Deutsche Reich und der Zweite Weltkrieg*, vol. 9/1, ed. Jörg Echternkamp (Munich: DVA, 2004), pp. 99–193, here p. 103. The exact number given by Nolzen is 1,329,448. However, because of the constant changes in the SA's organization and the territory in which it operated, all estimates on the membership of the late SA can only be plausible approximations.

99. On the extensive historiographical debate about the analytical value of the concept of a German *Volksgemeinschaft*, see Martina Steber and Bernhard Gotto (eds), *Visions of Community in Nazi Germany: Social Engineering and Private Lives* (Oxford: Oxford University Press, 2014); Steuwer, 'Was meint und nützt das Sprechen von der "Volksgemeinschaft"?'; Dietmar von Reeken and Malte Thießen (eds), *'Volksgemeinschaft' als soziale Praxis: Neue Forschungen zur NS-Gesellschaft vor Ort* (Paderborn: Schöningh, 2013); Detlef Schmiechen-Ackermann (ed.), *'Volksgemeinschaft': Mythos, wirkungsmächtige soziale Verheißung oder soziale Realität im 'Dritten Reich'* (Paderborn: Schöningh, 2012); Frank Bajohr and Michael Wildt (eds), *Volksgemeinschaft: Neue Forschungen zur Gesellschaft des Nationalsozialismus* (Frankfurt am Main: Fischer, 2009).

100. Such a broader perspective is all the more necessary as historians of Nazi Germany are increasingly challenged by the prevailing 'obsessive post-national historiography' that has raised new questions about the importance of their subject. Historicization of the Third Reich more than ever means the attempt to determine its place not only in the course of a rather narrowly defined German national history, but also in the wider development of capitalist modernity; Ulrich Herbert, 'Nach dem Postnationalismus', paper presented at the conference on 'Transformationen der Geschichtswissenschaft: Hans-Ulrich Wehler und der Wandel der akademischen Felder seit den 1960er Jahren', Bielefeld, 10–12 September 2015.

101. See in particular the pioneering books by Hans Schafranek, *Söldner für den Anschluss: Die Österreichische Legion 1933–1938* (Vienna: Czerzin, 2011); and his *Sommerfest mit Preisschießen: Die unbekannte Geschichte des NS-Putsches im Juli 1934* (Vienna: Czernin, 2006).

102. Dietrich Beyrau, 'Eastern Europe as a "Sub-Germanic Space": Scholarship on Eastern Europe under National Socialism', in *Kritika: Explorations in Russian and Eurasian History* 13:3 (2012), pp. 685–723; Rolf-Dieter Müller, *Hitlers Ostkrieg und die deutsche Siedlungspolitik: Die Zusammenarbeit von Wehrmacht, Wirtschaft und SS* (Frankfurt am Main: Fischer, 1991); Valdis O. Lumans, *Himmler's Auxiliaries: The Volksdeutsche Mittelstelle and the German National Minorities of Europe 1933–45* (Chapel Hill, NC, and London: University of North Carolina Press, 1993); Michael Wildt, *Generation des Unbedingten: Das Führungskorps des Reichssicherheitshauptamtes* (Hamburg: Hamburger Edition, 2002); Michael A. Hartenstein, *Neue Dorflandschaften: Nationalsozialistische Siedlungsplanung in den 'eingegliederten Ostgebieten' 1939 bis 1944* (Berlin: Dr. Köster, 1998); Isabel Heinemann, *'Rasse, Siedlung, deutsches Blut': Das Rasse- und Siedlungshauptamt der SS und die rassenpolitische Neuordnung Europas* (Göttingen: Wallstein, 2003); Isabel Heinemann and Patrick Wagner (eds), *Wissenschaft – Planung – Vertreibung: Neuordnungskonzepte und Umsiedlungspolitik im 20. Jahrhundert* (Stuttgart: Steiner, 2006); Markus Leniger, *Nationalsozialistische "Volkstumsarbeit" und Umsiedlungspolitik 1933–1945: Von der Minderheitenbetreuung zur Siedlerauslese* (Berlin: Frank & Timme, 2006); Gerhard Wolf, *Ideologie und Herrschaftsrationalität: Nationalsozialistische Germanisierungspolitik in Polen* (Hamburg: Hamburger Edition, 2012).

103. Christian Gerlach, *Extremely Violent Societies: Mass Violence in the Twentieth-Century World* (Cambridge: Cambridge University Press, 2010); Jörg Baberowski, *Verbrannte Erde: Stalins Herrschaft der Gewalt* (Munich: Beck, 2012); Donald Bloxham and Dirk A. Moses (eds), *The Oxford Handbook of Genocide Studies* (Oxford: Oxford University Press, 2010); Arjun Appadurai, *Fear of Small Numbers: An Essay on the Geography of Anger* (Durham, NC, and London: Duke University Press, 2006).

104. See Georg Elwert, 'Gewaltmärkte: Beobachtungen zur Zweckrationalität der Gewalt', in *Soziologie der Gewalt*, ed. Trutz von Trotha (Opladen: Westdeutscher Verlag, 1997), pp. 86–101, esp. pp. 87–91.

105. Jan Philipp Reemtsma, 'Gewalt als attraktive Lebensform betrachtet', *Mittelweg 36* 24:4 (2015), pp. 4–16, here pp. 12–14.

106. On violence as pleasure, see in particular the influential sociological study of Randall Collins, *Violence: A Micro-Sociological Theory* (Princeton, NJ, and Oxford: Princeton University Press, 2008), pp. 242–81.

107. Karl Marx, *Das Kapital. Kritik der politischen Ökonomie*, vol. 1 (Berlin: Dietz, 1983), p. 779; Friedrich Engels, 'Herrn Eugen Dührings Umwälzung der Wissenschaft', in *Marx-Engels-Werke*, vol. 20 (Berlin: Dietz, 1962), pp. 1–303, here p. 171; both as quoted in Felix Schnell, 'Gewalt und Gewaltforschung', version 1.0, *Docupedia-Zeitgeschichte*, 8 November 2014, http://docupedia.de/zg/Gewalt_und_Gewaltforschung, p. 7.

108. Reemtsma, 'Gewalt als attraktive Lebensform betrachtet', pp. 12–14. See also the seminal studies by Collins, *Violence*; Peter Imbusch, *Moderne und Gewalt: Zivilisationstheoretische Perspektiven auf das 20. Jahrhundert* (Wiesbaden: VS Verlag, 2005); Hans Joas, *War and Modernity* (Cambridge: Polity, 2003); Sofsky, *Traktat über die Gewalt*; Heinrich Popitz, *Phänomene der Macht*, 2nd edn (Tübingen: Siebeck, 1992), esp. pp. 43–78.

109. On 'mobilization' as a key concept for the analysis of social dynamics in the Third Reich, see Oliver Werner, 'Mobilisierung im Nationalsozialismus – eine Einführung', in *Mobilisierung im Nationalsozialismus: Institutionen und Regionen in der Kriegswirtschaft und der Verwaltung des 'Dritten Reiches' 1936 bis 1945*, ed. Oliver Werner (Paderborn: Schöningh, 2013), pp. 9–26; Jürgen John, 'Mobilisierung als Charakteristikum des NS-Systems?', in Werner, *Mobilisierung im Nationalsozialismus*, pp. 29–57. On the importance of 'discipline' in interwar Germany, see also Ulrich Bröckling, *Disziplin: Soziologie und Geschichte militärischer Gehorsamsproduktion* (Munich: Fink, 1997), pp. 241–71.

110. For recent survey articles on the booming field of the history of violence, see Schnell, 'Gewalt und Gewaltforschung'; Jan C. Behrends, 'Gewalt und Staatlichkeit im 20. Jahrhundert: Einige Tendenzen zeithistorischer Forschung', *Neue Politische Literatur* 58 (2013), pp. 39–58; Elissa Mailänder, 'Geschichtswissenschaft', in *Gewalt: Ein interdisziplinäres Handbuch*, ed. Christian Gudehus and Michaela Christ (Stuttgart and Weimar: Metzler, 2013), pp. 323–31; Maike Christadler, 'Gewalt in der Frühen Neuzeit – Positionen der Forschung', *Gesnerus* 64 (2007), pp. 231–45.

111. Ernst Nolte, *Der Europäische Bürgerkrieg 1917–1945: Nationalsozialismus und Bolschewismus* (Frankfurt am Main: Propyläen, 1987); Enzo Traverso, *Im Bann der Gewalt: Der Europäische Bürgerkrieg* (Munich: Siedler, 2007).

112. Michael Mann, *Fascism* (New York: Cambridge University Press, 2004), quotation on p. 353. From the recent literature, see António Costa Pinto and Aristotle Kallis (eds), *Rethinking Fascism and Dictatorship in Europe* (Basingstoke: Palgrave Macmillan, 2014); António Costa Pinto (ed.), *Rethinking the Nature of Fascism: Comparative Perspectives* (Basingstoke: Palgrave Macmillan, 2011); Roger Griffin, *Modernism and Fascism: The Sense of a Beginning under Mussolini and Hitler* (Basingstoke: Palgrave Macmillan, 2007). See also the pioneering study of Ernst Nolte, *Three Faces of Fascism: Action Française, Italian Fascism, National Socialism* (New York: Holt, Rinehart and Winston, 1966).

113. Chris Millington and Kevin Passmore (eds), *Political Violence and Democracy in Western Europe, 1918–1940* (Basingstoke: Palgrave Macmillan, 2015); Donald Bloxham and Robert Gerwarth (eds), *Political Violence in Twentieth-Century Europe* (Cambridge, Cambridge University Press 2011); Enzo Traverso, *L'histoire comme champ de bataille: Interpréter les violences du XXe siècle* (Paris: Editions La Découverte, 2012); Alf Lüdtke and Bernd Weisbrod (eds), *No Man's Land of Violence: Extreme Wars in the 20th Century* (Göttingen: Vandenhoeck & Ruprecht, 2006); Bernd Weisbrod, 'Gewalt in der Politik. Zur politischen Kultur in Deutschland zwischen den beiden Weltkriegen', *Geschichte in Wissenschaft und Unterricht* 43 (1992), pp. 391–404.

114. For critical and contrasting summaries of this debate, see Geoff Eley, *Nazism as Fascism: Violence, Ideology, and the Ground of Consent in Germany 1930–1945* (London and New York: Routledge, 2013), pp. 198–225; Jürgen Kocka, 'Nach dem Ende des Sonderweges. Zur Tragfähigkeit eines Konzepts', in *Die Bielefelder Sozialgeschichte: Klassische Texte zu einem geschichtswissenschaftlichen Programm und seinen Kontroversen*, ed. Bettina Hitzer and Thomas Welskopp (Bielefeld: transcript, 2010), pp. 263–75.

115. See *pars pro toto*, the masterful synthesis of Saul Friedländer, *Nazi Germany and the Jews*, 2 vols (New York: HarperCollins, 1997/2007).

116. A similar classification was first suggested by Andreas Werner, *SA und NSDAP: 'Wehrverband', 'Parteitruppe' oder 'Revolutionsarmee'? Studien zur Geschichte der SA und der*

NSDAP 1920–1933, diss., Friedrich Alexander Universität zu Erlangen-Nürnberg, 1964. This book is still a major reference for the early organizational history of the SA.

117. See in particular Reichardt's methodological clarifications in his 'Praxeologie und Faschismus', pp. 129–35.

118. As made in ibid., pp. 136, 141; Reichardt, *Faschistische Kampfbünde*, pp. 22–6. In challenging Reichardt's view, I rely on recent praxis-based theoretical approaches as formulated by Schatzki and others: Theodore R. Schatzki, *Social Practices: A Wittgensteinian Approach to Human Activity and the Social* (Cambridge: Cambridge University Press, 1996); idem, 'Practice Mind-ed Orders', in *The Practice Turn in Contemporary History*, ed. Theodore R. Schatzki, Karin Knorr Cetina, and Eike von Savigny (London and New York: Routledge, 2001), pp. 42–55.

119. Gertrud Nunner-Winkler, 'Überlegungen zum Gewaltbegriff', in *Gewalt: Entwicklungen, Strukturen, Analyseprobleme*, ed. Wilhelm Heitmeyer and Hans-Georg Soeffner (Frankfurt am Main: Suhrkamp, 2004), pp. 21–61, here pp. 21–4; Schnell, 'Gewalt und Gewaltforschung', pp. 1–3, with further references. For an elaborate discussion of the forms of violence involved in the street violence of the 1920s, see Dirk Schumann, *Politische Gewalt in der Weimarer Republik 1918–1933: Kampf um die Straße und Furcht vor dem Bürgerkrieg* (Essen: Klartext, 2001), pp. 15–22.

120. For different conceptualizations of these forms of violence and their problems, see Trutz von Trotha, 'Zur Soziologie der Gewalt', in idem (ed.), *Soziologie der Gewalt* (Opladen: Westdeutscher Verlag, 1997), pp. 9–56; Schnell, 'Gewalt und Gewaltforschung', pp. 1–4; Raphael van Riel, 'Gedanken zum Gewaltbegriff: Drei Perspektiven', IPW-Working Paper no. 5, Hamburg University, 2005, https://www.wiso.uni-hamburg.de/fileadmin/sowi/akuf/Text_2010/Gewalt-Riel-2005.pdf; Imbusch, *Moderne und Gewalt*, pp. 20–35; Pierre Bourdieu, *Grundlagen einer Theorie der symbolischen Gewalt* (Frankfurt am Main: Suhrkamp, 1973).

121. The concept of the 'bystander' has recently come under criticism. Here, the term simply designates those individuals who are physically present in a particular situation but do not regard themselves as actively involved in it, either as perpetrators or as victims. This definition does not imply any statement about the effects of 'bystanderism'. For a critical perspective on the concept of the 'bystander', see the contributions to the conference on 'Probing the Limits of Categorization: The "Bystander" in Holocaust History', Amsterdam, 24–26 September 2015.

122. As Hans-Gerd Jaschke and Martin Loiperdinger have demonstrated, the Nazis' 'aesthetic occupation' and 'physical terror' were intrinsically linked. See Hans-Gerd Jaschke and Martin Loiperdinger, 'Gewalt und NSDAP vor 1933: Ästhetische Okkupation und physischer Terror', in *Faszination der Gewalt: Politische Strategie und Alltagserfahrung*, ed. Reiner Steinweg (Frankfurt am Main: Suhrkamp, 1983), pp. 123–55, here pp. 132–3, 146–7. See also Detlef Schmiechen-Ackermann, *Nationalsozialismus und Arbeitermilieus: Der nationalsozialistische Angriff auf die proletarischen Wohnquartiere und die Reaktionen in den sozialistischen Vereinen* (Bonn: Dietz, 1997), pp. 312–35; Gerhard Paul, *Aufstand der Bilder: Die NS-Propaganda vor 1933* (Bonn: Dietz, 1990), pp. 133–42; Reichardt, *Faschistische Kampfbünde*, pp. 101–19. I hereby disagree with Dirk Schumann whose otherwise excellent study pays little attention to such 'structural' aspects of violence, a consequence of his basic methodological choices. See Schumann, *Politische Gewalt in der Weimarer Republik*, pp. 15–16.

123. For this concept, which encompasses physical and psychological forms of violence, see Popitz, *Phänomene der Macht*, pp. 43–7.

124. Thomas Kühne, *Belonging and Genocide: Hitler's Community, 1918–1945* (New Haven, CT, and London: Yale University Press, 2010). Kühne's argument has provoked disagreement. In particular, his pointed emphasis on the genocidal aspects of Nazi community formation have been criticized as exaggerated; see Jürgen Matthäus's review in the *American Historical Review* 117:2 (2012), pp. 626–7. Yet Kühne is not alone in seeing such a connection. For example, the military sociologist Anthony King has likewise stressed that bonds based on feelings of belonging and comradeship are a central precondition for good performance in combat; see Anthony King, *The Combat Soldier: Infantry Tactics and Cohesion in the Twentieth and Twenty-First Centuries* (Oxford: Oxford University Press, 2013), pp. 7–23.

125. Jörg Baberowski, 'Einleitung: Ermöglichungsräume exzessiver Gewalt', in *Gewalträume: Soziale Ordnungen im Ausnahmezustand*, ed. Jörg Baberowski and Gabriele Metzler (Frankfurt am Main: Campus, 2012), pp. 7–27, esp. pp. 25–7.

126. Jan Philipp Reemtsma, 'Tötungslegitimationen: Die mörderische Allianz von Zivilisation und Barbarei', in *Bruchlinien: Tendenzen der Holocaustforschung*, ed. Gertrud Koch (Cologne: Böhlau, 1999), pp. 85–103, here p. 99.

127. However, in recent months two important studies have been published that summarize the violence in the early SA concentration camps: Nikolaus Wachsmann, *KL: A History of the Nazi Concentration Camps* (London: Little, Brown, 2015), here pp. 23–78; Wünschmann, *Before Auschwitz*.

128. Sara Ahmed, *The Cultural Politics of Emotion* (Edinburgh: Edinburgh University Press, 2004). Pioneering and still thought-provoking in this respect is David Schoenbaum, *Hitler's Social Revolution: Class and Status in Nazi Germany 1933–1939* (New York and London: Norton, 1980 [1966]).

129. See in particular the recent analysis by Thomas Rohkrämer, *Die fatale Attraktion des Nationalsozialismus: Zur Popularität eines Unrechtsregimes* (Paderborn: Schöningh, 2013), pp. 27–56, 178–217; Thomas Mergel, 'Führer, Volksgemeinschaft und Maschine: Politische Erwartungsstrukturen in der Weimarer Republik und dem Nationalsozialismus 1918–1936', in *Politische Kulturgeschichte der Zwischenkriegszeit 1918–1939*, ed. Wolfgang Hardtwig (Göttingen: Vandenhoeck & Ruprecht, 2005), pp. 91–127; Michael Wildt, 'Volksgemeinschaft und Führererwartung in der Weimarer Republik', in *Politische Kultur und Medienwirklichkeiten in den 1920er Jahren*, ed. Ute Daniel, Inge Marszolek, Wolfram Pyta, and Thomas Welskopp (Munich: Oldenbourg, 2010), pp. 181–204; Wolfgang Hardtwig, 'Volksgemeinschaft im Übergang: Von der Demokratie zum rassistischen Führerstaat', in *Gemeinschaftsdenken in Europa: Das Gesellschaftskonzept 'Volksheim' im Vergleich 1900–1938*, ed. Detlef Lehnert (Cologne: Böhlau, 2013), pp. 227–53.

130. In doing so, the NSDAP, as well as other Fascist and extreme nationalist parties, was not alone. In an instructive article, the historian Moritz Föllmer has recently argued that the idea of strong leadership in interwar Europe should not necessarily be regarded as a symptom of a 'crisis of democracy', as many moderate and left-wing politicians also favoured a highly personalized leadership. See Moritz Föllmer, 'Führung und Demokratie in Europa', in *Normalität und Fragilität: Demokratie nach dem Ersten Weltkrieg*, ed. Tim B. Müller and Adam Tooze (Hamburg: Hamburger Edition, 2015), pp. 177–97.

131. On the 'democratic' aspect of the leadership ideal in Germany after 1918, see also Wildt, 'Volksgemeinschaft und Führererwartung in der Weimarer Republik', pp. 196–8. As Christina Benninghaus and others have rightly emphasized, these concepts, which were popular among the intellectual leaders of the self-declared 'young generation', nearly exclusively addressed men. This is why, in the sentence above, I have used the male form only. See Christina Benninghaus, 'Das Geschlecht der Generation: Zum Zusammenhang von Generationalität und Männlichkeit um 1930', in *Generationen: Zur Relevanz eines wissenschaftlichen Grundbegriffs*, ed. Ulrike Jureit and Michael Wildt (Hamburg: Hamburger Edition, 2005), pp. 127–58. In reality, members of the middle and upper classes occupied by far the majority of the leadership ranks in the SA, to the detriment of those stormtroopers who originated from the lower classes; see Mühlberger, *Hitler's Followers*, p. 165; and, with regard to Hamburg, Wackerfuss, *Stormtrooper Families*, pp. 48–9.

132. This example is taken from Felix Römer, *Kameraden: Die Wehrmacht von innen* (Munich: Piper, 2012), pp. 85–6. The findings of Alexander W. Hoerken's recent study on the political attitudes of German prisoners of war during the Second World War confirm the appeal of the idea of a people's community – in contrast to the frequent and often bold criticism of the party and its personnel, including the SA. See Alexander W. Hoerkens, *Unter Nazis? Die NS-Ideologie in den abgehörten Gesprächen deutscher Kriegsgefangener von 1939 bis 1945* (Berlin: Be.bra, 2014), pp. 308–12, 336.

133. In this respect see also Malte Thießen, 'Schöne Zeiten? Erinnerungen an die "Volksgemeinschaft" nach 1945', in *Volksgemeinschaft: Neue Forschungen zur Gesellschaft des Nationalsozialismus*, ed. Bajohr and Wildt, pp. 165–87.

Chapter 1

1. As quoted in Othmar Plöckinger, *Unter Soldaten und Agitatoren: Hitlers prägende Jahre im deutschen Militär 1918–1920* (Paderborn: Schöningh, 2013), p. 5.
2. See recently Robert Gerwarth, 'The Central European Counter-Revolution: Paramilitary Violence in Germany, Austria and Hungary after the Great War', *Past and Present* 200 (2008), pp. 175–209, here p. 177; idem, 'Rechte Gewaltgemeinschaften und die Stadt nach dem Ersten Weltkrieg: Berlin, Wien und Budapest im Schatten von Kriegsniederlage und Revolution', in *Kollektive Gewalt in der Stadt: Europa 1890–1939*, ed. Friedrich Lenger (Munich: Oldenbourg, 2013), pp. 103–21; Béla Bodó, 'Heroes or Thieves? Nepotism, Clientage and Paramilitary Violence in Hungary, 1919–1921', *Centre. Journal for Interdisciplinary Studies of Central Europe in the 19th and 20th Centuries* 1 (2015), pp. 66–114.
3. For Germany, see among others the contributions in Gerhard Krumeich (ed.), *Nationalsozialismus und Erster Weltkrieg* (Essen: Klartext, 2010). For a European perspective, see Angelo Ventrone, 'Fascism and the Legacy of the Great War', in *The Legacies of Two World Wars: European Societies in the Twentieth Century*, ed. Lothar Kettenacker and Torsten Riotte (New York: Berghahn, 2011), pp. 90–119; Michael Mann, *Fascists* (New York: Cambridge University Press, 2004), pp. 31–91.
4. From the extensive literature on the topic, see Kathleen Canning, 'Claiming Citizenship: Suffrage and Subjectivity in Germany after the First World War', in *Weimar Publics / Weimar Subjects: Rethinking the Political Culture of Germany in the 1920s*, ed. Kathleen Canning, Kerstin Barndt, and Kristin McGuire (New York and London: Berghahn, 2010), pp. 116–37; Julia Sneeringer, *Winning Women's Votes: Propaganda and Politics in Weimar Germany* (Chapel Hill, NC, and London: University of North Carolina Press, 2002); Matthew Stibbe, 'Anti-Feminism, Nationalism and the German Right, 1914–1920: A Reappraisal', *German History* 20:2 (2002), pp. 185–210.
5. Jörn Leonhard, 'Means of Propaganda, Tools of Loyalty? Experience and Language in the First World War', paper presented at the 17th International Conference, 'History of Concepts: Communicating Concepts – Conceptualizing Communication', Bielefeld University, 28–30 August 2014.
6. On the languages and forms of politics in interwar Germany, see in particular Thomas Mergel, *Parlamentarische Kultur in der Weimarer Republik: Politische Kommunikation, symbolische Politik und Öffentlichkeit im Reichstag* (Düsseldorf: Droste, 2002); Kirsten Heinsohn, *Konservative Parteien in Deutschland 1912–1933: Demokratisierung und Partizipation in geschlechterhistorischer Perspektive* (Düsseldorf: Droste, 2010).
7. On the early Reichswehr and its clandestine paramilitary forces, the so-called 'Black Reichswehr', see Bergien, *Die bellizistische Republik*, pp. 107–30; Francis L. Carsten, *Reichswehr und Politik* (Cologne: Kiepenheuer and Witsch, 1964), pp. 168–173; Franz von Gaertner, *Die Reichswehr in der Weimarer Republik: Erlebte Geschichte* (Darmstadt: Fundus, 1969), pp. 129–35. For partisan views on the extremely controversial topic of the 'Black Reichswehr' in the 1920s and 1930s, see the 'defence statements' by Bruno Ernst Buchrucker, *Im Schatten Seeckt's: Die Geschichte der 'Schwarzen Reichswehr'* (Berlin: Kampf-Verlag, 1928); Friedrich Wilhelm von Oerzen, *Die Deutschen Freikorps 1918–1923* (Munich: Bruckmann, 1938), pp. 462–73; for a critical voice of the 1920s, see Emil Julis Gumbel, *Verschwörer* (Vienna: Malick, 1924), pp. 100–17.
8. The historian Peter Keller has recently argued that the use of *Freikorps* as a catch-all term for those military units that operated with the consent of the German government, but were not officially part of the Reichswehr, largely stems from a tradition invented in the 1930s. Instead of *Freikorps*, Keller prefers the term *Regierungstruppen* – government forces. See Peter Keller, *'Die Wehrmacht der Deutschen Republik ist die Reichswehr': Die deutsche Armee 1918–1921* (Paderborn: Schöningh, 2014), pp. 81–101. See also Sprenger, *Landsknechte*; Perry Biddiscombe, 'The End of the Freebooter Tradition: The Forgotten *Freikorps* Movement of 1944/45', *Central European History* 32:1 (1999), pp. 53–90, here p. 58; Kai Uwe Tapken, *Die Reichswehr in Bayern von 1919 bis 1924* (Hamburg: Kovač, 2002), p. 115; Schulze, *Freikorps und Republik*, pp. 35–47.
9. Richard Bessel, 'Militarismus im innenpolitischen Leben der Weimarer Republik: Von den Freikorps zur SA', in *Militär und Militarismus in der Weimarer Republik: Beiträge eines*

internationalen Symposiums an der Hochschule der Bundeswehr Hamburg am 5. und 6. Mai 1977, ed. Klaus-Jürgen Müller and Eckardt Opitz (Düsseldorf: Droste, 1978), pp. 193–222, here pp. 200–3.

10. Jan-Philipp Pomplun, 'Freikorps als personelle und organisatorische Keimzellen des Nationalsozialismus? Eine sozial- und politikgeschichtliche Untersuchung am Beispiel süddeutscher Einheiten', speech delivered at the conference 'Wegbereiter des Nationalsozialismus: Personen, Organisationen, Netzwerke des völkisch-antisemitischen Aktivismus 1919–1933', Gelsenkirchen, 30 September–2 October 2013. According to Pomplun, 1 per cent of former *Freikorps* members later joined the SS, and 17 per cent became members of the NSDAP. The previously dominant perspective emphasized the continuity in membership between *Freikorps* units and the Nazi Party; see Robert G. L. Waite, *Vanguard of Nazism: The Free Corps Movement in Postwar Germany* (Cambridge, MA: Harvard University Press, 1970); Bernhard Sauer, 'Freikorps and Antisemitismus in der Weimarer Republik', *Zeitschrift für Geschichtswissenschaft* 56:1 (2008), pp. 5–29, here p. 29; Bessel, 'Militarismus im innenpolitischen Leben der Weimarer Republik', p. 202.

11. After the failed Kapp Putsch in March 1920, Hermann Ehrhardt moved his brigade from Berlin to Munich, where Bavarian authorities welcomed him and his men. He then set up a secret terror organization, the Organization Consul (OC), under the guise of the *Bayerische Holzverwertungsgesellschaft*, literally the 'Bavarian Forest and Wood Company'. For details, see Gabriele Krüger, *Die Brigade Ehrhardt* (Hamburg: Leibnitz, 1971), pp. 68–99.

12. The *Freikorps* Epp, named after its leader Franz Xaver Ritter von Epp (1868–1947), was founded in Thuringia as the Bavarian Free Corps for the Protection of the Eastern Frontier in the spring of 1919. It participated in the toppling of the Munich Soviet Republic in May 1919 and later that month was integrated into the provisional Reichswehr as the *1. Bayerisches Schützenregiment*, literally the 'First Bavarian Shooters Regiment'. Later leading National Socialist politicians Rudolf Hess, Ernst Röhm, and Gregor and Otto Strasser were all members of the *Freikorps* Epp. See Bruno Thoß, 'Freikorps Epp', in *Historisches Lexikon Bayerns*, http://www.historisches-lexikon-bayerns.de/artikel/artikel_44494; Katja-Maria Wächter, *Die Macht der Ohnmacht: Leben und Politik des Franz Xaver Ritter von Epp (1868–1946)* (Frankfurt am Main: Lang, 1999), pp. 53–113.

13. On the *Freikorps Oberland* that in 1921 was renamed *Bund Oberland*, see Hans Fenske, *Konservatismus und Rechtsradikalismus in Bayern nach 1918* (Berlin and Zurich: Gehlen, 1969), pp. 53–6, 159–64; Reinhold Friedrich, *Spuren des Nationalsozialismus im bayerischen Oberland: Schliersee und Hausham zwischen 1933 und 1945* (Norderstedt: Books on Demand, 2011), pp. 76–90; Rüdiger Ahrens, *Bündische Jugend: Eine neue Geschichte 1918–1933* (Göttingen: Wallstein, 2015), p. 56.

14. The best book that provides a comprehensive picture of Munich society during the war and post-war years is Martin Geyer, *Verkehrte Welt: Revolution, Inflation und Moderne. München 1914–1924* (Göttingen: Vandenhoeck & Ruprecht, 1998), here esp. pp. 94–129.

15. David Clay Large, *The Politics of Law and Order: A History of the Bavarian Einwohnerwehr, 1918–1921* (Philadelphia, PA: The American Philosophical Society, 1980), pp. 3–4, 20–6; 'Ein "Bund der erwachenden Bayern"', *Das Jüdische Echo* 9:11, 17 March 1922, p. 146. On the Bavarian *Einwohnerwehren*, see also the older but still relevant accounts by Fenske, *Konservatismus und Rechtsradikalismus*, pp. 76–112; Werner Gabriel Zimmermann, *Bayern und das Reich 1918–1923* (Munich: R. Pflaum Verlag, 1953), pp. 98–104.

16. Large, *The Politics of Law and Order*, pp. 25–31, 39, 43. In contrast to Large, Dirk Schumann has argued that the *Einwohnerwehr* movement had only a limited influence on the radicalization of the middle classes, at least in Saxony: Schumann, *Politische Gewalt in der Weimarer Republik*, p. 361. For Bavaria, however, this nexus is irrefutable.

17. On the *Orgesch*, see Christoph Hübner, 'Organisation Escherich (Orgesch), 1920/21', in *Historisches Lexikon Bayerns*, http://www.historisches-lexikon-bayerns.de/artikel/artikel_44558.

18. Dietrich Orlow, *Weimar Prussia 1918–1925: The Unlikely Rock of Democracy* (Pittsburgh, PA: University of Pittsburgh Press, 1986). See also his second volume: *Weimar Prussia 1925–1933: The Illusion of Strength* (Pittsburgh, PA: University of Pittsburgh Press, 1991); as well as Hans-Peter Ehni, *Preußen-Regierung, Reich-Länder-Problem und Sozialdemokratie 1928–1932* (Bonn: Neue Gesellschaft, 1975). For a first-hand account, see the memoirs of the

former Prussian Minister of the Interior, Albert C. Grzesinski, *Inside Germany* (New York: E. P. Dutton, 1939).

19. Revealing in this context is that the Bavarian government did not accept the Reich laws designed to protect the democratic order after the murder of the Foreign Minister, Walther Rathenau, on 24 June 1922, which was the most prominent of a series of political murders between 1919 and 1922 that were meant to punish those whom the nationalist right branded as appeasement politicians, traitors to the German cause, and Jews. See Martin Sabrow, *Die verdrängte Verschwörung: Der Rathenau-Mord und die deutsche Gegenrevolution* (Frankfurt am Main: Fischer, 1999); Ulrike Claudia Hofmann, *'Verräter verfallen der Feme!' Fememorde in Bayern in den zwanziger Jahren* (Cologne: Böhlau, 2000); Gumbel, *Verschwörer*.

20. Maurice, born in 1897 in Westermoor near Itzehoe in Schleswig-Holstein, had come to Munich in October 1917. There, he briefly worked as a watchmaker, his learned profession, before he was drafted into the military, where he was wounded but apparently never deployed in combat. He was released from the army on 25 January 1919 and returned to his former employer. Apparently aided by the introduction of the eight-hour workday, which gave him more spare time, Maurice became involved in politics and the world of paramilitarism over the course of 1919. He joined the new *Deutsche Arbeiterpartei* (DAP) in late 1919, played leading roles in the SA and later the SS, and in 1923 participated in the Beer Hall Putsch. Protected by Hitler, with whom he was on an intimate footing beginning in the early 1920s, Maurice became a Munich city councilman in 1933 and president of the Munich Chamber of Crafts in 1936. On his early life, see the Bavarian police's note about him from 3 November 1921 in StA München, Pol. Dir. 6804, pp. 1–2; on his later life, see Anna Maria Sigmund, *Des Führers bester Freund: Adolf Hitler, seine Nichte Geli Raubal und der 'Ehrenarier' Emil Maurice – eine Dreiecksbeziehung* (Munich: Heyne, 2003).

21. StA München, Pol. Dir. 6803, pp. 1–7, here p. 2: Memorandum of the Bavarian Police on the Self-Defence Leagues, undated.

22. Longerich, *Geschichte der SA*, p. 23; Fenske, *Konservatismus und Rechtsradikalismus*, pp. 77–8; Werner, *SA und NSDAP*, pp. 19–27; Jeremy Noakes, *The Nazi Party in Lower Saxony, 1921–1933* (London: Oxford University Press, 1971), pp. 24–5.

23. Paul Hoser, 'Nationalsozialistischer Deutscher Arbeiterverein e.V. (NSDAV), 1920–1923/1925–1935', *Historisches Lexikon Bayerns*, http://www.historisches-lexikon-bayerns.de/artikel/artikel_44775.

24. Auer acted as Minister of the Interior in the revolutionary government in 1918–19 and was from 1919 until 1933 the leader of the Bavarian SPD. See Markus Schmalzl, *Erhard Auer – Wegbereiter der parlamentarischen Demokratie in Bayern* (Laßleben: Kallmünz, 2013), pp. 468–79. While the SPD in exile in 1934 still knew that the Nazis had 'stolen' the term 'SA' from the Bavarian Social Democrats, this knowledge came to be forgotten later. See Sopade, *Deutschland-Berichte*, vol. 1 (1934), p. 262.

25. On Valley, see Friedrich Hitzer, *Anton Graf Arco: Das Attentat auf Kurt Eisner und die Schüsse im Landtag* (Munich: Knesebeck and Schuler, 1988).

26. Wilhelm Buisson (1892–1940) had studied pharmacy science in Munich between 1913 and 1920, with an interruption for his military service. With the help of Auer, he was able to open his own pharmacy in 1924. Two years later he started to volunteer as 'leisure warden' (*Vergnügungswart*) for the Bayern Munich sports club. He was sentenced to death because of his anti-Fascist activities in the 1930s, and the Nazis executed him on 6 September 1940 in Berlin-Plötzensee. His role as a Social Democrat activist in the early 1920s is virtually unknown. For biographical details, see Dietrich Schulze-Marmeling, *Der FC Bayern und seine Juden: Aufstieg und Zerschlagung einer liberalen Fußballkultur* (Göttingen: Die Werkstatt, 2011), pp. 190–1, 239; 'Erinnerungstag 2015 – Wilhelm Buisson – FC Bayern-Funktionär und Widerstandskämpfer', *Südkurvenbladdl Onlinemagazin*, http://suedkurvenbladdl.org/erinnerungstag-2015-wilhelm-buisson-fc-bayern-funktionaer-und-widerstandskaempfer.

27. StA München, Pol. Dir. 6803, pp. 13–15: Memorandum of the Bavarian Police on the SA of the NSDAP, undated (but after 3 February 1923); Robert Hofmann, 'Auergarde, 1919–1924', *Historisches Lexikon Bayerns*, http://www.historisches-lexikon-bayerns.de/artikel/artikel_44656; Günther Gerstenberg, *Freiheit! Sozialdemokratischer Selbstschutz im München der zwanziger und frühen dreißiger Jahre* (Munich: Eulenspiegeldruck, 1997), vol. 1, p. 75.

28. On the origins and first years of the *Reichsbanner*, see Benjamin Ziemann, *Contested Commemorations: Republican War Veterans and Weimar Political Culture* (Cambridge and New York: Cambridge University Press, 2013), pp. 60–94; idem, *Die Zukunft der Republik? Das Reichsbanner Schwarz-Rot-Gold 1924–1933* (Bonn: Friedrich-Ebert-Stiftung, 2011), pp. 13–20; Carsten Voigt, *Kampfbünde der Arbeiterbewegung: Das Reichsbanner Schwarz-Rot-Gold und der Rote Frontkämpferbund in Sachsen 1924–1933* (Cologne: Böhlau, 2009).

29. See StA München, Pol. Dir. 6804, p. 52: Memorandum from Bauerreiter of the Munich police, 3 November 1921.

30. Given the overwhelming evidence on this point, it is striking that the Bavarian police under Pöhner in a memo from 1923 still claimed that the National Socialist stormtroopers had never taken the offensive. See StA München, Pol. Dir. 6803, pp. 13–15, here p. 13: Memorandum from the Bavarian Police on the SA of the NSDAP, undated (but after 3 February 1923).

31. Johannes Schwarze, *Die bayrische Polizei und ihre historische Funktion bei der Aufrechterhaltung der öffentlichen Sicherheit in Bayern von 1919–1933* (Munich: Wölfle, 1977), p. 151.

32. BayHStA, MInn, no. 71712, pp. 32–4, here p. 33: Letter from the Bavarian Ministry of the Interior to the Police Headquarters in Munich, 11 February 1921.

33. StA München, Pol. Dir. 6803, p. 8: Note by the Bavarian police, 24 September 1921.

34. BayHStA, MInn, no. 71712, pp. 32–4: Letter from the Bavarian Ministry of the Interior to the Police Headquarters in Munich, 11 February 1921.

35. StA München, Pol. Dir. 6803, pp. 13–15: Memorandum of the Bavarian Police on the SA of the NSDAP, undated (but after 3 February 1923).

36. On the early SA in Bavaria, see above all Longerich, *Geschichte der SA*, pp. 9–44; Eric G. Reiche, *The Development of the SA in Nürnberg, 1922–1934* (London and New York: Cambridge University Press, 1986), pp. 1–49; Werner Maser, *Der Sturm auf die Republik: Frühgeschichte der NSDAP* (Munich: DVA, 1973), pp. 284–464; Werner, *SA und NSDAP*; Heinrich Bennecke, *Hitler und die SA* (Munich and Vienna: Günter Olzog Verlag, 1962), pp. 25–103.

37. StA München, Pol. Dir. 6803, pp. 1–7, here p. 2: Memorandum from the Bavarian Police on the Self-Defence Leagues, undated; 'An unsere deutsche Jugend!', *Völkischer Beobachter*, 11 August 1921 (trans. Heiden, *History of National Socialism*, pp. 82–3); Werner, *SA und NSDAP*, pp. 38–40.

38. Krüger, *Brigade Ehrhardt*, pp. 105–7; Hans-Günter Richardi, *Hitler und seine Hintermänner: Neue Fakten zur Frühgeschichte der NSDAP* (Munich: Süddeutscher Verlag, 1991), p. 368; Werner, *NSDAP und SA*, 23; HA-Spiegel, Personal Papers of Heinz Höhne, no. 242: Letter from the SA-Gruppe Hansa, 9 July 1936. For Johannes Paul Klintzsch (1861–1920), see the entry in *Evangelisches Pfarrerbuch für die Mark Brandenburg seit der Reformation*, ed. Brandenburgischer Provinzialsynodalverband, vol. 2 (Berlin: Mittler, 1941), p. 417.

39. Krüger, *Brigade Ehrhardt*, pp. 105–6. For a biographical sketch of Klinzsch's life, see Friedrich Walsdorff, 'Hans-Ulrich Klintzsch', in *Alma Mater Joachimica: Zeitschrift der Vereinigung Alter Joachimsthaler e.V.* 53 (1981), pp. 1,253–7.

40. It is telling that in Friedrich Freksa (ed.), *Kapitän Ehrhardt: Abenteuer und Schicksale* (Berlin: Scherl, 1924), a popular but authorized account of Ehrhardt's life, all references to the illegality of the SA and NSDAP are omitted.

41. 'Kritische Zeit', *Das Jüdische Echo* 9:32, 11 August 1922, pp. 403–4. On Ludendorff and his 'movement' in the 1920s, see Bettina Amm, *Die Ludendorff-Bewegung: Vom nationalistischen Kampfbund zur völkischen Weltanschauungssekte* (Hamburg: Ad Fontes, 2006); Bruno Thoß, *Der Ludendorff-Kreis 1919–1923: München als Zentrum der mitteleuropäischen Gegenrevolution zwischen Revolution und Hitler-Putsch* (Munich: Woelfle, 1978).

42. See the instructive article 'Kapitän Ehrhardt', *Das Jüdische Echo* 9:49, 8 December 1922, p. 607.

43. Bessel, 'Militarismus im innenpolitischen Leben der Weimarer Republik', p. 208.

44. On Hitler's life and political development between 1918 and 1921, see the exemplary Ian Kershaw, *Hitler 1889–1936* (Stuttgart: DVA, 1998), pp. 149–276; Evans, *Coming of the Third Reich*, pp. 161–75; Plöckinger, *Unter Soldaten und Agitatoren*; Thomas Weber, *Hitler's First War: Adolf Hitler, the Men of the List Regiment, and the First World War* (Oxford: Oxford University Press, 2011), pp. 227–87.

45. Richardi, *Hitler und seine Hintermänner*, p. 369. After the Second World War, Klintzsch likewise claimed that he had only been responsible to Ehrhardt, but not Hitler. He even denied that there ever was a formal affiliation between the Ehrhardt men and the organizations under Hitler's command; Landeskirchliches Archiv Stuttgart (LKA Stuttgart), A 127, no. 1293: Letter from Klintzsch to a Protestant *Oberkirchenrat* in Württemberg, 25 March 1948.

46. StA München, Pol. Dir. 6803, pp. 174–83: an early list of SA members (from Maurice), presumably intercepted by the police in September 1921. A newspaper report from October 1922 likewise gave the age of the stormtroopers involved in public appearances as 'between 18 and 25 years'; see 'Bayerischer Skandal', *Oberfränkische Volkszeitung*, no. 295, 20 October 1922, in BayHStA, MInn, no. 81589. As the SA was, at least between 1921 and the first half of 1922, divided into two categories – Category A comprising those between seventeen and twenty-three and Category B comprising the more 'senior gentlemen' – it is possible that the total number of stormtroopers was actually slightly higher than estimated, so that Longerich's number of 300 seems plausible; Longerich, *Geschichte der SA*, p. 26. In light of these sources, Rösch's claim that the SA in November 1921 comprised 1,500 men seems exaggerated; Mathias Rösch, *Die Münchner NSDAP 1925–1933: Eine Untersuchung zur inneren Struktur der NSDAP in der Weimarer Republik* (Munich: Oldenbourg, 2002), p. 80. See also StA München, Pol. Dir. 6803, pp. 20–1: Letter from the Munich police to the Bavarian Ministry of the Interior, 25 June 1923.

47. It remained a characteristic of the SA until the early 1930s that its rank and file as well as *Führer* were often of very young age. See Bessel, 'Militarismus im innenpolitischen Leben der Weimarer Republik', pp. 216–17.

48. See the documents in Klintzsch's investigation file, in LArch Freiburg, F 179/4 no. 110.

49. Hermann Göring (1893–1946), a well-known fighter pilot during the First World War, had spent most of the years 1919–21 in Denmark and Sweden, before he moved to Bavaria in 1922 and enrolled in the Faculty of Arts at Ludwig Maximilians University (at least for the winter term of 1922–3). He suffered from morphine addiction for most of his life and – perhaps because of it – at times behaved so violently that he eventually spent several weeks in a psychiatric hospital in Stockholm in 1925. Within the Third Reich, Göring, as Hitler's deputy, served in several influential positions, most notably as Prussian Minister of the Interior in 1933 and later as Reich Minister for the Four-Year Plan. Sentenced to death by the International Military Tribunal in Nuremberg, Göring committed suicide by ingesting a potassium cyanide capsule prior to his execution. On Göring's drug-related physical violence, see Hermann Weber et al. (eds), *Deutschland, Russland, Komintern. II. Dokumente (1918–1943). Nach der Archivrevolution: Neuerschlossene Quellen zu der Geschichte der KPD und den deutsch-russischen Beziehungen* (Berlin: de Gruyter, 2015), pp. 958–9.

50. For details on the biographies of the early SA leaders, see the excellent analysis by Bruce Campbell, *The SA Generals and the Rise of Nazism* (Lexington, KY: University of Kentucky Press, 2004), esp. pp. 7, 29–48, 62–79.

51. See the comprehensive article by Malinowski and Reichardt, 'Die Reihen fest geschlossen?'

52. The membership list cited earlier contains a total of 241 names, 144 of them with professional status. It is included in StA München, Pol. Dir. 6803, pp. 174–83. See also 'Die bayrischen Nationalsozialisten', *Frankfurter Zeitung*, 8 November 1922, in BayHStA, MInn, no. 81589; 'Beim Überfall auf das Deutsche Theater', *Münchener Post*, 18 October 1922, in ibid. As early as late 1920, a *Studentensturm*, or 'SA Student Storm', co-founded and initially led by Rudolf Hess, who later became Hitler's proxy, is said to have existed. See Michael S. Steinberg, *Sabers and Brown Shirts: The German Students' Path to National Socialism, 1918–1935* (Chicago, IL, and London: The University of Chicago Press, 1977), pp. 73–4; Hans Peter Bleuel and Ernst Klinnert, *Deutsche Studenten auf dem Weg ins Dritte Reich: Ideologien – Programme – Aktionen, 1918–1935* (Gütersloh: Mohn, 1967), p. 196. I have not been able to verify this claim.

53. See Benjamin Ziemann, 'Germany after the First World War: A Violent Society? Results and Implications of Resent Research on Weimar Germany', *Journal of Modern European History* 1 (2003), pp. 80–95; Klaus Schönhoven, 'Die Entstehung der Weimarer Republik aus dem Krieg: Vorbelastungen und Neuanfang', in *Weimar im Widerstreit: Deutungen der ersten deutschen Republik im geteilten Deutschland*, ed. Heinrich August Winkler (Munich:

Oldenbourg, 2002), pp. 13–32; Andrew Donson, *Youth in the Fatherless Land: War Pedagogy, Nationalism, and Authority in Germany, 1914–1918* (Cambridge, MA: Harvard University Press, 2010). The classical study is George Mosse, *Fallen Soldiers: Reshaping the Memory of the World Wars* (Oxford: Oxford University Press, 1990). For a short summary of the debate, see Gerwarth, 'Rechte Gewaltgemeinschaften und die Stadt nach dem Ersten Weltkrieg', pp. 106–7.

54. StA München, Pol. Dir. 6804, pp. 4, 6: Transcripts of SA announcements from 26 August and 19 October 1921.

55. StA München, Pol. Dir. 6803: Police report about the SA meeting on 5 October 1921 in the Högerbräu.

56. Ibid.: Police report about the SA meeting in Corneliusstraße on 25 January 1922.

57. Ibid.: Police report about the SA meeting in the Hofbräuhaus on 6 April 1922.

58. Ibid.: Police report about the SA meeting in the restaurant Liebherr on 30 November 1921.

59. 'An alle Schaffenden! Die wahren Verräter und Würger der Deutschen!', in Bayerische Staatsbibliothek München, *Sammlung von Flugblättern betreffend die Münchener Räterepublik 1919*, http://www.bayerische-landesbibliothek-online.de/flugblaetter-1919.

60. On the rise of antisemitism during the First World War and in the early years of the Weimar Republic, see Christoph Jahr, *Antisemitismus vor Gericht: Debatten über die juristische Ahndung judenfeindlicher Agitation in Deutschland (1879–1960)* (Frankfurt am Main: Campus, 2011), pp. 245–76; Daniel Siemens, 'Konzepte des nationaljüdischen Körpers in der frühen Weimarer Republik', *Zeitschrift für Geschichtswissenschaft* 56:1 (2008), pp. 30–54, here pp. 30–2; Cornelia Hecht, *Deutsche Juden und Antisemitismus in der Weimarer Republik* (Bonn: Dietz, 2003); Avraham Barkai, *'Wehr Dich!' Der Centralverein deutscher Staatsbürger jüdischen Glaubens (C.V.) 1893–1938* (Munich: Beck, 2002), pp. 55–66; Dirk Walter, *Antisemitische Kriminalität und Gewalt: Judenfeindschaft in der Weimarer Republik* (Bonn: Dietz, 1999).

61. Hofmann, *'Verräter verfallen der Feme!'*, pp. 108, 112–13.

62. On the reception of juvenile criminality during the war years and in the Weimar Republic, see Sarah Bornhorst, 'Bad Boys? Juvenile Delinquency during the First Word War in Wilhelmine Germany', in *Juvenile Delinquency and the Limits of Western Influence, 1850–2000*, ed. Heather Ellis (London and New York: Palgrave Macmillan, 2014), pp. 121–44; Daniel Siemens, *Metropole und Verbrechen: Die Gerichtsreportage in Berlin, Paris und Chicago* (Stuttgart: Steiner, 2007), pp. 129–35.

63. BayHStA, MInn, no. 81589: 'Mussolini – Beherrscher Italiens', *Bayerische Staatszeitung*, 28–29 October 1922.

64. Hitler's speech in the Hofbräuhaus on the occasion of the first anniversary of the SA, as quoted in 'Unsere Sturmabteilung', *Völkischer Beobachter*, 5 August 1922, in BayHStA, MInn, no. 81589; 'Aufruf! Deutsche Volksgenossen, Hand- und Kopfarbeiter!', *Völkischer Beobachter*, 9 November 1921; HA-Spiegel, Personal Papers of Heinz Höhne, no. 242: Letter from the SA-Gruppe Hansa, 9 July 1936.

65. Paradigmatic for the tone and style of this glorification is Karl W. H. Koch, *Männer im Braunhemd: Vom Kampf und Sieg der SA* (Berlin: Stubenrauch, 1936), pp. 11–17. Consequently, the Nazis used the events of 4 November 1921 in further propaganda. Three days later, on 7 November, they published a second call to join the SA in the *Völkischer Beobachter*, entitled 'Hinein in die Sturmabteilungen!' See StA München, Pol. Dir. 6803, pp. 1–7, here p. 2: Memorandum from the Bavarian Police on the Self-Defence Leagues, undated.

66. BayHStA, MInn, no. 81589: 'Aus der politischen Kinderstube', *Münchener Post*, 29 June 1922.

67. Ibid.: 'Hakenkreuz und Ettstraße', *Münchener Post*, 14 July 1922.

68. StA München, Pol. Dir. 6803, p. 8: Note of the Bavarian Police from 24 September 1921; StA München, Pol. Dir. 6803, pp. 13–15, here p. 14: Memorandum from the Bavarian Police on the SA of the NSDAP, undated (but after 3 February 1923); Westernhagen, *Von der Herrschaft zur Gefolgschaft*, p. 49.

69. StA München, Pol. Dir. 6804, pp. 175–92: Interrogation of Adolf Modes, 8 February 1923.

70. For details, see Torsten Homberger, *Fashioning German Fascism: Constructing the Image of Hitler's Storm Troopers, 1924–1933*, PhD diss., Washington State University, 2014, pp. 56–73.

71. Richardi, *Hitler und seine Hintermänner*, p. 372.

72. BayHStA, MInn, no. 81589: 'Aus der Bewegung', *Völkischer Beobachter*, 2 August 1922.

73. For an overview of the SA's organizational structure in 1933, see Julius M. Ruhl and Carl B. Starke (eds), *Adolf Hitlers Braunhemden: Organisation, Einteilung, Bekleidung und Ausrüstung der Nationalsozialistischen Sturm-Abteilungen, Schutz-Staffeln, der Hitler-Jugend, des Deutschen Jungvolkes sowie der Politischen Organisation usw.* (Leipzig: Moritz Ruhl, 1933). For the organization of the SA's subdivisions in 1938, see Ernst Bayer, *Die SA: Geschichte, Arbeit, Zweck und Organisation der Sturmabteilungen des Führers und der Obersten SA-Führung* (Berlin: Junker and Dünnhaupt, 1938).

74. StA München, Pol. Dir. 6804, pp. 15–16: 'Flame letter' from the O[ber]k[ommando] Transportleitung, a certain Herr Streck, to the leader of the SA (Göring), 14 July 1923.

75. StA München, Pol. Dir. 6803, pp. 230–1: Constable Pfeilschifler, Report to the Municipal Council of Bad Tölz, 16 August 1922.

76. StA München, Pol. Dir. 6803, p. 232: Memo by the Munich police on the interrogation of Hans Ulrich Klintzsch, 20 September 1922. The Zionist weekly *Das Jüdische Echo* in May 1922 remarked that 'Upper Bavaria is for its most part antisemitic', thanks not least to the antisemitic agitation of the local newspaper *Miesbacher Anzeiger*. As a matter of self-respect, the author of the *Das Jüdische Echo* article urged his Jewish brothers in faith to no longer vacate in this area: Hans Guggenheimer, 'Bayerische Sommerfrischen', *Das Jüdische Echo* 9:21, 26 May 1922, pp. 268–9. See also Karl Glaser, 'Antisemitismus und kleine Gemeinden', *Das Jüdische Echo* 9:13, 31 March 1922, pp. 167–8.

77. Nunner-Winkler, 'Überlegungen zum Gewaltbegriff', p. 53.

78. 'Kritische Zeit', *Das Jüdische Echo* 9:32, 11 August 1922, pp. 403–4, here p. 403.

79. StA München, Pol. Dir. 6803, pp. 1–7, here p. 2: Memorandum from the Bavarian Police on the Self-Defence Leagues, undated.

80. Ernst Röhm, *The Memoirs of Ernst Röhm*, trans. Geoffrey Brooks (London: Frontline, 2012), p. 126.

81. The journalist Hermann Esser (1900–81) joined the DAP, the later NSDAP, in 1919. In the same year he became editor-in-chief of the *Völkischer Beobachter*. In the early 1920s, Esser made a name for himself in Bavaria as a fervently antisemitic demagogue. In 1923 he stated that all Jews in Germany should be interned in concentration camps, and that if the Allied occupation of the Ruhr region did not stop, 50,000 Jews would be 'sent to a better afterworld' (*einem besseren Jenseits zugeführt*) – that is, murdered. After becoming a member of the Bavarian *Landtag* in 1932, Esser was promoted to the head of the Bavarian State Chancellery in 1933. See 'Die Sturmarmee', *Das Jüdische Echo* 10:14, 6 April 1923, in StA München, Pol. Dir. 6803, p. 319; Kurt G. W. Ludecke, *I Knew Hitler: The Lost Testimony by a Survivor from the Night of the Long Knives*, ed. Bob Carruthers (Barnsley: Pen & Sword, 2013), p. 81; Thomas Fürst, *Karl Stützel. Ein Lebensweg in Umbrüchen: Vom Königlichen Beamten zum Bayerischen Innenminister der Weimarer Zeit (1924–1933)* (Frankfurt am Main: Lang, 2007), p. 454, n. 1,735.

82. BayHStA, MInn, no. 81589: 'Zur Psychologie der Nationalsozialisten', *Münchener Post*, 17 August 1922.

83. On the European dimension of this political event, which inspired Fascist movements throughout Europe, see Arnd Bauerkämper, 'Transnational Fascism: Cross-Border Relations between Regimes and Movements in Europe, 1922–1939', *East Central Europe* 37 (2010), pp. 214–46, here pp. 217–22. On the National Socialist admiration for Italian Fascism in the 1920s, see also Patrick Bernhard, 'Konzertierte Gegnerbekämpfung im Achsenbündnis. Die Polizei im Dritten Reich und im faschistischen Italien 1933 bis 1943', *Vierteljahrshefte für Zeitgeschichte* 59:2 (2011), pp. 229–62, esp. pp. 230–7.

84. BayHStA, MInn, no. 81589: Clipping from *Bayerischer Kurier*, 19 June 1922.

85. Ibid.: 'Eine Justizkomödie', *Münchener Post*, 29 November 1922.

86. 'Antisemitisches aus Bayern: "Nieder mit den Juden!"', *Das Jüdische Echo* 9:37, 15 September 1922, p. 466.

87. BayHStA, MInn, no. 81589: 'Deutscher Tag in Koburg', *Bayerische Zeitung* (Munich), 22 October 1922. On the National Socialist memory of this particular meeting, see BArch Berlin, NS 26/371: *Auf nach Coburg! Einladung zur Nationalsozialistischen Kundgebung in Coburg am 8. und 9. Mai 1929.*

88. BayHStA, MInn, no. 81589: 'Die bayerischen Faschisten treten auf den Plan!', *Fränkische Tagespost*, 17 October 1922.

89. 'Deutschvölkische Radauhelden', *Das Jüdische Echo* 9:40, 6 October 1922, p. 501; BayHStA, MInn, no. 81589: 'Beim Überfall auf das Deutsche Theater', *Münchener Post*, 18 October 1922.
90. 'Vom bayerischen Kriegsschauplatz: Nationalsozialistischer Hausfriedensbruch und anderes', *Das Jüdische Echo* 10:1, 5 January 1923, p. 5.
91. BayHStA, MInn, no. 81589: 'Nationalsozialistische Skandalmethoden', *Münchener Post*, 2 October 1922.
92. Maser, *Der Sturm auf die Republik*, pp. 380–2. Klintzsch never returned to the SA. He married on 8 September 1923 and in the following two years struggled to earn a living for his quickly growing family. In 1925 he became an instructor at the Hanseatic Yacht School (*Hanseatische Yacht-Schule*) in Neustadt in Holstein. From 1929 onward Klinzsch worked as an instructor at the German School of Aviation in Warnemünde and on the island of Sylt. He entered the ranks of the Luftwaffe in 1936. In 1938 he was the commander of the Airforce School of Navigation (*Navigationsschule der Luftwaffe*) in the city of Anklam in Pomerania, and from 1942 onward he served as Chief of Staff in the airforce sea-rescue forces in the German Bight; Walsdorff, 'Hans-Ulrich Klintzsch', p. 1257; LKA Stuttgart, A 127, no. 1293: Personal information form Hans-Ulrich Klintzsch (1949/50).
93. StA München, Polizeidirektion München, Personalakten, no. 10020 (Wilhelm Brückner), p. 25: Testimony of Wilhelm Brückner to the Bavarian Police, 9 May 1923. In early 1923 several SA *Hundertschaften* formed a *Bezirk*, or 'group'. Starting on 28 January 1923 each group disposed of its own 'Standarte'. The first groups were said to have been Munich I, Munich II, Landshut, and Nuremberg.
94. Ibid., p. 40: Testimony of Wilhelm Brückner to the Bavarian Police, 19 May 1923. On the origins of the SS, see Bastian Hein, *Elite für Volk und Führer? Die Allgemeine SS und ihre Mitglieder 1925–1945* (Munich: Oldenbourg, 2012), pp. 39–75; idem, *Die SS. Geschichte und Verbrechen* (Munich: Beck, 2015), pp. 7–14.
95. StA München, Pol. Dir. 6803, p. 6: Memorandum from the Bavarian Police on the Self-Defence Leagues, undated; StA München, Pol. Dir. 6803, pp. 19–20: Report by Hans Lechner from the Austrian SA to SA headquarters in Munich, 1 September 1923; StA München, Pol. Dir. 6804: Report about a meeting of the Munich SA on 11 April 1923; Noakes, *The Nazi Party in Lower Saxony*, pp. 24–5; Wackerfuss, *Stormtrooper Families*, p. 81; Daniel Schmidt, *Schützen und Dienen: Polizisten im Ruhrgebiet in Demokratie und Diktatur 1919–1939* (Essen: Klartext, 2008), p. 283.
96. On Baur, a factotum of the early NSDAP who later served as a nurse in the Dachau concentration camp, see Daniela Andre, 'Eleonore Baur – "Blutschwester Pia" oder "Engel von Dachau"', in *Rechte Karrieren in München: Von der Weimarer Zeit bis in die Nachkriegsjahre*, ed. Marita Krauss (Munich: Volk, 2010), pp. 166–85. On the biography of Ernst von Westernhagen, see von Westernhagen, *Von der Herrschaft zur Gefolgschaft*, pp. 45–66.
97. All information on this incident, if not noted otherwise, is taken from Karl-Heinz Rueß, 'Die "Schlacht am Walfischkeller": Aus der politischen Niederlage entsteht die Göppinger SA', in *Göppingen unterm Hakenkreuz*, ed. Konrad Plieninger and Karl-Heinz Rueß (Göppingen: Stadtarchiv Göppingen, 1994), pp. 12–21, here pp. 13–15.
98. Figures from the police show the participation of 1,300 SA men, 200 *Reichsflagge* men, 400 *Bund Blücher* men, 800 *Bund Oberland* men, and members of some other even smaller groups. See BayHStA, MInn, no. 81594: Letter from the Munich Police to the Bavarian Ministry of the Interior, 3 May 1923.
99. Ibid.: Letter from the Munich Police to the Bavarian Ministry of the Interior, 28 May 1923; 'Dokumente gegen "bedenkenlose Geschichtsfälschung"', *Münchener Post*, 7 January 1932.
100. Ibid.: Letter from the Munich Police to the Bavarian Ministry of the Interior, 3 May 1923.
101. Idid.: Letter from Wehrkreiskommando VIII to Reichswehrministerium, 6 May 1923.
102. Ibid.: Letter from the Munich Police to the Bavarian Ministry of the Interior, 3 May 1923.
103. Ibid.: 'Das Feldlager auf Oberwiesenfeld', *Münchener Post*, 3 May 1923.
104. One reason for von Lossow's benevolence toward the SA in 1923 was the threat of a possible German war with the French, who together with Belgian troops had occupied the demilitarized Ruhr area in January 1923. In such circumstances Röhm suggested to von

Lossow that only a close cooperation between the paramilitary leagues and the Reichswehr would allow for suitable national defence. See Eleanor Hancock, *Ernst Röhm: Hitler's SA Chief of Staff* (Houndsmills, Basingstoke: Palgrave Macmillan, 2008), pp. 51–2.

105. BayHStA, MInn, no. 81594: Letter from Wehrkreiskommando VIII to Reichswehrministerium, 6 May 1923.

106. Ibid.: 'Kurze Anfrage Nr. 664 an das Bayerische Kultusministerium', 2 May 1923. See also chapter 3.

107. Ventrone, 'Fascism and the Legacy of the Great War', p. 111.

108. Kurt Jackmush, in *Boxwoche* 1 (1923), as quoted in Erik N. Jensen, *Body by Weimar: Athletes, Gender, and German Modernity* (New York: Oxford University Press, 2010), p. 63.

109. BayHStA, MInn, no. 81594: Speech of Schweyer in the Bayerischer Landtag, 8 June 1923, in *Stenographischer Bericht über die Verhandlungen des Bayerischen Landtags*, no. 195, vol. 8, pp. 378–9. On Schweyer's perception of the early Nazi movement, see also his book *Politische Geheimverbände* (Freiburg/Breisgau: Herder, 1925).

110. Collins, *Violence*, pp. 2–4 and *passim*.

111. StA München, Pol. Dir. 6803: Police report about the meeting of the NSDAP in the Hotel Adelmann on 19 October 1921.

112. The situation was particularly chaotic in Nuremberg; see Reiche, *Development of the SA in Nürnberg*, pp. 36–40; Herbert Linder, *Von der NSDAP zur SPD: Der politische Lebensweg des Dr. Hemuth Klotz (1894–1943)* (Konstanz: UKV, 1998), pp. 48–81.

113. Konrad Heiden, *A History of National Socialism* (Abingdon: Routledge, 2010 [1934]), p. 103.

114. BayHStA, MInn, no. 81594: Confidential report, 'Aus der Rechtsbewegung', 2 June 1923; Westernhagen, *Von der Herrschaft zur Gefolgschaft*, p. 57; Andreas Hofer, *Kapitänleutnant Hellmuth von Mücke: Marineoffizier – Politiker – Widerstandskämpfer. Ein Leben zwischen den Fronten* (Marburg: Tectum, 2003), p. 51. Mücke broke with the Nazis in 1929 and committed himself to preventing Hitler from coming to power. After the Second World War he campaigned against the rearmament of the Federal Republic of Germany. On the complex biography of this forgotten but highly interesting man, see Hofer, *Kapitänleutnant Hellmuth von Mücke*; StA München, Polizeidirektion München, Personalakten, no. 10119 (Hellmuth von Mücke).

115. Hancock, *Ernst Röhm*, pp. 32–3. On the relationship between Röhm and von Epp, see Wächter, *Die Macht der Ohnmacht*, pp. 79–82.

116. Heiden, *A History of National Socialism*, pp. 8–9.

117. Nigel Jones, *Mosley* (London: Haus Publishing, 2004), p. 12.

118. For the characterization of Röhm as a 'military desperado', see Otis, *Hitler's Stormtroopers*, pp. 25–6; for a more nuanced portrayal that stresses his roots as a royalist, see Hancock, *Ernst Röhm*, pp. 7–35. On Röhm's biography, see also the literary collage by Norbert Marohn, *Röhm: Ein deutsches Leben. Romanbiografie* (Leipzig: Lychatz, 2011); Marcus Mühle, *Ernst Röhm: Eine biografische Skizze* (Berlin: Wissenschaftlicher Verlag, 2016). For biographical studies on important leaders of the extreme right in interwar Europe, see Martyn Rady and Rebecca Haynes (eds), *In the Shadow of Hitler: Personalities of the Right in Central and Eastern Europe* (London: I. B. Tauris, 2011).

119. Hancock, *Ernst Röhm*, p. 1. Her perspective is partly influenced by the writings of the German historian and former SA-*Führer* Heinrich Bennecke; see Bennecke, *Hitler und die SA*, p. 23. Othmar Plöckinger likewise stresses that Röhm was of 'utmost importance' for the early SA; see Plöckinger, *Unter Soldaten und Agitatoren*, p. 175. For more on this perspective, established very early, see Heiden, *A History of National Socialism*, p. 39.

120. Ernst Röhm, *Geschichte eines Hochverräters* (Munich: Eher, 1928, with several editions to follow). The first abbreviated English edition was published only in 2012: Ernst Röhm, *The Memoirs of Ernst Röhm* (London: Frontline, 2012). Although Röhm's book gives a reliable picture of his political philosophy, it is less trustworthy when it comes to his role in the early Nazi movement.

121. Hanns H. Hofmann, *Der Hitlerputsch: Krisenjahre deutscher Geschichte 1920 bis 1924* (Munich: Nymphenburger, 1961), p. 75; Hancock, *Ernst Röhm*, pp. 37–45.

122. Röhm, *The Memoirs of Ernst Röhm*, p. 87.

123. See among others Evans, *The Coming of the Third Reich*, pp. 176–94; Kershaw, *Hitler 1889–1936*, pp. 253–67; Hoffmann, *Der Hitlerputsch*, pp. 142–217; Otis, *Hitler's Stormtroopers*, pp. 72–82.

124. Conan Fischer convincingly argues that the failure of the German passive-resistance campaign had a very negative impact on the population's acceptance of the Republic well beyond 1923. Even if the Weimar Republic had lasted for another decade, the 'emotional engagement with the new republican order was as good as dead and buried', he claimed. See Conan Fischer, *The Ruhr Crisis* (Oxford and New York: Oxford University Press, 2003), p. 290.

125. Evans, *The Coming of the Third Reich*, p. 194.

126. On Hitler's arrest, see Ludecke, *I Knew Hitler*, p. 135.

127. It is not without irony that the majority of those killed on 9 November were members of the *Bund Oberland* and Röhm's *Reichskriegsflagge*, but not genuine members of the SA. See Hofmann, *Der Hitler-Putsch*, p. 271.

128. On the cult of the martyrs of 9 November 1923, see the excellent analysis by Behrenbeck, *Der Kult um die toten Helden*, pp. 299–313; on Wessel's life and the cult that was established at his death, see Siemens, *Making of a Nazi Hero*. On SA 'martyrdom', see also Reichardt, *Faschistische Kampfbünde*, pp. 548–60.

129. Paradigmatic in this respect is Koch, *Männer im Braunhemd*, p. 41; for a recent analytical discussion of how (National Socialists') sacrifice and violence were linked, see David Pan, *Sacrifice in the Modern World: On the Particularity and Generality of Nazi Myth* (Evanston, IL: Northwestern University Press, 2012).

130. Röhm, *The Memoirs of Ernst Röhm*, p. 209. Göring, who at the time was suffering from a badly healed leg wound he had received in November 1923, soon left for Italy, where he attempted to intensify the contacts between the Italian Fascists and the German National Socialists. See Michael Palumbo, 'Goering's Italian Exile 1924–1925', *Journal of Modern History* 50:1 (1978), pp. D1035–D1051.

131. Röhm, *The Memoirs of Ernst Röhm*, pp. 209–10.

132. On the *Frontbann*, see Hancock, *Ernst Röhm*, pp. 71–81; Werner, *SA und NSDAP*, pp. 175–293; Röhm, *Memoirs of Ernst Röhm*, pp. 210–35.

133. For an overview, see Bruno Thoß, 'Deutscher Notbann, 1924–1926', *Historisches Lexikon Bayerns*, http://www.historisches-lexikon-bayerns.de/Lexikon/Deutscher Notbann. For an inside glimpse into the state's calculations, see BayHStA IV, Bestand Bayern und Reich, no. 65: highly confidential letter from the State Minister of the Interior, Franz Schweyer, to Dr Essel in Ebersberg, 10 April 1924.

134. Hancock, *Ernst Röhm*, pp. 75–6.

135. The 'National Socialist Freedom Party' existed only from 1924 to 1925. It was a merger of the more traditional *Deutschvölkische Freiheitspartei*, or 'German Völkisch Freedom Party' (DVFP), with the 'National Socialist Freedom Movement', a successor organization to the banned NSDAP.

136. Werner, *SA und NSDAP*, pp. 187–9.

137. On this lack of accord between Hitler and Röhm, see Hancock, *Ernst Röhm*, pp. 72–5, 79–81.

138. Adolf Hitler, Proclamation to refound the NSDAP, *Völkischer Beobachter*, 26 February 1925, as quoted in Hein, *Elite für Volk und Führer?*, pp. 40–1. For a very early critical assessment of this 'turn', see Schweyer, *Politische Geheimverbände*, pp. 118–19.

139. Werner, *SA und NSDAP*, pp. 299–304.

140. Adolf Hitler, *Mein Kampf*, 851st edn (Munich: Eher, 1943), pp. 604–5, 611, 620.

141. Ibid., pp. 603–4.

142. On the history of the Red Front Fighters League, see Kurt G. P. Schuster, *Der Rote Frontkämpferbund: Beiträge zur Geschichte und Organisationsstruktur eines politischen Kampfbundes* (Düsseldorf: Droste, 1975); Sara Ann Sewell, 'Bolshevizing Communist Women: The Red Women and Girls' League in Weimar Germany', *Central European History* 45 (2012), pp. 268–305.

143. BArch Berlin, NS 23/510: Decree 'An die gesamte nationalsozialistische Presse', 28 September 1926.

144. Noël O'Sullivan, *Fascism* (London and Melbourne: J. M. Dent, 1983), p. 43.
145. HA-Spiegel, Personal Papers of Heinz Höhne, no. 242: Letter from Franz Pfeffer von Salomon to the regional party leaders of the NSDAP, 1 October 1926.

Chapter 2

1. Franz Neumann, *Behemoth: The Structure and Practice of National Socialism, 1933–1944*, with an introduction by Peter Hayes (Chicago, IL: Ivan R. Dee, 2009), p. 436.
2. See, for example, Rösch, *Die Münchner NSDAP*, pp. 122–3.
3. Longerich, *Geschichte der SA*, pp. 52–3.
4. On the origins of the unusual name, see Mark A. Fraschka, *Franz Pfeffer von Salomon: Hitlers vergessener Oberster SA-Führer* (Göttingen: Wallstein, 2016), pp. 229–32.
5. For biographical details on von Pfeffer, see ibid. and Hermann Weiß, 'Pfeffer von Salomon, Franz', *Neue Deutsche Biographie* 20 (2001), pp. 310ff, http://www.deutsche-biographie.de/pnd124769810.html.
6. Heiden, *A History of National Socialism*, p. 123. On Kaufmann, see Frank Bajohr, 'Gauleiter in Hamburg: Zur Person und Tätigkeit Karl Kaufmanns', *Vierteljahrshefte für Zeitgeschichte* 43:2 (1995), pp. 267–95.
7. See also Longerich, *Geschichte der SA*, p. 54.
8. On the early HJ and its members, see Peter D. Stachura, *Nazi Youth in the Weimar Republic* (Santa Barbara, CA: Clio, 1975); Michael H. Kater, *Hitler Youth* (Cambridge, MA, and London: Harvard University Press, 2004), pp. 15–28.
9. Hein, *Elite für Volk und Führer?*, pp. 47–50, 65; RGVA, Osobyi Archives, Fond 720, Opis 1, no. 47, p. 200: Adolf Hitler, Order from 7 November 1930.
10. From 1931 onward, SA groups were termed *Scharen*, which is best translated as 'hordes' or 'bands'.
11. The SA's new structure is here described according to a transcript of *Vorwärts* from 21 December 1926 and to Der Oberste SA-Führer, *Erlaß Nr. 2* (Gliederung der SA), 20 February 1931, both in StA München, Pol. Dir. 6805. For an overview of the organizational changes within the SA between 1923 and 1935, see Campbell, *SA Generals and the Rise of Nazism*, pp. 161–2.
12. Bessel, 'Militarismus im innenpolitischen Leben der Weimarer Republik', p. 210; Helge Matthiesen, *Greifswald in Vorpommern: Konservatives Milieu in Kaiserreich, in Demokratie und Diktatur 1900–1990* (Düsseldorf: Droste, 2000), p. 270.
13. For an illustrated overview of these insignias and their corresponding ranks and units, see Ruhl and Starke (eds), *Adolf Hitlers Braunhemden*.
14. StA München, Pol. Dir. 6805: Transcript of the *Lagebericht* from the Berlin Police, no. 128, 20 February 1929; 'SA-Versicherung der NSDAP', *Völkischer Beobachter*, 12 December 1928.
15. For details on these commercial activities, see chapter 3; for an extensive summary of Pfeffer von Salomon's reforms, see also Fraschka, *Franz Pfeffer von Salomon*, pp. 342–64.
16. StA München, Pol. Dir. 6805: Transcript of the *Lagebericht* from the Berlin Police, no. 128, 20 February 1929.
17. Werner, *SA und NSDAP*, p. 412. A Nazi newspaper account in May 1931 provides the number of 2,055 reported cases for the five-month period between 1 January and 6 May 1931; see RGVA, Osobyi Archives, Fond 720, Opis 1, no. 44, p. 19: 'Achtung, Parteigenossen!', *Völkischer Beobachter*, 12 May 1931.
18. Joachim C. Häberlen, *Vertrauen und Politik im Alltag: Die Arbeiterbewegung in Leipzig und Lyon im Moment der Krise 1929–1933/38* (Göttingen: Vandenhoeck & Ruprecht, 2013), p. 31.
19. See, above all, Schmiechen-Ackermann, *Nationalsozialismus und Arbeitermilieus*, pp. 108–435. On the SA in Hamburg, see in particular Wackerfuss, *Stormtrooper Families*; Anthony McElligott, *Contested City: Municipal Politics and the Rise of Nazism in Altona, 1917–1937* (Ann Arbor, MI: University of Michigan Press, 1998); idem, '". . . und so kam es zu einer schweren Schlägerei": Straßenschlachten in Altona und Hamburg am Ende der Weimarer Republik', in *'Hier war doch alles nicht so schlimm': Wie die Nazis in Hamburg den Alltag eroberten*, ed. Maike Bruhns, Thomas Krause, and Anthony McElligott (Hamburg: VSA, 1984), pp. 58–87; Thomas Krause, *Hamburg wird braun: Der Aufstieg der NSDAP 1921–1933*

(Hamburg: Ergebnisse Verlag, 1987); idem, 'Von der Sekte zur Massenbewegung: Die Hamburger NSDAP von 1922 bis 1933', in *Hier war doch alles nicht so schlimm*', pp. 18–51; Werner Jochmann, *Nationalsozialismus und Revolution: Ursprung und Geschichte der NSDAP in Hamburg 1922–1933. Dokumente* (Frankfurt am Main: Europäische Verlagsanstalt, 1963).

20. Wackerfuss, *Stormtrooper Families*, p. 34; Daniel Siemens, 'Prügelpropaganda: Die SA und der nationalsozialistische Mythos vom "Kampf um Berlin"', in *Berlin 1933–1945*, ed. Michael Wildt and Christoph Kreutzmüller (Munich: Siedler, 2013), pp. 33–48, here p. 40.

21. On the development of the Nazi movement in Berlin and, in particular, the violent 'street politics' that occurred there, see Eve Rosenhaft, *Beating the Fascists? The German Communists and Political Violence, 1929–1933* (Cambridge: Cambridge University Press, 1983); Pamela E. Swett, *Neighbors and Enemies: The Culture of Radicalism in Berlin* (Cambridge and New York: Cambridge University Press, 2004); Anders G. Kjøstved, 'The Dynamics of Mobilisation: The Nazi Movement in Weimar Berlin', *Politics, Religion & Ideology* 14:3 (2013), pp. 338–54; Benjamin C. Hett, *Burning the Reichstag: An Investigation into the Third Reich's Enduring Mystery* (Oxford: Oxford University Press, 2014), pp. 38–59; Andreas Wirsching, *Vom Weltkrieg zum Bürgerkrieg? Politischer Extremismus in Deutschland und Frankreich, 1918–1933/39: Berlin und Paris im Vergleich* (Munich: Oldenbourg, 1999), pp. 437–67; Wildt and Kreutzmüller (eds), *Berlin 1933–1945*; Rüdiger Hachtmann, Thomas Schaarschmidt, and Winfried Süß (eds), *Berlin im Nationalsozialismus: Politik und Gesellschaft 1945* (Göttingen: Wallstein, 2011). For detailed local studies on particular neighbourhoods, see Oliver Reschke, *Kampf um den Kiez: Der Aufstieg der NSDAP im Zentrum Berlins 1925–1933* (Berlin: Trafo, 2014); idem, *Der Kampf um die Macht in einem Berliner Arbeiterbezirk: Nationalsozialisten am Prenzlauer Berg 1925–1933* (Berlin: Trafo, 2008); idem, *Der Kampf der Nationalsozialisten um den roten Friedrichshain (1925–1933)* (Berlin: Trafo, 2004).

22. See Ziemann, 'Germany after the First World War'; Dirk Schumann, 'Einheitssehnsucht und Gewaltakzeptanz: Politische Grundpositionen des deutschen Bürgertums nach 1918 (mit vergleichenden Überlegungen zu den britischen middle classes)', in *Der Erste Weltkrieg und die europäische Nachkriegsordnung: Sozialer Wandel und Formveränderung der Politik*, ed. Hans Mommsen (Cologne: Böhlau, 2000), pp. 83–105.

23. Rudy Koshar, 'From Stammtisch to Party: Nazi Joiners and the Contradictions of Grass-Roots Fascism in Weimar Germany', in *The Journal of Modern History* 59:1 (1987), pp. 1–24, here p. 2. On the rise of National Socialism in the countryside, see in particular Wolfram Pyta, *Dorfgemeinschaft und Parteipolitik 1918–1933: Die Verschränkung von Milieu und Parteien in den protestantischen Landgebieten Deutschlands in der Weimarer Republik* (Düsseldorf: Droste, 1996), pp. 324–432; Frank Bösch, *Das konservative Milieu: Vereinskultur und lokale Sammlungspolitik in ost- und westdeutschen Regionen (1900–1960)* (Göttingen: Wallstein, 2002); Zdenek Zofka, *Die Ausbreitung des Nationalsozialismus auf dem Lande: Eine regionale Fallstudie zur politischen Einstellung der Landbevölkerung in der Zeit des Aufstiegs und der Machtergreifung der NSDAP 1928–1936* (Munich: Wölfle, 1979), pp. 93–132. For work on Weimar elections, see Jürgen W. Falter, *Hitlers Wähler* (Munich: Beck, 1991); idem, *Zur Soziographie des Nationalsozialismus: Studien zu den Wählern und Mitgliedern der NSDAP* (Cologne: Gesis, 2013); on the electoral behaviour of women in particular, see Helen Boak, 'Mobilising Women for Hitler: The Female Nazi Voter', in *Working Towards the Führer: Essays in Honour of Sir Ian Kershaw*, ed. Anthony McElligott and Tim Kirk (Manchester: Manchester University Press, 2004), pp. 68–92.

24. Exemplary local and regional studies include Andrew Stewart Bergerson, *Ordinary Germans in Extraordinary Times: The Nazi Revolution in Hildesheim* (Bloomington and Indianapolis, IN: Indiana University Press, 2004); Michael Schepua, *Nationalsozialismus in der pfälzischen Provinz: Herrschaftspraxis und Alltagsleben in den Gemeinden des heutigen Landkreises Ludwigshafen 1933–1945* (Mannheim: Palatium, 2000), pp. 71–165; Szejnmann, *Nazism in Central Germany*; Johnpeter Horst Grill, *The Nazi Movement in Baden 1920–1945* (Chapel Hill, NC: University of North Carolina Press, 1983); Volker Franke, *Der Aufstieg der NSDAP in Düsseldorf: Die nationalsozialistische Basis in einer katholischen Großstadt* (Essen: Die Blaue Eule, 1987); Klaus Tenfelde, *Proletarische Provinz: Radikalisierung und Widerstand in Penzberg/Oberbayern 1900–1945* (Munich and Vienna: Oldenbourg, 1982); Rainer Hambrecht, *Der Aufstieg der NSDAP in Mittel- und Oberfranken (1925–1933)* (Nuremberg:

Stadtarchiv, 1976); Thomas Schnabel (ed.), *Die Machtergreifung in Südwestdeutschland: Das Ende der Weimarer Republik in Baden und Württemberg, 1928–1933* (Stuttgart: Kohlhammer, 1982); Eberhart Schön, *Die Entstehung des Nationalsozialismus in Hessen* (Meisenhein am Glan: Anton Hain, 1972); Frank Bajohr (ed.), *Norddeutschland im Nationalsozialismus* (Hamburg: Ergebnisse-Verlag, 1993).

25. In Berlin the SA in 1926 comprised about 400–450 men, see Bernd Kessinger, *Die Nationalsozialisten in Berlin-Neukölln 1925–1933* (Berlin: Vergangenheitsverlag, 2013), p. 92; Bennecke, *Hitler und die SA*, p. 126; Martin Schuster, *Die SA in der nationalsozialistischen 'Machtergreifung' in Berlin und Brandenburg 1926–1934*, university diss., Technische Universität Berlin, 2005, pp. 39–41. In Hamburg the local SA, which after the party ban of November 1923 initially operated as the Blücher Gymnastic, Sports, and Hiking Club, attracted only 30–40 men in 1924, 60 men in early 1926, and some 350 in the summer of 1927: see Wackerfuss, *Stormtrooper Families*, pp. 90, 96, 101, 105; Krause, *Hamburg wird braun*, pp. 96–7. SA membership figures for several other large German cities are provided in Reichardt, *Faschistische Kampfbünde*, p. 271.

26. Rösch, *Die Münchner NSDAP*, pp. 122–5.

27. BArch Berlin, R 9361/II, no. 16746: Memorandum from Otto Herzog on the history of the SA in Frosen.

28. For a similar estimate, see Mühlberger, *Hitler's Followers*, p. 159. For the number of SA men present at the NSDAP party rally in Weimar in 1927, see Werner von Fichte, Typescript of a booklet on the SA: RGVA, Osobyi Archives, Fond 720, Opis 1, no. 47, pp. 372–437, here p. 380. Michael Kater gives a membership number for the SA of 15,000 for early 1929: see Kater, 'Ansätze zu einer Soziologie der SA bis zur Röhm-Krise', in *Soziale Bewegung und politische Verfassung: Beiträge zur Geschichte der modernen Welt*, ed. Ulrich Engelhardt et al. (Stuttgart: Klett, 1976), pp. 798–831, here p. 799.

29. Longerich, *Geschichte der SA*, p. 93; Reichardt, *Faschistische Kampfbünde*, p. 258. In slight contrast, SA General Curt von Ulrich in January 1929 overestimated the total number of stormtroopers as 50,000–60,000. See GStA PK, I. HA, Rep. 77, Titel 4043, no. 309, pp. 313–17, here p. 316: SA-Führer Ober-West Curt von Ulrich, 'Wehrhaftmachung', 21 January 1929.

30. GStA PK, VI. HA, NL Daluege, no. 9, pp. 20–4, here p. 23: Regierungsrat Bach (Darmstadt), 'Die Entwicklung der nationalsozialistischen Bewegung in Hessen, besonders im Odenwald'.

31. V. S. Khristoforov, Institut rossiĭskoĭ istorii (Rossiĭskaya akademiya nauk), Glavnoe arkhivnoe upravlenie goroda Moskvy, and Tsentralnyĭ arkhiv FSB Rossii (eds), *Oberfiurer SA Villi Redel'. Dokumenty iz arkhivov FSB Rossii* (Moscow: Izdatelstvo Glavnogo arkhivnogo upravleniya goroda Moskvy, 2012), pp. 46–7; Schön, *Die Entstehung des Nationalsozialismus in Hessen*, p. 120. For similar figures and problems in Dortmund, see the case study by Daniel Schmidt, 'Terror und Terrainkämpfe: Sozialprofil und soziale Praxis der SA in Dortmund 1925–1933', *Beiträge zur Geschichte Dortmunds und der Grafschaft Mark* 96/97 (2007), pp. 251–92; for Danzig, see Hans Sponholz, *Danzig – deine SA! Einsatz und Bewährung im Polenfeldzug* (Munich: Eher, 1940), pp. 26–7.

32. Gerhard Paul, *Die NSDAP des Saargebietes 1920–1935: Der verspätete Aufstieg der NSDAP in der katholisch-proletarischen Provinz* (Saarbrücken: Saarbrücker Druckerei und Verlag, 1987), p. 121.

33. Schmidt, *Schützen und Dienen*, p. 283; Thomas Schnabel, 'Die NSDAP in Württemberg 1928–1933: Die Schwäche einer regionalen Parteiorganisation', in *Die Machtergreifung in Südwestdeutschland*, ed. Thomas Schnabel, pp. 49–81, here pp. 53–4.

34. Christian Peters, *Nationalsozialistische Machtdurchsetzung in Kleinstädten: Eine vergleichende Studie zu Quakenbrück und Heide/Holstein* (Bielefeld: transcript, 2015), pp. 376, 447–9; Mühlberger, *Hitler's Followers*, p. 176; Oded Heilbronner, *Catholicism, Political Culture, and the Countryside: A Social History of the Nazi Party in South Germany* (Ann Arbor, MI: Michigan University Press, 1998), pp. 113–14.

35. Schumann, *Political Violence in the Weimar Republic*, pp. 186–204, here p. 187.

36. Longerich, *Geschichte der SA*, pp. 65–72; Campbell, *SA Generals*, pp. 71–6, 142–8. For Berlin, see Schuster, *Die SA in der nationalsozialistischen 'Machtergreifung'*, pp. 27–36.

37. Wackerfuss, *Stormtrooper Families*, pp. 104–5; BArch Berlin, NS 23/1239: Letter from the Hamburg SA to the Gausturm Nordmark, 5 April 1929.
38. Schuster, *Die SA in der nationalsozialistischen 'Machtergreifung'*, pp. 31–6; GStA PK, I. HA, Rep. 84a (Justizministerium), no. 55212.
39. For details, see Wirsching, *Vom Weltkrieg zum Bürgerkrieg?*, pp. 442–7, 589–94.
40. See, for example, *Die Tagebücher von Joseph Goebbels*, Teil 1, Band 1/II, p. 149 (entry from 15 November 1926).
41. As quoted in Noakes, *The Nazi Party in Lower Saxony*, p. 186.
42. Instructive in this respect is an SA-*Standartenbefehl* from the early 1930s which straightforwardly demands that 'more than ever before, it is necessary to rope the police in for our purposes [...] Every SA man needs to know the telephone number of his police station by heart. We have to convince those officers on duty that we don't fight for our idea out of rowdiness or by misguided activism, but that we only defend our naked lives' (GStA PK, I. HA, Rep. 219, no. 20, pp. 31–2: Typescript of an SA-*Standartenbefehl*, undated).
43. *Die Tagebücher von Joseph Goebbels*, Teil 1, Band 1/II, p. 153 (entry from 28 November 1926).
44. Gailus and Siemens, '*Hass und Begeisterung bilden Spalier*', p. 110; Siemens, *The Making of a Nazi Hero*, p. 60.
45. As quoted in Wackerfuss, *Stormtrooper Families*, pp. 78–9.
46. On this point, see in particular Reichardt, *Faschistische Kampfbünde*, pp. 416–18, 435–68; Wackerfuss, *Stormtrooper Families*, pp. 173–199; Swett, *Neighbors and Enemies*, pp. 237–60. For a detailed case study, see Reschke, *Der Kampf der Nationalsozialisten um den roten Friedrichshain*.
47. RGVA, Osobyi Archives, Fond 720, Opis 1, no. 47, pp. 143–53, here p. 145: Memorandum of the Baden police, *Die SA und SS der NSDAP*, Karlsruhe, 15 May 1931.
48. Kjøstved, 'Dynamics of Mobilisation', pp. 350–2; Krause, *Hamburg wird braun*, pp. 146–8; Longerich, *Geschichte der SA*, pp. 136–44.
49. Thomas Welskopp, *Das Banner der Brüderlichkeit: Die deutsche Sozialdemokratie vom Vormärz bis zum Sozialistengesetz* (Bonn: Dietz, 2000); Klaus Tenfelde (ed.), *Streik: Zur Geschichte des Arbeitskampfes in Deutschland während der Industrialisierung* (Munich: Beck, 1981).
50. Kjøstved, 'Dynamics of Mobilisation', pp. 343–6; Rudy Koshar, 'Political Gangsters and Nazism: Some Comments on Richard Hamilton's Theory of Fascism. A Review Article', *Comparative Studies in Society and History* 28:4 (1986), pp. 785–93; Felix Schnell, 'Gewalt und Gewaltforschung', p. 19.
51. Clayton A. Hartjen, 'Review of Hazen, Jennifer M; Rodgers, Dennis (eds): *Global Gangs: Street Violence across the World*', *H-Socialisms, H-Net Reviews*, August 2014, https://www.h-net.org/reviews/showrev.php?id=42245. For the gang-like character of Hungarian paramilitary violence after the First World War, see Bodó, 'Heroes or Thieves?', pp. 72, 83–9.
52. Ernst Haffner, *Jugend auf der Landstraße Berlin* (Berlin: Cassirer, 1932). For a contemporary critique, see Siegfried Kracauer, 'Großstadtjugend ohne Arbeit: Zu den Büchern von Lamm und Haffner', in *Essays, Feuilletons, Rezensionen*, vol. 5:4 (Frankfurt am Main: Suhrkamp, 2011), pp. 240–3. A new edition of Haffner's novel was published in 2013: Ernst Haffner, *Blutsbrüder: Ein Berliner Cliquenroman* (Berlin: Walde + Graf, 2013).
53. Eberhard Knödler-Bunte, 'Exkurs: Die Binnenstruktur der NSDAP und SA', *Ästhetik & Kommunikation* 26 (1976), pp. 35–7, here p. 35.
54. On the 'Captain of Köpenick' episode and its effects, see Philipp Müller, *Auf der Suche nach dem Täter: Die öffentliche Dramatisierung von Verbrechen im Berlin des Kaiserreichs* (Frankfurt am Main: Campus, 2005), pp. 173–354; on the relevance of Heinrich Mann's novel, see Georg Bollenbeck, 'Ein beweglicher Er-Erzähler, komplexe Erzählhaltungen und epochale Repräsentanz: Heinrich Mann, *Der Untertan*', in *Psyche und Epochennorm: Festschrift für Heinz Thomas zum 60. Geburtstag*, ed. Henning Krauss et al. (Heidelberg: Winter, 2005), pp. 499–519.
55. On the SA uniform and its effects, see Reichardt, *Faschistische Kampfbünde*, pp. 579–89; Noakes, *Nazi Party in Lower Saxony*, pp. 185–6; Homberger, *Fashioning German Fascism*; Balister, *Gewalt und Ordnung: Kalkül und Faszination der SA* (Münster: Westfälisches Dampfboot, 1989), pp. 96–102; Rohkrämer, *Die fatale Attraktion des Nationalsozialismus*, p. 152.

56. Hitler's orders to Pfeffer von Salomon are quoted according to the transcript of an article in *Vorwärts*, no. 54, 4 February 1927, in StA München, Pol. Dir. 6805.

57. RGVA, Osobyi Archives, Fond 720, Opis 1, no. 47, pp. 143–53, here p. 146: Memorandum of the Baden police, *Die SA und SS der NSDAP*, Karlsruhe, 15 May 1931.

58. On membership numbers of the *Stahlhelm*, see Volker R. Berghahn, *Der Stahlhelm: Bund der Frontsoldaten 1918–1935* (Düsseldorf: Droste, 1966), pp. 85, 286–7.

59. On the Red Front Fighters League, see Sewell, 'Bolshevizing Communist Women'; Voigt, *Kampfbünde der Arbeiterbewegung*; Kurt Finker, *Geschichte des roten Frontkämpferbundes* (Berlin: Dietz, 1981); Schuster, *Der Rote Frontkämpferbund*.

60. It is noteworthy, however, that an insider like the former Berlin police president Albert C. Grzesinski in retrospect spoke of an 'incipient civil war' when describing the situation in the German capital in 1930. See Grzesinski, *Inside Germany*, p. 130. At around this time the branch of the NSDAP located in the capital considered itself to be already 'in the thick of a civil war'. See GStA PK, I. HA, Rep. 77 titl. 4043, no. 302, pp. 221–6, here p. 224: Transcript of a speech by Martin Löpelmann, 12 August 1931.

61. LArch Berlin, A-Rep. 358-01, no. 2165, p. 37: 'Schlagt die Faschisten, wo ihr sie trefft!', *Die Rote Fahne*, 23 January 1930; LArch Berlin, A-Rep. 358-01, no. 2165, pp. 4–6: 'Nieder mit den faschistischen Mördern!', *Die Rote Fahne*, 29 August 1929.

62. Unlike the Communists and the Nazis, which both categorically opposed the 'system of Weimar', the *Reichsbanner* leadership defended the state monopoly on violence. Whereas the rank-and-file *Reichsbanner* men repeatedly engaged in violent attacks on their opponents, their regional leaders – among them the Hamburg police president Adoph Schönfelder and the young circuit judge Fritz Bauer in Stuttgart – urged their men to stage powerful demonstrations but to abstain from physical violence. See McElligott, '. . . und so kam es zu einer schweren Schlägerei', pp. 66–7; Ronen Steinke, *Fritz Bauer oder Auschwitz vor Gericht* (Munich and Zurich: Piper, 2013), pp. 89–91; Michael Trauthig, *Im Kampf um Glauben und Kirche: Eine Studie über Gewaltakzeptanz und Krisenmentalität der württembergischen Protestanten zwischen 1918 und 1933* (Leinfelden-Echterdingen: DRW-Verlag, 1999), pp. 53–4.

63. Hubert R. Knickerbocker, *The German Crisis* (New York: Farrar & Rinehart, 1932), p. 130; Jacques Decour, *Philisterburg* (Berlin: Die Andere Bibliothek, 2014), p. 70.

64. 'Kütemeyer – "geräuschlose Gegenarbeit des CV"', in *Anti-Anti: Tatsachen zur Judenfrage*, ed. CV-Verein (Berlin: Philo, 1932), p. 35 a–b.

65. Schuster, *Die SA in der nationalsozialistischen 'Machtergreifung'*, pp. 113–14.

66. 'Der Begräbnis-Umzug der Hakenkreuzler verboten', *Tempo*, 23 November 1928, p. 1.

67. See the official directive in GStA PK, I. HA, Rep. 77, Titel 4043, no. 309, p. 145.

68. In 1930 the authorities of Hesse, Bavaria, Prussia, Baden, and Hamburg prohibited the public wearing of the SA uniform for some time but likewise met with limited success; see Reichardt, *Faschistische Kampfbünde*, pp. 231–2.

69. Paul Hoser, 'Sturmabteilung (SA), 1921–1923/1925–1945', *Historisches Lexikon Bayerns*, http://www.historisches-lexikon-bayerns.de/artikel/artikel_44621.

70. Maik Hattenhorst, *Magdeburg 1933: Eine rote Stadt wird braun* (Halle an der Saale: Mitteldeutscher Verlag, 2009), p. 100.

71. GStA PK, XX. HA, Rep. 240 B 31 c, pp. 179–90, here p. 183: 'Erste Anfänge der SA in Ostpreußen'.

72. GStA PK, I. HA, NL Daluege, no. 9, pp. 32–42: Verdict of the Kammergericht, 13 March 1931.

73. There is a long debate on the political leanings of the German judiciary in the 1920s and its contribution to the misery of the Republic that cannot be dealt with here. See Ralph Angermund, *Deutsche Richterschaft 1919–1945: Krisenerfahrung, Illusion, politische Rechtsprechung* (Frankfurt am Main: Fischer, 1990); Daniel Siemens, 'Die "Vertrauenskrise der Justiz" in der Weimarer Republik', in *Die 'Krise' der Weimarer Republik: Zur Kritik eines Deutungsmusters*, ed. Moritz Föllmer and Rüdiger Graf (Frankfurt am Main: Campus, 2005), pp. 139–63, with further references.

74. Siemens, 'SA-Gewalt, nationalsozialistische "Revolution" und Staatsräson: Der Fall des Chemnitzer Kriminalamtschefs Albrecht Böhme 1933/34', in *Die Linke im Visier: Zur Errichtung der Konzentrationslager*, ed. Nikolaus Wachsmann and Sybille Steinbacher

(Göttingen: Wallstein, 2014), pp. 191–213, here p. 191. For Saxony, see also Andreas Peschel (ed.), *Die SA in Sachsen vor der 'Machtübernahme': Nachgelassenes von Heinrich Bennecke (1902–1972)* (Markkleeberg: Sax, 2012), pp. 41–4, 66, 75. For a general analysis, see Schmidt, *Schützen und Dienen*, pp. 250–310. For the relation between the German police and National Socialism, see Joachim Schröder, *Die Münchner Polizei und der Nationalsozialismus* (Essen: Klartext, 2013); KZ-Gedenkstätte Neuengamme (ed.), *Polizei, Verfolgung und Gesellschaft im Nationalsozialismus* (Bremen: Edition Temmen, 2013); Thomas Roth, *'Verbrechensbekämpfung' und soziale Ausgrenzung im nationalsozialistischen Köln: Kriminalpolizei, Strafjustiz und abweichendes Verhalten zwischen Machtübernahme und Kriegsende* (Cologne: Emons, 2010); Patrick Wagner, *Volksgemeinschaft ohne Verbrecher: Konzeptionen und Praxis der Kriminalpolizei in der Zeit der Weimarer Republik und des Nationalsozialismus* (Hamburg: Christians, 1996).

75. Andreas Wagner, *'Machtergreifung' in Sachsen: NSDAP und staatliche Verwaltung, 1930–1935* (Cologne: Böhlau, 2004), pp. 31–69.

76. Arno Schreiber, Speech in the Saxon *Landtag*, 26 April 1932, *Verhandlungen des Sächsischen Landtags*, 5. Wahlperiode, vol. 3, Dresden 1932, p. 2,991. In the Ruhr the NSDAP in early 1932 claimed that about 35 per cent of all police officers were sympathetic to the Nazi movement; GStA PK, I. HA, Rep. 77 titl. 4043, no. 311, pp. 25–6: Report from the Berlin Police President to the Regierungspräsident in Düsseldorf, 4 February 1932.

77. Wagner, *Volksgemeinschaft ohne Verbrecher*, pp. 180–7. See also 'Wegen Hochverrats verhaftet. Nationalsozialistische Spionage in der Polizei', *Vossische Zeitung*, 10 March 1932, p. 1; 'Grzesinski erklärt', *Vossische Zeitung*, 12 March 1932, p. 3.

78. Karl Gerlach, speech in the Saxon *Landtag*, 26 April 1932, *Verhandlungen des Sächsischen Landtags*, 5. Wahlperiode, vol. 3, Dresden 1932, pp. 2,946–7.

79. GStA PK, VI. HA, NL Daluege, no. 9, pp. 20–4, here p. 23: Regierungsrat Bach (Darmstadt), 'Die Entwicklung der nationalsozialistischen Bewegung in Hessen, besonders im Odenwald.'

80. 'Hat man Ihnen schon zugeflüstert, dass . . .', *Ulk*, 18 December 1930.

81. Siegfried Kracauer, 'Zertrümmerte Fensterscheiben', *Frankfurter Zeitung*, 16 October 1930, as quoted in idem, *Essays, Feuilletons, Rezensionen*, 5:3 (1928–31), ed. Inka Mülder-Bach (Frankfurt am Main: Suhrkamp, 2011), pp. 348–50, here p. 348.

82. Erich Kästner, *Fabian: The Story of a Moralist*, trans. Cyrus Brooks (London: Libris 1990), p. 48.

83. Jürgen W. Falter, Thomas Lindenberger, and Siegfried Schumann, *Wahlen und Abstimmungen in der Weimarer Republik: Materialien zum Wahlverhalten 1919–1933* (Munich: Beck, 1986), p. 41; GStA PK, I. HA, Rep. 219, no. 20, pp. 196–9: Circular from the leadership of the KPD at the Ruhr, 12 December 1931.

84. For careful discussions, see Paul, *Aufstand der Bilder*, pp. 133–42; Balister, *Gewalt und Ordnung*, in particular pp. 55–62, 198–204; Thomas Childers and Eugene Weiss, 'Voters and Violence: Political Violence and the Limits of National Socialist Mass Mobilisation', *German Studies Review* 13:3 (1990), pp. 481–98.

85. Malinowski, *Vom König zum Führer: Sozialer Niedergang und politische Radikalisierung im deutschen Adel zwischen Kaiserreich und NS-Staat*, 3rd edn (Berlin: Akademie, 2003), p. 476.

86. This is one of the central findings of Timothy S. Brown, *Weimar Radicals: Nazis and Communists between Authenticity and Performance* (New York and Oxford: Berghahn, 2009).

87. Statement of the former SA Brigade Leader Franz Bock at the Nuremberg trials, Monday, 12 August 1946, http://www.nizkor.org/hweb/imt/tgmwc/tgmwc-21/tgmwc-21-201-08.shtml.

88. Roger Griffin, 'Political Modernism and the Cultural Production of "Personalities of the Right" in Inter-War Europe', in *In the Shadow of Hitler*, ed. Rady and Haynes, pp. 20–37, here p. 23; idem, 'Fixing Solutions: Fascist Temporalities as Remedies for Liquid Modernity', *Journal of Modern European History* 13:1 (2015) pp. 5–22.

89. *Die Tagebücher von Joseph Goebbels*, Teil 1, Band 1/II, p. 147 (entry from 11 November 1926).

90. The official crime statistics, as published by the Reich justice minister, are only of limited use, as they contain only those crimes that were punished and furthermore do not identify the political affiliation of those condemned as criminals. Overall, criminality did not increase considerably in 1931 and 1932, and it even remained lower in those years than in those immediately following the First World War. However, convictions for high treason and

for violations of the Reich president's decrees on political terrorism sharply increased. See Reichsjustizministerium und Statistisches Reichsamt (ed.), *Kriminalstatistik für das Jahr 1932*: Statistik des Deutschen Reichs 448 (Berlin: Verlag für Sozialpolitik, 1935), p. 20.

91. McElligott, '". . . und so kam es zu einer schweren Schlägerei"', pp. 60–4, 69. For similar forms of violence in Leipzig, see Häberlen, *Vertrauen und Politik im Alltag*, pp. 53–61; for Dortmund, see Schmidt, 'Terror und Terrainkämpfe', pp. 275–80.

92. BArch Berlin, R1501, no. 20234, p. 16: Reichsministerium des Innern, Mis I A 2000/13.5, 13 May 1932, as quoted in Camiel Oomen, *'Wir sind die Soldaten der Republik!' Das Berliner Reichsbanner und die Politische Gewalt 1930–1933*, doctoral diss., Universiteit Utrecht, 2007, p. 21.

93. Noakes, *The Nazi Party in Lower Saxony*, p. 186.

94. IfZ Archive, ED 414, vol. 181: 'Statistik der Gewalt', *Vossische Zeitung*, 19 December 1931.

95. Häberlen, *Vertrauen und Politik im Alltag*, p. 44.

96. As quoted in Schumann, *Politische Gewalt in der Weimarer Republik*, pp. 306–7.

97. Rosenhaft, *Beating the Fascists?*, p. 6.

98. See, among others, GStA PK, I. HA, Rep. 77 titl. 4041, no. 302, pp. 69–70: Letter from the Berlin Police President to the Prussian Minister of the Interior on the search of weapons at an NSDAP meeting, 9 May 1930.

99. Grzesinski, *Inside Germany*, p. 132.

100. For details, see Ulrich Herbert, *Best: Biographische Studien über Radikalismus, Weltanschauung und Vernunft, 1903–1989* (Bonn: Dietz, 1996), pp. 112–19.

101. Schepua, *Nationalsozialismus in der pfälzischen Provinz*, pp. 87–91; 'Bomben für Boxheim', *Vossische Zeitung*, 10 March 1932, p. 1. On Eicke, see the detailed biographical study by Niels Weise, *Eicke: Eine SS-Karriere zwischen Nervenklinik, KZ-System und Waffen-SS* (Paderborn: Schöningh, 2013), particularly pp. 95–176 on the Palatinate bombings.

102. Herbert, *Best*, pp. 116, 118.

103. For examples, see Häberlen, *Vertrauen und Politik im Alltag*, pp. 69–72.

104. Christian Goeschel, 'The Criminal Underworld in Weimar and Nazi Germany', *History Workshop Journal* 75:1 (2013), pp. 58–80; Siemens, *Horst Wessel*, pp. 25–6, with further references.

105. Kessinger, *Die Nationalsozialisten in Berlin-Neukölln 1925–1933*, p. 98.

106. Sven Reichardt, 'Violence and Community: A Micro-Study on Nazi Storm Troopers', *Central European History* 46:2 (2013), pp. 275–97; reprinted in slightly modified form as Sven Reichardt, 'Vergemeinschaftung durch Gewalt: Der SA-"Mördersturm 33"in Berlin-Charlottenburg', in *SA-Terror als Herrschaftssicherung*, ed. Hördler, pp. 110–29.

107. StA München, Pol. Dir. 6805: Extract from Munich Police's *Lagebericht*, no. 101, Munich, 9 June 1931; Helmut von Klotz, *Wir gestalten durch unser Führerkorps die Zukunft!* (Berlin: Arbeiter-Parteikorrespondenz, 1932), p. 4.

108. Chris Bowlby, 'Blutmai 1929: Police, Parties and Proletarians in a Berlin Confrontation', *Historical Journal* 29:1 (1986), pp. 137–58; Thomas Kurz, *'Blutmai': Sozialdemokraten und Kommunisten im Brennpunkt der Berliner Ereignisse von 1929* (Bonn: Dietz, 1988); Léon Schirmann, *Altonaer Blutsonntag, 17. Juli 1932: Dichtungen und Wahrheit* (Hamburg: Ergebnisse, 1994); McElligott, *Contested City*, pp. 192–4; Trauthig, *Im Kampf um Glauben und Kirche*, p. 54.

109. Robert Gerwarth emphasizes that throughout the 1920s a cross-party consensus that the use of violence was a legitimate if not necessary tool of politics survived among the young and radical political activists that came to the fore in the latter part of the decade and into the 1930s. See Gerwarth, 'Rechte Gewaltgemeinschaften und die Stadt nach dem Ersten Weltkrieg', p. 115.

110. Grzesinski, *Inside Germany*, p. 130.

111. As quoted in Reschke, *Kampf um den Kiez*, p. 100.

112. University and City Library of Cologne, Archives (UAK), Zugang 386, no. 294: Public Prosecution Office of Cologne, Bill of indictment against Toni Winkelnkemper et al., 24 April 1931.

113. Josef Frings, later the Archbishop of Cologne and a cardinal, acted as parish priest of St Joseph in Cologne-Braunsfeld between 1928 and 1937. He gained wider popularity in post-war Germany when he defended the frequent stealing of food and coal out of necessity in the extraordinarily cold winter of 1946–7. Such acts became known as *fringsen*, meaning 'to whip' or to 'snitch' by leave of Frings. See Norbert Trippen, *Joseph Kardinal Frings (1887–1978). Band 1: Sein Wirken für das Erzbistum Köln und für die Kirche in Deutschland* (Paderborn: Schöningh, 2003).

114. See the letter from the Public Prosecution Office of Cologne to the President of the University of Cologne, 21 July 1931. On this second verdict, see in particular 'Keine Sühne für den Nazi-Überfall in Braunsfeld!', *Lokalanzeiger*, 10 October 1931 (morning edition). Both in UAK, Zugang 386, no. 294.

115. Gerhard Nebel, *'Alles Gefühl ist leiblich': Ein Stück Autobiographie*, ed. Nicolai Riedel (Marbach am Neckar: Deutsche Schillergesellschaft, 2003), pp. 130–31.

116. Paul, *Aufstand der Bilder*, pp. 133–4.

117. The Nazis at times referred to this shopping mile as 'Kohnfürstendamm', alluding to the pretended high presence of Jews there. See Kjøstved, 'Dynamics of Mobilisation', p. 341.

118. Walter, *Antisemitische Kriminalität und Gewalt*, pp. 211–21; Hecht, *Deutsche Juden und Antisemitismus in der Weimarer Republik*, pp. 236–68.

119. Herbert Linder, *Von der NSDAP zur SPD*, pp. 152–3.

120. For statistical details on unemployment in Germany at this time, see *Statistiken zu Detlev Humann: 'Arbeitsschlacht': Arbeitsbeschaffung und Propaganda in der NS-Zeit 1933–1939* (Göttingen: Wallstein, 2011), pp. 10–20, www.wallstein-verlag.de/Statistiken_Humann_AS.pdf. For the high number of unemployed in the SA, see Theodor Geiger, *Die soziale Schichtung des deutschen Volkes: Soziographischer Versuch auf statistischer Grundlage* (Stuttgart: Enke, 1932), pp. 110–11.

121. Kessinger, *Die Nationalsozialisten in Berlin-Neukölln*, p. 99; Reschke, *Kampf um den Kiez*, p. 128; Longerich, *Die braunen Bataillone*, p. 85.

122. Grant, *Stormtroopers and Crisis in the Nazi Movement*, p. 31. On 1 February 1933 the SA in the city reported a 75 per cent unemployment rate (Fischer, *Stormtroopers*, p. 48).

123. NSDAP party members contributed to the SA's budget by paying 10 and, from September 1930 onward, 20 pfennig to the group on a monthly basis. The SA therefore had a clear financial interest in its members also joining the party. See Longerich, *Geschichte der SA*, p. 134; Mühlberger, *Hitler's Followers*, p. 160. On the high turnover rates in the SA in the early 1930s, see Jamin, 'Zur Rolle der SA im nationalsozialistischen Herrschaftssystem', pp. 331–3.

124. Mann, *Fascists*, p. 168. For a more detailed discussion of this subject, see Bessel, *Political Violence and the Rise of Nazism*, pp. 45–9; Hattenhorst, *Magdeburg 1933*, pp. 106–10.

125. Walter Struve, 'Arbeiter und Nationalsozialismus in Osterode am Harz bis 1933', in *Norddeutschland im Nationalsozialismus*, ed. Frank Bajohr (Hamburg: Forschungsstelle für die Geschichte des Nationalsozialismus in Hamburg, 1993), pp. 67–82, here p. 75.

126. Bessel, *Political Violence and the Rise of Nazism*, p. 46.

127. There is extensive older research on the social composition of the SA, partly driven by the desire to demonstrate that the SA did not really take hold in working-class areas, despite its partial successes there. More recent studies, however, suggest that the SA indeed appealed to workers as the economic situation began to deteriorate starting in 1929. See Longerich, *Geschichte der SA*, pp. 81–5; Reichardt, *Faschistische Kampfbünde*, pp. 310–23; Schmiechen-Ackermann, 'Nationalsozialismus und Arbeitermilieus', pp. 268–9, 322–35; Mann, *Fascists*, pp. 167–8.

128. On the decline of alcohol consumption between 1929 and 1933 and its social and fiscal consequences, see Thomas Welskopp, 'Halbleer oder halbvoll? Alkoholwirtschaft, Alkoholkonsum und Konsumkultur in den Vereinigten Staaten und im Deutschen Reich in der Zwischenkriegszeit: Biergeschichte(n)', in *Die vielen Gesichter des Konsums: Westfalen, Deutschland und die USA 1850–2000*, ed. Michael Prinz (Paderborn: Schöningh, 2016), pp. 183–207, here pp. 201–5. For a comprehensive analysis of the SA storm taverns, see Reichardt, *Faschistische Kampfbünde*, pp. 449–68.

129. Longerich, *Geschichte der SA*, pp. 130–1; GStA PK, I. HA, Rep. 77 titl. 4043, no. 311, p. 4: Der Oberste SA-Führer on 'Arbeitsdienstpflicht', 31 December 1931.
130. Gesamtverband der christlichen Gewerkschaften Deutschlands (ed.), *Jahrbuch der christlichen Gewerkschaften 1932: Bericht über das Jahr 1931* (Berlin: Christlicher Gewerkschaftsverlag, 1932), pp. 76–7.
131. These figures are taken from the synopsis provided by Reichardt in *Faschistische Kampfbünde*, pp. 258–9.
132. BArch Berlin, NS 26/2521: Letter from Hellmuth v. Mücke to Herr Friedrich, 29 August 1929 (emphasis in original). Mücke's anger was partly motivated by his personal quarrels with the Saxon NSDAP leader Mutschmann and the SA-*Obergruppenführer* von Killinger, but his letter also attests to more widespread criticism of the party's propaganda, which played on short-lived emotions without providing lasting intellectual guidance. On this subject, see Paul, *Aufstand der Bilder*, pp. 51–2. For similar criticism from a disappointed former Nazi activist who had joined the ranks of the SPD, see Helmut von Klotz, *Wir gestalten durch unser Führerkorps die Zukunft!*; Linder, *Von der NSDAP zur SPD*, pp. 140–89.
133. In October 1927 Stennes was promoted to the position of OSAF-Ost, 'the leader of the SA in East Germany'. See Patrick Moreau, *Nationalsozialismus von links. Die 'Kampfgemeinschaft Revolutionärer Nationalsozialisten' und die 'Schwarze Front' Otto Straßers 1930–1935* (Munich: Deutsche Verlags-Anstalt, 1984), pp. 12–101; Reinhard Kühnl, *Die nationalsozialistische Linke 1925–1930* (Meisenheim am Glan: Anton Hain, 1966).
134. RGVA, Osobyi Archives, Fond 720, Opis 1, no. 43, p. 6: 'Wo stehen wir?', *Das Sprachrohr. Organ der Berliner NSDAP*, November 1930. For a clearsighted 1930 analysis of the incommensurate nature of the Nazis' economic and social positions, see Decour, *Philisterburg*, pp. 88–9.
135. RGVA, Osobyi Archives, Fond 720, Opis 1, no. 43, pp. 61: 'Politische Schulung der SA: Was trennt uns von der NSDAP?', typescript, 6 October 1931; Siemens, 'Prügelpropaganda', p. 36.
136. For details, see Hancock, *Ernst Röhm*, pp. 105–10.
137. One reason for the dissatisfaction of these men was that they had requested to be considered as candidates for parliament in the upcoming elections but after initial concessions were bypassed by Hitler and Goebbels. For details, see Sauer, 'Goebbels "Rabauken". Zur Geschichte der SA in Berlin-Brandenburg', in *Berlin in Geschichte und Gegenwart*, ed. Uwe Schaper (Berlin: Jahrbuch des Landesarchivs, 2006), pp. 107–64, here pp. 121–2; Moreau, *Nationalsozialismus von links*, pp. 71–81; Bernhard Fulda, *Press and Politics in the Weimar Republic* (Oxford and New York: Oxford University Press, 2009), pp. 159–62.
138. BArch Berlin, NS 23/510: Ernst Röhm, Decree of 31 March 1931.
139. GStA PK, I. HA, Rep. 77 titl. 4043, no. 32, pp. 147–9: Police President Berlin, Abt. IA, on the NSDAP in the capital, 27 November 1930.
140. On these events, see the excellent memorandum (most likely provided by the Berlin police): 'Gründe und Auswirkungen des Zwists Hitler-Stennes', in RGVA, Osobyi Archives, Fond 720, Opis 1, no. 47, pp. 97–110.
141. The new name of this joint group was *Nationalsozialistische Kampfgemeinschaft Deutschland*. See RGVA, Osobyi Archives, Fond 720, Opis 1, no. 43, pp. 13–14: NSKD (*Nationalsozialistische Kampfgemeinschaft Deutschland*), Die Oberste SA-Führung, SABE 6 [= SA-*Befehl* 6] from 6 June 1931. For a characteristic impression of this group's self-image as working-class militants, see also their song 'Arbeiter, Bauern, Soldaten', which was sung to the tune of 'Brüder aus Zechen und Gruben', itself a National Socialist reworking of the famous Socialist 'Brüder, zur Sonne, zur Freiheit'; ibid., p. 40.
142. RGVA, Osobyi Archives, Fond 720, Opis 1, no. 43, pp. 20–2, here p. 20: Nationalsozialistische Kampfbewegung, SA-Befehl No. 4, undated. Against this background, Jamin's verdict that 'socialist' or 'revolutionary' ideas were only of secondary importance in the two Stennes revolts should be revised; see Jamin, 'Zur Rolle der SA im nationalsozialistischen Herrschaftssystem', p. 334.
143. RGVA, Osobyi Archives, Fond 720, Opis 1, no. 43, p. 14: NSKD, Die Oberste SA-Führung, SABE 6 from 6 June 1931.

144. RGVA, Osobyi Archives, Fond 720, Opis 1, no. 43, pp. 7–8: G. Kübler, *Die 'R.K.'* *(Revolutionäre Kämpfer)*, transcript of the second letter 'Schulungsbriefe der Kampfgemeinschaft Revolutionärer Nationalsozialisten', March 1931.

145. RGVA, Osobyi Archives, Fond 720, Opis 1, no. 43, p. 55: Mitteilung Nr. 18 des Landeskriminalamts IA Berlin der Preußischen Polizei, 15 September 1931; Gailus and Siemens, *'Hass und Begeisterung bilden Spalier'*, pp. 107, 142; Krüger, 'Die Brigade Ehrhardt', p. 122.

146. RGVA, Osobyi Archives, Fond 720, Opis 1, no. 43, pp. 20–2, here p. 20: Nationalsozialistische Kampfbewegung, SA-Befehl Nr. 4, undated; Moreau, *Nationalsozialismus von links*, pp. 41–71, 102–99. On the organization of the regional groups of the Stennes SA, see also 'Anlage 1 zu Sabe 7', in RGVA, Osobyi Archives, Fond 720, Opis 1, no. 43, pp. 30–1. On Stennes's post-1934 biography, see Charles Drage, *The Amiable Prussian* (London: Blond, 1958), pp. 105–92; Mechthild Leutner (ed.), *Deutschland und China 1937–1949: Politik – Militär – Wirtschaft – Kultur. Eine Quellensammlung* (Berlin: Akademie, 1998), pp. 67, 108.

147. Open letter to Hitler, published in *Nachrichten für Stadt und Land*, 10 September 1931, as quoted in Noakes, *The Nazi Party in Lower Saxony*, pp. 184–5.

148. For a recent survey of the most prominent 'corruption scandals' in the Weimar Republic, see Annika Klein, *Korruption und Korruptionsskandale in der Weimarer Republik* (Göttingen: V&R unipress, 2014).

149. RGVA, Osobyi Archives, Fond 720, Opis 1, no. 47, pp. 97–110, here p. 101: 'Gründe und Auswirkungen des Zwists Hitler-Stennes'.

150. *Die Tagebücher von Joseph Goebbels*, Teil 1, Band 2/II, p. 361 (entry from 11 September 1932).

151. BArch Berlin, NS 23/510: Transcript of the Munich police's *Lagebericht* from 20 October 1932.

152. BArch Berlin, NS 23/337, p. 228: Development of SA membership between July 1932 and January 1933.

153. Mühlberger, *Hitler's Followers*, pp. 166–80; Reichardt, *Faschistische Kampfbünde*, pp. 267–9.

154. Mechthild Hempe, *Ländliche Gesellschaft in der Krise: Mecklenburg in der Weimarer Republik* (Cologne: Böhlau, 2002), pp. 57–128, 181–99.

155. Schuster, *Die SA in der nationalsozialistischen 'Machtergreifung'*, pp. 94–5.

156. See Geiger, *Die soziale Schichtung des deutschen Volkes*, p. 114; as well as the historical studies cited below.

157. Matthiesen, *Greifswald in Vorpommern*, p. 221.

158. Heinrich Schoene, born on 25 November 1889 in Berlin, had a remarkable career in the Third Reich. In February 1934 he was appointed Police President of the city of Königsberg as well as SA-*Gruppenführer Ostmark*. Starting 1 September 1941 he served as the General Commissar for the Volhynia and Podolia general district in the *Reichskommissariat* Ukraine. Schoene died in April 1945. For details of his biography, see BArch Berlin, SA 400003464 (Schoene, Heinrich). On his involvement in the mistreatment of civilians in Ukraine, see Karel C. Berkhoff, *Harvest of Despair: Life and Death in Ukraine under Nazi Rule* (Cambridge, MA, and London: Belknap, 2004), pp. 267–8.

159. GStA PK, I. HA, Rep. 77, titl. 4043, no. 309, pp. 337–8: Report on speeches of the leader of the SA-Gruppe Ober-Nord, Major a.d. Dinglage [Karl Dincklage] and his adjutant Schöhne [Heinrich Schoene], 8 March 1929.

160. BArch Berlin, NS 23/1239: Heinrich Schoene, *Gaubefehl*, 10 May 1929.

161. See in particular Alexander Otto-Morris, *Rebellion in the Province: The Landvolkbewegung and the Rise of National Socialism in Schleswig-Holstein* (Frankfurt am Main: Peter Lang, 2013); idem, '"Bauer, wahre dein Recht!" Landvolkbewegung und Nationalsozialismus 1928/30', in *'Siegeszug in der Nordmark': Schleswig-Holstein und der Nationalsozialismus 1925–1950. Schlaglichter – Studien – Rekonstruktionen*, ed. Kay Dohnke et al. (Kiel: Arbeitskreis zur Erforschung des Nationalsozialismus in Schleswig-Holstein, 2009), pp. 55–74; Gerhard Stoltenberg, *Politische Strömungen im schleswig-holsteinischen Landvolk 1918–1933: Ein Beitrag zur politischen Meinungsbildung in der Weimarer Republik* (Düsseldorf: Droste, 1962), pp. 128–81; Rudolf Heberle, *Landbevölkerung und Nationalsozialismus: Eine soziologische Untersuchung der politischen Willensbildung in*

Schleswig-Holstein 1918–1932 (Stuttgart: Deutsche Verlags-Anstalt, 1963). For a similar development in Western Pomerania, see Matthiesen, *Greifswald in Vorpommern*, pp. 220–38.

162. Pyta, *Dorfgemeinschaft und Parteipolitik 1918–1933*, pp. 472–8; Gerhard Reifferscheid, 'Die NSDAP in Ostpreußen: Besonderheiten ihrer Ausbreitung und Tätigkeit', *Zeitschrift für die Geschichte und Altertumskunde Ermlands* 39 (1978), pp. 61–85, here pp. 64, 67; Schnabel, 'Die NSDAP in Württemberg 1928–1933'; GStA PK, VI. HA, NL Daluege, no. 9, pp. 20–4: Regierungsrat Bach (Darmstadt), 'Die Entwicklung der nationalsozialistischen Bewegung in Hessen, besonders im Odenwald'; GStA PK, I. HA, Rep. 77 titl. 4043, vol. 311, p. 318: Racliffe (Polizeimajor), 'Denkschrift über Kampfvorbereitung und Kampfgrundsätze radikaler Organisationen', 1931. On the NSDAP's rural campaigns in Bavaria, see Geoffrey Pridham, *Hitler's Rise to Power: The Nazi Movement in Bavaria, 1923–1933* (London: Hart-Davis, 1973), pp. 224–36.

163. Pridham, *Hitler's Rise to Power*, p. 229.

164. Bösch, *Das konservative Milieu*, pp. 116–32. For similar processes in small towns, see Koshar, 'From *Stammtisch* to Party'; Bergerson, *Ordinary Germans in Extraordinary Times*.

165. Pyta, *Dorfgemeinschaft und Parteipolitik 1918–1933*, pp. 324–432; Adelheid von Saldern, 'Sozialmilieus und der Aufstieg des Nationalsozialismus in Norddeutschland (1930–1933)', in *Norddeutschland im Nationalsozialismus*, ed. Frank Bajohr (Hamburg: Ergebnisse, 1993), pp. 20–52, here p. 36.

166. Mühlberger, *Hitler's Followers*, p. 164. In rural Bavaria, the situation was markedly different from that in the north of Germany. In the south, members of the lower classes, both skilled and unskilled labourers, prevailed. See ibid., pp. 165–6.

167. Bösch, *Das konservative Milieu*, p. 119.

168. Pridham, *Hitler's Rise to Power*, p. 131.

169. Pyta, *Dorfgemeinschaft und Parteipolitik 1918–1933*, pp. 324–9.

170. Hans-Helmuth Krenzlin, *Das NSKK: Wesen, Aufgaben und Aufbau des Nationalsozialistischen Kraftfahrkorps, dargestellt an einem Abriß seiner geschichtlichen Entwicklung* (Berlin: Junker und Dünnhaupt, 1939), p. 7.

171. RGVA, Osobyi Archives, Fond 720, Opis 1, no. 47, pp. 143–53, here pp. 148–9: Memorandum of the Baden police, *Die SA und SS der NSDAP*, Karlsruhe, 15 May 1931; Hochstetter, *Motorisierung und 'Volksgemeinschaft'*, pp. 21–39; Krenzlin, *Das NSKK*, pp. 9–11. On working-class youth's excitement about the NSKK, see Michael Zimmermann, 'Ausbruchshoffnung: Junge Bergleute in den Dreißiger Jahren', in *'Die Jahre weiß man nicht, wo man die heute hinsetzen soll': Faschismuserfahrungen im Ruhrgebiet*, ed. Lutz Niethammer (Bonn: Dietz, 1983), pp. 97–132, here pp. 101–2.

172. In those parts of the countryside with a predominantly Catholic population, the organization of the SA largely happened later and recruited followers less successfully, even if local varieties were considerable. See Heilbronner, *Catholicism, Political Culture and the Countryside*, pp. 112–15, with further references.

173. Benjamin Schröder, 'Stately Ceremony and Carnival: Voting and Social Pressure in Germany and Britain between the World Wars', *Comparativ: Zeitschrift für Globalgeschichte und vergleichende Gesellschaftsforschung* 23:1 (2013), pp. 41–63, here pp. 61, 63.

174. For a more detailed analysis of this subject, see Daniel Siemens, 'Gegen den "gesinnungs-schwachen Stimmzettelträger": Emotion und Praxis im Wahlkampf der späten Weimarer Republik', in *Kultur und Praxis der Wahlen: Eine Geschichte der modernen Demokratie*, ed. Hedwig Richter and Hubertus Buchstein (Wiesbaden: Springer, 2017), pp. 215–36.

175. On von Obernitz, see Utho Grieser, *Himmlers Mann in Nürnberg. Der Fall Benno Martin: Eine Studie zur Struktur des Dritten Reiches in der 'Stadt der Reichsparteitage'* (Nuremberg: Stadtarchiv, 1974), pp. 44–61.

176. On the sympathies of considerable parts of the East German nobility toward the NSDAP in the late 1920s and early 1930s, see Bergien, *Die bellizistische Republik*, pp. 308–23; Malinowski and Reichardt, 'Die Reihen fest geschlossen?'

177. GStA PK, I. HA, Rep. 77, titl. 4013, no. 311, pp. 210–14: SA-Untergruppe Oberschlesien, 'Besondere Anordnung: Propagandastürme für die Wahlarbeit', 22 March 1932.

178. GStA PK, I. HA, Rep. 77, titl. 4013, no. 311, p. 65: Report of Regierungsrat Dr Müller.

179. GStA PK, I. HA, Rep. 77, titl. 4043, no. 311, p. 5: Der Oberste SA-Führer on propaganda marches, 7 January 1932. As the discussions among Red Front Fighters about the participation of women in street marches demonstrate, such a prohibition was not unique to the NSDAP, but was a characteristic element of the 'masculine' character of Weimar's street politics. For a detailed discussion of this problem, see Daniel Siemens, 'Erobern statt Verführen: Die Kategorie Geschlecht in der Politik der Straße der Weimarer Republik', in *Geschlechter(un)ordnung und Politik in der Weimarer Republik*, ed. Gabriele Metzler and Dirk Schumann (Bonn: Dietz, 2016), pp. 255–77.

180. Moritz Föllmer has recently argued that Nazism allowed for more room for individual development than previously claimed. However, he largely concentrates his analysis on German men and women originating from the middle classes, broadly defined. While I agree with Föllmer's general conclusion that the Nazi regime promoted individual self-transformation, aspects of class should be given stronger emphasis in such an examination. The history of the stormtroopers, as provided in this study, clearly elucidates the limits of inter-class dynamics and individual empowerment. See Moritz Föllmer, 'The Subjective Dimension of Nazism', *Historical Journal* 56:4 (2013), pp. 1,107–32.

181. Stefan Jonsson, *Crowds and Democracy: The Idea and Image of the Masses from Revolution to Fascism* (New York: Columbia University Press, 2013), p. 250.

182. Siegfried Kracauer, 'The Mass Ornament', in *The Mass Ornament: Weimar Essays*, trans. and ed. Thomas Y. Levin (Cambridge and London: Cambridge University Press, 1995), pp. 75–86, here esp. pp. 75–6, 84–6.

183. Ibid., pp. 76, 79.

184. Theweleit, *Male Fantasies*.

185. This observation is also in line with the sociological findings of Lewis A. Coser, who observed that 'greedy' organizations 'tend to consider stable sexual ties a threat to total allegiance and commitment which they require of all or of some of their members'. See Coser, *Greedy Institutions*, p. 136.

186. RGVA, Osobyi Archives, Fond 720, Opis 1, no. 47, pp. 372–437, here p. 386: Werner von Fichte, typescript of a booklet on the SA, untitled and undated, sixty-five pages.

187. Ferdinand Tuohy, *Craziways, Europe* (London: Hamish Hamilton, 1934), p. 18, as quoted in Angela Schwarz, 'British Visitors to National Socialist Germany', *Journal of Contemporary History* 28:3 (1993), pp. 487–509, here pp. 490–1. The guidelines for SA physicians from 20 April 1931 requested that they regularly lecture the rank and file on personal hygiene, nourishment, and sexual diseases. To prevent acquiring the latter, physicians were urged to propagate beliefs about sexual abstinence. See BArch Berlin, NS 23/510: [Reichsarzt] Paul Hocheisen, 'Anweisung betr. Aufgaben und Tätigkeit der SA-Ärzte', 20 April 1931.

188. Kracauer, 'Mass Ornament', pp. 85–6.

189. Speech of Joseph Goebbels on the occasion of the opening of the Berlin Auto Show, 17 February 1939, as quoted in Jeffrey Herf, *Reactionary Modernism: Technology, Culture, and Politics in Weimar and the Third Reich* (Cambridge: Cambridge University Press, 1984), p. 196.

190. Goebbels, Speech in the Heidelberg Civic Centre on 7 July 1943, as quoted in ibid., p. 196.

191. This tendency even dominated much of the historiography on the 'rise' of National Socialism until the 1980s; see Oded Heilbronner, 'The Role of Nazi Antisemitism in the Nazi Party's Activity and Propaganda: A Regional Historiographical Study', *Year Book of the Leo Baeck Institute* 35 (1990), pp. 397–439.

192. Centralverein deutscher Staatsbürger jüdischen Glaubens (ed.), *Eine Aussprache über die Judenfrage zwischen Dr. Margarete Adam (mit einem Nachwort: Warum habe ich nationalsozialistisch gewählt) und Dr. Eva Reichmann-Jungmann* (Berlin: Centralverein, 1930/1931), pp. 19, 23.

193. For details on this meeting, see Heinrich August Winkler, *Der Weg in die Katastrophe: Arbeiter und Arbeiterbewegung in der Weimarer Republik* (Berlin and Bonn: Dietz, 1987), pp. 432–4.

194. Letter from Ernst Brandi to his son F. H. Brandi from 7 March 1932, as quoted in Werner Abelshauser, *Ruhrkohle und Politik: Ernst Brandi 1875–1933. Eine Biographie* (Essen: Klartext, 2009), p. 71.

195. Ibid., p. 90.
196. Siegfried Kracauer, 'Die deutschen Bevölkerungsschichten und der Nationalsozialismus', in Kracauer, *Essays, Feuilletons, Rezensionen* 5:4, pp. 433–45, here p. 439.
197. Reichardt, *Faschistische Kampfbünde*, pp. 110–11.
198. Letter from Ernst Brandi to his son F. H. Brandi from 7 March 1932, as quoted in Abelshauser, *Ruhrkohle und Politik*, p. 71.
199. On the industry's support of the NSDAP and its limits, see Henry Ashby Turner, Jr., '"Alliance of Elites" as a Cause of Weimar's Collapse and Hitler's Triumph?', in *Die deutsche Staatskrise 1930–1933*, ed. Heinrich August Winkler (Munich: Oldenbourg, 1992), pp. 205–14; Jürgen John, 'Zur politischen Rolle der Großindustrie in der Weimarer Staatskrise. Gesicherte Erkenntnisse und strittige Meinungen', in *Die deutsche Staatskrise 1930–1933*, pp. 215–37.
200. *Hamburger Echo*, no. 250 from 18 October 1932, as quoted in McElligott, '". . . und so kam es zu einer schweren Schlägerei"', p. 72.
201. This term is used by Grzesinski, *Inside Germany*, p. 130.
202. Deutsche Hochschule für Politik (ed.), *Seminar für SA-Führer: Winter-Lehrgang 1937/38* (Berlin: Deutsche Hochschule für Politik, 1937), p. 16.
203. Friedrich Lenger, *Metropolen der Moderne: Eine europäische Stadtgeschichte seit 1850* (Munich: Beck, 2013), p. 393. The studies mentioned are Schumann, *Politische Gewalt in der Weimarer Republik*; Blasius, *Weimars Ende*; and Fulda, *Press and Politics*.
204. For different angles on this development, see Michael Wildt, *Volksgemeinschaft als Selbstermächtigung: Gewalt gegen Juden in der deutschen Provinz 1919 bis 1939* (Hamburg: Hamburger Edition, 2007); Szejnmann, *Nazism in Central Germany*; Bergien, *Die bellizistische Republik*; Schmidt, *Schützen und Dienen*.
205. Winkler, *Der Weg in die Katastrophe*, pp. 646–80.
206. Several SA leaders, among them Wilhelm Stegmann in Nuremberg, were advocating by late 1932 for a return to the *Wehrverband* strategy should Hindenburg continue to refuse to appoint Hitler as chancellor. After internal disagreements, Stegmann in early 1933 left the NSDAP and organized the *Freikorps* Franken, which grew to between 2,000 and 3,000 men strong. The events of 30 January 1933 prepared the ground for further agitation by this and similar groups. See Longerich, *Geschichte der SA*, pp. 163–4.
207. Fulda, *Press and Politics*, p. 201; Lenger, *Metropolen der Moderne*, p. 393.
208. Sebastian Ulrich, *Der Weimar-Komplex: Das Scheitern der ersten deutschen Demokratie und die politische Kultur der frühen Bundesrepublik* (Göttingen: Wallstein, 2009), esp. pp. 79–143, 376–535.
209. According to Heinrich Bennecke, SA Chief of Staff Röhm was not present on this occasion. Instead, he attended a social evening at the SA-*Reichsführerschule* in Munich and followed the events on the radio; Peschel (ed.), *Die SA in Sachsen vor der 'Machtübernahme'*, p. 76.
210. Peter Fritzsche, *The Turbulent World of Franz Göll: An Ordinary Berliner Writes the Twentieth Century* (Cambridge, MA, and London: Harvard University Press, 2011), p. 149.
211. As quoted in Bernt Engelmann, *Im Gleichschritt marsch: Wie wir die Nazizeit erlebten 1933–1939* (Cologne: Kiepenheuer & Witsch, 1982), p. 51. For a detailed, yet slightly exaggerated, description of the 'magnitude' of this parade, based on later memoirs and Nazi newspaper coverage, see Peter Fritzsche, *Germans into Nazis* (Cambridge, MA, and London: Harvard University Press, 1998), pp. 139–41.

Chapter 3

1. First printed in *Encyclopedia Italiana*, vol. 14 (1932), as quoted in Benito Mussolini, 'The Doctrine of Fascism', in his *Fascism: Doctrine and Institutions* (Rome: Ardita, 1935), pp. 5–42, here p. 8.
2. Ernst Bloch, 'Reminder: Hitler's Force', in *Heritage of Our Times* (Berkeley and Los Angeles, CA: University of California Press, 1990), pp. 145–8, here p. 147 (originally published as 'Erinnerung: Hitlers Gewalt', *Das Tage-Buch* 5:15 [1924], 12 April, pp. 474–7).
3. Ibid., p. 146.

4. Martin Blinkhorn, *Fascism and the Right in Europe, 1919–1945* (Harlow: Pearson, 2000), pp. 19–24.
5. Patrizia Dogliani, 'Propaganda and Youth', in *The Oxford Handbook of Fascism*, ed. R. J. B. Bosworth (Oxford and New York: Oxford University Press, 2009), pp. 185–202, here p. 186.
6. See Michael Geyer, 'The Militarization of Europe 1914–1945', in *The Militarization of the Western World*, ed. John R. Gillis (New Brunswick, NJ: Rutgers University Press, 1989), pp. 65–102. Rüdiger Bergien has lately criticized the rather loose use of the term 'militarization' in many studies and has instead suggested 'bellicism' as a substitute; Bergien, *Die bellizistische Republik*, pp. 33–7. I nevertheless prefer the established 'militarization' as long as a very narrow understanding of this term is avoided that equates militarization exclusively with preparation for conventional war.
7. See, in particular, Merkl, *Political Violence under the Swastika*, pp. 231–310.
8. For a recent summary, see Rohrkrämer, *Die fatale Attraktion des Nationalsozialismus*, pp. 151–60.
9. See, among others, O'Sullivan, *Fascism*, pp. 33–84.
10. See Kater, 'Ansätze zu einer Soziologie der SA', pp. 815–17; Campbell, *SA Generals*, pp. 29–79. However, other researchers have emphasized that the SA was not always such a 'young' organization as the party propaganda portrayed it. In the Black Forest, for example, the early SA activists were predominantly in their mid- to late thirties. See Heilbronner, *Catholicism, Political Culture and the Countryside*, pp. 62–3.
11. For a critical position, see Benninghaus, 'Das Geschlecht der Generation'.
12. Ernst Günther Gründel, *Die Sendung der jungen Generation* (Munich: Beck, 1932). The phenomenon of this self-declared 'war youth generation' has been analysed extensively; see Andrew Donson, *Youth in the Fatherless Land: War Pedagogy, Nationalism, and Authority in Germany, 1914–1918* (Cambridge, MA: Harvard University Press, 2010), pp. 59–107; Herbert, *Best*; Helmut Lethen, *Cool Conduct: The Culture of Distance in Weimar Germany* (Berkeley, CA, and London: University of California Press, 2002); Daniel Siemens, 'Kühle Romantiker: Zum Geschichtsverständnis der "jungen Generation" in der Weimarer Republik', in *Die Kunst der Geschichte: Historiographie, Ästhetik, Erzählung*, ed. Martin Baumeister, Moritz Föllmer, and Philipp Müller (Göttingen: Vandenhoeck & Ruprecht, 2009), pp. 189–214; Christian Ingrao, *Believe and Destroy: Intellectuals and the SS War Machine* (Cambridge: Polity, 2013), pp. 3–16.
13. Gerwarth, 'Central European Counter-Revolution', p. 181.
14. Ibid.
15. Weisbrod, 'Gewalt in der Politik', p. 393. However, at least in Erlangen, students' excitement for such units was limited. Only a minority of those students who had received military training during the war years or had actively fought in battle registered for these 'student companies'. See Manfred Franze, *Die Erlanger Studentenschaft 1918–1945* (Würzburg: Schöningh, 1972), pp. 29–31.
16. Othmar Plöckinger, 'Adolf Hitler als Hörer an der Universität München im Jahr 1919: Zum Verhältnis zwischen Reichswehr und Universität', in *Die Universität München im Dritten Reich: Aufsätze. Teil II*, ed. Elisabeth Kraus (Munich: Utz, 2008), pp. 13–47, here pp. 14–17; von Oerzen, *Die deutschen Freikorps 1918–1923*, pp. 422–31 (in particular the sections on Leipzig and Würzburg).
17. In Budapest the membership of highly violent student battalions that perceived themselves as auxiliary police forces increased from 3,000 men in 1919 to 10,000 men in the summer of the following year. See Bodó, 'Heroes or Thieves?', pp. 94–5; Gerwarth, 'Rechte Gewaltgemeinschaften und die Stadt nach dem Ersten Weltkrieg', pp. 118–19.
18. Chris Millington, 'Political Violence in Interwar France', *History Compass* 10:3 (2013), pp. 246–59, here p. 249; Dominique Borne and Henri Dubief, *La crise des années 30: 1929–1928* (Paris: Éditions du Seuil, 1989), p. 93; Xavier Cheneseau, *Camelots du Roi: Les troupes de choc royalistes (1908–1936)* (Boulogne: Éditions Défi, 1997), pp. 46–7.
19. Plöckinger, 'Adolf Hitler als Hörer an der Universität München', pp. 15–16.
20. The Bavarian *Einwohnerwehren* also integrated members of the *Reichswehr-Zeitfreiwilligen* units after the latter were dissolved under the Versailles Peace Treaty on 1 April

1920. See BayHStA IV, Bestand Reichswehr, Brigade 23: Letter from the Reichswehrgruppenkommando no. 4 on 'Auflösung der Reichswehr-Zeitfreiwilligen', 9 March 1920.

21. StA München, Pol. Dir. 6803, pp. 174–83: An early list of SA members (from Maurice), presumably intercepted by the police in September 1921.

22. Hambrecht, *Der Aufstieg der NSDAP in Mittel- und Oberfranken*, pp. 45–6.

23. Geoffrey Giles, *Students and National Socialism in Germany* (Princeton, NJ: Princeton University Press, 1985), p. 26; Steinke, *Fritz Bauer oder Auschwitz vor Gericht*, p. 54. In the early 1930s SA units that consisted exclusively of students mushroomed in German university towns. In Cologne, for example, the law student Heinz Siepen was appointed the first leader of the local SA university *Sturm*, see GStA PK, I. HA, Rep. 77, titl. 4043, vol. 311, p. 52.

24. On the *'Heißsporn'* Klintzsch, see the characterization of the writer Ferdinand Lindner from September 1921 in LArch Freiburg, F 179/4 Nr. 110, p. 9.

25. Frank Bajohr, *'Unser Hotel ist judenfrei': Bäder-Antisemitismus im 19. und 20. Jahrhundert* (Frankfurt am Main: Fischer, 2003), pp. 73–88.

26. Heinz Wegener, *Das Joachimsthalsche Gymnasium – Die Landesschule Templin: Ein berlin-brandenburgisches Gymnasium im Mahlstrom der deutschen Geschichte 1607–2007* (Berlin: Berlin Story, 2007), pp. 113–15; Walsdorff, 'Hans-Ulrich Klintzsch'.

27. LArch Freiburg, F 179/4 no. 110, pp. 15–22, here p. 17: Offenburg regional court, Record of interrogation of Hans Ulrich Klintzsch, 16 September 1921.

28. Email from the archive of the Technical University (TU) of Munich to the author from 7 June 2016; LKA Stuttgart, A 127, no. 1293: Personal information form Hans-Ulrich Klintzsch (1949/50). I have also checked with Ludwig Maximilian University of Munich (LMU) student registers for the years 1921 to 1925–6, but to no avail. Digitized registers with the names of professors and students are available from LMU's university library website, epub.ub.uni-muenchen.de/view/lmu/pverz.html.

29. LArch Freiburg, F 179/4 no. 153, pp. 81–3, here p. 83: Tübingen local court, Record of interrogation of Dietrich von Jagow, 2 February 1922; Brigitte Riethmüller and Hermann-Arndt Riethmüller, *Osiander. Die Geschichte einer Buchhandlung*, http://www.osiander.de/download/Osiander_Geschichte_Stand_2013.pdf.

30. Barbara Hachmann, 'Der "Degen". Dietrich von Jagow, SA-Obergruppenführer', in *Die Führer der Provinz: NS-Biographien aus Baden und Württemberg*, ed. Michael Kißener and Joachim Scholtyseck (Konstanz: UVK, 1997), pp. 267–87, here pp. 271–2; Ernst Piper, *Alfred Rosenberg: Hitlers Chefideologe* (Munich: Blessing, 2005), p. 52; Rafael Binkowski, *Die Entwicklung der Parteien in Herrenberg 1918–1933: Ausprägungen der Parteienentwicklung auf lokaler Ebene in der Weimarer Republik am Beispiel der Stadt Herrenberg und anderer südwestdeutscher Vergleichsstädte*, university diss., Universität Stuttgart, 2007, http://elib.uni-stuttgart.de/opus/volltexte/2007/3273/, pp. 296–7, 313–14.

31. Hermann Schützinger, 'Tübingen', *Die Weltbühne* 22:2 (1926), no. 32, 10 August, pp. 207–10, here 209–10. Actual historical research has come to very similar conclusions, and not only for Tübingen: 'The cultural political milieu that operated at German universities tended toward the political Right, and like their professors, German students tended to be nationalists, anti-Communists, and anti-Semitic, a perfect match for the burgeoning Nazi party'; see Hilary Earl, '"Bad Nazis and Other Germans": The fate of SS-*Einsatzgruppen* Commander Martin Sandberger in Postwar Germany', in *A Nazi Past: Recasting German Identity in Postwar Europe*, ed. David A. Messenger and Katrin Paehler (Lexington, KY: University of Kentucky Press, 2015), pp. 57–82, here pp. 60–1. For a balanced assessment that emphasizes the widespread sympathy for the Nazi movement at Tübingen University but at the same time points to the fact that Nazi organizations for a long time did not recruit there more easily than elsewhere, see Hans-Joachim Lang, 'Die Universität Tübingen im Nationalsozialismus', in *Forschung – Lehre – Unrecht: Die Universität Tübingen im Nationalsozialismus*, ed. Ernst Seidl (Tübingen: MUT, 2015), pp. 33–49.

32. The students were led by the *Hochschulring deutscher Art* under the young Theodor Eschenburg. See Benigna Schönhagen, 'Stadt und Universität Tübingen in der NS-Zeit', in *Die Universität Tübingen im Nationalsozialismus*, ed. Urban Wiesing et al. (Stuttgart: Steiner,

2010), pp. 731–58, here p. 743; Uwe Dietrich Adam, *Hochschule und Nationalsozialismus: Die Universität Tübingen im Dritten Reich* (Tübingen: Mohr, 1977), p. 22; Trauthig, *Im Kampf um Glauben und Kirche*, p. 64. On Gumbel, see in particular Christian Jansen, *Emil Julius Gumbel: Porträt eines Zivilisten* (Heidelberg: Wunderhorn, 1991).

33. Adam, *Hochschule und Nationalsozialismus*, pp. 22–3. Initially, however, the SA did not allow for the formation of genuine student *Stürme*, as this was perceived to be a new form of elitism that ran contrary to the party's ideal of a *Volksgemeinschaft* transgressing class boundaries. The situation changed fundamentally in 1932 with the establishment of the new *Studentenbundorganisation* that attempted to intensify the paramilitary training offered at German universities. See BArch Berlin, NS 23/510: Transcript of the Munich police's *Lagebericht* from 20 October 1932.

34. By the Nazis' own accounting, forty-eight SA leaders and between 600 and 700 rank-and-file SA men were members of the National Socialist Student League as early as 1929; see Baldur von Schirach, *Wille und Weg des Nationalsozialistischen Deutschen Studentenbundes* (Munich: NSDAP, 1929), p. 11. Historians' opinions on this issue differ considerably. Michael Kater in the 1970s argued that student activism in the SA remained limited, despite the prominent place that the union of 'brain and hand' – that is, of students and workers – occupied in Nazi propaganda. In reality, Kater claimed, no more than 40 per cent of all students who were members of the National Socialist Student League also became members of the SA. Yet whether or not this is a small number – given the importance of the National Socialist Student League in many German universities starting in 1928 – seems highly debatable; Michael Kater, *Studentenschaft und Rechtsradikalismus in Deutschland 1918–1933: Eine sozialgeschichtliche Studie zur Bildungskrise in der Weimarer Republik* (Hamburg: Hoffmann & Campe, 1975), pp. 186–97. Contrary to Kater, contemporaries like Theodor Geiger identified middle-class male youth and in particular students as the 'pillars of national activism'; Geiger, *Die soziale Schichtung des deutschen Volkes*, p. 115. On the rise of the National Socialist Student League and its relation to the SA, see also Giles, *Students and National Socialism in Germany*, pp. 44–100; Michael Grüttner, *Studenten im Dritten Reich* (Paderborn: Schöningh, 1995), pp. 19–61; Schön, *Die Entstehung des Nationalsozialismus in Hessen*, pp. 104–16.

35. As an example of such reasoning, see LArch Freiburg, F 179/4 Nr. 110, pp. 15–22, here p. 19: Offenburg regional court, Record of interrogation of Hans Ulrich Klintzsch, 16 September 1921. Students with more liberal tendencies likewise stressed that they felt called to shape the people's community; see Fritz Söhlmann, 'Akademiker und Volksgemeinschaft. Die Aufgabe einer studentischen Selbstverwaltung', *Der Jungdeutsche*, 27 June 1929, in GStA PK, I. HA, Rep. 77, titl. 4043, no. 160, p. 90.

36. RGVA, Osobyi Archives, Fond 720, Opis 1, no. 47, pp. 372–437, here p. 374: Werner von Fichte, Typescript of a booklet on the SA, untitled and undated, sixty-five pages.

37. On the development of and positions within the German youth movement, see the recent publications by Ahrens, *Bündische Jugend*, and Barbara Stambolis (ed.), *Die Jugendbewegung und ihre Wirkungen: Prägungen, Vernetzungen, gesellschaftliche Einflussnahmen* (Göttingen: V&R unipress, 2015). For examples of the biographical overlap of the youth movement and the NSDAP, see BArch Berlin, NS 26/370: Letter from Rudolf Schmidt, 'Anschriften Egerland', undated.

38. Instructive in this respect is a travel report from the SA-*Sturmführer* Horst Wessel, who cycled from Berlin to an NSDAP party rally held in Nuremberg in 1927. He interwove his description of the German landscape and its people with political deliberations. See Gailus and Siemens (eds), *'Hass und Begeisterung bilden Spalier'*, pp. 157–183.

39. RGVA, Osobyi Archives, Fond 720, Opis 1, no. 47, pp. 372–437, here pp. 374–5: Werner von Fichte, Typescript of a booklet on the SA.

40. Stefan Vogt, 'Strange Encounters: Social Democracy and Radical Nationalism in Weimar Germany', *Journal of Contemporary History* 45:2 (2010), pp. 253–81; idem, *Nationaler Sozialismus und Soziale Demokratie: Die sozialdemokratische Junge Rechte 1918–1945* (Bonn: Dietz, 2006).

41. Carl Mierendorff, 'Republik', in *Sozialistische Monatshefte* 38:2, 1932, p. 793, as quoted in Vogt, *Nationaler Sozialismus und Soziale Demokratie*, p. 222.

42. Alfred Weber uses the term 'authoritarian democracy' approvingly in *Das Ende der Demokratie? Ein Vortrag* (Berlin: Junker & Dünnhaupt, 1931), p. 23. See also Carl Mierendorff, 'Wahlreform, die Losung der jungen Generation', *Neue Blätter für den Sozialismus* 1 (1930), pp. 342–9. The most elaborate and influential manifestos are Edgar J. Jung, *Die Herrschaft der Minderwertigen: Ihr Zerfall und ihre Ablösung durch ein Neues Reich* (Berlin: Verlag Deutsche Rundschau, 1930); and the less idealistic Ernst Jünger, *Der Arbeiter: Herrschaft und Gestalt* (Hamburg: Hanseatische Verlags-Anstalt, 1932).

43. August Rathmann, 'Neuer Anfang sozialdemokratischer Politik?', *Neue Blätter für den Sozialismus* 1 (1930), pp. 388–95, here p. 390. In similar terms the German jurist Karl Loewenstein in exile noted a few years later that 'the emotional past of early liberalism and democracy cannot be revived. Nowadays, people do not want to die for liberty'; Karl Loewenstein, 'Militant Democracy and Fundamental Rights', *The American Political Science Review* 31:3 (1937), pp. 417–32, here p. 428.

44. For a more detailed discussion, see Elizabeth Harvey, 'The Cult of Youth', in *A Companion to Europe 1900–1945*, ed. Gordon Martel (Malden, MA, and Oxford: Blackwell, 2006), pp. 66–81, esp. pp. 75–8; Kater, *Hitler Youth*, p. 10.

45. Kater, *Hitler Youth*, p. 382.

46. StA München, Pol. Dir. 6803: Transcript of a blank form of an SA declaration of engagement (*Verpflichtungsschein*).

47. Wackerfuss, *Stormtrooper Families*, pp. 190–1. See also Reichardt, *Faschistische Kampfbünde*, pp. 673–9. Nazi propaganda likewise emphasized the importance of women for the SA. The SA-*Obergruppenführer* and police president of Frankfurt am Main, Adolf-Heinz Beckerle, in 1940 praised the contribution of women to the SA, particularly their highly active role in spreading Nazi propaganda from mouth to mouth during the *Kampfzeit* and their provision of comfort to their husbands and partners in times of crisis. See Adolf-Heinz Beckerle, 'Unsere Frauen', *Die SA* 1:34 (1940), pp. 5–6.

48. StA München, Pol. Dir. 6805: Paragraph 6 of the *Satzung der Sturmabteilung der Nationalsozialistischen Deutschen Arbeiterpartei*, 17 September 1926, modified on 31 May 1927.

49. BayHStA IV, Bestand Stahlhelm, no. 97: Stahlhelm-Führerspiegel (draft from September 1931), paragraph XIV.

50. For a similar conclusion, see Eley, *Nazism as Fascism*, pp. 92–3. By 1930 the *Frauenabteilung*, or 'Women's Department', was no longer under the control of the SA. See RGVA, Osobyi Archives, Fond 720, Opis 1, no. 47, pp. 143–53, here p. 143: Memorandum of the Baden police, *Die SA und SS der NSDAP*, Karlsruhe, 15 May 1931.

51. See also Axel Fehlhaber, Detlef Garz, and Sandra Kirsch, '"Wie ich Nationalsozialistin wurde" – Erste Annäherungen an eine Typologie weiblichen Engagements in der nationalsozialistischen Bewegung auf Basis der Abel-Collection', *sozialersinn* 8:2 (2007), pp. 357–83.

52. Hoover Institution Library and Archives, Stanford, CA (HILA), Theodore Fred Abel Papers, Box 1, no. F44: Hilde Boehm-Stoltz, *Warum und wie ich zum Nationalsozialismus kam* (1933). By 1932, Boehm-Stoltz had already published an article in the Nazi press: see Hilde Boehm-Stoltz, 'Die Nationalsozialistin und die Familie', *Völkischer Beobachter*, 20 January 1932, as quoted in Leila J. Rupp, *Mobilizing Women for War: German and American Propaganda, 1939–1945* (Princeton, NJ: Princeton University Press, 1978), p. 32.

53. HILA, Theodore Fred Abel Papers, Box 1, no. F36: Hertha von Reuß, 'Wie ich zur NSDAP kam' (1933).

54. Ibid., Box 1, no. F41: Marlene Heder, 'Wie es kam, daß wir zwei Schwestern mit 19 und 20 Jahren schon zu den alten oder wenigstens älteren Kämpfern der Bewegung gehören' (1933).

55. See also Lara Hensch: '"Wir aber sind mitten im Kampf aufgewachsen" – Erster Weltkrieg und "Kampfzeit" in Selbstdarstellungen früher SA-Männer', in *Bürgerkriegsarmee*, ed. Müller and Zilkenat, pp. 331–53.

56. In this respect a recent attempt by Joachim C. Häberlen to identify women as actors in Weimar's violent street politics is only partly convincing. He provides compelling evidence for Communist women's activities but does not prove that National Socialist women were equally active. See Joachim C. Häberlen, '"Weiter haben sich zwei Frauenpersonen besonders hervorgetan": Zur Rolle von Frauen in der Straßenpolitik am Ende der Weimarer Republik', *L'Homme: Europäische Zeitschrift für feministische Geschichtswissenschaft* 23:1 (2012),

pp. 91–105. On the persistent gender imbalance within the Communist Party, see Sewell, 'Bolshevizing Communist Women'.

57. On women's motives for joining the NSDAP prior to 1933, see also Marit A. Berntson and Brian Ault, 'Gender and Nazism: Women Joiners of the Pre-1933 Nazi Party', *American Behavioral Scientist* 49:9 (1998), pp. 1,193–1,218; Boak, 'Mobilising Women for Hitler'.

58. Lore Snyckers, 'Wie SA-Frauen', *Die SA* 1:34 (1940), p. 7. For a short biographical sketch of her husband, see 'SA-Sturmbannführer Dr. Hans Snyckers', *Die SA* 2:9 (1941), p. 12. Hans Snyckers later served as *Kulturreferent* for the German Embassy in Bratislava; Frank-Rutger Hausmann, *'Auch im Krieg schweigen die Musen nicht': Die Deutschen Wissenschaftlichen Institute im Zweiten Weltkrieg* (Göttingen: Vandenhoeck & Ruprecht, 2001), p. 322.

59. Hattenhorst, *Magdeburg 1933*, p. 110.

60. Riccardo Bavaj, *Die Ambivalenz der Moderne im Nationalsozialismus: Eine Bilanz der Forschung* (Munich: Oldenbourg, 2003). On the increasing number of female students beginning in the second half of the 1930s, see Grüttner, *Studenten im Dritten Reich*, pp. 119–26; on women's room for (professional) development in the Third Reich, see the pioneering work by Kirsten Heinsohn, Barbara Vogel, and Ulrike Weckel (eds), *Zwischen Karriere und Verfolgung: Handlungsspielräume von Frauen im nationalsozialistischen Deutschland* (Frankfurt am Main: Campus, 1997); for recent overviews on gender and National Socialism, see Matthew Stibbe, 'In and Beyond the Racial State: Gender and National Socialism, 1933–1955', *Politics, Religion & Ideology* 13:2 (2012), pp. 159–78; Johanna Gehmacher and Gabriella Hauch (eds), *Frauen- und Geschlechtergeschichte des Nationalsozialismus: Fragestellungen, Perspektiven, neue Forschungen* (Innsbruck: Studien Verlag, 2007).

61. Schweyer, *Politische Geheimverbände*, p. 108.

62. Hermann Schützinger, *Bürgerkrieg* (Leipzig: Oldenburg, 1924), pp. 56, 59. See also BArch Berlin, R1501/20234: 'Auch ein Reichsbannerführer: Aus der Vergangenheit des Herrn Schützinger', *Berliner Börsenzeitung*, 1 May 1932.

63. On the diverse political youth organizations of this period, see Wolfgang Krabbe, *Die gescheiterte Zukunft der Ersten Republik: Jugendorganisationen bürgerlicher Parteien im Weimarer Staat (1918–1933)* (Opladen: Westdeutscher Verlag, 1995); Irmtraud Götz von Olenhusen, 'Die Krise der jungen Generation und der Aufstieg des Nationalsozialismus: Eine Analyse der Jugendorganisationen der Weimarer Zeit', *Jahrbuch des Archivs der Deutschen Jugendbewegung* 12 (1980), pp. 53–86.

64. For an introduction, see Jan Plamper, *Geschichte und Gefühl: Grundlagen der Emotionsgeschichte* (Munich: Siedler, 2012), with further references.

65. Pioneering in this respect was Wolfgang Schieder (ed.), *Faschismus als soziale Bewegung: Deutschland und Italien im Vergleich*, 2nd edn (Göttingen: Vandenhoeck & Ruprecht, 1983).

66. On Behrendt's biography, see Katja Windisch, *Gestalten sozialen Wandels: Die Entwicklungssoziologie Richard F. Behrendts* (Bern: Lang, 2005), pp. 19–31.

67. Richard F. Behrendt, *Politischer Aktivismus: Ein Versuch zur Soziologie und Psychologie der Politik* (Leipzig: Hirschfeld, 1932). For a more detailed analysis of this book, see Daniel Siemens, 'Politische Gewalt als emotionale Befriedigung', *Zeithistorische Forschungen/ Studies in Contemporary History* 13:1 (2016), pp. 172–8.

68. It was Georg Lukácz who originally coined the term 'transcendental homelessness' in his *Die Theorie des Romans* (Berlin: Cassirer, 1920).

69. Behrendt, *Politischer Aktivismus*, pp. 57–61.

70. In line with such deliberations are the memoirs of the teacher and intellectual Gerhard Nebel, who, as a radical socialist, in late 1932 participated in several clashes with ideological opponents 'with deep satisfaction'; Nebel, *'Alles Gefühl ist leiblich'*, p. 130.

71. This was the main idea proposed by Herman Schmalenbach, 'Die soziologische Kategorie des Bundes', *Die Dioskuren: Jahrbuch für Geisteswissenschaften* 1 (1922), pp. 35–105. This essay influenced Behrendt's writing tremendously. On Schmalenbach's concept, see also Reichardt, *Faschistische Kampfbünde*, pp. 390–3.

72. Behrendt, *Politischer Aktivismus*, pp. 62, 80–1, 96–103, 106. Independently of Behrendt, Thomas Rohkrämer recently came to a similar conclusion; see Rohkrämer, *Die fatale Attraktion des Nationalsozialismus*, pp. 148–9.

73. Ludwig Holländer, 'Klarheit, Arbeit, Mut!', *CV-Zeitung*, 19 September 1930, p. 1.

74. For the concept of 'emotional communities', see Barbara H. Rosenwein, *Emotional Communities in the Early Middle Ages* (Ithaca, NY: Cornell University Press, 2006), pp. 1–31; and, recently, idem, *Generations of Feelings: A History of Emotions, 600–1700* (Cambridge, MA: Cambridge University Press, 2015), pp. 4–6. For the current debate on the difference between affects and emotions and the social relevance of both, see Edward J. Lawler, 'An Affect Theory of Social Exchange', *American Journal of Sociology* 107:2 (2001), pp. 321–52; Anna M. Parkinson, *An Emotional State: The Politics of Emotion in Postwar West German Culture* (Ann Arbor, MI: University of Michigan Press, 2015), pp. 10–24.

75. Joachim Raschke, *Soziale Bewegungen: Ein historisch-systematischer Grundriß*, 2nd edn (Frankfurt am Main: Campus, 1988), p. 77.

76. Ibid., pp. 54, 305–7.

77. Reichardt, *Faschistische Kampfbünde*, p. 32.

78. Ibid.

79. The terms *Bund* and Fascism are also semantically closely connected, as the Italian word *fascio* that gave Fascism its name originally meant 'bundle' or 'bunch'. See ibid., p. 390.

80. Hans-Ulrich Wehler, *Der Nationalsozialismus: Bewegung, Führerherrschaft, Verbrechen* (Munich: Beck, 2009); Arif Dirlik, 'Mao Zedong: Charismatic Leadership and the Contradictions of Socialist Revolution', in *Charismatic Leadership and Social Movements: The Revolutionary Power of Ordinary Men and Women*, ed. Jan Willem Stutje (New York: Berghahn, 2012), pp. 117–37; Richard R. Fagan, 'Charismatic Authority and the Leadership of Fidel Castro, Part 1', *Western Political Quarterly* 18:2 (1965), pp. 275–84.

81. Thomas Welskopp, 'Incendiary Personalities: Uncommon Comments on Charisma in Social Movements', in Stutje, *Charismatic Leadership and Social Movements*, pp. 164–79, here pp. 164, 169.

82. Welskopp, 'Incendiary Personalities', p. 165. Already in the early 1920s the German philosopher Helmuth Plessner came to similar conclusions; see his *Grenzen der Gemeinschaft: Eine Kritik des sozialen Radikalismus* (Frankfurt am Main: Suhrkamp, 2002 [1924]), pp. 43–8.

83. StA München, Pol. Dir. 6803: Guidelines for the formation of a stormtrooper unit, 16 May 1922.

84. StA München, Pol. Dir. 6805: OSAF, Decree no. 2. See also Noakes, *Nazi Party in Lower Saxony*, p. 182.

85. BArch Berlin, R 9361/II, no. 16746: Letter from Otto Herzog to the Reichsuschla, 26 August 1932.

86. Welskopp, 'Incendiary Personalities', p. 171.

87. Gehrig, *Im Dienste der nationalsozialistischen Volkstumspolitik in Lothringen*, p. 33. See also Reichardt, *Faschistische Kampfbünde*, pp. 418–21, 468–74; Wacherfuss, *Stormtrooper Families*, pp. 164–87.

88. RGVA, Osobyi Archives, Fond 720, Opis 1, no. 44, p. 2: 'Eine Dankespflicht', *Der Nationale Sozialist*, 17 May 1930.

89. Ibid., Fond 720, Opis 1, no. 44, p. 9: Extract from the 'Mitteilungen des Landeskriminalamts (IA) Berlin', 15 November 1930.

90. Ibid., p. 18: 'SA-Befehl Nr. 6', *Völkischer Beobachter*, 6 May 1931.

91. Ibid., p. 22: Proclamation of the NSDAP Leipzig (typescript), April 1931.

92. One of these women was Marie von Trotha, who regularly accepted stormtroopers into her house in the beach resort of Groß-Möllen in Pomerania, today's Polish Mielno. A collection of stormtroopers' letters to her is stored in BArch Berlin, NS 26/326.

93. RGVA, Osobyi Archives, Fond 720, Opis 1, no. 44, p. 26: Ernst Röhm, Order from 12 March 1931.

94. StA München, Pol. Dir. 6805: OSAF, Erlaß Nr. 2. The Communists pursued a very similar strategy; see BArch Berlin, NS 23/431: Typescript of 'Communist Fighting Principles' (1931/1932).

95. Geiger, *Die soziale Schichtung des deutschen Volkes*, p. 115.

96. In the previous two years all SA equipment had had to be ordered from the so-called SA-*Wirtschaftsstelle* in Munich, which was run by a party member named Rottenberg. See StA München, Pol. Dir. 6805: Extract from the *Lagebericht* of Berlin Police, no. 128, 20 February 1929.

97. StA München, Pol. Dir. 6805: Extracts from the *Lagebericht* of Munich Police, no. 77, 7 May 1929.

98. BArch Berlin, NS 26/372: Letter from the Danzig HJ to Rudolf Schmidt, 31 August 1930.

99. This aspect is cleverly exploited in early SA films, particularly *S.A. Mann Brand* from 1933.

100. His official entry date was 1 April 1931, and his membership number was 508,889. See Elisabeth Timm, *Hugo Ferdinand Boss (1895–1948) und die Firma Hugo Boss: Eine Dokumentation* (Metzingen: 1999), http://www.metzingen-zwangsarbeit.de/hugo_boss.pdf, p. 4.

101. Unless noted otherwise, all information in this paragraph is taken from Roman Köster, *Hugo Boss, 1924–1945: Die Geschichte einer Kleiderfabrik zwischen Weimarer Republik und 'Drittem Reich'* (Munich: Beck, 2011), pp. 24–33.

102. According to a survey from 1942, approximately half of the German textile industry was Jewish-owned. Four years later these companies represented less than 1 per cent of the industry; Köster, *Hugo Boss*, p. 39.

103. Irene Guenther, *Nazi Chic? Fashioning Women in the Third Reich* (Oxford and New York: Berg, 2004).

104. Timm, *Hugo Ferdinand Boss*, p. 31; Köster, *Hugo Boss*, p. 30.

105. Petra Bräutigam, *Mittelständische Unternehmer im Nationalsozialismus: Wirtschaftliche Entwicklungen und soziale Verhaltensweisen in der Schuh- und Lederindustrie Badens und Württembergs* (Munich: Oldenbourg, 1997), pp. 147–50.

106. As early as 1924 the Communist daily *Die Rote Fahne* ran an advertisement for the *Klassen-Kampf Zigarette* (KKZ) – literally 'class struggle cigarettes' – and promised that Red Aid, the Communist self-defence organization, would obtain a 'certain percentage' of the monthly sales. Unfortunately, no further information is available on this apparently short-lived attempt to fuse consumption and politics. The original advertisement from *Die Rote Fahne*, no. 147 from 2 November 1924, is reprinted in Gert-Joachim Glaessner, Detlef Lehnert, and Klaus Sühl (eds), *Studien zur Arbeiterbewegung und Arbeiterkultur in Berlin* (Berlin: Colloquium Verlag, 1989), p. 11.

107. Sandra Schünemann, 'Bilderwelten, Markengesichter und Marktgesetze: Werbung und Produktpolitik der Reemtsma Cigarettenfabriken zwischen 1920 und 1960', in *Wirtschaft – Kultur – Geschichte: Positionen und Perspektiven*, ed. Susanne Hilger and Achim Landwehr (Stuttgart: Steiner, 2011), pp. 111–32, here pp. 116–18, 123–4.

108. Ibid., p. 118.

109. This sentiment is best reflected in Hans Fallada's 1932 novel *Kleiner Mann, was nun?*, published in English as *Little Man, What Now?* (New York: Grosset & Dunlap, 1933).

110. Schünemann, 'Bilderwelten', pp. 119–21.

111. Holger Starke, 'Dampfschokolade, Neumünchner Bier und allerfeinster Korn', in *Dresdner Geschichtsbuch*, ed. Stadtmuseum Dresden (Altenburg: DZA-Verlag, 1995), pp. 119–50, here pp. 137–42.

112. Thomas Grosche, 'Arthur Dressler: Die Firma Sturm – Zigaretten für die SA', in *Braune Karrieren: Dresdner Täter und Akteure im Nationalsozialismus*, ed. Christine Piper, Mike Schmeitzner, and Gerhard Nader (Dresden: Sandstein, 2012), pp. 193–9, here p. 193; Erik Lindner, *Die Reemtsmas: Geschichte einer deutschen Unternehmerfamilie* (Hamburg: Hoffmann und Campe, 2007), pp. 69–70; Grant, *Stormtroopers and the Crisis in the Nazi Movement*, pp. 99–106.

113. One central reason why the SA engaged in business affairs was its lack of financial independence from the NSDAP. Every stormtrooper was expected to join the party and pay membership duties, which in part were used by the NSDAP to finance the SA. See Lindner, *Die Reemtsmas*, p. 70.

114. Grosche, 'Dressler', p. 193. Bettenhausen had made a fortune in the previous decades through his flourishing chain of station bookshops, which operated under both the former Habsburg monarchy and the German Reich. His credit seems to have been high and quite risky, given the marginal status of the NSDAP in 1929–30. However, it seems to have paid off in several forms later: Bettenhausen's company was one of the major distributors of newspapers and magazines in the Third Reich, and the Nazis even entrusted him with organizing the bookselling industry in occupied Poland. See Christine Haug, *Reisen und Lesen im Zeitalter der Industrialisierung: Die Geschichte des Bahnhofs- und Verkehrsbuchhandels*

in Deutschland von seinen Anfängen um 1850 bis zum Ende der Weimarer Republik (Wiesbaden: Harrassowitz, 2007), pp. 155–7.

115. Grosche, 'Dressler', pp. 193–4.
116. Lindner, *Die Reemtsmas*, p. 70.
117. Grosche, 'Dressler', pp. 194–6.
118. Lindner, *Die Reemtsmas*, p. 70.
119. Ibid., pp. 78, 81.
120. See several regional reports to the OSAF from the summer and autumn of 1932, in BArch Berlin, NS 23/474.
121. BArch Berlin, NS 23/474, p. 105,070: Report of the SA-Gruppe West, 21 September 1932; ibid., p. 105,188: Report of the SA-Untergruppe Oberschlesien, 22 September 1932.
122. BArch Berlin, NS 23/474, p. 105,178: Letter from the Gruppenführer of the SA-Gruppe Schlesien to OSAF, 22 September 1932.
123. GStA PK, XX. HA, Rep. 240 B 31 c, pp. 191–201, here p. 191: Typescript of 'Wie kam es nun zum 1. August 1932?'
124. The brands of this company, which were actually produced by the Gera-based cigarette company Mahalesi (led by Paul Rother), were named 'Spielman' ($3\frac{1}{3}$ pfennig), 'Kommando' (4 pfennig), 'Staffel' (5 pfennig), and 'Neue Arena' (6 pfennig). See BArch Berlin, NS 23/474, p. 105,144: Letter from SA-Standartenführer Heinrich Löwenstein, Kassel, to Sturmbann I – V/83, 14 July 1932; ibid., p. 105,151: Letter from NSDAP Gera, 20 May 1932.
125. BArch Berlin, NS 23/474, p. 105,174: Letter from SA-Mittelschlesien Süd to OSAF, 26 September 1932.
126. Grosche, 'Dressler', p. 194.
127. Thomas Grosche, *Die Zigarettenindustrie in Dresden – Von den Anfängen bis zum zweiten Weltkrieg*, MA diss. (unpublished), TU Dresden, 2009, pp. 71–2. I am grateful to Thomas Grosche for providing me with a copy of his work.
128. Industrie- und Handelskammer Dresden, *Chronik*, http://www.dresden.ihk.de/150jahre/chronik.html.
129. Lindner, *Die Reemtsmas*, pp. 91–2.
130. Ibid., pp. 72–141, esp. pp. 88–90.
131. Ibid., pp. 92, 114–19. According to National Socialist sources, the largest German cigarette producers had invested 3 million reichsmark on advertising in party newspapers and magazines in 1932 alone; BArch Berlin, NS 23/474, p. 105,123: Letter from the Führer of the SA-Gruppe Franken, W. Stegmann.
132. Grosche, *Die Zigarettenindustrie*, pp. 76–7, with further references.
133. Grosche, 'Dressler', p. 198.
134. Schünemann, 'Bilderwelten', p. 125.
135. On the interrelations between the Christian churches and the Nazi stormtroopers, see Bergen, *Twisted Cross*, in particular pp. 70–81; Gailus, *Protestantismus und Nationalsozialismus*; Steigmann-Gall, *The Holy Reich*; Klauspeter Reumann (ed.), *Kirche und Nationalsozialismus: Beiträge zur Geschichte des Kirchenkampfes in den evangelischen Landeskirchen Schleswig-Holsteins* (Neumünster: Karl Wachholtz, 1988); Siemens, *The Making of a Nazi Hero*, pp. 126–7.
136. GStA PK, I. HA, Rep. 77, titl. 4043, no. 423, p. 79: Prussian Minister of the Interior, Notation from 20 August 1931 (signed Dr Gräser).
137. See his lengthy (and querulous) letter to the East Prussian *Gauleiter* Koch, 22 April 1932, in GStA PK, XX. HA, Rep. 240 B 27 d+e, pp. 168–77. On the Nazis' 'deadly hate' for the Centre Party, see Geiger, *Die soziale Schichtung des deutschen Volkes*, p. 112; on their problem of winning over Catholic voters, see Falter, *Hitlers Wähler*, pp. 177–88.
138. According to the historian Richard Steigmann-Gall, in 1930 only about 120 out of 18,000 Protestant pastors in Germany were members of the Nazi Party. However, he argues that the number of supporters was certainly much bigger, particularly given the fact that the churches 'discouraged their clergy from formally joining any political party'; Steigmann-Gall, *Holy Reich*, p. 76.
139. All facts and quotations in this paragraph are taken from Trauthig's excellent study on Württemberg's Protestants, *Im Kampf um Glauben und Kirche*, pp. 55–67. Benedikt Brunner

has recently demonstrated to what extent such 'male' rhetoric of religious battle even shaped the autobiographies of Protestant theologians in the first two decades after 1945; Benedikt Brunner, 'Geschlechterordnung im Kirchenkampf: Konstruktion von Gender in der auto-biographischen Verarbeitung der Zeit des Nationalsozialismus', in 'sichtbar unsichtbar: *Geschlechterwissen in (auto-)biographischen Texten*', ed. Maria Heidegger et al. (Bielefeld: transcript, 2015), pp. 103–17.

140. A telling example is the provost Ernst Szymanowski, who later changed his surname into Biberstein. In his parish in Bad Segeberg he would hold church services in front of entire SA units and dressed in the brown shirt himself on these occasions. He even put pressure on other pastors who did not conform to his views by sending stormtroopers to disturb their services. See Stephan Linck, 'Eine mörderische Karriere: der Schleswig-holsteinische Theologe Ernst Szymanowski/Biberstein', in Manfred Gailus and Clemens Vollnhals (eds), *Für ein artgemäßes Christentum der Tat: Völkische Theologie im 'Dritten Reich'* (Göttingen: V&R unipress, 2016), pp. 239–59, here pp. 244, 246.

141. Heinrich Rendtorff, 'Kirche und Nationalsozialismus', *Das evangelische Hamburg* 25 (1931), pp. 166–7 (first published in *Mecklenburgische Zeitung*, 23 April 1931).

142. Trauthig, *Im Kampf um Glauben und Kirche*, pp. 60–1. Wurm was a central figure of German Protestantism in the twentieth century. On his fierce opposition to Allied denazification procedures after the Second World War, see his *Memorandum by the Evangelical Church in Germany on the Question of War Crimes Trials before American Military Courts* (Waiblingen-Stuttgart: Stürner, 1949); Jon David K. Wyneken, 'Memory as Diplomatic Leverage: Evangelical Bishop Theophil Wurm and War Crimes Trials, 1948–1952', *Kirchliche Zeitgeschichte* 19:2 (2006), pp. 368–88.

143. Manfred Gailus, '1933 als protestantisches Erlebnis: emphatische Selbsttransformation und Spaltung', *Geschichte und Gesellschaft* 29:4 (2003), pp. 481–511.

144. Kurt Hutten, *Nationalsozialismus und Christentum* (Stuttgart: Evangelischer Volksbund, 1932), p. 31. On the Protestants' generally welcoming attitude to the Nazis between 1930 and 1934, see also Hans-Ulrich Wehler, *Deutsche Gesellschaftsgeschichte, Vierter Band: Vom Beginn des Ersten Weltkriegs bis zur Gründung der beiden deutschen Staaten 1914–1949* (Munich: Beck, 2003), pp. 797–804.

145. Hansjörg Buss, '"Für arteigene Frömmigkeit – über alle Konfessionen und Dogmen hinweg". Gerhard Meyer und der Bund für Deutsche Kirche', in Gailus and Vollnhals (eds), *Für ein artgemäßes Christentum der Tat*, pp. 119–33, here pp. 121, 124.

146. Ralf Czubatynski, 'Domprediger Ernst Martin (1885–1974) im Spannungsfeld von Politik und Kirchenpolitik in der Zeit der Weimarer Republik und des Nationalsozialismus', in *Sachsen-Anhalt: Beiträge zur Kultur und Landesgeschichte* 15 (Halle: Mitteldeutscher Verlag, 1999), pp. 101–24, here pp. 112–13; Hattenhorst, *Magdeburg 1933*, pp. 120–3.

147. Czubatynski, 'Domprediger Ernst Martin', pp. 114–23.

148. Franz Tügel, 'Kirche und Nationalsozialismus', *Das evangelische Hamburg* 26 (1932), pp. 52–6, here pp. 53–4.

149. Wackerfuss, *Stormtrooper Families*, pp. 26–32, 220–3.

150. Stehn, 'Über die politische Betätigung der Pastoren', *Das evangelische Hamburg* 25 (1931), p. 357.

151. In Württemberg the Protestant Church temporarily prohibited their pastors from participating in political party activities on 29 September 1932; Trauthig, *Im Kampf um Glauben und Kirche*, p. 58. In reaction to such orders, the liberal press in November 1932 reported that Röhm had requested every SA group in the Reich to appoint an 'SA cler-gyman' to consecrate party flags and provide pastoral care for the stormtroopers. Such pastors, the newspapers reported, were required to be party members and were to be supervised by Ludwig Münchmeyer, a notorious antisemite and former Protestant pastor who since 1930 represented the NSDAP in the Reichstag. Two weeks later, however, the Nazi paper *Der Völkische Beobachter* disclaimed such rumours. With the appointment of Hitler to the position of *Reichskanzler* soon afterwards, the Nazi Party no longer needed to rely on specially chosen pastors. Some upright dissenters notwithstanding, local cler-gymen now happily performed services for the party – another indicator that National Socialism had struck a chord with many Protestant pastors in the previous years. See 'Pfarrer als Sturmbannführer', *Vossische Zeitung*, 4 November 1932, p. 2; Kater, 'Ansätze

zu einer Soziologie der SA', p. 807. On Münchmeyer, see Gerhard Lindemann, *'Typisch jüdisch': Die Stellung der Ev.-luth. Landeskirche Hannovers zu Antijudaismus, Judenfeindschaft und Antisemitismus 1919–1949* (Berlin: Duncker & Humblot, 1998), pp. 136–220.

152. In Holzkirchen, a market town south of Munich, the local priest reported that four-fifths of his believers were National Socialist; Pridham, *Hitler's Rise to Power*, p. 157.

153. Ibid., p. 168.

154. Ibid., pp. 166–9, 177.

155. Hastings, *Catholicism and the Roots of Nazism*, pp. 107–42, 168–70. See also idem, 'How "Catholic" Was the Early Nazi Movement? Religion, Race, and Culture in Munich, 1919–1924', *Central European History* 36:3 (2003), pp. 383–433; Thomas Forstner, 'Braune Priester – Katholische Geistliche im Spannungsfeld von Katholizismus und Nationalsozialismus', in *Täter und Komplizen in Theologie und Kirchen 1933–1945*, ed. Manfred Gailus, 2nd edn (Göttingen: Wallstein, 2015), pp. 113–39.

156. Pridham, *Hitler's Rise to Power*, pp. 164–5.

157. On 28 April, SA Chief of Staff Röhm was among those present in the church, and he met at least twice with the archbishop. See the entries from 27 and 29 April 1933 in Faulhaber-Edition, *Critical Online Edition of the Diaries of Michael Kardinal von Faulhaber (1911–1952)*: http://p.faulhaber-edition.de/exist/apps/faulhaber/dokument.html?collid=1933&sortby=year&doctype=bb&docidno=BB_06393_0542r; http://p.faulhaber-edition.de/exist/apps/faulhaber/dokument.html?collid=1933&sortby=year&doctype=bb&docidno=BB_09263_0030s.

158. GStA PK, I. HA, Rep. 77 titl 4043, no. 311, pp. 275–85: Hans Georg Hofmann (ed.), *Pflichtenlehre des Sturm-Abteilungsmannes (SA-Katechismus)* (Dießen: Huber, undated [1934]), p. 10.

159. Werner Betcke (ed.), *Der kleine Katechismus Dr. Martin Luthers für den braunen Mann* (Gütersloh: Bertelsmann, 1934), pp. 4, 24.

160. Klintzsch's father, the pastor Johannes Paul Klintzsch, had died on 11 September 1920, at the age of fifty-nine. The father of Horst Wessel, the pastor Ludwig Wessel, had died on 9 May 1922, at the age of forty-two; Stadt Lübbenau, Letter to the author from 8 May 2015; Siemens, *Making of a Nazi Hero*, p. 27.

161. Walsdorff, 'Hans Ulrich Klintzsch', p. 1,257; LKA Stuttgart, A 127, no. 1293 (personnel file of Hans Ulrich Klintzsch). His appointment by the Evangelical-Lutheran Church in Württemberg was partly financed with donations from the Evangelical-Lutheran churches in the USA. Klintzsch quit the job as a catechet in 1952 when he was granted an officer pension. He died in Berlin on 17 August 1959.

162. Emil Maurice, Letter to the pastor of Gettorf, dated 3 June 1924, as quoted in Sigmund, *Des Führers bester Freund*, p. 29.

163. Andrew Wackerfuss in his case study of the Hamburg SA likewise stresses the importance of religious beliefs for understanding the stormtrooper mentality. See Wackerfuss, *Stormtrooper Families*, pp. 218–23.

164. StA München, Pol. Dir. 6804: Police report from the NSDAP's Christmas Party in the Bürgerbräukeller, 18 December 1922. On this occasion, the well-known Bavarian humorist Weiß Ferdl also contributed to the popularity of the event.

165. Ibid.

166. Joseph Berchtold, 'Auferstehung', *S.A.-Mann*, March 1929, as cited in StA München, Pol. Dir. 6805: Extracts from Munich's Police *Lagebericht*, no. 77, 7 May 1929. On the biography of Berchtold, see Hein, *Elite für Volk und Führer?*, pp. 42–3, 69–70.

167. See Jürgen W. Falter, 'The Young Membership of the NSDAP between 1925 and 1933: A Demographic and Social Profile', *Historical Social Research*, Supplement 25 (2013), pp. 260–79, here pp. 271–2; Jörg Thierfelder and Eberhard Röhm, 'Die evangelischen Landeskirchen von Baden und Württemberg in der Spätphase der Weimarer Republik und zu Beginn des Dritten Reiches', in *Die Machtergreifung in Südwestdeutschland*, ed. Thomas Schnabel, pp. 219–56, here p. 229.

168. Otto Wagener, *Hitler: Memoirs of a Confidant*, ed. Henry Ashby Turner (New Haven, CT: Yale University Press, 1985), pp. 19–21, as cited in Steigmann-Gall, *Holy Reich*, p. 66.

169. Ibid.

170. See Charlotte Tacke, *Denkmal im sozialen Raum: Nationale Symbole in Deutschland und Frankreich im 19. Jahrhundert* (Göttingen: Vandenhoeck & Ruprecht, 1995); Rudy Koshar, *From Monuments to Traces: Artifacts of German Memory, 1870–1990* (Berkeley, CA: University of Berkeley Press, 2000), pp. 35–40.

171. The idea of a 'muscular Christianity' was popular in the first half of the twentieth century in North America and western Europe alike. In Germany its proponents usually referred to such ideas as a 'Germanization of the Christian faith'. See Clifford Puttney, *Muscular Christianity: Manhood and Sports in Protestant America, 1880–1920* (Cambridge, MA: Harvard University Press, 2003); Arthur Bonus, *Von Stöcker zu Naumann: Ein Wort zur Germanisierung des Christentums* (Heilbronn: Salzer, 1896); Rainer Lächele, 'Protestantismus und völkische Religion im deutschen Kaiserreich', in *Handbuch zur 'Völkischen Bewegung' 1871–1918*, ed. Uwe Puschner, Walter Schmitz, and Justus H. Ulbricht (Munich: Saur, 1999), pp. 149–63. Such ideas even resonated among the Catholic priesthood in interwar Germany; see Forstner, 'Braune Priester', pp. 131–3. For an instructive case study on the Protestant pastor Gustav von Bodelschwingh, who in the Third Reich recruited SA students of Protestant theology to his settlement project in Dünne near Bielefeld using similar arguments, see Ulrich Rottschäfer, 'Gustav von Bodelschwingh und die Gründung des Sammelvikariats in Dünne', *Jahrbuch für Westfälische Kirchengeschichte* 89 (1995), pp. 216–47, here pp. 223–31. I am grateful to Johannes Lübeck, Tangermünde, for pointing me to this article.

172. See the instructive contributions in Matthew Feldman and Marius Turda (eds), *Clerical Fascism in Interwar Europe* (London and New York: Routledge, 2008).

173. From the recent literature, see Dylan Riley, *The Civic Foundations of Fascism in Europe: Italy, Spain, and Romania, 1870–1945* (Baltimore, MD: Johns Hopkins University Press, 2010), as well as the contributions in Alejandro Quiroga and Miguel Angel des Arco (eds), *Right-Wing Spain in the Civil War Era: Soldiers of God and Apostles of the Fatherland, 1914–1945* (London: Continuum, 2012).

174. Rory Yeomans, 'Militant Women, Warrior Men and Revolutionary Personae: The New Ustasha Man and Woman in the Independent State of Croatia, 1941–1945', *Slavonic and East European Review* 83:4 (2005), pp. 685–732, here p. 705.

175. As quoted in Stephen Fischer-Galati (ed.), *Man, State, and Society in East European History* (London: Pall Mall, 1970), p. 330. For a comparative investigation into the religious elements of the Romanian and Croatian Fascist movements, see the excellent study by Radu Harald Dinu, *Faschismus, Religion und Gewalt in Südosteuropa: Die Legion Erzengel Michael und die Ustaša im historischen Vergleich* (Wiesbaden: Harrassowitz, 2013), pp. 204–52.

176. Hofmann, *Pflichtenlehre des Sturm-Abteilungsmannes*, p. 11. Irrespective of those promises, the relations between the National Socialist regime and the churches soon became complicated.

177. Bergen, *Twisted Cross*, p. 71.

178. The printmaker Schwarzkopf was born on 11 April 1893 in Bonn, educated in the 1910s at the *Kunstgewerbeschule Düsseldorf*, and, in 1933, appointed professor at the *Kunstakademie Düsseldorf*. In 1937 he became a leader in the National Socialist German Lecturers League and was also elected president of the Malkasten artists' association, a position he held until 1945. He served again as its president beginning in 1956. Schwarzkopf died on 31 May 1963 in Düsseldorf. On his biography and works, see Dietrich Grünewald, 'Der Totentanz bei Rethel, Ille und Schwarzkopf', *Deutsche Comicforschung* 5 (2009), pp. 21–32, here pp. 30–2; Sabine Schroyen, *Bildquellen zur Geschichte des Künstlervereins Malkasten in Düsseldorf. Künstler und ihre Werke in den Sammlungen* (Düsseldorf: Grupello, 2001), pp. 34–6, 316–18.

179. See in particular the reproductions in Oberste SA-Führung, *... wurde die SA eingesetzt: Politische Soldaten erzählen von wenig beachteten Frontabschnitten unserer Zeit* (Munich: Eher, 1938), pp. 43, 55, 91.

180. For details, see Grünewald, 'Der Totentanz bei Rethel'; Alfred Rethel, *Auch ein Todtentanz*, 11th edn (Leipzig, Schlicke, 1879); Hans Jürgen Imiela, 'Alfred Rethel und der Tod', in *Der Tod in Dichtung, Philosophie und Kunst*, 2nd edn, ed. Hans Helmut Jansen (Darmstadt: Steinkopff, 1989), pp. 371–9.

181. Grünewald, 'Der Totentanz bei Rethel', p. 27.

182. *Der Kampf der SA: Eine Bildfolge nach 6 Holzschnitten von Prof. Richard Schwarzkopf* (advertising brochure), in LArch Ludwigsburg, PL 505 Bü 12. For earlier versions in which Life defeats Death, see Grünewald, 'Der Totentanz bei Rethel', p. 32.

183. Besides *German Passion*, the series was also referred to as *The Fight of the SA* and *Totentanz der SA*; Schroyen, *Bildquellen zur Geschichte des Künstlervereins Malkasten*, p. 35.
184. Fest, 'Ernst Röhm und die verlorene Generation', p. 190.
185. Ibid., pp. 191, 193.
186. Emre Sencer, 'Fear and Loathing in Berlin: German Military Culture at the Turn of the 1930s', *German Studies Review* 37:1 (2014), pp. 19–39, here p. 22. In reality, this erosion of authority began during the last two years of the war.
187. Horst von Metzsch, 'Nie wieder ein solches Jahrzehnt!', *Militär-Wochenblatt*, 4 July 1929, as quoted in Sencer, 'Fear and Loathing in Berlin', p. 23.
188. Until 1928 the relationship between the Reichswehr and the NSDAP was distant – partly as a result of long-term mutual antagonism between the two in the wake of the failed November 1923 putsch, and partly because of the consolidation of Weimar democracy in the mid-1920s. On 5 December 1928 Hitler even formally prohibited members of his party from joining the Reichswehr, thereby indirectly acknowledging the military's self-image as an institution 'above politics'. See Peter Bucher, *Der Reichswehrprozeß: Der Hochverrat der Ulmer Reichswehroffiziere 1929/30*, Militärgeschichtliche Studien 4 (Boppard am Rhein: Boldt, 1967), p. 9.
189. Bucher, *Der Reichswehrprozeß*, p. 11.
190. Timothy S. Brown, 'Richard Scheringer, the KPD and the Politics of Class and Nation in Germany, 1922–1969', *Contemporary European History* 14:3 (2005), pp. 317–46, here pp. 323–5; Bucher, *Der Reichswehrprozeß*, pp. 110–13.
191. Sencer, 'Fear and Loathing in Berlin', p. 25.
192. For a detailed discussion of Ludin's biography and later career, see the following note and chapter 10.
193. Bucher, *Der Reichswehrprozeß*, p. 130; Brown, 'Richard Scheringer', pp. 323, 337.
194. Ernst Niekisch, *Erinnerungen eines deutschen Revolutionärs. Erster Band: Gewagtes Leben 1889–1945* (Cologne: Wissenschaft und Politik, 1974), p. 185.
195. Eckart Kehr, 'Zur Soziologie der Reichswehr', *Neue Blätter für den Sozialismus* 1 (1930), pp. 156–64, here p. 163.
196. On the complex relationship between the German nobility and the SA, see Malinowski and Reichardt, 'Die Reihen fest geschlossen?'
197. Peter Hoffmann, *Claus Schenk Graf von Stauffenberg und seine Brüder* (Stuttgart: DVA, 1992), p. 101. On the 'George circle' and George's ideas of a 'secret Germany', see Thomas Karlauf, *Stefan George: Die Entdeckung des Charisma* (Munich: Blessing, 2007); Robert E. Norton, *Secret Germany. Literary Modernism and Visual Culture: Stefan George and His Circle* (Ithaca, NY: Cornell University Press, 2002).
198. Hoffmann, *Claus Schenk Graf von Stauffenberg*, p. 103. Eberhard Zeller in his biography of Stauffenberg likewise mentions the man's sympathy toward Scheringer, Ludin, and Wendt, but insists that this sympathy should not be taken as a political endorsement of the Nazi Party. See Eberhard Zeller, *Oberst Claus Graf Stauffenberg: Ein Lebensbild* (Paderborn: Schöningh, 2008 [1994]), p. 25.
199. Hans Roschmann, *Erinnerungen eines 'Kämpferischen Schwaben'* (Überlingen: self-published, undated [1985]), pp. 37–8.
200. RGVA, Osobyi Archives, Fond 720, Opis 1, no. 47, p. 201: Röhm, SABE (SA-Befehl) from 13 January 1931. On the collaboration of the Reichswehr and the SA in border-protection efforts, see also IfZ Archive, ED 414, vol. 181: 'Stabschef Röhm im Kieler Hitler-Prozeß', *Hamburger Tageblatt*, 11 July 1932, p. 12.
201. For details, see in particular RGVA, Osobyi Archives, Fond 720, Opis 1, no. 47, pp. 352–62: 'Material zur Frage der Militarisierung der SA', September 1931.
202. GStA PK, I. HA, Rep. 77 titl. 4043, no. 311, pp. 25–6: Report from the Berlin Police President to the Regierungspräsident in Düsseldorf, 4 February 1932.

Chapter 4

1. Ernst Röhm, *Die Geschichte eines Hochverräters* (1928), as translated and quoted in Röhm, *The Memoirs of Ernst Röhm*, p. 237.
2. Erich Koch-Weser, 'Der deutsche Mensch', *Vossische Zeitung*, 1 February 1933 (morning edition), pp. 1–2.

3. Gustave Le Bon, *Psychologie des foules* (Paris: F. Alcan, 1895); for the English version, see *The Crowd: A Study of the Popular Mind* (London: Unwin, 1897).

4. Several years after Koch-Weser's statement, British historians put forth a very similar argument to explain the German psyche. In 1941, Lewis B. Namier wrote: 'It is the lack of moral self-courage, self-assurance, and independence in the individual German which makes him seek safety, self-assertion and superlative power in and through his State and nation, and which makes him glorify them beyond all bounds of sense and reason.' Lewis B. Namier, 'Both Slaves and Masters', *Time & Tide*, 5 July 1941, as quoted in Jörg Später, *Vansittart: Britische Debatten über Deutsche und Nazis 1902–1945* (Göttingen: Wallstein, 2003), p. 220.

5. The literature on this topic is exhaustive. From the most recent publications, see Wachsmann, *KL*, pp. 23–78; Irene Mayer-von Götz, *Terror im Zentrum der Macht: Die frühen Konzentrationslager in Berlin* (Berlin: Metropol, 2008); as well as the contributions in Nikolaus Wachsmann and Sybille Steinbacher (eds), *Die Linke im Visier: Zur Errichtung der Konzentrationslager 1933* (Göttingen: Wallstein, 2014); and those in Hördler (ed.), *SA-Terror als Herrschaftssicherung*. For overviews of the political history of 1933, see in particular Andreas Wirsching (ed.), *Das Jahr 1933: Die nationalsozialistische Machteroberung und die deutsche Gesellschaft* (Göttingen: Wallstein, 2009); Richard Bessel, 'The Nazi Capture of Power', *Journal of Contemporary History* 39:2 (2004), pp. 169–88, as well as the literature in the following notes.

6. Elias Canetti, *Crowds and Power* (New York: Noonday Press, 1998), p. 17.

7. RGVA, Osobyi Archives, Fond 720, Opis 1, no. 43, p. 80: Letter from the Bavarian Minister of the Interior, Adolf Wagner, to the Reich Ministry of the Interior, 26 April 1933 (typescript); BArch Berlin, R1501/20234: 'Reichsbanner nun auch in Sachsen verboten', *Der Montag*, 13 March 1933.

8. GSt PK, I. HA, Rep. 77, titl. 4043, no. 14, pp. 2–3: SA-Gruppenführer Schlesien (Edmund Heines), Gruppenbefehl no. 32, Breslau, 24 April 1933, and draft of a telegram from the Prussian Minister President sent to all SA, SS, and *Stahlhelm* formations in East Prussia, Silesia, and the Grenzmark, undated; German Foreign Ministry, Political Archives (PAAA), R 99246, p. 90: Order of Ernst Röhm on matters of 'Auslandsdeutsche' in the SA, 27 November 1933.

9. Klaus Schwabe and Rolf Reichardt (eds), *Gerhard Ritter: Ein politischer Historiker in seinen Briefen* (Boppard am Rhein: Boldt, 1984), p. 66.

10. Alexander Mitscherlich, *Ein Leben für die Psychoanalyse: Anmerkungen zu meiner Zeit* (Frankfurt am Main: Suhrkamp, 1980), p. 111, as quoted in Tobias Freimüller, 'Verdrängung und Bewältigung: Alexander Mitscherlich und die NS-Vergangenheit', in Freimüller (ed.), *Psychoanalyse und Protest: Alexander Mitscherlich und die 'Achtundsechziger'* (Göttingen: Wallstein, 2008), pp. 118–32, here p. 121.

11. As quoted in Fritzsche, *Turbulent World of Franz Göll*, p. 147.

12. Röhm did not approve of such demands, because he regarded them as attempts to organize private interests under the umbrella of the SA. See BArch Berlin, NS 23/510: Oberster SA-Führer, Circular Letter on 'Sondergliederungen', 5 July 1933.

13. BArch Berlin, NS 1/388, pp. 126–8, here p. 126: Letter from Elfriede Conti to Martin Bormann, 3 March 1933.

14. LArch Berlin, A Rep. 003-04-01, p. 101: Letter from Karl Ernst to the Staatskommissar of the capital city of Berlin (Julius Lippert), 26 July 1933.

15. Detlev Humann, '"Alte Kämpfer" in der neuen Zeit: Die sonderbare Arbeitsvermittlung für NS-Parteigänger nach 1933', *Vierteljahrschrift für Sozial- und Wirtschaftsgeschichte* 98:2 (2011), pp. 173–94, here pp. 174–5.

16. Ibid., pp. 176–7.

17. Ibid., pp. 178–83.

18. Ulrich Klein, 'SA-Terror und Bevölkerung in Wuppertal 1933/34', in Detlev Peukert and Jürgen Reulecke (eds), *Die Reihen fast geschlossen: Beiträge zur Geschichte des Alltags unterm Nationalsozialismus* (Wuppertal: Peter Hammer, 1986), pp. 45–61, here p. 56.

19. Christian Meyer, *Semantiken des Privaten in autobiographischen Deutungen des Nationalsozialismus 1939/1940*, PhD diss., Bielefeld University, 2015, pp. 154–7.

20. According to official reports, SA unemployment had been reduced by up to 80 per cent by the spring of 1934. For examples, see Humann, '"Alte Kämpfer" in der neuen Zeit', pp. 185–6, 192.

The situation in the southwest was less promising, as there only a third of all unemployed 'Old Fighters' had been placed in jobs by the end of 1933; Gunter Mai, 'Die Nationalsozialistische Betriebszellen-Organisation: Zum Verhältnis von Arbeiterschaft und Nationalsozialismus', *Vierteljahrshefte für Zeitgeschichte* 31:4 (1981), pp. 573–613, here p. 601.

21. Humann, '"Alte Kämpfer" in der neuen Zeit', p. 185.
22. Frank Bajohr appropriately characterized the NSDAP as the party of 'organized self-pity'; see Frank Bajohr, *Parvenüs und Profiteure: Korruption in der NS-Zeit* (Frankfurt am Main: Fischer, 2001), pp. 13, 22–4.
23. On the SA-*Hilfswerklager* and their funding, see Detlev Humann, 'Verwahranstalten mit Fantasiegehältern?: Die Hilfswerklager der SA für arbeitslose "alte Kämpfer"', *Vierteljahrschrift für Sozial- und Wirtschaftsgeschichte* 97:4 (2010), pp. 425–36; Fischer, *Stormtroopers*, pp. 130–3.
24. Peter Schyga, *Goslar 1918–1945: Von der nationalen Stadt zur Reichsbauernstadt des Nationalsozialismus* (Bielefeld: Verlag für Regionalgeschichte, 1999), p. 137.
25. The stormtroopers of the 'Austrian Legion' were particularly notorious in this respect; see Schafranek, *Söldner für den 'Anschluss'*, pp. 174–205; Humann, 'Verwahranstalten mit Fantasiegehältern?', p. 426, n. 4.
26. The original advertisement is included in BArch Berlin, NS 23/204.
27. BArch Berlin, NS 23/204: Letter from Müller to Rudolf Hess, 23 April 1934.
28. On the social gulf between the SA leadership and 'ordinary' SA men, see Kater, 'Ansätze zu einer Soziologie der SA'. On the widespread corruption in the Third Reich, see Bajohr, *Parvenüs und Profiteure*. On the SA, see here esp. pp. 17–34.
29. Fritz Tobias, *Der Reichstagsbrand: Legende und Wirklichkeit* (Rastatt: Grote, 1962); Hans Mommsen, 'Der Reichstagsbrand und seine politischen Folgen', *Vierteljahrshefte für Zeitgeschichte* 12:4 (1964), pp. 351–413.
30. Hett, *Burning the Reichstag*, pp. 318–23. Hett's book is the latest in a list of contributions to the so-called Reichstag fire controversy over which historians of twentieth-century German history in particular have fought bitterly. For critical interventions against the Tobias/Mommsen faction, see Hans Schneider (ed.), *Neues vom Reichstagsbrand? Eine Dokumentation* (Berlin: BWV, 2004); Alexander Bahar and Wilfried Kugel, *Der Reichstagsbrand: Wie Geschichte gemacht wird* (Berlin: edition q, 2001); Jürgen Schmädeke, Alexander Bahar, and Wilfried Kugel, 'Der Reichstagsbrand in neuem Licht', *Historische Zeitschrift* 269:3 (1999), pp. 603–51. As was to be expected, Hett's work provoked a defence of the single-perpetrator thesis; see Richard J. Evans, 'The Conspiracists', *London Literary Review of Books* 36:9 (2014), pp. 3–9; also Hett's and Evans's subsequent replies, both published in the *London Literary Review of Books* 36:11 (2014).
31. Häberlen, *Vertrauen und Politik*, p. 186; Hermann Weber, 'Zum Verhältnis von Komintern, Sowjetstaat und KPD', in Hermann Weber, Jakov Drabkin, and Bernhard H. Bayerlein (eds), *Deutschland, Russland, Komintern I: Überblicke, Analysen, Diskussionen. Neue Perspektiven auf die Geschichte der KPD und die Deutsch-Russischen Beziehungen (1918–1943)* (Berlin: de Gruyter, 2014), pp. 9–139, here p. 102, with further references.
32. For a particularly dreadful case, see GSt PK, XX. HA, Rep. 240 B 29 a–g, p. 153: Letter from Fräuling Itzig, the daughter of a Jewish cattle dealer, to Hermann Göring, 15 March 1933. On the anti-Jewish boycott actions, see Hannah Ahlheim, *'Deutsche, kauft nicht bei Juden!' Antisemitismus und politischer Boykott in Deutschland 1924 bis 1935*, 2nd edn (Göttingen: Wallstein, 2012), pp. 241–62; Christoph Kreutzmüller, *Ausverkauf: Die Vernichtung der jüdischen Gewerbetätigkeit in Berlin 1930–1945* (Berlin: Metropol, 2012), pp. 123–45, 219–38.
33. BArch Berlin, NS 23/409: 'Schacht Issues Debt Warning', *Evening Sun* (New York), 7 April 1933.
34. Johannes Tuchel, 'Organisationsgeschichte der "frühen" Konzentrationslager', in Wolfgang Benz and Barbara Distel (eds), *Instrumentarium der Macht: Frühe Konzentrationslager 1933–1937* (Berlin: Metropol, 2003), pp. 9–26, here p. 11; Karin Orth, *Das System der nationalsozialistischen Konzentrationslager: Eine politische Organisationsgeschichte* (Hamburg: Hamburger Edition, 1999), p. 23; Wünschmann, *Before Auschwitz*, p. 68. The peak of the arrests occurred in the spring of 1933. Between February and April of that year alone 45,000 people were held in confinement.

35. For an overview of the different types of early concentration camps, see Tuchel, 'Organisationsgeschichte der "frühen" Konzentrationslager', pp. 13–15; Jan Erik Schulte, 'Das KZ-System in der Region: Konzentrationslager im Rheinland und in Westfalen 1933–1945', in his (ed.), *Konzentrationslager im Rheinland und in Westfalen 1933–1945: Zentrale Steuerung und regionale Initiative* (Paderborn: Schöningh, 2005), pp. xi–xli. On the importance of Dachau as a 'model camp', see Wünschmann, *Before Auschwitz*, pp. 133–5; and Christopher Dillon, *Dachau and the SS: A Schooling in Violence* (Oxford: Oxford University Press, 2015).

36. Irene von Götz, 'Die frühen Konzentrationslager in Berlin', in *Bürgerkriegsarmee*, ed. Müller and Zilkenat, pp. 131–46, here p. 132.

37. A particularly drastic example of SA violence in Berlin was the so-called 'Köpenick murder week', or 'Köpenick's blood week'. Between 21 and 26 June 1933 stormtroopers arrested up to 500 people and killed at least 23 of them. See in particular Stefan Hördler, 'Ideologie, Machtinzenierung und Exzess: Taten und Täter der Köpenicker Blutwoche', in Stefan Hörder (ed.), *SA-Terror als Herrschaftssicherung*, ed. Hördler, pp. 83–104. On the local knowledge of the early concentrations camps with regard to those in the Rhineland and Westphalia, see also Schulte, 'Das KZ-System in der Region', p. xxiii.

38. See, for example, the case of the quarryman Hugo Rappenhöner, who hanged himself after being released from internment in the SA Porz prison; BArch Berlin, NS 23/889: Report from the Oberstaatsanwalt Cologne to the Prussian Minister of Justice, 13 December 1933.

39. Irene von Götz, 'Die Errichtung der Konzentrationslager in Berlin 1933: Entfesselter SA-Terror in der Reichshauptstadt', in *Die Linke im Visier: Zur Errichtung der Konzentrationslager 1933*, ed. Nikolaus Wachsmann and Sybille Steinbacher (Göttingen: Wallstein, 2014), pp. 70–83, here p. 73.

40. Sascha Münzel and Eckart Schörle, *Erfurt Feldstraße: Ein frühes Lager im Nationalsozialismus* (Erfurt: Landeszentrale für politische Bildung Thüringen, 2012), p. 50.

41. Julia Pietsch, 'Stigmatisierung von Juden in frühen Konzentrationslagern: Die "Judenkompanie" des Konzentrationslagers Oranienburg 1933/34', in Marco Brenneisen et al. (eds), *Stigmatisierung–Marginalisierung–Verfolgung: Beiträge des 19. Workshops zur Geschichte und Gedächtnisgeschichte der nationalsozialistischen Konzentrationslager* (Berlin: Metropol, 2015), pp. 99–120, here pp. 109–13; Veronika Springmann, *Gunst und Gewalt: Sport in nationalsozialistischen Konzentrationslagern*, diss., Carl von Ossietzky University of Oldenburg, 2015; Will Greif [Peter Blachstein], 'Juden', *Freies Deutschland*, 6 April 1939, as reprinted in Peter Blachstein, *'In uns lebt die Fahne der Freiheit': Zeugnisse zum frühen Konzentrationslager Burg Hohnstein*, ed. Norbert Haase and Mike Schmeizner (Dresden: Stiftung Sächsische Gedenkstätten zur Erinnerung an die Opfer politischer Gewaltherrschaft, 2005), pp. 126–8.

42. Gebhard Aders, 'Terror gegen Andersdenkende: Das SA-Lager am Hochkreuz in Köln-Porz', in *Instrumentarium der Macht: Frühe Konzentrationslager 1933–1937*, ed. Wolfgang Benz and Barbara Distel (Berlin: Metropol, 2003), pp. 179–88, here p. 184.

43. Norbert Haase, 'Das Konzentrationslager Hohnstein 1933/34 und seine Überlieferung in der deutschen Emigration', in Blachstein, *'In uns lebt die Fahne der Freiheit'*, pp. 8–22, here p. 15; Mike Schmeizner, 'Diktaturerfahrung und politische Konsequenz: Zur Biographie des deutsch-jüdischen Sozialisten Peter Blachstein, 1911–1977', in ibid., pp. 23–55, here p. 33.

44. Prior to 1939, women never constituted more than 10 per cent of all prisoners in the Third Reich. See Jane Caplan, 'Gender and the Concentration Camps', in Jane Caplan and Nikolaus Wachsmann (eds), *Concentration Camps in Nazi Germany: The New Histories* (London and New York: Routledge, 2010), pp. 82–107, here p. 83; Wünschmann, *Before Auschwitz*, p. 7.

45. Häberlen, *Vertrauen und Politik*, p. 186.

46. See also the pioneering article by Caplan, 'Gender and the Concentration Camps', esp. pp. 86–95.

47. Kim Wünschmann observed similar effects in her analysis of the strategies employed by Jewish men interned in Germany after 9 November 1938, and Brian Feltman has recently identified an analogous process adopted by the German prisoners of war during and after the First World War. See Kim Wünschmann, 'Die Konzentrationslagererfahrungen

deutsch-jüdischer Männer nach dem Novemberpogrom 1938: Geschlechtergeschichtliche Überlegungen zu männlichem Selbstverständnis und Rollenbild', in Susanne Heim, Beate Meyer, and Francis R. Nicosia (eds), '*Wer bleibt, opfert seine Jahre, vielleicht sein Leben': Deutsche Juden 1938–1941* (Göttingen: Wallstein, 2010), pp. 39–58; Brian K. Feltman, *The Stigma of Surrender: German Prisoners, British Captors, and Manhood in the Great War and Beyond* (Chapel Hill, NC: University of North Carolina Press, 2015).

48. Pietsch, 'Stigmatisierung von Juden in frühen Konzentrationslagern'; Kim Wünschmann, 'Cementing the Enemy Category: Arrest and Imprisonment of German Jews in Nazi Concentration Camps 1933–8/9', *Journal of Contemporary History* 45:3 (2010), pp. 576–600; Jürgen Matthäus, 'Verfolgung, Ausbeutung, Vernichtung: Jüdische Häftlinge im System der Konzentrationslager', in Günter Morsch and Susanne zur Nieden (eds), *Jüdische Häftlinge im Konzentrationslager Sachsenhausen 1936–1945* (Berlin: Hentrich, 2004), pp. 64–89; Caplan, 'Gender and the Concentration Camps', p. 87. On the Jewish welfare home in Wolzig, see Claudia Prestel, *Jugend in Not: Fürsorgeerziehung in deutsch-jüdischer Gesellschaft (1901–1933)* (Cologne: Böhlau, 2003), pp. 313–40, and for the SA raid of March 1933 and its consequences, pp. 336–7; as well as the detailed report by the CV-Verein, available in English in Jürgen Matthäus and Mark Roseman, *Jewish Responses to Persecution*, vol. 1: *1933–1938* (Lanham, MD: AltaMira, 2010), pp. 75–7.

49. Gerhart Seger, *Oranienburg: Erster authentischer Bericht eines aus dem Konzentrationslager Geflüchteten, mit einem Geleitwort von Heinrich Mann* (Karlsbad: Graphia, 1934), reprinted in Irene A. Diekmann and Klaus Wettig (eds), *Konzentrationslager Oranienburg: Augenzeugenberichte aus dem Jahre 1933: Gerhart Seger, Reichstagsabgeordneter der SPD; Max Abraham, Prediger aus Rathenow* (Potsdam: Verlag für Berlin-Brandenburg, 2003), pp. 15–89. A few months later Werner Schäfer, the ambitious commandant of the Oranienburg camp, replied with the book *Konzentrationslager Oranienburg: Das Anti-Braunbuch über das erste deutsche Konzentrationslager* (Berlin: Buch- und Tiefdruck-Gesellschaft, 1934). See the instructive article by Paul Moore, '"The Truth about the Concentration Camps": Werner Schäfer's Anti-Brown Book and the Transnational Debate on Early Nazi Terror', in *German History* 34 (2016), advanced access, published 3 October 2016.

50. Diekmann and Wettig, *Konzentrationslager Oranienburg*, pp. 62–5, here p. 64. Seger's negative characterization of his guards at least helped him uphold his own masculine identity. On this psychological coping mechanism, see also Wünschmann, 'Die Konzentrationslagererfahrungen deutsch-jüdischer Männer nach dem Novemberpogrom 1938', pp. 49–50.

51. Diekmann and Wettig, *Konzentrationslager Oranienburg*, p. 65.

52. Will Greif, 'Handwerker', *Freies Deutschland*, 27 April 1939, as reprinted in Blachstein, '*In uns lebt die Fahne der Freiheit*', pp. 132–4.

53. Diekmann and Wettig, *Konzentrationslager Oranienburg*, pp. 64–5; Will Greif, 'Rekruten', *Freies Deutschland*, 23 March 1939, as reprinted in Blachstein, '*In uns lebt die Fahne der Freiheit*', pp. 121–3.

54. Günter Morsch and Agnes Ohm (eds), *Terror in der Provinz Brandenburg: Frühe Konzentrationslager 1933/34* (Berlin: Metropol, 2014), p. 70; Haase, 'Das Konzentrationslager Hohnstein 1933/34', pp. 13–14.

55. Volker Bendig, 'Unter Regie der SA: Das Konzentrationslager Börnicke und das Nebenlager Meissnershof im Osthavelland', in *Instrumentarium der Macht*, ed. Wolfgang Benz and Barbara Diestel, pp. 97–101.

56. Eike Wolgast, 'Die Studierenden', in Wolfgang U. Eckart, Volker Sellin, and Eike Wolgast (eds), *Die Universität Heidelberg im Nationalsozialismus* (Heidelberg: Springer, 2006), pp. 57–94, here p. 60; Axel W. Bauer, Karin Langsch, and Wolfgang U. Eckart, 'Die Universitätsklinik und Poliklinik für Mund-, Zahn- und Kiefernkrankheiten', in ibid., pp. 1,031–41, here pp. 1,033–4.

57. Julia Deinert, *Die Studierenden der Universität Rostock im Dritten Reich*, PhD diss., Universität Rostock, 2010, pp. 72–3. For other examples of the SA's public display of its captives, see Wünschmann, *Before Auschwitz*, pp. 32–4.

58. Volker Friedrich Drecktrah, 'Die "Verbrechen gegen die Menschlichkeit" der Marine-SA Cuxhaven von 1933 und deren Ahndung nach 1945', in Alfred Gottwaldt et al. (eds),

NS-Gewaltherrschaft: Beiträge zur historischen Forschung und juristischen Aufarbeitung (Berlin: Hentrich, 2005), pp. 118–34, here pp. 131–3.

59. To provide just one example, in the Upper Silesian town of Beuthen a group of SA men on 22 July 1935 paraded a female Christian hairdresser who was engaged to a Jewish man through the streets of the town. The woman had to carry a sign that identified her as a 'race defiler'; her hair was cut short, and she is said to have been blackened with bitumen. See RGVA, Fond 721, Opis 1, no. 2604, p. 2: Letter from the CV-Verein, Landesverband Oberschlesien, to CV-Verein, Berlin, 23 July 1935. For similar examples, see Sopade, *Deutschland-Berichte* 2 (1935), p. 811.

60. Dorothee Wierling, *Eine Familie im Krieg: Leben, Sterben und Schreiben 1914–1918* (Göttingen: Wallstein, 2013), pp. 394–5.

61. Julie Braun-Vogelstein (ed.), *Otto Braun aus nachgelassenen Schriften eines Frühvollendeten* (Stuttgart: Deutsche Verlags-Anstalt, 1919). This book was reprinted several times before 1931 and sold approximately 100,000 copies; Wierling, *Eine Familie im Krieg*, pp. 380, 383–9.

62. On Litten, see Hett, *Crossing Hitler*; on Kronheim, see Andrea Löw and Hubert Schneider, 'Dr. Walter Kronheim', in Bochumer Anwalt- und Notarverein (ed.), *Zeit ohne Recht: Justiz in Bochum nach 1933* (Recklinghausen: Bitter, 2002), pp. 140–1; Schmidt, *Überwachen und Dienen*, p. 327. For an overview of the Jewish lawyers in the capital, see Simone Ladwig-Winters, *Anwalt ohne Recht: Das Schicksal jüdischer Rechtsanwälte in Berlin nach 1933*, 2nd edn (Berlin: be.bra, 2007).

63. Ludwig Foerder, who according to Alfred Wiener refused to compromise in his pursuit of right and justice, fled Germany in 1933 and temporarily settled in Prague, where he and his wife were 'found wandering in a demented state' in the spring of 1934. Foerder later emigrated to Palestine, where he died in relative isolation. His wife was arrested in the German-occupied Netherlands and subsequently murdered in the Holocaust. For insight into Foerder's political activities, see his two pamphlets *Antisemitismus und Justiz* (Berlin: Philo, 1924) and *Die Stellung des Centralvereins zu den innerjüdischen Fragen in den Jahren 1919–1926: Eine Denkschrift für Vereinsmitglieder* (Breslau: Volkswacht, 1927). On Foerder's life, see Joseph Walk, *Kurzbiographien zur Geschichte der Juden 1918–1945* (Munich: Saur, 1988), p. 94; Alfred Wiener, 'In Memory of Ludwig Foerder', *AJR Information* 9:8 (1954), p. 4; and the article 'Dr. Foerder, Wife Return to Health', originally published 1 June 1934 and here quoted in *JTA Archive*, http://www.jta.org/1934/06/01/archive/dr-foerder-wife-return-to-health.

64. Abraham Ascher, *A Community Under Siege: The Jews of Breslau under Nazism* (Stanford, CA: Stanford University Press, 2007), p. 76–7.

65. By 30 April 1934, 574 Jewish judges and prosecutors had left their jobs. In Prussia alone more than 700 Jewish lawyers had been denied admission to the courts by late 1933. See Wolfgang Benz, 'Jüdische Juristen unter dem nationalsozialistischen Regime: Von der Entrechtung zur Verfolgung und Vernichtung', in *Justiz und Judentum*, ed. Gerhard Pauli (Düsseldorf: Justizministerium des Landes NRW, 1999), pp. 19–36, here pp. 23–6.

66. Stephan A. Glienke, *Die NS-Vergangenheit späterer niedersächsischer Landtagsabgeordneter: Abschlussbericht zu einem Projekt der Historischen Kommission für Niedersachen und Bremen im Auftrag des Niedersächsischen Landtages* (Hannover: Niedersächsischer Landtag, 2012), p. 64.

67. For details, see Uwe Lohalm, '"Bis in die letzten Kriegstage intakt und voll funktionsfähig": Der öffentliche Dienst in Hamburg 1933 bis 1945', in Detlef Schmiechen-Ackermann and Steffi Kaltenborn (eds), *Stadtgeschichte in der NS-Zeit: Fallstudien aus Sachsen-Anhalt und vergleichende Perspektiven* (Münster: Lit, 2005), pp. 53–65, esp. pp. 55–6.

68. For a short biographical sketch of Werner von Fichte, a great-grandson of the philosopher Johann Gottlieb Fichte and former leader of the *Bund Wiking*, see Münzel and Schörle, *Erfurt Feldstraße*, pp. 23–4.

69. Ted Harrison, '"Alter Kämpfer" im Widerstand: Graf Helldorff, die NS-Bewegung und die Opposition gegen Hitler', *Vierteljahrshefte für Zeitgeschichte* 45 (1997), pp. 385–423, here p. 395.

70. Glienke, *Die NS-Vergangenheit späterer niedersächsischer Landtagsabgeordneter*, p. 65.

71. Klein, 'SA-Terror und Bevölkerung in Wuppertal', pp. 47–8.

72. On Helldorff, who later joined the men of the (predominantly) military resistance group led by Claus Schenk Graf von Stauffenberg and was executed in 1944, see Harrison, '"Alter Kämpfer" im Widerstand'.

73. Schmidt, *Schützen und Dienen*, pp. 323–32; Götz, 'Die Errichtung der Konzentrationslager', p. 70; Tuchel, 'Organisationsgeschichte der "frühen" Konzentrationslager', p. 12.

74. 'Röverstaat Oldenburg!', *Vorwärts*, 31 July 1932; 'S.A.-Leute werden Polizisten', *Vorwärts*, 29 July 1932, both in GSt PK, I. HA, Rep. 77, titl. 4043, no. 311, pp. 418–20. With this move Röver nearly doubled the regular police forces, which previously were only 320 men strong.

75. Abraham Ascher, *Was Hitler a Riddle? Western Democracies and National Socialism* (Stanford, CA: Stanford University Press, 2012), p. 22.

76. Schmidt, *Schützen und Dienen*, pp. 324–5.

77. In Bavaria even two types of auxiliary police were introduced by order of *Reichskommissar* Franz von Epp: a 'political auxiliary police' to be recruited exclusively from the ranks of the SS, and a 'security auxiliary police', consisting of SA and *Stahlhelm* men. See BayHStA IV, Stahlhelm, no. 392: The Commissarial State Minister of the Bavarian Ministry of the Interior on 'Einberufung und Verwendung von Hilfspolizei in Bayern', 27 March 1933.

78. See Michael Schneider, *Unterm Hakenkreuz: Arbeiter und Arbeiterbewegung 1933 bis 1939* (Bonn: Dietz, 1999); idem, 'Verfolgt, unterdrückt und aus dem Land getrieben: Das Ende der Arbeiterbewegung im Frühjahr 1933', in Wachsmann and Steinbacher, *Die Linke im Visier*, pp. 31–51, here pp. 43–6; Schmidt, *Schützen und Dienen*, pp. 332–6.

79. Frank Boblenz and Bernhard Post, *Die Machtübernahme in Thüringen 1932/33* (Erfurt: Landeszentrale für politische Bildung Thüringen, 2013), p. 36.

80. BayHStA, StK, no. 5256: Bavarian Ministry of Finance, Letter on 'Sonderbeauftragte bei den Bezirksämtern und Sonderbevollmächtigte bei den Regierungen', undated.

81. See Wolfgang Edler von Zander, *Das SA-Feldjägerkorps: Eine vergessene Einheit der Geschichte* (Wolfenbüttel: Melchior, 2014), p. 26.

82. Schepura, *Nationalsozialismus in der pfälzischen Provinz*, p. 282.

83. See, for example, Klein, 'SA-Terror und Bevölkerung in Wuppertal', pp. 47–8.

84. BayHStA, StK, no. 5256: Letter from Hanns Günther von Obernitz to the Bavarian Ministry of the Interior, 20 July 1933.

85. On Martin's biography, see in particular Grieser, *Himmlers Mann in Nürnberg*.

86. BayHStA, StK, no. 5256: Letter from Dr Benno Martin to the Bavarian Minister President, 20 July 1933.

87. In the years prior to 1933, Nazi leaders had threatened to carry out severe reprisals against policemen after the takeover of power. Wilhelm Loeper, the *Gauleiter* of Magdeburg-Anhalt, even boasted in 1932 that policemen who would not toe the party line were to be 'gunned down with Reichswehr cannons'; Schumann, *Politische Gewalt in der Weimarer Republik*, p. 345.

88. Schyga, *Goslar 1918–1945*, pp. 139, 142–6; Ingo von Münch, *Gesetze des NS-Staates: Dokumente eines Unrechtssystems* (Paderborn: Schöningh, 2004), p. 93.

89. Schyga, *Goslar 1918–1945*, p. 147.

90. BArch Berlin, NS 23/708: Letter from Röhm on SA-Feldpolizei, 11 August 1933.

91. BArch Berlin, NS 23/708: Letter from Röhm on Feldjägerkorps in Prussia, 31 October 1933; GSt PK, I. HA, Rep. 84a, no. 12004, pp. 134–6: OSAF on Feldjägerkorps in Prussia, 7 October 1933; Schmidt, *Schützen und Dienen*, pp. 328–9. For a collection of documents related to the *Feldjägerkorps*, see Zander, *Das SA-Feldjägerkorps*.

92. Several eyewitnesses later claimed that Walter Fritsch was directly involved in the executions that took place between 30 June and 2 July 1934 in Berlin; Rainer Orth, *'Der Amtssitz der Opposition?': Politik und Staatsumbaupläne im Büro des Stellvertreters des Reichskanzlers in den Jahren 1933/1934*, diss., Humboldt Universität zu Berlin, 2016, ch. 6.3.1 with further references.

93. BArch Berlin, NS 23/708: Letter from Röhm on Feldjägerkorps in Bavaria, 27 February 1934.

94. Ibid.: SA-Gruppe Hansa, 'Standort-Befehl 14/35', 8 March 1935.

95. Ibid., NS 23/708: Letter from Lutze to the Reich Minister of the Interior, 23 May 1935.

96. Klaus Wisotzky, 'Zwischen Integration und Opposition: Aspekte des Arbeiterverhaltens im Nationalsozialismus', in Anselm Faust (ed.), *Verfolgung und Widerstand im Rheinland und Westfalen 1933–1945* (Cologne: Landeszentrale für politische Bildung, 1992), pp. 137–51, here p. 140. This feeling of humiliation was aggravated by the tendency of the SA men to undertake their raids when drunk; see Monika Hinterberger, 'Menschen wie wir', in Marlene Zinken (ed.), *Der unverstellte Blick: Unsere Mütter (aus)gezeichnet durch die Zeit 1938 bis 1958: Töchter erinnern sich* (Opladen and Farmington Hills: Barbara Budrich, 2008), pp. 106–10, here p. 108.

97. Häberlen, *Vertrauen und Politik im Alltag*, pp. 9–12, 50–62, 82–92.

98. This argument was common as early as 1931. See, for example, Knickerbocker, *German Crisis*, p. 46.

99. On the strategy of the men who rallied around von Papen, see Orth, *'Der Amtssitz der Opposition?'*, and Roshan Magub, *A Life Cut Short: Edgar Julius Jung (1894–1934): Political Theorist and Man of Action. A Political Biography* (Rochester, NY: University of Rochester Press/Camden House, forthcoming).

100. The following paragraph on Böhme and the SA violence that occurred in Chemnitz is based on my article 'SA-Gewalt, nationalsozialistische "Revolution" und Staatsräson', in *Die Linke im Visier*, ed. Wachsmann and Steinbacher, pp. 191–213.

101. See Albrecht Böhme, *Psychotherapie und Kastration: Die Bedeutung der Psychotherapie als Erziehungs- und Ausscheidungsmethode für sexuell Abwegige und Sittlichkeitsverbrecher, dargestellt an Fällen aus der Kriminalpraxis, unter Heranziehung der Graphologie als Hilfswissenschaft; mit Einführung in das Sterilisations- und Kastrationsrecht sowie in Fragen der Vorbeugung gegen das Verbrechen, mit Ausblick auf Fragen der Gesetzgebung und Strafrechtspflege* (Munich: Lehmanns, 1935).

102. Siemens, 'SA-Gewalt, nationalsozialistische "Revolution" und Staatsräson', pp. 195–6, with further references.

103. Albrecht Böhme, *Wider den Rechtsbruch der Staatsführung*, unpublished manuscript, Munich 1958, pp. 9, 21.

104. World Committee for the Victims of German Fascism (ed.), *The Brown Book of the Hitler Terror and the Burning of the Reichstag, with an introduction by Lord Marley* (London: Gollancz, 1933), pp. 341–51.

105. Siemens, 'SA-Gewalt, nationalsozialistische "Revolution" und Staatsräson', p. 197.

106. IfZ, Archives, F 92, pp. 98, 101: Albrecht Böhme, Polizeilicher Gesamtbericht über die Vorfälle in Chemnitz für die Zeit von April bis Mitte Juni 1933.

107. Siemens, 'SA-Gewalt, nationalsozialistische "Revolution" und Staatsräson', pp. 202–6.

108. Letter from Friedrich von Bodelschwingh to a Jewish physician, April 1933, as quoted in Barbara Degen, *Bethel in der NS-Zeit: Die verschwiegene Geschichte* (Waldkirchen: VAS, 2014), p. 262.

109. For the very similar position of Martin Niemöller, another prominent representative of the Protestant churches, see Matthew D. Hockenos, 'Pastor Martin Niemöller, German Protestantism, and German National Identity, 1933–1937', in John Carter Wood (ed.), *Christianity and National Identity in Twentieth-Century Europe: Conflict, Community, and the Social Order* (Göttingen: Vandenhoeck & Ruprecht, 2016), pp. 113–30, here pp. 115–18.

110. GSt PK, XX. HA, Rep. 240 B 27 d+e, pp. 88–9: Typescript of three Easter cards, April 1933.

111. All quotations are taken from Trauthig, *Im Kampf um Glauben und Kirche*, pp. 296–8. For a more in-depth discussion of the positions taken by the Protestant churches in 1933, see also Hermann Beck, 'Anti-Semitic Violence "From Below": Attacks and Protestant Church Responses in Germany in 1933', *Politics, Religion & Ideology* 14:3 (2013), pp. 395–411, esp. pp. 407–9; Gailus, '1933 als protestantisches Erlebnis'.

112. On this ambivalence, see in particular Peter Reichel, *Der schöne Schein des Dritten Reiches: Gewalt und Faszination des deutschen Faschismus* (Hamburg: Ellert & Richter, 2006 [1991]).

113. Schwarz, 'British Visitors', pp. 499–500.

114. Ascher, *Was Hitler a Riddle?*, p. 42.

115. BayHStA IV, Stahlhelm, no. 181: Report from the SA special representative in Bad Aibling to the SA, Brigade Chiemgau, 24 August 1933.

116. BayHStA IV, Stahlhelm, no. 108: Letter from the Stahlhelm-Ortsgruppe Rosenheim to Bezirksführer Willmer in Prien, 20 June 1933.

117. RGVA, Osobyi Archives, Fond 500, Opis 4, no. 268, p. 6: Letter from the SA-Gruppe Berlin-Brandenburg to the Geheime Staatspolizeiamt, 20 October 1933.

118. Lothar Gruchmann, *Justiz im Dritten Reich 1933–1940: Anpassung und Unterwerfung in der Ära Grüttner* (Munich: Oldenbourg, 1988), p. 329; Michael Grüttner, *Brandstifter und Biedermänner: Deutschland 1933–1939* (Stuttgart: Klett-Cotta, 2015), p. 101. The German authorities learned of the exact wording of this decree only in June 1935. On the problem of keeping the decree hidden from the general public, see BArch Berlin, NS 23/889: Letter from the lawyer and 'SA-Rechtsberater' Walter Luetgebrune to Ernst Röhm, 5 March 1934.

119. BArch Berlin, NS 23/889: Typescript of Röhm's decree from 31 July 1933.

120. Reichsjustizministerium und Statistisches Reichsamt (ed.), *Kriminalstatistik für das Jahr 1932*, p. 12.

121. Instructive in this respect is GSt PK, I. HA, Rep. 84a, no. 12004, p. 49: Hellmuth Türpitz, 'Etwas vom Recht der SA', *Deutsche Zeitung*, 6 January 1934. Plans for an 'SA disciplinary law' were ultimately abandoned in the summer of 1934. On 20 July 1934 the Reich Minister of Justice, Franz Gürtner, informed the German legal bodies that 'a special SA judiciary does not exist and will not be introduced'; GSt PK, I. HA, Rep. 84a, no. 12,004, p. 115.

122. On Schoene, see also chapter 2.

123. For a detailed account of the negotiations and scoldings that occurred behind the scenes, see Gruchmann, *Justiz im Dritten Reich 1933–1940*, pp. 337–45.

124. GSt PK, I. HA, Rep. 84a, no. 12004, p. 5: Letter from Heinrich Schoene to the Oberlandesgerichtspräsident Kiel, 10 July 1933.

125. Ibid., p. 6: Letter from Heinrich Schoene to Hanns Kerrl, 10 July 1933. Both letters are also quoted in Gruchmann, *Justiz im Dritten Reich*, p. 339.

126. BayHStA, StK, no. 5256: Decree of the Prussian Minister President from 30 October 1933, printed in *Ministerialblatt für die Preußische Innere Verwaltung* 1933, Part 1, no. 56, pp. 1,303–4; ibid.: OSAF, Decree of 12 March 1933.

127. BayHStA, StK, no. 5256: Confidential Order of Röhm, 20 March 1933.

128. Ibid.: Extract from *Schwäbischer Merkur*, 30 May 1933.

129. For details on this development in Prussia, see Schuster, *Die SA*, pp. 261–4.

130. BayHStA, StK, no. 5256: Letter from the Reich Minister of the Interior to the Länder governments, 16 August 1933.

131. Ibid.: Letter from OSAF to the Bavarian Minister President, 9 March 1934.

132. Until 1 September 1933, they were called 'special commissioners' (*Sonderkommissare*); see Hoser, 'Sturmabteilung (SA)'.

133. BayHStA, StK, no. 5256: Letter from the Bavarian Ministry of Finance on 'Sonderbeauftragte bei den Bezirksämtern und Sonderbevollmächtigte bei den Regierungen', undated.

134. Ibid.: Protocol of the Meeting of Siebert, Wagner, Frank, Himmler, and Röhm, 20 October 1933.

135. BayHStA, StK, no. 7579: Letter from the Bavarian State Bank, Munich branch, to the directorate of the Bavarian Staatsbank, 5 July 1934.

136. Longerich, *Geschichte der SA*, pp. 159, 184.

137. On the history of the *Stahlhelm*, see Anke Hoffstadt, 'Eine Frage der Ehre – zur "Beziehungsgeschichte" von "Stahlhelm: Bund der Frontsoldaten" und SA', in *Bürgerkriegsarmee*, ed. Müller and Zilkenat, pp. 267–96; Joachim Tautz, *Militaristische Jugendpolitik in der Weimarer Republik: Die Jugendorganisationen des Stahlhelm, Bund der Frontsoldaten: Jungstahlhelm und Scharnhorst, Bund deutscher Jungmannen* (Regensburg: Roderer, 1998); Remco Schaumann, 'Der Stahlhelm, Bund der Frontsoldaten, in Bielefeld und im Regierungsbezirk Minden 1918–1935', *Jahresbericht des Historischen Vereins für die Grafschaft Ravensberg* 83 (1996), pp. 139–98. Still indispensable are also the pioneering study by Berghahn, *Der Stahlhelm*, and idem., 'Das Ende des "Stahlhelm"', *Vierteljahrshefte für Zeitgeschichte* 13:4 (1965), pp. 446–51.

138. Berghahn, *Der Stahlhelm*, pp. 55–63; Schaumann, *Der Stahlhelm*, p. 139.

139. Schaumann, *Der Stahlhelm*, p. 164.

140. Hoffstadt, 'Eine Frage der Ehre', pp. 273–7.

141. BArch Berlin, NS 23/474: Report from SA-*Standartenführer* Gottlob Berger, SA-*Untergruppe* Württemberg, from 21 September 1932.
142. 'Ein Sündenregister: Düsterberg über die Nationalsozialisten', *Berliner Tageblatt*, 8 February 1933, as quoted in British Library (London), *Stahlhelmberichte 1933*, vol. 2, unpaginated.
143. On Seldte's career in 1933, see Rüdiger Hachtmann, 'Seldte, Franz', in *Neue deutsche Biographie*, vol. 24 (Berlin: Duncker & Humblot, 2010), pp. 215–16.
144. BayHStA IV, Stahlhelm, no. 99: Letter from Major Mündel, Constance, to Franz Seldte, 18 April 1933. In turn, the Nazis suspected that former 'Marxists' had successfully infiltrated regional *Stahlhelm* units; see BArch Berlin, NS 23/409: Note of the SA-*Untergruppe* Hamburg, 4 July 1933.
145. Schaumann, *Der Stahlhelm*, p. 167.
146. BayHStA IV, Stahlhelm, no. 365: 'Bundesbefehl für die Neugliederung des Stahlhelms, B.d.F.', 18 July 1933.
147. In light of the post-Second World War debates it is important to note that the transfers from the *Stahlhelm* to the SA-R I and II were optional. See BayHStA IV, Stahlhelm, no. 109: Letter from the Landesamt to the Stahlhelm Ortsgruppe Vilsbiburg, 20 August 1934.
148. BArch Berlin NS 23/510: Der Oberste SA-Führer, 'Betr. Gliederung der gesamten SA', 6 November 1933; Hermann-J. Rupieper and Alexander Sperk (eds), *Die Lageberichte der Geheimen Staatspolizei zur Provinz Sachsen 1933–1936*, vol. 2: *Regierungsbezirk Merseburg* (Halle: Mitteldeutscher Verlag, 2004), p. 121. In 1936 all men aged between eighteen and forty-five were part of the 'active' SA, divided into an 'active SA I' (18–35) and an 'active SA II' (36–45). See BArch Berlin, NS 23/510: Oberste SA-Führung, On the organization of the SA, 15 December 1936. In 1935, by the latest, the SA-R II was referred to as the SA-*Landsturm* (SA-L); see BArch Berlin, NS 23/510: Der Oberste SA-Führer, 'Aufgaben und Gliederung der SA', 22 January 1935.
149. For the perspective of the *Stahlhelm* is BayHStA IV, Stahlhelm, no. 109: Letter from the Stahlhelm Landesverband [Bavaria] to the Bavarian Political Police, 3 October 1934.
150. Patrick Leigh Fermor, *A Time of Gifts: On Foot to Constantinople: From the Hook of Holland to the Middle Danube* (London: John Murray, 2002), p. 31.
151. Ibid., p. 33.
152. Ibid., p. 34.
153. On the activities of the SA at universities, see in particular Grüttner, *Studenten im Dritten Reich*; Giles, *Students and National Socialism in Germany*; Stefan Rückel and Karl-Heinz Noack, 'Studentischer Alltag an der Berliner Universität 1933 bis 1945', in Christoph Jahr (ed.), *Die Berliner Universität in der NS-Zeit*, vol. 1: *Strukturen und Personen* (Stuttgart: Steiner, 2005), pp. 115–42. On the burning of books in May 1933, see Hans-Wolfgang Strätz, 'Die geistige SA rückt ein: Die studentische "Aktion wider den undeutschen Geist" im Frühjahr 1933', in Ulrich Walberer (ed.), *10 Mai 1933: Bücherverbrennung in Deutschland und die Folgen* (Frankfurt am Main: Fischer, 1983), pp. 84–114.
154. On Bennecke's time as leader of the SA-Hochschulamt, see Peschel (ed.), *Die SA in Sachsen vor der 'Machtübernahme'*, pp. 17–18.
155. BayHStA, StK, no. 7350: Letter from the Chef SA-*Ausbildungswesen*, Krüger, to the Minister President of Bavaria, 14 September 1933.
156. BayHStA, MInn, no. 81589: Speech of Adolf Hitler from 28 July 1922, as quoted in the Supplement of the *Völkischer Beobachter*, no. 63/65, *Freistaat oder Sklaventum?*
157. Deinert, *Die Studierenden der Universität Rostock*, pp. 329–30.
158. Karl Gengenbach was a model Nazi activist. Born into a middle-class family in Pforzheim on 9 November 1911, he joined the NSDAP at the age of eighteen, shortly after receiving his *Abitur* with honorable mention. He then studied law and politics (*Staatswissenschaften*) in Munich. Gengenbach quickly developed into one of the city's most influential student functionaries and as such was a leading organizer of the burning of books that occurred there in May 1933. Shortly after his time in the SA-*Hochschulamt* came to an end in the summer of 1934, he joined the SS and its *Sicherheitsdienst*, the SD. From 1939 onward, Gengenbach held a leading position in the Reich Security Main Office and was an SD representative in the German-occupied Netherlands. He died in a car accident on 25 January 1944. See Volker Bendig and Jürgen Kühnert, 'Die Münchner Bücherverbrennung

vom 10 Mai 1933 und der NS-Studentenführer Karl Gengenbach', in Christine Haug and Lothar Poethe (eds), *Leipziger Jahrbuch zur Buchgeschichte 18* (Wiesbaden: Harrassowitz, 2009), pp. 347–64, esp. pp. 349, 358–64; Wildt, *Generation des Unbedingten*, pp. 88, 380–91, 511, and *passim*.

159. BayHStA, StK, no. 7350: Letter from the leader of the SA University Office in Munich to the Minister Hermann Esser, 24 January 1934, and further correspondence in file.

160. For an introduction, see Monika Marose, *Unter der Tarnkappe: Felix Hartlaub: Eine Biographie* (Berlin: Transit, 2005).

161. Felix Hartlaub in a letter to his father from 29 April 1934, as quoted in Felix Hartlaub, *Aus Hitlers Berlin 1934–1938*, ed. Nikola Herweg and Harald Tausch (Frankfurt am Main: Suhrkamp, 2014), p. 104. See also his letter to his father from March 1934, in Erna Krauss and G. F. Hartlaub (eds), *Felix Hartlaub in seinen Briefen* (Tübingen: Rainer Wunderlich Verlag, 1958), p. 134.

162. Grüttner, *Studenten im Dritten Reich*, pp. 252–60.

163. The German version, as quoted in BayHStA, MK, no. 11247, reads: 'Wetzt die langen Messer / Auf dem Bürgersteig! / Lasst die Messer flutschen / In den Judenleib / Blut muss fließen knüppelhageldick / Wir scheißen auf die Freiheit der Judenrepublik / Kommt einst die Stunde der Vergeltung / Sind wir zu jedem Massenmord bereit // Hoch die Hohenzollern / Am Laternenpfahl / Lasst die Hunde baumeln / Bis sie runterfalln! / Blut muss fließen . . . // In der Synagoge / Hängt ein schwarzes Schwein / In die Parlamente / Schmeisst ne Handgranate rein! / Blut muss fließen . . . // Reisst die Konkubine / Aus dem Fürstenbett / Schmiert die Guillotine / Mit dem Judenfett / Blut muss fließen . . . //.'

164. For a detailed analysis of the different variants of this song, see the excellent analysis by Michael Kohlstruck and Simone Scheffler, 'Das "Heckerlied" und seine antisemitische Variante: Zur Geschichte und Bedeutungswandel eines Liedes', in Michael Kohlstruck and Andreas Klärner (eds), *Ausschluss und Feindschaft: Studien zu Antisemitismus und Rechtsextremismus* (Berlin: Metropol, 2011), pp. 135–58.

165. BayHStA, MK 11247: Letter from the General Vicar of the Archdiocese of Munich and Freising to the Bavarian Ministry of Education and Culture, 9 June 1934; Letter from the SA-Sturmführer Springer to the Directorate of the Bavarian Academy for Agriculture and the Brewing Trade in Weihenstephan, 4 June 1934. See also Johann Neuhäusler, *Kreuz und Hakenkreuz: Der Kampf des Nationalsozialismus gegen die katholische Kirche und der kirchliche Widerstand: Erster Teil* (Munich: Verlag der Katholischen Kirche Bayerns, 1946), pp. 316–17.

166. BArch Berlin, NS 23/1239: Letter from SA-Gruppenführer W. C. Meyer to SA-Brigadeführer Paul Ellerhusen, 31 May 1929. The only knowledge of the song we have from Meyer's letter is that it contained the words 'Und wer kein Haar am Arschloch hat, der ist noch kein Soldat' ('One is simply not yet a soldier without hair around one's asshole').

167. BayHStA, MK 11247: Letter from the SA University Office Munich to the Bavarian Ministry of Education and Culture, 19 June 1934.

168. Ibid.: Letter from the SA-Hochschulamt Munich to the Reichs SA-Hochschulamt, 31 August 1934.

169. See, for example, Sopade, *Deutschland-Berichte*, vol. 2 (1935), p. 704, and vol. 3 (1936), p. 214.

170. Instructive in this respect is the example of the gifted jurist Ernst Forsthoff, who in the early 1930s publicly turned to National Socialism and was rewarded with professorships at the German universities of Frankfurt am Main and Hamburg in 1933 and 1935, respectively. See Florian Meinel, *Der Jurist in der industriellen Gesellschaft: Ernst Forsthoff und seine Zeit* (Berlin: Akademie, 2011), pp. 48–54.

171. Christoph Cornelißen, *Gerhard Ritter: Geschichtswissenschaft und Politik im 20. Jahrhundert* (Düsseldorf: Droste, 2001), p. 164.

172. Emanuel Hirsch, *Die gegenwärtige geistige Lage im Spiegel philosophischer und theologischer Besinnung* (Göttingen: Vandenhoeck & Ruprecht, 1934), p. 4.

173. Deinert, *Die Studierenden der Universität Rostock*, pp. 336–8; Matthiesen, *Greifswald in Vorpommern*, p. 403.

174. Nicola Willenberg, '"Der Betroffene war nur Theologe und völlig unpolitisch": Die Evangelisch-Theologische Fakultät von ihrer Begründung bis in die Nachkriegszeit', in Hans-Ulrich Thamer, Daniel Droste, and Sabine Happ (eds), *Die Universität Münster im Nationalsozialismus: Kontinuitäten und Brüche zwischen 1920 und 1960*, vol. 1 (Münster: Aschendorff, 2012), pp. 251–308, here pp. 269–70. See also Ulrich Rottschäfer, *100 Jahre Predigerseminar in Westfalen 1892–1992* (Bielefeld: Luther-Verlag, 1992), pp. 102–11.

175. Willenberg, '"Der Betroffene war nur Theologe und völlig unpolitisch"', pp. 270–2.

176. Grüttner, *Studenten im Dritten Reich*, p. 442.

177. Deinert, *Die Studierenden der Universität Rostock*, pp. 338–9. In the following year Martin Bormann decreed that from July 1938 on it was no longer acceptable for clergymen to hold leadership positions in the NSDAP and its organizations, and that they should be replaced as soon as 'suitable replacements' were available. GSt PK, XX. HA, Rep. 240 A 1 a–e, p. 77: Secret Decree of Martin Bormann (no. 104/38), 27 July 1938.

178. By the late 1930s the number of students affiliated with the SA comprised only 10 per cent of the total student population. See Deinert, *Die Studierenden der Universität Rostock*, pp. 330–1, with further references.

179. UAK, Zugang 244: Wehner, Report on his activities as 'SA-Verbindungsführer' in the winter term 1937/38.

180. There was nevertheless no shortage of obligations for the students: Reich Labour Service, mandatory participation in state-sponsored sporting events, general military service (introduced in 1935), and, beginning in 1937, the completion of auxiliary work service in either industry or agriculture. See Deinert, *Die Studierenden der Universität Rostock*, p. 74, n. 48.

181. Morsch and Ohm, *Terror in der Provinz Brandenburg*, p. 40.

182. Klein, 'SA-Terror und Bevölkerung in Wuppertal', p. 59.

183. Fischer, *Stormtroopers*, p. 111. Fischer's chapter on 'The SA and its Sources of Financial and Welfare Assistance' (pp. 110–42) provides a detailed analysis of the financial situation of the SA up to 1935.

184. Ibid., pp. 113–35.

185. BArch Berlin, R2/11913a, vol. 1: Rechnungshof of the German Reich, 'Bericht über die Prüfung der Vereinnahmung der Obersten SA-Führung (OSAF) vom Reichministerium des Innern im Rechnungsjahr 1933 [. . .] überwiesenen Reichsgelder', 8 June 1934.

186. Ibid.: Rechnungshof of the German Reich, 'Bericht über die Prüfung der Einnahmen und Ausgaben der SA-Gruppe Berlin-Brandenburg', 30 June 1934.

187. Ibid.: Letter from the Rechnungshof of the German Reich to the Reich Minister of Finance, 8 August 1934.

188. Ibid.: Letter from the Reich Treasurer Schwarz to the President of the Reich Court of Auditors, 23 July 1934.

189. Ibid.: Letter from the Reich Treasurer Schwarz to the Reich Ministry of Finance, 8 August 1934.

190. BArch Berlin, SA 400003178 (Personal SA File of Erich Reimann): Letter from Lutze to the Reich Treasurer of the SA (Georg Mappes), 4 November 1938.

191. Most revealing in this context is BArch Koblenz, ZSG 158/40: Erich Bandekow, 'Über steuerliche Korruptionsfälle von Reichsministern, Reichsleitern etc', 2 July 1945. For a more recent overview, see Bajohr, *Parvenüs und Profiteure*.

192. BArch Koblenz, ZSG 158/40, p. 8: Bandekow, 'Über steuerliche Korruptionsfälle'.

193. BArch Berlin, R 43 II/1206, pp. 50–4: Correspondence between Lutze's testamentary executor Bodo Beneke and Hans Lammers, the head of the Reich Chancellery; BArch Koblenz, ZSG 158/40, p. 4: Bandekow, 'Über steuerliche Korruptionsfälle'.

194. Friedrich-Ebert-Stiftung, Bonn/Archiv der sozialen Demokratie (FES), Viktor Lutze Papers, Political Diary of Viktor Lutze, p. 228. Bandekow very likely misdated the donation in question to the year 1939.

195. Information provided by Karl Lutze to the author on 14 October 2015.

196. Röhm's speech is quoted in the online edition of the diaries of Michael Kardinal von Faulhaber (1911–52); see EAM, NL Faulhaber 09263, p. 40, http://p.faulhaber-edition.de/exist/apps/faulhaber/dokument.html?collid=1933&sortby=year&doctype=bb&docidno=BB_09263_0040s.

197. Fest, 'Röhm', p. 204.

Chapter 5

1. Thomas Mann, journal entry from 4 July 1934, in his *Tagebücher 1933–1934*, ed. Peter de Mendelsohn (Frankfurt am Main: Fischer, 1977), p. 458.

2. Whereas the English-speaking world refers to the events in question as the 'Night of the Long Knives', German historians usually speak of them as the 'Röhm purge' or the 'Röhm affair'. All three terms are questionable. In particular, the German label 'Röhm purge' echoes the perspective of the regime, obscuring the fact that this event was a purge *of* Röhm and his followers, not a purge *by* them. Even 'Purge of the SA' is not fully correct, as the SA constituted just one group of victims on this occasion. For a more elaborate discussion, see Eleanor Hancock, 'The Purge of the SA Reconsidered: "An Old Putschist Trick"'?, *Central European History* 44:4 (2011), pp. 669–83, here pp. 682–3.

3. For thorough discussions of this problem, see Brown, 'SA in the Radical Imagination', pp. 248–74; Udo Grashoff, 'Erst rot, dann braun? Überläufer von der KPD zu NS-Organisationen im Jahr 1933', in Günther Heydemann, Jan Erik Schulte, and Francesca Weil (eds), *Sachsen und der Nationalsozialismus* (Göttingen: Vandenhoeck & Ruprecht, 2014), pp. 215–36.

4. BArch Berlin, NS 23/431: Circular letter from OSAF on KPD infiltrations, 8 December 1932.

5. Rudolf Diels, *Lucifer ante portas: Es spricht der erste Chef der Gestapo* (Stuttgart: Deutsche Verlags-Anstalt, 1950), p. 207.

6. Grashoff points to the fact that the 50,000 Communists who allegedly joined the SA in 1933 constituted only 1.7 per cent of the SA's overall membership but roughly 15 per cent of the strength of the Communist Party; Grashoff, 'Erst rot, dann braun?', pp. 230–4.

7. Kirstin A. Schäfer, *Werner von Blomberg: Hitlers erster Feldmarschall. Eine Biographie* (Paderborn: Schöningh, 2006), p. 135.

8. Hancock, 'Purge of the SA Reconsidered', pp. 673–8; idem, *Ernst Röhm*, pp. 141–51.

9. Schäfer, *Werner von Blomberg*, pp. 136–7.

10. For summaries of these developments in the spring of 1934, see Kershaw, *Hitler 1889–1936*, pp. 629–44; Evans, *Third Reich in Power*, pp. 20–31; Karl Martin Graß, *Edgar Jung: Papenkreis und Röhm-Krise 1933/34* (Edingen: Self-Publishing, 1967), pp. 156–98; and the popular yet carefully researched and in many respects reliable book by the journalist Heinz Höhne, *Mordsache Röhm: Hitlers Durchbruch zur Alleinherrschaft 1933–1934* (Reinbek bei Hamburg: Rowohlt, 1984). For a contemporary analysis, see Sopade, *Deutschland-Berichte*, vol. 1 (1934), pp. 261–71.

11. Linder, *Von der NSDAP zur SPD*, pp. 168–89. For Heimsoth's interest in homosexuality, see in particular his medical dissertation *Hetero- und Homophilie: Eine neuorientierende An- und Einordnung der Erscheinungsbilder, der 'Homosexualität' und der 'Inversion' in Berücksichtigung der sogenannten 'normalen Freundschaft' auf Grund der zwei verschiedenen erotischen Anziehungsgesetze und der bisexuellen Grundeinstellung des Mannes* (Dortmund: Schmidt & Andernach, 1924). Although Röhm suffered from the fact that he was forced to hide his homosexuality from the public, he became a member of Friedrich Radszuweit's *Bund für Menschenrecht*, a homosexual lobby group.

12. Andreas Dornheim, *Röhms Mann fürs Ausland: Politik und Ermordung des SA-Agenten Georg Bell* (Münster: Lit, 1998), pp. 117–41; Hancock, *Ernst Röhm*, pp. 115–16.

13. John Wheeler-Bennett, *The Nemesis of Power: The German Army in Politics, 1918–1946* (London: Macmillan, 1954), pp. 320–32. For a critical evaluation of the arguments in question, see Schäfer, *Werner von Blomberg*, pp. 137–9.

14. Röhm and his followers quickly got wind of such plans. On 16 May 1934, Röhm in a confidential letter to SA leaders claimed that 'enemies of the SA' were at work, but that a direct intervention against them was not possible at the moment. However, for a later settling of scores, Röhm requested all SA-*Standarten* to collect evidence on cases of 'animosity towards the SA'. For the stormtroopers who received the letter, it was clear that Röhm was referring to the activities of the Reichswehr; HA-Spiegel, Personal Papers of Heinz Höhne, no. 42: Typescript of Röhm's letter from 16 May 1934.

15. 'The Rule of the Inferior' was also the title of Edgar J. Jung's magnum opus, published first in 1927 and again, in a revised and extended form, in 1930.

16. On this group and its activities, see in particular Orth's dissertation *Der Amtssitz der Opposition?*' See also the forthcoming book by Roshan Magub, *A Life Cut Short – Edgar Julius Jung (1894–1934): A Political Biography* (Lake Placid, NY: Camden House). For a dated yet still impressive summary, see Graß, *Edgar Jung*, in particular pp. 199–236.

17. Extracts of von Papen's speech at Marburg on 17 June 1934 are available in English translation in Roderick Stackelberg and Sally A. Winkle (eds), *The Nazi Germany Sourcebook: An Anthology of Texts* (London and New York: Routledge, 2002), pp. 170–2, here p. 171.

18. Orth, *'Der Amtssitz der Opposition?'*, ch. 6.1.4.

19. HA-Spiegel, Personal Papers of Heinz Höhne, no. 42: Minutes of the meeting in the Ministry of the Interior, 19 June 1934. Schmidt, whose wife was Jewish, was forced to resign in November 1938 after several thousand members of the HJ and the SA publicly requested his resignation. See Horst Romeyk, *Düsseldorfer Regierungspräsidenten 1918 bis 1945*, *Rheinische Vierteljahrsblätter* 44 (1980), pp. 237–99, here pp. 285–6. Lüninck was executed in the wake of the 20 July 1944 plot.

20. HA-Spiegel, Personal Papers of Heinz Höhne, no. 121: Confidential report of U.S. ambassador William E. Dodd on the 'internal political situation' in Germany from 20 June 1934.

21. For a recent summary of the positions in the relevant literature, see Hancock, 'Purge of the SA Reconsidered'.

22. Kurt Gossweiler, *Die Röhm-Affäre: Hintergründe – Zusammenhänge – Auswirkungen* (Cologne: Pahl-Rugenstein, 1983 [1963]), here p. 417.

23. Such accusations were made, for example, by Roschmann, *Erinnerungen eines kämpferischen Schwaben*, pp. 37–8.

24. Not surprisingly, Röhm's opponents later did their best to obscure the prefabricated nature of the accusations against him and instead stressed the latter's alleged revolutionary determination. A typical example of such a strategy was that adopted by Werner von Blomberg, who when being interrogated by the U.S. Seventh Army Interrogation Center on 24 September 1945 characterized Röhm as an 'anarchist who strove for power. Neither did he defend a particular ideal nor did he have any precise plans for a German government. His main purpose was to obtain control of the army. For this reason, he had planned to eliminate me and some other generals, maybe even Hitler'; HA-Spiegel, Personal Papers of Heinz Höhne, no. 42: Extract of the interrogation of Werner von Blomberg, 24 September 1945.

25. Next to the secondary literature already mentioned, see also Evans, *Third Reich in Power*, pp. 31–41; Wackerfuss, *Stormtrooper Families*, pp. 319–44; Otto Gritschneder, *'Der Führer hat Sie zum Tode verurteilt . . .': Hitlers 'Röhm-Putsch'-Morde vor Gericht* (Munich: Beck, 1993); Susanne zur Nieden and Sven Reichardt, 'Skandale als Instrument des Machtkampfes in der NS-Führung', in Martin Sabrow (ed.), *Skandal und Diktatur: Öffentliche Empörung im NS-Staat und in der DDR* (Göttingen: Wallstein, 2004), pp. 33–58; Charles Bloch, *Die SA und die Krise des NS-Regimes 1934* (Frankfurt am Main: Suhrkamp, 1970), pp. 96–116; Max Gallo, *The Night of the Long Knives: Hitler's Purge of Roehm and the S.A. Brown Shirts* (Godalming and Surrey: Fontana, 1972).

26. The political diary of Viktor Lutze is today stored in the archives of the Friedrich-Ebert-Stiftung, Bonn (FES). The story of how it landed there is worth a chapter of its own. In the final stages of the Second World War the Lutze family in Bevergern – allegedly out of fear of Allied confiscations – handed over the diary to friends who lived in the city of Werne and had promised to keep an eye on it. Yet, in November 1945, the diary was in possession of the U.S. journalist William Chester, who had come to Germany to cover the proceedings of the International Military Tribunal in Nuremberg. Unsure of the diary's authenticity, Chester showed it in the same month to the former Nuremberg police president and SS-*Obergruppenführer* Benno Martin, who was in Allied internment. Martin confirmed the authenticity of the diary and provided a handwritten 'expert opinion' on the notebook's blank pages. In 1957 the above-mentioned extracts of the diary were published in the *Frankfurter Rundschau*. Subsequently, Anton Hoch, the archivist of the Institute for Contemporary History in Munich (IfZ), attempted to buy the diary for the institute's library and contacted Chester, who was then living in Togo, offering $1,000 for the diary. However, all attempts by the IfZ to get hold of the diary were unsuccessful. Instead, in early 1959, Chester gave it to Georges Spénale, at the time the French *Haut Commissaire Spéciale* for Togo. Eleven years

later Spénale – who had become a member of the French *Assemblée Nationale* – travelled to Bonn and presented the diary to the FES. Since then it has been held in the special collections of the FES archive and can only be consulted with the consent of Karl Lutze, a nephew of Viktor who represents the family's interests. See the Viktor Lutze Papers at FES. Additional information was provided by Karl Lutze and Anja Kruke at the FES.

27. For a short biographical sketch of Lutze, see Marcus Weidner, 'Lutze, Viktor', in *Die Straßenbenennungspraxis in Westfalen und Lippe während des Nationalsozialismus: Datenbank der Straßenbenennungen 1933–1945*, http://www.lwl.org/westfaelische-geschichte/nstopo/strnam/Begriff_211.html, with further references.

28. Bloch, *Die SA und die Krise des NS-Regimes*, p. 155.

29. Schafranek, *Söldner für den Anschluss*, p. 358.

30. Niekisch, *Das Reich der niederen Dämonen*, p. 167.

31. Hans Rudolf Wahl, 'Antisemitismus in der NS-Wochenzeitung *Der SA-Mann*', in Michael Nagel and Moshe Zimmermann (eds), *Judenfeindschaft und Antisemitismus in der deutschen Presse über fünf Jahrhunderte: Erscheinungsformen, Rezeption, Debatte und Gegenwehr*, vol. 2 (Bremen: edition lumière, 2013), pp. 671–90, here p. 676.

32. A day before, on 21 June, Hitler had met with General Blomberg and Reich President Hindenburg in Gut Neudeck. It seems likely that it was at this meeting that the decisive actions against the SA were discussed and coordinated. See Orth, *'Der Amtssitz der Opposition?'*, ch. 6.3, with further references.

33. FES, Viktor Lutze Papers, Political Diary of Viktor Lutze, pp. 31–5.

34. According to the post-war testimony of Karl Schreyer, Röhm had heard rumours that Hitler planned to replace him with Lutze as early as 26 June 1934 but was lulled into a false sense of security by later reports. See HA-Spiegel, Personal Papers of Heinz Höhne, no. 42: Letter from Karl Schreyer to the Munich Police about the events of 30 June 1934, 27 May 1949.

35. FES, Viktor Lutze Papers, Political Diary of Viktor Lutze, pp. 28–30. Lutze's verdict on Röhm was largely negative. In Lutze's eyes, 'besides his sexual predisposition', Röhm was 'too militaristic' and not enough of a politician. He regarded him as a troublemaker who threatened the political unity of the Nazi camp.

36. FES, Viktor Lutze Papers, Political Diary of Viktor Lutze, pp. 39–41.

37. Ibid., pp. 41–51.

38. On Röhm's execution, see Hancock, *Ernst Röhm*, pp. 160–1; Gritschneder, *'Der Führer hat Sie zum Tode verurteilt'*, pp. 29–36.

39. HA-Spiegel, Personal Papers of Heinz Höhne, no. 42: Letter from Karl Schreyer to the Munich Police about the events of 30 June 1934, 27 May 1949.

40. FES, Viktor Lutze Papers, Political Diary of Viktor Lutze, pp. 59–79.

41. Ibid., p. 65. On the night of 1–2 July, Lutze made Erich Reimann, who later became the commander of the SA-*Standarte* Feldherrnhalle, his adjutant; see BArch Berlin, SA 400003178 (Reimann, Erich): Erich Reimann, Curriculum Vitae, 21 March 1942.

42. Lutze claimed to have personally seen these lists, which provided the basis for Hitler's ultimate decision of life or death on 30 June 1934. See FES, Viktor Lutze Papers, Political Diary of Viktor Lutze, p. 62.

43. In this paragraph I follow the detailed reconstruction of events by Orth, *'Der Amtssitz der Opposition?'*, chs 6.3.1 and 6.3.2. For an instructive case study on the planned *Feme* murder of Paul Schulz – who in 1934 narrowly escaped execution, not for the first time – see Anke Hoffstadt and Richard Kühl, '"Dead Man Walking": Der "Fememörder" Paul Schulz und seine "Erschießung am 30. Juni 1934"', *Historische Sozialforschung* 34:4 (2009), pp. 273–285.

44. As quoted in Mathilde Jamin, 'Das Ende der "Machtergreifung": Der 30. Juni 1934 und seine Wahrnehmung in der Bevölkerung', in Wolfgang Michala (ed.), *Die nationalsozialistische Machtergreifung* (Paderborn: Schöningh, 1984), pp. 207–19, here p. 212.

45. ÖstA/AdR, Bürckel/Materie, Karton 206, Mappe 4605: Decree of Adolf Hitler to Chief of Staff Lutze, 30 June 1934 (typescript).

46. HA-Spiegel, Personal Papers of Heinz Höhne, no. 121: Werner von Blomberg, Order to the Army, translated by the *Deutsches Nachrichtenbüro*, 1 July 1932.

47. Published in *Reichsgesetzblatt* I 1934, p. 529. See also Gritschneder, *'Der Führer hat Sie zum Tode verurteilt'*, pp. 46–51.

48. FES, Viktor Lutze Papers, Political Diary of Viktor Lutze, pp. 66–8. On the tension between the SA and the SS during the 'Röhm purge', see also BArch Berlin, NS 26/2540: Report of the SA-Sturmführer Hermann Baecke about the comportment of the SS man Fritz Völker on the night of 30 June–1 July 1934.

49. HA-Spiegel, Personal Papers of Heinz Höhne, no. 121: Report from Jacob W. S. Wuest, U.S. Military Attaché in Berlin, to the U.S. Department of State, 2 July 1934.

50. BayHStA, StK, no. 7579: Bavarian Ministry of the Interior, situational report, 2 July 1934.

51. Dietmar Schulze, 'Der "Röhm-Putsch" in der Provinz Sachsen', in *Hallische Beiträge zur Zeitgeschichte*, ed. Jana Wüstenhagen and Daniel Bohse (Halle/Saale: Martin-Luther-Universität Halle-Wittenberg, 2005), pp. 9–33, here pp. 9 and 21.

52. StA München, Bestand Polizeidirektion München, Personalakten, Nr. 10007 (Otto Ballerstädt): Testimony of Paul Zell, 18 June 1949.

53. BayHStA, StK, no. 7579: Letter from the Bavarian Minister President, 5 July 1934. Röhm's mother died on 6 January 1936.

54. FES, Viktor Lutze Papers, Political Diary of Viktor Lutze, p. 88. See also Gritschneder, *'Der Führer hat Sie zum Tode verurteilt'*, pp. 38–9.

55. Orth, *'Der Amtssitz der Opposition?'*; idem, *Der SD-Mann Johannes Schmidt* (Marburg: Tectum, 2012), pp. 102–12.

56. Schulze, 'Der "Röhm-Putsch" in der Provinz Sachsen', pp. 25–6.

57. BArch Berlin, NS 23/475: List of the victims of the 'Röhm purge', undated.

58. On the 'Röhm purge' in Silesia, see Schmidt, 'Der SA-Führer Hans Ramshorn', pp. 233–5.

59. Mann, journal entries of 5 July and 11 July 1934, in his *Tagebücher 1933–1934*, pp. 460–1, 467. Such reasoning is substantiated by Bloch, *Die SA und die Krise des NS-Regimes*, pp. 165–72. See also Hett, *Burning the Reichstag*, pp. 122–39.

60. On the case of Wilhelm Schmid, see Gritschneder, *'Der Führer hat Sie zum Tode verurteilt'*, pp. 37–9.

61. Ludecke, *I Knew Hitler*, p. 554.

62. Nikolai Tolstoy, *Night of the Long Knives* (New York: Ballantine Books, 1972), p. 145.

63. BArch Berlin, NS 23/434: Letter from SA-*Obersturmbannführer* Lothar Schiedlausky, with two anonymous reports attached, 9 August 1934. See also the detailed information available in HA-Spiegel, Personal Papers of Heinz Höhne, no. 42: Letter from Karl Schreyer to the Munich Police about the events of 30 June 1934, 27 May 1949.

64. BArch Berlin, NS 26/2048: Article in the *Lübbener Kreisblatt*, 18 or 19 August 1934.

65. BArch Berlin, NS 23/204: Letter from Walter Buch to the Führer's deputy (Rudolf Hess), 2 August 1934.

66. BArch Berlin, NS 23/508: Letter from the Silesian SA to the OSAF, 26 July 1934.

67. In the years to come 'moral failings' remained a common accusation in many of the disciplinary proceedings carried out against members of the SA. See Campbell, 'SA after the Röhm Purge', p. 660.

68. As quoted in Max Domarus, *Hitler: Reden und Proklamationen 1932–1945*, vol. 1: *Triumph, Erster Halbband 1932–1934* (Munich: Süddeutscher Verlag, 1965), pp. 423–4.

69. BArch Berlin, NS 23/508: Report of SS-Hauptsturmführer Helmut Willich, Stettin, 21 August 1935. This document is also used by Bessel, *Political Violence and the Rise of Nazism*, pp. 144–5.

70. PAAA, Personal Papers of Siegfried Kasche, vol. 24, pp. 25 and 45.

71. BArch Berlin, NS 23/508: 'Geflüster um das Morden', *Neuer Vorwärts: Sozialdemokratisches Wochenblatt*, no. 57, 15 July 1934. 'Hitlerjunge Knax' was a reference to the feature film *Hitlerjunge Quex*. Based on a novel by the writer Karl Aloys Schenzinger, the propaganda film was first shown in September 1933 and became a big success in the German cinemas. See Kurt Schilde, ' "Hitlerjunge Quex" – Eine Welturaufführung am 11. September 1933 in München: Blick hinter die Kulissen des NS-Propagandafilms', *Geschichte in Wissenschaft und Unterricht* 59:10 (2008), pp. 540–50.

72. BArch Berlin, NS 23/508: Der Führer der Leibstandarte [König], Munich, 30 June 1934.

73. For a recent example, see Wackerfuss, *Stormtrooper Families*, p. 323.

74. For a list of other homosexual SA leaders, see Reichardt, *Faschistische Kampfbünde*, pp. 679–80.
75. As quoted in Hancock, *Ernst Röhm*, p. 107.
76. Linder, *Von der NSDAP zur SPD*, pp. 135–89.
77. Helmuth Klotz, *Der Fall Röhm* (Berlin-Tempelhof: Self-Publishing, 1932).
78. For a detailed reconstruction of the incident as well as public reactions to it, see Laurie Marhoefer, *Sex and the Weimar Republic: German Homosexual Emancipation and the Rise of the Nazis* (Toronto: University of Toronto Press, 2015), pp. 146–73; Wackerfuss, *Stormtrooper Families*, pp. 200–8. The nicknames are quoted according to FES, Viktor Lutze Papers, Political Diary of Viktor Lutze, p. 71. See also Reichardt, *Faschistische Kampfbünde*, pp. 681–2.
79. For a detailed analysis of the press coverage, see Marhoefer, *Sex and the Weimar Republic*, pp. 160–73. In contrast to Marhoefer, Susanne zur Nieden and Sven Reichardt have argued that homophobic arguments were widespread among the mainstream press coverage of the 'Röhm scandal'; Susanne zur Nieden and Sven Reichardt, 'Skandale als Instrument des Machtkampfes in der NS-Führung', pp. 37–8. Hans Rudolf Wahl has emphasized that Social Democrats in particular in the early 1930s attempted to 'disclose' the Nazis' identity as a genuine homosexual movement; Wahl, 'Männerbünde, Homosexualitäten und politische Kultur', pp. 221–2.
80. Ignaz Wrobel [Kurt Tucholsky], 'Bemerkungen: Röhm', *Die Weltbühne*, no. 17 from 26 April 1932, p. 641.
81. Marhoefer, *Sex and the Weimar Republic*, p. 154; Alexander Zinn, *Die soziale Konstruktion des homosexuellen Nationalsozialisten: Zu Genese und Etablierung eines Stereotyps* (Frankfurt am Main: Lang, 1997); idem, 'SA, Homosexualität und Faschismus', p. 410; Andreas Pretzel, 'Schwule Nazis: Narrative und Desiderate', in *Homosexuelle im Nationalsozialismus*, ed. Michael Schwartz (Munich: de Gruyter Oldenbourg, 2014), pp. 69–76. In many of the early anti-Nazi novels published in the first years of the Third Reich, the homosexuality of the higher-ranking SA leadership figured prominently. See Jörn Meve, ' "Homosexuelle Nazis": Zur literarischen Gestaltung eines Stereotyps des Exils bei Ludwig Renn und Hans Siemsen', *Forum Homosexualität und Literatur* 11 (1991), pp. 79–100.
82. This view is also advanced by Marhoefer, *Sex and the Weimar Republic*, p. 155. See also Wahl, 'National-Päderasten?', which provides a careful discussion of this aspect based on the assumption that there are only two mutually exclusive positions: that the SA was marked by homosexuality or that it was not. In the view advanced here, by contrast, the SA is seen as an organization that had homosexual men in its ranks but was less shaped by male homosexual subcultures than Wahl suggests.
83. Wackerfuss, *Stormtrooper Families*, pp. 163–209.
84. Reichardt, *Faschistische Kampfbünde*, p. 683. On the persecution of male homosexuals in the Third Reich, see Stefan Micheler and Patricia Szobar, 'Homophobic Propaganda and the Denunciation of Same-Sex-Desiring Men under National Socialism', *Journal of the History of Sexuality* 11: 1–2 (2002), pp. 95–130; as well as the pioneering study by Burckhard Jellonnek, *Homosexuelle unter dem Hakenkreuz* (Paderborn: Schöningh, 1990).
85. For these continuities, see in particular Claudia Bruns and Susanne zur Nieden, ' "Und unsere germanische Art ruht bekanntlich zentnerschwer auf unserem Triebleben . . .": Der "arische" Körper als Schauplatz von Deutungskämpfen bei Blüher, Heimsoth und Röhm', in Paula Diehl (ed.), *Körper im Nationalsozialismus: Bilder und Praxen* (Munich: W. Fink, 2006), pp. 111–28. For a critical view of Blüher's influence in the SA, see Reichardt, 'Homosexualität und SA-Führer', p. 739.
86. For a detailed discussion, see Jason Crouthamel, ' "Comradship" and "Friendship": Masculinity and Militarisation in Germany's Homosexual Emancipation Movement after the First World War', *Gender & History* 23:1 (2011), pp. 111–29, esp. pp. 118–26. See also Marhoefer, *Sex and the Weimar Republic*, pp. 151–2, as well as above, chapter 4.
87. On the homosexual networks in the Silesian SA prior to the summer of 1934, see Schmidt, 'Der SA-Führer Hans Ramshorn', pp. 226–7; on Karl Ernst and his 'entourage', see Wahl, 'National-Päderasten?' On homosexual networks in the SA more generally, see Reichardt, *Faschistische Kampfbünde*, p. 680.
88. See also Pretzel, 'Schwule Nazis', p. 69.

89. HA-Spiegel, Personal Papers of Heinz Höhne, no. 121: Letter from George S. Messersmith, Legation of the United States of America, to William Philipps, Under Secretary of State, 18 August 1934.

90. Werner Otto Müller-Hill, journal entry from 21 July 1944, in his *'Man hat es kommen sehen und ist dennoch erschüttert': Das Kriegstagebuch eines deutschen Richters 1944/45* (Munich: Siedler, 2012), p. 59.

91. 'Hitler: Ich warte nicht bis 11.00 Uhr', *Frankfurter Rundschau*, 14 May 1957, p. 3.

92. Sopade, *Deutschland-Berichte*, vol. 1 (1934), pp. 191–5.

93. Jamin, 'Das Ende der "Machtergreifung"', p. 215.

94. HA-Spiegel, Personal Papers of Heinz Höhne, no. 127: Manuskript 'Betr.: Adolf Hitler', Kopenhagen, 17 March 1949, p. 6.

95. Mann, journal entry from 13 July 1934, in his *Tagebücher 1933–1934*, p. 470. For the text of Hitler's speech, see Domarus, *Hitler: Reden und Proklamationen*, pp. 410–24.

96. Bösch, *Das konservative Milieu*, p. 138. For similar examples, see Bessel, *Political Violence and the Rise of Nazism*, p. 143.

97. HA-Spiegel, Personal Papers of Heinz Höhne, no. 42: Maximilian Fretter-Pico, Memorandum on the relationship between the Wehrmacht and the Nazi Party.

98. Carl Schmitt, 'Der Führer schützt das Recht', *Deutsche Juristen Zeitung*, 1 August 1934, pp. 945–50, here pp. 946–7.

99. Ibid., p. 947.

100. Carl Schmitt, 'Nationalsozialismus und Rechtsstaat', *Juristische Wochenschrift* 63 (no. 12/13, 24 and 31 March 1934), pp. 713–18.

101. Ibid., pp. 716–17.

102. Ernst Fraenkel, *The Dual State: A Contribution to the Theory of Dictatorship* (New York: Octagon Books, 1969), p. xiii.

103. Adam Tooze, *The Wages of Destruction: The Making and Breaking of the Nazi Economy* (London: Allan Lane, 2006), p. 101. The view that the 'Röhm purge' was first and foremost an attempt to repress the growing resistance of the German working classes is advocated by Gossweiler, *Die Röhm-Affäre*, pp. 523–4.

104. BayHStA, StK, no. 5256: Letter from the Bavarian Minister of the Interior to the Bavarian Minister President, 14 August 1934.

105. Ibid.: Decree of the Bavarian Minister of the Interior Adolf Wagner, 19 July 1934.

106. Carsten Schröder, 'Der NS-Schulungsstandort Lockstedter Lager: Von der "Volkssportschule" zur SA-Berufsschule "Lola I"', *Informationen zur schleswig-holsteinischen Zeitgeschichte* 37 (2000), pp. 3–26, here p. 12.

107. HA-Spiegel, Personal Papers of Heinz Höhne, no. 121: Confidential report of U.S. ambassador William E. Dodd, 13 July 1934; BArch Berlin, NS 23/508: 'Das Schicksal der SA', *Neuer Vorwärts: Sozialdemokratisches Wochenblatt* (Karlsbad), 15 July 1934.

108. For this view, see Jamin, 'Das Ende der "Machtergreifung"', p. 207.

Chapter 6

1. Sopade, *Deutschland-Berichte*, vol. 2 (1935), p. 610.

2. PAAA, Personal Papers of Siegfried Kasche, vol. 34: Letter from SA-*Obersturmbannführer* Wilhelm Blessing, Schönlanke, to SA-*Gruppenführer* Siegfried Kasche, 24 November 1934.

3. On this 'Nazi morality', see Wolfgang Bialas, *Moralische Ordnungen des Nationalsozialismus* (Göttingen: Vandenhoeck & Ruprecht, 2014), in particular pp. 9–62; Raphael Groß, *Anständig geblieben: Nationalsozialistische Moral* (Frankfurt am Main: Fischer, 2010).

4. GSt PK, I. HA, Rep. 90 Annex P, Geheime Staatspolizei, no. 79/1, p. 84: 'Lagebericht für die Provinz Berlin-Brandenburg', October 1934.

5. Bessel, *Political Violence*, p. 148.

6. Ibid.; Hochstetter, *Motorisierung und 'Volksgemeinschaft'*, p. 73.

7. Sopade, *Deutschland-Berichte*, vol. 1 (1934), pp. 761–7, here p. 762.

8. Jürgen Matthäus and Frank Bajohr (eds), *Alfred Rosenberg: Die Tagebücher von 1934 bis 1944* (Frankfurt am Main: Fischer, 2015), p. 182 (entry from 27 April 1936).

9. HA-Spiegel, Personal Papers of Heinz Höhne, no. 183: J. C. White, Chargé d'Affaires ad interim at the American Embassy in Berlin, 'The Present Position of the S.A. in the National Socialist Organization', 31 December 1934.

10. See Karl Joachim Warnecke, *Rechtliche Entwicklung und Stellung der nationalsozialistischen Sturmabteilungen (SA)*, inaugural diss., Georg-August Universität zu Göttingen, 1935, p. 28.

11. Longerich, *Geschichte der SA*, pp. 222–3. From March 1935 on, this court was called *Disziplinargericht der Obersten SA-Führung*. See Jamin, 'Zur Rolle der SA im nationalsozialistischen Herrschaftssystem', p. 344.

12. Jamin, 'Zur Rolle der SA im nationalsozialistischen Herrschaftssystem', pp. 344–53.

13. Longerich, *Geschichte der SA*, p. 223.

14. For an instructive collection of cases, see Oberste SA-Führung (ed.), *Das Jahr der SA: Vom Parteitag der Ehre zum Parteitag der Arbeit* (Munich: Eher, 1939), pp. 70–80; Sopade, *Deutschland-Berichte*, vol. 3 (1936), p. 851. For the official SA discourse, see Viktor Lutze, *Wesen und Aufgaben der SA: Rede des Stabschefs vor dem Diplomatischen Korps und den Vertretern der ausländischen Presse am 24 Januar 1936* (Munich: Eher, 1939), in particular pp. 20–1. On the stormtroopers as the 'little guardians of the people's community', see Frank Werner, 'Die kleinen Wächter der "Volksgemeinschaft": Denunzianten, Boykotteure und Gewaltakteure aus Schaumburg', in Frank Werner (ed.), *Schaumburger Nationalsozialisten: Täter, Komplizen, Profiteure* (Bielefeld: Verlag für Regionalgeschichte, 2009), pp. 521–83.

15. OSAF (ed.), . . . *wurde die SA eingesetzt*, pp. 12, 30–3, 37.

16. See, for example, the information provided in Sopade, *Deutschland-Berichte*, vol. 2 (1935), pp. 946–8.

17. Merkl, *Political Violence under the Swastika*, pp. 530–1.

18. Schafranek, *Söldner*, p. 361.

19. PAAA, Personal Papers of Siegfried Kasche, vol. 34: Letter from SA-*Gruppenführer* Siegfried Kasche to Adolf-Heinz Beckerle, 18 November 1940.

20. Eugen Kogon, *Der SS-Staat: Das System der deutschen Konzentrationslager* (Munich: Alber, 1946).

21. As quoted in GSt PK, I. HA, Rep. 90 Annex P, no. 36/1, pp. 19–22: Letter from the Regierungspräsident in Stade to the Prussian Minister President, 21 August 1935. The original German text reads: 'Die Roten sind bezwungen / Am Boden liegt das ganze Bonzenpack / Und schon erhebt sich frech der fette Spießer / Der nie gekämpft und nie geblutet hat // Ihr Spießer und Bonzen, wir sind auf der Wacht / Wir sind die Alten noch heut / Wir haben geblutet, gekämpft und geschafft / Für Deutschland, doch niemals für Euch // Drum vorwärts, drum vorwärts, die Straße frei / Ihr Spießer, schert Euch nach Haus! / Ihr Spießer, schert Euch nach Haus! / Wir schlagen Euch sämtliche Knochen entzwei / Und räuchern die Tempel Euch aus!' Another radical SA song of the time is provided in Sopade, *Deutschland-Berichte*, vol. 2 (1935), p. 608.

22. Fritz Stern, 'Five Germans I Have Known', *European Review* 10:4 (2002), pp. 429–45, here p. 432.

23. Gottfried Oy and Christoph Schneider (eds), *Die Schärfe der Konkretion: Reinhard Strecker, 1968 und der Nationalsozialismus in der bundesdeutschen Historiografie* (Essen: Westfälisches Dampfboot, 2014), 42–3. On the booming field of the history of sound, see the recent dissertation by Huw D. Hallam, *National Socialism and Its Musical Afterlife*, PhD diss., King's College London, 2013, esp. pp. 50–87.

24. Marlene Zinken, 'Ein dehnbares Haus', in Marlene Zinken (ed.), *Der unverstellte Blick*, pp. 30–9, here p. 33. For an example of an SA march turned violent attack on passers-by, see GSt PK, I. HA, Rep. 90 Annex P, no. 36/1, p. 34: 'Ereignismeldung', 12 September 1935.

25. All information in the previous paragraph is taken from BayHStA, MInn, no. 73686: 'Bericht über die Vorfälle in Weildorf', undated. Cases of local SAs mounting *Der Stürmer* showcases were common; see GSt PK, I. HA, Rep. 90 Annex P, no. 36/1, pp. 48–50: 'Auszug aus dem Lagebericht des Regierungspräsidenten in Wiesbaden vom 30 August 1935'.

26. Letter from Josef Gruber, Markt Teisendorf, from 27 May 2015 to the author, referring to the record in Rainer Wilfinger, *Heimatbuch Teisendorf: Markt und Land* (Teisendorf: Markt Teisendorf, 2001), p. 456. 'Resistance' is used here according to the definition of the pioneering 'Bavarian project', which in the 1970s analysed life under National Socialism from a bottom-up perspective. See Michael Wildt, 'Das "Bayern-Projekt", die

Alltagsforschung und die "Volksgemeinschaft"', in Norbert Frei (ed.), *Martin Broszat, der 'Staat Hitlers' und die Historisierung des Nationalsozialismus* (Göttingen: Wallstein, 2007), pp. 119–29.

27. See Friedemann Bedürftig, 'Hitlers braune Bataillone: Vom Kampfverband zum Parteifluchtweg', *Die Zeit*, 1 December 1989, p. 55.

28. Alan E. Steinweis, *Kristallnacht 1938* (London: Belknap, 2009), p. 4. On the problems of the competing terms to describe these events (*Kristallnacht*, November Pogrom, or *Reichspogromnacht*), see ibid., pp. 1–4.

29. For an overview, see the excellent studies by Wildt, *Volksgemeinschaft als Selbstermächtigung*; Ahlheim, *'Deutsche, kauft nicht bei Juden!'*, pp. 319–403; Saul Friedländer, *Das Dritte Reich und die Juden* (Munich: dtv, 2008), pp. 129–91; Peter Longerich, *Holocaust: The Nazi Persecution and Murder of the Jews* (Oxford and New York: Oxford University Press, 2010), pp. 70–89; as well as the more specialized literature discussed below.

30. BArch Berlin, NS 23/515: Report of the Breslau Police President to the District President of Lower Silesia, 9 July 1935.

31. LArch Berlin, A Pr. Br. Rep. 030, tit. 95, no. 21617: Kripo-Tagebuch Berlin-Schöneberg, 'Zwischenfall mit SA-Angehörigen', 10 October 1935. According to a Gestapo report from the summer of 1934, between 80 and 90 per cent of all crimes committed by stormtroopers were carried out in a state of intoxication. See GSt PK, I. HA, Rep. 90 Annex P Geheime Staatspolizei, no. 76/2, p. 24: 'Lagebericht für die Provinz Berlin-Brandenburg', July 1934.

32. LArch Berlin, A Pr. Br. Rep. 030, tit. 95, no. 21638: Berliner Schutzpolizei, 'Ungerechtfertigtes Verhalten von Volksgenossen gegen Polizeibeamte', 22 July 1935.

33. This argument was most forcefully established by Wildt, *Volksgemeinschaft als Selbstermächtigung*. For a critical discussion of the range of Wildt's argument, in particular with regard to rural milieus, see Jill Stephenson, 'The *Volksgemeinschaft* and the Problems of Permeability: The Persistence of Traditional Attitudes in Württemberg Villages', *German History* 34:1 (2016), pp. 49–69.

34. Lutze, *Wesen und Aufgaben der SA*, p. 16.

35. Wünschmann, *Before Auschwitz*, pp. 168–210; Faludi, *Die Juni-Aktion*, pp. 35–54.

36. As quoted in Paul Jandl, 'Statt zu bezahlen, wurde ausgespuckt', *Die Welt*, 26 October 2013, p. 26. See also Vilma Neuwirth, *Glockengasse 29: Eine jüdische Arbeiterfamilie in Wien* (Vienna: Milena Verlag, 2008).

37. Michael Wildt, 'Einleitung', in: Hans Reichmann, *Deutscher Bürger und verfolgter Jude: Novemberpogrom und KZ Sachsenhausen 1937 bis 1939*, ed. Michael Wildt (Munich: Oldenbourg, 1998), pp. 1–37, here p. 17.

38. Reichssicherheitshauptamt – Amt V (ed.), *Vorbeugende Verbrechensbekämpfung* (Erlaßsammlung), Berlin, undated [1943], pp. 81–2.

39. Christian Faludi, 'Die "Juni-Aktion" im Kontext der Judenpolitik 1938', in Christian Faludi (ed.), *Die 'Juni-Aktion' 1938: Eine Dokumentation zur Radikalisierung der Judenverfolgung* (Frankfurt am Main: Campus, 2013), pp. 9–102, here p. 64.

40. Franz Alfred Six, 'Report on the "Jew Action" in Berlin between 17 June and 21 June 1938', in Faludi, *Die 'Juni-Aktion' 1938*, pp. 298–301, here p. 299.

41. See diverse articles of Paris newspapers, 14–16 June 1938, in Faludi, *Die 'Juni-Aktion' 1938*, pp. 225–7, here p. 226. For photographs of vandalized Jewish shops in the eastern districts of Berlin, see Christoph Kreutzmüller, Hermann Simon, and Elisabeth Weber (eds), *Ein Pogrom im Juni: Fotos antisemitischer Schmierereien in Berlin, 1938* (Berlin: Hentrich & Hentrich, 2013).

42. Faludi, 'Die "Juni-Aktion" im Kontext der Judenpolitik 1938', pp. 65–7.

43. Hans Reichmann, *Deutscher Bürger und verfolgter Jude*, p. 75.

44. BArch Berlin, NS 23/1174: Letter from the Bavarian Minister of the Interior, Adolf Wagner, to the Gauleiter Wächtler, Streicher, Helmuth, Wahl, and Bürckel, 31 October 1938.

45. Götz Aly et al. (eds), *Die Verfolgung und Ermordung der europäischen Juden durch das nationalsozialistische Deutschland 1933–1945*, vol. 2: *Deutsches Reich 1938–August 1939*, ed. Susanne Heim (Munich: Oldenbourg, 2009), p. 415; Sopade, *Deutschland-Berichte*, vol. 5 (1938), p. 1,187; Stefanie Fischer, *Ökonomisches Vertrauen und antisemitische Gewalt: Jüdische Viehhändler in Mittelfranken* (Göttingen: Wallstein, 2014), pp. 286–7.

46. Much has been written about *Kristallnacht* and its background on the national, regional, and local levels. For an excellent recent survey, see Steinweis, *Kristallnacht 1938*, with further references. On the participation of women and children, see Aly et al. (eds), *Die Verfolgung und Ermordung der europäischen Juden*, vol. 2, p. 377; Sopade, *Deutschland-Berichte*, vol. 5 (1938), p. 1,191. For a collection of eyewitness accounts, see Matthäus and Roseman, *Jewish Responses*, vol. 1, pp. 341–78; and Uta Gerhard and Thomas Karlauf (eds), *Nie mehr zurück in dieses Land: Augenzeugen berichten über die Novemberpogrome 1938* (Berlin: List, 2009). On the visual aspects of the violence, see in particular Christoph Kreutzmüller and Bjoern Weigel, *Kristallnacht? Bilder der Novemberpogrome 1938 in Berlin* (Berlin: Kulturprojekte Berlin, 2013). On its international repercussions, see Colin McCullough and Nathan Wilson (eds), *Violence, Memory, and History: Western Perceptions of Kristallnacht* (New York and London: Routledge, 2015).
47. BArch Berlin 23/515: Joachim Meyer-Quade, Report of the SA-*Gruppe* Nordmark on the action of the night of 9–10 November 1938. Additional information is taken from Christa Geckeler, 'Novemberpogrom in Kiel', https://kiel.de/kultur/stadtarchiv/erinnerungstage/index.php?id=95.
48. See Frank Bajohr and Christoph Strupp (eds), *Fremde Blicke auf das 'Dritte Reich': Berichte ausländischer Diplomaten über Herrschaft und Gesellschaft in Deutschland 1933–1945* (Göttingen: Wallstein, 2011), pp. 501–20.
49. Monika Hinterberger, 'Menschen wie wir', in Zinken, *Der unverstellte Blick*, pp. 106–10, here p. 108.
50. Bernd Wagner, *Psychiatrie und Gesellschaft in der Moderne: Geisteskrankenfürsorge in der Provinz Westfalen zwischen Kaiserreich und NS-Regime* (Paderborn: Schöningh, 1996), p. 460.
51. Peter Schyga, *NS-Macht und evangelische Kirche in Bad Harzburg* (Wolfenbüttel: Landeskirchenamt, 2013), pp. 98–9.
52. FES, Viktor Lutze Papers, Political Diary of Viktor Lutze, p. 124.
53. Aly et al. (eds), *Die Verfolgung und Ermordung der europäischen Juden*, vol. 2, p. 387; Fischer, *Ökonomisches Vertrauen und antisemitische Gewalt*, p. 285; Sopade, *Deutschland-Berichte*, vol. 5 (1938), p. 1,198; ÖStA/AdR/'Bürckel'-Nachträge: Karton rot 5: Letter from the *Ortsgruppenleiter* Untere Donaustraße/Vienna to the Gestapo, 9 February 1939.
54. Aly et al. (eds), *Die Verfolgung und Ermordung der europäischen Juden*, vol. 2, p. 401.
55. Gerhard Ritter, Letter to his mother, Freiburg, 24 November 1938, in *Gerhard Ritter: Ein politischer Historiker in seinen Briefen*, p. 339. Foreign diplomats repeatedly noticed that many Germans were appalled by the pogrom; see Bajohr and Strupp, *Fremde Blicke auf das 'Dritte Reich'*, pp. 503, 509–12. For the widespread negative reactions of the population in the newly integrated Sudetenland, see Volker Zimmermann, *Die Sudetendeutschen im NS-Staat: Politik und Stimmung der Bevölkerung im Reichsgau Sudetenland (1938–1945)* (Essen: Klartext, 1999), pp. 106–7; Jörg Osterloh, *Nationalsozialistische Judenverfolgung im Reichsgau Sudetenland 1938–1945* (Munich: Oldenbourg, 2006), pp. 218–21.
56. See the detailed introduction by Thomas Vogel, 'Wilm Hosenfeld – ein deutsches Leben', in Wilm Hosenfeld, *'Ich versuchte jeden zu retten': Das Leben eines deutschen Offiziers in Briefen und Tagebüchern*, ed. Thomas Vogel and Militärgeschichtliches Forschungsamt (Munich: Deutsche Verlags-Anstalt, 2004), pp. 1–146, in particular pp. 21–36. On the NSDAP's appeal to the German elementary teachers, see Pyta, *Dorfgemeinschaft und Parteipolitik*, pp. 421–32. On the significance to the SA of teachers and pastors in the countryside, see also Sopade, *Deutschland-Berichte*, vol. 2 (1935), p. 611.
57. Hosenfeld, *'Ich versuchte jeden zu retten'*, p. 208. Otmar Welck, who in 1940 became the adjutant of the 'Higher SS and Police Leader' Josef Berkelmann in German-annexed Lorraine, remembered his time as an SA-*Truppführer* between 1931 and 1935 in a similarly positive way; see Gehrig, *Im Dienste der nationalsozialistischen Volkstumspolitik in Lothringen*, pp. 29–36.
58. On the pogroms in Hesse that began on 7 November, see Steinweis, *Kristallnacht 1938*, pp. 22–35. One of Hosenfeld's very few remarks on the Jews during these years is from 25 November 1936: 'In the evening I attended a political meeting on the Jews. Very modest deliberations'; Hosenfeld, *'Ich versuchte jeden zu retten'*, p. 217.
59. Hosenfeld, *'Ich versuchte jeden zu retten'*, pp. 210, 219, 234.

60. Ibid., pp. 214–15, 229, 235–6.
61. Ernst Klee, *Die SA Jesu Christi: Die Kirchen im Banne Hitlers* (Frankfurt am Main: Fischer, 1989); Siemens, *The Making of a Nazi Hero*, pp. 132–4.
62. Riley, *The Civic Foundation of Fascism in Europe*, pp. 72–112.
63. More popular were only football and athletics, see Henning Borggräfe, *Schützenvereine im Nationalsozialismus: Pflege der 'Volksgemeinschaft' und Vorbereitung auf den Krieg (1933–1945)* (Münster: Ardey, 2010), p. 20.
64. The *Deutsche Reichsbund Kyffhäuser*, an umbrella organization for the diverse veterans' organizations, comprised 2.5 million members in 1929. See Frank Bösch, 'Militante Geselligkeit: Formierungsformen der bürgerlichen Vereinswelt zwischen Revolution und Nationalsozialismus', in Wolfgang Hardtwig, *Politische Kulturgeschichte der Zwischenkriegszeit 1918–1939* (Göttingen: Wallstein, 2005), pp. 151–82, here p. 164.
65. Borggräfe, *Schützenvereine im Nationalsozialismus*, pp. 18–23; Bösch, 'Militante Geselligkeit', here p. 159.
66. Bösch, 'Militante Geselligkeit', p. 172.
67. For details, see Borggräfe, *Schützenvereine im Nationalsozialismus*, pp. 29–39. The attraction of 'SA sports' is also emphasized by Szejnmann, *Nazism in Central Germany*, pp. 151–2.
68. Borggräfe, *Schützenvereine im Nationalsozialismus*, p. 41.
69. The SA's 'mass sports' built on the *Wehrsport* of the Weimar years. Physical training, particularly boxing and jiu jitsu, but also skiing, handball, and motorcycling were popular; see Christiane Eisenberg, *'English sports' und deutsche Bürger: Eine Gesellschaftsgeschichte 1800–1939* (Paderborn: Schöningh, 1999), pp. 327–30, 389–91; Berno Bahro, *Der SS-Sport: Organisation – Funktion – Bedeutung* (Paderborn: Schöningh, 2013), pp. 27–2, 37–8; Michael B. Barrett, *Soldiers, Sportsmen, and Politicians: Military Sport in Germany, 1924–1935*, PhD diss., University of Massachusetts–Amherst, 1977; Arnd Krüger and Frank von Lojewski, 'Ausgewählte Aspekte des Wehrsports in Niedersachsen in der Weimarer Zeit', in Hans Langenfeld and Stefan Nielsen (eds), *Beiträge zur Sportgeschichte Niedersachsens*, vol. 2: *Weimarer Republik* (Göttingen, NISH, 1998), pp. 124–47. Regional studies suggest that the SA's influence on mass sports between 1933 and 1939 differed substantially from region to region; see, for example, Florian Lueke, *Geschichte des Sports in Lippe: Menschen – Vereine – Politik: Eine vergleichende regionalgeschichtliche Studie* (Lage: Lippe Verlag, 2015), pp. 302–7.
70. Borggräfe, *Schützenvereine im Nationalsozialismus*, p. 48.
71. Eisenberg, *'English sports' und deutsche Bürger*, p. 393.
72. Borggräfe, *Schützenvereine im Nationalsozialismus*, p. 50.
73. On the SA rider storms, see Schuster, *Die SA*, pp. 171–2; Bahro, *Der SS-Sport*, p. 225; GSt PK, I. HA, Rep. 77 titl. 4043, vol. 311, p. 321: Racliffe (Polizeimajor), 'Denkschrift über Kampfvorbereitung und Kampfgrundsätze radikaler Organisationen'. For an early example of the fight between the SA and the SS over such rider units, see Christiane Rothländer, *Die Anfänge der Wiener SS* (Vienna: Böhlau, 2012), pp. 160–2.
74. *Deutsche Reiter Zeitung*, no. 7 (1934), p. 122, as quoted in Nele Maya Fahnenbruck, '... reitet für Deutschland': Pferdesport und Politik im Nationalsozialismus* (Göttingen: Verlag die Werkstatt, 2013), p. 238.
75. Publications like *Der Stürmer* blended existing prejudices against 'professional sports' with antisemitism, claiming that 'foreign races' had seized control over German riding activities, and horseracing in particular. See Fahnenbruck, '... reitet für Deutschland'*, pp. 238–9; Bayer, *Die SA*, pp. 26–7.
76. In this respect I follow Fahnenbruck's interpretation and disagree with Bahro, who in his study on SS sports comes to a somewhat contradictory conclusion. Bahro stresses that the *Reichssportführer* and the SS managed to refute the leadership claims of the SA prior to 1936, only to acknowledge two pages later the SA's 'numerical ascendance' with regard to the distribution of the obligatory *Reiterscheine*, or 'rider's permits'. In 1935 more than 88,000 riders were organized in the SA, compared to only 12,000 in the SS; Bahro, *Der SS-Sport*, pp. 231, 233, 236.
77. Fahnenbruck, '... reitet für Deutschland'*, p. 240.
78. Ibid., pp. 246–7. The OSAF attempted to maintain its influence over the riders' clubs in the countryside well into the war years; see BArch Berlin, NS 23/98: Note of SA-Obergruppenführer Max Jüttner, 5 November 1940.

79. PAAA, Personal Papers of Siegfried Kasche, vol. 34: Report on 'Veranstaltung der SA-*Gruppe* Hansa und der Schützenvereine des Standortes Groß-Hamburg', 1 December 1938.

80. This is the unanimous conclusion of Borggräfe, Fahnenbruck, and Bösch in their respective studies: Borggräfe, *Schützenvereine im Nationalsozialismus*, pp. 53–6, 96–102; Fahnenbruck, '... *reitet für Deutschland'*, pp. 157–8; Bösch, 'Militante Geselligkeit'.

81. For several examples of SA violence directed against non-Jewish Germans on the occasion of the (mock) Reichstag elections of 10 April 1938, see Sopade, *Deutschland-Berichte*, vol. 5 (1938), pp. 415–24.

82. Borggräfe, *Schützenvereine im Nationalsozialismus*, pp. 47–53, 81–6.

83. Sven Reichardt even claimed that, for the stormtroopers, it was a kind of 'character test to be opposed to all sorts of middle-class culture'; Reichardt, *Faschistische Kampfbünde*, pp. 643–6. But what seems plausible for the urban 'Old Fighters' is less convincing for those men living in small-town and rural Germany.

84. Hosenfeld, *'Ich versuchte jeden zu retten'*, p. 219.

85. Ibid., p. 236. The SA units in the Palatinate were called on to perform similar collections in the late 1930s; see Schepua, *Nationalsozialismus in der pfälzischen Provinz*, p. 284.

86. Hosenfeld, *'Ich versuchte jeden zu retten'*, p. 234.

87. Fritz Otto Böhmig, *Briefe aus dem Felde 15.8.1939–15.8.1943* (unpublished typescript), p. 18. I am grateful to Stephanie Bird, London, who provided me with a copy of this correspondence.

88. Ibid., p. 69.

89. Hosenfeld, *'Ich versuchte jeden zu retten'*, pp. 429 and 696.

90. Ibid., p. 754.

91. For introductory overviews of this entangled history, see John T. Lauridsen, *Nazism and the Radical Right in Austria 1918–1934* (Copenhagen: Royal Library, 2007), in particular pp. 296–312; Bruce F. Pauley, *Hitler and the Forgotten Nazis: A History of Austrian National Socialism* (London: Macmillan, 1981). For a comprehensive analysis of political violence in Austria during the interwar years, see Gerhard Botz, *Gewalt in der Politik: Attentate, Zusammenstöße, Putschversuche, Unruhen in Österreich 1918 bis 1938* (Munich: Wilhelm Fink, 1983). For further literature, see Schafranek, *Söldner für den Anschluss*, pp. 19–23.

92. For recent general surveys, see Florian Wenninger and Lucile Dreidemy (eds), *Das Dollfuß-Schuschnigg-Regime 1933–1938: Vermessung eines Forschungsfeldes* (Vienna: Böhlau, 2013); Ilse Raither-Zatloukal, Christiane Rothländer, and Pia Schölnberger (eds), *Österreich 1933–1938: Interdisziplinäre Annäherungen an das Dollfuß-/Schuschnigg-Regime* (Vienna: Böhlau, 2012). On the putsch of July 1934, see Schafranek, *Sommerfest mit Preisschießen*; Hans Schafranek and Herbert Blatnik (eds), *Vom NS-Verbot zum 'Anschluss': Steierische Nationalsozialisten 1933–1938* (Vienna: Czernin, 2015), with further references. On the internment of Nazis in Austria, see Pia Schölnberger, '"Ein Leben ohne Freiheit ist kein Leben": Das "Anhaltelager" Wöllersdorf 1933–1938', in Raither-Zatloukal, Rothländer, and Schölnberger, *Österreich 1933–1938*, pp. 94–107. For the perspective of the illegal Nazis, see Edgar Traugott, *Elisabethpromenade 7/9* (Brünn: Rohrer, 1940).

93. Rothländer, *Die Anfänge der Wiener SS*, pp. 451–7.

94. Instructive in this respect is ÖStA/AdR, MGH Wien, MHv 61/34, pp. 7–39: Verdict of the Vienna Military Tribunal against the Viennese SA leader Fritz Hamburger, 13 February 1935.

95. This number was the total for the five years between 1933 and 1938 and comprised long-standing legionaries as well as those who were only briefly in the Austrian Legion. The actual number of legionaries at any given moment was thus always below 10,000. For details, see Schafranek, *Söldner für den Anschluss*, pp. 46–60.

96. ÖStA/AVA, Justiz, Allgemein, Sig. 6 A 3236 (NSDAP, Österreichische Legion 1934–1936): Bundeskanzleramt, Information on the Austrian Legion, 23 March 1936.

97. On the Austrian Legion, see in particular the comprehensive monograph by Schafranek, *Söldner für den Anschluss*; idem, 'Die steirischen Angehörigen der Österreichischen Legion: Regionale und lokale Herkunft, Alters- und Berufsstruktur, NSDAP- und SA-Mitgliederentwicklung, Führungspersonal (Biografien)', in Schafranek and Blatnik, *Vom NS-Verbot zum 'Anschluss'*, pp. 83–124; idem, 'Österreichische Nationalsozialisten in der

Illegalität 1933–1938: Ein Forschungsbericht', in *Das Dollfuß-Schuschnigg-Regime 1933–1938: Vermessung eines Forschungsfeldes*, ed. Wenninger and Dreidemy, pp. 105–37. For the official National Socialist historiography, see Otto Bokisch and Gustav A. Zirbs (eds), *Der Österreichische Legionär: Aus Erinnerungen und Archiv, aus Tagebüchern und Blättern* (Vienna: Österreichische Verlagsgesellschaft, 1940).

98. Schafranek, *Söldner für den Anschluss*, p. 168.
99. Ibid., pp. 193–205 (example on p. 199).
100. Ibid., pp. 132–46, 156–8.
101. Ibid., p. 157.
102. ÖStA/AVA, Justiz, Allgemein, Sign. 6 A 3627, Mappe 6682: Letter from the BKA in the criminal case of Josef Artur Fischer, born 25 November 1914 in Wolfurt. The German-Austrian agreement of 11 July 1936 facilitated such returns; see Schafranek, *Söldner für den Anschluss*, pp. 315–19.
103. BArch Berlin, NS 23/892: Durchführungsbestimmungen der Österreichischen SA-*Brigade* 2.
104. ÖStA/AdR, NS-Vermittlungsstelle, Karton 43, Mappe 200: Letter from the NS-Vermittlungsstelle to Dr Hammerschmid, 25 August 1938; SA Austria, 'Lagebericht über die Liquidierung der Österr. Legion', 22 June 1938.
105. Schafranek, *Söldner für den Anschluss*, pp. 351–8.
106. Bajohr and Strupp (eds), *Fremde Blicke auf das 'Dritte Reich'*, pp. 481–2; Schafranek, *Söldner für den Anschluss*, p. 42.
107. ÖStA/AdR, Gauakt 245.169 (Kurt Barisani): Claim to the NS-Betreuungs- und Wiedergutmachungsstelle des Gaues Wien, 1 December 1938; ÖStA/AdR, Gauakt 92.698 (Alexander Cseri): Letter from the Polizeidirektion Wien to Bundesministerium des Inneren, 4 April 1948.
108. ÖstA/AdR, 'Bürckel'/Nachträge: Karton rot 9, Nr. 60 (Korrespondenz Oberste SA-Führung 1938–1939: Anonymous letter from an 'SA man of Sturm III', May 1938).
109. A letter from the National Socialist Placement Bureau in Vienna (NS-*Vermittlungsstelle Wien*) from 10 March 1939 is particularly instructive in this respect. In it the *Vermittlungsstelle* supported the 'Aryanization request' (*Arisierungsantrag*) of the stormtrooper Wilhelm Walliczek using the argument that because Walliczek would only be capable of work to a limited extent, 'it would be highly advisable to provide him with a new existence by the way of Aryanization'; ÖStA/AdR, NS-Vermittlungsstelle, Karton 43, Mappe 197: Letter from the NS-Vermittlungsstelle Wien to Vermögensverkehrsstelle Wien, 10 March 1939; Schafranek, *Söldner für den Anschluss'*, pp. 390–1.
110. 'Mitteilung der Gruppe (Legionsdienstanrechnung)', in *SA in Feldgrau: Feldpostbriefe der SA-Gruppe Südmark*, no. 14/15 (July/August 1941).
111. Whereas the role of the SA in the destabilization of Austria prior to March 1938, as well as its behaviour in the months that followed, is well established, its contribution to the annexation of the Sudeten and the Memel regions in 1938–9 has rarely been touched upon (a notable exception is Dölling, 'Grenzüberschreitende Gewalttätigkeit'). From the perspective of the stormtroopers, the SA's activities in these regions signified a relative comeback of the SA on the domestic scene as well as a successful performance test abroad. Its increased paramilitary activities not only brought new credit to the stormtrooper propaganda that – as we have seen – had started to sound shallow to the ears of many SA men from the Reich but also contributed to an increasingly eastward turn by the OSAF.
112. On the early Nazi organizations in the region, see Dölling, 'Grenzüberschreitende Gewalttätigkeit', pp. 242–4.
113. See the paradigmatic remarks in Günther Wolff, *Großfahrt vogtländischer Jungen zu den deutschen Siedlungen in Ostgalizien. Sommer 1936* (Plauen: Das junge Volk, 1936), pp. 5 and 35; as well as Andreas Peschel, 'Die Bündische Jugend', *Dresdner Hefte: Beiträge zur Kulturgeschichte* 26 (2007), pp. 35–42, here pp. 40–1.
114. See Schmidt's extensive correspondence between 1928 and 1933 in BArch Berlin, NS 26/370-372. With regard to the early SA in the Sudetenland, see in particular the letter from Albert Umlauf, Brüx, of 18 September 1929 in BArch Berlin, NS 26/372; with regard to the problems of the uniform abroad, see Schmidt's letter to Alfred Günzel, 13 February 1931, in BArch Berlin, NS 26/370. On the continuity of such student travels,

see Elizabeth Harvey, 'Emissaries of Nazism: German Student Travellers in Romania and Yugoslavia in the 1930s', *Österreichische Zeitschrift für Geschichtswissenschaft* 22:1 (2011), pp. 135–60.

115. Despite this development it is important to note that Henlein's *Heimatbund* acted quite independently of the NSDAP in the Reich until 1935. The popular narrative of the German 'fifth column' is to an important degree an ex post facto construction that oversimplifies the actual tensions within the German camp. See Mark Cornwall, '"A Leap into Ice-Cold Water": The Manoeuvres of the Henlein Movement in Czechoslovakia, 1933–1938', in Mark Cornwall and R. J. W. Evans (eds), *Czechoslovakia in a Nationalist and Fascist Europe 1918–1948* (Oxford: Oxford University Press, 2007), pp. 123–42. For a general picture, see Ronald Smelser, *Das Sudetenproblem und das Dritte Reich, 1933–1938: Von der Volkstumspolitik zur nationalsozialistischen Außenpolitik* (Munich: Oldenburg, 1980).

116. Caitlin Murdock, 'Central Policy and Local Practice: The Changing Dynamics of the Saxon-Bohemian Borderlands after 1933', *Zeitschrift für Osteuropa-Forschung* 53 (2004), pp. 184–99.

117. On the development of the *Deutscher Turnverband*, see Andreas Luh, *Der Deutsche Turnverband in der ersten Tschechoslowakischen Republik: Vom völkischen Vereinsbetrieb zur volkspolitischen Bewegung* (Munich: Oldenbourg, 2006). On the founding of the FS, see Werner Röhr, 'September 1938: Diversion und Demagogie bei der Erzeugung einer Kriegspsychose durch den Hitlerfaschismus und seiner Fünften Kolonne in der CSR', in Dietrich Eichholtz and Kurt Pätzold (eds), *Der Weg in den Krieg: Studien zur Geschichte der Vorkriegsjahre (1935/36 bis 1939)* (Cologne: Pahl-Rugenstein, 1989), pp. 211–77, here p. 218; as well as idem, 'Der "Fall Grün" und das Sudetendeutsche Freikorps', in Hans Henning Hahn (ed.), *Hundert Jahre sudetendeutsche Geschichte: Eine völkische Bewegung in drei Staaten* (Frankfurt am Main: Lang, 2007), pp. 241–56, here p. 245.

118. Detlef Brandes, *Die Sudetendeutschen im Krisenjahr 1938*, 2nd edn (Munich: Oldenbourg, 2010), pp. 252–87.

119. Dölling, 'Grenzüberschreitende Gewalttätigkeit', pp. 247–8.

120. The text of this proclamation is included in 'Die sudetendeutsche Befreiung: Vom Nürnberger Parteitag bis zum Münchner Abkommen', *Nation und Staat: Deutsche Zeitschrift für das europäische Nationalitätenproblem* 12:1 (1938), pp. 33–43, here pp. 36–7. On the Sudeten German Free Corps, see in particular Röhr, 'Der "Fall Grün"'; Dölling, 'Grenzüberschreitende Gewalttätigkeit'.

121. BArch Berlin, NS 23/477: Letter from the SA-Gruppe Sachsen to the Erziehungshauptamt of the SA, September 1938; Stefan Dölling, *Henleins Bürgerkrieger: Das Sudetendeutsche Freikorps zwischen Eigenmobilisierung und Fremdsteuerung durch das 3. Reich*, unpublished MA diss., Humboldt University Berlin, 2010, pp. 12–13.

122. Dölling, *Henleins Bürgerkrieger*, p. 1.

123. Zimmermann, *Die Sudetendeutschen im NS-Staat*, p. 128. Many leaders of the Sudeten German Free Corps were integrated into the SS; see Dölling, 'Grenzüberschreitende Gewalttätigkeit', p. 260.

124. Zimmermann, *Die Sudetendeutschen im NS-Staat*, p. 127.

125. An example is Toni Sandner, who from the autumn of 1938 onward served as Franz May's adjutant. Building on his former role in the *Deutscher Turnverband*, he also occupied the position of 'SA sports warden'; Zimmermann, *Die Sudetendeutschen im NS-Staat*, p. 127.

126. Osterloh, *Nationalsozialistische Judenverfolgung im Reichsgau Sudetenland*, pp. 209–10; Zimmermann, *Die Sudetendeutschen im NS-Staat*, p. 104; Ralf Gebel, *'Heim ins Reich!' Konrad Henlein und der Reichsgau Sudetenland (1938–1945)* (Munich: Oldenburg, 1999), pp. 69–80.

127. Franz May was born on 24 January 1903 in Warnsdorf, Sudeten, at that time part of the Habsburg monarchy, and studied from 1920 to 1923 at the University of Halle-Wittenberg. A landscape architect by training, he was elected on the ticket of the Sudeten German Party into the Czech parliament in 1935. Around the same time he clandestinely began working for the *Abwehr* of the German *Wehrmacht*. On May's biography prior to 1939, see the documents in BArch Berlin, SA 4000002816 (May, Franz). On his activities during the Second World War, see chapter 8. After being released from Czechoslovakian detention, May lived in Bavaria and

committed himself to German expellee organizations (*Sudetendeutsche Landsmannschaft* and the *Bund der Vertriebenen*).

128. BArch Berlin, SA 4000002816: Letter from Konrad Henlein to Viktor Lutze, 22 November 1941.

129. Zimmermann, *Die Sudetendeutschen im NS-Staat*, p. 128, n. 57.

130. For details on the political and military developments in Lithuania between 1918 and 1919, see Tomas Balkelis, 'Demobilization and Remobilization of German and Lithuanian Paramilitaries after the First World War', *Journal of Contemporary History* 50:1 (2015), pp. 38–57.

131. See Ernst-Albert Plieg, *Das Memelland 1920–1939: Deutsche Autonomiebestrebungen im litauischen Gesamtstaat* (Würzburg: Holzner, 1962). Unfortunately, the account by Tomas Balkelis (*The Making of Modern Lithuania* [Basingstoke: Routledge, 2009]) ends in the years 1918–19.

132. Lithuanian Central State Archive (LCVA), Collection no. 383, inventory no. 7, no. 1773, pp. 146–54: Memo of the Lithuanian Minister of Foreign Affairs, Stasys Lozoraitis, to the director of the political department of the Ministry of Foreign Affairs, Juozas Urbšys, 26 January 1935.

133. The National Socialist press characteristically spoke of a 'state of war'. See BArch Berlin, NS 23/227: 'SA-Appell und Marsch der SA', *Memelwacht* (Tilsit), 11 January 1940.

134. 'Die Lage: Litauen', *Nation und Staat: Deutsche Zeitschrift für das europäische Nationalitätenproblem*, 12:4 (1939), pp. 245–51, here p. 248.

135. Ian Kershaw, *Hitler 1936–1945: Nemesis* (Stuttgart: DVA, 2000), p. 228.

136. Martin Broszat, 'Die Memeldeutschen Organisationen und der Nationalsozialismus', *Vierteljahrshefte für Zeitgeschichte* 5:3 (1957), pp. 273–8, here p. 274.

137. Broszat, 'Die Memeldeutschen Organisationen', pp. 274–5. For details of the complicated relationship between the CSA and the SOVOG, see PAAA, R 84874, pp. 64–90: 'Anklageschrift in dem Verfahren gegen Dr. Neumann, v. Saß und Genossen (deutsche Übersetzung)'.

138. 'Dr. Ernst Neumann †', *Memelländer Dampfboot: Die Heimatzeitung aller Memelländer*, no. 11, 5 June 1955, pp. 3–4.

139. PAAA, R 84874, pp. 58–112: 'Anklageschrift in dem Verfahren gegen Dr. Neumann, v. Saß und Genossen'.

140. Broszat, 'Die Memeldeutschen Organisationen', p. 275; PAAA, R 84874, pp. 105–38: 'Anklageschrift in dem Verfahren gegen Dr. Neumann, v. Saß und Genossen'.

141. LCVA, Collection no. 383, inventory no. 7, no. 1773, pp. 146–54, here pp. 151–2: Memo of the Lithuanian Minister of Foreign Affairs, Stasys Lozoraitis, to the director of the political department of the Ministry of Foreign Affairs, Juozas Urbšys, 26 January 1935; PAAA, R 84875: 'Aufzeichnung v. Grundherr für das Auswärtige Amt vom 27 Oktober 1934'; PAAA, R 84874, pp. 39–45, 56–8: 'Anklageschrift in dem Verfahren gegen Dr. Neumann, v. Saß und Genossen'.

142. For a German perspective on this trial, see Helmut Jenkis, 'Der Neumann-Sass-Kriegsgerichtsprozess in Kaunaus 1934/35: Aus deutscher Sicht', *Annaberger Annalen* 17 (2009), http://annaberger-annalen.de/jahrbuch/2009/6_Jenkis.pdf. For a Lithuanian perspective, see Algimantas Taskunas, 'The World's First Nazi Trial', *Lithuanian Papers* 22 (2008), http://jloughnan.tripod.com/lithuania.htm.

143. BArch Berlin, NS 23/227: 'Memel-SA steht am 30. Januar 1939', *Der Alemanne* (Freiburg), 20 January 1939.

144. Ibid.: 'Die braune Uniform in Memel', *Stuttgarter NS-Kurier*, 26 January 1939.

145. Ibid.: 'Memeldeutsche Sicherheitsabteilung gebildet', *Königsberger Allgemeine Zeitung*, 10 January 1939.

146. Broszat, 'Die Memeldeutschen Organisationen', p. 278.

147. 'Die Lage: Litauen', *Nation und Staat* 12:5 (1939), p. 299.

148. There are many indications that even well-informed contemporaries did not know precisely the ways in which these two organizations differed from one other. See BArch Berlin, NS 23/227: 'Kowno fragt: Wird die SA gefährlich sein?', *Preußische Zeitung* (Königsberg), 12 January 1939.

149. Ralf Meindl, *Ostpreußens Gauleiter: Erich Koch – eine politische Biographie* (Osnabrück: Fibre, 2007), pp. 243–4.

150. As quoted in 'Der Wortlaut des Abkommens zwischen Litauen und dem Reich über die Rückgabe Memels', *Nation und Staat: Deutsche Zeitschrift für das europäische Nationalitätenproblem*, 12:8 (1939), pp. 560–1.

151. Broszat, 'Die Memeldeutschen Organisationen', p. 278.

152. See in particular Götz Aly, *Hitler's Beneficiaries: Plunder, Racial War, and the Nazi Welfare State* (London and New York: Verso, 2007).

153. For a similar assessment, see Campbell, 'SA after the Röhm Purge'.

154. Sopade, *Deutschland-Berichte*, vol. 5 (1938), p. 849.

Chapter 7

1. Sopade, *Deutschland-Berichte*, vol. 2 (1935), p. 1,498.

2. See Müller, *Hitlers Ostkrieg*; Czesław Madajczyk (ed.), *Vom Generalplan Ost zum Generalsiedlungsplan* (Munich: K. G. Saur, 1994); Mechthild Rössler and Sabine Schleiermacher (eds), *Der 'Generalplan Ost': Hauptlinien der nationalsozialistischen Planungs- und Vernichtungspolitik* (Berlin: Akademie Verlag, 1993); Lumans, *Himmler's Auxiliaries*; Wildt, *Generation des Unbedingten*; Hartenstein, *Neue Dorflandschaften*; Heinemann, *'Rasse, Siedlung, deutsches Blut'*; David Blackbourn, *Die Eroberung der Natur: Eine Geschichte der deutschen Landschaft* (Munich: Siedler, 2006), pp. 319–39; Heinemann and Wagner, *Wissenschaft – Planung – Vertreibung*; Leniger, *Nationalsozialistische 'Volkstumsarbeit' und Umsiedlungspolitik*; Wolf, *Ideologie und Herrschaftsrationalität*. On the academic forerunners of the German expansionist policies in the east, see Piper, *Alfred Rosenberg*, pp. 448–56; Eduard Mühle, 'Putting the East in Order: German Historians and their Attempts to Rationalise German Eastward Expansion during the 1930s and 1940s', in Robert L. Nelson (ed.), *Germans, Poland, and Colonial Expansion to the East: 1850 Through the Present* (New York: Palgrave Macmillan, 2009), pp. 95–120; Beyrau, 'Eastern Europe as a "Sub-Germanic Space"'; Ulrich Prehn, *Max Hildebert Boehm: Radikales Ordnungsdenken vom Ersten Weltkrieg bis in die Bundesrepublik* (Göttingen: Wallstein, 2013).

3. See Armin Nolzen's article, 'Organizing the People's Community during the Second World War: The NSDAP and the Ethnic Germans in Nazi-Occupied Territories', submitted for publication in a forthcoming special issue of the *Journal of Genocide Research* on 'Lebensraum and Volksgemeinschaft' (expected for 2017).

4. Ute Peltz-Dreckmann, *Nationalsozialistischer Siedlungsbau: Versuch einer Analyse der die Siedlungspolitik bestimmenden Faktoren am Beispiel des Nationalsozialismus* (Munich: Minerva, 1978). On the SA settlements as a sub-category of the *Kleinsiedlung* (small-scale settlements), see Jörn Düwel and Niels Gutschow, *Städtebau in Deutschland im 20 Jahrhundert: Ideen – Projekte – Akteure* (Stuttgart: Teubner, 2001), pp. 96–105.

5. 'Gesetz über die Neubildung deutschen Bauerntums', 14 June 1933, in *Reichsgesetzblatt* 1933, vol. 1, p. 517.

6. Heinz Franz, *Der Mensch in der Siedlungsbewegung*, university diss., Ruprecht-Karls-Universität of Heidelberg, 1937, p. 40. On the NSDAP's strategies in rural Germany, see in particular Pyta, *Dorfgemeinschaft und Parteipolitik*; Hempe, *Ländliche Gesellschaft in der Krise*; Otto-Morris, *Rebellion in the Province*.

7. BArch Berlin, NS 23/222: 'Im Kampf gegen die Landflucht: SA schafft neues Bauerntum', *NSK*, Series 164, 15 July 1939, p. 1; 'Richtlinien für die Neubildung deutschen Bauerntums', 1 June 1935, in Gustavo Corni and Horst Gies, *'Blut und Boden': Rassenideologie und Agrarpolitik im Staat Hitlers* (Idstein: Schulz-Kirchner, 1994), p. 121.

8. On the German settlement movement as part of the life-reform movement, see Anne Feuchter-Schawelka, 'Siedlungs- und Landkommunebewegung', in Diethard Kerbs and Jürgen Reulecke (eds), *Handbuch der deutschen Reformbewegungen, 1880–1933* (Wuppertal: Hammer, 1998), pp. 227–44. On the National Socialist settlement movement, see Uwe Mai, *'Rasse und Raum': Agrarpolitik, Sozial- und Raumplanung im NS-Staat* (Paderborn: Schöningh, 2002); Corni and Gies, *'Blut und Boden'*; Roland Baier, *Der deutsche Osten als soziale Frage: Eine Studie zur preußischen und deutschen Siedlungs- und Polenpolitik in den Ostprovinzen während des Kaiserreichs und der Weimarer Republik* (Cologne: Böhlau, 1980).

9. At this time earlier dissonances between the Supreme SA Command and the *Reichsnährstand* had been overcome. See BArch Berlin, R 43 II, no. 207, p. 118ff: Letter from the SA's Führungsamt to Darré, 24 May 1934, as quoted in Corni and Gies, *'Blut und Boden'*, p. 121. Since 1935 the guidelines of the Reich labour minister had specified that 'combat veterans and fighters of the national revolution' were to be given preference in the distribution of settlement patches; Peltz-Dreckmann, *Nationalsozialistischer Siedlungsbau*, pp. 139–40. Consequently, we can assume that SA men prior to 1937 benefited disproportionately from the state-sponsored construction of small housing estates (*Kleinsiedlungsbau*).

10. BArch Berlin, NS 23/222: 'Sturmabteilungsmänner packen an', *Bremer Zeitung*, 27 November 1939; PAAA, Personal Papers of Siegfried Kasche, no. 41, pp. 59–77, here p. 70: 'Bericht über die Arbeiten in der SA hinsichtlich ihrer Beteiligung bei der Neubildung deutschen Bauerntums'. This document is also included in BArch Berlin, NS 23/688.

11. SA-Oberführer Holtz, 'SA-Dankopfersiedlung "Glaubensstatt"', *Die SA* 2:17 (1941), pp. 14–16.

12. On the close cooperation between the SA and the German shooting associations, see Borggräfe, *Schützenvereine im Nationalsozialismus*, as well as the previous chapter.

13. Barbara Wolf, 'Wohnungs- und Siedlungsbau', in Michael Cramer-Fürtig and Bernhard Gotto (eds), *'Machtergreifung' in Augsburg: Anfänge der NS-Diktatur 1933–1937* (Augsburg: Wißner, 2008), pp. 179–88 (quotation on p. 180).

14. BArch Berlin, NS 23/222: 'Zinsfrei und kapitallos', *NSK*, Series 77, 5 April 1937, p. 1.

15. Ibid., p. 2.

16. Holtz, 'SA-Dankopfersiedlung "Glaubensstatt"', p. 14.

17. Jan (Johannes) G. Smit, *Neubildung deutschen Bauerntums: Innere Kolonisation im Dritten Reich: Fallstudien in Schleswig-Holstein* (Kassel: Gesamthochschul-Bibliothek, 1983), p. 184.

18. Wolfram Pyta, '"Menschenökonomie": Das Ineinandergreifen von ländlicher Sozialraumgestaltung und rassenbiologischer Bevölkerungspolitik im NS-Staat', *Historische Zeitschrift* 273:1 (2001), pp. 31–94, here p. 39; Franz, *Der Mensch in der Siedlungsbewegung*, p. 30; Müller, *Hitlers Ostkrieg*, pp. 11–12.

19. Smit, *Neubildung deutschen Bauerntums*, p. 186.

20. Klaus Kiran Patel, 'The Paradox of Planning: German Agricultural Policy in a European Perspective, 1920s to 1970s', *Past and Present* 212:1 (2011), pp. 239–69, here p. 245.

21. On the actual mood of the German peasants at the end of the 1930s, see Timothy W. Mason, *Arbeiterklasse und Volksgemeinschaft: Dokumente und Materialien 1936–1939* (Opladen: Westdeutscher Verlag, 1975), pp. 865–7; J. E. Farquharson, 'The Agrarian Policy of National Socialist Germany', in Robert G. Moeller (ed.), *Peasants and Lords in Modern Germany* (Boston: Allen & Unwin, 1986), pp. 233–59.

22. R. Walther Darré, 'Bauern und Soldaten', in *Der SA-Führer* 8 (1938), reprinted in R. Walther Darré, *Um Blut und Boden: Reden und Aufsätze* (Munich: Eher, 1942), pp. 158–61.

23. On the importance of 'male comradeship' in the National Socialist movement as well in the Third Reich, see Thomas Kühne, *Belonging and Genocide: Hitler's Community, 1918–1945* (New Haven, CT, and London: Yale University Press, 2010).

24. Smit, *Neubildung deutschen Bauerntums*, p. 185. Darré in October 1939 made a very similar argument; see Peter Longerich, *Heinrich Himmler: Biographie* (Munich: Siedler, 2008), p. 450.

25. Historical research so far has mentioned Kasche only with regard to his role as German envoy in Croatia (1941–5). See most recently Alexander Korb, *Im Schatten des Weltkriegs: Massengewalt der Ustaša gegen Serben, Juden und Roma in Kroatien 1941–1945* (Hamburg: Hamburger Edition, 2013).

26. On Kasche's biography, see his detailed responses while interned to questions by the Yugoslav authorities on 7 March 1947 in Croatian State Archives, Zagreb (HDA), HR-HDR-1561, Sg 013.0.47 (Slavko Kvaternik), III DIO, pp. 280–1. See also BArch Berlin, R 9354/601: 'Der deutsche Gesandte in Agram/Kroatien: SA-Obergruppenführer Kasche', *Illustrierter Beobachter*, 14 August 1941.

27. Prestien, 'Die SA bei der Neubildung deutschen Bauerntums', *Die SA* 2:17 (1941), pp. 10–13, here p. 11.

28. BArch Berlin, NS 23/222: 'Zinsfrei und kapitallos', *NSK*, Series 77, 5 April 1937, p. 1.

29. BArch Berlin, NS 23/688: Siegfried Kasche, 'Richtlinien für die Beteiligung der SA bei der Neubildung deutschen Bauerntums', 8 September 1938. See also Kasche, 'Bericht über die Arbeiten in der SA', pp. 59–60.

30. BArch Berlin, NS 23/688: 'Merkblatt betreffend den Erwerb des Neubauernscheins' (1938).

31. Ibid.: Siegfried Kasche, 'Besondere Anordnung Nr. 1', 4 November 1940.

32. Kasche, 'Richtlinien für die Beteiligung der SA'.

33. Alexander Prusin, '"Make This Land German Again!" The Nazi Population Policies in the Wartheland, 1939–1941', in Aleksandr Dyukov and Olesya Orlenko (eds), *Divided Eastern Europe: Border and Population Transfer, 1938–1947* (Newcastle upon Tyne: Cambridge Scholars Publishing, 2012), pp. 74–91, here pp. 75–7; Smit, *Neubildung deutschen Bauerntums*, pp. 30–60.

34. PAAA, Personal Papers of Siegfried Kasche, no. 34: SA-Oberführer Udo von Alvensleben, 'Die Bedeutung der Grenzlandsiedlung: Vortrag vor den Neubauernsiedlungsreferenten und der Obersten SA Führung am 12 Mai 1939 in Schlochau'. Alvensleben, born on 4 May 1895, was an East Elbian aristocrat who was attracted to National Socialism already prior to 1933. After the First World War he initially joined the *Stahlhelm*, but in September 1930 he became a member of the NSDAP and soon was promoted to leader of the local SA-*Standarte*. In 1933 he was appointed head of the district authority in Schlochau/Pomerania and in the following years tried to reconcile local customs and religious traditions with the National Socialist ideology. On his biography and political views, see the documents in his SA personal file in BArch Berlin, SA 4000000027 (Alvensleben, Udo von).

35. Christoph Dieckmann, 'Plan und Praxis: Deutsche Siedlungspolitik im besetzten Litauen 1941–1944', in *Wissenschaft – Planung – Vertreibung*, ed. Heinemann and Wagner, pp. 93–118, here p. 94.

36. Prusin, '"Make This Land German Again!"' pp. 75–6. Among the important literature on the influence of colonial fantasies and experiences on Nazi rule, see Patrick Bernhard, 'Hitler's Africa in the East: Italian Colonialism as a Model for German Planning in Eastern Europe', *Journal of Contemporary History* 51:1 (2016), pp. 61–90; Benjamin Madley, 'From Africa to Auschwitz: How German South West Africa Incubated Ideas and Methods Adopted and Developed by the Nazis in Eastern Europe', *European History Quarterly* 35:3 (2005), pp. 429–64; Jürgen Zimmerer, 'Die Geburt des "Ostlandes" aus dem Geist des Kolonialismus: Die nationalsozialistische Eroberungs- und Beherrschungspolitik in (post-) kolonialer Perspektive', *Sozial.Geschichte* 19:1 (2004), pp. 10–43.

37. Kasche, 'Bericht über die Arbeiten in der SA', pp. 62–4.

38. Longerich, *Heinrich Himmler*, pp. 449–51; Robert L. Koehl, *RKFDV: German Resettlement and Population Policy 1939–1945: A History of the Reich Commission for the Strengthening of Germandom* (Cambridge, MA: Harvard University Press, 1957), pp. 49–70.

39. BArch Berlin, NS 23/688: Kasche, 'Schreiben betr. der Beteiligung der SA'.

40. In contrast to the situation in Upper Silesia, no detailed planning with regard to rural settlements existed for the Warthegau and Danzig district in late 1939.

41. BArch Berlin, NS 23/688: SA-Obersturmbannführer Prestin, Summary of all important questions on the settlement of new peasants (*Neubauernsiedlung*) in the former Polish territories, 8 December 1939.

42. BArch Berlin, NS 23/688: Circular of the leader of SA-Gruppe Hessen, 4 December 1939.

43. Kasche, Letter on the SA's contribution to the new formation of German peasantry.

44. BArch Berlin, NS 23/688: Siegfried Kasche, 'Besondere Anordnung', 20 January 1941; Kasche, 'Bericht über die Arbeiten in der SA', p. 73. Remarkably, there is no mention of Kasche in the relevant book by Lumans, *Himmler's Auxiliarie*. From the multitude of studies on the ethnic Germans and their experiences, see in particular Doris L. Bergen, 'The "Volksdeutschen" of Eastern Europe, World War II and the Holocaust: Constructed Ethnicity, Real Genocide', in Keith Bullivant et al. (eds), *Germany and Eastern Europe: Cultural Identities and Cultural Differences* (Amsterdam and Atlanta, GA: Rodopi, 1999), pp. 70–93; idem, 'Die Volksdeutschen in German Propaganda', *German Studies Review* 31:3 (2008), pp. 447–70.

45. See Kasche's personal papers, deposited in a Berlin safe-deposit locker in the final months of the war and today stored in the Political Archive of the German Foreign Ministry, as well as the extensive files on SA settlement policies in the German Federal Archives.

46. BArch Berlin, NS 23/510: OSAF (Jüttner), Urgent letter [*Schnellbrief*] on the set-up of the SA in the German territories of the former Polish state, 30 October 1939.

47. Kasche, 'Bericht über die Arbeiten in der SA', pp. 61 and 75.

48. Ibid., p. 75.

49. BArch Berlin, NS 23/98: Remarks on the speech of the SA Reich Treasurer, 13 September 1940.

50. Kasche, 'Bericht über die Arbeiten in der SA', p. 75. Błonie Castle was the birthplace of the later commander of the Polish army in the Soviet Union, Władysław Anders. On Anders, see Joanna Pyłat et al. (eds), *General Władysław Anders: Soldier and Leader of the Free Poles in Exile* (London: Polish University Abroad, 2008).

51. BArch Berlin, SA 4000001265 (Hacker, Heinrich): Letter from Hacker to Viktor Lutze, 25 September 1941; BArch Berlin, NS 23/98: Note from Siegele (Oberführer) on a meeting with SA-Obergruppenführer Litzmann, Berlin, 9 October 1940. According to Hacker, the Wehrmacht and the SS had also expressed a vivid interest in *Freihufen*, 'one of the most profitable country estates in the whole Warthegau'.

52. BArch Berlin, NS 23/688: Siegfried Kasche, 'Besondere Anordnung Nr. 3', 8 January 1941.

53. Ibid.: Beauftragter des Stabschefs für die Beteiligung der SA bei der Neubauernsiedlung, Merkblatt 1, 2 January 1940.

54. BArch Berlin, NS 23/688: 'Zahlenmäßige Aufstellung über die Neubauernbewerber in den Gruppen nach dem Stand vom 20. Juni 1940'.

55. Kasche, 'Bericht über die Arbeiten in der SA', p. 67.

56. Ibid., p. 68.

57. On Kasche's tainted relations with Himmler, see Edmund Glaise von Horstenau, *Ein General im Zwielicht: Die Erinnerungen Edmund Glaises von Horstenau. Bevollmächtigter General in Kroatien und Zeuge des Untergangs des Tausendjährigen Reiches*, ed. Peter Broucek, vol. 3 (Vienna: Böhlau, 1988), pp. 188–9.

58. Kasche, 'Bericht über die Arbeiten in der SA', p. 68.

59. Joachim Wolschke-Bulmahn, 'Gewalt als Grundlage nationalsozialistischer Stadt- und Landschaftsplanung in den "eingegliederten Ostgebieten"', in *Der 'Generalplan Ost'*, ed. Rössler and Schleiermacher, pp. 328–38, here p. 330.

60. See Heinemann, *'Rasse, Siedlung, deutsches Blut'*; and the ongoing project on the SS by Jan Erik Schulte.

61. Siegfried Kasche, 'Besondere Anordnung Nr. 3', 8 January 1941. For a thorough discussion of the general problem of reconciling the idea of a *Volksgemeinschaft* with the elitist self-understanding of the German nobility, see Malinowski, *Vom König zum Führer*, pp. 531–52. On those members of the German gentry who occupied leadership positions in the SA prior to 1934, see Malinowski and Reichardt, 'Die Reihen fest geschlossen?', pp. 146–9.

62. Ernst Jünger, *Der Arbeiter: Herrschaft und Gestalt* (Cotta: Stuttgart, 1981 [1932]), p. 246.

63. Longerich, *Heinrich Himmler*, pp. 401–11, 427–32.

64. On the German conduct of war, which often did not respect the standards of international law, see Wolf, *Ideologie und Herrschaftsrationalität*, pp. 76–90.

65. Christopher R. Browning, 'Unterstaatssekretaer Martin Luther and the Ribbentrop Foreign Office', *Journal of Contemporary History* 12:2 (1977), pp. 313–44. For Rosenberg's good relations with SA leaders, see Piper, *Rosenberg*, p. 471; Matthäus and Bajohr, *Alfred Rosenberg*, pp. 181–2, 237.

66. Siegfried Kasche, 'Besondere Anordnung Nr. 3', 8 January 1941.

67. This shows a remarkable parallel to the settlement praxis of former members of the Wehrmacht in the newly conquered European east, with actual settlements there likewise remaining the exception. The majority of the '*Wehrbauern* to be' was supposed to be provided with land only after the final military victory. Nevertheless, many members of the military behaved as colonizers during the war. For details, see Müller, *Hitlers Ostkrieg*, pp. 25–48.

68. Max Otto Luyken was born on 16 October 1885 in Wesel in the Lower Rhine province. A professional soldier from 1905 until 1920, he became active with the Organization Escherich in Saxony and in the Black Reichswehr in the early 1920s before entering the agriculture business in 1926. In 1929, Luyken joined the NSDAP. He subsequently led the SA in the *Gau* Essen and then the SA-*Gruppe* Niederrhein before being transferred to the SA-*Gruppe*

Kurpfalz in the autumn of 1934. Starting in early 1937 he was the director of the SA's Reich Leadership School in Munich and *Inspekteur der Obersten SA-Führung für das Erziehungs- und Ausbildungswesen*. From September 1939 onward, Luyken served in the Wehrmacht with the military rank of a major. He was released from military service in late 1940 in order to help establish SA units in Alsace and Lorraine. On Luyken's biography, see BArch Berlin, VBS 1/1070053842 (Luyken, Max); BArch Berlin, SA 4000002767 (Luyken, Max); Joachim Lilla, 'Luyken, Max', in Joachim Lilla, *Staatsminister, leitende Verwaltungsbeamte und (NS-) Funktionsträger in Bayern 1918 bis 1945*, http://verwaltungshandbuch.bayerische-landesbibliothek-online.de/luyken-max.

69. Karl Rothmann, 'Das Reich der Zukunft – ein Bauernreich: Was der SA-Mann über die Neubauernsiedlung wissen muß', in *SA in Feldgrau: Feldpostbriefe der SA-Gruppe Südmark*, no. 22/23 (March/April 1942), pp. 2–3.

70. BArch Berlin, NS 23/688: 'Führungsbefehl der Obersten SA-Führung, Bestandsübersicht über Neubauernbewerber', 20 February 1943.

71. Ibid.: Circular of the leader of the SA-Gruppe Hessen on 'Neubauerntum. Mitarbeit in der Propaganda', 1 April 1942.

72. Ibid.: 'Führungsbefehl der Obersten SA-Führung', 15 August 1942.

73. Ibid.: Der Oberste SA-Führer, 'Schnellbrief betr. Stillegung der Inspektion für Neubauerntum und Volkstumspflege', 16 February 1943. At around the same time Lutze glumly noted in his diary: 'Some persons and institutions of the NSDAP no longer endure the word SA'; FES, Viktor Lutze Papers, Political Diary of Viktor Lutze, p. 302.

74. PAAA, Gesandtschaft Sofia, vol. 59/2, p. 69: Personal Notes of the Ambassador Adolf-Heinz Beckerle I, 4 October 1941; 'Memorandum of a meeting of Hitler, Rosenberg, Göring and Field Marshal Keitel in the Führer's Headquarters on 16 July 1941', in U.S. Government Printing Office (ed.), *Documents on German Foreign Policy 1918–1945: Series D (1937–1945)*, vol. 13: *The War Years, June 23–December 11, 1941* (Washington, DC: U.S. Government Printing Office, 1954), pp. 149–56, here p. 154; Alex J. Kay, *Exploitation, Resettlement, Mass Murder: Political and Economic Planning for German Occupation Policy in the Soviet Union, 1940–1941* (New York und Oxford: Berghahn, 2006), p. 182; Götz Aly et al., *Biedermann und Schreibtischtäter: Materialien zur deutschen Täter-Biographie* (Berlin: Rotbuch, 1987), p. 137.

75. Kay, *Exploitation, Resettlement, Mass Murder*, p. 85.

76. Kasche was by no means the only SA leader who was considered for or appointed to prominent positions in the German-occupied east. SA-*Obergruppenführer* (General) Karl-Siegmund Litzmann was made General Commissioner for Estonia in late 1941, and SA-*Obergruppenführer* Heinrich Schoene, the longtime SA leader in Schleswig-Holstein, was appointed General Commissioner for Volhynia-Podolia. Furthermore, no fewer than five SA generals were sent as German envoys to south-eastern Europe between 1940 and 1941 – next to Kasche these were Manfred von Killinger, Gottfried von Jagow, Hanns Elard Ludin, and Adolf-Heinz Beckerle. For details on these SA diplomats, see chapter 9.

77. For a biographical sketch of Deuchler, see Hans-Peter de Lorent, 'Gustaf Adolf Deuchler, Ordinarius in SA-Uniform', *HLZ: Zeitschrift der GEW Hamburg*, 12 (2007), pp. 38–42 (part 1) and 3–4 (2008), pp. 46–50 (part 2).

78. IfZ Archive, ED 149, vol. 2, pp. 10–13: Gustaf Deuchler, 'Denkschrift-Entwurf: Über die Notwendigkeit und die Aufgabe eines Kolonialsturmes (K.-Sturmes)'. A few weeks later Deuchler even fantasized about a new *Kolonialpädagogisches Institut*, literally the 'Institute for Colonial Pedagogy', that was allegedly planned to be established at Hamburg University; IfZ Archive, ED 149, vol. 2, pp. 14–15: Letter from Gustaf Deuchler to Siegfried Kasche, 26 July 1941.

79. 'Planungsgrundlagen der SS für den Aufbau der Ostgebiete (April–Mai 1940)', in Madajczyk (ed.), *Vom Generalplan Ost zum Generalsiedlungsplan*, pp. 3–14, here p. 5.

80. Ibid., pp. 3–5.

81. Ibid., pp. 6–7.

82. Note from Alexander Dolezalek from the planning department of the SS-*Ansiedlungsstab* Litzmannstadt on the *Generalsiedlungsplan*, 19 August 1941, in Madajczyk (ed.), *Vom Generalplan Ost zum Generalsiedlungsplan*, pp. 19–20, here p. 19; Prusin, '"Make This Land German Again!"'; Birthe Kundrus, 'Regime der Differenz: Volkstumspolitische Inklusionen

und Exklusionen im Warthegau und im Generalgouvernement 1939–1944', in Bajohr and Wildt, *Volksgemeinschaft*, pp. 105–23. On the limited excitement for the 'German east', see Mai, *'Rasse und Raum'*, pp. 319–31.

83. Mai, *'Rasse und Raum'*, p. 320.
84. Geraldine von Frijtag Drabbe Künzel, 'Die niederländische Ostkolonisation (1941–1944)', in Friso Wielenga and Loek Geeraedts (eds), *Jahrbuch des Zentrums für Niederlande Studien*, vol. 22 (Münster: Aschendorff, 2011), pp. 81–101 (quotation p. 89).
85. See Elizabeth Harvey, *Women and the Nazi East: Agents and Witnesses of Germanisation* (New Haven, CT: Yale University Press, 2003); Aly, *Hitler's Beneficiaries*; Sönke Neitzel and Harald Welzer, *Soldaten: Protokolle vom Kämpfen, Töten und Sterben* (Frankfurt am Main: Fischer, 2011).
86. Patel, 'The Paradox of Planning', p. 245; Müller, *Hitlers Ostkrieg*, p. 8.
87. For details, see Pyta, 'Menschenökonomie', pp. 46–52. In contrast to Pyta, who emphasizes that this plan was ready for implementation by 1943, I would argue that by then there was no longer any chance of pushing such measures through because of the growing discontent on the 'home front'. As early as November 1941 the party-chancellery of the NSDAP informed Nazi functionaries that the 'resettlement' of peasants from the Old Reich would only take place after the war. See GSt PK, XX. HA, Rep. 240 B 8 a–e, pp. 105–6: Gauleitung Ostpreußen, Supplement to the information on 'Settlement of the new territories in the East', November 1941.
88. Sven Oliver Müller, 'Nationalismus in der deutschen Kriegsgesellschaft', in Militärgeschichtliches Forschungsamt and Jörg Echternkamp (eds), *Die Deutsche Kriegsgesellschaft 1939 bis 1945: Zweiter Halbband: Ausbeutung, Deutungen, Ausgrenzung* (Munich: DVA, 2005), pp. 9–92, here pp. 67–9; Harvey, *Women and the Nazi East*; Helmut Heiber, 'Dokumentation: Der Generalplan Ost', *Vierteljahrshefte für Zeitgeschichte* 6:3 (1958), pp. 281–325, here pp. 288–9; Blackbourn, *Die Eroberung der Natur*, pp. 320–4.
89. Herbert Backe, 'Die Neubildung des deutschen Bauerntums im eroberten Europa', *NS-Landpost*, 7 July 1942, as quoted in Corni and Gies, *'Blut und Boden'*, p. 207.
90. Karl Rothmann, 'Das Reich der Zukunft – ein Bauernreich: Was der SA-Mann über die Neubauernsiedlung wissen muß', *SA in Feldgrau: Feldpostbriefe der SA-Gruppe Südmark*, 22/23 (March/April 1942), pp. 2–3.
91. Michael Wildt, 'The Individual and the Community: New Research on the History of National Socialism' (Lecture at the German Historical Institute, London, 25 May 2014).
92. Both terms are used in Kasche, 'Bericht über die Arbeiten in der SA', p. 72.
93. Ibid., p. 77.
94. Reinhart Koselleck, '"Erfahrungsraum" und "Erwartungshorizont" – zwei historische Kategorien', in Reinhart Koselleck, *Vergangene Zukunft: Zur Semantik geschichtlicher Zeiten* (Frankfurt am Main: Suhrkamp, 1989), pp. 349–75.
95. Kasche, 'Bericht über die Arbeiten in der SA', p. 72.
96. See the detailed analysis in the previous chapter.
97. Barbara Wolf, 'Wohnungs- und Siedlungsbau', in *'Machtergreifung' in Augsburg*, ed. Cramer-Fürtig and Gotto, pp. 179–88, here p. 180.
98. BArch Berlin, NS 23/501, pp. 114–20: Typescript 'Die Wehrschützenbereitschaft im Gen[eral]-Gouvernement', probably from October 1942, here p. 120.
99. Ibid.: 'Die SA als Vorbild im Generalgouvernement', *Krakauer Zeitung*, 21 April 1942; 'Die Aufstellung der SA-Einheit General-Gouvernement' (Typescript).
100. For details, see Bergien, *Die bellizistische Republik*, pp. 82–7, 107–20, as well as above, introduction.
101. Christoph Rass, '"Volksgemeinschaft" und "Wehrgemeinschaft"', in *'Volksgemeinschaft als soziale Praxis'*, ed. von Reeken and Thießen, pp. 309–22.

Chapter 8

1. BArch Berlin, NS 23/515: Wilhelm Schepmann, 'Weltanschauliche Ausrichtung für den totalen Einsatz' (topic 3: 'Jeder SA-Mann ein fanatischer Träger des äußersten und totalen Widerstandswillens'), 6 December 1944.

2. The number of studies that have hitherto dealt with such aspects of the SA's history is very limited. See Campbell, 'SA after the Röhm Purge'; Longerich, *Geschichte der SA*, pp. 237–45; Jamin, 'Zur Rolle der SA im nationalsozialistischen Herrschaftssystem', pp. 353–8; Müller, 'Wilhelm Schepmann'; Müller/Reiner Zilkenat, '... der Kampf wird über unserem Leben stehe [sic!], solange wir atmen!' Einleitung, in idem (eds), *Bürgerkriegsarmee*, pp. 21–4.

3. Michael Mann, *The Dark Side of Democracy: Explaining Ethnic Cleansing* (Cambridge and New York: Cambridge University Press, 2005), p. 198; Merkl, *Political Violence under the Swastika*, pp. 634–5.

4. Wilhelm Rehm, 'Willensträger deutscher Wehrgemeinschaft!', in *SA in Feldgrau: Feldpostbriefe der SA-Gruppe Südmark* 13 (May 1941). The same argument, phrased slightly differently, is also found in Wilhelm Rehm, 'Zwei Jahre Kriegsbewährung der SA', in *SA in Feldgrau: Feldpostbriefe der SA-Gruppe Südmark* 16/17 (September/October 1941). On Rehm's importance to the DC, see Helmut Baier, *Die Deutschen Christen Bayerns im Rahmen des bayerischen Kirchenkampfes* (Nürnberg: Selbstverlag des Vereins für bayerische Kirchengeschichte, 1968). For a short biographical sketch of Rehm, see Nora Andrea Schulze (ed.), *Verantwortung für die Kirche: Stenographische Aufzeichnungen und Mitschriften von Landesbischof Hans Meiser 1933–1955*, vol. 3: *1937* (Göttingen: Vandenhoeck & Ruprecht, 2010), p. 1,069.

5. For biographical information about Schepmann, see IfZ Archive, ED 467, vol. 51, pp. 1–24: Testimony of Wilhelm Schepmann in the Landgerichtsgefängnis Lüneburg, 6 May 1949; Müller, 'Wilhelm Schepmann'.

6. BArch Berlin, VBS 264, no. 4001006602 (Sponholz, Hans): 'Programm der 2: Arbeitstagung der Dienststelle Berlin der Obersten SA-Führung vom 4–6 März 1944 in Posen'.

7. Ibid.: 'Merkblatt für die Tagungsteilnehmer', Posen, 3 March 1944.

8. On the SA Sports Badge, which was issued by the SA's *Amt für Ausbildungswesen* under SA-*Obergruppenführer* Friedrich Wilhelm Krüger, see Eisenberg, *'English sports' und deutsche Bürger*, pp. 390–1; Bahro, *Der SS-Sport*, pp. 96–9.

9. In a formal sense the men in the *Wehrmannschaften* did not automatically become members of the SA, even if the stormtroopers hoped to recruit among them. Consequently, the SA-*Wehrmannschaften* did not dress in the traditional Nazi brown shirt but trained in civil clothes. See Max Jüttner, 'SA an allen Fronten', *Die SA* 2:2 (1941) (10 January), pp. 9–10.

10. BArch Berlin, NS 23/98: Letter from OSAF, Georg Mappes, to the Oberkommando des Heeres on the budget for the Wehrmannschaften (classified), 18 July 1939.

11. Ibid.: Note from SA-Oberführer Siegele on a meeting with the Oberkommando des Herres on 26 October 1939.

12. 'Täglich wächst Deutschlands Wehrkraft', in *Die SA* 1:25 (1940) (12 July).

13. Borggräfe, *Schützenvereine im Nationalsozialismus*, pp. 88–9. Because of war-related censorship, the only statistics available are those compiled and published by the OSAF. A validation of these figures is therefore difficult.

14. BArch Berlin, NS 23/166: Max Luyken, 'Bericht über den 6. Sonderlehrgang in Schliersee'.

15. The best account of the creation and consequences of this organizational structure is still Manfred Messerschmidt, *Die Wehrmacht im NS-Staat: Zeit der Indoktrination* (Hamburg: R. v. Decker's Verlag, 1969), pp. 226–32. See also Rudolf Absolon, *Die Wehrmacht im Dritten Reich, Band IV: 5 Februar 1938 bis 31 August 1939* (Boppard am Rhein: Boldt, 1979), p. 35.

16. For an extract of this speech, see Volker Dahm et al. (eds), *Die tödliche Utopie. Bilder, Texte, Dokumente, Daten zum Dritten Reich* (Munich: IfZ, 2008), p. 272.

17. The *Nationalsozialistische Parteikorrespondenz* (NSK) even reported that von Brauchitsch had advanced these developments on his own initiative; Messerschmidt, *Die Wehrmacht im NS-Staat*, p. 227.

18. Otto Herzog, born 30 October 1900 in Zeiskam in the Palatinate, had received military training in Fürstenfeldbruck in 1917. After the war, he joined the *Freikorps* Epp and later became a member of the Reichswehr and the *Reichskriegsflagge*. Herzog participated and was severely wounded in the suppression of the Bavarian Soviet Republic in May 1919. Later, in 1923, he took part in the Hitler Purge. He joined the NSDAP and the SA in June 1926 and was promoted to the leader of the SA-*Brigade* Weser-Ems in November 1930,

to the leader of the SA-*Gruppe* Nordsee in August 1933, and to the leader of the SA-*Gruppe* Schlesien in July 1934. On Herzog's biography, see Werner Vahlenkamp, 'Herzog, Otto', in Hans Friedl (ed.), *Biographisches Handbuch zur Geschichte des Landes Oldenburg* (Oldenburg: Isensee, 1992), pp. 308–9; for his close relationship with Lutze, see in particular Herzog's letter to Lutze from 15 July 1932, in BArch Berlin, SA 4000001586 (Herzog, Werner).

19. FES, Viktor Lutze Papers, Political Diary of Viktor Lutze, pp. 125–6.
20. Ibid., p. 126.
21. Messerschmidt, *Die Wehrmacht im NS-Staat*, p. 229; FES, Viktor Lutze Papers, Political Diary of Viktor Lutze, pp. 126–7. Georg von Neufville, born 27 October 1883, descended from one of the most distinguished families of Frankfurt am Main. A member of the General Staff in the First World War, he subsequently led a *Freikorps* unit and joined the *Stahlhelm* before becoming a member of the NSDAP on 1 May 1933. A protégé of Reichenau, Neufville was initially regarded by the SA with extreme suspicion, as a representative of the old elite who had switched sides for personal benefit just in time. For biographical details, see his SA file in BArch Berlin, SA 400002962 (Neufville, Georg von); as well as Tobias Picard, 'Neufville, Familie de', in Wolfgang Klötzer (ed.), *Frankfurter Biographie: Personengeschichtliches Lexikon*, vol. 2: *M–Z* (Veröffentlichungen der Frankfurter Historischen Kommission 19/2) (Frankfurt am Main: Kramer, 1996), pp. 94–6.
22. Messerschmidt, *Die Wehrmacht im NS-Staat*, p. 231.
23. BArch Berlin, NS 23/515: Letter from SA-Gruppenführer Lehmann to OSAF Dienststelle Schrifttum, undated (probably spring 1941). In September 1943 the SA claimed that more than 75 per cent of its membership was serving in the Wehrmacht; see BArch Berlin, NS 23/518: NSDAP 'Aufklärungs- und Redner-Informationsmaterial on "Feldherrnhalle"', September 1943.
24. SA-Standartenführer Speer, 'Unsere größere Pflicht!', *SA in Feldgrau: Feldpostbriefe der SA-Gruppe Südmark*, 35/36 (September/October 1943).
25. BArch Berlin, SA 400002962 (Neufville, Georg von): 'Oberst v. Neufville gefallen', *Fränkische Tageszeitung*, 24 November 1941.
26. BArch Berlin, NS 23/515: Letter from Max Jüttner to SA-Obergruppenführer Mappes, 29 April 1941.
27. BArch Berlin, NS 23/98: Brigadeführer Kömpf, judge at the Oberste SA-Gericht, on 'Aufklärungsdienst der SA' (classified), 3 October 1941.
28. BArch Berlin, NS 23/166: 'Der Einsatz der SA im Kriege'.
29. As we are dealing here with up to a million men with different backgrounds, experiences of socialization, and ambitions, it is impossible to generalize about such issues before detailed empirical investigations are available. Further, it is beyond the scope of this study to provide a clear and representative picture that would do justice to this very large group. On the basis of the few existing case studies and my own archival findings, it is, however, possible to come to conclusions that are more than just tentative. These conclusions can be considered 'fragments floating out of a theoretical whole', to borrow a formulation of Raul Hilberg, thus allowing the discernment of contours and insights into a wider phenomenon that is theoretically imaginable even while empirically not (yet) fully accessible. See Raul Hilberg, 'Review of *Entscheidungsjahr 1932: Zur Judenfrage in der Endphase der Weimarer Republik*', *American Historical Review* 72:4 (1967), pp. 1,425–6, here p. 1,426.
30. Christoph Rass, *'Menschenmaterial': Deutsche Soldaten an der Ostfront: Innenansichten einer Infanteriedivision 1939–1945* (Paderborn: Schöningh, 2003), pp. 122–3.
31. Ibid., pp. 124–5.
32. Ibid., pp. 125–6, provides a similar conclusion.
33. For details, see also 'Verein zur militärhistorischen Forschung e.V.', http://www.lexikon-der-wehrmacht.de/Gliederungen/Infanteriedivisionen/253ID.htm.
34. For detailed insight into the confusion of many SA generals in reaction to the decree of 19 January 1939, see BArch Berlin, NS 23/166: Max Luyken, 'Bericht über den 6. Sonderlehrgang in Schliersee'.
35. PAAA, Personal Papers of Siegfried Kasche, vol. 35: SA-Oberführer Moock, Report, 15 September 1939. On the glorification of this 'front-line experience' since the late 1920s, see Matthias Schöning, *Versprengte Gemeinschaft: Kriegsroman und intellektuelle Mobilmachung in*

Deutschland 1914–1933 (Göttingen: Vandenhoeck & Ruprecht, 2009); Sprenger, *Landsknechte auf dem Weg ins Dritte Reich?*

36. A characteristic text for the ideological and historical worldview of the stormtroopers in the early 1940s can be found in BArch Berlin, NS 23/166: Obersturmführer Karl Bauer, 'Menschen und Mächte deutscher Geschichte: Eine Rede zur Weihnachtsfeier des SA-Sturmes 21/16 L', 20 December 1941.

37. See, for example, BArch Berlin, NS 23/166: Letter from Viktor Hölscher to Hans Sponholz at OSAF, 15 June 1942. For a broader discussion, see Hensch, 'Wir aber sind mitten im Kampf aufgewachsen'.

38. GSt PK, XX. HA Rep. 240 B 8 b, no. 21, pp. 88–91: 'Förderungsbestimmungen für Politische Leiter und Gliederungsführer'; RGVA, Osobyi Archives, Fond 1212, Opis 2, no. 68: 'Ausbildung ungedienter SA-Führer und SA-Unterführer durch das Heer', 17 March 1939. I am grateful to Yves Müller for pointing me to the latter document.

39. Ibid.

40. Konrad H. Jarausch and Klaus Jochen Arnold (eds), *'Das stille Sterben . . .': Feldpostbriefe von Konrad Jarausch aus Polen und Rußland, 1939–1942* (Paderborn: Schöningh, 2008), p. 187 (diary entry from 7 March 1940).

41. Officially, von Brauchitsch in January 1940 ordered that previous service in the SA be registered in the military service record. See GSt PK, XX. HA Rep. 240 B 8 b, no. 21, pp. 88–91: 'Förderungsbestimmungen für Politische Leiter und Gliederungsführer'.

42. For details, see SA-*Obersturmbannführer* Jaeger, 'Der Einsatz der Danziger SA', *Danziger Vorposten*, 5 September 1940; 'So kämpften Danzig's Soldaten', *Danziger Vorposten*, 19 September 1943. I am grateful to Jan Daniluk for kindly providing me with copies of these articles.

43. BArch Berlin, NS 23/166: 'Der Einsatz der SA im Kriege'.

44. The figure is taken from Sponholz, *Danzig – deine SA!*, p. 5.

45. BArch Berlin, NS 23/166: 'Der Einsatz der SA im Kriege'.

46. 'Tagesbericht über den 7./8. September 1939 (nachts)', in Stephan Lehnstaedt and Jochen Böhler (eds), *Die Berichte der Einsatzgruppen aus Polen 1939: Vollständige Edition* (Berlin: Metropol, 2013), pp. 62–4, here p. 64.

47. As one of his first actions, Schröder appointed Ulrich Uhle, since 1935 the *Gauleiter* in Posen, as the Führer of the organization of the ethnic German formations; Lehnstaedt and Böhler, *Die Berichte der Einsatzgruppen aus Polen*, p. 127. This suggests that the work of registering the Germans of occupied Poland was carried out more by the SS than by the SA, not least because the SA was initially prohibited from establishing a proper infrastructure in the region.

48. Jochen Böhler, *Der Überfall: Deutschlands Krieg gegen Polen*, 2nd edn (Frankfurt: Eichborn, 2009), pp. 137–40.

49. See BArch Berlin, NS 23/238: 'Stabschef der SA Lutze in Pressburg', *Grenzbote: Deutsches Tagblatt für die Karpathenländer*, 69. Jg., no. 286; BArch Berlin, NS 23/166: 'Der Einsatz der SA im Kriege'; Max Jüttner, 'SA an allen Fronten', in *Die SA* 1:2 (1940) (9 March). On Leo Bendak, see Luh, *Der Deutsche Turnverband in der Ersten Tschechoslowakischen Republik*, p. 432. On stormtroopers as concentration camp guards, see the IMT's examination of Max Jüttner on 14 August 1946 (morning session), http://avalon.law.yale.edu/imt/08-14-46.asp.

50. BArch Berlin, NS 23/166: 'Der Einsatz der SA im Kriege'.

51. Georg Wagner, *Sudeten SA in Polen: Ein Bildbericht vom Einsatz sudetendeutscher SA-Männer im polnischen Feldzug* (Karlsbad and Leipzig: Adam Kraft Verlag, 1940).

52. SA-*Gruppenführer* May, 'Preface', in Wagner, *Sudeten SA in Polen*, unpaginated.

53. The literature on this region is sparse, particularly for the interwar years. On the German minority there, see Nikolaus G. Kozauer, *Die Karpaten-Ukraine zwischen den beiden Weltkriegen unter besonderer Berücksichtigung der deutschen Bevölkerung* (Esslingen: Langer, 1979).

54. StA München, Bestand Staatsanwaltschaften München, Nr. 34835, vol. 1, p. 8: Verdict of the Bratislava People's Court, 22 June 1948, p. 4.

55. FES, Viktor Lutze Papers, Political Diary of Viktor Lutze, p. 159.

56. The soldier and former SA man Kurt Pfau provided a telling example in his war diaries. On 1 September, the first day of the war, Pfau approvingly noted that his unit had burned alleged

Polish snipers alive in the first village they had reached on their advance. See Udo Rosowski (ed.), *Glückauf zum Untergang: Die Kriegstagebücher des Feldwebels Kurt Pfau 1939–1945* (Brüggen: Literates, 2012), pp. 19–20. For general information on German warfare in Poland, see Jochen Böhler, *Auftakt zum Vernichtungskrieg: Die Wehrmacht in Polen 1939* (Frankfurt am Main: Fischer, 2006); Michael Alberti, '"Niederträchtige Perfidie, gemeine, unermessliche Gier und kalte, berechnende Grausamkeit …": Die "Endlösung der Judenfrage" im Reichsgau Wartheland', in Jacek Andrzej Młynarczyk and Jochen Böhler (eds), *Der Judenmord in den eingegliederten polnischen Gebieten 1939–1945* (Osnabrück: Fibre, 2010), pp. 117–42, here pp. 118–20. On the economic exploitation of the Poles, see Lehnstaedt, 'Das Generalgouvernement als Mobilisierungsreserve'.

57. FES, Viktor Lutze Papers, Political Diary of Viktor Lutze, pp. 160–1.
58. Few scholars have written on this particular SA unit. The most detailed account is from Erich Jainek, *Standarte Feldherrnhalle: Bewährung an den Brennpunkten des Zweiten Weltkriegs* (Rosenheim: Deutsche Verlagsgesellschaft, 1997). Jainek was a former member of the *Standarte* and as such provides first-hand information. His book suffers from an overtly apologetic tendency but is useful for determining the course of the Feldherrnhalle's combat operations and gaining insight into the worldview of its members. For basic information on its organization and deployment, see BArch Berlin, NS 23/518: 'Übersichtsblatt über die Entwicklung der Standarte Feldherrnhalle' (classified), 1943; Georg Tessin, *Verbände und Truppen der deutschen Wehrmacht und Waffen-SS im Zweiten Weltkrieg 1939–1945*, vol. 8: *Die Landstreitkräfte 201–280* (Osnabrück: Biblio, 1979), pp. 302–6; Rudolf Absolon, *Die Wehrmacht im Dritten Reich*, vol. 5: *1. September 1939 bis 18. Dezember 1941* (Boppard am Rhein: Boldt, 1988), pp. 27–8.
59. Rudolf Absolon, *Die Wehrmacht im Dritten Reich*, vol. 4: *5. Februar bis 31. August* (Boppard am Rhein: Boldt, 1979), p. 40.
60. BArch Berlin, NS 23/518: Recruitment guidelines for the SA-Wachstandarte, 20 April 1936.
61. Absolon, *Die Wehrmacht*, vol. 4, pp. 41–2; Deutsche Dienststelle, Berlin (WASt), Personal-Kartei M-1334/024 (Herbert M.). According to Jainek, there existed between seven and twelve 'Feldherrnhalle' branches between 1936 and 1945; see his *Soldaten der Standarte Feldherrnhalle*, p. 32.
62. Oberste SA-Führung (ed.), *Das Jahr der SA*, p. 53.
63. Against the backdrop of this involvement, Göring's merits as leader of the SA in 1923 did not matter much.
64. Absolon, *Die Wehrmacht*, vol. 4, p. 42.
65. Karl-Heinz Golla, *The German Fallschirmtruppe 1936–1941: Its Genesis and Employment in the First Campaigns of the Wehrmacht* (Solihull: Helion, 2012), pp. 39–40, 42.
66. FES, Viktor Lutze Papers, Political Diary of Viktor Lutze, p. 122.
67. Letter from Erich Reimann to Viktor Lutze, 5 May 1940, in BArch Berlin, SA 400003178 (Reimann, Erich). Erich Reimann was the Feldherrnhalle regimental commander from 20 June 1938 onward. He was born on 17 June 1903 in Berlin and served in the Hamburg police between 1925 and 1930 and again from 1935 to 1936. From 1926 to 1930 he was a member of the *Stahlhelm*. In 1929 he faced disciplinary proceedings because of the suspicion that he had been involved in politically motivated bombings in Schleswig-Holstein. Reimann was expelled from the police and joined the SA in Altona on 1 May 1930, at a time when his economic situation had deteriorated to such an extent that he accepted work as a travelling salesman. In July 1934, Lutze appointed him his adjutant general. See Reimann's SA files in BArch Berlin, SA 4000003178 (Reimann, Erich); Absolon, *Die Wehrmacht*, vol. 4, pp. 42–3.
68. Golla, *The German Fallschirmtruppe 1936–1941*, p. 45; Wilhelm Rehm, 'Zwei Jahre Kriegsbewährung der SA', *SA in Feldgrau: Feldpostbriefe der SA-Gruppe Südmark*, no. 16/17 (September/October 1941).
69. BArch Berlin, NS 23/166: 'Der Einsatz der SA im Kriege'.
70. See, for example, ibid.; 'Männer der Standarte "Feldherrnhalle" über Kreta', in *Die SA* 2:30 (1941) (25 July), p. 4. On the battle of Crete, see Golla, *The german Fallschirmtruppe 1936–1941*, pp. 403–536; Anthony Beevor, *Crete: The Battle and the Resistance* (London: Penguin, 1991).

71. In this respect it is noteworthy that the Luftwaffe in June 1943 began preparing for the formation of a '*Fallschirmjäger*-regiment Feldherrnhalle (*Fallschirmjäger*-Regiment 2)', to be recruited from SA volunteers. See BArch Berlin, NS 23/518: Oberkommando der Wehrmacht on Division Feldherrnhalle, 21 June 1943.

72. Werner Präg and Wolfgang Jacobmeyer (eds), *Das Diensttagebuch des deutschen Generalgouverneurs in Polen, 1939–1945* (Stuttgart: DVA, 1975), p. 292 (entry from 18 October 1940).

73. 'Aus Dienst und Leben der SA', *Die SA* 1:40 (1940), p. 14. In Cracow the Feldherrnhalle guarded the Wawel, which during the time of German occupation served as the headquarters of General Governor Frank. See BArch Berlin, NS 23/501, pp. 173–5, here p. 173: 'Die Aufstellung der SA-Einheit General-Gouvernement'; Präg and Jacobmeyer (eds), *Das Diensttagebuch des deutschen Generalgouverneurs*, p. 386 (entry from 17 July 1941).

74. Stephan Lehnstaedt, *Okkupation im Osten: Besatzeralltag in Warschau und Minsk* (Munich: Oldenbourg, 2010), p. 251.

75. I am grateful to Stephan Lehnstaedt for kindly providing me with his excerpts of this verdict.

76. Friedrich Fromm's Chief of Staff in his *Diensttagebüchern* gives a figure of 700 men for the Feldherrnhalle's membership (entry from 2 September 1939). From 1939 onward, Fromm served as the Chief of Army Armour and as commander of the Replacement Army in the Wehrmacht. The diaries of his Chief of Staff are scheduled for publication in 2016–17 by a group of military historians under the leadership of Bernhard Kroener at the University of Potsdam (in the following cited as 'Fromm's *Diensttagebücher*'). I thank Alexander Kranz for providing me with extracts of the unpublished manuscript and for further advice.

77. August Raben was born on 2 December 1892 in Tarming-Gaard. A fighter pilot in the First World War (leader of the 'Raben squadron'), he later worked for the *Afrikanische Frucht Compagnie* and spent some time in Cameroon. He died as battalion commander with the rank of major on 15 June 1940 in Barst-Marienthal, in one of the regiment's most costly battles, and was buried in the German Soldiers' Graveyard in Niederbronn-les-Bains. See Thorsten Pietsch, *Frontflieger: Die Soldaten der Deutschen Fliegertruppe 1914–1918*, http:// www.frontflieger.de/3-r-f.html.

78. SA Chief of Staff Lutze repeatedly met with members of the Feldherrnhalle, behind the front lines as well as in the Reich. See Lutze's report, 'Besichtigungsfahrt an der Westfront', *Die SA* 1:9 (1940) (29 March); 'Mit dem Stabschef an der Westfront', in *Die SA* 1:10 (1940) (5 April).

79. Herbert Böhme was born on 21 April 1898 in Rattwitz in Lower Silesia. He died on 27 December 1943 on the eastern front. See BArch Berlin, NS 23/1408, pp. 19–21, here p. 19: 'Liste der Ritterkreuzträger, welche der SA angehören bzw. der SA angehört haben'; 'Kurznachrichten', in *Die SA* 1:25 (1940) (12 July); Jainek, *Soldaten der Standarte Feldherrnhalle*, p. 22.

80. Jörg Ganzenmüller, *Das belagerte Leningrad 1941–1944: Die Stadt in den Strategien von Angreifern und Verteidigern* (Paderborn: Schöningh, 2005); Harrison E. Salisbury, *The Siege of Leningrad* (London: Seckler & Warburg, 1969) – neither of which make any explicit reference to the 271st Regiment.

81. 'Des verpflichtenden Namens würdig', in *SA in Feldgrau: Feldpostbriefe der SA-Gruppe Südmark*, no. 24/25 (May/June 1942); BArch Berlin, NS 23/518: 'Das Regiment "Feldherrnhalle" hält in zähem Späh- und Stoßtruppkrieg einen Abschnitt der deutschen Hauptlinie in der Sumpfhölle am Wolchow'.

82. Tessin, *Verbände und Truppen*, vol. 8, p. 303.

83. BArch Berlin, VBS 264, no. 4001006602 (Sponholz, Hans): Typescript of Hitler's order from 4 May 1943 to integrate the SA-Regiment Feldherrnhalle into the 60th Infantry Division (mot.); Jainek, *Soldaten der Standarte Feldherrnhalle*, pp. 25–32. Previously, losses were replaced using men from the Infantry Replacement Battalion 203, stationed in Berlin-Spandau, and, from 1942 onward, using soldiers from the Infantry Replacement Battalion 9, under the command of SA-*Oberführer* August Ritter von Eberlein and based in Potsdam. For details, see http://www.lexikon-der-wehrmacht.de/Gliederungen/InfErsBat/InfErsBatFHH-R.htm.

84. The fact that he was later awarded the Medal of Remembrance for 13 March 1938, the date of the *Anschluss* of Austria, suggests that he might have joined the SA just before that event.

85. For the biographical information on Karl A., see Deutsche Dienststelle, Personal-Kartei A-259/0553.
86. For the biographical information on Herbert M., see Deutsche Dienststelle, Personal-Kartei M-1334/024.
87. At about the same time, still only twenty years old, Kurt M. agreed to serve for an unlimited time in the Wehrmacht. As he was still underage, his father, an accountant (*Rechnungsinspekteur*), had to approve this decision.
88. For the biographical information on Kurt M., see Deutsche Dienststelle, Personal-Kartei M-1643/588.
89. The OSAF's description of the Feldherrnhalle is instructive in this respect. On the one hand, its propagandists insisted that the Feldherrnhalle was open to all men aged eighteen or older who were of good health and of proper race (*rassische Eignung*) and had not been subject to prosecution (with the exception of charges for 'politically motivated' misdoings). On the other hand, they repeatedly emphasized that the Feldherrnhalle's political education was deliberately simple and 'artless' (*natürlich*), as a purely academic approach would only cause confusion among the men of the Feldherrnhalle who were deemed 'simple minded and feeling' (*einfach denkende und empfindende Menschen*). Oberste SA-Führung (ed.), *Das Jahr der SA*, pp. 49–50.
90. Carola Tischler, 'Von Geister- und anderen Stimmen: Der Rundfunk als Waffe im Kampf gegen "die Deutschen" im Großen Vaterländischen Krieg', in Karl Eimermacher and Astrid Volpert (eds), *Verführungen der Gewalt: Russen und Deutsche im Ersten und Zweiten Weltkrieg* (Munich: Fink, 2005), pp. 467–506, here p. 467.
91. Brown, 'SA in the Radical Imagination', pp. 258–68. On the KPD's infiltration tactics, see also BArch Berlin, NS 23/431: Circular from OSAF on the Communist Movement, 24 April 1933.
92. Tischler, 'Von Geister- und anderen Stimmen', p. 473; Fritz Erpenbeck, 'Hier spricht der Sender der SA-Fronde ...', *Beiträge zur Geschichte des Rundfunks: deutscher demokratischer Rundfunk* 4 (1974), pp. 7–15, here pp. 8–9. On GS1, see Jerome S. Berg, *On the Short Waves 1923–1945: Broadcast Listening in the Pioneer Days of Radio* (Jefferson, NC: McFarland, 2007), p. 220.
93. Patrick Merziger, 'Humour in the *Volksgemeinschaft*: The Disappearance of Destructive Satire in National Socialist Germany', in Martina Kessel and Patrick Merziger (eds), *The Politics of Humour: Laughter, Inclusion, and Exclusion in the Twentieth Century* (Toronto: University of Toronto Press, 2012), pp. 131–52.
94. Erpenbeck, 'Hier spricht der Sender der SA-Fronde', pp. 12–14.
95. Ibid., pp. 13–14. It is impossible to verify the truth of these accounts, but in light of what we know about the German mentality at war, they do not seem to have been totally exaggerated.
96. On this (largely unsuccessful) strategy, see the documents in Hermann Weber, Jakov Drabkin, and Bernhard H. Bayerlein (eds), *Deutschland, Russland, Komintern. II: Dokumente (1918–1943): Nach der Archivrevolution: Neuerschlossene Quellen zu der Geschichte der KPD und den deutsch-russischen Beziehungen* (Berlin: de Gruyter, 2015), pp. 989–95, 1,080–1, 1,097–1,100.
97. Annette Weinke, *Die Verfolgung von NS-Tätern im geteilten Deutschland: Vergangenheitsbewältigungen 1949–1969, oder: Eine deutsch-deutsche Beziehungsgeschichte im Kalten Krieg* (Paderborn: Schöningh, 2002), pp. 63–75. The generation that particularly benefited from these politics was that born in the 1920s or early 1930s. These individuals often became staunch adherents of the GDR; see Thomas Ahbe and Rainer Gries, 'Gesellschaftsgeschichte als Generationengeschichte', in Annegret Schüle, Thomas Ahbe, and Rainer Gries (eds), *Die DDR aus generationsgeschichtlicher Perspektive: Eine Inventur* (Leipzig: Leipziger Universitäts-Verlag, 2006), pp. 475–571, here pp. 502–18.
98. BArch Berlin, NS 23/510: Die Oberste SA-Führung, 'Aufbau der SA im deutschen Gebiet des früheren polnischen Staates', 30 October 1939. On an order from Jüttner on 10 November 1939, the SA-*Gruppe* Sudeten lost 'its' share in the operation. Instead, the SA-*Gruppe* Schlesien was made the only group permitted to operate in Upper Silesia.
99. BArch Berlin, NS 23/510: Der Oberste SA-Führer, 'Betr. Gliederung der SA im deutschen Gebiet des früheren polnischen Staates', 25 January 1940.

100. BArch Berlin, NS 23/98: Note from SA-Gruppenführer Georg Mappes, 18 November 1939.

101. Heinrich Hacker, born on 16 June 1892 in Würzburg in Franconia, had attended grammar school, served in the German army in the First World War, and studied at Würzburg University until 1922, when he was forced to abandon his studies, allegedly for financial reasons. He then worked as a salesman for pumice and leather goods. Originally a member of the *Stahlhelm* and then of the *Frontbann*, he entered the ranks of the NSDAP in 1925 but quickly left. He became a member of the party again in 1929 and was elected into the Bavarian *Landtag* in the same year. From 1931 onward, Hacker led the SA-*Untergruppe* Franken. From 1933 to 1934 he served as one of the SA's special representatives in Bavaria. He then led the SA-*Brigade* 6 until 1939. For his biography, see BArch Berlin, SA 4000001265 (Hacker, Heinrich); 'Kurznachrichten', *Die SA* 1:8 (1940) (22 March).

102. Wilhelm Rehm, 'Aufbau im deutschen Osten', *Die SA* 1:2 (1940) (9 February); Baumgärtner, 'Sturmdienst im Wartheland', *Die SA* 2:28 (1941) (11 July); 'Bassarabiendeutsche in den SA-Wehrmannschaften', *Die SA* 2:20 (1941) (16 May).

103. A forthcoming study on the SA by the historian Yves Müller aspires to demonstrate more in detail that these Baltic Germans played an important role in the SA in the newly German-annexed and occupied territories.

104. Baumgärtner, 'Sturmdienst im Wartheland', *Die SA* 2:28 (1941) (11 July). The SA in Southern Styria likewise taught its men German language, history, and geography; see Franz Glatzer, '"Sie bauen das Morgen", Wehrmannschaftsdienst in der Untersteiermark', in ibid.

105. BArch Berlin, SA 4000001265 (Hacker, Heinrich): Note of SA-Gruppenführers Lehmann, 2 September 1941. On Greiser, see in particular Catherine Epstein, *Model Nazi: Arthur Greiser and the Occupation of Western Poland* (New York: Oxford University Press, 2010).

106. BArch Berlin, SA 4000001265 (Hacker, Heinrich): Letter from Hacker to Lutze, 25 September 1941. For Hacker's view on the SA's mission in the east, see his essay 'Pioniere des Ostens', *Die SA* 2:25/26 (1941) (20/27 June), pp. 1–3.

107. Jill Stephenson, *The Nazi Organisation of Women* (Abingdon: Routledge, 2013), p. 191.

108. FES, Viktor Lutze Papers, Political Diary of Viktor Lutze, p. 171. Lutze's official speech on this occasion was broadcast live on German radio; see 'Kurznachrichten aus Dienst und Leben der SA', *Die SA* 1:5 (1940) (1 March).

109. BArch Berlin, NS 23/510: OSAF, 'Änderung des Anschriftenverzeichnisses', 17 May 1940. The development of the SA farther west, in Alsace and Lorraine, mirrored the build-up of the SA in the former Polish territories but was less successful. Beginning in February 1941, two SA-*Brigaden* (Elsaß-Nord, based in Straßburg, and Elsaß-Süd, headquartered in Colmar) were created. They belonged to the SA-*Gruppe* Oberrhein and initially comprised eight regular *Standarten*, two *Reiterstandarten*, and one *Marinestandarte*; BArch Berlin, NS 23/510: Oberste SA-Führung, Gliederung der SA im Elsaß, 19 February 1941. On 27 March 1941 one SA-*Brigade* based in Metz was assigned to Lorraine and became part of the SA-*Gruppe* Kurpfalz; BArch Berlin NS 23/510: Die Oberste SA-Führung, Neuaufstellung von SA-Einheiten in Lothringen, 27 March 1941. Finally, the formation of two SA-*Standarten* for Luxembourg was approved, taking effect on 1 April 1941. They became part of the SA-*Gruppe* Westmark, headquartered in Koblenz; BArch Berlin, NS 23/510: OSAF on 'Neugliederung', 25 April 1941. See also Lothar Kettenacker, *Nationalsozialistische Volkstumspolitik im Elsaß* (Stuttgart: DVA, 1973), pp. 207–16; Dieter Wolfanger, *Die nationalsozialistische Politik in Lothringen (1940–1945)*, university diss., Universität des Saarlandes (Saarbrücken), 1976, pp. 84–6.

110. Zilich, 'SA im Protektorat', in *Die SA* 2:1 (1941) (3 January), p. 18.

111. Präg and Jacobmeyer (eds), *Das Diensttagebuch des deutschen Generalgouverneurs*, p. 292 (entry from 26 October 1940).

112. BArch Berlin, NS 23/510: Letter from the leader of the Wehr- und Schützenbereitschaften in the General Government, Peltz, to OSAF, 7 November 1941.

113. Dieter Schenk, *Krakauer Burg: Die Machtzentrale des Generalgouverneurs Hans Frank 1939– 1945* (Berlin: Links, 2010), p. 136.

114. See Daniel Brewing, '"Wir müssen um uns schlagen": Die Alltagspraxis der Partisanenbekämpfung im Generalgouvernement 1942', in *Gewalt und Alltag im besetzen Polen 1939–1945*, ed. Böhler and Lehnstaedt, pp. 497–520, with further references.

115. On the rivalry between Frank and Himmler, see Schenk, *Krakauer Burg*, pp. 130–3.

116. In the spring of 1944, Peltz was called up to the Wehrmacht and was succeeded by SA-*Brigadeführer* Wilhelm Kühnemund.

117. Gerhard Eisenblätter, *Grundlinien der Politik des Reichs gegenüber dem Generalgouvernement, 1939–1945*, inaugural diss., Johann Wolfgang Goethe-Universität, 1969, pp. 241–2; BArch Berlin, NS 23/98: Hans Frank, Decree on the establishment of the Wehrschützenbereitschaften, 19 December 1941.

118. BArch Berlin, NS 23/510: NSDAP and Arbeitsbereich General Gouvernement (Stahl), Anordnung 17/42 (SA, SS und NSKK-Einheiten im Generalgouvernement), 23 April 1942; Eisenblätter, *Grundlinien der Politik*, pp. 255–6.

119. BArch Berlin, NS 23/98: Letters from SA-Oberführer Peltz to OSAF, 21 March 1942, and to the General Government, 5 May 1942.

120. For details of Frank's position, see Präg and Jacobmeyer (eds), *Das Diensttagebuch des deutschen Generalgouverneurs*, pp. 474–5 (entry from 17 March 1942).

121. BArch Berlin, NS 23/510: Hans Frank, 'Erlaß über die Überführung der Wehrschützenbereitschaften in SA-Wehrbereitschaften', 16 April 1942; BArch Berlin, NS 23/510: Die Oberste SA-Führung (Jüttner), 'SA im Generalgouvernement', 18 May 1942. In return, Frank promised to provide the OSAF with two convalescent homes in the General Government; see BArch Berlin, NS 23/98: Cable from SA-Obersturmbannführer Schänzlin to Georg Mappes, 18 April 1942.

122. BArch Berlin, NS 23/501, pp. 114–20, here p. 120: 'Die Wehrschützenbereitschaft im Gen[eral]-Gouvernement', undated, presumably from October 1942.

123. Eisenblätter, *Grundlinien der Politik*, p. 257.

124. BArch Berlin, NS 23/510: Die Oberste SA-Führung (Ohrt), 'An den Aufbaustab der SA im Generalgouvernement', 16 September 1942. These SA-*Standarten* were based in Cracow, Warsaw (Warschau, Warschau-Süd, and Warschau-Land), Radom, Lublin, Lemberg, Reichshof, Neu-Sandez, Kielce, and Petrikau-Tomaschow.

125. Eisenblätter, *Grundlinien der Politik*, pp. 257–8.

126. On the security problems of the years 1942–4 see Präg and Jacobmeyer (eds), *Das Diensttagebuch des deutschen Generalgouverneurs*, pp. 642–7, 686–91 (entries from 15 April and 18 June 1943); Brewing, 'Wir müssen um uns schlagen', pp. 502–18; Stephan Lehnstaedt, 'Deutsche in Warschau: Das Alltagsleben der Besatzer 1939–1944', in *Gewalt und Alltag im besetzten Polen 1939–1945*, ed. Böhler and Lehnstaedt, pp. 205–28, here pp. 223–7.

127. Präg and Jacobmeyer (eds), *Das Diensttagebuch des deutschen Generalgouverneurs*, p. 624 (entry from 22 February 1943).

128. Central'nyj archiv Minoborony Rossii (CAMO), Collection 500, Finding Aid 12450, File 161, p. 11: stenograph of a meeting of Hitler, Keitel, and others on the Berghof on 8 June 1943, http://wwii.germandocsinrussia.org/de/nodes/2297-akte-161-stenogramm-der-besprechung-bei-a-hitler-in-berghof-uber-die-behandlung-der-kriegsgefa#page/1/mode/grid/zoom/1.

129. BArch Berlin, SA 4000003047 (Peltz, Kurt): Letter from Kurt Peltz to Leonhard Gontermann, 22 December 1943.

130. Eisenblätter, *Grundlinien der Politik*, p. 298. According to an internal SA document, storm-troopers from nineteen SA groups during the war participated in police operations. Five SA groups were also involved in border control activities. See BArch Berlin, NS 23/166: 'Der Einsatz der SA im Kriege', undated. See also BArch Berlin, NS 23/501, pp. 176–8, here p. 177: Report of Hauptsturmführer Behrenbrock about his journey to Vienna, Kracow, and other places, August 1944.

131. See the respective documents in Peltz's SA file in BArch Berlin, SA 4000003047 (Peltz, Kurt).

132. BArch Berlin, SA 400003178: Letter from Reimann to the Reich Ministry of Foreign Affairs, 23 April 1940.

133. BArch Berlin, NS 23/98: Note of SA-Oberführer Siegele, 9 December 1939.

134. Präg and Jacobmeyer (eds), *Das Diensttagebuch des deutschen Generalgouverneurs*, pp. 643, 704 (entries from 15 April and 16 July 1943); Władysław Bartoszewski, *Der Todesring um Warschau 1939–1944* (Cracow: Interpress, 1969), pp. 189–90.

135. Präg and Jacobmeyer (eds), *Das Diensttagebuch des deutschen Generalgouverneurs*, p. 898 (entry from 5 August 1944).

136. A well-known example of SA violence in this region was the murder of the prior of the Cloister Czerna by SA men in September 1944; see Präg and Jacobmeyer (eds), *Das Diensttagebuch des deutschen Generalgouverneurs*, p. 915 (entry from 26 September 1944). See also the IMT's examination of Max Jüttner on 14 August 1946 (morning session), http://avalon.law.yale.edu/imt/08-14-46.asp.

137. 'Der Dienst der SA im Grenzland', *SA in Feldgrau: Feldpostbriefe der SA-Gruppe Südmark*, no. 12 (March 1941), p. 4; Helmuth Ruschnig, 'Bericht über fünf Monate Arbeit des Kärnter Volksbundes', as printed in Tone Ferenc (ed.), *Quellen zur nationalsozialistischen Entnationalisierungspolitik in Slowenien 1941–1945 / Viri o nacistični raznarodovalni politiki v Sloveniji 1941–1945* (Maribor: Založba Obzorja, 1980), document no. 168.

138. BArch Berlin, NS 23/234: SA-Obertruppführer Schmidt, 'Die Südmark im deutschen Freiheitskampf'.

139. 'Sie haben ihre Aufgabe restlos erfüllt!', *SA in Feldgrau: Feldpostbriefe der SA-Gruppe Südmark*, no. 13 (May 1941), p. 1.

140. Schm[idt], 'Grenzwacht gegen Banditen', *Illustrierter Beobachter* (Feldpostausgabe), no. 31 (1942).

141. Lorenz Ohrt, 'Grundsätzliche Weisung Nr. 1 der SA-Gruppe Südmark für die Organisation und Ausbildung der Wehrmannschaften in den besetzten slowenischen Gebieten', 25 June 1941, in Ferenc, *Quellen zur nationalsozialistischen Entnationalisierungspolitik in Slowenien*, document no. 94.

142. For similar attempts in Alsace, see Kettenacker, *Nationalsozialistische Volkstumspolitik im Elsaß*, pp. 163–84. Bilingual stormtroopers speaking French in public was enough for a formal warning. 'The use of the French language is unworthy' for an SA man, an SA leader from Lorraine reasoned; BArch Berlin, NS 45/162: Circular from SA-Standarte Metz on the use of the French language, 28 May 1941.

143. Hans Baron and Franz Tscheligi, 'Report on the situation in Southern Styria', 1 May 1942, in Ferenc, *Quellen zur nationalsozialistischen Entnationalisierungspolitik in Slowenien*, document no. 218.

144. Ruschnig, 'Bericht über fünf Monate Arbeit des Kärnter Volksbundes', in Ferenc, *Quellen zur nationalsozialistischen Entnationalisierungspolitik in Slowenien*, document no. 168.

145. Joachim Hösler, 'Sloweniens historische Bürde', *Aus Politik und Zeitgeschichte* 46 (2006), http://www.bpb.de/apuz/29421/sloweniens-historische-buerde?p=all.

146. PAAA, Personal Papers of Siegfried Kasche, vol. 35: SA-Oberführer Moock, Report, 15 September 1939.

147. Richard Overy, *The Bombing War: Europe 1939–1945* (London: Allen Lane, 2013), pp. 327–38; Jörg Friedrich, *Der Brand: Deutschland im Bombenkrieg 1940–1945* (Berlin: Ullstein, 2004), pp. 192–5.

148. BArch Berlin, NS 23/227: Gustaf Deuchler, 'Die Bewährung der SA bei der Groß-Katastrophe Hamburgs', 16 December 1943.

149. Hans Erich Wagner, 'SA-Kameradschaft im Kriege', *SA in Feldgrau: Feldpostbriefe der SA-Gruppe Südmark*, no. 18/19 (November/December 1941); Wilhelm Rehm, 'Zwei Jahre Kriegsbewährung der SA', *SA in Feldgrau: Feldpostbriefe der SA-Gruppe Südmark*, no. 16/17 (September/October 1941).

150. See, for example, NS 23/227: 'SA an der Front', *Essener Volkszeitung*, 10 October 1939; 'Aus Dienst und Leben der SA', *Die SA* 2:23/24 (1941) (6/13 June), p. 26.

151. For these figures (although without reference to the SA), see Christian Kretschmer, 'Kriegsgefangene im Visier von Werkschutz, Kriminalpolizei und Landwacht: Bewachung, Fluchtprävention und Kriegsfahndung', in KZ-Gedenkstätte Neuengamme (ed.), *Polizei, Verfolgung und Gesellschaft im Nationalsozialismus* (Bremen: Edition Temmen, 2013), pp. 147–55. For an instructive case study, see NS 23/227: SA-Sturm 14/5 in Hirschaid/Franconia, Report on the murder of an SA-*Rottenführer*, 8 June 1943.

152. BArch Berlin, NS 6/857: Decree of the OSAF (Jüttner), 24 April 1942; Letter from his deputy Ohrt, 25 June 1942.

153. BArch Berlin, NS 23/227: 'Zwölfhundert Herde wurden geborgen', *Hannoversche Zeitung*, 15 December 1943.

154. Wilhelm Rehm, 'Zwei Jahre Kriegsbewährung der SA', *SA in Feldgrau: Feldpostbriefe der SA-Gruppe Südmark* 16/17 (September/October 1941).

155. BArch Berlin, NS 23/227: Gustaf Deuchler, 'Die Bewährung der SA bei der Groß-Katastrophe Hamburgs', 16 December 1943.

156. PAAA, Personal Papers of Siegfried Kasche, vol. 34: Letter from SA-Sturmführer Fritz Hancke to SA-Gruppenführer Siegfried Kasche, 25 August 1941.

157. BArch Berlin, NS 23/166: Letter from Viktor Hölscher to Hans Sponholz, 15 June 1942.

158. BArch Berlin, NS 23/234: Hans Sponholz, secret mood report from Munich, 23 September 1942.

159. Since the second half of the 1930s, the OSAF had glorified the stormtroopers as the bearers of the 'traditional male virtues' that allegedly distinguished the German people from others. See, among others, BArch Berlin, NS 23/238: Radio speech by Viktor Lutze, 3 July 1939.

160. Mai, 'Die Nationalsozialistische Betriebszellen-Organisation', here pp. 600–2. A well-known example of temporary cooperation between Nazi and Communist unionists was the strike by workers from Berlin's public transport company in the autumn of 1932; see Klaus Rainer Röhl, *Nähe zum Gegner: Kommunisten und Nationalsozialisten im Berliner BVG-Streik von 1932* (Frankfurt am Main: Campus, 1994).

161. See in particular Humann, 'Verwahranstalten mit Fantasiegehältern?'

162. For an overview of the history of these schools, see BArch Berlin, NS 23/70: Herbert Merker, 'SA-Berufsschulen'; Martin Kipp, 'Privilegien für "alte Kämpfer": Zur Geschichte der SA-Berufsschulen', in Manfred Heinemann (ed.), *Erziehung und Schulung im Dritten Reich*, vol. 1: *Kindergarten, Schule, Jugend, Berufserziehung* (Stuttgart: Klett-Cotta, 1980), pp. 289–300. The school in Lockstedter Lager provided training for members of the *Nordmark* SA as early as 1931; Schröder, 'Der NS-Schulungsstandort', p. 9.

163. BArch Berlin, NS 23/515: Public Notice of the SA-Berufsschule Lockstedter Lager, October 1939.

164. On the SA professional schools, see also Kipp, 'Privilegien für "alte Kämpfer"'; Volker Herrmann, *Vom Arbeitsmarkt zum Arbeitseinsatz: Zur Geschichte der Reichsanstalt für Arbeitsvermittlung und Arbeitslosenversicherung 1929 bis 1939* (Frankfurt am Main: Lang, 1993), p. 291.

165. Schröder, 'Der NS-Schulungsstandort', p. 12.

166. For details, see ibid., pp. 15–17.

167. BArch Berlin, NS 23/70: Letter from the Reichsarbeitsministerium to OSAF, 24 January 1939; Letter from the Reichsarbeitsministerium to OSAF, 16 April 1940.

168. Kipp, 'Privilegien für "alte Kämpfer"', p. 298; 'Kurznachrichten', *Die SA* 1:8 (1940) (22 March); 'Kurznachrichten aus Dienst und Leben der SA', *Die SA* 1:13/14 (1940) (26 April).

169. BArch Berlin, NS 23/70: OSAF decree from 15 October 1942; Schröder, 'Der NS-Schulungsstandort', p. 13. The plans for Westerstede, which included a cinema and a large gathering hall, were deemed 'exemplary'. Similar buildings were also planned for Schulitz.

170. Kipp, 'Privilegien für "alte Kämpfer"', p. 297.

171. The contract between the *Industriegemeinschaft* and the SA was signed on 1 July 1941; see BArch Berlin, NS 23/70: Protocol of the meeting of the *Industriegemeinschaft* and OSAF in Berlin, 22 January 1942.

172. BArch Berlin, NS 23/515: Letter from the *Einstellungszentrale* for the SA professional schools, 12 December 1941.

173. BArch Berlin, NS 23/70: Protocol of the meeting of the *Industriegemeinschaft* and OSAF in Berlin, 22 January 1942.

174. At least in theory, the period of schooling was meant to serve as a probation period, with successful graduates automatically accepted into the SA as regular members. If and to what extent these principles were practically applied, however, is not known. There were also plans to create 'SA shipyard storms' that would be allowed to meet during working hours. See BArch Berlin, NS 23/70: Protocol of the meeting of the *Industriegemeinschaft* and OSAF in Berlin, 22 January 1942.

175. BArch Berlin, NS 23/515: Letter from the head of the SA-*Gruppe* Nordmark, October 1939.
176. BArch Berlin, NS 23/70: Letter from the OSAF to Middendorff, 4 June 1942.
177. The SA also regarded the schools as a way to increase its budget: the shipbuilding industry was required to pay 3.20 reichsmark per day per man to the SA, while the apprentices were only paid 0.50 reichsmark per day. See BArch Berlin, NS 23/515: Administrative directive of the SA leadership, 14 July 1941.
178. BArch Berlin, NS 23/70: Report from the OSAF's 'Inspektion Erziehung und Führerausbildung' (Merker), 4 July 1942.
179. Ibid.: Letter from Middendorff to the OSAF, 25 June 1942.
180. Ibid.: Report from the OSAF's 'Inspektion Erziehung und Führerausbildung' (Merker), 4 July 1942.
181. Herbert Merker, born on 15 June 1901 in Bornstedt near Potsdam, joined the NSDAP in 1925. Previously a member of the *Freikorps* Hülsen (1919), the *Stahlhelm* (1922–3), and the *Frontbann* (1924), he served as a local and regional NSDAP leader in Westphalia between 1925 and 1927 before returning to his home region. On 25 September 1930 he was promoted to *Organisationsleiter* in Brandenburg and assumed other party functions in the years to come. He was sentenced for various political offences several times between 1931 and 1933. Imprisoned from 30 June to 3 August 1934 in the notorious Columbia House Prison in Berlin, Merker narrowly survived the 'Röhm purge' and on 28 February 1937 was promoted to SA-*Brigadeführer*. See BArch Berlin, SA 4000002858 (Merker, Herbert).
182. As quoted in 'Befehl ausgeführt!', *SA in Feldgrau: Feldpostbriefe der SA-Gruppe Südmark* 13 (May 1941).
183. The name change from 'school' to 'camp' was due to internal rivalries and was also a consequence of the fact that as ever more forced labourers were recruited, the character of the schools changed from that of a 'camp' to that of a 'prison'. See the correspondence on these matters from the summer and autumn of 1942 in BArch Berlin, NS 23/70.
184. Ibid.: Report from the OSAF's 'Inspektion Erziehung und Führerausbildung' (Merker), 4 July 1942.
185. Goebbels commented in his diary that 'unfortunately' Schepmann's speech had been only of secondary importance and that even the Führer had been informed about Schepmann's failure. 'The SA is extremely unlucky. Never in its existence did it possess a leader of stature'; Goebbels, diary entry from 27 October 1943, as quoted in Müller, 'Wilhelm Schepmann', p. 525, n. 61.
186. It is telling that Schepmann shortly after his appointment as Chief of Staff formally prohibited the term 'SA spirit' from being used in SA correspondence and propaganda. He likewise dissolved the 'Cultural Circle of the SA' (*Kulturkreis der SA*) on the argument that there was no particular SA culture, but only a German culture influenced by National Socialism. See BArch Berlin, NS 19/2119: Speech of Wilhelm Schepmann in Posen, 6 October 1943.
187. Ibid. On Schepmann's 'servility' toward Himmler, see also Müller, 'Wilhelm Schepmann', p. 524.
188. This figure is provided by Jamin, 'Zur Rolle der SA im nationalsozialistischen Herrschaftssystem', p. 357.
189. BArch Berlin, NS 23/515: Wilhelm Schepmann, 'Weltanschauliche Ausrichtung für den totalen Einsatz', 6 December 1944, here topic 6, 'Kampf gegen Nörgler und Gerüchtemacher'. For a more detailed discussion of this point, see Wagner, 'Die letzte Schlacht der "alten Kämpfer"', pp. 31–40.
190. Müller-Hill, *'Man hat es kommen sehen und ist dennoch erschüttert'*, p. 28 (diary entry from 5 April 1944).
191. On the developments that occurred prior to this appointment as well as its consequences, see Franz W. Seidler, *'Deutscher Volkssturm': Das letzte Aufgebot 1944/45* (Munich: Herbig, 1989), pp. 35–47; Müller, 'Wilhelm Schepmann', pp. 528–30.
192. BArch Berlin, NS 23/227: 'Zweiter Großeinsatz des Volkskriegs', *Front und Heimat* 49 (October 1944).
193. Willy Timm, *Freikorps 'Sauerland' im Deutschen Volkssturm: Südwestfalens letztes Aufgebot 1944/45* (Unna: Hellweg, 1993), pp. 22 and 29.

194. BArch Berlin, NS 23/510: Decree no. 3/44 from the leader of the SA-Brigade 94 Oberdonau, SA-Standartenführer Faller, 21 September 1944.
195. Seidler, *Deutscher Volkssturm*, pp. 142–5.
196. BArch Berlin, NS 23/227: 'Die Bedeutung der SA im Volkssturm', *Nürnberger Neueste Nachrichten*, 21 October 1944.
197. Timm, *Freikorps 'Sauerland' im Deutschen Volkssturm*, p. 34.
198. BArch Berlin, NS 23/515: Wilhelm Schepmann, 'Weltanschauliche Ausrichtung für den totalen Einsatz', 6 December 1944, here topic 8, 'Der SA-Mann ist immer im Dienst'.
199. Schepmann thereby followed the official propaganda, which urged leaders to draw this historical parallel as often as possible. See Seidler, *Deutscher Volkssturm*, pp. 261–3.
200. BArch Berlin, NS 23/515: Wilhelm Schepmann, 'Weltanschauliche Ausrichtung für den totalen Einsatz', 6 December 1944, including topic 3, 'Jeder SA-Mann ein fanatischer Träger des äußersten und totalen Widerstandswillens'.
201. See also Saul K. Padover, *Lügendetektor: Vernehmungen im besetzten Deutschland 1944/45* (Munich: Econ, 2001), esp. pp. 278–9 (first published in English in 1946 under the title *Experiment in Germany: The Story of an American Intelligence Officer*).
202. See, for example, 'SA Geist schlägt den Bolschewismus', *Die SA* 2:34 (1941) (22 August), p. 4; Walther Nibbe, 'Den Kampf, den Horst Wessel begonnen, im braunen Gewand der SA . . .', *SA in Feldgrau: Feldpostbriefe der SA-Gruppe Südmark* 16/17 (September/October 1941), pp. 1–2. On the Nazi interpretation of the Second World War as an eschatological battle from 1941 onwards, see Behrenbeck, *Der Kult um die toten Helden*, pp. 534–48.
203. See the published quotations from (alleged) war letters: 'Feldpostbriefe', *SA in Feldgrau: Feldpostbriefe der SA-Gruppe Südmark* 16/17 (September/October 1941); 'Streiflichter aus dem Sowjetparadies', *SA in Feldgrau: Feldpostbriefe der SA-Gruppe Südmark* 18/19 (November/December 1941); 'Streiflichter aus dem Sowjetparadies', *SA in Feldgrau: Feldpostbriefe der SA-Gruppe Südmark* 20/21 (January/February 1942). Even those soldiers who did not buy into such cheap Nazi propaganda, like the teacher Konrad Jarausch, insisted on categorical differences between 'Russians' and 'Bolshevists'. The ordinary Russian people, Jarausch noted, are 'still human beings as ourselves', whereas the 'Bolshevist element proper' (*das Eigentlich-Bolschewistische*) and the 'Jewish element' needed to be mercilessly eradicated. See Jarausch and Arnold, *Das stille Sterben*, pp. 330–1, 335.
204. BArch Berlin, NS 23/515: Wilhelm Schepmann, 'Weltanschauliche Ausrichtung für den totalen Einsatz', 6 December 1944, including topic 3, 'Jeder SA-Mann ein fanatischer Träger des äußersten und totalen Widerstandswillens'.
205. On the widespread war-weariness in 1944–5, see Keller, *Volksgemeinschaft am Ende*; Kershaw, *The End*. On the violence exercised by fanatical National Socialists in the last months of the war, see Wagner, 'Die letzte Schlacht der "alten Kämpfer"', and Jens-Christian Wagner, 'Kriegsende und Befreiung 1945 in Niedersachsen', in his (ed.) *70 Tage Gewalt, Mord, Befreiung: Das Kriegsende 1945 in Niedersachsen* (Göttingen: Wallstein, 2015), pp. 6–12.
206. Patricia Heberer, 'The American Military Commission Trials of 1945', in Nathan Stoltzfus and Henry Friedlander (eds), *Nazi Crimes and the Law* (New York: Cambridge University Press, 2008), pp. 43–62, here pp. 46–8. On the lynchings committed by stormtroopers, see also Overy, *Bombing War*, pp. 480–1.
207. BArch Berlin, NS 23/515: Wilhelm Schepmann, 'Weltanschauliche Ausrichtung für den totalen Einsatz', 6 December 1944, here topic 5, 'Verhalten gegenüber Fremdvölkischen'.
208. Heide Nowitzki, *Wer waren die Zwangsarbeiter in der Herforder Landwirtschaft 1939–1945? Eine exemplarische Untersuchung*, unpublished MA thesis, Bielefeld University, 2016, pp. 30, 42–3.
209. Wagner, 'Die letzte Schlacht der "alten Kämpfer"', p. 38.
210. It is not without irony that in 1946–7 several hundred Jewish DPs (displaced persons) were temporarily housed in this building. See 'Schliersee – Jüdisches DP-Lager', http://www.after-the-shoah.org/index.php?id=25&tx_aftertheshoah_aftertheshoah[object]=160&tx_after-theshoah_aftertheshoah[action]=show&tx_aftertheshoah_aftertheshoah[controller]=Object&cHash=209684030cd2f4f5f097c0aa9c4098f4.
211. For details on this SA school, see Friedrich, *Spuren des Nationalsozialismus im bayerischen Oberland*, pp. 56–71.

212. Until February 1945, Schepmann and his family lived in Dresden. After they were 'bombed out', they moved to Caputh near Potsdam and arrived in Schliersee in early April; IfZ Archive, ED 467, vol. 51, p. 5.

213. Wagner, 'Die letzte Schlacht der "alten Kämpfer"', p. 27.

214. Jens-Christian Wagner, 'Kriegsende und Befreiung 1945 in Niedersachsen', p. 7.

215. Daniel Blatman, *The Death Marches: The Final Phase of Nazi Genocide* (Cambridge and London: Belknap, 2011), pp. 228–33; Eleonore Lappin-Eppel, 'Die Todesmärsche ungarischer Jüdinnen und Juden durch die Steiermark', in Heimo Halbrainer, Gerald Lamprecht, and Ursula Mindler (eds), *NS-Herrschaft in der Steiermark: Positionen und Diskurse* (Vienna: Böhlau, 2012), pp. 385–410, here pp. 401–10; idem, *Ungarisch-jüdische Zwangsarbeiter und Zwangsarbeiterinnen in Österreich 1944/45: Arbeitseinsatz – Todesmärsche – Folgen* (Wien: Lit, 2010).

216. Biddiscombe, 'End of the Freebooter Tradition', pp. 70–1. For details on the military action of the *Freikorps* Sauerland, including cases of violence against civilians, see Timm, *Freikorps 'Sauerland' im Deutschen Volkssturm*, pp. 49–69.

217. Biddiscombe, 'End of the Freebooter Tradition', pp. 71–2. The total death toll on this night was sixteen. On the 'Penzberg murder night' and its background, see also Tenfelde, *Proletarische Provinz*, pp. 369–82.

218. As quoted in Friedrich, *Spuren des Nationalsozialismus*, p. 70.

219. As quoted in Mathias Brüggemann, 'In der Weser schwammen SA-Uniformen', *Neue Westfälische*, 6 April 2015, http://www.nw.de/lokal/kreis_hoexter/hoexter/hoexter/20424355_In-der-Weser-schwammen-SA-Uniformen.html.

220. For similar ideas, see the statement of Thomas Kühne at the conference 'Der Ort der "Volksgemeinschaft"' in Hanover in June 2015, here quoted according to Johannes Hürter and Matthias Uhl, 'Hitler in Vinnica: Ein neues Dokument zur Krise im September 1942', *Vierteljahrshefte für Zeitgeschichte* 63:4 (2015), pp. 581–639, here p. 598.

221. Blatman, *The Death Marches*, p. 419.

Chapter 9

1. SA-*Rottenführer* Schwalke, 'Wir sind das ordnende unter den Völkern', *Die SA* 2:28 (1941) (11 July), pp. 1–2.

2. This hotel, situated at Wilhelmsplatz, had also been Hitler's choice of accommodation in the capital in the years leading up to 1933.

3. PAAA, Gesandtschaft Sofia, vol. 59/2 (Personal Notes of the Ambassador Adolf-Heinz Beckerle I: 20 July 1941–16 February 1943), pp. 1–2 (entry from 20 July 1941).

4. Klaus Thörner, *'Der ganze Südosten ist unser Hinterland': Deutsche Südosteuropapläne von 1840 bis 1945*, university diss., University of Oldenburg, 2000, pp. 421–5, 447, 496–7, http://oops.uni-oldenburg.de/409/1/442.pdf.

5. For short biographies of these men, see the respective entries in Auswärtiges Amt (ed.), *Biographisches Handbuch des deutschen Auswärtigen Dienstes* (Paderborn: Schöningh, 2000–8), vol. 1, pp. 88–9 (Beckerle); vol. 2, pp. 414–15 (von Jagow); vol. 2, p. 480 (Kasche); vol. 2, p. 532 (von Killinger); vol. 3, p. 131 (Ludin). On Beckerle, see also Susanne Meinl, 'Adolf Heinz Beckerle, Frankfurter SA-Führer, Polizeipräsident und Diplomat', http://www.ffmhist.de/ffm33–45/portal01/mitte.php?transfer=t_ak_beckerle_01. For a general introduction to the German envoys with SA backgrounds, see Eckart Conze et al., *Das Amt und die Vergangenheit: Deutsche Diplomaten im Dritten Reich und in der Bundesrepublik* (Munich: Blessing, 2010), pp. 165–6; Sebastian Weitkamp, 'Kooperativtäter – die Beteiligung des Auswärtigen Amtes an der NS-Gewaltpolitik jenseits der "Endlösung"', in Hürter and Mayer, *Das Auswärtige Amt und die NS-Diktatur*, pp. 197–217, here pp. 213–15; Browning, 'Unterstaatssekretär Martin Luther', pp. 327–8; Weinke, *Die Verfolgung von NS-Tätern*, pp. 258–86.

6. For the recent controversies on continuities and change in the German Foreign Service before and after 1945, see Conze, *Das Amt und die Vergangenheit*; Martin Sabrow and Christian Mentel (eds), *Das Auswärtige Amt und seine umstrittene Vergangenheit: Eine deutsche Debatte* (Frankfurt am Main: Fischer, 2013); Johannes Hürter and Michael Mayer (eds), *Das Auswärtige Amt in der NS-Diktatur* (Berlin: De Gruyter Oldenbourg, 2014);

Thomas W. Maulucci, 'German Diplomats and the Myth of the Two Foreign Offices', in David Messenger and Katrin Paehler (eds), *A Nazi Past: Recasting German Identity in Postwar Europe* (Lexington, KY: University of Kentucky Press, 2015), pp. 139–67. In all four publications the SA diplomats are dealt with in a few footnotes, if they are mentioned at all.

7. In this respect it is worth remembering that for Hitler and his generation the establishment of a military dictatorship during the First World War under the two Supreme Army Commanders Paul von Hindenburg and Erich Ludendorff had constituted a central element of their political socialization. Hitler consistently tried to avoid situations that could lead to greater independence of the military to the detriment of the NSDAP's ideological goals.

8. PAAA, Gesandtschaft Sofia, vol. 59/2, p. 98 (entry from 13 November 1941). Luther was promoted to the rank of SA-Brigade General in 1942. For details about Luther and his central role at the Foreign Office, see Christopher Browning, *The Final Solution and the German Foreign Office: A Study of Referat D III of Abteilung Deutschland 1940–1943* (New York: Holmes & Meier, 1978); idem, 'Unterstaatssekretär Martin Luther'; Hans-Jürgen Döscher, *Das Auswärtige Amt im Dritten Reich: Diplomatie im Schatten der 'Endlösung'* (Berlin: Siedler, 1987), pp. 205–7; idem, 'Martin Luther – Aufstieg und Fall eines Unterstaatssekretärs', in Ronald Smelser, Enrico Syring, and Rainer Zitelmann (eds), *Die braune Elite II* (Darmstadt: Wissenschaftliche Buchgesellschaft, 1993), pp. 179–92.

9. PAAA, Gesandtschaft Sofia, vol. 59/2, p. 9 (entry from 27 July 1941). For early career diplomats' criticism of 'party mercenaries', see also Maulucci, 'German Diplomats and the Myth of the Two Foreign Offices', p. 146.

10. After the war Beckerle emphasized his family, religious, and patriotic background. See Weinke, *Die Verfolgung von NS-Tätern im Geteilten Deutschland*, p. 264.

11. See, for example, his diary entries from 25 January 1942, 5 February 1942, and 6 March 1943: PAAA, Gesandtschaft Sofia, vol. 59/2, pp. 143 and 150; idem, vol. 59/3 (Personal Notes of the Ambassador Adolf-Heinz Beckerle II: 17 February 1943–9 August 1944), p. 9. Similarly, Siegfried Kasche had a golden notebook in which he noted his maxims and reflections, covering the years 1938 to 1944; PAAA, Personal Papers of Siegfried Kasche, vol. 24.

12. Heinz Edelmann [Adolf-Heinz Beckerle], *Wir wollten arbeiten: Erlebnisse deutscher Auswanderer in Südamerika* (Frankfurt am Main: Diesterweg, 1942). This book tells the story of one individual's fate while also charting the general political developments of the time: the main character decides to return to Germany precisely when he receives the news of Hitler's release from prison.

13. Email from Henning von Jagow to the author, 5 April 2015.

14. On these journeys von Killinger was accompanied by Edmund Veesenmayer, who later became his rival, and by his SA comrade Willy Roedel, who would later become his right-hand man in Bratislava and Bucharest. In Romania, Roedel also built the national branch of the *Deutscher Informationsdienst III*, von Ribbentrop's personal intelligence service within the Foreign Office. See Igor-Philip Matić, *Edmund Veesenmayer: Agent und Diplomat der nationalsozialistischen Expansionspolitik* (Munich: Oldenbourg, 2002), pp. 91–4; Khristoforov, *Oberfiurer SA Villi Redel*, pp. 48–55.

15. Strictly speaking, von Killinger only partly belonged to the group of SA diplomats appointed to their posts for political reasons in 1940–1, as he seems to have been a *Versorgungsfall*, an accomplished party leader in need of a suitable position who kept aloof from politics. He was born in 1886 and was therefore, on average, fifteen years older than his fellow SA generals. His publications from the Weimar years testify to his mercenary mentality; see Manfred von Killinger, *Ernstes und Heiteres aus dem Putschleben* (Berlin: Vormarsch, 1928); idem, *Die SA in Wort und Bild* (Leipzig: Kittler, 1933). For details on von Killinger's political career in Saxony during the 1930s, see Andreas Wagner, *Mutschmann gegen von Killinger: Konfliktlinien zwischen Gauleiter und SA-Führer während des Aufstiegs der NSDAP und der 'Machtergreifung' im Freistaat Sachsen* (Beucha: Sax, 2001); on other aspects of his life, see the detailed but overly sympathetic portrait by Bert Wawrzinek, *Manfred von Killinger (1886–1944): Ein politischer Soldat zwischen Freikorps und Auswärtigem Amt* (Preußisch Oldendorf: Deutsche Verlagsgesellschaft, 2003).

16. They thus formed a particular kind of 'elite network' that Rüdiger Hachtmann has recently referred to as the 'lubricating oil of the NS system'. See Rüdiger Hachtmann, 'Allerorten Mobilisierung? Vorschläge, wie mit Schlagworten in der Sozial- und Wirtschaftsgeschichte der NS-Diktatur umzugehen ist', in Oliver Werner (ed.), *Mobilisierung im Nationalsozialismus: Institutionen und Regionen in der Kriegswirtschaft und der Verwaltung des 'Dritten Reiches' 1936 bis 1945* (Paderborn: Schöningh, 2013), pp. 69–85, here pp. 79–83.

17. Henning von Jagow remembers a trip his family took to Styria with the Kasche family in the early 1940s, as well as family holidays with the Ludin children after the Second World War. Erla Ludin was his godmother. He also remembers that Kasche's widow later repeatedly visited the von Jagow family in Dingelsdorf on Lake Constance.

18. See the correspondence in PAAA, Personal Papers of Siegfried Kasche, vol. 3.

19. See also the memorandum of a meeting between Hitler, Rosenberg, Göring, and Field Marshal Keitel in the Führer's headquarters on 16 July 1941 in U.S. Government Printing Office (ed.), *Documents on German Foreign Policy 1918–1945: Series D (1937–1945)*, vol. 13: *The War Years, June 23–December 11, 1941* (Washington, DC: U.S. Government Printing Office, 1954), pp. 149–56, here p. 154.

20. PAAA, Gesandtschaft Sofia, vol. 59/2, p. 69 (entry from 4 October 1941). According to Rosenberg's diary, he had initially recommended Erich Koch, the *Gauleiter* of East Prussia, for this post. See Matthäus and Bajohr (eds), *Alfred Rosenberg: Die Tagebücher*, pp. 397–9 (entry from 20 July 1941). Rosenberg and Kasche met 'for a first detailed conference on the future Reichskommissariat Russland' in late September. See ibid., p. 424.

21. PAAA, Gesandtschaft Sofia, vol. 59/2, p. 73 (entry from 10 October 1941). In contrast, von Jagow's son Henning von Jagow, born in 1934, remembers the years in Hungary as 'happy times' for his parents. However, because of the many social obligations of the German ambassador, he and his siblings 'often missed their parents' and were raised primarily by a governess; email from Henning von Jagow to the author, 5 April 2015.

22. Ibid.

23. See Michael Wildt, *An Uncompromising Generation: The Nazi Leadership of the Reich Security Main Office* (Madison, WI: University of Wisconsin Press, 2010) (first published in German as *Generation des Unbedingten: Das Führungskorps des Reichssicherheitshauptamtes*, Hamburg: Hamburger Edition, 2002).

24. BArch Berlin, NS 19/2798, pp. 1–3: Letter from SS-Brigadeführer Gottlob Berger to Himmler, 17 April 1941. On this point, see also Döscher, *Das Auswärtige Amt im Dritten Reich*, pp. 205–6; Browning, 'Unterstaatssekretär Martin Luther', p. 327.

25. After the war, Fritz von Twardowsky was appointed vice-director of the *Bundespresseamt* (Federal Press Office) in 1950 and served as ambassador to Mexico from 1952 to 1955. Noteworthy in this context is a book that von Twardowsky published shortly before his death, at the age of eighty: Fritz von Twardowsky, *Anfänge der deutschen Kulturpolitik im Ausland* (Bonn: Inter Nationes, 1970).

26. The memoirs of Edmund Glaise von Horstenau, a Wehrmacht general, former vice-chancellor of Austria, and plenipotentiary general in the Independent State of Croatia, confirm this information. According to von Horstenau, Lutze had complained to von Ribbentrop that only SS men were being enlisted in the service of the Foreign Office. Von Ribbentrop had then agreed to appoint four high-ranking SA men as envoys. See Horstenau, *Ein General im Zwielicht*, vol. 3, p. 91. On Horstenau, see also Georg Christoph Berger Waldenegg, '"From My Point of View, I Never Ceased Being a Good Austrian": The Ideology and Career of Edmund Glaise von Horstenau', in Martyn Rady and Rebecca Haynes (eds), *In the Shadow of Hitler: Personalities of the Right in Central and Eastern Europe* (London: I. B. Tauris, 2011), pp. 313–28.

27. BArch Berlin, NS 19/3872, pp. 1–2: Letter from SS-Brigadeführer Gottlob Berger to Himmler, 26 April 1941.

28. For a detailed analysis, see chapter 7.

29. Horstenau, *Ein General im Zwielicht*, vol. 3, pp. 188–9. Theodor Habicht, the former NSDAP *Landesinspektor* for Austria, confirmed this view. In a diary entry he noted that Himmler and Rosenberg would have an 'open conflict' because of the latter's 'leaning' on the SA (BArch-Militärarchiv, Freiburg im Breisgau, MSg 2/12955, Diary of Theodor Habicht, entry from

7 July 1941). I am grateful to Felix Römer, London, for providing me with extracts of Habicht's diaries. On the continuing close relations between Rosenberg and the SA, see also RGVA, Osobyi Archives, Fond 1212, Opis 2, no. 17, pp. 47–50: Protocol of a meeting between SA-Obergruppenführer Luyken and Dr Stellrecht in the Dienststelle Reichsleiter Rosenberg, 19 July 1943.

30. An English translation of this memorandum (Nuremberg document 221-L) is printed in full in U.S. Government Printing Office, *Documents on German Foreign Policy 1918–1945: Series D, vol. 13*, pp. 149–56.

31. Memorandum of a meeting between Hitler, Rosenberg, Göring, and Field Marshal Keitel in the Führer's headquarters, 16 July 1941, p. 150.

32. On Schepmann's and Bennecke's biographies, see the information provided in the previous chapters. On Manthey, see Joachim Lilla, Martin Döring, and Andreas Schulz (eds), *Statisten in Uniform: Die Mitglieder des Reichstags 1933–1945: Ein biographisches Handbuch: Unter Einbeziehung der völkischen und nationalsozialistischen Reichstagsabgeordneten ab Mai 1924* (Düsseldorf: Droste, 2004), p. 399. On Drechsler, see Sven Jüngerkes, 'Bürokratie als Stabilisierungs- und Destabilisierungsmechanismus: Das "Reichskommissariat für das Ostland"1941–1944', in Sven Reichardt and Wolfgang Seibel (eds), *Der prekäre Staat: Herrschen und Verwalten im Nationalsozialismus* (Frankfurt am Main: Campus, 2010), pp. 275–98, here p. 279, with further references.

33. Memorandum of a meeting between Hitler, Rosenberg, Göring, and Field Marshal Keitel in the Führer's headquarters, 16 July 1941, p. 153.

34. BArch Berlin, NS 23/166: Dr Otto, 'SA-Obergruppenführer und Diplomat' (autumn 1941). Mark Mazower has recently argued that the Nazi idea of a European 'community of peoples' has to be seen as a deliberate attempt to overcome the contractions of the League of Nations when it came to matters of minority rights and national sovereignty, and that it was more strongly rooted in traditional ideas of international law than is usually claimed; Mark Mazower, 'National Socialism and the Search for International Order', *Bulletin of the GHI* 50 (2012), pp. 9–26.

35. BArch Berlin, NS 23/166: Letter from SA-Gruppenführer Thomas Girgensohn to OSAF Schrifttum, 10 November 1941.

36. This view was shared by von Horstenau, who saw Kasche's appointment as envoy to Croatia as a herald of the '*Reichskommissariat Kroatien*'. See Horstenau, *Ein General im Zwielicht*, vol. 3, p. 90.

37. Memorandum of a meeting between Hitler, Rosenberg, Göring, and Field Marshal Keitel in the Führer's headquarters, 16 July 1941, p. 150.

38. On von Jagow's activities in the spring of 1933, see HStA Stuttgart (Hauptstaatsarchiv Stuttgart), E 130 b Bü 1859.

39. On von Jagow as *Reichskommissar* in Württemberg, see Jill Stephenson, *Hitler's Home Front: Württemberg under the Nazis* (London: Hambledon Continuum, 2006), pp. 42–3; Hachmann, 'Der "Degen"', pp. 277–9. On Beckerle as police president, see Meinl, 'Adolf Heinz Beckerle'.

40. As quoted in von Horstenau, *Ein General im Zwielicht*, vol. 3, p. 90.

41. In addition to the following landmark studies (Raul Hilberg, *The Destruction of the European Jews* [London: W. H. Allen, 1961]; Saul Friedländer, *Nazi Germany and the Jews*, vol. 1: *The Years of Persecution, 1933–1939* [New York: HarperCollins, 1997], vol. 2: *The Years of Extermination* [New York: HarperCollins, 2007]; Peter Longerich, *Politik der Vernichtung: Eine Gesamtdarstellung der nationalsozialistischen Judenverfolgung* [Munich: Piper, 1998]), notable exceptions include the comparative studies by Martin Dean, *Robbing the Jews: The Confiscation of Jewish Property in the Holocaust, 1933–1945* (Cambridge and New York: Cambridge University Press, 2008); Christopher Browning, *Die 'Endlösung' und das Auswärtige Amt: Das Referat D III der Abteilung Deutschland 1940–1943* (Darmstadt: Wissenschaftliche Buchgesellschaft, 2010) [first published in English as *The Final Solution and the German Foreign Office*]; Eduard Nižňanský, 'The Discussions of Nazi Germany on the Deportation of Jews in 1942 – The Examples of Slovakia, Rumania and Hungary', in *Historický časopis* 59 (2011), Supplement, pp. 111–36. See also Max Münz's pioneering but nowadays forgotten dissertation dealing with the legal consequences of German policies toward its eastern European allies: *Die*

Verantwortlichkeit für die Judenverfolgungen im Ausland während der nationalsozialistischen Herrschaft, inaugural diss., Johann Wolfgang Goethe-Universität zu Frankfurt am Main, 1958.

42. See esp. Tatjana Tönsmeyer, *Das Dritte Reich und die Slowakei 1939–1945: Politischer Alltag zwischen Kooperation und Eigensinn* (Paderborn: Schöningh, 2003), pp. 335–9.
43. Dean, *Robbing the Jews*, pp. 317–22.
44. Nižňanský, 'The Discussions of Nazi Germany on the Deportation of Jews in 1942', p. 112.
45. See esp. Browning, *Die 'Endlösung' und das Auswärtige Amt*, pp. 143–74.
46. Jozef Tiso, *Die Wahrheit über die Slowakei: Verteidigungsrede gehalten am 17. und 18. März 1947 vor dem 'National'-Gericht in Bratislava*, ed. by Jon Sekera (published 'in exile', 1948), p. 48.
47. Lotte Weiss, *Meine zwei Leben: Erinnerungen einer Holocaust-Überlebenden* (Münster: Lit, 2010), pp. 176–7.
48. Tiso, *Die Wahrheit über die Slowakei*, p. 167.
49. Dean, *Robbing the Jews*, pp. 319–20.
50. StA München, Staatsanwaltschaften, no. 34835, vol. 1, pp. 52–6, here p. 54: Testimony made under oath by Aron Grünhut, 13 January 1960; Oskar Neumann, *Im Schatten des Todes: Vom Schicksalskampf des slowakischen Judentums* (Tel Aviv: Olamenu, 1956), p. 53.
51. Cable of Ludin to the German Foreign Office, 4 December 1941, in Nižňanský (ed.), *Holokaust na Slovensku*, vol. 4, pp. 111–12.
52. Neumann, *Im Schatten des Todes*, pp. 67, 96–8. In August 1944 the FS was integrated into the *Heimatschutz Slowakei*; StA München, Staatsanwaltschaften, no. 34835, vol. 4, p. 780: Testimony of Walter Postl, 23 June 1967.
53. StA München, Staatsanwaltschaften, no. 21808, pp. 103–5: Testimony of Ferdinand Durcansky, 28 February 1964; StA München, Staatsanwaltschaften, no. 34835, vol. 1, p. 86: Verbal note from the Deutsche Gesandtschaft Bratislava to the Slovakian Ministry of the Interior, 1 May 1942.
54. Cable from Ludin to the German Foreign Office, 6 April 1942, in Nižňanský (ed.), *Holokaust na Slovensku*, vol. 4, p. 127.
55. Nižňanský, 'The Discussions of Nazi Germany on the Deportation of Jews in 1942', p. 119.
56. Ibid., p. 120.
57. StA München, Staatsanwaltschaften, no. 21808, pp. 34–6: Letter from Franz Karmasin to Heinrich Himmler, 29 July 1942.
58. Ibid., p. 135: Notation of the Staatsanwaltschaft München, 10 July 1964. Wisliceny's counterpart in Slovakia was the 'Jew king' Anton Vosek, head of Department XIV of the Slovak Ministry of the Interior; Neumann, *Im Schatten des Todes*, p. 65. On the role of the SS advisors in Slovakia – but without any reference to Ludin – see Tatjana Tönsmeyer, 'The German Advisors in Slovakia, 1939–1945: Conflict of Co-operation?', in Mark Cornwall and R. J. W. Evans (eds), *Czechoslovakia in a Nationalist and Fascist Europe 1918–1948* (Oxford: Oxford University Press, 2007), pp. 169–84.
59. PAAA, Personalakten, no. 9246, p. 40: Cable from the Foreign Office to Ludin, 26 July 1944. It is not clear when precisely this meeting took place.
60. Dean, *Robbing the Jews*, p. 324; StA München, Staatsanwaltschaften München, no. 34835, vol. 2, pp. 257–8: Notation of the Bavarian Landeskriminalamt München, 8 January 1965.
61. In October 1938 the party changed its name to *Deutsche Partei*.
62. After 1945, Karmasin took refuge in the American sector of occupied Germany, initially living under a false name. The Bratislava People's Court sentenced him to death (in absentia) on 22 June 1948. However, the German authorities did not hand him over, and in the West, Karmasin made a second career as a journalist and a functionary of the *Sudetendeutsche Landsmannschaft*, an expellee organization of the Slovakian Germans. Rumours in post-war Germany claimed that he had received substantial help from former SA-*Obersturmbannführer* Hans Gmelin, Ludin's adjutant at the German Embassy in Bratislava between 1941 and 1945 and from 1954 to 1974 the elected mayor of Tübingen. Karmasin, who was also a member of the revanchist *Witikobund*, escaped punishment and died a free man on 25 June 1970. For details on his life, see Lubomir Lipták, *Franz Karmasin opät na scene* (Bratislava: Vyd-vo Polit. Lit., 1962), as well as the extensive files of the Munich prosecutor in StA München, Staatsanwaltschaften, no. 34835, vols 1–33.

63. Wagner, *Sudeten SA in Polen*.

64. StA München, Staatsanwaltschaften, no. 21808, pp. 12–19: BDC-Documents of Franz Karmasin.

65. In this respect, see also StA München, Staatsanwaltschaften, no. 34835, vol. 1, pp. 52–6: Testimony made under oath by Aron Grünhut, 13 January 1960.

66. StA München, Staatsanwaltschaften, no. 21808, pp. 34–6: Letter from Franz Karmasin to Heinrich Himmler, 29 July 1942.

67. Such an interpretation is in line with Ludin's defence strategy after the war; see StA München, Staatsanwaltschaften, no. 34835, vol. 3, p. 560: Testimony of Norbert Münz, 14 October 1965. For Karmasin's view, see StA München, Staatsanwaltschaften, no. 34835, vol. 5, pp. 1,215–16: Testimony of Franz Karmasin, 28 October 1969.

68. StA München, Staatsanwaltschaften, no. 34835, vol. 1, p. 86: Verbal note from the Deutsche Gesandtschaft Bratislava to the Slovakian Ministry of the Interior, 1 May 1942.

69. Ibid., vol. 6, p. 1,290: Testimony of Josef Hotovy, 14 November 1969. Contrary to my findings, Ludin's proxy Hans Gmelin in 1970 claimed that Ludin had threatened to resign and volunteer for service at the front lines once Tiso had informed him about the systematic killing of the Jews in 1942. See StA München, Staatsanwaltschaften, no. 34835, vol. 6, p. 1,454: Testimony of Hans Gmelin, 5 March 1970.

70. Korb, *Im Schatten des Weltkriegs*, pp. 111–12. For a contrary judgement, see Conze et al., *Das Amt und die Vergangenheit*, p. 280.

71. Conze et al., *Das Amt und die Vergangenheit*, p. 280. Such literary comparisons were not limited to Kasche, however. Rudolf Rahn in Italy, for example, was known as the 'Karl May of the diplomats'; see Lutz Klinkhammer, *Zwischen Bündnis und Besatzung: Das nationalsozialistische Deutschland und die Republik von Salò 1943–1945* (Tübingen: Niemeyer, 1993), p. 142. For Hitler's and Kasche's views on Croatian politics, views that slowly drifted apart in 1943 and 1944, see in particular Kasche's memos on his meetings with Hitler on 29 October 1943, 30 March 1944, and 16 September 1944, in PAAA, Personal Papers of Siegfried Kasche, vol. 23, pp. 5–17.

72. Conze et al., *Das Amt und die Vergangenheit*, pp. 280–1; Korb, *Im Schatten des Weltkriegs*, pp. 195–6. For a detailed discussion of the nature of the Ustaša regime's antisemitism, see ibid., pp. 136–46.

73. A detailed discussion of the Ustaša regime's atrocities and Kasche's benevolence toward the Croatian position is beyond the reach of this study. See the excellent analysis by Jozo Tomasevich, *War and Revolution in Yugoslavia, 1941–1945: Occupation and Collaboration* (Stanford, CA: Stanford University Press, 2001); Ivo Goldstein, *The Holocaust in Croatia* (Pittsburgh, PA: The University of Pittsburgh Press, 2016); and Korb, *Im Schatten des Weltkriegs*, as well as the more partisan account of Lazo M. Kostich, *The Holocaust in the 'Independent State of Croatia': An Account Based on German, Italian and Other Sources* (Chicago, IL: Liberty, 1981), pp. 6–7, 43–6, 145–6.

74. For Kasche's perspective on this meeting, see his telegram to the Foreign Office of 4 June 1941, in *Akten zur Deutschen Auswärtigen Politik 1918–1945, Series D*, vol. XII: *1937–1941* (Göttingen: Vandenhoeck & Ruprecht, 1969), pp. 796–8.

75. Korb, *Im Schatten des Weltkriegs*, p. 204, with further references.

76. Browning, *The Final Solution and the German Foreign Office*, p. 93.

77. Münz, *Die Verantwortlichkeit für die Judenverfolgungen im Ausland*, p. 209.

78. Korb, *Im Schatten des Weltkriegs*, p. 413.

79. Ibid., p. 419.

80. Conze et al., *Das Amt und die Vergangenheit*, pp. 280–1.

81. For a detailed discussion (with slightly lower figures for those deported and killed in Auschwitz), see Tomislav Dulić, 'Mass Killing in the Independent State of Croatia, 1941–1945: A Case for Comparative Research', *Journal of Genocide Research* 8:3 (2006), pp. 255–81.

82. Gerhard Köpernik, *Faschisten im KZ: Rumäniens Eiserne Garde und das Dritte Reich* (Berlin: Frank & Timme, 2014), pp. 97–103; Andrej Angrick, 'Rumänien, die SS und die Vernichtung der Juden', in Mariana Hausleitner, Brigitte Mihok, and Juliane Wetzel (eds), *Rumänien und der Holocaust: Zu den Massenverbrechen in Transnistrien 1941–1944* (Berlin: Metropol, 2001), pp. 113–38, here p. 122; Michael Kroner, 'Ahnungslosigkeit oder

Hochverrat? Manfred von Killinger in Bukarest 1941–1944', *Südostdeutsche Vierteljahresblätter: Zeitschrift für Literatur und Kunst, Geschichte und Zeitgeschichte* 43 (1994), pp. 123–32.

83. *Akten zur Deutschen Auswärtigen Politik 1918–1945, Series D*, vol. XII: *1937–1941*, pp. 11, 18–20, 140–4. See also Antonescu's letter to von Killinger from 25 February 1941, in IfZ Archiv, Bestand Reichsführer-SS, MA 325, vol. 1, pp. 9,017–19.

84. Wawrzinek, *Manfred von Killinger*, p. 210.

85. Ion Georghe, *Rumäniens Weg zum Satellitenstaat* (Heidelberg: Vowinckel, 1952), pp. 124–8; Kroner, 'Ahnungslosigkeit oder Hochverrat?', p. 124.

86. Based on, among other things, the diary entries of Romanian politicians, the German-Romanian historian Michael Kroner has suggested that von Killinger might have been involved in negotiations between the Romanian government and the Allies, and therefore may have deliberately misinformed the Foreign Office. However, this thesis seems largely based on unsubstantiated speculation. See Kroner, 'Ahnungslosigkeit oder Hochverrat?', pp. 124–8.

87. Münz, *Die Verantwortlichkeit für die Judenverfolgungen im Ausland*, p. 144.

88. On Richter, Lecca, and their relationship, see Dennis Deletant, *Hitler's Forgotten Ally: Ion Antonescu and His Regime, Romania, 1940–1944* (Basingstoke: Palgrave, 2006), pp. 113, 121–2.

89. Münz, *Die Verantwortlichkeit für die Judenverfolgungen im Ausland*, p. 164.

90. Wolfgang Benz, 'Der "vergessene Holocaust": Der Sonderfall Rumänien: Okkupation und Verfolgung von Minderheiten im Zweiten Weltkrieg', in Hausleitner, Mihok, and Wetzel, *Rumänien und der Holocaust*, pp. 9–13.

91. Jews were not the only victims of this policy of forced homogenization. Up to 30,000 Romani people were also deported to Transnistria, the majority of whom did not survive. See Brigitte Mihok, 'Die Verfolgung der Roma: Ein verdrängtes Kapitel der rumänischen Geschichte', in Hausleitner, Mihok, and Wetzel, *Rumänien und der Holocaust*, pp. 25–31.

92. Mariana Hausleitner, 'Großverbrechen im rumänischen Transnistrien 1941–1944', in Hausleitner, Mihok, and Wetzel, *Rumänien und der Holocaust*, pp. 15–24; Dalia Ofer, 'The Holocaust in Transnistria: A Special Case of Genocide', in Lucjan Dobroszycki and Jeffrey S. Gurock (eds), *The Holocaust in the Soviet Union: Studies and Sources on the Destruction of the Jews in the Nazi-occupied Territories of the USSR, 1941–1945* (New York: Sharpe, 1993), pp. 133–54. Ofer also discusses the fate of the local Jews of Transnistria, the vast majority of whom were killed by German *Einsatzgruppen* in the first days of the occupation.

93. Münz, *Die Verantwortlichkeit für die Judenverfolgungen im Ausland*, p. 165.

94. Browning, *Die 'Endlösung' und das Auswärtige Amt*, pp. 163–4; Deletant, *Hitler's Forgotten Ally*, pp. 205–29.

95. Deletant, *Hitler's Forgotten Ally*, pp. 213–14.

96. Richter had used this term as early as April 1942 in an article in the *Bukarester Tageblatt*; see Lya Benjamin, 'Die "Judenfrage" in Rumänien im Spiegel des "Bukarester Tageblatts"', in Hausleitner, Mihok, and Wetzel (eds), *Rumänien und der Holocaust*, pp. 139–52, here p. 141.

97. As quoted in Deletant, *Hitler's Forgotten Ally*, pp. 210–11.

98. However, in the spring of 1943, von Killinger intervened on behalf of the Reich to prevent the emigration of Jewish children from Romania; see Deletant, *Hitler's Forgotten Ally*, p. 216.

99. PAAA, Gesandtschaft Sofia, vol. 59/2, p. 156 (entry from 19 February 1942).

100. IfZ Archiv, Bestand Befehlshaber Serbien, MA 512, pp. 917–18: Cable from Beckerle to the Foreign Office, 27 July 1941.

101. Frederick B. Chary, *The Bulgarian Jews and the Final Solution* (Pittsburgh, PA: University of Pittsburgh Press, 1972), p. 48.

102. Stefan Troebst, 'Rettung, Überleben oder Vernichtung? Geschichtspolitische Kontroversen über Bulgarien und den Holocaust', *Südosteuropa: Zeitschrift für Politik und Gesellschaft* 59:1 (2011), pp. 97–127, here pp. 104–5; Browning, *Die 'Endlösung' und das Auswärtige Amt*, p. 172.

103. Dean, *Robbing the Jews*, pp. 335–7.

104. Chary, *The Bulgarian Jews and the Final Solution*, pp. 51 and 69.

105. Browning, *Die 'Endlösung' und das Auswärtige Amt*, pp. 172–3; Chary, *The bulgarian Jews and the Final Solution*, pp. 72–3.
106. PAAA, Gesandtschaft Sofia, vol. 59/2, p. 313 (entry from 16 February 1943).
107. Dean, *Robbing the Jews*, p. 339.
108. Beckerle's diary entry from 3 March 1943, in which he summarizes a talk with Dannecker, makes it plain that he had been informed about these deportation plans and approved of them: 'Starting on 15 March, eight trains shall leave, deporting 20,000 Jews (2,500 per train). As it will not completely work out, 2,000 Jews from Sofia shall be included. It is thought best to deport the most influential Jews who always create trouble when it comes to Aryanizations. I disapprove of resorting to Sofia, as this will make a lot of noise and endangers the whole action for the future. First, away with the other Jews, and afterwards, [we deport] all Jews from Sofia together!'; PAAA, Gesandtschaft Sofia, vol. 59/3, p. 7 (entry from 3 March 1943).
109. Todorov Tzvetan, *The Fragility of Goodness: Why Bulgaria's Jews Survived the Holocaust* (London: Weidenfeld & Nicolson, 2001), pp. 8–11.
110. PAAA, Gesandtschaft Sofia, vol. 59/3, p. 48 (entry from 10 May 1943).
111. Todorov, *The Fragility of Goodness*, p. 13; PAAA, Gesandtschaft Sofia, vol. 59/3, p. 80 (entry from 21 July 1943).
112. Christian Neef, 'Die schlimmste Stunde', *Der Spiegel*, 24 October 2011, http://www.spiegel.de/spiegel/print/d-81136856.html.
113. 'Streiflichter aus Litzmannstadt', in Rudolf von Elmayer-Veestenbrugg (ed.), *SA-Männer im feldgrauen Rock: Taten und Erlebnisse von SA-Männern in den Kriegsjahren 1939–1940* (Leipzig: v. Hase & Koehler, 1941), pp. 30–4, here pp. 31–2. Beckerle's obsession with 'Jewish dirt' did not prevent him from moving into an 'Aryanized' villa in Frankfurt by the end of the 1930s; see Meinl, 'Adolf Heinz Beckerle'.
114. PAAA, Gesandtschaft Sofia, vol. 59/2, pp. 150 and 217 (entries from 4 February and 20 August 1942).
115. PAAA, Gesandtschaft Sofia, vol. 59/3, p. 67 (entry from 19 June 1943).
116. PAAA, Gesandtschaft Sofia, vol. 59/2, pp. 86 and 235 (entries from 26 October 1941 and 15 September 1942). According to his diaries, Beckerle often slept late and spent whole days sunbathing on his terrace.
117. PAAA, Personalakten, no. 647, pp. 27–9: SD-Report to the Foreign Office on the flight of the Germans from Bulgaria, 18 December 1944.
118. On von Jagow's biography, see the very well-informed article by Hachmann, 'Der "Degen"', pp. 267–87.
119. Even in wartime, life as a German diplomat in Hungary between 1941 and early 1944 was not unpleasant. In late August 1941 von Jagow demanded additional funds to buy 'greater amounts of food, drinks and tobacco' from one of the free ports of Hamburg, Lisbon, or Trieste, as luxury goods of sufficient quality were not available in Hungary; PAAA, Personalakten, no. 6681, p. 15: Letter from von Jagow to the Foreign Office, 30 August 1941.
120. Hachmann, 'Der "Degen"', p. 284.
121. The German deliberations on this matter also included financial considerations. A partial deportation – in which all 'illegal' Jews in Hungary were deported – would require as many resources as a total deportation, Eichmann argued. See Longerich, *Politik der Vernichtung*, p. 524.
122. Münz, *Die Verantwortlichkeit für die Judenverfolgungen im Ausland*, pp. 180–95. See also Veesenmayer's memorandum from April 1943, in *Akten zur Deutschen Auswärtigen Politik 1918–1945, Series E*, vol. XI: *1941–1945*, pp. 78–80.
123. There were important exceptions, however, as Hungary deported Jews who did not hold Hungarian citizenship as early as 1941. Best-known in this regard is the Kamianets-Podilskyi massacre of late August 1941, in which German *Einsatzgruppen* and SS forces in Ukraine murdered more than 20,000 Jews previously deported from Hungary. See Andrej Angrick, *Besatzungspolitik und Massenmord: Die Einsatzgruppe D in der südlichen Sowjetunion 1941–1943* (Hamburg: Hamburger Edition, 2003), pp. 196–206; Randolph L. Braham, 'The Kamenets Podolsk and Délvidék Massacres: Prelude to the Holocaust in Hungary', *Yad Vashem Studies* 9 (1973), pp. 133–56.

124. Margit Szöllösi-Janze, *Die Pfeilkreuzlerbewegung in Ungarn: Historischer Kontext, Entwicklung und Herrschaft* (Munich: Oldenbourg, 1989), pp. 426 and 432.

125. Longerich, *Politik der Vernichtung*, p. 530; Randolph L. Braham, *The Destruction of Hungarian Jewry: A Documentary Account* (New York: Pro Arte, 1963), p. 160. This was a consequence of von Ribbentrop's demand that diplomatic efforts to start the deportation of all Jews from Hungary, Bulgaria, and Denmark be intensified; see the note from Luther to Weizäcker from 24 September 1942, in ibid., p. 133.

126. Ibid., pp. 165–71; Longerich, *Politik der Vernichtung*, p. 530.

127. See the information provided in Veesenmayer's personnel file at the Foreign Office in PAAA, Personalakten, no. 15789. When paying his first official visit to the king, Veesenmayer expressed the expectation that the Hungarians would fight side by side with the Germans and, after the 'elimination of all subversive elements that threatened the people of Hungary and its state' (*nach Ausschaltung aller staats- und volkszersetzender Elemente*), a phrase referring to the Jews, would ultimately win the war. See ibid., p. 30.

128. Krisztian Ungváry, 'Robbing the Dead: The Hungarian Contribution to the Holocaust', in Beata Kosmala and Feliks Tych (eds), *Facing the Nazi Genocide: Non-Jews and Jews in Europe* (Berlin: Metropol, 2004), pp. 231–61, here pp. 231–3.

129. Figures according to Szöllösi-Janze, *Die Pfeilkreuzlerbewegung in Ungarn*, p. 426.

130. After leaving Hungary in the spring of 1944, von Jagow's wife and seven children, including a recently born baby, moved from Budapest to the shores of Lake Balaton and then to the more secure Groß-Münche in the Warthegau. It seems likely that the mansion the family inhabited there was one of the estates the SA had acquired in the early 1940s with the intent of transforming it into an SA leadership school after the war (see also chapter 7), but further research is needed to verify this. With the Russian troops approaching, the von Jagow family in late 1944 or early 1945 fled to Berlin and then to the city of Constance in March 1945. I would like to thank Henning von Jagow for his patience in answering my questions on his family's history in the last months of the war.

131. Erich Murawski, *Der deutsche Wehrmachtsbericht 1939–1945: Ein Beitrag zur Untersuchung der geistigen Kriegsführung: Mit einer Dokumentation der Wehrmachtsberichte vom 1.7.1944 bis zum 9.5.1945* (Boppard am Rhein: Boldt, 1962), pp. 443–4.

132. Klinkhammer, *Zwischen Bündnis und Besatzung*, pp. 148–50.

133. Hachmann, 'Der "Degen"', p. 286; Rudolf Rahn, *Ruheloses Leben: Aufzeichnungen und Erinnerungen* (Stuttgart and Zurich: Europäischer Buchklub, 1951), p. 440; email from Henning von Jagow to the author, 5 April 2015.

134. Moshe Zimmermann, 'Das Auswärtige Amt und der Holocaust', in Johannes Hürter and Michael Mayer (eds), *Das Auswärtige Amt in der NS-Diktatur* (Berlin: De Gruyter Oldenbourg, 2014), pp. 165–76, here p. 173.

135. Rahn, *Ruheloses Leben*, p. 390.

136. Horstenau, *Ein General im Zwielicht*, vol. 3, p. 90. See also Döscher, *Das Auswärtige Amt im Dritten Reich*, p. 206, with further references.

137. Horstenau, *Ein General im Zwielicht*, vol. 3, p. 91.

138. An extensive discussion of this topic is beyond the scope of this book. See the instructive remarks on the necessity of such an approach in Magnus Brechtken, 'Auswärtiges Amt, Sicherheitsdienst und Reichssicherheitshauptamt 1933 bis 1942', in *Das Auswärtige Amt in der NS-Diktatur*, ed. Hürter and Mayer, pp. 151–64, here pp. 163–4.

139. See, among others, the detailed analysis of Adolf-Heinz Beckerle, 'Die Neuordnung in Rumänien und die Legionärsbewegung Codreanus', *Die SA* 1:38 (1940), pp. 6–12.

140. Wagner, *Sudeten SA in Polen*, unpaginated.

141. IfZ Archiv, Bestand Sicherheitsdienst Reichsführer-SS, MA 650, pp. 4,982–8: SD-Report from SS-Hauptsturmführer Dr Börsch on the political situation in Slovakia, 1943.

142. PAAA, Gesandtschaft Sofia, vol. 59/2, p. 156 (entry from 19 February 1942).

143. See Kasche's detailed justification of his position in a letter to von Ribbentrop from 5 November 1943, in PAAA, Personal Papers of Siegfried Kasche, vol. 23, pp. 26–30, esp. pp. 27–8.

144. As quoted in Chary, *The Bulgarian Jews and the Final Solution*, p. 75. For Beckerle's naive trust in his Bulgarian counterparts, see PAAA, Gesandtschaft Sofia, vol. 59/3, p. 4 (entries from 23 and 24 February 1943).

145. See Aly, *Hitler's Beneficiaries.*
146. Döscher, *Das Auswärtige Amt im Dritten Reich*, pp. 256–61.
147. PAAA, Personalakten, no. 9246, pp. 54–6: Göpfert to the German Foreign Office, 27 October 1944.
148. Kroner, 'Ahnungslosigkeit oder Hochverrat?', p. 131.
149. For the verdict, see USHMM, RG-57.004: *Selected Records of Trials of the National Court of Slovakia, Including the Jozef Tiso Trial, 1910–1975.* On these trials, see also Bradley Abrams, 'The Politics of Retribution: The Trial of Jozef Tiso in the Czechoslovak Environment', in István Deák, Jan T. Gross, and Tony Judt (eds), *The Politics of Retribution in Europe: World War II and Its Aftermath* (Princeton, NJ: Princeton University Press, 2000), pp. 252–89.
150. For the verdict against Kasche, see HDA, HR-HDA-1561, Sg 013.0.47, File Slavko Kvaternik and others. The bill of indictment against Kasche, written by Jakov Blazevic, the chief prosecutor of the People's Republic of Croatia, accused him of having contributed to 'the physical destruction of our peoples and the looting of our property'. More precisely, it mentioned his role in the infamous conference held at the German Embassy on 4 June 1941, as well as his contribution to the 'organization of terror, arrest and torture of the Yugoslav Jews'. Kasche was also held responsible for his collaboration with the Ustaša in the persecution of Communists and for the formation of so-called volunteer brigades that fought on the side of the Germans in the Second World War. I am grateful to Bojan Aleksov in London for his help in translating relevant passages of these documents.
151. PAAA, Personalakten, no. 647, pp. 23–4: Information provided by the Swiss Embassy, 5 October 1944; 'Russians Arrest Nazi Ministers', *Manchester Guardian*, 22 September 1944, p. 5.
152. Meinl, 'Adolf Heinz Beckerle'; Neef, 'Die schlimmste Stunde'.
153. For details on Beckerle's trials, see Weinke, *Die Verfolgung von NS-Tätern*, pp. 258–86; Meinl, 'Adolf Heinz Beckerle'.
154. The surviving members of the von Jagow and Ludin families still keep in touch today. After the war, the Ludin children spent several summer holidays at the von Jagow family home near Dingelsdorf on Lake Constance, and the von Jagows visited the Ludins at the (now demolished) Schlösslehof near Ostrach in Upper Swabia; email from Henning von Jagow to the author, 5 April 2015.
155. Malte Ludin, *2 oder 3 Dinge, die ich von ihm weiß*, BRD, 2005. See also Régine-Mihal Friedman, 'All About My Mother – On Malte Ludin's Film *2 oder 3 Dinge, die ich von ihm weiß (2005)*', in José Brunner (ed.), *Mütterliche Macht und väterliche Autorität: Elternbilder im deutschen Diskurs* (Göttingen: Wallstein, 2008), pp. 152–81.
156. For the long-term impact of this 'family heritage', see also the book by Ludin's grand-daughter Alexandra Senfft, *Schweigen tut weh: Eine deutsche Familiengeschichte* (Hamburg: Classen, 2007).
157. Ernst von Salomon, *Der Fragebogen*, 19th edn (Reinbek bei Hamburg: Rowohlt, 2011), pp. 635–68.
158. Malte Ludin, 'Hanns Elard Ludin'. For a detailed and convincing analysis of Salomon's novel and the reasons for its success in the early 1950s, see Parkinson, *An Emotional State*, pp. 73–111 (on Ludin, see pp. 102–3). For a general analysis of this intergenerational phenomenon, see Harald Welzer, *Opa war kein Nazi: Nationalsozialismus und Holocaust im Familiengedächtnis* (Frankfurt am Main: Fischer, 2002). Interestingly, even recent historical scholarship tends to see Ludin as a comparatively 'moderate' figure, ignoring his vital role in the Holocaust in Slovakia. See Tatjana Tönsmeyer, 'Von der Schutzfreundschaft zur Okkupationsmacht: Die Wahrnehmung des deutschen Einflusses durch die slowakische Elite', in Monika Glettler, Ľubomír Lipták, and Alena Míškova (eds), *Geteilt, besetzt, beherrscht: Die Tschechoslowakei 1938–1945: Reichsgau Sudetenland, Protektorat Böhmen und Mähren, Slowakei* (Essen: Klartext, 2004), pp. 311–25, here p. 316.
159. Letter from Dr Carola Wolf to Henning von Jagow, 23 January 2003, as quoted in an email from Henning von Jagow to the author, 5 April 2015.
160. In this context Ernst von Weizäcker is the most prominent case. For a balanced assessment, see Lars Lüdicke, 'Offizier und Diplomat: Ernst von Weizäcker im Kaiserreich, Weimarer Republik und "Drittem Reich"', in Jan Erik Schulte and Michael Wala (eds), *Widerstand und Auswärtiges Amt: Diplomaten gegen Hitler* (Munich: Siedler, 2013), pp. 225–49.

161. PAAA, B 83, no. 761: Letter from Hans Kasche to the Ministry of Justice of the Federal Republic of Germany, 10 January 1954. I am grateful to Annette Weinke, Friedrich Schiller University Jena, for directing me to this document.

162. StA München, Spruchkammerakten, K 843, p. 70: Letter from Hans Kasche to Berufungskammer München, 16 September 1954.

163. See the two verdicts from 1954 in StA München, Spruchkammerakten, K 843. For the German authorities, the 1947 verdict of the Croatian State Court was irrelevant. In such cases, 'substantial legal guarantees' of the defendants had not been granted, the Foreign Office informed the Kasche family. See StA München, Spruchkammerakten, K 843, p. 67: Letter from the Foreign Office to Hans Kasche, 23 February 1954.

164. On Kiesinger's time in the Foreign Office, see Philipp Gassert, *Kurt Georg Kiesinger 1904– 1988: Kanzler zwischen den Zeiten* (Munich: DVA, 2006), pp. 105–49.

165. PAAA, B 83, no. 761: Letter from Hans-Günther Kasche to Willy Brandt, 16 May 1968.

Chapter 10

1. Hans Rosenthal, 'Das gibt's nur einmal – Noten, die verboten wurden', as quoted in Thomas Henschke, *Hans Rosenthal: Ein Leben für die Unterhaltung* (Berlin: Schwarzkopf und Schwarzkopf, 1999), p. 161.

2. See Almut Giesecke, 'Nachwort', in Hans Fallada, *Jeder stirbt für sich allein* (Berlin: Aufbau, 2013), pp. 687–99; Carsten Gansel and Werner Liersch (eds), *Zeit vergessen, Zeit erinnern: Hans Fallada und das kulturelle Gedächtnis* (Göttingen: V & R Unipress, 2008).

3. This holds true even if one considers that Fallada had actually written his novel accepting a suggestion by Johannes R. Becher, the president of the 'Kulturbund zur demokratischen Erneuerung Deutschlands' and, from 1954, the GDR's first culture secretary (Minister für Kultur).

4. For a general assessment of this aspect of post-war (West) Germany, see Norbert Frei, *Adenauer's Germany and the Nazi Past: The Politics of Amnesty and Integration* (New York: Columbia University Press, 2002), first published in German as *Vergangenheitspolitik: Die Anfänge der Bundesrepublik und die NS-Vergangenheit* (Munich: Beck, 1996).

5. UAK, Archives, Zugang 726 (Theodor Klefisch), File 2, no. 11: Affidavit of the merchant and former SA man Dietrich Bölken, 8 June 1946; File 3, no. 37: Affidavit of the railroad employee and former SA man Reiner Pittinger, 7 June 1946.

6. See also the introduction to this book.

7. This title alludes to Eugen Kogon's eye-opening 1946 analysis, *Der SS-Staat*.

8. See, above all, the expert opinions of Buchheim and Broszat in *Anatomie des SS-Staates*, pp. 218–25, 336–51.

9. Lawrence Douglas, 'The Didactic Trial: Filtering History and Memory into the Courtroom', *European Review* 14:4 (2006), pp. 513–22, here p. 514.

10. Article 6 of the Agreement for the Prosecution and Punishment of the Major War Criminals of the European Axis, and Charter of the International Military Tribunal, London, 8 August 1945; http://www.icrc.org/ihl.nsf/FULL/350. On the legal aspects of the 'crimes against humanity' category, see also the detailed analysis by Daniel Marc Segesser, 'Der Tatbestand Verbrechen gegen die Menschlichkeit', in Kim C. Priemel and Alexa Stiller (eds), *NMT: Die Nürnberger Militärtribunale zwischen Geschichte, Gerechtigkeit und Rechtsschöpfung* (Hamburg: Hamburger Edition, 2013), pp. 586–604.

11. Initially, only those members of the SA who by the end of the war held the rank of *Sturmbannführer* or higher were to be arrested and detained by the Allied forces. By late 1944 the number of those stormtroopers was expected to total about 30,000 men; US Army Center of Military History, Fort McNair: Supreme Headquarters of the Allied Expeditionary Force (ed.), *Handbook for Military Government in Germany prior to Defeat or Surrender* (December 1944), unpaginated, http://www.history.army.mil/reference/Finding%20Aids/ Mil_gov.pdf.

12. Statement of the President of the IMT, Geoffrey Lawrence, 30 September, in Secretariat of the Tribunal under the Jurisdiction of the Allied Control Authority for Germany (ed.) (hereafter Secretariat of the Tribunal), *Trial of the Major War Criminals before the International*

Military Tribunal, Nuremberg, 14 November 1945–1 October 1946, The Blue Series (Nuremberg, 1947–8), vol. 22, p. 413.

13. IfZ Archive, ZS 251/1: Max Jüttner, 'Führung, Aufgaben und Tätigkeit der SA und Nürnberger Prozess'.

14. Ibid., pp. 3–4. Dr Robert Servatius defended the Thuringian *Gauleiter* Fritz Sauckel and the NSDAP leadership corps before the IMT and later also served as the defence lawyer for Adolf Eichmann in Jerusalem; Priemel and Stiller, *NMT*, pp. 761–2.

15. IfZ Archive, ZS 251/1, pp. 11–12, 22: Max Jüttner, 'Führung, Aufgaben und Tätigkeit der SA'.

16. Dorothea Gaitner, 'Robert Gerhard Storey, a Prosecution Counsel at Nuremberg Trials', *The New York Times*, 18 January 1981, http://www.nytimes.com/1981/01/18/obituaries/robert-gerard-storey-a-prosecution-counsel-at-nuremberg-trials.html.

17. Statement of Robert G. Storey, 18 December 1945, in Secretariat of the Tribunal, *Trial of the Major War Criminals*, vol. 4, p. 124.

18. Ibid., p. 125.

19. Ibid., p. 151.

20. Statement of Robert G. Storey, 19 December 1945, in Secretariat of the Tribunal, *Trial of the Major War Criminals*, vol. 4, p. 138.

21. Soviet Chief Prosecutor Roman Rudenko made a similar point on 2 March 1946; see Secretariat of the Tribunal, *Trial of the Major War Criminals*, vol. 8, p. 473.

22. See chapter 6.

23. On Schellenberg, see Reinhard R. Doerries, *Hitler's Last Chief of Foreign Intelligence: Allied Interrogations of Walter Schellenberg* (London and New York: Routledge, 2007).

24. Statement of Robert G. Storey, 19 December 1945, in Secretariat of the Tribunal, *Trial of the Major War Criminals*, vol. 4, p. 158.

25. Ibid., p. 159.

26. The biography of Georg Boehm (1900–52), a Nuremberg-based lawyer since 1929, is virtually unknown. Martin Löffler (25 January 1905–4 February 1987) was a member of the DVP between 1927 and 1933 and received his PhD in law from Tübingen University in 1928. He opened a solicitor's office in Stuttgart in 1933 and joined the Reiter-SA. In Nuremberg he thus also acted in a kind of self-defence. During the Second World War, Löffler served in the Wehrmacht in, among other places, Africa, before he was appointed a military judge in 1944. After the Third Reich fell, he became one of the leading authorities in press law in the Federal Republic. For a short biographical sketch, see his entry in the Munzinger archive, as well as the information provided on the homepage of the solicitor's office he founded, at http://www.rae-loeffler.de/geschichte.php. At the IMT, Klefisch acted as the lawyer of Gustav Krupp von Bohlen und Halbach, at least until 15 November 1945; Christoph Safferling and Philipp Graebke, 'Strafverteidigung im Nürnberger Hauptkriegsverbrecherprozess: Strategien und Wirkung', *Zeitschrift für die gesamte Strafrechtswissenschaft* 123:1 (2011), pp. 47–81, here p. 49; Hubert Seliger, *Politische Anwälte? Die Verteidiger der Nürnberger Prozesse* (Baden-Baden: Nomos, 2016), pp. 191–3.

27. So far no biographical study of Theodor Klefisch exists. On his reputation in Weimar Germany, see Ismar Lachmann, 'Die Größen der Berliner Advocatur', *Das Kriminal-Magazin* 3:29 (August 1931), http://www.anwaltsgeschichte.de/kriminal-magazin/kriminal-magazin.html.

28. Seliger, *Politische Anwälte?*, pp. 192–3; Statement of Geoffrey Lawrence, 15 August, in Secretariat of the Tribunal, *Trial of the Major War Criminals*, vol. 21, p. 175.

29. For details, see Hoffstadt, 'Stahlhelm und SA', pp. 270–7.

30. Statement of Georg Boehm, 28 August 1946, in Secretariat of the Tribunal, *Trial of the Major War Criminals*, vol. 22, p. 157.

31. This number was the estimate given by Dr Kuboschok, the defence lawyer for the former *Reichsregierung*, at the Nuremberg hearings on 28 February 1946; see ibid., vol. 8, p. 392.

32. Statement of Martin Löffler, 1 March 1946, in ibid., vol. 8, p. 415. It remains unclear whether this statement was correct and, if so, how many former SA men were actually elected.

33. Statement of Justice Jackson, 28 February 1946, in ibid., vol. 8, p. 370.

34. Statement of Martin Löffler, 1 March 1946, in ibid., vol. 8, p. 409.

35. Ibid., p. 410.

36. Ibid., p. 411.
37. See the 'canonical' work by Karl Jaspers, *Die Schuldfrage* (Heidelberg: Lambert Schneider, 1946). For a recent discussion, see Barbara Wolbring, 'Nationales Stigma und persönliche Schuld: Die Debatte über Kollektivschuld in der Nachkriegszeit', *Historische Zeitschrift* 289:2 (2009), pp. 325–64; Markus Urban, 'Kollektivschuld durch die Hintertür? Die Wahrnehmung der NMT in der westdeutschen Öffentlichkeit, 1946–1951', in Priemel and Stiller, *NMT*, pp. 684–718. For a broader discussion of resentment in post-war Europe, see Frank Biess, 'Feelings in the Aftermath: Toward a History of Postwar Emotions', in Frank Biess and Robert G. Moeller (eds), *Histories of the Aftermath: The Legacies of the Second World War in Europe* (New York: Berghahn, 2010), pp. 30–48, esp. pp. 40–2.
38. Verdict of the International Military Tribunal, 30 September 1946, in Secretariat of the Tribunal, *Trial of the Major War Criminals*, vol. 22, p. 518.
39. Ibid., vol. 22, p. 519. On the Jewish ghetto in Kaunas, see Jürgen Matthäus, 'Das Ghetto Kaunas und die "Endlösung" in Litauen', in Wolfgang Benz and Marion Neiss (eds), *Judenmord in Litauen* (Berlin: Metropol, 1999), pp. 97–112; Christoph Dieckmann, 'Das Ghetto und das Konzentrationslager in Kaunas, 1941–1944', in Ulrich Herbert, Karin Orth, and Christoph Dieckmann (eds), *Die nationalsozialistischen Konzentrationslager – Entwicklung und Struktur*, vol. 1 (Göttingen: Wallstein, 1998), pp. 439–71.
40. Verdict of the IMT, in Secretariat of the Tribunal, *Trial of the Major War Criminals*, vol. 22, p. 519.
41. Donald Bloxham, 'Prosecuting the Past in the Postwar Decade', in David Bankier and Dan Michman (eds), *Holocaust and Justice: Representation and Historiography of the Holocaust in Post-War Trials* (Jerusalem and New York: Yad Vashem, 2010), pp. 23–43, esp. pp. 37–9. On the methodological problems of assessing the German reactions to the IMT, see H. Krösche, 'Abseits der Vergangenheit: Das Interesse der deutschen Nachkriegsöffentlichkeit am Nürnberger Prozess gegen die Hauptkriegsverbrecher 1945/46', in Jörg Osterloh and Clemens Vollnhals (eds), *NS-Prozesse und deutsche Öffentlichkeit: Besatzungszeit, frühe Bundesrepublik und DDR* (Göttingen: Vandenhoeck & Ruprecht, 2011), pp. 93–105.
42. The lawyers of the SS adopted a similar defence strategy, but – hardly surprisingly – failed to achieve comparable results. See Kim C. Priemel, 'Beyond the Saturation Point of Horror: The Holocaust at Nuremberg Revisited', *The Journal of Modern European History* 14:4 (2016), pp. 522–47.
43. UAK, Archives, Zugang 726, File 2: Letter from Theodor Klefisch to an unknown addressee, 5 November 1946.
44. See the comprehensive collection of cases in Edith Raim, *Justiz zwischen Diktatur und Demokratie: Wiederaufbau und Ahndung von NS-Verbrechen in Westdeutschland 1945–1949* (Munich: Oldenbourg, 2013), pp. 659–944, as well as the database *Nazi Crimes on Trial: German Trial Judgements Concerning National Socialist Homicidal Crimes 1945–2012*, ed. Christiaan F. Rüter and Dick W. de Mildt, http://www1.jur.uva.nl/junsv.
45. Carina Baganz, '"Milde gegen die Verbrecher wäre Verbrechen gegen die Opfer": Die Hohnstein-Prozesse 1949', in Osterloh and Vollnhals, *NS-Prozesse und deutsche Öffentlichkeit*, pp. 207–20.
46. Weinke, *Die Verfolgung von NS-Tätern im geteilten Deutschland*; Andreas Eichmüller, 'Die strafrechtliche Verfolgung von NS-Verbrechern und die Öffentlichkeit in der frühen Bundesrepublik Deutschland 1949–1958', in Osterloh and Vollnhals, *NS-Prozesse und deutsche Öffentlichkeit*, pp. 53–73, here p. 54.
47. Carina Baganz, 'Vom Wachmann zum Inoffiziellen Mitarbeiter: Täter der frühen sächsischen Konzentrationslager und ihr Wirken für die Staatssicherheit', in Günther Heydemann, Jan Erik Schulte, and Francesca Weil (eds), *Sachsen und der Nationalsozialismus* (Göttingen: Vandenhoeck & Ruprecht, 2014), pp. 351–64.
48. As quoted in Margarete Mitscherlich-Nielsen, 'Erinnern, Vergessen und Verdrängen – Überlegungen zur *Unfähigkeit zu trauern*', in Sibylle Drews (ed.), *Freund in der Gegenwart: Alexander Mitscherlichs Gesellschaftskritik* (Frankfurt am Main: Brandes & Apsel, 2006), pp. 23–34, here p. 23.
49. The tendency of many Germans to deny any emotional or deliberate involvement in the National Socialist 'project' was evident as early as 1945. Committed Nazis seem to have disappeared overnight, with only disappointed or embittered 'victims' of the regime remaining

who now turned against the previously much-loved Führer. For a very early analysis of this phenomenon, see Saul Padover, *Experiment in Germany: The Story of an American Intelligence Officer* (New York: Duell, Sloan, and Pearce, 1946). For the term 'little guardians of the people's community', see Werner, 'Die kleinen Wächter der "Volksgemeinschaft"'.

50. Eichmüller, 'Die strafrechtliche Verfolgung von NS-Verbrechen', p. 55.

51. See chapter 9.

52. LArch NRW-Westfalen (Landesarchiv NRW, Abt. Westfalen), Staatsanwaltschaft Dortmund, nos 1293–1305, 1542–6.

53. LArch Hannover (Niedersächsisches Landesarchiv, Hauptstaatsarchiv Hannover), Nds. 171, no. 25522.

54. LArch Freiburg, V 1, Nr. 2473: Badisches Staatskommissariat für politische Säuberung, Verdict of the Spruchkammer Freiburg in the proceedings against Dietrich von Jagow, 13 February 1950.

55. Bernhard Gotto, 'Die Erfindung eines "anständigen Nationalsozialismus": Vergangenheitspolitik der schwäbischen Verwaltungsbeamten in der Nachkriegszeit', in Peter Fassl (ed.), *Das Kriegsende in Bayerisch-Schwaben 1945: Wissenschaftliche Tagung der Heimatpflege des Bezirks Schwaben in Zusammenarbeit mit der Schwabenakademie Irsee am 8/9 April 2005* (Augsburg: Wißner, 2006), pp. 263–83, esp. pp. 282–3.

56. 'Otto Straßer und der Solidarismus', *Arbeiter-Zeitung* (Vienna), no. 9, 12 January 1949, p. 2, http://www.arbeiter-zeitung.at/cgi-bin/archiv/flash.pl?seite=19490112_A02;html=1.

57. 'Senat stellt Strafantrag', *Hamburger Abendblatt*, 12 March 1952, p. 3. I am grateful to Christoph Strupp for providing me with a copy of this article.

58. BayHStA, MSo, Nr. 1929: Letter from the Treuchtlingen Municipal Council to the Bavarian Ministry of Justice, 17 August 1956. In this case the municipal council had demanded clemency for Andreas Güntner, who from 1933 to 1944 had served as mayor of Treuchtlingen. In 1950 he was sentenced to a prison term of three and a half years because of his participation in the 'anti-Jewish pogrom in Treuchtlingen'.

59. On Gmelin's education and his professional and political career in the 1930s, see the information provided in his SA files, in BArch Berlin, SA 4000001096; as well as in his personnel file with the Reich Ministry of Justice, in BArch Berlin, R/3001/57470 and 57471.

60. BArch Berlin, R/3001/57470, p. 41: Letter from the Reich Minister of Justice to the Foreign Office, 23 April 1941. In 1944, Gmelin praised his boss as an 'outstanding personage'; IfZ Archiv, MA 650, pp. 4,995–5,000, here p. 4,999: SD note on Gmelin's lecture at a party leadership meeting in Vienna, 14 January 1944. On the relationship of Ludin and Gmelin, see also Tönsmeyer, *Das Dritte Reich und die Slowakei*, pp. 89–90. According to Gmelin's daughter, her father 'took care' of Ludin's widow Erla and her children after the war; email from Dr Herta Däubler-Gmelin to the author, 26 February 2015.

61. Information provided by Niklas Krawinkel, Marburg, who is currently writing his PhD thesis on Gmelin under the supervision of Eckart Conze. I am also grateful to Krawinkel for providing me with a copy of Gmelin's denazification file.

62. IfZ Archiv, MA 650, pp. 4,995–5,000, here p. 4,999: SD note on Gmelin's lecture at a party leadership meeting in Vienna, 14 January 1944.

63. BArch Berlin, R 9354/601: Letter from R. Brandt to SS-Standartenführer Leg. Rat Wagner in the Foreign Office, 4 December 1944.

64. On the living conditions in these camps, which ultimately did not 're-educate' the former National Socialist leadership but instead provided an echo chamber for their reconstruction of the past, see Christof Strauß, 'Zwischen Apathie und Selbstrechtfertigung: Die Internierung NS-belasteter Personen in Württemberg-Baden', in Paul Hoser and Reinhard Baumann (eds), *Kriegsende und Neubeginn: Die Besatzungszeit im schwäbisch-alemannischen Raum* (Konstanz: UVK, 2003), pp. 287–313.

65. LArch Sigmaringen, Wü13 T 2, Nr. 2108/068: Verdict against Hans Gmelin, 13 July 1948.

66. This argument was frequently voiced in German politics post-Second World War. The best-known case is that of Chancellor Willy Brandt who, as a young Socialist, had escaped Nazi persecution by going into exile in Sweden and Norway and later had to defend himself against accusations of not having been a patriot. See Mergel, *Propaganda nach Hitler*, pp. 217–18.

67. StA Tübingen (Stadtarchiv Tübingen), ZGS-1: Hans Gmelin, election speech from 24 September 1954, *Schwäbisches Tagblatt*, 2 October 1954.

68. Gerhard Ebeling, 'Wiederkehr des Nationalsozialismus', in *Schwäbisches Tagblatt*, 27 October 1954.

69. 'Thema des Tages: Wiederkehr des Nationalsozialismus', in *Schwäbisches Tagblatt*, 28 October 1954. Such accusations and demands to stop the current denazification proceedings were common; see Strauß, 'Zwischen Apathie und Selbstrechtfertigung', pp. 310–13.

70. 'Fortsetzung der Debatte über "Wiederkehr des Nationalsozialismus": Sind wir in Tübingen schon wieder so weit?' in *Schwäbisches Tagblatt*, 30 October 1954.

71. 'Die meisten Einsender sagen: Nein', in *Schwäbisches Tagblatt*, 2 November 1954.

72. For Gmelin's post-war career, see also the instructive account by Hans-Joachim Lang, 'Die rechte Hand des Botschafters', *Schwäbisches Tagblatt*, 28 April 2005.

73. Critics, however, argue that Gmelin's involvement in the Holocaust should prevent him from being labelled an 'honorary citizen', an honour bestowed on him by the Tübingen city council in 1975. See Gerlind Strasdeit, 'Stellungnahme für die Fraktion DIE LINKE in Tübingen', 18 December 2014, http://www.die-linke-bw.de/nc/magazin/aus_den_kreis_und_ortsverbaenden/detail/zurueck/magazin/artikel/solange-hans-gmelin-ehrenbuerger-von-tuebingen-ist-bleibt-die-scheefstrassen-umbenennung-ein-ink.

74. Email from Dr Herta Däubler-Gmelin to the author, 26 February 2015.

75. On Bennecke's activities in the SA, see esp. chapter 4 as well as Peschel, *Die SA in Sachsen vor der 'Machtübernahme'*, pp. 7–22. Mike Schmeitzner of the Hannah-Arendt-Institut für Totalitarismusforschung at the TU Dresden is currently preparing a biographical study of Bennecke that will provide further details of his life both prior to and after 1945.

76. Documents from the *Hausarchiv*, the internal archive of the IfZ, demonstrate that critical collaborations with formerly high-ranking National Socialists were common. For example, the files that contain the institute's correspondence with Bennecke also enclose similar and usually extremely polite correspondence with former SS heavyweights Werner Best and Gottlob Berger. Researchers with the IfZ certainly aimed at and in many cases succeeded in extracting inside knowledge from these figures for use in critical historical scholarship. However, it also seems vital to analyse if, when, and why the former Nazis were successful in giving their partisan views on the Nazi past the stamp of scholarly excellence. See Nicolas Berg, *Der Holocaust und die westdeutschen Historiker: Erforschung und Erinnerung* (Göttingen: Wallstein, 2003), pp. 270–321; Hett, *Burning the Reichstag*, pp. 283–308. On the formation of the IfZ, see also Winfried Schulze, *Deutsche Geschichtswissenschaft nach 1945* (Munich: Oldenbourg, 1989), pp. 229–42; and John Gimbel, 'The Origins of the *Institut für Zeitgeschichte*: Scholarship, Politics and American Occupation', *American Historical Review* 70:3 (1964–5), pp. 714–31.

77. See, for example, Bennecke's interviews with the former SA leader Franz Pfeffer von Salomon and the Nazi writer Hans Zöberlein in IfZ Archive, ZS 177 and ZS 319. For Bennecke's memorandum of the Reich SA-*Hochschulamt*, see IfZ Archive, ZS 1685-1, pp. 21–4.

78. IfZ Archive, ID 200/177: Letter from Anton Hoch to Heinrich Bennecke, 25 May 1962; IfZ Archive, ID 300/23: Internal note by Thilo Vogelsang, 17 November 1958.

79. IfZ Archive, ID 200/177: Contract signed by Bennecke and Helmut Krausnick, director of the IfZ, 5 July 1963.

80. The surviving documents do not provide a clear explanation for this decision, but it doesn't seem unreasonable to assume that the appointment of a former Nazi functionary had the potential to harm the institute's reputation. IfZ Archive, ID 300/23: Internal note of the IfZ, 8 May 1963. The same document is also included in IfZ Archive, ID 103/85, p. 127.

81. Heinrich Bennecke, *Hitler und die SA* (Munich and Vienna: Olzog, 1962); idem, *Die Reichswehr und der 'Röhm-Putsch'* (Munich and Vienna: Olzog, 1964). After the publication of *Hitler und die SA*, Bennecke intended to send one copy to IfZ director Krausnick with the dedication 'To Dr Krausnick with many thanks for the help of the Institute for Contemporary Research'; IfZ Archive, ID 300/23: Letter from Bennecke to Thilo Vogelsang, 2 November 1962. In a letter to Krausnick, Bennecke remarked that his book was 'basically produced in the Institute' (*Sie entstand ja im wesentlichen im Institut für Zeitgeschichte*); IfZ Archive, ID 103/85, p. 128: Letter from Bennecke to Krausnick, 25 November 1962.

82. IfZ Archive, ID 200/177: Internal note from the IfZ, 13 February 1963.
83. Peschel, *Die SA in Sachsen vor der 'Machtübernahme'*, pp. 23–77. The IfZ files include an unsigned draft contract between the Federal Archives and Bennecke for a study on the SA in Saxony prior to the Nazi takeover of power; IfZ Archive, ID 200/177.
84. IfZ Archive, ID 300/23: 'Entwurf eines Vorworts'. Bennecke distinguished between 'four distinct periods' of the SA's history: The period up to 1923, the one between 1926 and April 1932, the one between June 1932 and 30 June 1934, and the one after 30 June 1934.
85. Peschel, *Die SA in Sachsen vor der 'Machtübernahme'*, p. 21.
86. Bennecke, *Hitler und die SA*, pp. 28–30.
87. Ibid., p. 194.
88. Instructive in this respect is Schmerbach, *Der Kampf der Kommunistischen Partei*, pp. 118–20.
89. Bennecke, *Hitler und die SA*, pp. 197–200.
90. For the rather ambivalent reviews, see ibid., pp. 78–82.
91. For a lucid discussion of this important problem, see Habbo Knoch, 'Review of Nicolas Berg, *Der Holocaust und die westdeutschen Historiker: Erforschung und Erinnerung*, H-Soz-Kult', 4 February 2004, http://www.hsozkult.de/publicationreview/id/rezbuecher-2433.
92. See the examples in Klaus Große-Kracht, *Die zankende Zunft: Historische Kontroversen in Deutschland nach 1945* (Göttingen: Vandenhoeck & Ruprecht, 2005).
93. Höhne, *Mordsache Röhm*.
94. On the long-lived myth of the 'clean Wehrmacht', see Ben Shepherd, 'The Clean Wehrmacht, the War of Extermination, and Beyond', *Historical Journal* 52:2 (2009), pp. 455–73; Hamburger Institut für Sozialforschung, Hannes Heer, and Birgit Otte (eds), *Vernichtungskrieg: Verbrechen der Wehrmacht 1941–1944* (Hamburg: Hamburger Edition, 1996).
95. Karsten Wilke, *Die 'Hilfsgemeinschaft auf Gegenseitigkeit' (HIAG), 1950–1990: Veteranen der Waffen-SS in der Bundesrepublik* (Paderborn: Schöningh, 2011).
96. Hans Hermann Karl Sponholz, born 9 April 1902 in Kolberg, volunteered for a *Jungmannenkommando* in his home town in the last year of the First World War, at the age of sixteen. After falling severely ill in a prisoner-of-war camp, he spent two years in the sickbay. Sponholz's health remained fragile for the rest of his life. From 1921 to 1923 he was a member of the *Verband nationalgesinnter Soldaten*, and from 1924 to 1931 he belonged to the *Stahlhelm*. On 1 July 1931 he joined the SA in Flatow and three months later entered the ranks of the NSDAP. Sponholz was exempt from regular SA duty but fought very effectively with words. Struggling to make a living from his modestly successful novels, he became a full-time SA leader on 15 January 1934. From 1937 onward the father of five children lived in Munich, where he rose to become one of the principal propagandists of the SA. On his biography, see BArch Berlin, VBS 264, no. 4001006602 (Sponholz, Hans) and SA 4000003627 (Sponholz, Hans).
97. Hans Sponholz, 'Naturschutz in der Defensive', *Natur und Landschaft: Zeitschrift für Freunde und Schützer der Deutschen Heimat* 41:9 (1966), pp. 191–3, here p. 193. For more on the 'brown heritage' of the West German environmentalist movement after the Second World War, see the pioneering Joachim Radkau and Frank Uekötter (eds), *Naturschutz und Nationalsozialismus* (Frankfurt am Main: Campus, 2003); Franz-Josef Brüggemeier and Jens Ivo Engels (eds), *Natur- und Umweltschutz nach 1945: Konzepte, Konflikte, Kompetenzen* (Frankfurt am Main: Campus, 2005).
98. Michael Seeholzer, 'Hans Sponholz – von Nazivergangenheit eingeholt', *Merkur*, 5 October 2013, http://www.merkur.de/lokales/ebersberg/ebersberg/hans-sponholz-nazi-vergangenheit-eingeholt-3148688.html. On Lorenz and National Socialism, see Benedikt Föger and Klaus Taschwer (eds), *Die andere Seite des Spiegels: Konrad Lorenz und der Nationalsozialismus* (Vienna: Czernin, 2001).
99. 'Hans Sponholz', in *Wikipedia.org*, https://de.wikipedia.org/wiki/Hans_Sponholz, date accessed: 28 October 2015.
100. For paradigmatic statements as well as self-critical reflections, see the contributions in Hannes Heer and Volker Ullrich (eds), *Geschichte entdecken: Erfahrungen und Projekte der neuen Geschichtsbewegung* (Reinbek bei Hamburg: Rowohlt, 1985) and Alf Lüdtke, *Alltagsgeschichte: Zur Rekonstruktion historischer Erfahrungen und Lebensweisen* (Frankfurt am Main: Campus, 1989); idem, 'Arbeiten und Dabeisein: Wie Alltagsgeschichte den

Nationalsozialismus erklärt', in Axel Lubinski (ed.), *Historie und Eigen-Sinn: Festschrift für Jan Peters zum 65. Geburtstag* (Weimar: Böhlau, 1997), pp. 75–86.

101. For the discovery of this place and its early exploration, see Kurt Schilde, Rolf Scholz, and Sylvia Walleczek (eds), *SA-Gefängnis Papestraße: Spuren und Zeugnisse* (Berlin: Overall Verlag, 1996). More recently, see Irene von Götz and Petra Zwaka (eds), *SA-Gefängnis Papestraße: Ein frühes Konzentrationslager in Berlin* (Berlin: Metropol, 2013). For information on Berlin's central institution for the remembrance of the Nazi terror, the *Stiftung Topographie des Terrors*, see Reinhard Rürup (ed.), *10 Jahre Topographie des Terrors* (Berlin: Topographie des Terrors, 1997).

102. For a historical sketch of 'Köpenick's blood murder week', see Yves Müller, 'Vom Traditionskabinett zur Gedenkstätte Köpenicker Blutwoche', in *SA-Terror als Herrschaftssicherung*, ed. Hördler, pp. 232–45.

103. See Stephan Buchloh, *'Pervers, jugendgefährdend, staatsfeindlich': Zensur in der Ära Adenauer als Spiegel des gesellschaftlichen Klimas* (Frankfurt am Main: Campus, 2002), pp. 142–5, here p. 144.

104. See, in particular, Nationalrat der Nationalen Front des Demokratischen Deutschland (ed.), *Braunbuch: Kriegs- und Naziverbrecher in der Bundesrepublik: Staat, Wirtschaft, Armee, Verwaltung, Justiz, Wissenschaft* (Berlin: Staatsverlag der DDR, 1968); there were several editions under slightly different titles between 1959 and 1981.

105. *Der Spiegel*, no. 34, 5 May 1968, quoted in Varon, *Bringing the War Home*, p. 39.

106. Lorenz Jäger, *Adorno: A Political Biography* (New Haven, CT, and London: Yale University Press, 2004), p. 192.

107. Interview of Ernst Fraenkel with the *Berliner Morgenpost*, 11 November 1967, as quoted in Thomas Pegelow Kaplan, '"Den mörderischen Alltag bei seinem richtigen Namen nennen": Linke Protestbewegungen, jüdische Remigranten und die Erinnerung an Massenverbrechen in den 1960er Jahren', *Zeitschrift für Geschichtswissenschaft* 62:7/8 (2014), pp. 600–19, here p. 612. In turn, the most radical students denounced Fraenkel as a 'reactionary'; see ibid. and Simone Ladwig-Winters, *Ernst Fraenkel: Ein politisches Leben* (Frankfurt am Main: Campus, 2009), pp. 318–25.

108. Uwe Siemon-Netto, 'The 68er Regime in Germany', *Orbis* 48:4 (2004), pp. 641–56, here p. 645.

109. *Berliner Extra-Dienst*, April 1968, quoted in Varon, *Bringing the War Home*, p. 40.

110. For a summary of these events, including the quote from Schmalz-Jacobsen, see Human Rights Watch Helsinki (ed.), *'Germany for Germans': Xenophobia and Racist Violence in Germany* (Helsinki: Human Rights Watch 1995), http://www.hrw.org/reports/1995/Germany.htm.

111. For an overview of the actual situation and the historical references of current neo-Nazis, see Alexander Häusler and Jan Schedler (eds), *Autonome Nationalisten: Neonazismus in Bewegung* (Wiesbaden: VS Verlag, 2011); Ulli Jentsch and Frank Metzger, 'Die "Blutzeugen der Bewegung" im Blick des heutigen Neonazismus', in *Bürgerkriegsarmee*, ed. Müller and Zilkenat, pp. 417–32.

Conclusion

1. Peter Sachse, *SA-Männer von Leipzig: Ein Beitrag zur Rassenkunde Deutschlands* (Leipzig: Werkgemeinschaft, 1934), pp. 7–12, 21, 29, 50, 55, 60. As Sachse informed his readers, his dissertation supervisor Professor Otto Reche had suggested this topic to him in the spring of 1932, precisely at a time when the authorities had banned the SA. He thus deliberately subverted the government's attempts to diminish the public prominence of the storm-troopers. Reche had also taken care to obtain the consent of the NSDAP's Reich Leadership Office, and, in 1933, had contrived the patronage of the new Minister President, SA-*Obergruppenführer* Manfred von Killinger.

2. Gerhard Wolf, 'Negotiating Germanness: National Socialist Germanisation Policy in the Wartheland', *Journal of Genocide Research*, forthcoming; idem, *Ideologie und Herrschaftsrationalität*.

3. In this respect it is instructive to take earlier ideas of a new 'German race' into account, as formulated between 1932 and 1934 by the SA men and academics Friedrich Merkenschlager, a biologist, and the anthropologist Karl Saller. Both men challenged the paradigm of the superiority of an allegedly 'pure' and 'nordic' race and instead advocated for a 'racial mixture' (*Rassenmischung*). They did not perceive the German race as an absolute given, but as a fragile equilibrium that could only be maintained by allowing for constant variation. See Cornelia Essner, *Die 'Nürnberger Gesetze' oder Die Verwaltung des Rassenwahns 1933–1945* (Paderborn: Schöningh, 2002), pp. 62–75. I am grateful to Stefan Boberg, Berlin, for directing me to this study.

4. Jonsson, *Crowds and Democracy*, p. xvi.

5. On 'individuality' and 'personality', see the pioneering work by Warren I. Susman, '"Personality" and the Making of Twentieth-Century Culture', in *New Directions in American Intellectual History*, ed. John Higham and Paul K. Conkin (Baltimore, MD: Johns Hopkins University Press, 1979), pp. 212–26; for the importance of individual empowerment in the Nazi 'people's community', see also Moritz Föllmer, *Individuality and Modernity in Berlin: Self and Society from Weimar to the Wall* (Cambridge: Cambridge University Press, 2013), esp. pp. 105–31.

6. Steuwer, 'Was meint und nützt das Sprechen von der "Volksgemeinschaft"?', p. 520.

7. Stefan Kühl, *Ganz normale Organisationen: Zur Soziologie des Holocausts* (Frankfurt am Main: Suhrkamp, 2014), pp. 102–3.

8. See already Harold D. Lasswell, 'The Garrison State', *American Journal of Sociology* 46:4 (1941) 4, pp. 455–468, here p. 461.

9. See above, chapter 8.

10. Loewenstein, 'Militant Democracy', p. 418.

11. Pendas, 'Explaining the Third Reich', p. 595. For an elaborate discussion of this point, see Robert Gellately, *Backing Hitler: Consent and Coercion in Nazi Germany* (Oxford: Oxford University Press, 2001); for a more sceptical view of the persuasiveness of the appeal of the Nazi *Volksgemeinschaft*, see Geoff Eley, *Nazism as Fascism*, pp. 13–58, here p. 28.

INDEX

Erklärung der Grenzen:

Grenze des Deutschen Reiches
Ehemalige Grenze des Deutschen Reiches
Ländergrenze von Bayern, Sachsen, Braunschweig
Tirol, Steiermark, Kärnten usw.
Provinzgrenze in Preußen Lds.-Komm.-Bez. i. Baden
Regierungsbezirksgrenze in Preußen und Bayern
Kreisgrenze in Baden
Kreishauptmannschaftsgrenze in Sachsen
Kreisgrenze in Preußen
Bezirksamtsgrenze in Bayern
Oberamtsgrenze in Württemberg
Amtsbezirksgrenze in Baden
Amtshauptmannschaftsgrenze in Sachsen
Bezirkshauptmannschaftsgrenze in Österreich
Grenze des Saargebietes
Grenze der Stadtkreise, kreisunmittelbare,
kreisfreie Städte usw.

GRUPPE NORDMARK

GRUPPE HANSA

GRUPPE NORDSEE
OBERGRUPPE VI

GRUPPE BERLIN
OBERGRUPPE

BRANDENBURG

GRUPPE WESTFALEN
OBERGRUPPE X

GRUPPE MITTE

GRUPPE NIEDERRHEIN

GRUPPE HESSEN

OBERGRUPPE IX

OBERGRUPPE IV

GRUPPE SACHSEN

GRUPPE THÜRINGEN

GRUPPE WESTMARK

GRUPPE FRANKEN

GRUPPE KURPFALZ

OBERGRUPPE

GRUPPE SÜDWEST

GRUPPE
BAYR. OSTMARK
OBERGRUPPE VII

GRUPPE HOCHLAND

BRIGADE 88
OBERGRUPPE

BRIGADE